The Psychology of Women

The *Psychology* of *Women*

Ongoing Debates

Edited by MARY ROTH WALSH

YALE UNIVERSITY PRESS
New Haven and London

Designed by Winston Potter and set in Bulmer type
by Composing Room of Michigan, Grand Rapids, Michigan.
Printed in the United States of America by
Vail-Ballou Press, Inc., Binghamton, New York.

Library of Congress Cataloging-in-Publication Data

The Psychology of women.

        Includes bibliographies and index.
        1. Women—Psychology.   I. Walsh, Mary Roth.
[DNLM: 1. Women—psychology.   HQ 1206 P9738]
HQ1206.P769   1987   155.6'33   87–6167
ISBN 0–300–03965–4 (alk. paper)
ISBN (pbk) 0–300–03966–2 (alk. paper)

The paper in this book meets the guidelines for permanence
and durability of the Committee on Production Guidelines
for Book Longevity of the Council on Library Resources.

                    10   9   8   7   6   5   4   3

Contents

Contents

Contents

Acknowledgments

This is the first book to consist entirely of debates in the psychology of women. My choice of a title reflects the fact that the issues and controversies addressed herein continue even as I write this preface. The search for answers to these questions has engaged a whole army of scholars, both women and men. Although this book is titled *The Psychology of Women,* some of these debates have contributed to the development of a psychology of men and a psychology of gender. Nonetheless, the questions here are about women and their answers have important political implications for the quality of women's lives. Many of the authors whose work is included in this book have devoted years, some almost their entire professional careers, to developing an area of specialization important to the psychology of women. We all owe these scholars an enormous debt of gratitude for expanding the frontiers of knowledge.

I owe a personal debt to my own mentor in the psychology of women, Matina Horner, now president of Radcliffe College. I belong to a small but fortunate generation of women scholars who began graduate work when the second wave of twentieth-century feminism was just beginning to enrich our lives with new ideas and new possibilities for academic work. In 1970, I was enrolled in a Radcliffe College seminar and I remember walking through Harvard Square and seeing Kate Millet's pathbreaking book, *Sexual Politics,* prominently displayed in bookstore windows. I also remember browsing in the library and being surprised to find a reserve reading list for a new course on the psychology of women. I immediately went to the psychology department and found the office of the instructor, Matina Horner, then a new assistant professor of clinical psychology at Harvard. I can still remember her warm spirit and generous reception. Research on tokenism in the work environment was just beginning to emerge, and I did not yet know how difficult it was to be a faculty woman at Harvard or elsewhere in the early 1970s, but Matina's presence signaled new opportunities for women students. Her kindness opened new doors for me and for many others.

x   I enrolled in Matina Horner's seminar on the psychology of women the following year and each session reinforced my view that I wanted to do research in this area. Matina generously shared reams of unpublished papers with me and she became a member of my Ph.D. examining committees and the sponsor of my post-doctoral training grant in the psychology of women. I am proud to include her 1972 article in this book. Her work on fear of success has stimulated almost twenty years of research on female achievement barriers. I am also deeply indebted to Joyce Lazar at the National Institute of Mental Health for research support and to the Bunting Institute for its Fellowship during 1974–76.

Soon afterward, I began working with a project sponsored by the American Medical Women's Association and directed by Marlys Hearst Witte with funding from the Women's Educational Equity Act and the National Institute of Education. I served as director of curriculum, and my visits to medical schools all over the country planted the seeds for this book. My work involved facilitating programs and making research in women's studies available to an unusual audience: medical school students, faculty, administrators, and deans. Our classrooms were hotbeds of debate; discussions continued long after the sessions were over. I am grateful that I had the chance to participate in such an exciting intellectual program and that I have been able to continue my association with such outstanding physicians and national leaders as Lila A. Wallis, Constance U. Battle, and Kathryn E. McGoldrick.

Sam Bass Warner and Nathan Glazer are both scholars in quite different fields but in 1980 they helped me prepare grant proposals so I could begin the research for this book. Their help enabled me to win two separate awards from the National Endowment for the Humanities—a summer grant and a College Teacher's Award. Although the awards were a major source of support, I am especially grateful to these two men for their confidence in me.

I met Carolyn Wood Sherif, now deceased, in the spring of 1980, and she, along with Ruth Hubbard, wrote letters of support for me for several successful fellowship applications. In the years that followed, all of the following people shared information and reactions which helped me, in numerous ways, to do research related to this book and to see it through the publication process: Pamela Adelman, Judith Alpert, Susan Basow, Nancy Bifano, Phyllis Bronstein, Alice Brown-Collins, Paula Caplan, Faye Crosby, Florence Denmark, Myra Marx Ferree, Mary Ellen Foti, Laurel Furumoto, Lucia Gilbert, Judith A. Hall, Karen Howe, Nancy Henley, Janet Hyde, Randi Koeske, Bernice Lott, Neil Malamuth, Margaret Matlin, Vicki Mays, Kathleen McCartney, Sonja M. McKinlay, Martha Mednick,

Jean Baker Miller, Mary Parlee, Joseph Pleck, Kathryn Quina, Patricia Rieker, Shula Reinharz, Abigail Stewart, and Michele Wittig.

In February 1982, I visited Brendan A. Maher at Harvard University, who had a special interest in the history of psychology. Brendan's enthusiasm for the work I was doing on the history of the psychology of women helped me obtain concrete institutional support when he, along with Sheldon White, sponsored my appointment as a Visiting Scholar in the Psychology Department of Harvard University from 1983 to 1985. This validation of my work in the psychology of women was very important and it helped speed my research and work on this book.

Beginning in 1983, the Wellesley College Center for Research on Women provided a very supportive environment with seminars for feminist scholars in the social sciences. Peggy McIntosh was responsible for obtaining funding for this innovative program and I am grateful to her and to the Andrew Mellon Foundation for a national fellowship I received in the spring of 1984. She also obtained funding allowing several of us to continue meeting for two more years as the Anna Wilder Phelps Social Science Seminar. I discussed the early outlines of this book with faculty in that seminar: Emily Steir Adler, Laurie Crumpacker, Katheleen Dunn, Laurel Furumoto, Michele Hoffnung, Ruth Harriet Jacobs, Sukie Magraw, Frances Maher, Robin Roth, Jane Torrey, and Eleanor Vander Haegen. I appreciate their enthusiasm for my work.

Radcliffe College has two very special institutions which supported me at various points while I was working on this book. I am grateful for a Henry Murray Research Center Award which enabled me to hire Heidi Peddell as my research assistant during 1984–85. I am also grateful to Radcliffe directors Ann Colby and Patricia King for the confidence they had in my work. I would like especially to thank Barbara Haber, the dynamic and creative Curator of Printed Books at the Arthur and Elizabeth Schlesinger Library on the History of Women in America, a marvelous resource which I always knew I could count on when other university libraries disappointed me with their slim holdings in women's studies.

The library of the Boston Women's Health Book Collective in Watertown, Massachusetts, and the authors of *The New Our Bodies, Ourselves* were important sources of information for me for several research topics. The library has books and articles on women's health issues found in none of the four medical school libraries in the area. Judy Norsigian, Norma Swenson, and Esther Rome shared with me references and the names of researchers I might never have discovered, including Diane Laskin Siegal and Paula Duress, who showed me material from their Midlife and Older Women Book Project.

xii   Several years ago, Irene Hanson Frieze suggested that I organize national sessions on teaching of the psychology of women at several major conferences: the Association for Women in Psychology, the American Psychological Association, and the American Educational Research Association. These meetings proved to be a splendid opportunity to learn about the progress and problems of faculty who were teaching courses related to the psychology of women. At one of these meetings, serendipity played a role and I met Gladys Topkis, Senior Editor at Yale University Press. Her lovely note asking about my work was the catalyst that finally set this book in motion. I am grateful for her editorial guidance and her knowledge of the publishing world. Since we met, I have read many acknowledgments of her editorial skill and her friendship with other scholars, and I feel fortunate to belong to this circle. Charles Grench at Yale University Press opened the first door for me there, and now Gladys Topkis has opened the second. And I cannot begin to describe how hard Manuscript Editor Stephanie Jones worked on this manuscript and how carefully she went over each page with her sharp editorial eyes. This book is much better because of her efforts.

Patricia M. Stano, a computer consultant from Marlborough, Massachusetts, helped me master my computer. Without her assistance I could not possibly have completed the final production of this book in such a short period of time. I have taught two seminars based on this book and the support and enthusiasm of my students at the University of Lowell have been very important to me. The university has also awarded me Research Scholar status this semester. This, and the university funding for my student research assistant, E. Alice Moore, are making the final preparation of this book much easier.

Most of all, I wish to thank my husband, Frank. I cannot remember a time when he was not supportive and loving throughout the long process of research for and editing of this book. His contribution to my work has been immeasurable.

The Psychology of Women

Introduction

A Brief History of the Psychology of Women

In 1968, psychologist Naomi Weisstein charged: "Psychology has nothing to say about what women are really like, what they need and what they want, essentially, because psychology does not know" (p. 268). Ironically, just as Weisstein was making this charge, the rebirth of the feminist movement was stimulating a massive reappraisal of the entire field of psychology. The result was the development of a new research field: the psychology of women.

This is not to say that the topic of women had previously been completely ignored. The problem lies rather in how earlier psychologists, psychoanalysts, and psychiatrists had approached the topic. In the early 1970s, feminist social scientists directed much of their attention to refuting what had passed for a psychology of women in the past.

The feminist challenge encompassed almost every aspect of psychology, from broad conceptual issues to specific research methodologies and therapeutic practices. Freud's view of female personality development, for example, was dismissed as misogynist and based on biological determinism. Critics also claimed that therapists were ignoring the social causes of women's distress, encouraging women to adjust to a sexist society. "As far as the woman is concerned," commented Germaine Greer (1971), "psychiatry is an extraordinary confidence trick: the unsuspecting creature seeks aid because she feels unhappy, anxious and confused, and psychology persuades her to seek the cause in *herself*" (p. 82).

Neither could feminist critics derive any satisfaction from the work of academic psychologists. At best, social scientists relegated female subjects to the periphery of their research interests. As Mary Brown Parlee commented, the result was "distorted facts" and "omitted problems" which, in turn, "perpetuated pseudoscientific data relevant to women" (1975, p. 124). More often than not, researchers ignored women's existence entirely,

2   viewing male behavior as the prototype of human behavior. All of this falls into what Nancy Henley has characterized as "psychology against women" (1974, p. 20).

There were, however, efforts to steer a different course. Earlier in the century, a small number of psychologists launched an attack on the Victorian notion of sex differences. In the process, they did succeed in narrowing the scientific definition of differences between men and women. One of the leaders in this struggle was Helen Thompson [Woolley]. Her research at the University of Chicago, involving a detailed study of the motor skills and sensory abilities of fifty male and female undergraduate students, demonstrated that the intellectual similarities between the two sexes far outweighed the differences (Thompson, 1903). The noted sociologist William Isaac Thomas, who had earlier defended the notion that there were significant differences between men and women, hailed her findings as "probably the most important contribution to this field" (Rosenberg, 1982, p. 81).

Leta Stetter Hollingworth, another brilliant pioneer, coauthored several articles with Thompson and established a remarkable record for herself in this field. Before she received her Ph.D. from Columbia University in 1916, Hollingworth had already published a book and nine scientific papers on the psychology of women. Her research and writing have a strikingly modern flavor. In one of her articles, she criticized the social forces that pressured women into becoming mothers, a situation that later feminists would label "the motherhood mandate" (Hollingworth, 1916; Russo, 1979, p. 7).

Hollingworth also rejected the notion, widely accepted by leading psychologists of her time, that men tended to have a wider range of intellectual abilities than women, an idea known as "the variability thesis." In her research, she also attacked the popular view that women's cognitive abilities declined during menstruation (Hollingworth, 1914a, 1914b).

Although Hollingworth shifted the focus of her research when she took a teaching position at Columbia University in child psychology, her interest in the psychology of women continued. Hollingworth hoped to see the time when a psychology of women would be written "based on truth, not opinion; on precise, not on anecdotal evidence; on accurate data, rather than on remnants of magic" (1914b, p. 99). She also had a plan, which she never realized, to write a book on the psychology of women entitled "Mrs. Pilgrim's Progress," reflecting her emphasis on women's self-determination (Shields, 1975, p. 857).

Meanwhile, a new controversy concerning the psychology of women began to take shape, arising out of Freud's work on female psychosexual development (Fliegel, 1986). Three of the five protagonists involved in the ensuing debate were women. Helene Deutsch and Jeanne Lampl-de Groot supported Freud's position while Karen Horney dissented. In her critique of Freud's views, Horney struck a note that feminists of the 1970s would respond to: she insisted that psychoanalytic theories about women evolved from a male point of view (Horney, 1926; Westkott, 1986).

Positions on both sides of the debate quickly hardened. At one point, Freud dismissed criticisms of his work on women as the "denials of the feminists, who are anxious to force us to regard the two sexes as completely equal in position and worth" (1925, p. 258). As Zenia Odes Fliegel (1986) has noted, after Horney's break with Freud in the 1920s the criticism of Freud's views on women disappeared almost entirely from the mainstream of psychoanalytic literature.

Other women psychologists also experienced difficulty in making their voices heard (Scarborough & Furumoto, 1987). Although women made up one-third of the membership of the American Psychological Association by the 1930s, women psychologists were largely relegated to clinical and counseling work, then considered lower in status than teaching and research positions. Consequently, they remained outside the academic circles where most of the research and theory building was taking place (Furumoto, 1987; Furumoto, in press).

In 1941, in an effort to improve their status within the profession, a number of women psychologists banded together to form the National Council of Women Psychologists (later the International Council of Women Psychologists). Although the council sponsored a number of projects, including a newsletter and efforts to expand job opportunities, that prefigured the efforts of women psychologists in the 1970s, its leaders were able to effect only minimal changes in the profession's treatment of women (Walsh, 1985c).

When the council voted to eliminate the word *women* from the title of their organization in 1959, they brought to a close its role as a lobbyist for women within the profession. Cynthia Deutsch, who once had unsuccessfully attempted to persuade the council to sponsor a study of sex discrimination against women psychologists in the late 1950s, later described the forces working against professional women in those years. Deutsch argued that a good deal of the blame for the dearth of professional training and career opportunities for women could be traced to psychoanalytic theory, which assigned women a dependent and passive role vis-á-vis men. The psychoanalytic movement also identified women with the concept of "Mom," thus confirming the attitudes of male psychologists who continued to treat women colleagues as "dependent and subordinately

4   nurturing, rather than as fully equal scientists" (Deutsch, 1986, p. 187).

Ironically, within a decade of the disappearance of the International Council of Women Psychologists as an interest group for women, efforts to improve the status of women in psychology again took shape. Spurred on by the civil rights and social reform movements of the late 1960s, women psychologists not only demanded a larger role within the profession but also called for a new approach to the study of women. The psychology of women was formally recognized as an official division of the American Psychological Association (APA) in 1973 (Denmark, 1977; Mednick, 1978; Walsh, 1985c). The APA also established an office for women's programs and a committee on women in psychology, both of which are still in existence. Special task forces have issued reports on a number of topics ranging from "Sex Bias and Sex Role Stereotyping in Psychotherapeutic Practice" to the development of guidelines for nonsexist research. (Brodsky & Hare-Mustin, 1980; McHugh, Koeske & Frieze, 1986).

An APA task force was called in 1972 to evaluate the status of women in the profession. One of its first actions was to conduct a national survey of courses focusing on the female life experience. The task force located thirty-two departments that offered courses on the female life experience. Fifteen years later, this number has swelled to more than two hundred. Further evidence of change is the fact that APA evaluates graduate programs in clinical, counseling, and school psychology on the basis of whether they include courses on sex roles. Even the Graduate Record Exam Advanced Test in psychology contains questions on the psychology of women and experts on women's issues are recruited to serve on the test evaluation committee (Walsh, 1985a; Walsh, 1985b).

Similarly, psychology has been transformed from a profession that, in Naomi Weisstein's words, had "nothing to say about women" to one that has a great deal to say. In 1975, the journal *Sex Roles* began publication, followed a year later by the *Psychology of Women Quarterly*. Since then, practically every psychology journal has increased the number of articles it publishes dealing with the psychology of women (Deaux, 1984; Lott, 1985; Lykes & Stewart, 1986). Margaret Matlin (1987), the author of a recent introductory college textbook on the psychology of women, estimates that the number of articles and books potentially relevant to the topic and published in the last fifteen to twenty years is close to one hundred thousand. Bibliographies on the psychology of women no longer claim to be comprehensive and now carefully select their focus (Dilling & Claster, 1985; Golub & Freedman, 1987).

The four most recent textbooks for college courses on the psychology of

women represent still another dimension of this knowledge explosion
(Hyde, 1985; Matlin, 1987; Lott, 1987; Williams, 1987). In 1985, Janet
Hyde noted in the preface to the third edition of her textbook that ten years
earlier, when she began the first edition, her problem had been that "the
field was too new" and the research was "too thin." Now, in this latest
edition, she found that she had more information than could possibly be
included in one textbook and that it was difficult to make decisions on
which topics to eliminate and where to abbreviate discussions (p. viii).

The changes that have taken place in psychology over the past twenty
years do not, of course, constitute a panacea. Critics have pointed out that
we still have a long way to go if our goal is to conduct truly nonsexist
research (McHugh, Koeske, & Frieze, 1986; Lykes & Stewart, 1986).
Nevertheless, it is clear that the psychology of women has come of age.

About This Book

My goal in this book is to confront the reader with some of the diverse
viewpoints which exist in the psychology of women. I hope that this book
will break new ground both for those just beginning their study in this field
and also for those who have been involved in the field for some time. Each
of the fourteen controversies I have identified is represented by two opposing points of view. There is, of course, nothing new in employing debates
as a learning device. The Socratic method is some twenty-four hundred
years old. But this book is different because it puts women at center stage,
acknowledging the incredible growth of knowledge in the field. I also want
this book to serve as a springboard to encourage further debate and controversy and stimulate the evaluation of information from different perspectives. I hope some readers will want to expand (or refute) the arguments
presented in this book and add to the published literature in the field.

As I have already indicated, the field of the psychology of women has
expanded rapidly in recent years. Clearly the two "voices" I have selected
are not the only ones that speak on the specific issues. Sometimes it was very
difficult for me to choose between two excellent articles on a given position.
One measure of the increased maturity of the field is that the debates are no
longer just between feminists and nonfeminists: several issues, though not
all, involve a conflict of feminist perspectives. I view this growing diversity
of perspectives within the field of the psychology of women as a very
positive development. A continued flow of new ideas and rival claims is
essential to growth in any field. The psychology of women is dependent on

6   conflict and dissent for its very life energy. Viewed from this perspective, the different voices represented in this collection are a sign of great hope for the future.

From the very beginning of the recent renaissance in feminist studies, the psychology of women has been an interdisciplinary field. Consequently, the authors in this book span a number of different disciplines—psychology, sociology, psychoanalysis, psychiatry, and medicine—and the issues in the debates are of even broader interest than the authors' diverse disciplines suggest. I hope this book will appeal to students in other fields as well, particularly education, anthropology, history, American Studies, philosophy, social work, and literature. In fact, a recent reassessment of feminist scholarship points to three of these fields, anthropology, history and literature, as academic areas where the most impressive feminist conceptual shifts have occurred in the past decade (Stacey & Thorne, 1985).

I do not claim that the two selections for each question always represent the definitive position on either side of a given question. On the contrary, one of the underlying assumptions of this book is that research is a continuous dialogue where dissent and difference of opinion are essential. As Virginia Woolf noted, "When a subject is highly controversial—and any question about sex is that—one cannot hope to tell the truth. One can only show how one came to hold whatever opinion one does hold. One can only give one's audience a chance of drawing their own conclusions as they observe the limitations, the prejudices, the idiosyncrasies of the speaker" (1929, p. 4).

I hope that this book will provide some understanding of how we arrive at what is defined as psychological knowledge. In order to place each controversy in perspective, I have written a brief introduction to each topic. And because all of the following questions represent ongoing controversies within the field of the psychology of women, I have also included suggestions for further reading in each case.

Clearly, not every controversy within the field found its way into this book. Space limitations forced me to choose from a number of possibilities. In making these difficult decisions, I have used four criteria: (1) the controversy should deal with a significant question; (2) the controversy should be an ongoing one; (3) it should have relevance to some larger social issue involving women; and (4) most important, the debate should involve strongly divergent points of view. For example, I did not include the topic of whether married women are physically or mentally healthier as a result of working outside the home because it did not satisfy the fourth criterion. Although the topic of women's combined work and family roles is a significant social issue that has stimulated more than 150 studies in the past thirty years, researchers appear to have reached the consensus that, on balance, married women do benefit by working outside the home (Adelman, 1986; Froberg, Gjerdingen, & Preston, 1986).

Another topic of great importance in the psychology of women and one that is not represented in this book involves racial and ethnic differences among women. Although there are a growing number of publications on the psychology of black and Hispanic women (two recent bibliographies [Mays, 1986; Amaro, 1986] sum up the research in this field), it is extremely difficult to identify issues involving race and ethnicity where behavioral scientists have articulated sharply divided views on gender. This may be due to the fact that the topic is still in a formative research period. It takes time for intellectual conflict to emerge. As Nancy Henley (1985) put it: "The psychology of women of racial and ethnic minorities is in a stage of development similar to that of psychology of gender in its early years" (p. 117).

I hope that the questions examined in this book will do more than provide insight into the process of psychological research. I also hope that this collection will generate discussions about how the field of the psychology of women has developed in the past decade. I want readers, in looking at the controversies that have emerged in the psychology of women, to get a sense of the excitement engendered by this still relatively new field of study.

The Debates

Perhaps no topic has produced more passion within the field of the psychology of women than Freudian theory. Since psychoanalytic views played such an important role in shaping both popular and psychological concepts of the female personality, it is not surprising that efforts to repudiate the Freudian paradigm constituted a central component of the feminist counterattack on mainstream psychology in the late 1960s and early 1970s. Nevertheless, in spite of the broad-based rejection of Freud's work, his theories have exhibited a remarkable resiliency. Beginning in the early 1970s, feminists such as Jean Baker Miller (1973), Juliet Mitchell (1974), Jean Strouse (1974), and Helen Lewis (1976, 1986) sought a rapprochment between psychoanalysis and feminism.

Shahla Chehrazi, in the first essay in this book, maintains that current psychoanalytic views offer valuable insights into female development. Hannah Lerman, on the other hand, expresses the view of many feminist psychologists who argue that Freud's understanding of the female personality is so riddled with errors that it is beyond repair (question 1).

Feminists who use psychoanalytic theory as a starting point for their own work are fully aware of the misogyny that runs through Freud's writing on women. Nevertheless, they believe that his views should not be rejected out of hand. The growing recognition in the 1970s of the problems of rape, incest, and battering, for example, has led some mental health professionals, including Natalie Shainess, to argue that it is a mistake not to consider Freud's concept of masochism. Opponents of this position, among them Paula Caplan, characterize masochism as an approach that "blames the victim" and contend that the behavior of victimized women can be explained in other ways (question 2).

The resurgence of feminism involved not only the initial repudiation of psychoanalysis but also a protest against the entire mental health delivery system. Germaine Greer (1971), after describing how psychologists tried to persuade women that they were mentally ill, concluded, "Psychologists cannot fix the world so they fix women" (p. 83). Phyllis Chesler (1972) saw this as a power play: women were being driven mad by men who were trying to keep them in their place. The debate on this topic contrasts the views of Walter Gove, who argues that there actually is a higher incidence of mental illness in women, and Marilyn Johnson, who challenges both Gove's data and his concept of what constitutes appropriate therapy (question 3).

Psychotherapy is just one of several methods of treatment for women that have come under attack. The health care system has also been charged with medicalizing women's lives to the point where normal female life events, such as menstruation, pregnancy, childbirth, and the menopause, are transformed into diseases. The premenstrual syndrome, popularly known as PMS, is often cited as a prime example of this phenomenon. Premenstrual syndrome attracted a great deal of popular interest when it was used as a defense a few years ago in several murder trials. According to Katharina Dalton, the English gynecologist who is credited with coining the term, the accused women in these cases and a significant number of women in the larger society are simply suffering from a hormonal deficiency that could be treated with progesterone. Opponents such as Randi Koeski have voiced a number of concerns about PMS, ranging from reservations about Dalton's research methodology and treatment to questions about the very existence of the syndrome (question 4).

Equally controversial is the question of whether menopause is the beginning of a disease requiring medical intervention and treatment. Historically, the American Psychiatric Association Diagnostic and Statistical Manual of Mental Disorders (DSM-II, 1968) even had a term for depressions occurring in the menopausal years: *involutional melancholia*

(Weissman, 1979). Once considered a neurotic reaction to the aging process, the menopause was redefined as a "deficiency disease" in the 1960s when synthetic estrogen came into use on a wide scale (McCrea, 1983). Critics have charged that medical practitioners have needlessly put women at risk in order to "cure" a natural phenomenon.

Penny Wise Budoff, however, argues that it is the misuse of estrogen rather than the estrogen itself that is the problem. While not denying that some women do experience depression and physical symptoms during the menopause period, critics of estrogen replacement therapy, such as John McKinley and Sonja McKinley, have argued that women's problems during this transition in the life cycle are largely the result of factors unrelated to hormonal changes (question 5).

A great deal of controversy also surrounds the search for new theoretical models within the psychology of women. In the late 1960s, a new line of research opened up when Matina Horner suggested the concept that women have a motive to avoid success because they associate it with negative consequences. Her findings quickly attracted the attention of psychologists and popular writers alike. The appeal of "fear of success" was its relative simplicity: a single variable, easily tested, offered a readily understandable explanation of why women had not succeeded in the world of work and the professions. While the "fear of success" continues to appeal to some psychologists on an intuitive level, a number of researchers, such as Michele Paludi, have challenged Horner's methodology and findings (question 6).

As criticism of Horner's work mounted in the mid- to late 1970s, attention switched to another theory, Sandra Bem's concept of androgyny. Bem made it clear from the beginning that her interest in sex roles was political even though she was an empirical scientist whose research involved the construction of a test to measure androgyny, the Bem Sex Role Inventory. In the first of her two essays reprinted in this book, Bem notes that the major purpose of her research was a feminist one: "to free the human personality from the restricting prison of sex-role stereotyping."

Initially hailed as a major contribution to the psychology of women, Bem's theory soon ran into difficulties. As Kay Deaux (1985) has noted, a backlash against the concept of androgyny developed in the 1980s as criticism of Bem's methods and conclusions grew. Bem, too, began to have second thoughts about the implications of her research. Shifting the focus of her earlier work on androgyny, she went on to develop a new paradigm, "gender schema theory." A comparison of Bem's two theories presents a rare example of a major theorist critiquing her own work (question 7).

The fear of success and androgyny are both examples of the use of a single variable which in turn rests on a single testing instrument to explain

10   much of the female condition. Nancy Chodorow (1978) also turned to a single variable, mothering, to explain the behavior of women and men. But in contrast to the relatively straightforward typologies of the fear of success and androgyny, Chodorow's work is a complex fusion of psychoanalytic and sociological theory with feminism.

According to Chodorow, mothering prepares boys and girls for their respective roles in society and the economy. Relationships with the mother evolve along different lines for the two sexes. As a consequence, girls learn to relate to the world of mothering and the family (in Chodorow's terms, mothering reproduces itself) while boys become men who devalue women and orient themselves to the external world. In order to break this cycle, Chodorow argues that fathers must participate equally in childcare. Chodorow's work has been hailed as "perhaps the most important and impressive feminist interpretation of Freudian theory" (Donovan, 1985, p. 109). However, a number of critics, including Alice Rossi, have challenged everything from Chodorow's methodology and choice of evidence to her solutions (question 8).

One measure of a theory is its influence on other theorists. Carol Gilligan, currently perhaps the most widely discussed author in the psychology of women, has used Chodorow's description of sex role socialization as a springboard for her own study, *In a Different Voice* (1982). According to Gilligan, developmental theories depict men as advancing to more mature levels of moral reasoning than women. Gilligan argues that women do reason in a different, but no less mature, way than men. More specifically, women see morality as a matter of care and relationships, while men view moral issues in terms of a system of law or impartial justice.

Gilligan's work presents an interesting paradox. On the one hand, her approach is part of the feminist critique of the male bias in psychology. Some feminist psychologists, however, have expressed concern that her conclusions can be used to support traditional sex-role stereotypes (Henley, 1985). Others, such as Anne Colby and William Damon, have questioned whether her evidence is strong enough to bear the weight of her theory (question 9).

While some psychologists have focused on larger theoretical issues, most of the work within the psychology of women has been devoted to discrete areas of research. Probably the subject that has received the most attention is that of sex differences. In 1974, Maccoby and Jacklin concluded that the data indicated only four areas of sex differences: verbal ability, aggression, visual-spatial ability, and mathematical ability.

Although investigators have been busy testing Maccoby and Jacklin's conclusions ever since the publication of their book, the topic of mathematical ability has received the greatest popular attention. Research in the early 1970s indicated that lack of mathematical preparation in high school seriously limited women's choice of a major in college (Sells, 1978). As a result, there was a proliferation of courses and books on overcoming women's "math anxiety." Camilla Benbow and Julian Stanley have questioned the assumption that the sex differences in mathematical knowledge are merely a matter of preparation. They attribute the superior performance of boys on the College Board's Scholastic Aptitude Test (SAT) for mathematics to "superior male mathematical ability," an inborn talent. Not surprisingly, Benbow and Stanley's findings have drawn a great deal of criticism from scholars such as Jacqueline Eccles and her associates, who charge that they fail to consider other factors that might better explain the differences in test scores (question 10).

Another question that has received a considerable amount of recent attention from social scientists as well as from the public at large is whether mothers of young children should work outside the home. The popular view that mothers should stay home was reinforced by the early research of Spitz (1946) and Bowlby (1951) on the adverse effects of repeated separations of infants and mothers.

In the 1970s, the number of working mothers increased, which sparked reconsideration of the effect this would have on their children. Nevertheless, as the two articles by Burton White and Joanne Curry O'Connell demonstrate, there is still considerable disagreement over how much parenting infants need. Moreover, since it is still the norm for fathers to remain in the workforce, the question of homecare versus daycare is a major issue for many mothers of small children (question 11).

The topic of abortion on demand is an even more highly charged issue (Nadelson, 1978). Several studies prior to the legalization of abortion in 1973 concluded that there were serious psychological consequences for women who had abortions. However, research since the liberalization of the abortion laws, such as that of Joy Osofsky and Howard Osofsky, has consistently reported that the psychological aftereffects are negligible. Nevertheless, there is some concern that minimizing the negative effects of abortion overlooks the needs of the small number of women who do experience difficulties. The issue is obviously fraught with political implications. Pro-choice social scientists and clinicians, such as Karen Lodl, Ann McGerttigan, and Janette Bucy, fear that by raising this issue they may provide anti-abortion forces with additional ammunition in the battle. Within the field, the debate revolves around the question of how many women need help after the abortion and what kind of help they require (question 12).

The 1970s also brought new insights into lesbianism. Prior to the late 1960s, most mental health professionals labeled lesbianism as a developmental disorder for which heterosexuality was the cure. Recognizing the methodological weaknesses of the early research on this subject and responding to the changing social climate, the American Psychiatric Association voted in 1973 that "homosexuality per se" should no longer be viewed as a "psychiatric disorder" in its official guide to mental disorders.

It is, of course, one thing to remove a particular mental disorder from a diagnostic manual and another thing to change the attitude of therapists. Although a majority of therapists, such as Nanette Gartrell, agree with the position of the American Psychiatric Association, there are still some, such as Charles Socarides, who regard lesbianism as pathological (question 13).

The changing political and social climate of the past two decades has also led to changing views on the effects of pornography. Early research on the effects of explicit erotic stimuli on behavior was limited (Byrne & Kelley, 1984, p. 1). In 1970 the President's Commission on Obscenity and Pornography concluded that there was no evidence that exposure to or use of explicit sexual materials is harmful in any significant way (Barnes, 1970). The growth of the women's movement has led to renewed attention on the subject of pornography and its relationship to the sexual abuse of women. Since the early 1970s, a steady stream of research has tested the connection between pornography and sexual aggression.

Although the 1986 Report of the Attorney General's Commission on Pornography states that there is a causal link between pornography and both the degradation of women and aggressive behavior toward women, there is widespread disagreement on the topic among behavioral scientists. Richard Green's testimony before the Attorney General's Commission rejected any direct causal relationship between pornography and sexual crimes. Neil Malamuth, however, believes there is value in pursuing the investigation of indirect effects of pornography on human behavior (question 14).

There are, of course, more than two sides to all of these questions. I hope, however, that the debate format provides some sense of the complexity of these issues. In some cases, both points of view will appear unsatisfactory. This might be the most beneficial result of this approach. As historian C. Vann Woodward (1986) has pointed out, "Questions have to be asked before they can be even wrongly answered. Answers have to be ventured even before we are sure that they are addressed to the right questions. Errors have to be made before they can be corrected and contrary answers provoked. All of which leads to controversy, to be sure; but controversy is

one of the ways we have of arriving at what we assign the dignity of truth" *13*
(p. 33).

References

Adelman, P. K. (Ed.) (1986). Meta-analysis bibliography for study of multiple role literature. Unpublished manuscript.

Amaro, H. (Ed.) (1986). *Bibliographical guide to research materials on Hispanic women in psychology: American Psychological Association, division 35 project.* (Available from Hortensia Amaro, Ph.D., Dept. of Pediatrics, Boston University School of Medicine, Boston, Mass. 02118).

Barnes, C. (1970). Introduction. *The report of the commission on obscenity and pornography.* New York: Bantam Books, 1970.

Bowlby, J. (1951). *Maternal Care and Mental Health.* New York: Schocken Books, 1966.

Brodsky, A. M., & Hare-Mustin, R. T. (Eds.) (1980). *Women and psychotherapy: An assessment of research and practice.* New York: Guilford Press.

Byrne, D., & Kelley, K. (1984). Pornography and sex research. In N. Malamuth & E. Donnerstein (Eds.), *Pornography and sexual aggression.* Orlando, Fla.: Academic Press.

Chesler, P. (1972). *Women and madness.* Garden City, N.Y.: Doubleday.

Chodorow, N. (1978). *The reproduction of mothering.* Berkeley: University of California Press.

Deaux, K. (1984). From individual differences to social categories: analysis of a decade's research on gender. *American Psychologist, 39* (2), 105–16.

Deaux, K. (1985). Sex and gender. *Annual Review of Psychology, 36,* 49–81.

Denmark, F. L. (1977). The psychology of women: An overview of an emerging field. *Personality and Social Psychology Bulletin, 3,* 356–67.

Deutsch, C. (1986). Gender discrimination as an intergroup issue: Comment on Capshew and Laszlo, *Journal of Social Issues, 42* (1), 181–84.

Dilling, C., & Claster, B. L. (Eds.) (1985). *Female psychology: A partially annotated bibliography.* New York: New York Coalition for Women's Mental Health.

Donovan, J. (1985). *Feminist theory.* New York: Frederick Ungar.

Fliegel, Z. O. (1986). Women's development in analytic theory. In J. L. Alpert (Ed.), *Psychoanalysis and women: Contemporary reappraisals.* New York: Lawrence Erlbaum, Analytic Press.

Freud, S. (1925). Some psychological consequences of the anatomical distinction between the sexes. *Standard Edition, 19,* (pp. 248–58). London: Hogarth Press, 1961.

Froberg, D., Gjerdingen, D., & Preston, M. (1986). Multiple roles and women's mental and physical health: What have we learned? *Women and Health, 11* (2), 79–96.

Furumoto, L. (1987). Shared knowledge: The Experimentalists: 1904–1929. In J. G. Morawski (Ed.), Exploring inner space: The rise of experimentation in American psychology. Unpublished manuscript.

Furumoto, L. (in press). On the margins: women and the professionalization of psychology in the United States, 1890–1940. In M. G. Ash and W. R. Woodward (Eds.), *Psychology in twentieth-century thought and society.* New York: Cambridge University Press.

Gilligan, C. (1982). *In a different voice: psychological theory and women's development.* Cambridge: Harvard University Press.

Golub, S., & Freedman, R. (Eds.) (1987). *Psychology of women: Resources for a core curriculum.* New York: Garland.

14 Greer, G. (1971). *The female eunuch.* New York: McGraw-Hill.

Henley, N. (1974). Resources for the study of psychology and women. *R. T.: Journal of Radical Therapy, 4,* 20–21.

Henley, N. (1985). Psychology and gender. *Signs: Journal of Women in Culture and Society, 11*(1), 101–19.

Hollingworth, L. S. (1914a). Variability related to sex differences in achievement. *American Journal of Sociology, 19,* 510–30.

Hollingworth, L. S. (1914b). Functional periodicity: An experimental study of the mental and motor abilities of women during menstruation. *College Contributions to Education, 69.* New York: Teacher's College, Columbia University.

Hollingworth, L. S. (1916). Social devices for impelling women to bear and rear children. *American Journal of Sociology, 22,* 19–29.

Horney, K. (1926). The flight from womanhood. In H. Kelman (Ed.), *Feminine psychology.* New York: Norton, 1967.

Hyde, J. (1985). *Half the human experience: The psychology of women* (3d ed.). Lexington, Mass.: D. C. Heath.

Lewis, H. B. (1976). *Psychic war in men and women.* New York: New York University Press.

Lewis, H. B. (1986). Is Freud an enemy of women's liberation? In T. Bernay & D. W. Cantor (Eds.), *The psychology of today's woman: New psychoanalytic visions.* New York: Lawrence Erlbaum, Analytic Press.

Lott, B. (1985). The potential enrichment of social/personality psychology through feminist research and vice versa. *American Psychologist, 40* (2), 155–64.

Lott, B. (1987). *The psychology of women.* Monterey, Calif.: Brooks/Cole.

Lykes, B. & Stewart, A. (1986). Evaluating the feminist challenge to research in personality and social psychology: 1963–1983. *Psychology of Women Quarterly.*

Maccoby, E. E. & Jacklin, C. N. (1974). *The psychology of sex differences.* Stanford: Stanford University Press.

Matlin, M. (1987). *The psychology of women.* New York: Holt.

Mays, V. (In press). *Bibliographic guide to research materials on black women in the social sciences and mental health.* New York: Praeger.

McHugh, M., Koeske, R., & Frieze, I. H. (1986). Issues to consider in conducting nonsexist psychological research: A guide for researchers. *American Psychologist, 41* (8), 879–90.

McCrea, F. B. (1983). The politics of menopause: The "discovery" of a deficiency disease, *Social Problems, 31,* 111–23.

Mednick, M. T. S. (1978). Now we are four: What should we be when we grow up? *Psychology of Women Quarterly, 3* (2), 123–38.

Miller, J. B. (Ed.) (1973). *Psychoanalysis and women.* New York: Penguin Books.

Mitchell, J. (1974). *Psychoanalysis and feminism.* New York: Random House.

Nadelson, C. C. (1978). The emotional impact of abortion. In M. T. Notman & C. C. Nadelson (Eds.), *The woman patient: Medical and psychological interfaces.* New York: Plenum Press.

Osofsky, J. D., & Osofsky, H. (1972). The psychological reaction of patients to legalized abortion. *American Journal of Orthopsychiatry, 42* (1), 48–61.

Parlee, M. B. (1975). Review essay: Psychology. *Signs: Journal of Women in Culture and Society, 1* (1), 119–58.

Rosenberg, R. (1982). *Beyond separate spheres: Intellectual roots of modern feminism.* New Haven: Yale University Press.

Russo, N. F. (Ed.) (1979). The motherhood mandate. (Special issue.) *Psychology of Women Quarterly, 4* (1).

Scarborough, E., & Furumoto, L. (1987). *Untold lives: The first generation of American women psychologists.* New York: Columbia University Press.

Sells, L. (1978). Mathematics—a critical filter, *The Science Teacher, 45* (2), 28–29.

Shields, S. A. (1975). Ms. Pilgrim's progress: the contributions of Leta Stetter Hollingworth to the psychology of women. *American Psychologist, 30,* 852–57.

Spitz, R. (1945). Hospitalism: An inquiry into the genesis of psychiatric conditions in early childhood. *The Psychoanalytic Study of the Child, Vol. 1.* New York: International Universities Press.

Stacey, J. & Thorne, B. (1985). The missing feminist revolution in sociology. *Social Problems, 32* (4), 301–16.

Strouse, J. (Ed.) (1974). *Women and analysis: Dialogues on psychoanalytic views of femininity.* New York: Dell.

Thompson, H. *See* [Woolley], H. T.

Walsh, M. R. (1985a). The psychology of women course: A continuing catalyst for change. *Teaching of Psychology, 12* (4), 198–203.

Walsh, M. R. (1985b). The psychology of women course and clinical psychology. *The Clinical Psychology of Women, 1* (2), 4–7.

Walsh, M. R. (1985c). Academic professional women organizing for change: The struggle in psychology. *Journal of Social Issues, 41* (4), 17–28.

Weissman, M. (1979). The myth of involutional melancholia. *Journal of American Medical Association, 242* (8), 742–744.

Weisstein, N. (1968, October). "Kinder, Küche, Kirche" as scientific law: Psychology constructs the female. Paper presented at the American Studies Association Meeting, University of California, Davis. Reprinted in R. Morgan, (Ed.), *Sisterhood is powerful: An anthology of writings from the women's liberation movement,* 1970, (pp. 205–20). New York: Vintage Books.

Westkott, M. (1986). The feminist legacy of Karen Horney. New Haven: Yale University Press.

Williams, J. H. (1987). *Psychology of women: Behavior in a biosocial context* (3d ed.). New York: Norton.

Woodward, C. Vann (1986, February 3). Between Little Rock and a hard place. *New Republic,* 29–33.

Woolf, V. (1929). *A room of one's own.* New York: Harcourt, Brace, & World, 1957.

[Woolley], H. T. (1903). *The mental traits of sex: An experimental investigation of the normal mind in men and women.* Chicago: University of Chicago Press.

PART I

Psychoanalytic Theory and the Psychology of Women

Question 1

Is Psychoanalytic Theory Relevant to
the Psychology of Women?

It is safe to say that no theorist has been the target of more feminist criticism than Sigmund Freud. Josephine Donovan (1985) recently remarked that what Betty Friedan called the "feminine mystique" could just as easily be called the "Freudian mystique" (p. 105). In fact, feminist criticism of Freud began long before the rebirth of feminism in the 1960s, dating back to the early twentieth century, when Charlotte Perkins Gilman dismissed his work as a revival of "phallic worship" (Donovan, p. 101).

The first major critique of Freud's theory of female psychology came to light in the mid-1920s when Karen Horney, one of Freud's early disciples, charged that his ideas about women grew out of masculine narcissism. In rejecting his view that penis envy played a critical role in female development, Horney turned Freudian theory on its head with her notion that some men were jealous of the reproductive capacity of women—in other words, that they suffered from womb envy (Horney, 1926/1967).

In a similar vein, Clara Thompson declared that so-called penis envy simply reflected the greater prestige and power of men in our society. If women envied the penis, it was an understandable reaction to men's superior position. Thompson went on to note that if we lived in a matriarchal society, the breast, not the penis, might be the symbol of power (Thompson, 1964).

In a discussion of the Freud-Horney controversy, Zenia Odes Fliegel (1973) suggests that diagnosis of Freud's cancer in the period 1925–33, when he wrote his essays on female development, in combination with the polemical nature of the debates within the psychoanalytic movement of the time made Freud more doctrinaire on this topic than he might have been under different conditions. In any case, in 1941, both Horney and Thomp-

20 son experienced the usual punishment for apostates—excommunication—in this instance, from the New York Psychoanalytic Institute, the mother church of American Freudianism.

The rebirth of feminism in the late 1960s appeared to bring a consensus among feminist writers and psychologists that psychoanalysis was a means of social control and dangerous to women's mental health. Nevertheless, this initial rejection of Freudian theory was reconsidered by some feminist psychologists.

In 1974, for example, Juliet Mitchell attempted to build a bridge between psychoanalysis and feminism, arguing that Freud's theories had an important descriptive power, explaining male and female development within a patriarchal society. Twelve years later, Helen Block Lewis (1986) concluded that "feminist themes have always been intrinsic in Freud's work" (p. 30). Janet Sayers (1986) has taken Lewis' observation one step further; she contends that psychoanalysis is a necessary building block for feminism's focus on social change. She sees Freud's work as uniquely suited to the task of energizing women to move beyond their social subordination.

Can the psychoanalytic view of female development, as Shahla Chehrazi describes it, be revised into a new framework for the psychology of women? Or is Hannah Lerman correct when she states that women cannot benefit from any attempt to revive a theory that is "fundamentally flawed"?

References

Donovan, J. (1985). *Feminist theory*. New York: Ungar.

Fliegel, Z. O. (1973). Feminine psychosexual development in Freudian theory: A historical reconstruction. *Psychoanalytic Quarterly, 42* (3), 385–407.

Horney, K. (1967). The flight from womanhood. In H. Kelman (Ed.), *Feminine Psychology*. New York: W. W. Norton. (Original work published 1926)

Lewis, H. (1986). Is Freud an enemy of women's liberation? Some historical considerations. In T. Bernay and D. W. Cantor (Eds.), *The psychology of today's woman* (pp. 7–35). New York: Erlbaum, Analytic Press.

Mitchell, J. (1974). *Psychoanalysis and feminism*. New York: Random House.

Sayers, J. (1986). *Sexual contradictions: Psychology, psychoanalysis, and feminism*. London: Tavistock.

Thompson, C. (1964). Penis envy. In M. Green (Ed.), *On women* (pp. 73–78). New York: Basic Books.

Additional Reading

Alpert, J. L. (Ed.) (1986). *Psychoanalysis and women: Contemporary reappraisals*. New York: Erlbaum, Analytic Press.

Eisenstein, H. (1983). *Contemporary feminist thought.* Boston: G. K. Hall.

Fliegel, Z. O. (1982). Half a century later: the current status of Freud's controversial views on women. *Psychoanalytic Review, 69,* 7–28.

Mitchell, J. (1984). *Women: The longest revolution.* New York: Pantheon Books.

Notman, M. T., Zilbach, J. J., Baker-Miller, J., & Nadelson, C. C., (1986). Themes in psychoanalytic understanding of women: Some reconsiderations of autonomy and affiliation. *Journal of the American Academy of Psychoanalysis, 14* (2), 241–53.

Person, E. S. & Ovesey, L., (1983). Psychoanalytic theories of gender identity. *Journal of the American Academy of Psychoanalysis, 11* (2), 203–26.

Person, E. S. (1983). The influence of values in psychoanalysis: The case of female psychology. *Psychoanalytic Inquiry, 3* (4), 623–46.

Sayers, J. (1982). Freud and feminism. In *Biological politics: Feminist and anti-feminist perspectives* (pp. 125–46). New York: Methuen.

Yes

Female Psychology: A Review

SHAHLA CHEHRAZI

Over the past twenty years, research studies and substantial clinical material have provided new information regarding female psychology and development. The recent findings have significant implications for psychoanalytic treatment of women and often lead to a different outcome in the clinical situation. However (in spite of recent suggested revisions regarding the theory of female development), it is my impression from seminars and clinical conferences that our diagnostic formulations and dynamic conceptualizations remain more or less the same.

This apparent lag between our knowledge of female psychosexual development and its clinical application might be due in part to the lack of a revised theoretical framework. If the various suggested revisions are put together in a systematic manner and integrated with our earlier views, then they might offer a preliminary, updated, and revised theoretical framework.

Understandably, there is strong resistance to any revision of our theory, a problem that seems inherent in our field. I see this not as specific to female psychology, but to all theoretical revisions in psychoanalysis. Freud himself repeatedly stated that his ideas regarding female psychology were incomplete and required further investigation. However, in spite of his caution, the early theory became solidified. If we push aside all the recent contributions and suggested revisions of the theory of female psychology, as either insignificant or political (Lampl-de Groot, 1982), we are not adhering to an objective scientific position. The issue is not that Freud valued and respected women, but that, in spite of his genius and invaluable contributions, he did not have enough information regarding early preoedipal development in girls, something that he pointed out himself

"Female Psychology" by Shahla Chehrazi, *Journal of the American Psychoanalytic Association*, 1986, *34* (1), 111–162. Copyright 1986 by the International Universities Press, Inc. Reprinted by permission.

Dr. Chehrazi is a psychiatrist and Assistant Clinical Professor, Department of Psychiatry, University of California, San Francisco.

(1933). The sociocultural attitudes and the phallocentric orientation that prevailed during Freud's time contributed to his theory of female psychology. The issue, however strong the possibilities for politicizing it are, is essentially a clinical one. That is, we seem to arrive at very different clinical formulations and conceptualizations depending on which views we adhere to. As a result, the outcome of psychoanalytic treatment of women can differ markedly (Grossman & Stewart, 1976).

One example is the clinical management of penis envy, which remains a controversial and ambiguous issue. In the context of the current or revised views, penis envy is clinically regarded as a complex and symptomatic attitude in women, which not only serves multiple defensive functions but is also a reflection of particular versions of self- and object representation. In the early views, penis envy is considered a basic concept that is not susceptible to further analysis. This oversimplified and reductionistic interpretation of penis envy in the analysis of women often leads to a lowering of their self-esteem and an intensification of the neurotic image of themselves as deficient and damaged (Lerner, 1980; Karme, 1981).

In this paper I shall examine the inconsistencies and differences between the early psychoanalytic views of female development and the recent ones. In addition, I shall discuss the clinical implications of the recent views or suggested revisions.

Beginning developmentally, there is now research that confirms early preoedipal genital awareness in little girls (Galenson & Roiphe, 1971; Kleeman, 1976). This observation was already offered by Horney (1924, 1926, 1932), Jones (1935), Greenacre (1950), Harley (1961), and Chasseguet-Smirgel (1976).

Kleeman (1971, 1976) and others report their observation that the little girl discovers her external genitalia and her vagina some time before the age of two. This discovery is part of her body exploration and follows discovery and recognition of other body parts, such as eyes, nose, fingers, etc. The assumption is made that mental representation of genitals, even though incompletely defined at this stage of development, becomes integrated into the little girl's body image. Genital play during the first two years of life appears to be in the service of body schematization and the formation of body image, and is differentiated from masturbation (which requires associated fantasies, and at this early age we have as yet no evidence of them).

The little girl's awareness and understanding of her genitals between the ages of two and four is vague and incomplete. This is so because of lack of the visual modality, cognitive immaturity, and inability to fully comprehend the complexity of her internal and external organs. As a result, the girl's mental representation of her genitals at an early age (2–3) is less well

24 established than a boy's at the same age, whose visible and protuberant genitals lead to a clearer mental representation (Lerner, 1976). However, no matter how vague and incompletely defined the little girl's mental representation might be, it seems to reflect her awareness that she has "something there." That "something" is pleasurable and will later, under optimal conditions, become cathected and highly valued.

This early vaginal awareness during the preoedipal years, from fifteen months on, seems to contradict the earlier notion that vaginal awareness is absent in girls until the time of puberty (Freud, 1933). Furthermore, recent work suggests that early genital awareness is accompanied by an early or primary sense of femaleness. A variety of factors converge to establish the little girl's early sense of femaleness: Money and Ehrhardt (1972) emphasize the genetic, hormonal, central nervous system patterning and anatomical-physiological factors, while Kleeman (1971) emphasizes cognitive maturity, learning experiences, and verbal and nonverbal modes of communication with significant adults and other children. Stoller's work (1968, 1976), however, integrates both views and offers the concept of core gender identity, an early (preoedipal) sense of femaleness or maleness that is established by age two or three.

As Freud pointed out, the observation of anatomical differences remains a significant event for children of both sexes and usually occurs between the ages of eighteen and twenty-four months. Observation of anatomical differences in little girls can provoke a penis envy reaction which has been described by Galenson and Roiphe (1976), Mahler (1966), and others. This penis envy is experienced as a narcissistic injury and as "wanting something the little girl sees she does not have." According to early psychoanalytic views, the little girl seldom recovers from this narcissistic injury, and her subsequent female development always remains secondary to penis envy (Freud, 1925). By contrast, penis envy in the context of the recent views is considered a phase-specific developmental phenomenon.

To put it differently, the early theory emphasized what the little girl does not have rather than what she indeed has (Chasseguet-Smirgel, 1976). If, however, we reverse our focus, then it becomes evident that penis envy reaction may be a phase-specific reaction, since the little girl will soon come to value what she herself has and relinquish the envy of what she does not have. Within this framework one could suggest a reemergence and reworking of penis envy at each developmental stage.

To appreciate the differing views we need to pay attention to the context in which the observation of anatomical differences occurs. Early views hypothesize that because the little girl sees herself as a little boy she is traumatized when she begins to observe her anatomical differences. Cur-

rent views do not underestimate the trauma of observation of an
differences and penis envy, but they do suggest that at the ti
occurrence the little girl already sees herself as a girl and has sor
ness of her femaleness and her genitals. Her wish to have a penis,
does not necessarily imply that she wants to be a boy, but that she wants the
penis in addition to the vagina and clitoris she already has. (Later, I shall
refer to the ubiquitous wish for having both male and female genitals,
which occurs not only in little boys and girls, but may be present in adults
as well.)

The reworking of the penis envy reaction is aided by the little girl's
cognitive growth and her full awareness and appreciation of her external
and internal genitalia. Following the libidinal cathexis of her own complex
genitalia and its purported child-bearing capacity, the little girl comes to
value what she has, which gradually diminishes her envy of the penis she
does not have. It may be that the concomitant deidealization of the penis is
also necessary as part of the process of partial or complete mastery and
resolution of penis envy. We are familiar with how idealization is an
essential part of the envy. There are not only numerous references to this in
the literature (Torok, 1970), but it is also a common clinical phenomenon
in the psychoanalytic treatment of women. The idealization of men and the
relation between their superior "capabilities" and their having a penis is
often readily brought up by women patients. Needless to say, attention to
the defensive function of this idealization is necessary.

The current views differ from early views in yet another aspect: the later
views emphasize the little girl's (or the adult woman patient's) fantasy of
being damaged or defective, while the early views tend to focus on the
acceptance of her defectiveness or her position of inferiority. Silverman
(1981) suggests:

Major narcissistic injuries including humiliating oedipal defeats and disap-
pointments can become interwoven with the early *fantasy* of genital inferiority.
When the latter remains uncorrected, it persists as an emotionally charged illusion
that is thereafter embroiled in intense narcissistic and sexual conflicts. If parents
and other significant adults express and live out their lives in accordance with
societal attitudes that portray women as inferior, second-rate, or of secondary
importance, this too will tend to reinforce and fixate the little girl's *fantasy* of
genital inferiority. (Pp. 594–95; italics added)

The erroneous fantasy of being damaged or defective needs reworking and
correction during subsequent development or in the course of psychoanalytic treatment. Even though this distinction between fact and fantasy
might seem obvious or even unnecessary, it has significant technical and

26 clinical implications. Furthermore, in the early literature, there are references to the "fact" of genital inferiority in women (Freud, 1925). I am certain that Freud did not consider women inferior; however, in reading some of his early writings the reader can be easily impressed with this mistaken notion.

The current views pay special attention to environmental factors. For example, the prevailing notion is that the little girl will value her own genitals and her femininity only if the parental attitude (conscious and unconscious) supports this development. Furthermore, it has been noted that girls who grow up in the context of a culture where women are devalued rarely value their bodies or develop a sense of pride in their femininity. We also need to raise the question of whether and how the past ten years of important sociocultural changes have influenced the dynamics of the little girl's development.

Summarizing the recent contributions, if we view penis envy in a developmental context (Settlage, 1971), we might hypothesize a gradual process of reworking of penis envy during the course of normal development. This process begins between the ages of three and six and continues during subsequent development. The factors that assist the reworking or attempted resolution of penis envy are: good enough relationship with the mother; awareness and appreciation of one's genitals; further cognitive development, which aids comprehension of the complex inner and outer genitals; and, most important, the resolutions of oedipal conflict, and identification with the mother.

Thus, according to the current views, the real question is what can go awry in the development of the little girl to cause failure of mastery and resolution of penis envy, which then results in regression to pathological traits or symptom formation. Even when there is a partial resolution of penis envy reaction, it still tends to reemerge at each subsequent developmental stage. This reemergence needs to be understood in terms of the various defensive functions that it serves. The reworking of penis envy provides the little girl with an opportunity for further negotiation and resolution of the penis envy reaction. Under optimal conditions this would foster further development of a stable sense of her gender. The female developmental line is enriched by two additional developmental events which act as organizers of development: menarche and pregnancy. Both enhance and promote female development at the same time that they can trigger regressive trends contributing to defensive and regressive constellations. However, the emphasis here is on normal development, a more or less normal female developmental line, which can lead to a healthy adult female identity.

Besides the controversy surrounding penis envy, our current knowledge also contradicts the previous notion that regards the clitoris as a "truncated penis," and that insists the little girl has to give up her "masculine clitoris" and masturbatory activities as a prerequisite to feminine development. Earlier Bornstein (1953) and more recently Fraiberg (1972) and Clower (1976) showed that girls continue to masturbate during latency and that the clitoris is an integral part of the female genitals and the adult woman's sexuality.

Recent studies also question a number of other notions, such as entry into the oedipal phase as triggered by penis envy, automatic equation of baby with penis, and the onset and nature of the little girl's relationship with her father. The entry into the oedipal phase was formerly thought to be a secondary formation preceded by the castration complex. This was considered a reaction to the trauma of penis envy; within the context of an ambivalent and rivalrous relationship to the mother, the little girl turns to her father in the hope of getting the penis (penis-baby) she lacks. Research by Parens and his co-workers (1976) suggests a reformulation of the girl's entry into the oedipal phase. They observed variable pathways by which girls enter the oedipal phase—not necessarily the castration complex. A psychobiological gender-related force is considered to be the primary factor characterizing entry into the oedipal phase.

Current views reject a reductionistic equation of the wish for a baby with the wish for a penis. The wish for the baby can be seen prior to the penis envy reaction and is often an expression of identification with the mother as well as an inborn gender characteristic. This was initially pointed out by Jacobson (1950), later by Kestenberg (1956), and more recently by Parens et al. (1976). The original preoedipal pregnancy wishes may gradually transform and relate to fantasies about the father in the oedipal stage. Therefore the baby-penis equation observed in the analysis of adult women is already a secondary formation. We also know more regarding the little girl's preoedipal relationship to her father. Her turning to her father as a significant other at the age of eight to eighteen months, preceding the oedipal stage, seems to contradict the earlier notion that her turning to the father is only secondary to penis envy (Abelin, 1971).

Finally, the notion of the defective structure of superego in women has been critically examined by Schafer (1974), Blum (1976), Applegarth (1976), and others. Applegarth (1976) states, "Freud may have failed to distinguish clearly enough between superego content and the basic superego structure or function." She adds, "Women often seem to have as a superego content the value that they should be responsive to the wishes and opinions of others. Such a value system will certainly result in behavior that

28   will at first glance appear to reflect, as Freud says, a less inexorable, independent superego. Furthermore, the areas that men and women regard as matters for the superego may vary somewhat" (p. 264).

We now know that girls can develop strong superegos based on preoedipal precursors and the oedipal anxiety secondary to oedipal wishes, fears, and guilt. Genital anxiety—the wish for penetration by the paternal penis along with the fear of genital and bodily injury—also plays a significant part in the repression and resolution of oedipal conflict and the subsequent development of superego. In brief, the development of the structure of the superego and the factors contributing to its structure formation are similar in boys and girls, while the content of the superego is different. As Schafer (1974) pointed out, it is not that women's superego is inferior or that men's superego is superior, but that they are different. Furthermore, the moral values and ego ideals are often different in men and women (Gilligan, 1982). On the basis of her research study, Gilligan suggests that women impose a distinctive construction on moral problems, seeing moral dilemmas in terms of conflicting responsibilities: "In women a more complex understanding of the relationship between self and others represents a critical reinterpretation of the moral conflict between selfishness and responsibility" (p. 515). She criticizes Kohlberg's stages of moral development for presenting a single configuration (the responses of adolescent males to hypothetical dilemmas of conflicting rights) as the basis for a universal stage sequence. She then attempts to illustrate an inherently feminine value system, independent of and different from, but not inferior to, the masculine value system. Here I have emphasized only the distinction between superego structure and its contents; a discussion of the complex processes of superego development is beyond the scope of this paper.

The following list summarizes the differences between early theory and current views.

Early Psychoanalytic Views	*Current Psychoanalytic Views*
1. Absence of vaginal awareness until puberty.	1. Vaginal awareness between 14 and 24 months.
2. Absence of gender identity and assumption that the little girl sees herself as a little boy.	2. Core gender identity formation contributes to sense of femaleness in preoedipal years.
3. Observation of anatomical differences results in penis envy.	3. Observation of anatomical differences results in penis envy reaction.

4. Penis envy and castration complex as bedrock phenomena in female development.

4. Penis envy as a developmental phenomenon in females invites re-working and resolution during subsequent stages of development.

5. Entry into oedipal phase as reaction to castration complex.

5. Entry into oedipal phase as innately feminine process.

6. Wish for baby is a substitute for penis envy.

6. Wish for the baby is not *necessarily* a substitute for penis envy. Wish for baby is observed preoedipally as part of identification with mother.

7. Lack of castration anxiety leads to faulty and defective superego development.

7. Adequate superego development, apparently similar in structure but different in content.

8. Woman can seldom overcome "fact of her castration" and remains envious of superior genital of men.

8. Girl's penis envy reemerges during each subsequent stage of development and is reworked in context of recognition and appreciation of her complex inner and outer genital—recognizing what she has is different, yet valuable.

9. Penis envy and castration complex, observed commonly in women, are often intractable to analytic treatment.

9. Penis envy is result of faulty development due either to lack of resolution of early penis envy with excessive vulnerability to narcissistic injuries, or regression from the oedipal conflict. Analytic treatment often can help correct neurotic distortions regarding body image, sense of femininity, and self-esteem.

In the following section I shall demonstrate the clinical application of the current views. Cases 1 and 2 reflect the defensive functions of penis envy and its management in the clinical situation. Case 3 illustrates the male child's wish for a baby. The wish for a baby in boys, a possible counterpart to the wish for the penis in girls, has received very little attention in the literature (Jacobson, 1950).

Clinical Material

Case I

L., aged two, stood in the middle of my consulting room in the second hour of consultation, pulling her dress up and referring to her umbilicus as 29

30   "broken." Severe separation anxiety and excessive temper tantrums were the reason L.'s mother consulted me. L., a bright and verbally precocious child, was also responding to her parents' divorce six months earlier. Through a joint custody arrangement, the father continued to be very available to L. In her play, she was intrigued by broken crayons. She would take them to me and say "fix it." Another repetitive game was undoing her shoelaces and turning to her mother and me, saying "fix it." It seemed clear that L. had experienced her lack of penis as a punishment and persistently hoped for reparation. I interpreted to L. that she thought she had a penis and that it was broken because she had done something wrong. Needless to say, the father's absence in spite of biweekly visits only intensified L.'s early penis envy reaction and dovetailed with her feeling that she had done something wrong. We explored L.'s fantasy that if her body could be fixed, her parents' problems could also be fixed, and Daddy would come home. In other words, penis envy was also used to defend against separation anxiety. I also had to help L.'s young feminist mother gain an understanding of how L. was experiencing her not having a penis. Within two months L.'s repetitive "fix it" play diminished and ceased. It was then replaced by hide-and-seek games and its various derivatives. L's treatment was terminated after six months due to her mother's geographical move. On a follow-up visit three years later, L. was progressing developmentally and continued to be intellectually advanced for her age. In her play and fantasy material there was no evidence of any residue of penis envy. L.'s further cognitive development had aided her in the recognition that "good things can come in small boxes."

Case 2

Miss M., a twenty-nine-year-old woman, entered analysis for depression and what she called "failure to succeed." She was the oldest of three children raised in a rural area of the East Coast. In school, even though she did not apply herself for fear that if she were too smart she would become unpopular, her performance was above average, and she graduated with a degree in English literature. An attractive and intelligent woman, Miss M. presented herself as highly motivated and worked hard at being a "good patient." She was unhappy about her job but felt she could not do anything about it. She worked as an insurance clerk, a job clearly beneath her intellectual abilities. Two years before seeking treatment she was promoted to a managerial position, but she had "messed up" so much that she was later demoted. Feeling "stuck" at her current job, she was struggling to find a more satisfying and stimulating career for herself.

Derivatives of castration complex and penis envy were evident from the beginning of the analysis. Her brother, B., only one year her junior, appeared early in the analysis with numerous examples of how he was treated more favorably by their mother. She recalled how she got a "second-hand bicycle" for her sixth birthday, while her brother got a "shiny and new bicycle." This significant memory and its derivatives seemed to represent Miss M.'s image of herself as "second-hand" and inferior to her brother and men. Her image of herself as second-hand was also expressed in the transference. Since she was a low-fee case, she felt inferior to my other patients. I interpreted her fantasy that I saw her as second-hand, not only because of her fee but because of her other deficiencies. She complained bitterly about her mother's lack of interest in any intellectual pursuit on her part, yet she encouraged her brother to become a scientist. In exploring her anger and envy toward her brother, I interpreted Miss M.'s idealization of men in general. It was not only her mother who thought her brother had superior capabilities compared to her, but Miss M.'s perception was indeed identical to her mother's or, more correctly, to the way the patient perceived her mother. We then addressed Miss M.'s relationship to her boss and how her sexual affair with him (a married man) was partly intended to make up for her perceived "incompetence and inadequacy." In fact, she was highly competent at her work and often did more than her share.

Miss M.'s aggression toward men was disguised by the masochistic stance of seeing herself as oppressed and victimized. It took a couple of years before analysis of her promiscuous sexual behavior with men made it possible for her to see her own mistreatment of men. A masturbation fantasy of having intercourse with a man without reaching orgasm and reaching orgasm with his dog while the dog was engaged in oral sex with her revealed her feeling that "men are inferior to dogs" or "even dogs are better than men." However, it soon became clear that her manifest penis envy of her brother and other men was mainly in the service of defending against her own aggression toward men. Technically, rather than interpreting penis envy, I paid attention to its defensive function and interpreted the patient's anger and contempt for men. She was highly resistant to seeing herself as the aggressor and was more interested in acting out her image of herself as the helpless victim. The emergence of numerous dreams and fantasies and tactful analytic work gradually diminished her resistances. As Miss M. became less afraid of her own aggression, she was able to observe the two shifting images of herself as victim and as aggressor.

Toward the end of the second year of analysis, Miss M. decided to go back to school and pursue a career in counseling. At school, she became interested in feminist therapy, a discipline highly critical of analysis. Now

32   she perceived me, the Freudian analyst, as her oppressor and as one who could not appreciate her plight as a woman in a patriarchal society. It soon became clear that her interest in feminist therapy, on top of its obvious rebellious qualities, was a defense against an emerging homosexual transference. This stormy period in the analysis subsided when she became aware of her homosexual fears and fantasies. Now her promiscuous sexual behavior, particularly prior to my vacation and interruptions in treatment, could also be understood in the light of her homosexual anxiety, which was warded off by her acting out of her defensive heterosexuality. In brief, I persistently interpreted the various defensive and regressive meanings and functions of penis envy whenever it emerged in the analysis and in particular in the transference.

In the fourth year of analysis, unresolved penis envy was evidenced in Miss M.'s unconscious fantasy of having a penis. This was revealed following the exploration of her particular form of masturbation. During latency she would put a pillow between her legs and masturbate with the fantasy that the pillow was a giant penis and she was rocking on it. It was later revealed that her counterphobic, promiscuous sexual behavior as an adult woman was also in part an acting out of this fantasy by being the aggressor during intercourse. This unconscious fantasy was present concurrently with a transference wish for phallic penetration by me. A dream of her getting injections from a doctor reflected this wish.

In the same year, Miss M. purchased a new car, in contrast to her old second-hand car; this provoked a re-emergence of the second-hand bicycle memory. However, at this time the patient was accessible to further analytic work. It became evident that her brother's shiny new bicycle represented mobility, independence, mastery, and finally, his penis. The second-hand bicycle represented her fantasized castrated state. In further exploration of her brother's "superior abilities" I interpreted Miss M.'s unconscious association of penis with capability and competence, what she imagined she lacked in competition with her brother.

Clinically, in addressing the various regressive and defensive meanings of penis envy in women, there is a tendency to overlook genital anxiety. Horney (1926) stated: "Undoubtedly the familiar fantasies that an excessively large penis is effecting forcible penetration, producing pain and haemorrhage and threatening to destroy something, go to show that the little girl bases her oedipus fantasies most realistically (in accordance with the plastic concrete thinking of childhood) on the disproportion in size between father and child" (p. 334). She added, "The female genital anxiety, like the castration-dread of boys, invariably bears the impress of feelings of guilt and it is to them that it owes its lasting influence" (p. 335). I have been repeatedly surprised when my male colleagues overlook genital anxiety in the analysis of women. The fear of injury and damage to one's genitals by a big penis, which is a residue of oedipal stage anxiety, is often confused with castration anxiety in women. Castration anxiety, a problematic term in the psychology of women, refers to the anxiety about losing the fantasized phallus.

A dream presented by Miss M. expressed both genital anxiety and penis envy: She was in a restaurant with her boyfriend. She was told that he had found ten million dollars. On leaving the restaurant, she realized she had lost her purse. Embarrassed, she started looking for it and was aware of feeling how unfair it was that her boyfriend found all that money when she lost her purse. Her association "Men have it a lot better than women," led to her thoughts of her brother, whom she had perceived as her mother's favorite.

Money (ten million dollars) symbolized power and achievement, something she felt she lacked. I added, something she *thought* she had lost—the lost purse in her dream not only represented her lost genitals but the money inside it stood for her fantasized penis. She then noted that, in contrast to the dream, she never uses the word "purse" and always refers to her purse as her pocketbook. She associated that a pocketbook has a firmer structure and often has a zipper or a lock, in contrast to a purse, which has a soft structure with an opening that, at times, cannot be locked. I interpreted that her conscious use of the word "pocketbook" was indeed a reaction to her anxiety about her genitals—an opening she cannot lock. At this point Miss M. recalled some memories reflecting her genital anxiety as an adolescent girl. As an adult woman, her feeling of lack of control over her vaginal opening and genital, of lack of a firm and tangible boundary, was acted out counterphobically in her promiscuous behavior—as if she had no control over her body openings within the context of her sexual relationships.

Another clinical problem is the denial of the significance of penis envy and avoidance of interpretation of its various defensive functions along with exclusive emphasis on the extrapsychic or sociocultural determinants of penis envy.

Case 3

S., four years old, was in the midst of responding to his mother's pregnancy. He played out having babies with his doll with no seeming recognition that he could not have a baby. S.'s mother reported that he takes one of his old dolls to bed and talks to it, calling it his baby. S. had already been confronted with the anatomical sexual differences and was well aware of boys and girls as being different. He had a close and loving relationship with his father, but his mother was clearly his preferred love object. Even

34   though the initial intense separation anxiety that brought him to treatment
had diminished, he continued to be anxious about his mother's whereabouts and at times reacted to her leaving with manifest anxiety. S.'s
vulnerability to separation anxiety was provoked by an abrupt separation
from his mother when she left the country briefly some six months before.

S.'s core gender identity was well established; he saw himself as a boy
and there was evidence of his identification with his father. Yet he maintained that he was going to have a baby like Mommy. His denial was not
only in the service of warding off his feelings of rejection and betrayal by his
mother for preferring his oedipal rival, his father, but was additionally in
the service of his narcissistic needs. Since we are more familiar with the
injury of oedipal defeat or the regressive identification with the mother,
maybe we tend to minimize the impact of the narcissistic injury to the little
boy when he is confronted with the reality that he is not able to have babies
like Mommy. It was indeed an added injury for S. to accept that he could
not do something that Mommy or girls could do. Inability to have babies is
a narcissistic injury for girls as well. We often observe strong feelings of
betrayal and sadness secondary to this oedipal defeat, with renewed interest
in doll play and in playing Mommy. However, it seems plausible that in the
case of the little girl the awareness that she can have babies when she grows
up is comforting to her and might help to diminish the narcissistic injury.

S.'s father had patiently explained to him that he could not have babies
like Mommy. The persistence of the boy's stance that "he can have babies
too" and his play with his doll was somewhat alarming to his father. He
overtly discouraged S.'s doll play, saying, "Boys don't do that," and with
seemingly renewed interest supported his son's masculine identification
and interests. S.'s interest in babies was soon replaced by his new interest in
cowboys. He walked around in his new cowboy boots and hat, imitating
hypermasculine gestures and manners. S. clearly wanted me to admire his
new boots and how he walked in them. S.'s mother reported that he was at
times reluctant to take off his boots at night and always wanted them at his
bedside before going to bed. The weakening of S.'s defensive denial and the
narcissistic injury of recognizing he could not have babies was soon coun-
teracted by the hypercathexis of his masculinity and masculine pursuits. In
this case I had the opportunity to observe the process in a tangible and clear
manner. The hypercathexis of his masculinity represented by his interest in
cowboy boots soon came to replace S.'s loss or narcissistic injury.

We are well aware of the universality of the fantasy of bisexuality in
children (Fast, 1979). It is usually given up prior to entry into the positive
oedipal phase. This is done partly by the hypercathexis of one's own genital
and gender as well as by devaluation of the other sex. We are more familiar

with the little boy's devaluation of his mother and femaleness in this
process and as part of the resolution of the oedipal conflict. Is this partly
because the devaluation of women is a more culturally acceptable attitude?
A similar process occurs during the little girl's development. The relinquishment of fantasies of bisexuality, of having both penis and vagina, and
resolution of penis envy reaction can be facilitated by hypercathexis of her
own genitalia and her femininity. Here I am referring to a model for normal
development. In the clinical situation we often observe a failure of this
process.

The following example might help to clarify further the clinical implications of the current views. I would like to illustrate the contrast between the
two types of interpretation in addressing penis envy in the psychoanalytic
treatment of women. A type I interpretation is based on the view of penis
envy as a primary concept and addresses the patient's wish to acquire a
penis. A type II interpretation views the penis envy as secondary, a defensive structure, and addresses the anxiety inherent in those various defensive
functions. The following vignette is from a case that was presented to a
supervisory seminar. The treating analyst offered a type I interpretation;
my suggestion was type II interpretation.

G. is a twenty-year-old adolescent girl with tomboyish characteristics
and a conscious wish to be a boy. In this particular hour she presents the
analyst with a gift she has made for him. This follows an hour that seemed
particularly meaningful to her, when she indirectly revealed one of her old
symptoms, stealing. In response to her bringing the present, the analyst
makes an interpretation that she is giving him a present with the wish for
reciprocity. Her giving him a present is an expression of the wish to get
something from him; namely, she wishes him to grant her wish to become a
boy or to help her change into a boy. The depressive response to the
analyst's interpretation on the part of the patient is no surprise. Such an
interpretation, after all, not only reinforces the patient's low self-esteem but
inadvertently confirms her neurotic perception that having a penis will
solve her conflicts. Following our discussion of the case in the seminar, the
analyst offered a type II interpretation, such as: G. has many fears and
anxieties about being a girl and somehow finds it safer to wish to be a boy.
Following this interpretation, the patient reveals her fears about wearing
skirts as opposed to pants, and material concerning her anxiety about
menstruation and genital injury emerges.

In conclusion, I would like to say a few words about the terminology we
use to describe female development, which frequently perpetuates some of
the earlier and mistaken notions—for example, reference to the "phallic

36 phase" of the girl's psychosexual development. Phallic phase applied to the development of girls is a reflection of the earlier notion that the little girl has no awareness of her genitals, specifically, her vagina, and that because of the necessity to relinquish her libidinal cathexis of her clitoris, which is masculine in nature, she is left with a feeling that she has nothing. "Phallic phase" ignores our present knowledge and treats the little girl as if she had no genitals, or sees herself as a little boy, while in fact she not only sees herself as a girl and is aware of her vagina, but fantasizes having a penis as well. In other words, she is both vaginal and phallic (Greenacre, 1950). Therefore, it might be more accurate to substitute the term "genital phase" for the so-called "phallic phase" of development in girls (Parens et al., 1976). Although the term "phallic phase" beautifully describes that particular phase of development in boys, it has indeed very little to say regarding normal development in girls. However, because the term "genital phase" is reserved for a later period—namely, adolescence—perhaps a more specific term would be "early genital phase." Glover and Mendell (1982) suggest yet another term, "preoedipal genital phase." During the "preoedipal genital phase" or the "early genital phase," the genitals in both sexes become libidinally cathected and exhibitionistic impulses are observed in both boys and girls. The achievement of the "preoedipal genital phase" in both boys and girls prepares and aids them in their entry into the oedipal phase.

Another term that needs repair in our terminology is "phallic strivings" in reference to women. Abraham (1920) suggested that relinquishment of phallic strivings is a prerequisite for healthy female development. The woman's strivings for mastery, achievement, and competence are at times mistakenly referred to as "phallic strivings." The equation of intellectual strivings with phallic strivings in women is an error, reflecting a neurotic distortion we often observe in our women patients. Obviously, cultural attitudes and stereotypes beyond the scope of our terminology have contributed to these misconceptions. Because of the present ambiguity and confusion associated with the term "phallic strivings" in relation to female development, perhaps more specific terms, such as "intellectual strivings" or "competitive strivings," would be conceptually and clinically more helpful. They also help to clarify that these strivings are not necessarily a defensive reaction to penis envy.

Currently, we need further observation, clarification, and examination of the different developmental lines for men and women, which earlier were thought to be identical. Further research in this area will sharpen our knowledge of differences as well as similarities between the two developmental lines for sexes.

References

Abelin, E. (1971). The role of the father in the separation-individuation process. In *Separation-Individuation*, ed. J. B. McDevitt & C. F. Settlage. New York: Int. Univ. Press, pp. 229–52.

Abraham, K. (1920). Manifestations of the female castration complex. *Selected Papers on Psychoanalysis*. New York: Basic Books, 1971, pp. 338–69.

Applegarth, A. (1976). Some observations on work inhibitions in women. *J. Amer. Psychoanal. Assn.*, 24 (Suppl.):251–68.

Blum, H. P. (1976). Masochism, the ego ideal and the psychology of women. *J. Amer. Psychoanal. Assn.*, 24 (Suppl.):157–92.

Bornstein, B. (1953). Masturbation in the latency period. *Psychoanal. Study Child*, 8:65–78.

Chasseguet-Smirgel, J. (1976). Freud and female sexuality: the consideration of some blind-spots in the exploration of the "dark continent." *Int. J. Psychoanal.*, 57:275–86.

Clower, V. (1976). Theoretical implications of current views on masturbation in latency girls. *J. Amer. Psychoanal. Ass.*, 24 (Suppl.):109–26.

Fast, I. (1979). Developments in gender identity: gender differentiation in girls. *Int. J. Psychoanal.*, 60:443–53.

Fraiberg, S. (1972). Some characteristics of genital arousal and discharge in latency girls. *Psychoanal. Study Child*, 27:439–76.

Freud, S. (1925). Some psychical consequences of the anatomical distinction between the sexes. *S. E.*, 19.

———— (1933). Femininity. *S.E.*, 22.

Galenson, E. & Roiphe, M. (1971). The impact of early sexual discovery on mood, defensive organization, and symbolization. *Psychoanal. Study Child*, 26:195–216.

———— (1976). Some suggested revisions concerning early female development. *J. Amer. Psychoanal. Assn.*, 24 (Suppl.):24–58.

Gilligan, C. (1982). In a Different Voice. Cambridge: Harvard Univ. Press.

Glover, L. & Mendell, D. (1982). A suggested developmental sequence for a preoedipal genital phase. In *Early Female Development—Current Psychoanalytic Views*, ed. D. Mendell. New York: Spectrum, pp. 127–74.

Greenacre, P. (1950). Special problems of early female sexual development. *Psychoanal. Study Child*, 5:122–38.

Grossman, W. & Stewart, W. (1976). Penis envy: from childhood wish to developmental metaphor. *J. Amer. Psychoanal. Assn.*, 24 (Suppl.):93–126.

Harley, M. (1961). Masturbation conflict. In *Adolescents. Psychoanalytic Approach to Problems and Therapy*, ed. L. Schneer. New York: Harper, pp. 51–78.

Horney, K. (1924). On the genesis of the castration complex in women. In *Feminine Psychology*, ed. H. Kelman. New York: Norton, 1967, pp. 37–53.

———— (1926). Flight from womanhood. *Int. J. Psychoanal.*, 7:329–39.

———— (1932). The dread of women. *Int. J. Psychoanal.*, 13:348–60.

Jacobson, E. (1950). Development of the wish for a child in boys. *Psychoanal. Study Child*, 5:139–52.

Jones, E. (1935). Early female sexuality. *Int. J. Psychoanal.*, 16:263–73.

Karme, L. (1981). A clinical report on penis envy: its multiple meanings and defensive functions. *J. Amer. Psychoanal. Assn.*, 29:427–47.

Kestenberg, J. (1956). On the development of maternal feelings in early childhood. *Psychoanal. Study Child*, 11:257–91.

Kleeman, J. A. (1971). The establishment of core gender identity in normal girls. *Arch. Sex. Behav.*, 1:103–29.

38   ———— (1976). Freud's views on early sexuality in the light of direct child observation. *J. Amer. Psychoanal. Assn.*, 24 (Suppl.):3–28.

Lampl-de Groot, J. (1982). Thoughts on psychoanalytic views of female psychology, 1927–1977. *Psychoanal.*, 51:1–18.

Lerner, H. (1976). Parental mislabeling of female genitals as a determinant of penis envy and learning inhibitions in women. *J. Amer. Psychoanal. Assn.*, 24 (Suppl.):269–84.

———— (1980). Penis envy: underlying conceptual issues. *Bull. Menninger Clin.*, 44:39–48.

Mahler, M. S. (1966). Notes on the development of basic moods: the depressive affect. In *Psychoanalysis—A General Psychology*, ed. R. M. Loewenstein, L. Newman, M. Scheur & A. J. Solnit. New York: Int. Univ. Press, pp. 156–68.

Money, J. & Ehrhardt, A. A. (1972). *Man and Woman, Boy and Girl*. Baltimore: Johns Hopkins Univ. Press.

Parens, H., Pollock, L., Stern, J. & Kramer, S. (1976). On the girl's entry into the Oedipus complex. *J. Amer. Psychoanal. Assn.*, 24 (Suppl.):79–108.

Schafer, R. (1974). Problems in Freud's psychology of women. *J. Amer. Psychoanal. Assn.*, 22:459–85.

Settlage, C. (1971). On the libidinal aspect of early psychic development and the genesis of infantile neurosis. In *Separation-Individuation*, ed. J. B. McDevitt & C. F. Settlage. New York: Int. Univ. Press, pp. 131–54.

Silverman, M. (1981). Cognitive development and female psychology. *J. Amer. Psychoanal. Assn.*, 29:5–81.

Stoller, R. (1968). The sense of femaleness. *Psychoanal.*, 37:42–55.

———— (1976). Primary femininity. *J. Amer. Psychoanal. Assn.*, 24 (Suppl.):59–78.

Torok, M. (1970). *Female Sexuality*. Ann Arbor: Univ. of Michigan Press.

From Freud to Feminist Personality Theory: Getting Here From There

HANNAH LERMAN

I have been studying Sigmund Freud's life experiences as well as the culture in which he lived in order to learn as much as possible about where his theories about women came from (Lerman, 1986). I have also been trying to figure out just why Freud's particular set of theories has had and continues to have such a hold on our consciousness. In this paper I will start with this issue and progress toward formulating some guidelines that suggest a potential direction for theorizing about female personality development. I begin with the assumption that you, my readers, are reasonably familiar with both the content of Freud's theories about female psychosexual development and the critiques that feminist theorists have made of his position.

You also probably know that attempts are being made within the psychoanalytic camp to remedy the grossest problems that his original theory poses. Few now accept, for example, Freud's preposterous idea that women have less fully developed superegos than men do. Psychoanalytic thinking now generally sidesteps the subject entirely or else pulls in new ideas from outside, such as those of Carol Gilligan (1982), who has suggested a new way to conceptualize differences in moral development between males and females. Some psychoanalysts are extremely eager to have the glaring problems of psychoanalysis with female development rehabilitated without recognizing that the problems lie at the very heart of the theory. A year and a half ago, I heard Robert Wallerstein, a prominent analyst, say at a conference that if you eliminate Freud's notion that the libido is inherently masculine, you have removed all the sexism that exists within psychoanalysis (Wallerstein, 1984). Freud's ideas about female superego, though,

"From Freud to Feminist Personality Theory: Getting Here from There" by Hannah Lerman, *Psychology of Women Quarterly*, 1986, *10* (1), 1–18. Copyright © 1986 by Division 35, American Psychological Association. Reprinted by permission of Cambridge University Press. This essay contains a version of material that appears in Hannah Lerman, *A Mote in Freud's Eye: From Psychoanalysis to the Psychology of Women* (New York: Springer, 1986).

Dr. Lerman is a clinical psychologist in private practice in Los Angeles.

40   do not have much to do directly with the concept of libido. More importantly, practically no aspect of the Oedipal theory in its application to women has been verified by psychological research (Fisher & Greenberg, 1977; Sherman, 1971). Nevertheless, these ideas continue to be used and still influence our thinking about the psychological development and psychotherapy of women.

Despite this, Freud would be hard put to recognize his theory in what is today practiced under the name of psychoanalysis. In 1922, he said definitively:

> The assumption that there are unconscious mental processes, the recognition of the theory of resistance and repression, the appreciation of the importance of sexuality and of the Oedipus complex—these constitute the principal subject-matter of psycho-analysis and the foundations of its theory. No one who cannot accept them *all* [emphasis added] should count himself a psycho-analyst. (Freud, 1922/1955, p. 247)

A hodgepodge of diverse theoretical positions sit together under the psychoanalytic umbrella today—despite the clarity of both Sigmund Freud's statement and Anna Freud's views on the subject. Jeffrey Masson has quoted Anna Freud to the effect that the very basis of psychoanalysis was in its Oedipal theory. She stated that if it was removed from psychoanalytic theory, "the whole importance of phantasy life, conscious or unconscious phantasy" would also be gone (Masson, 1984, p. 113). In her view, little if anything about psychoanalytic theory would be left to salvage.

In the years since Freud's death, the Oedipal constellation has moved out of the mainstream of psychoanalytic theorizing. Although the broad outlines of Oedipal theory remain in place, they are less and less directly utilized in theoretical discussions. More and more, theorists are emphasizing earlier periods of development, and seemingly incidentally Oedipal concepts are being downplayed and neglected. The earlier developmental phases are increasingly being viewed as more crucial for adult psychological development. This change has been taking place apart from the consideration of female development per se, but simultaneously many of the details of Oedipal theory are also being reinterpreted by those psychoanalysts who have specifically focused on women's development. Examples include the work of Moulton (1970), Grossman and Stewart (1977), Lerner (1980), Stoller (1977), Blum (1977), and Lester (1976), but there are many more as well. The reformation of Freudian thought has not been limited solely to theoretical issues, of course, nor even to Oedipal theory. The shifts have been much broader than that. Even the major elements of psycho-

analytic technique have not been spared, as can be seen by the changes   *41*
proposed and utilized by Kohut (1984, pp. 81–82 and n., for example) and
his followers.

Despite Freud's definitive statement, what unites the variegated views
that make up psychoanalysis today is not in full accord with the group of
theoretical elements he enumerated. While we find that the constructs of
the unconscious, repression, and resistance are still generally maintained,
support for the total nexus of Freud's emphasized concepts has become
quite weak today. In addition to the downgrading of the significance of
Oedipal theory that has taken place, most current versions of psychoanalysis give considerably less weight to the significance of sexuality than
Freud advocated or would have accepted.

If the views of Sigmund Freud and Anna Freud are not sufficient to mold
psychoanalytic theory to the form they espoused, there must be other
pivotal forces that bind the now-diverse theories and theoreticians together
under the psychoanalytic rubric. Any search for its essence, I believe, has to
concern itself more with the community and subculture of psychoanalysis,
particularly in the United States. Psychoanalysis has become enmeshed in
the very fabric of our society, in part because of the active early popularization of its precepts and ideas in the United States (see Hale, 1978). Whether
in status, consensual validation, financial gain, or something else entirely,
some mental health practitioners benefit by calling themselves psychoanalysts and remaining a part of the psychoanalytic community, however
far they have deviated from the ideal theoretical stance of Freud's 1922
statement. The psychoanalytic community also benefits when it can encompass persons with widely divergent views within the psychoanalytic
camp rather than having to cope with the influence of additional devia-
tionist movements.

I have suggested elsewhere (Lerman, 1982b, 1985) that particular social
and psychological elements enter into the maintenance of the status of
psychoanalysis in our society. The very extent and nature of the organiza-
tional structure of psychoanalysis are one. Psychoanalysis has always existed as a separate entity apart from all other scientific pursuits within the
social sciences and accountable to no external academic or other system of
checks. This has been especially true in the United States (Hale, 1978). No
other theoretical system here has ever been able to become as pervasive and
prestigious using such a strategy. The very early popularization helped
tremendously. In recent years, other psychotherapeutic systems, such as
Gestalt therapy, transactional analysis, psychodrama, and so on, have attempted to operate similarly—but it was too late. Psychoanalysis was too

42   firmly entrenched in the public (and professional) mind and similar tactics could not work again in the same way for another psychological system. Having been there first has turned out to be a tremendous advantage.

The historical hold that psychoanalytic theory was thus able to impose upon our consciousness as theorists and practitioners remains a crucial factor. Because of the longevity of psychoanalysis as the reigning theory of personality and the degree to which it has permeated our culture, we are often not aware of the grip that psychoanalysis has upon our thinking. Even the least psychoanalytically oriented among us implicitly accept certain concepts that, upon inspection, turn out to have come to us from psychoanalysis. We are little aware, for example, that the wish to explain or describe someone's behavior dynamically is in itself largely a result of having been imbued with the metapsychology of psychoanalysis. If we believe, as I think most clinicians do, that we are not consciously aware of the motivation behind all our behavior, we are also in the midst of this metapsychology. Accepting the idea of the unconscious, or at least of motivations hidden from ourselves, is just one small part of our social legacy from psychoanalysis. Not knowing the roots of our assumptions results in our being caught up unwittingly in psychoanalytic thought. Laura Brown (1984) stated the situation very well:

> The art, literature, and criticism of this century assume that there *is* an unconscious mind, that behavior *is* motivated and determined by early experiences, that there *is* an Oedipal struggle between father and son, that women *do* lack the objectivity bestowed by a successful resolution of the Oedipal conflict. Having internalized psychoanalytic thought in so many and subtle ways, and having learned to value the grandiose over the accurate, many feminist therapists, indeed most literate members of Western civilization, use psychoanalytic thinking as a standard against which the quality of other theories of human behavior can be measured. (p. 75)

The Nature of Psychoanalytic Theory

Another factor to reckon with is the nature of psychoanalytic theory itself. No other existing personality theory purports to explain so much of human nature and behavior. There are few if any real psychic unknowns for a psychotherapist to grapple with on a day-to-day basis when sticking to the basic premises of psychoanalysis. Psychoanalysis comes very close to providing a religious faith within which all is satisfactorily explained and put into its proper place in the universe (Rieff, 1966). Psychoanalytic theory is not simple-minded, whatever else it is. One aspect of its appeal to the public and the profession, however, is its appearance of simplicity. If everything in the human repertoire can be explained by one set of global and inclusive concepts, the result appears to be simple: A always equals B as long as C is accounted for, no matter what. What could look simpler than that?

If we accept as a given that in our society we all maintain unexamined psychoanalytic assumptions wittingly or unwittingly, another explanation is needed to account for those practitioners who have adopted the psycho-analytic label for their own. They have accepted far more than a theoretical structure. They have become a part of a vast psychoanalytic subcultural system that includes not only a very particular metapsychology and philo-sophical value system but also a social and intellectual community and set of norms. Psychoanalysis, as a system, has many of the characteristics that cults have. Adams (1984) has recently categorized *all* theoretical orienta-tions as cults and psycho-religions. He suggests that

The growth of professionalism and concerns with professional issues such as third party payment have resulted in a very casual and often hostile attitude toward science. If psychotherapy or behavior therapy or sex therapy or biofeedback are no more effective than placebo and our clinical predictions/diagnosis no better than chance, what happens to practitioners? If psychoanalysis is less effective than behavior therapy (or vice versa), what happens to the psychologists who have spent years practicing this approach? Research can become an emotionally and politi-cally volatile issue to the parochial clinician who has a personal investment in a particular orientation or set of clinical techniques. (p. 91)

If this is at least partially true for most psychotherapists, it is easy to see how entrenched this attitude has become within such an established theoretical orientation as psychoanalysis, particularly because a large segment of this establishment (the non-psychologists) was not at all trained to appreciate empirical research in the first place.

The characterization of psychoanalysis in particular as a cult is not a new one, but it usually has been inferred indirectly (see, for example, Frank, 1961/1973; Rieff, 1966; Rubins, 1974; Thompson, 1958). The label *cult* has especially negative connotations when attached to a purportedly scien-tific system, meaning as it does unverified and unverifiable belief systems that people hold on faith, something that scientists (even social scientists) are not supposed to do. But the holding of such beliefs helps individuals feel better about themselves (Galanter, 1978; Marx, 1980; Snow, Zurcher, & Ekland-Olson, 1980). Cults do represent one extreme result of organiza-

44 tional attempts to channel significant human needs. Is it possible to parcel out the useful part of how social movements create cohesiveness from those aspects of cultism that we consider destructive?

If, as has been suggested, the cohesive core of psychoanalysis and its appeal has relatively little to do with the theory's content or even its technique, other theories could presumably serve as an anchor for a group of practitioners if the other theories could offer comparable comprehensiveness of scope, social cohesiveness, psychic certainty, and social status.

It has become evident that theories are not accepted and promulgated solely or even primarily upon their scientific merit. We must look, therefore, for other criteria by which to accept or reject the theories now extant or those that will evolve. Very likely, social science will not become sufficiently more advanced during the near future to permit us to completely operationalize and empirically validate all of the tenets of any theory of personality. Progress toward that ideal remains useful, especially if evaluative concepts and measures of scientific thought are themselves broadened to take fuller account of the particular sociohistorical circumstances of life events (Sampson, 1978). To fill the breach, however, it behooves us to establish other criteria by which to judge and evaluate the suitability of any personality theory.

But suitability for what? I do not believe that Freud's original theories served women well. I also do not believe that the modern revisions of psychoanalytic theory further the health and well-being of the modern woman. After the initial feminist rejection of Freudian concepts in the early 1970s, some have reaccepted his ideas as having validity and applicability to women. I am not in that group because I see the theory as so fundamentally flawed in its thinking about women that it cannot be repaired, however extensive the tinkering with it. I suggest, moreover, that it is the philosophical stance that underpins the theory that cannot be rehabilitated. Assumptions about the inherent inferiority of women are embedded in the very core of psychoanalytic theory. These are not readily changed and are also not very amenable to patchwork repair. I remind you too that every time people use a term such as Oedipal, pre-Oedipal or pre-genital, they are implicitly accepting ideas whose validity has not been demonstrated despite years of trying. We need a theory that is likely to serve women's interests better and that would not build in such an inherent bias. Would it also be possible for us to manufacture our own consensually validating community within which to operate with such a theory?

Women are saying now that we know more about ourselves than men do. In the past, we have not spoken up with the clarity and determination with which we are now speaking. Whether our banner becomes a variant of

Freudian theory or some other theoretical framework, we are demanding and taking the right to define ourselves. This process is still very new. We have not gone far, perhaps, but we have started.

Criteria for a Woman-Based Theory of Personality

I offer here, then, the beginning nucleus of criteria by which a woman-based theory of personality and personality development could be evaluated. These are not the concepts of a theory per se but are, instead, meta-assumptions that a feminist personality theory would likely include, whatever form the actual theory were to take.[1] The criteria as listed are part of an unfinished and still growing statement. They could be called simple-minded in that they reflect primary assumptions, but in the past ideas such as these were not usually honored or even considered by theorists. The criteria suggested here are not all at the same level of generalization but are presented together to begin the process of explicating our own metapsychology.

1. Clinical Usefulness. The distinctions between theories of personality and theories of psychotherapy are necessarily blurred and indistinct. As a clinician, I assert that any worthwhile theory of personality development must be clinically useful—i.e., its concepts need to be readily translatable into what could and might take place in a therapy session. This idea is simple, but its implications are tricky because one person's view of what constitutes clinical usefulness is not necessarily the same as that of someone else. In the future, we may become able to be more specific and detailed about the kinds of subcriteria this general statement might encompass and about the nature of the clinical usefulness that is assumed. For some, usefulness might lie primarily in the nature of the personality constructs postulated, while for others the key might lie in the philosophy of the therapist-client relationship that a particular system promotes, and so forth. In addition to clinical usefulness within a therapy session, we must also include awareness about the value of what can be carried from such sessions into women's lives.

1. I wish to thank my sister colleagues at the Advanced Feminist Therapy Institute Conference in Washington, D.C. in May 1983 for their feedback when I initially offered the idea of criteria (Lerman, 1983). Many of their ideas have been incorporated into what is presented here. I am unable fully to thank all who contributed because the flow of ideas in response to my presentation was so free and open. Of the specific women whose contribution I was able to note, I should especially like to thank Laura Brown, Barbara Claster, Doris DeHardt, Sara Sharrett and Adrienne Smith.

46   *2. Encompassing the Diversity and Complexity of Women and Their Lives.*   I do not see how any theory could be truly called feminist or woman-based without providing for the inclusion of the broad array of female subgroups and issues that make up the female experience. Most theories that are currently available have not considered this point imperative. Perhaps in its beginnings a new theoretical system might not deal with all the possible permutations of women's lives, but in order to be of true heuristic value any budding theory would have to contain conceptual room for expansion and inclusion of the issues engaging all of diverse womankind.

3. Viewing Women Positively and Centrally.   Contrary to most previous theories, a woman-based theory would view women in a positive and explicit way rather than by indirect implication and negative connotations. While conceptually different, in actual practice this criterion is likely to be closely associated with the one that follows. A theory of woman's development needs to originate in a positive view of women's experience, and that experience must provide the central data from which the theory derives its philosophy, its attitude, and its view of reality.

4. Arising from Women's Experience.   As a feminist therapist, I am aware that our best work comes out of our experience as women working with women. Only if our theory remains close to and within the world of women can it be a truly woman-based theory. The viewpoint must be female rather than male, as it has usually been. The female eye relates psychic events to a different set of experiences and sees and/or interprets these events differently than the male. In addition, we must never forget that the client in therapy sees differently than the therapist. Her reality has to be acknowledged rather than ignored in the way many other theoretical systems ignore it. While women's experience as a whole has been bypassed in the process of theory construction, the views of the woman client even more often have been given short shrift.

5. Remaining Close to the Data of Experience.   Where women have previously entered into theory construction, our concepts have generally stayed fairly close to our experience. Therein is one of our strengths—as well as one of our weaknesses. We have not developed inclusive theories or even inclusive concepts. In part, this is a reaction against such theories as Freud's, in which concepts end up only minimally attached to the experience with which they began. It is also the result, however, of theoretical timidity related to our cultural (and thus internalized) idea that women are not objective and therefore not fully capable of theorizing. Balancing between the Scylla of overgeneralization and the Charybdis of theoretical timidity, we need to arrive at the level of discourse that is most fitting to our material. I envision the ideal theory as one not so distant from the experiential data that we lose touch with the data but also lifted far enough from the data so that it can encompass truly useful generalizations. We will only be able to find the appropriate level of generalization through some measure of trial and error. We would expect, moreover, that the usefulness of our concepts could be also reflected empirically to some measure. A presently existing theory that passed on this criterion would not ignore empirical data contradictory to it or not explained by it.

6. Recognizing that the Internal World Is Inextricably Intertwined with the External World.   I could not call a theory woman-based that recognized any other relationship than one of complicated interaction between internal reality and the social circumstances in which women live. We have already incorporated into feminist thinking generally the idea that the external world and the internal psychological world are intrinsically and intricately interrelated. Not new to *us,* this concept, nevertheless, is a significant change from most psychological theories from which psychotherapeutic systems develop. It is the psychological equivalent of the rallying cry, "The personal is political." Gilbert (1980) has expanded our understanding of this concept, pointing out that it implies the need for therapists to monitor their actions continually for the ways their internalized value systems operate upon the externality of their clients' lives. The necessity for social changes to promote women's mental health and well-being as well as internal psychological changes by individual women also arises intrinsically from this criterion.

7. Not Confining Concepts by Particularistic Terminology or in Terms of Other Theories.   Traditional theories use what will be referred to as particularistic language—i.e., terms like *mother*—as opposed to a broader view of what we might intend to convey. For example, instead of using *mother,* more appropriate terminology might convey something of what terms like *caretaker* and *caregiver* tell us. Use of such more general terms would help us to consider more easily the alternative family, network, and pairing possibilities that are being or could be used by the broad spectrum of women and men in broadly defined "families." A feminist theory would refer to developmental tasks and the adult helpers where appropriate.

48   When fully evolved, however, it would not use terms like *maternal* and *childish* to discuss behavior that is chronologically distant from the developmental situation. A feminist theory would recognize that adult needs, whether based in developmental issues or not, are different in character and require a different terminology. For example, while the importance of the mother-daughter relationship is crucial and has not been broadly recognized by many previous theorists, to derive all varieties of adult woman-woman pairing relationships from that context is conceptually limiting. One of the tasks, therefore, of a feminist theory would be to delineate the psychological dynamics of adult pairing relationships, of whatever gender, separately from a paradigm based solely upon the nuclear family. It is likely, moreover, that such theorizing would also fulfill criterion 2 (encompassing the diversity and complexity of women's lives) in that the resulting feminist theory could then more easily accommodate family and network groups from differing cultural contexts and not be based solely upon our society's typical (although mythical) nuclear family construction.

The language used in stating ideas is often as important as the concepts themselves. Rather than using the shorthand strategy of taking terms from another theory (usually psychoanalysis), we need to carefully study the implications of whatever concepts are used. Examples where such thinking has often not occurred are in the carryover of terms like *pre-Oedipal* and *transference*. As has been mentioned, more and more emphasis (within psychoanalysis proper as well as outside) is being placed on the significance of the child-caregiver relationship for personality development. The primary qualities of these relationships are unwittingly downgraded when they are referred to as pre-Oedipal, as if they were important only in terms of what is postulated to develop and not in their own right. The significance of the Oedipal situation thus is also implicitly accepted without further examination of the theoretical premises involved.

The problem with the concept of transference is different. The original Freudian use of the term referred to the projection onto the therapist of sexual material generated primarily from the relationship with the parents. Few would doubt that the client can and probably does project symbolically onto the therapeutic relationship from past experiences. Yet, the process is broader than the term *transference* signifies and is likely to involve layers of symbolism that originate from a variety of sources within the broad psychological and environmental sphere from which the client comes. This too requires new terminology rather than the continued shorthand use of the term *transference*, with its remaining implicit meaning of libidinal sexual projection.

8. Supporting Feminist (or at Minimum Nonsexist) Modes of Psychotherapy. Many theories of personality development do not speak directly to the nature of the psychotherapy that might evolve from their use. Frequently, however, the nature of the relationship between therapist and patient/client that fits the particular theory most easily can be inferred. Theories of psychotherapy, however, frequently do not have explicit theories of personality built into them (a primary exception is psychoanalysis). It might be possible to evaluate these theories on this criterion but not on some of the others. What is significant to explore are the various aspects of the therapeutic interaction which feminists have identified as nonsexist (i.e., the therapist listening to and validating the woman's experience and having knowledge about the psychology of women) and feminist (i.e., the therapist maintaining an egalitarian rather than authoritarian/expert stance toward the woman in therapy sessions and in other therapy-related issues such as fee setting). Sometimes, extrapolation is necessary to answer the question of whether nonsexist or feminist aspects of relating are enhanced or diminished by the form and content of a particular theory.

Can criteria such as these reliably differentiate between the kinds of theories that are acceptably woman-based and those that are not? I am trying to determine whether they can. I have indicated earlier that many partial theories exist which will be difficult to evaluate along all the criteria mentioned. Only Freudian psychoanalysis and other psychoanalytic derivatives profess a more global scope. These are obvious choices for evaluation, but other theories, including some that have been intended to build toward a feminist or woman-based theoretical system, can also be evaluated in terms of the criteria. So far I have limited my evaluations to theories rooted in psychoanalytic thinking and theories derived from a feminist perspective. There are, obviously, other groups of theories, such as those originating in humanistic or behavioral thinking, that could also be measured on these bases.

For a fuller discussion of what I have arrived at in measuring theories such as those of Horney, contemporary psychoanalytic views, Chodorow, and other feminist theorists against my criteria, I refer you to my book, *A Mote in Freud's Eye* (Lerman, 1986). In the remainder of this paper I will present my analysis of Freudian theory and a few feminist theories in order to demonstrate the process I have been using and to illustrate some of my conclusions. Consideration of Freudian psychoanalysis here may be anticlimactic since it has been used as a model by many feminist theorists for what a woman-based theory definitely is *not*. It may be instructive, nevertheless, to measure psychoanalysis against the criteria as an aid in demonstrating their potential utility.

Evaluation of Freudian Psychoanalysis

Freudian psychoanalysis could be considered clinically useful (criterion 1) because so many practitioners since Freud have proclaimed it to be so. I see that brand of clinical usefulness coming essentially from Freudian theory's providing the practitioner with an all-inclusive and therefore easy frame of reference in which to operate. Whether this is viewed as negative or positive depends upon whether one thinks the precepts used are appropriate to the broad spectrum of human experiences to which they are applied. I maintain that, despite its having been used extensively with women, psychoanalysis is not clinically useful for women because it neglects significant areas of women's lives and denigrates other areas. Its frame of reference is male and the uniqueness of female experience is not considered at all. In addition, it has become the prototypical antithesis of our criterion 8 (stance of the therapist in psychotherapy).

Psychoanalysis can be declared to encompass only marginally the variety of female subgroups and the complexity of women's issues (criterion 2). Freud did not deal significantly with such central women's issues as menstruation, childbirth, or, despite his sexual focus, female orgasm (Lerman, 1986). Also, as Chodorow and others have shown us, he did not even attempt to deal with the process by which mothering, a very significant endeavor, is fostered in women (Chodorow, 1978). Others (Brody, 1970, 1976) have pointed out that his clientele was the upper middle class and that his theory necessarily reflects that fact. He himself occasionally mentioned (Freud, 1916/1963) how his theories might apply to persons of lower-class upbringing, although he presumed the world of his middle- and upper-middle-class clientele to be a universal one.[2] Yet Freudian theory purports to be universally explanatory and to be applicable, therefore, to many and diverse cultural, class, and ethnic groups. Whether one considers Freud's views broad enough in terms of this criterion, then, depends upon the viewpoint with which one starts. I, however, am not alone in choosing to reject the proclamations of universality that Freudian psychoanalysis has made in the past and still, albeit in somewhat more muted tones, claims in the present day.

There can be relatively little dispute, however, about whether Freud's views of women are explicitly derived from his theoretical structure (criteri-

2. Based on his particular clinical experience he did, however, once comment to the effect that "proletarians and princes" (Freud, 1906/1962, p. 73) do not develop neuroses.

on 3). They are not explicit at all when compared to the theory of male development. Almost all the concepts used for women are developed as analogues with male experience. Many wish to claim that Freud's view of women was not negative. This is difficult to support if one looks at the available evidence—his writings. Separated from the experience of women's lives in his youth as well as in his mature life, Freud built a theoretical structure permeated with the residue of his fears and negativity toward women. The viewpoint toward women was definitely neither female nor sympathetic to female views of the world (criterion 4). The famous case known as Dora demonstrates the distance between Freud's views and those of his female patients, along with his lack of acceptance or even consideration of their views (Freud, 1905/1953).

Freudian concepts are theoretically complex, and many discussions in the theory take place at a conceptual level far removed from specific experience (criterion 5). Psychoanalytic theory in general has posed enormous problems and obstacles to attempts at empirical validation. Oedipal theory applied to female development in particular has received little confirmation outside the psychoanalytic consulting room. Psychoanalysis is also one of the prime proponents in our social world of the view that the internal psyche exists relatively independently of external realities (criterion 6). Freudian language is also, of course, particularistic (criterion 7). It presupposes that only mothers can be caregivers and describes adult behavior in terms that assume childhood development to be the basis for all development which could occur during the lifespan.

So, without much surprise, I conclude that Freudian psychoanalytic theory fails to meet the prerequisites for a feminist theory of personality. Without going into detail here, let me say that I have not found any more current perspective from within the psychoanalytic establishment—neither the work of current women's issues theorists nor that of the ego psychological and object relations theorists—that significantly improves upon the original Freudian formulations in terms of the criteria by which we are judging theoretical viewpoints.

Evaluation of Chodorow's Theory

Nancy Chodorow's work does not come from the psychoanalytic mainstream. The origins of her work are in feminist thought, although her ideas have catalyzed a partial rapprochement between the two viewpoints. Because her viewpoint has become so significant and because if offers us much that is new, Chodorow's work merits evaluation separately from

52 other feminist psychoanalytic work. Chodorow is not a clinician and her work has no direct connection to psychotherapeutic practice. Many women therapists, however, have found her view of mothering an avenue for useful clinical insights on separation-individuation issues in female development. Her theory does not offer any particular guidelines per se to the therapist for her therapeutic stance.

Chodorow discusses diversity and suggests that the processes she speaks of, although not their specific culture content, are probably universal or nearly so. The crucial variables, from her perspective, are the degree of father presence or absence and the degree of social isolation of the mother-and-child unit. She makes the categorical statement that "cross-culturally, the more father-absence (or absence of adult men) in the family, the more severe are conflicts about masculinity and fear of women" (Chodorow, 1978, p. 213). This is an intriguing idea if it is true. It is not, however, as self-evident as Chodorow seems to regard it. Pleck (1981) studied the evidence bearing upon the use of psychodynamic theories to account for the relationship between men's attitudes toward women and their self-esteem and did not find relevant data.

Chodorow's theory is based upon the essentially female phenomenon of mothering, around which she weaves our society's gender division of labor into public (masculine) and private (feminine) spheres. Women's experience is thereby central to her views. Prior discussions of mothering have often emphasized the mother's pathological contributions to the process without describing the pathological matrix in which mothers and children exist in our society. Chodorow moves between the internal psychological and the external social phenomena in ways that describe but do not assign blame or negate the position of women as mothers. Apart from her usage of such psychoanalytic concepts as Oedipal and pre-Oedipal to describe phases in development, she remains close to what individuals experience.

Chodorow points out that her view of developmental psychology is at odds with psychoanalysis over the nature of the process of identification in boys and girls, and then without further explanation she uses only the psychoanalytic view as her jumping-off point for further theorizing. It is in her acceptance of psychoanalytic theory, which she views as contributing positively, that she moves away from both the experiential level and empirical evidence. She comments in a footnote that her view of psychoanalysis "is as an interpretative theory and not as a behavioral science" (Chodorow, 1978, p. 41). I do not know all of what she means by that, but she does seem to say that concern about empirical validation plays no part in her acceptance of psychoanalytic theory. She also accepts the psychoanalytic case literature uncritically without any recognition that the ana-

lyst's view as written represents a level of abstraction and does not necessarily provide a veridical statement. For example, when analysts write that a
woman has demonstrated penis envy, they usually give no indication of
what observations of that particular woman's verbal and/or nonverbal
behavior led them to that conclusion. We can therefore see ample room for
the operation of individual and theoretical bias in such case material.
Chodorow ignores this possibility completely.

Throughout her book, Chodorow uses the term *mother* when referring to
a caregiver, but at the very end she expresses the need to be less particularistic and to separate the function from those who perform the function.
This is consistent with her cultural arguments, but since this point is
mentioned only in one seven-line paragraph, readers may quite easily miss
it and assume that she means to say that "mothering" is to be done by those
who are biologically mothers.

Since Chodorow's view is nonclinical in immediate focus, it does not tell
us anything directly about the therapy that anyone using her perspective
might offer. Because she thoroughly weaves psychoanalytic theory into her
account and has made it fashionable for feminists to reaccept psychoanalytic thinking, it is easy to assume that she would find the techniques of
psychoanalytic therapy acceptable although they do not generally accord
with a feminist or even a nonsexist stance.

Evaluation of Other Feminist Theories

The other feminist theorists whom I wish to discuss briefly are Jean Baker
Miller, Luise Eichenbaum and Suzy Orbach, and Miriam Greenspan. Jean
Baker Miller (1976) was the first to point the way and to suggest some of the
issues involved in looking at women's lives. Her work and the later work of
others from the Stone Center (Wellesley College) bear the psychoanalytic
label but show awareness of and sensitivity to all the issues raised in each of
our stated criteria. Miller and her associates have devoted themselves more
to specific clinical issues than to any overriding theory of personality or
personality development.

Eichenbaum and Orbach (1983) call themselves psychoanalytic feminist
therapists. Their theory is clearly derived most directly from their clinical
work with women. In speaking of how they have been drawn back to a
viewpoint that they label psychoanalytic, they say:

In turning to psychoanalysis, we were interested in three specific areas. We recognized the importance of Freud's discovery of the unconscious; we were trying to

54 understand the vicissitudes of a psychic life that was a powerful determinant in the politics of everyday experience; and we wanted to understand girls' psychological development. (p. 13)

While they accept some of the tenets of the object relations branch of psychoanalytic theory, they neither deal in Oedipal theorizing nor focus upon sexuality as the basis of all behavior. They derive female and male development from the mother-daughter relationship without emphasizing the more objectionable aspects of psychoanalytic theory or using psycho-analytic terminology carelessly. In a passage immediately prior to the one quoted above, they seem to be saying that they see psychoanalysis as the only alternative to working in therapy solely with the here and now. In other words, they see psychoanalysis as the only avenue through which they could operate with a psychodynamic perspective. They continue to use the term *transference* without thinking through its implications for their work, portray the mother as conveying negative self-messages to the daughter without fully incorporating the mother's place in the general society, and, like Chodorow, seem to ignore the reality of lesbian women and their lives (Zick, 1984). They have tried to eliminate most of the nonfeminist aspects of psychoanalysis from their theoretical formulation, but they have not been fully successful. Their work illustrates the problems involved in viewing behavior psychodynamically without accepting specific psycho-analytic concepts, an issue that I have discussed elsewhere (Lerman, 1982a).

There are also feminist theorists who are explicitly non-psychoanalytic in their orientation. The most prominent of this group is Miriam Green-span (1983). Deriving her viewpoint primarily from her clinical work with women, she focuses less upon theoretical constructs and personality devel-opment than on the relationship between therapist and client in therapy. Her book presents the clinical usefulness she sees as evolving from her different view of that relationship. That is, indeed, one of her major premises. Beginning, as she does, with a feminist perspective, it is clear that her ideas arise from women's own experience and that she views women positively and centrally. Clinically focused, her ideas remain close to the data of the experience upon which they are based. She specifically empha-sizes the need to react to the diversity and complexity of women's lives. In addition, her viewpoint encompasses the notion of the interaction of the external with the internal view of her women clients. Her language is neither particularistic nor borrowed from another theoretical framework. Implicitly and explicitly, her view is a feminist approach to the process of psychotherapy. Greenspan's work obviously meets all our criteria satis-factorily.

That viewpoints originating in psychoanalysis, such as Eichenbaum and Orbach's and Miller's, and that one which is in no way directly derived from psychoanalytic thinking, such as Greenspan's, can come close to meeting the above-mentioned criteria is most striking, if not downright revolutionary. Despite difficulties that arise when psychoanalytic theory is used as the basis for a feminist theory, the level of agreement among theoretical positions that begin from radically different frameworks could be said to be amazing if we in the women's movement had not already many times recognized the same kinds of ideas spontaneously emanating from a multitude of sources.

When the ideas that have been fomenting for fifteen years are brought together, we clearly see that we already have a coherent philosophy and set of values and beliefs. Although still relatively small in number, a group of women therapists who believe in the budding system and use its tenets daily in their work with other women already exists. We have organized ways of nurturing each other, supporting each other in our work, and working together on theory building.

The criteria stated in this paper come from my interaction with other feminist therapists. Their use here makes it clear that it is possible to develop coherent and useful theoretical structures. This also tells us that psychoanalytic theory need not be the only basis for our thought. It is difficult to develop a fully formed perspective on the psychological development of women that is psychodynamically based but that does not utilize psychoanalytic concepts, but it can be and is being done.

The specific symptoms of emotional illness and distress today are quite different from what they were in Freud's day. The changes in symptomatology since Freud's time tell us graphically about the changes that have taken place in our society during the twentieth century. It seemed to Freud and his followers that such acts as abortion, masturbation, and other sexual practices were, in and of themselves and without consideration of how society viewed them, sufficient to cause severe mental distress. We can see now that it was not perversion of the sexual instinct that was involved when people of Freud's day developed symptoms when they engaged in what were then considered deviant actions, but the impact of internalized social pressures. If we care to emulate Freud to the extent of wishing to suggest a single psychic root cause of emotional dysfunction, the most appropriate one that I can suggest is the conflict between basic human strivings (which no one has yet fully described) and the prohibitions imposed by a particular cultural milieu.

Chodorow and others have made it clear to us that the customs of our society are not geared toward the rearing of emotionally healthy human beings. We also receive that information from many other sources (see

56 Carmen, Rieker, & Mills, 1984, for a strong suggestion about the relationship of child sexual and physical abuse to psychiatric illness). The women's movement in general, by emphasizing the patriarchal biases in our culture, has been forcing our society to pay some, although not nearly enough, attention to the particular circumstances of women's lives. We wish fervently to work toward a theoretical framework that can actively participate in the process of increasing our understanding of and our ability to improve the quality of our own lives as women and those of our client

References

Adams, H. E. (1984). The pernicious effects of theoretical orientations in clinical psychology. *Clinical Psychologist, 37,* 90–94.

Blum, H. P. (1977). Masochism, the ego ideal, and the psychology of women. In H. P. Blum (Ed.), *Female psychology: Contemporary psychoanalytic views* (pp. 157–191). New York: International Universities Press.

Brody, B. (1970). Freud's case-load. *Psychotherapy: Theory, research and practice, 7,* 8–12.

Brody, B. (1976). "Freud's case-load" and social class: a rejoinder. *Psychotherapy: Theory, research and practice, 13,* 196–97.

Brown, L. S. (1984). Finding new language: Getting beyond analytic verbal shorthand in feminist therapy. *Women and Therapy, 3,* 73–80.

Carmen, E. H., Rieker, P. P., & Mills, T. (1984). Victims of violence and psychiatric illness. *American Journal of Psychiatry, 141,* 378–83.

Chodorow, N. J. (1978). *The reproduction of mothering: Psychoanalysis and the sociology of gender.* Berkeley: University of California Press.

Eichenbaum, L., & Orbach, S. (1983). *Understanding women: A psychoanalytic approach.* New York: Basic Books.

Fisher, S., & Greenberg, R. P. (1977). *The scientific credibility of Freud's theories and therapy.* New York: Basic Books.

Frank, J. D. (1973). *Persuasion and healing: A comparative study of psychotherapy.* Baltimore, MD: The Johns Hopkins University Press. (Originally published 1961)

Freud, S. (1953). Fragment of an analysis of a case of hysteria. In J. Strachey (Ed. and Trans.), *The standard edition of the complete psychological works of Sigmund Freud* (Vol. 7, pp. 7–122). London: Hogarth Press. (Originally published 1905)

Freud, S. (1955). Two encyclopaedia articles: (A) Psychoanalysis. In J. Strachey (Ed. and Trans.), *The standard edition of the complete psychological works of Sigmund Freud* (Vol. 18, pp. 235–54). London: Hogarth Press. (Originally published 1922)

Freud, S. (1962). Scientific meeting on December 5, 1906. In H. Nunberg & E. Federn (Eds. and Trans.), *Minutes of the Vienna psychoanalytic society* (Vol. I, pp. 69–80). New York: International Universities Press. (Originally published 1906)

Freud, S. (1963). Introductory lectures on psycho-analysis, parts I and II. In J. Strachey (Ed. and Trans.), *The standard edition of the complete psychological works of Sigmund Freud* (Vol. 15, pp. 15–239).London: Hogarth Press. (Originally published 1916)

Galanter, M. (1978). "The relief effect": A sociological model for neurotic distress and large-group therapy. *American Journal of Psychiatry, 135,* 588–91.

Gilbert, L. (1980). Feminist therapy. In A. M. Brodsky & R. Hare-Mustin (Eds.), *Women and psychotherapy: An assessment of research and practice* (pp. 245–65). New York: Guilford.

Gilligan, C. (1982). *In a different voice: Psychological theory and women's development.* Cambridge, MA: Harvard University Press.

Greenspan, M. (1983). *A new approach to women and therapy.* New York: McGraw-Hill.

Grossman, W. I., & Stewart, W. A. (1977). Penis envy: From childhood wish to developmental metaphor. In H. P. Blum (Ed.), *Female psychology: Contemporary psychoanalytic views* (pp. 193–212). New York: International Universities Press.

Hale, N. G., Jr. (1978). From Berggasse XIX to Central Park West: The Americanization of psychoanalysis, 1919–1940. *Journal of the History of the Behavioral Sciences, 14,* 299–315.

Kohut, H. (1984). *How does analysis cure?* (Ed. A. Goldberg & Paul Stepansky.) Chicago: University of Chicago Press.

Lerman, H. (1982a, August). *The relevance of psychoanalysis for psychotherapy with women.* Paper presented at the convention of the American Psychological Association, Washington, DC.

Lerman, H. (1982b, May). *The role of psychoanalytic theory in feminist therapy.* Position paper prepared for the Advanced Feminist Therapy Conference, Vail, CO.

Lerman, H. (1983, May). *Criteria for a feminist personality theory—and some rudimentary concepts.* Position paper prepared for the Advanced Feminist Therapy Conference, Washington, DC.

Lerman, H. (1985). Some barriers to the development of a feminist theory of personality. In Rosewater, L., & Walker, L. E. (Eds.), *Handbook of feminist therapy: Women's issues in psychotherapy* (pp. 5–12). New York: Springer.

Lerman, H. (1986). *A mote in Freud's eye: From psychoanalysis to the psychology of women.* New York: Springer.

Lerner, H. E. (1980). Penis envy: Alternatives in conceptualization. *Bulletin of the Menninger Clinic, 44,* 39–48.

Lester, E. P. (1976). On the psychosexual development of the female child. *Journal of the American Academy of Psychoanalysis, 4,* 515–27.

Marx, J. H. (1980). The ideological construction of post-modern identity models in contemporary cultural movements. In R. Robertson & B. Holnzer (Eds.), *Identity and authority: Explorations in the theory of society* (pp. 145–89). New York: St. Martin's.

Masson, J. (1984). *The assault on truth: Freud's suppression of the seduction theory.* New York: Farrar, Straus and Giroux.

Miller, J. B. (1976). *Toward a new psychology of women.* Boston: Beacon Press.

Moulton, R. (1970). A survey and reevaluation of the concept of penis envy. *Contemporary Psychoanalysis, 7,* 84–104.

Pleck, J. (1981). *The myth of masculinity.* Cambridge, MA: MIT Press.

Rieff, P. (1966). *The triumph of the therapeutic: Uses of faith after Freud.* New York: Harper and Row.

Rubins, J. L. (1974). The personality cult in psychoanalysis. *American Journal of Psychoanalysis, 34,* 129–33.

Sampson, E. E. (1978). Scientific paradigms and social values: Wanted—a scientific revolution. *Journal of Personality and Social Psychology, 36,* 1332–43.

Sherman, J. (1971). *On the psychology of women: A survey of empirical studies.* Springfield, IL: Charles C. Thomas.

Snow, D., Zurcher, L. A., Jr., & Ekland-Olson, S. (1980). Social networks and social movements: A microstructural approach to differential recruitment. *American Sociological Review, 45,* 787–801.

Stoller, R. J. (1977). Primary femininity, In H. P. Blum (Ed.), *Female psychology: Contemporary psychoanalytic views* (pp. 59–78). New York: International Universities Press.

Thompson, C. (1958). A study of the emotional climate of psychoanalytic institutes. *Psychiatry, 21,* 45–51.

Wallerstein, R. (1984, March). Changing psychoanalytic perspectives on women. In *Women*

58   *and Psychoanalysis: Historical and Clinical Perspectives.* Symposium conducted by the
        San Francisco Psychiatric Institute and the University of California, Berkeley, CA.
    Zick, T. (1984). *A look at the ideas of Susie Orbach and Luise Eichenbaum.* Unpublished
        paper, Antioch University, San Francisco.

Question 2

Are Women Masochistic?

Rooted in Freud's belief that "biology is destiny" is the notion of women's masochism. According to Freud, it is normal for women to exhibit masochistic tendencies. In a similar vein, Helene Deutsch (1944), a loyal disciple, contended that masochism, narcissism, and passivity are the three key characteristics of the female personality. How far one can extend the concept of female masochism is probably best illustrated by analyst Marie Bonaparte's characterization of coitus: "The woman, in effect, is subjected to a sort of beating by the man's penis. She receives its blows and often, even, loves the violence" (Bonaparte, 1953, p. 87).

In "The Problem of Feminine Masochism," Karen Horney (1935/1967) challenged Freud's concept of masochism, charging that the theory rested on a small number of studies of neurotic patients. Horney argued that female behavior labeled masochistic could be better explained as the result of cultural conditioning in a society that inhibits women's growth and views them as inferiors.

Despite the efforts of Horney and others, the belief that women derive some gain from being treated roughly by men has continued to find a place in the literature of both psychology and psychiatry. Hilberman (1984) argues that the clinical and psychiatric literature reinforces the popular notion that wife abuse is an isolated problem and that women are satisfying their own masochistic needs when they become victims. For example, in a study of twelve families in which the husbands had been charged with assault and battery and referred to a psychiatric clinic, the authors concluded that the wives were masochistic: "a husband's behavior may serve to fill a wife's needs even though she protests it" (Snell, Rosenwald, & Robey, 1964, p. 110). The victim, in this case the battered woman, is seen as the problem, a classic case of blaming the victim (Hirsch, 1981).

60   There are instances, some clinicians argue, in which victims seek out situations where they are mistreated or demeaned. This issue erupted into a major debate within the American Psychiatric Association in December 1985, when a committee reported its recommendations for revising the third edition of the Diagnostic and Statistical Manual of Mental Disorders (DSM-III). This manual serves as a guide not only for clinicians but also for government agencies and third-party insurance companies such as Blue Cross, which use it to determine payment for treatment.

Concerned about the possible misuse of the diagnosis labeled "masochistic personality disorder," a feminist coalition lobbied against several of the committee's recommendations. In June 1986, the board voted at first to include a new category called the "self-defeating personality disorder" in the DSM-III revision but, in response to another round of criticism, they finally decided to put it in an appendix clearly marked "controversial research categories" rather than in the main section of the manual. Feminist psychologists, psychiatrists, and other mental health workers continue their protests, arguing that the new diagnostic category does great harm to women whether it is in the main body of the manual or in the appendix. Listing the category in either location, they argue, legitimizes erroneous and unscientific conclusions about female behavior (Ahmann, 1987).

Lenore Walker has written that a misdiagnosis of self-defeating personality for a person who is a victim of abuse—for example, a battered women—can result "at best in no treatment, or at worst in an inadequate intervention which could perpetuate the impact from the abuse or even make it worse." Walker estimates that this decision would affect millions of women, many of whom are hospitalized for years because doctors do not recognize the cause of their problem (Walker, 1986, p. 21).

Feminist writers are not in agreement on this issue. Do some women, as Natalie Shainess suggests, contribute to their own victimization? Or is Paula Caplan correct when she argues that female masochism is both a matter of definition and a result of learned behavior?

References

Ahmann, S. (1987, January). Battle-scarred Diagnostic Manual gets APA approval. *Clinical Psychiatry News, 2,* 22.

Bonaparte, M. (1953). *Female sexuality.* New York: International Universities Press. (Reprinted 1965, New York: Grove Press).

Deutsch, H. (1944). *The psychology of women* (Vol. I). New York: Grune & Stratton.

Hilberman, E. (1984). Overview: The "wife-beater's wife" reconsidered. In P. P. Rieker & E. H. Carmen (Eds.), *The gender gap in psychotherapy: Social realities and psychological processes.* New York: Plenum.

Hirsch, M. (1981). *Women and Violence.* New York: Van Nostrand Reinhold.
Horney, K. (1967). The problem of feminine masochism. In H. Kelman (Ed.), *Karen Horney, M.D., Feminine Psychology* (pp. 214–33). New York: W. W. Norton. (Originally published 1935).
Snell, J. E., Rosenwald, R. J., & Robey, A. (1964). The wifebeater's wife: a study of family interaction. *Archives of General Psychiatry, 11,* 107–13.
Walker, L. E. (1986, August). Diagnosis and Politics: Abuse Disorders. Paper presented at the meeting of the American Psychological Association, Washington, D.C.

Additional Reading

Braude, M. (Ed.) (In press). *Women, power, and therapy.* Binghamton, N.Y.: Haworth Press.
Caplan, P. J. (1987). *The myth of women's masochism.* New York: New American Library.
Caplan, P. J. (In press). The psychiatric association's failure to meet its own standards: The dangers of "self-defeating personality disorder" as a category. *Journal of Personality Disorders.*
Janoff-Bulman, R. & Frieze, I. H. (1983). A theoretical perspective for understanding reactions. *Journal of Social Issues, 39* (2), 1–17.
Janoff-Bulman, R. & Frieze, I. H. (Eds.) (1983). Reactions to Victimization [Special issue]. *Journal of Social Issues, 39* (2).
Marcus, M. (1981). *A taste for pain: On masochism and female sexuality.* New York: St. Martin's Press.
Norwood, R. (1985). *Women who love too much.* Los Angeles: J. P. Tarcher.
Schad-Somers, S. (1982). *Sadomasochism: Etiology and treatment.* New York: Human Sciences Press.
Schafer, R. (1984). The pursuit of failure and the idealization of unhappiness. *American Psychologist, 39* (4), 398–405.
Shainess, N. (1984). *Sweet suffering: Woman as victim.* New York: Bobbs-Merril.
Waites, E. A. (1984). Female masochism and the enforced restriction of choice. In P. P. Rieker & E. Carmen (Eds.), *The gender gap in psychotherapy: Social realities and psychological processes* (pp. 139–50). New York: Plenum.

Yes

Vulnerability to Violence: Masochism as Process

NATALIE SHAINESS

If the credo of Descartes, "I think, therefore I am," were restated as "I suffer, therefore I am," this would express the masochist's position. However, a corollary must be added for a real understanding. It is not, as people (including professionals) commonly think, "I suffer because I *like* to suffer." It is "I suffer because that is the only way I know how to live." In short, I am talking about an all-pervasive cognitive style that characterizes some people—male and female—but more commonly female, for reasons I shall develop. In my psychiatric involvement of over thirty-five years, I have seen no decrease in the appearance of this personality type.

Let me turn to my reasons for interest in this area. The rise in the incidence, or greater recognition of the incidence, of violent crimes of all kinds, particularly rape and wife assault, has sparked great professional interest in these problems at long last. Yet in the various studies there is considerable difference of opinion not only of the personality traits and situational factors contributing to violent action, but of those which may make the victims contributors to their own distress.

Let us look at the broad picture for the moment, and at the varied gropings by those studying the problems of sudden, isolated eruptions of violence as well as ongoing intrafamilial assault. Studies have shown, first of all, that violence *does* occur more frequently in lower socioeconomic groups, but there is no clear indication of degree. Gelles (1972) has defined violence as "the illegitimate use of force." Of course, one could ask whether the use of force is ever "legitimate." It has also been observed that abused children are more likely to become violent adults. Here, Sullivan's (1953) observations of what he called the "malevolent transformation" of the person frustrated in his need for tenderness, and meeting with attack at

"Vulnerability to Violence: Masochism as Process" by Natalie Shainess, *American Journal of Psychotherapy*, 1979, *33* (2), 174–189. Copyright © 1979 by the *American Journal of Psychotherapy*. Reprinted by permission.
Dr. Shainess is a psychiatrist in private practice in New York City.

such times, are relevant. Martin (1976) asks: "What makes him (the batterer) a brute?" She observed that much of what is known comes from the victim, who often reports that the husband is outwardly a charming man and well liked by everybody. This brings to mind the character of Thorvald in Ibsen's *A Doll's House*. Of course, his violence to Nora was psychological rather than physical. Martin observed that, ironically, Eisaku Sato, once Prime Minister of Japan, was awarded the Nobel peace prize even though his wife publicly accused him of beating her. It was reported that his popularity rocketed after his wife said—in good masochistic style—"He's a good husband, he only beats me once a week." As an aside, I have often wondered why society accepts inconsistency between private and public life so willingly—perhaps there is a skeleton in almost every closet.

The Aggressor

But, returning to the personality of the batterer, he has been reported as a "loser" in some way, angry with himself and frustrated by life. He is therefore more volatile and proves himself by showing he is at least "master" in his home. In one example (Martin, 1976) in *Battered Wives* the husband, not inappropriately named Adam, hit his wife if he didn't like the way she dressed, if she said something "stupid," if she defied him in something. His wife has supported him through most of the marriage, enabling him to study for a career, but—and probably *because* of this—he complained that she did not keep the house clean and did not properly balance the budget. "I wanted her to take seriously the things I expected to be taken seriously," he is reported to have said. He made it clear on interview that he did not regret "slapping" her—but he pointed out that in the four years of their marriage he "never really 'damaged' her." Supporting him and keeping house for him, as well as keeping their books, were not sufficient, I presume, to prove that she was "serious."

Erin Pizzey (in Martin, 1976) observed that wife-beaters are alcoholics, psychotics, or "plain and simple bullies." Psychiatrists are reported as agreeing that most wife-beaters have a personality disorder. Whether considered psychopathic or not, the assaulter is "aggressive, dangerous, plausible and deeply immature."

Trigger Event

The batterer's actions are never warranted by the actual triggering event—which might be as trivial as his wife's breaking of an egg yolk when she was cooking breakfast, or fury that the first piece of birthday cake went to a guest

64   rather than to him, or because *his* driver's license was suspended. Others have reported that the wife's saying she didn't like a wallpaper pattern, or wearing her hair in a pony tail, resulted in a beating. Thus, on the surface, trivial actions evoked violent responses—some men have even beaten their sleeping wives. Obviously, most of these triggering actions—I stress the fact that "to trigger" does not mean "to be responsible for"—are simply a peg on which to hang the hat of rage. Ray Fowler, director of the American Association of Marriage Counsellors, described the wife-batterer as "a generally obsessional person who has learned how to trigger himself emotionally" (in Martin, 1976). Often such men interpret the most reasonable comments by their wives as nagging or whining complaints.

An important aspect of the violence is reported by wives: these husbands hit with fists, not with the open hand; they are expert in aiming blows at places that do now show—the breasts, stomach (even when, or probably *because*, the wife is pregnant). Gelles (1972) notes that such men are good at choking, shoving, punching, kicking, pushing their victims down stairs. Obviously, the underlying intent is murderous. He also observed that violent threats are typically used by such men to intimidate, but he found no instance of a wife threatening her husband with violence.

The Victim

Phelps and Austin (1975) have made a very important observation: while male psychiatrists often characterize the wife as a domineering shrew, those who operate shelters for battered wives have learned that these women are generally inhibited, passive, and helpless. "In anxiety-arousing situations, they are unable to act. They are at a loss to come up with an effective response—in fact, any response at all." They need to learn assertiveness, here defined as "behavior that allows a person to express honest feelings comfortably, to be direct and straightforward, and to exercise personal rights without denying the rights of others and without experiencing undue anxiety and guilt."

Interaction

In considering the interaction between marital partners where violence occurs, Gelles stresses that "it takes two." "Acts of intrafamilial violence are not sporadic outbursts of irrational violence . . . victims are not simply passive 'hostility-sponges,' or whipping-boys for their violent partners. On the contrary," Gelles asserts, "the role of the victim is an important and active one." Research by Wolfgang (1972) showed that "the victim was a direct, positive precipitator of the crime in 26 percent of the criminal homicides in Philadelphia for the 4-year period from 1948–52." Of course, this was before new insights were brought to bear. According to Gelles, conjugal violence, not including homicide, is often precipitated by the victim's verbal abuse—the victim is a tormenter. Characteristic incidents are, for example, interfering with the partner's attempt to punish the children, nagging, anger over drinking or gambling, criticisms of sexual performance.

Bach and Wyden (1968) in their book *The Intimate Enemy*, describe all-out fights in which all topics are thrown into the hopper as grist for the arguments—sooner or later a nerve is hit which produces violent retaliation. They make the important point that violence is brought into play when verbal resources are insufficient. Couples become experts at attacking each other's weak points and hurting each other effectively. In considering "the abuser" they state that "violent people were born into violent families"—nothing new, but it is helpful to be reminded that the violent person is often "imprinted" on violence. Gelles also considers the effects of television violence and concludes that its lessons are readily absorbed.

Factors Leading to Violence

Gelles (1972) shows the various factors that conspire to create intrafamily violence. The crucial factor is the *offender's identity*, marked by vulnerable self-concept and low self-esteem, which stem from his *family of orientation* and the forms of *socialization* he had been exposed to, i.e., violence, violent role models, and self-devaluing experiences.

Further factors enumerated by Gelles characterize the family headed by the offender. The *family structure* might be burdened by unwanted children, religious differences, and *structural stresses* caused by unemployment and financial and health problems, *social isolation*, and *situational factors* (such as gambling, drinking, and so on) plus the acceptance of violent behavior according to the *norms and values* of the family background and community or subculture. These lead inexorably to violence.

In my opinion, however, Gelles has omitted the other crucial factor in his construct: the *victim's personality and identity*.

Toch (1969), in a study of violent men, reported that violence was used as an ego-enhancing technique, and that these men were egocentric, their own needs being the only fact of social relevance to them—they were

66   bullies and exploiters. Yet at the same time, it was observed that situational factors rather than personality were important in predicting behavior. While there is no question but that situations and events trigger violence, I believe it would be a mistake to disregard personality factors. Toch makes the important statement that "violent men play violent games because their nonviolent repertoire is restricted . . . [the violent man] rarely knows what he could do instead . . . changing his needs is not enough; we must help him arrive at the discovery of new strategies for satisfying needs."

With this serving as background to indicate the interaction and kind of men to whom masochistic women relate, let me turn to consideration of a group of women who may play a part in their own misfortunes. I recognize that not all victims are masochists, but a goodly number are, in subtle ways. There is a special link between the battered wife and the victim of rape, although I hasten to say that not every rape victim has had a part in the outcome. For the rape victim, the violence—which may be a single, never-repeated encounter—includes sexual assault; for the battered wife, the violence may be the major link in an ongoing sexual and interpersonal relationship. For both, the sexual element creates a special vulnerability to hurt.

In recent literature on violence and spouse abuse, there is a tendency to deny the role of the woman or her masochistic predisposition. Lenore Walker (1978), in an excellent article on learned helplessness, is really using a cognitive euphemism for masochism. She says:

The myth of the masochistic woman who finds her appropriate mate has been the most popular explanation for the analytical and psychopathological viewpoints. Blaming the victim or her batterer and labeling either one or both mentally ill forms a cognitive set that prevents understanding of such violent love relationships. It is probable that a combination of sociological and psychological variables account for the existence of the battered woman syndrome.

While this is undoubtedly true, I feel it is a mistake to cast out Freud's concept of masochism—a term that has been in use a long time. Be it *learned helplessness* or *pain dependence,* it can be considered in terms of developmental and cultural influences rather than instinct as an undercurrent to libidinal concepts. Selkin (1975) has reported on a study of rape resisters, suggesting that women who resist are more flexible than those who do not, more likely to understand another's point of view, including the rapist's. He noted that the first act of resistance is refusal to stop or agree to help or be helped by strange men. He observed that rapists have a kind of sixth sense about women who are vulnerable and who live alone. In a sense, they test out their victims (Shainess, 1976). Of course, this is not to claim that every woman who is raped, beaten, or murdered is masochistic.

Freud, in *The Economic Problem of Masochism* (1959), pointed out in relation to men that "The masochist wants to be treated like a little, helpless, dependent child, but especially like a *naughty* child." He went on to say that "if one has the opportunity of studying cases in which the masochistic fantasies have undergone especially rich elaboration, one easily discovers that in them the subject is placed in a situation characteristic of womanhood, i.e., they mean that he is being castrated, is playing the passive part in coitus, or is giving birth." Alas for the fact that in Freud's view weakness and femininity were equated! Nonetheless, he was accurate, although he was observing something much more complex than he realized, for he was undoubtedly including the gender confusion of transsexuals and homosexuals in these observations. But returning to his views on masochism, he observed that if mental processes were governed by the pleasure-principle, so that avoidance of pain is the first aim, then masochism is in this light incomprehensible. He connected passivity with masochism and properly pointed out that it is the suffering itself that is important, not who passes the sentence (of course, it is really the masochist him/herself who passes sentence), and he added: "the true masochist always holds out his cheek wherever he sees a chance of receiving a blow." He noted that a person may give up one form of suffering for another— "the maintenance of suffering is all that matters. Feelings of guilt are traded in, as it were, for a need for punishment. Introjected persons, via the superego, become harsh, cruel, inexorable." He observed that masochistic persons seem to be dominated by an especially sensitive conscience. He equated all this with "the feminine wish to have passive sexual relations with the father," and felt that "the temptation to sinful acts forces the masochist to do something inexpedient, to act against his own interests, ruin the prospects which the real world offers, and possibly destroy his own existence." He observed the inconsistency of it—"one might expect that a person in the habit of avoiding aggressions . . . would have a *good* conscience as a result."

Now, if we eliminate the passive oedipal concept—and Waites (1978) also points to Freud's error in tying up masochism with erotic pleasure— and if we take into account Freud's naive image of parents as universally benign, then we can see that the person has introjected, or, in other words, become imprinted upon, not by persons who "have *become* harsh, cruel, inexorable," but by significant adults who *were* in fact harsh, cruel, and inexorable. The world of the masochist is peopled with such figures; every interaction is a special coping style, an intended defense against such figures, a specious and spurious survival mechanism based on a deeply held conviction of unworthiness. The masochistic woman (and happily, there are some women who are not) caught in the repetition compulsion—

68 one of Freud's great observations—unwittingly chooses a dangerous figure to relate to, because it is the only kind of figure appearing real to her, and then acts out her defensive style. The combination is deadly.

Freud also described a kind of hypnotic transference. Rioch (1943) spoke of this in considering transference phenomena, pointing out that transferences are like congealed posthypnotic suggestions in which there is a repetitive "naming" of the child by the parent: "you are naughty," "you are stupid," "how can mother love a bad girl?" She felt that the child was in a "chronic state of hypnosis."

According to Spiegel (1960), there is a compulsive triad relating to the posthypnotic suggestion: (1) carrying out of the command; (2) amnesia for the command; and (3) rationalization to account for carrying out of the command. The masochistic person is in fact carrying out long-range, posthypnotic suggestions from childhood—the effect of a particularly cruel parent, especially a mother, is the formation of what I will call "the masochistic style."

The double-bind phenomenon, as described by Weakland, Bateson, et al. (1960), also applies here: there is a type of communication in which one person (the less powerful) feels absolutely obliged to understand the communication of the other (the more powerful). Since the communication carries two contradictory statements no clarification is possible, and the less powerful person is left confused and frightened.

The helplessness, plasticity, and long period of dependency of the human infant make it particularly vulnerable. The fact that painful stimuli or experiences facilitate survival means that they make a deeper impression and have more durable effects, as Hess (1959) showed in his studies of human imprint phenomena. This shapes the quality of emotional dependency in the human being, and the masochistic person is, therefore, afraid to resist, refuse, offend, or insist on limits. She apologizes in advance for a fancied misdeed, excuses herself, is full of mea culpas. Her feeling of guilt is all-pervasive. As one patient put it: "I know I haven't done anything bad, but I am constantly expecting an accusation." An accusation or criticism will, like a magnet acting on iron filings, pull all kinds of unpleasant feelings about the self to the surface.

Contrary to Freud's view that the father is the most significant figure to the child, it seems certain that all persons giving the child its early care shape its feelings; but the first early and comprehensive caretaker, the mother, plays the most important role, especially with daughters. If the mother's self-hate makes it difficult or impossible for her to identify with her maternal role and project a positive feeling to the child, this rejection will play its part in the child's development. Further, the mother, more than any other person, mediates cultural attitudes to the child, especially to a daughter. Nothing very new is being said here, but the point permits a word about the sociocultural circumstances that shape feminine masochism.

Of course, awareness of superior masculine strength and lack of control over their reproductive processes, must have originally shaped women's submissiveness. As Shainess (1977) indicated, legal codes played a part in making a woman a man's chattel, as Shakespeare made clear in *The Taming of the Shrew*. Listen to Petrucchio, who of course feels no embarrassment about proclaiming that he has married the "horrible" Kate for her money: "I will be master of what is mine own. She is my goods, my chattels; she is my house [note the sexual innuendo], my household stuff, my field, my barn, my horse, my ox, my ass, my anything." As I have pointed out elsewhere (Selkin, 1975), in reviewing literary criticism of *The Shrew* I came across the fact that it was an accepted principle of common law in England that a man might beat his wife, provided that the stick he used was not thicker than his thumb. The ducking stool could be repeatedly soused in a pond or river to punish a scolding woman as late as 1809. John Taylor, one of the so-called Water Poets, counted sixty whipping-posts within one mile of London prior to 1630, and it was not until 1791 that the whipping of female vagrants was forbidden by statute. The brank—a particularly cruel gag—was in common use to punish "a certain sort of woman." This is most instructive. Winter (1892) has stated: "It is not that the gentlemen of England are tyrannical and cruel in their treatment of women; but the predominance of John Bull in any question between him and Mrs. Bull is a cardinal doctrine of British law." Thus, acceptance of brutality to women and wives is a cultural heritage, and women, having little resort to help, have done what the helpless do—succumbed and fitted into the expected mold, to avoid trouble. Hilberman (1976) has reported that juries have been known to acquit rapists, even when women were brutally beaten, because their victims "did not resist enough."

Of course Horney (1967), in "The Problem of Feminine Masochism," rejected the bio-instinctual psychoanalytic basis for masochism. She proposed many contributing factors for what was observable, including regarding the self as weak or helpless, in part from a social view of women as inferior; emotional dependency; the blocking of outlets for expansiveness and sexuality; economic dependence on men; restriction of women to the sphere of family life; the surplus of marriageable women, and so forth.

I believe that often the husband who assaults his wife is paranoid or he is a sadistic person for whom the ongoing destruction of another person is the central theme of relatedness. His wife aims at avoiding trouble by being "a

70   good little girl," but because she does not really understand the nature of their relationship, she cannot succeed. (Of course, he does not understand it either, but he *does* succeed!) His fault-finding stems from his inner mood and the degree of his anger or hate, *not* from her behavior, although some insignificant action of hers may trigger the violence. In the need "to be good" (although the feeling is that of "being naughty" in the orientation in which the other person—the husband—is the primary arbiter of what is proper behavior), it is obvious that, among other problems, such women have an unresolved symbiosis with the mother—they allow themselves to be engulfed like food particles surrounded by an amoeba. The all-pervasive feeling of badness and of guilt is so easily triggered in masochistic persons that they are magnetized into self-abasing behavior, into victimization. In threatening interchanges, they buy others off by submission and settle for living marginally in order to "survive." While it is recognized that a threatened wolf may save its life by offering the jugular to the near-victor of a battle, humans often fight (symbolically) to the death, so that the submissive efforts of the masochistic style are prone to failure.

Vignettes

As one patient reported: "Nothing I ever did was right—everything was bad or wrong. My outstanding work at school was ignored—except when I got less than a 95—then I was questioned and punished. The punishment was so unyielding—I was confined to my room for a whole week for being a half hour late one afternoon when I was in high school. Now, when anything goes wrong, no matter how small, I blow it up out of proportion. I realize what I am doing, I know it's wrong, but I can't help it."

Notice in this report the number of times the words "right" and "wrong" are used. The language of the masochist contains extremes; everything is black or white, right or wrong. Of course, our English language is so structured, as has been observed by general semanticists, that there is little ease in expressing degrees of moderation, shades of grey.

Here is another statement by a young woman: "If anything is wrong, I immediately think it has to do with me. I spend a lot of energy trying to see how to avoid trouble, and I can't because its unpredictable. I seem to be looking for the opportunity to make myself anxious. I get all upset about things that don't even happen. Any change is threatening to me. Yesterday, something happened that reminded me of my mother—or rather, how I used to feel with her. My boss wasn't enthused about a project I had finished. I immediately thought I would lose my job. Here, I just got a promotion, and a considerable increase in salary; I knew he was upset about something personal, and yet I reacted as if it was my fault. I feel as if whatever I do, it's never enough."

Of course, I do not advocate being unself-critical—appropriate self-appraisal is an important aspect of autonomy. But the statement just quoted is hypercritical and also reveals the centrality, and what might be called the "passive grandiosity," which is a compensatory development in masochism. Imperfection is always on view; criticism never means "you are doing all right but can still improve"; it means "you are inadequate, wrong, hopeless." As a result, the masochistic person spends time trying to "second-guess" authority figures instead of expressing the self; instant defense, instant apology is the style. It leads to trouble, because the bully cannot be assuaged by submission; the message of weakness promotes the victimization even more strongly.

The young woman just referred to recently received a car as part of her promotion. She was allowed to pick one to her liking, within a certain price range, and she chose a sporty two-seater. She went to see her mother and proudly showed the car. Her mother's response was: "Don't you think it's selfish of you to get a two-seater?" This attack becomes even clearer with one small additional piece of information: her mother lived in another state, and so was not in any way affected by the size of the car.

Let me give a few examples of masochistic interaction.

A young woman was given a large camelia plant for her birthday by her boyfriend, with whom she lived. It was ordered from a friend's florist shop. Within a day, the buds dropped off and she returned the plant to the florist, who said: "Look, keep it for a week, and if it does not have some blooms, I'll give you something else in its place." She lugged the heavy pot home again.

A week later, no blossoms having appeared, she brought it back to the florist. He was not there, but his assistant agreed to an exchange; she picked a plant she liked and carried it home. An hour later the florist called her angrily saying she must not have watered the plant, since the soil was dry, and in any event she could not keep the plant she had. She remarked to me that she had not watered the plant the day she returned it so that it would not be heavier than necessary. She brought the new plant back. The florist greeted her with annoyance and insisted that she take back the original, which she did.

Here, one can see that her back-and-forth trips were a submission to symbolic rape. Her fear was that since she saw the florist socially it might be embarrassing to run into him. It never occurred to her that *he* should feel some embarrassment; or that had she remained firm in the first place the

72 whole thing might have been resolved immediately. Further, I called her attention to the fact that it could be even *more* embarrassing to her on seeing him socially after letting herself be exploited than it would have been to be polite but firm. She commented, "The things that I am anxious about have little basis in reality, much of the time. I expect things to go wrong, I feel threatened and defensive. I can see that I make trouble for myself."

In another episode, this young woman's boss complained because one of her assistants had ordered a particular trade magazine. In a firm where thousands are spent with little thought, a fuss was made over a twelve-dollar subscription. She felt very threatened by her boss's annoyance. "You know," she told me, "this magazine is very useful. It is necessary to keep in touch with what is going on in the field. It's really not wasteful at all." I observed that that would have been a perfect reply to her boss. Her response was that it came out because she felt safe with me—she could not have said that to him.

Another young woman started her own business, which became quickly quite successful. She took in some partners because of the need for additional capital. It became evident that there would be a problem with one of them, as he took on the role of "boss" over her, interrogating her about her whereabouts and talking about *his* business and *his* success. It was part of his responsibility to place an ad, in which she had previously requested that her name as founder of the business and designer, be mentioned. He had "forgotten" once before. At a firm meeting, the following interchange took place: She: "Did you put my name in the ad?" He: "Oh, I forgot. Remind me (!) to call tomorrow morning at ten." She: "I'm not sure I'll be able to call you at that time." He: "Well, I hope I'll remember. Wait a minute, I think I did call—yes, I think I did." She: "All right, case closed."

This interchange is also ongoing acceptance of symbolic rape. Why had he forgotten something of importance to the firm, as well as to her? Her response to his demand that *she* shoulder the responsibility for remembering was a submission—her reply should have been "*You* better remember." His sudden memory of something he had apparently totally forgotten, taken in its context, can only be seen as a smokescreen, rather than a true recall, carrying the meta-message, "I am not going to tell *you* the truth." Her final statement, "Case closed" is total capitulation, conveying the message "I won't make trouble, I am a nice girl, I want to be liked, I won't fight." After due consideration, she arrived at the idea of calling him and telling him that on reflection, the case was *not* closed, that she was extremely dissatisfied with the discussion, that it was *his* responsibility to place the ad properly, and that she would regard it as malicious if her name did not appear.

Here is another session with the same young woman in which she reported a phone call from a young man to arrange for a "blind date." She commented that it had been a very long conversation. Not only had it interfered with some tasks she had planned to attend to, but she was very uncomfortable as she found a need to go to the bathroom increasingly urgent. I asked why she waited for *him* to end the conversation, and this led into a discussion of her "suffering passivity."

She reported that the young man in question had volunteered that she did not seem very aggressive, as so many were in her line of work. Her response? "I don't think of myself as aggressive, but I suppose I must be, in order to survive." (Note her acceptance of his premise, "clutching to her breast" a negative comment.) After some talk, he suggested that they go out. "I don't suppose there is anything much on the west side where you live?" he said. She hastened to assure him that there were places there, although she wished to go elsewhere.

"Do you like to get dressed up, or would you prefer to be more informal?" he asked. Although she had gotten a new dress recently and was longing to "go out in style," she agreed that informality was all right. They decided to meet at 8 P.M. at her apartment, but he then raised the question of whether he would have the time to go home and change to jeans. He said he would call her shortly before coming over, thus leaving her having to be ready but uncertain about when he would get in touch with her.

There were additional features of this initial conversation which indicate that from the very opening gambit, there was a series of moves in which he was the aggressor, she was on the defensive—the "game" was "lost" before the date even took place. One could restate this as a series of maneuvers leading to symbolic rape, with a compliant participant. At the end of the call, he said "Sorry to have kept you so long," and she responded, "Oh, that's all right." Had she been able to say, "You can bet your boots that it wouldn't have lasted so long if I hadn't wanted it to," she might have moved toward saving her position—her autonomy.

Going over salient points in the communication: Her response to his comment on the aggressiveness of women in her line of work might have been "Oh?" or, "Perhaps a few are, but certainly not most of the women I know;" or, "That's not very kind, is it?" or, "You certainly have the wrong idea." In response to "There isn't much on the west side" she might have said "My god, what about Lincoln Center and all the restaurants around"; or, "Where would *you* like to meet?" or, "I know a very nice place. . . ." In response to "Do you like to get dressed up or do you prefer being informal?" she might have replied "I certainly *do* like to get dressed up"; or, "I love to feel special on a date"; or, "I am informal so much of the time—it's fun to get dressed up now and then." Replying to "Where do you want to

74 meet?" she might have said "Why don't you decide that?" or, "If you insist, there's a very nice placed called . . ." When he proposed calling her when he was ready, she might have said "I'd like to settle it now," or, "I'll expect you at 8 o'clock."

The point of this analysis is that at every turn, with each aggressive move on his part, her defensive response was fear-motivated, indicating low self-esteem, and was basically a reenactment of the kind of response learned in relation to her tyrannical father, a carrying out of the triad connected with the posthypnotic suggestion.

While other ways of coping may be appropriate under some circumstances, there is only one way to respond when locked into a situation where only one's own resources are available. If the attitudinal set of the person with whom the masochistic one is involved is negative or hostile, submission promotes ultimate victory of the bully and never leads to positive change. Resistance and appropriate counterattack is the only effective tool, leading to reluctant respect for the initially victimized person.

It is interesting that the day after the New York Times had an article on Nobel prizewinner Rosaline Yalow,[1] my patients—especially my masochistic patients—were all agog about it. They unerringly picked out a statement Dr. Yalow had made, which they recognized as impossible for themselves. She was talking about the difficult time her husband was given when he took his doctorate exams. She said: "I took *my* doctorate exam in September, and the guy was stupid enough to try the same thing on me. And my answer was, 'Goldhaber and Nye taught it to me this way, and if there's anything wrong, you better talk to them about it.' " This was an audacious statement, and leads me to the proposition that self-certainty and audacity are the opposite of masochism. Dr. Yalow went on to say, "When a guy who was an authority told Aaron [her husband] he was wrong, Aaron worried [that] maybe he could have been." It is easy to guess who may be the masochist in that family!

Space permits only a brief word about the dreams, or, more accurately, the nightmares of the masochist. But metaphorically, they are filled with being chased and being paralyzed.

In her dream, a young woman is in a car, held by robbers, tearing along a road at breakneck speed. They come to an intersection with a red light, and the car stops. She feels a moment of excitement, of victory. She manages to get out of the car, only to find her legs paralyzed, and unable to move. She wakes up in a sweat.

1. "A Mme. Curie from the Bronx," by Elizabeth Stone, *New York Times Magazine*, April 9, 1978.

A brief word also about the sexual arena—a place where masochistic and submissive behavior is very much in evidence. In the past, unfortunately, women have been professionally coached to be submissive to their husbands' sexual demands, because that was considered "feminine" behavior. But submission to another's will is a negation of the self, and it causes trouble in the sexual arena as well as elsewhere.

A more extreme example of masochistic invitation to violence was revealed by a patient who was very hypnotizable, went to a hypnotist for help with an obesity problem, worked for him without salary, and also became his compliant sexual partner. She was rescued from this relationship in the therapy only to take up with another boyfriend, who had a particular sexual style: he liked to put his hands around her throat and squeeze, as orgasm was impending. It was not as easy to rescue her from this, but fortunately, with treatment, she gave up this relationship before anything seriously harmful occurred.

Another instance comes to mind of the start of a relationship which had a long sado-masochistic style and ended with wife battering, marital rape, and finally divorce.

The woman reported that at the end of the very first date, which was delightful, the young man took her home in a taxi. He took her hand in his, and held it on his lap. She was uncomfortable at the recognition that she seemed to be touching an erect penis. She was horribly embarrassed, didn't dare pull her hand away, because "what would he think of me, if I was wrong?" (Of course, you recognize that this took place before the "sexual revolution.") They were married fairly quickly, and she was dimly aware that they somehow seemed to focus on *his* needs, never hers.

In the first year, he had occasion to attend a conference in another city. She couldn't go with him, but arranged to meet him two days later. He was staying with friends while alone, but had a hotel reservation for her arrival and was to join her at a certain time. She arrived, filled with eagerness after their first "separation." She waited in the hotel room for several hours, becoming increasingly miserable and not knowing what might have happened or whom to call. Finally the phone rang. It was her husband. "Where have you been?" she inquired tearfully. "Oh," he replied, "the hotel made a mistake and put me in another room and I was waiting for you—I'll be right up." They embraced when he came in, and the unfortunate occurrence was over. But somewhere she registered the fact that there was something odd—*he* did not seem by far as upset as she had been. This came out when she was considering his dishonesty with her, and how successfully he could "pull the wool over my eyes." She recalled the

76   degrading details of her divorce in Juarez. But she reported that one thing had comforted her: she had seen a statue of Juarez, and at its base, in Spanish, were his words: "El respecto al derecho ajeno es la Paz." ("Respect for the rights of others is peace.")

Expecting, and demanding, respect for oneself as a person is an important aspect of psychological health. The failure to achieve this, to dare to throw the spotlight back upon the other person when he or she aggresses, is the major interactional problem of the masochistic person, based upon feelings of badness, guilt, unworthiness—all of which create fear.

In concluding, I want to point out that I have deliberately avoided presenting interchanges directly involving rape or battery, but every illustration came from a woman victim of one or both of these assaults. My aim was to isolate the kind of interaction, seen in its everyday context, which makes such women vulnerable.

Finally, here is an ad I came across in the "personals" column of a local newspaper, which was not only a set-up for masochism and violence but could only have appeared in a society grounded in these:

Aging, ugly, bitter, disenchanted,
poverty-stricken, antisocial fellow
(50s, 6'3, 185 lbs.) and the real me
is harder to get to know than the
surface statistics. If you're a
breathtakingly attractive girl
(we'll be a striking couple) who'd
care to try, call OR 3-1777—anytime."[2]

Summary

The recent growth of violence toward women, including rape, assault, wife-battering, and marital rape, has elicited much interest, particularly by women's self-help groups and police who see the victims. The type of violence often indicates that the offender is striking out against an incorporated, hated mother-image.

Freud elaborated on the concept of feminine masochism as a universal trait of women—this plays into the notion that they seek, or enjoy, the punishment they receive. His concept of masochism has been re-examined and translated into a more or less universal, culturally determined process that women use in dealing with certain situations, suggesting that their

2. *Our Town*, March 26, 1978

gender restriction in society has played a part in the evolution of a submissive and self-destructive style which does indeed increase their vulnerability to violence.

This tendency can be observed in many everyday interchanges, in which
the fear of men—particularly as authority figures—leads to difficulty. This
process was minutely examined in the effort to offer an effective counter-
process.

References

Bach, G. R., & Wyden, P. 1968. *The intimate enemy*. New York: Avon.
Fowler, R. 1976. In D. Martin, ed., *Battered wives*. San Francisco: Glide.
Freud, S. 1959. The economic problem of masochism. In *Collected papers*, Vol. 2. New
    York: Basic. (Original work published 1924.)
Gelles, R. J. 1972. *The violent home*. Beverly Hills: Sage.
Hess, E. H. 1959. Imprinting. *Science, 130:* 133.
Hilberman, E. 1976. *The rape victim*. New York: Basic.
Horney, K. 1967. The problem of feminine masochism. In H. Kelman, ed., *Feminine
    psychology*. New York: Norton.
Martin, D. (ed.) 1976. *Battered wives*. San Francisco: Glide.
Phelps, S., & Austin, N. A. 1975. *The assertive woman*. San Luis Obispo, Calif.: Impact.
Pizzey, E. 1976. In D. Martin, ed., *Battered wives*. San Francisco: Glide.
Rioch, J. McK. 1943. The transference phenomenon in psychoanalytic therapy. *Psychiatry,
    6:* 147.
Selkin, J. 1975. Don't take it lying down. *Psychology Today, 8* (January).
Shainess, N. 1976. Psychological significance of rape: Some aspects. *NY State J Med. 76:*
    2044.
Shainess, N. 1977. Psychological aspects of wife-battering. In M. Roy, ed., *The battered
    woman*. New York: Van Nostrand Reinhold.
Spiegel, H. 1960. Hypnosis and the psychotherapeutic process. *Compr Psychiatry, 1:* 174.
Sullivan, H. S. 1953. *Collected works*, Vol. 2. New York: Norton.
Toch, H. 1969. *Violent men: An inquiry into the psychology of violence*. New York: Aldine.
Waites, E. A. 1978. Female masochism and the enforced restriction of choice. *Victimology, 2:*
    535.
Walker, L. 1978. Battered women and learned helplessness. *Victimology, 2:* 525.
Weakland, J. H., Bateson, G. et al. 1960. The "double-bind" hypothesis of the schizo-
    phrenic and three-party interaction. In D. Jackson, ed., *The etiology of schizophrenia*.
    New York: Basic.
Winter, W. 1892. *Old shrines and ivy*. Boston: Macmillan.
Wolfgang, F. 1972. Patterns of criminal homicide. In R. J. Gelles, ed., *The violent home*.
    Beverly Hills: Sage.

The Myth of Women's Masochism

PAULA J. CAPLAN

The notion that women are innately, inevitably masochistic is an old one (e.g., see Deutsch, 1944), and it is still widely accepted by practicing clinicians. This has led to manifestations in women of healthy, human needs (such as a search for pleasure or for release from tension) being misinterpreted as manifestations of the need to suffer. Jean Baker Miller (1976) explained that this misinterpretation of women's behavior has been perpetuated by "a dominant group" in our society "despite overwhelming evidence" that women are not masochistic (p. 8). Jessie Bernard (1981) noted the important role that has been played in this process by language: "There seems to be in American English, in fact, a tendency . . . for words that designate women to become debased. . . . The love-and/or-duty ethos of the female world becomes 'masochism'" (p. 376).

In a general dictionary, *masochism* is defined as:

1. *Psychiatry.* the condition in which sexual gratification depends on suffering, physical pain, and humiliation. 2. gratification gained from pain, deprivation, etc. inflicted or imposed on oneself, either as a result of one's own actions or the actions of others, esp. the tendency to seek this form of gratification. 3. the act of turning one's destructive tendencies inward or upon oneself. 4. the tendency to find pleasure in self-denial, submissiveness, etc. (*Random House Dictionary of the English Language*, 1967)

According to Krafft-Ebing (1901/1950), who coined the term before the turn of the century (Lenzer, 1975), masochism is

the wish to suffer pain and be subjected to force. By masochism I understand a peculiar perversion of the psychical *vita sexualis* in which the individual affected, in sexual feeling and thought, is controlled by the idea of being completely and

"The Myth of Women's Masochism" by Paula J. Caplan, *American Psychologist*, *39* (2), 130–39. Copyright © 1984 by the American Psychological Association. Reprinted by permission of the publisher and author. Dr. Caplan is a clinical psychologist and Professor of Applied Psychology, Ontario Institute for Studies in Education, Toronto, Canada.

unconditionally subject to the will of a person of the opposite sex; of being treated by this person as by a master, humiliated and abused. . . . the essential and common element in all these cases is *the fact that the sexual instinct is directed to ideas of subjugation and abuse by the opposite sex.* (pp. 131, 133, italics in original)

In a contemporary article by Parkin (1980), one sees an example of clinicians' continuing interpretation of women's behavior as masochistic. Psychoanalyst Parkin gave only one case history in this article about masochism, but in that case history of "Miss C" he did not explicitly say, "Here is evidence of her masochism." He simply gave a brief description of her behavior and followed that with a discussion of the *etiology* of her masochism. Thus, the following appears to be what he regarded as evidence of Miss C's masochism:

There were also some indications that she felt herself to be abused and exploited by those with whom she had business or professional relationships: her physician who had prescribed a birth control pill was blamed for causing a malignant growth which was discovered in her breast, the mechanics who repaired her car defrauded her in ways to which she passively acquiesced, and merchants sold her goods which she frequently felt were not as represented. Occasionally she sought legal opinion about her rights but rarely proceeded to litigation. (pp. 309–10)

It is difficult to find signs that Miss C enjoyed the upsetting experiences described above. Furthermore, the description presents Miss C's experience with the physician, the birth control pill, and the tumor with the implications that, first of all, she had *sought out* such suffering and, second, that she somehow should have known (although there is no suggestion that the physician should have) that if she took the pill she would develop a malignant growth. In addition, for a female person to be defrauded by automobile mechanics is a depressingly common occurrence, and in the face of such treatment, unless one is very well-informed about automobile engines, one is hard put to do anything about it. Finally, many people of both sexes have been sold goods that were not as represented. However, this seems to be Parkin's attempt to describe a woman's masochistic behavior. Coming at the end of that paragraph, as though it were a final, convincing flourish, is Parkin's statement that Miss C rarely proceeded to litigation. One implication of this is that if one is *not* masochistic, one seeks legal redress and often proceeds to litigation—hardly a supportable assumption. Beyond that, given the history of many psychoanalytic writers, if Miss C *had* regularly proceeded to litigation, it is likely that she would have been diagnosed as hysterical (Wolowitz, 1972), castrating, and so on.

A second example of many current clinicians' attitudes is instructive. Newman and Caplan (1982) noted that enjoyment of pain and humiliation themselves—the heart of the definition of masochism and of its commonly

80 understood meaning—is very different from both the willingness to make do with less because one has never had more and the willingness to endure the bad in order to get the good. These last two patterns appeared to Newman and me to characterize the juvenile female prostitutes we studied, whereas "masochism" did not. One psychiatrist told us after a public presentation of this material that, although it did sound from our paper as though these girls said that they did *not* enjoy pain and humiliation, they were no doubt *un*consciously masochistic.

In the following examples of females' behavior, the first girl does not seek out pain but rather tries to make do with what she has and to endure unpleasantness in the hope that if she does, she will have a better future. Example 2 comes much closer to what might be legitimately considered the pursuit, although not the enjoyment, of pain. The crucial point is that the kinds of behavior in both examples have been called "masochistic."

1. A 13-year-old girl was raised by a young single mother who came from a problem-ridden family and was not able to offer her much in the way of love and emotional support. The girl's father left her mother when he learned that his child was a girl, and he sent her a Christmas card about every third year. When the girl reached puberty, she began working as a prostitute. Her pimp told her that she was his best girl and that he planned to set her up in a special apartment with him "very soon." She continued to believe his promises—although they were not kept—for eight months, when a new pimp took her away by making a similar promise.

2. A series of photos with text in *Chic* magazine [is] called "Columbine Cuts Up." Here, Columbine is shown stabbing herself in the vagina with a large butcher knife and cutting her labia with scissors. She is smeared with blood and on her face is a fixed smile. In a purported interview with this "panting mime" *Chic* has Columbine say, "I would much rather masturbate with a knife than a dildo. I guess, because I've always had an inferiority complex, I think of myself as deserving to be stabbed and killed. (Kreps, 1982. p. 12)

A particular concern is that, with one exception, a reading of major theories and clinical writings about women and masochism reveals that most of these writers are not describing masochism, even though they are applying that word to certain kinds of behavior. In the following section I will trace several important theories and attempt to show that (1) all but one are not really about masochism per se and (2) many of them are based on distorted or strangely misclassified aspects of women's behavior.

Psychoanalytic Theories of "Masochism"

The single theory in which the term masochism seems to have been used accurately in the strictest sense is Freud's work on the "death instinct." As

Lenzer (1975) points out, Krafft-Ebing described masochism, but it was left to Freud to inquire into its causes. When Freud became interested in what he called the masochistic repetition compulsion—the repeated placing of oneself in positions (or the emitting of certain kinds of behavior) that lead to one's own unhappiness—he was led to postulate that such behavior was caused by the death instinct. There were, he suggested, two primary instincts. One was Eros, the energy that drove humans to reproduce and try to survive; the other was Thanatos, the drive to return to the previous, inanimate state of matter (Freud, 1920/1959).

Keeping in mind that in *Beyond the Pleasure Principle,* where he articulated this theory, Freud by no means suggested that this applied more to women than to men, there are two points of interest with respect to the death-instinct explanation of masochism. One is that within the same book Freud said that the masochistic repetition compulsion was the person's attempt to prepare better for the repetition of a previously devastating occurrence. The other is that the masochistic repetition compulsion was a direct manifestation of the death instinct. He did not attempt to reconcile these two very different explanations of the repetition compulsion, and that is interesting because he thereby let stand one Thanatos explanation (the drive toward death) and one Eros explanation (the attempt to avoid pain) for the same "masochistic" behavior. Only if one accepted the Thanatos and rejected the Eros explanation could this be considered a description of genuine masochism—the seeking of the pain itself.

The second problem with Freud's death-instinct explanation of masochism is that, as Reich (1972) has pointed out, "to say that masochism consisted in the pleasure derived from *unpleasure* did not explain anything" (p. 234). Perhaps Freud's description of the death instinct is not much more than a way of saying that when one sees people hurting themselves or getting into upsetting situations, one should not be surprised, because self-harm is natural.

Several years later, in 1924, Freud addressed the issue of masochism from a different standpoint, proposing that there were three categories of masochism:

as a condition imposed on sexual excitation, as an expression of the feminine nature, and as a norm of behaviour. We may, accordingly, distinguish an *erotogenic,* a *feminine,* and a *moral* masochism. The first, the erotogenic, masochism—pleasure in pain—lies at the bottom of the other two forms as well. Its basis must be sought along biological and constitutional lines. . . . The third . . . form assumed by masochism . . . [is] a sense of guilt which is mostly unconscious. (Freud, 1924/1961, p. 16).

Sexual masochists' fantasies, Freud wrote, place them in a "characteristically female situation; they signify, that is, being castrated, or copu-

82   lated with, or giving birth to a baby" (Freud, 1924/1961, p. 162). Thus, he considered men's sexual masochism essentially feminine, and thus the feminine and the masochistic were presented as though they were equivalent. He might have said that certain men's behavior is "feminine" without calling it "masochistic," or vice versa, but he chose instead to identify the two with each other.

In this connection, it is instructive to note that although many theorists writing after Freud did not specifically identify masochism as feminine, others did, and this belief was so widely accepted among psychoanalytic theories that Horney (reprinted in Miller, 1978) referred to "the psychoanalytic belief that woman is masochistic by nature" (p. 36). The identification of masochism as feminine pervaded the literature and clinical practice so thoroughly that recent feminist writers (e.g., Chodorow, 1978; Cohen, 1978) have found it necessary to address that identification at some length. As Sherfey (1972) pointed out, "there have been no new psychoanalytic contributions to the understanding of female psychosexual development since Freud and the early analysts (cited by Chodoff, 1978, p. 184), and Bardwick (1971) noted that 'masochism, or the acceptance of pain, is seen as truly feminine'" (p. 7).

Freud said that the male masochist feels guilt that pain will expiate. Already, then, Freud has deviated from a discussion of genuine masochism (if indeed such a thing exists). To experience guilt is surely *un*pleasurable, and if one wants to be punished or hurt so that the guilt will be expiated, that is more properly regarded as a wish to *end* the unpleasure, not as enjoyment of it. In tracing the source of the male masochist's guilt, Freud claimed that the wish to be beaten by the father stands close to the wish to have what he called a "passive (feminine)" relation to him (Freud, 1924/1961).

In summary, then, in 1924 Freud was saying that masochism, even if in a male, is feminine behavior. Similarly, Freud's loyal disciple Helene Deutsch (1944) made the simple statement that women are *naturally* masochistic, narcissistic, and passive. However, elsewhere Deutsch (1930/1969) suggested that with reference to at least one activity from the standard list of masochistic ones—reproduction—women actually receive pleasure, or at least some gratification:

Women would never have suffered themselves throughout the epochs of history to have been withheld by social ordinances on the one hand from the possibilities of sublimation, and on the other from sexual gratification, were it not that in the function of reproduction they have found magnificent satisfaction for their urges. (p. 207)

It is not clear whether the "urges" she referred to in the above quotation were masochistic or pleasurable ones. In the paragraph just cited, she portrayed women as *not* wishing to be held back and held down, so it would seem bizarre if in the same sentence she had suggested that in reproduction "magnificent satisfaction" is found for masochistic, rather than pleasurable, urges. Thus, it may be that despite having authored the famous "feminine" triad of masochism–narcissism–passivity, Deutsch did not believe that women were naturally inclined to "enjoy pain," but rather that pleasure sometimes happened to go along with some situations that included pain.

Deutsch also said that what she called "abnormal masochism" in females was a consequence of the father's failure to encourage his daughter's aggressiveness, resulting in that aggressiveness being turned inward. It is not clear how Deutsch meant for these two theories to be reconciled. That is, if women are normally masochistic, then what is abnormal masochism in a woman? Is the difference between the two only quantitative? In any case, Deutsch's statement that women are naturally masochistic is probably the baldest known formulation of the inevitability of female masochism. Both Deutsch and Freud were protected in making such claims by Freud's (1925/1961) paper on "Negation." That paper is important because, once Freud's "negation" premise is accepted, the believer first reads the theoretical statements by Freud and his supporters, and these tell what human nature is "really" like. Then, when one observes human behavior, if it seems to support those theories, one is satisfied; if it seems to be the opposite of what those theories would predict, one interprets it as a reaction formation to the "real truth" as stated in the theory. If the behavior does not seem related in any way to the theory, one interprets it as a denial of the relevant material and feelings.

Wilhelm Reich (1972) disagreed with Freud's notion that masochism is a part of a death instinct and that as an instinct it is fundamental to us all. He wrote that "masochism represents a very late product of development. . . . It seldom emerges before the third or fourth year of life; for this very reason, therefore, it cannot be the manifestation of a primary biological instinct" (p. 278). Instead, Reich regarded "self-abasement" as "a defense mechanism because of the danger of castration . . . beating fantasies are the last possibilities of a guilt-free release" (p. 280). This formulation would seem to apply primarily to males and certainly fits within the traditional psychoanalytic model. However, his discussion ranged more broadly. He explained individuals' apparent bringing of suffering or pain upon themselves in the following way: When a person "senses the mounting of the pleasure as a danger of melting or bursting but naturally longs for the

84   pleasurable release, he [sic] develops the attitude of expecting and beseeching others to help him achieve release, i.e., to help him to burst, a sensation which he simultaneously fears and wards off" (p. 330). According to Reich, then, it sometimes happens that sexual pleasure is made to feel dangerous—perhaps through castration fears, perhaps through other occurrences—and so sexual pleasure can only be expressed in the presence of some pain; it becomes associated with pain. There are, then, the primary sexual pleasure and the learned fear of sexual pleasure, and the specter of sexuality elicits both feelings. It seems clear that as long as women are not supposed to be sexual creatures, this association of both pleasure and fear with sexuality might be an extremely common occurrence for them, within the framework of Reich's theory. In contrast to Freud's death-instinct formulation, Reich believed that the "masochistic striving" is in fact "striving toward the pleasurable goal which lies behind it or is concealed in it" (p. 332). Without examining whether this in fact happens, it is crucial to note that, if the striving is toward pleasure, then it is inaccurate, confusing, and potentially very damaging to call it masochism, which suggests that the striving is for pain itself rather than for the pleasure which will follow it. Horney (1978) pointed out that in what is called masochistic activity, "there is some gratification or relief of tension connected with it, and that is why it is striven for" (p. 31), and a similar notion is implicit in the following words of Krafft-Ebing (1901/1950):

The relation is not of such a nature that what causes physical pain is here simply perceived as physical pleasure; for the person in a state of masochistic ecstasy feels no pain, either because, by reason of his [sic] emotional state (like that of the soldier in battle), the physical effect on his cutaneous nerves is not apperceived, or because (as with religious martyrs and enthusiasts), in the preoccupation of consciousness with lustful emotion, the idea of maltreatment remains merely a symbol, without its quality of pain. (p. 210)

Parkin (1980), like Reich, disagreed with Freud's death-instinct explanation and suggested instead a different etiology. He wrote: "Most writers consider the rage or hate [which Parkin said is prominent in the masochistic character] to be a reaction to the hate or at least the withholding of love of an emotionally disturbed mother" (p. 308). He postulated that the growing girl deals with this in a three-layered way (pp. 308–12): (1) At the deepest level, the girl develops what Parkin calls a *unio mystica* (primary identification) with the mother, whom Parkin describes as "hugely aggressive" and having "prominent . . . phallic characteristics." The daughter behaves in as hateful, contemptuous, or withholding a way as her mother did toward her. This seems to me to be very close to Freud's discussion of introjection of the lost or dead "object." (2) The daughter shows hatred toward her mother, as seen in the hatred the daughter shows for her analyst as part of the transference. (3) At the most superficial level, the daughter adopts an "attitude of nobility in adversity," a "reaction formation" that Parkin says covers up her hatred and resentment. Her behavior at the deepest level is considered by Parkin to be her way of saying, "I am just as hateful and contemptuous as my mother—whom I love—so you should love me."

Parkin also described the view of another psychoanalyst, Eidelberg, who said that the patient's behavior at the first level would represent her attempt to convert the passively rejected daughter role into an active one. This is, of course, reminiscent of Freud's discussion of the repetition compulsion. Even if one considered Miss C to be somehow masochistic, however, no support for that belief would come from assuming that she was trying to convert a painful experience to a less painful one.

Parkin said that he would "stress the masochist's attempt to recover the lost omnipotence in fantasy through striving for the maternal self-ideal of the grandeur of power and the fascination of fury" (p. 309). Parkin offered this as an explanation of why some women arrange to be hurt, (i.e., what they stand to gain by such behavior). To put it another way, he did not describe enjoyment of the pain but rather suggested that, because the pain has become associated with something important and pleasurable, it is to be endured or even sought. When it is sought, it is because experience has taught the patient that with the pain comes pleasure in the form of a sense of omnipotence, a feeling of being with the mother, and so on.

Blum (1977) offered a striking exception to psychoanalytic theorists' practice of considering women as naturally masochistic. He wrote that "there is no evidence that the human female has a greater endowment to derive pleasure from pain" and that he "would not regard masochism as an essential or organizing attribute of mature femininity" (p. 187).

Feminist Contributions to Understanding Masochism in Women

In recent years, feminist theorists have made contributions to the understanding of so-called "masochism" in women, although not all have presented views that are very different from the ones that Freud had proposed. Thus, for example, Mitchell (1975) did not go beyond the traditional psychoanalytic definition of masochism as "pleasure in pain" and the claim that it "typifies the feminine predicament" (p. 114). She noted that the male

86   masochist "wants to be in a female situation" (p. 114), thereby identifying this serious male psychopathology with normal femaleness: "Masochism is 'feminine' in whatever sex it occurs" (p. 115).

In 1971, although Judith Bardwick pointed out the social origins of what is called feminine masochism, she then went on both to associate such behavior with biologically determined characteristics and to suggest that it was healthy for women to learn to suppress their aggression:

Because of their sexual constitution and because of societal pressure, women repress their aggressiveness and turn their aggression inward to the self. The healthy development is to bind these destructive impulses with erotic impulses. We see this as masochism, in this context necessary for the sublimation of a potentially destructive force into pleasure associated with the pain of reproduction (or, more parsimoniously, the acceptance of a certain inevitable amount of pain in the reproductive system). (pp. 7–8)

There are two further points worth noting about the above quotation. One is the failure to address the question of whether men's aggressiveness might not need to be suppressed as well, and how this might be done, since they do not bear children. Bardwick felt that women's aggressiveness must be suppressed because it is "a potentially destructive force," but she did not address the need for suppressing men's aggression. Second, the material in parentheses at the end of that paragraph—material that appears as if it were a side comment, an afterthought—makes a fundamental difference in how women's behavior is interpreted. Is one to regard women who suffer as experiencing "pleasure associated with pain" or, quite differently, as accepting "a certain inevitable amount of pain"?

A number of feminist theorists focus clearly on the social basis of masochism. Cavell (1974), for example, wrote that "the important distinction between what is the case and what could be the case, between human nature as we find it in a given situation or culture and human nature as it might be, is so often lacking in Freud's work" (p. 194). Thus, she disputed the assumption that "masochism" in women is natural, inevitable, and the basic feminine condition. Clara Thompson (1964) made a similar argument, saying that women's "masochism also often proves to be a form of adaptation to an unsatisfactory and circumscribed life" (p. 133). Thompson (1978a, 1978b) referred to women's learned denial of their sexuality; that denial is then interpreted as evidence of their "natural masochism." In a related vein, Bernard (1981) made the important general point that sociologists have demonstrated that considerable social pressure is placed on women to behave in altrustic ways and that they are often punished for deviating from such behavior (pp. 502–503). As I will discuss later in more detail, it is precisely this learned behavior that is taken to be a sign of "natural masochism." Chodorow (1978) echoed Bernard's point as she described the way society shapes females to become thoroughly absorbed in meeting their children's needs, and Miller (1976) did the same in regard to the meeting of both men's and children's needs.

Implicitly questioning the innateness of women's masochism, Cohen (1978) questioned its universality, saying that Freud's formulation of it "was based on a Victorian type of female who, when viewed from the twentieth century, looks like a rather hysterial specimen" (p. 181). Thompson (1964) reminded the reader that Freud's theory about feminine masochism was also based in part on the fantasies of "passive male homosexuals," and she suggested that Freud was wrong to equate such fantasies with the feelings of the average women, because "a healthy woman's sexual life is probably not remotely similar" to the fantasies of such men (p. 144).

Despite the fact that she, too, helped to debunk the notion that masochism is natural for all women, Ruth Moulton (1978) also used the word loosely, to describe women whose relationships include unhappy elements. Thus, she did not question whether the women actually *enjoy* the unhappiness (pp. 254–55) or whether they put up with it because of a low comparison level of alternatives (Thibaut & Kelley, 1978) or because of some pleasure or relief from tension that the relationships also provide. It is crucial to make this distinction, because if one does not it is then a short, easy step to saying, for example, that battered wives stay with their abusers *because of* the pain. Taking as subjects for study these battered wives who have been traditionally thought by many clinicians to enjoy or bring the beatings on themselves (which *would* be real masochism), Dutton and Painter (1981) have shown that these women stay with their abusers for quite different reasons. Using a traditional behaviorist model, they point out that the beatings leave the women exhausted, emotionally and physically hurt and drained, and thus in more than usual need of some human warmth and comfort. When the women are in this particularly needy state, the men who have just abused them are often still there and sometimes even feeling guilty. Thus, whatever warmth or affection these men offer tends to be accepted by the women, simply because they are in need. Dutton and Painter have called this a theory of "traumatic bonding," emphasizing that it is not the abusive side of their abusers to which these women bond but rather to the warmer, affectionate side that meets their needs to be loved and cared for.

Analyzing Historical Roots

Theories based on the notion that women are masochistic stem from one or both of two lines of reasoning. The first involves taking the psycho-analytically based assumption that biology is destiny as a starting point, and on this basis assuming that women are masochistic. In the second, some outstanding aspects of women's behavior have been observed and mis-labeled as "masochistic," and on this basis attempts have been made to understand why they became masochistic.

In regard to the first, Krafft-Ebing (1901/1950) wrote, "In women voluntary subjection to the opposite sex is a physiological phenomenon" (p. 195). It is interesting that in making what he seems to consider a clear case for the biological basis of female masochism, he also alluded to the effects of learning:

Owing to her passive role in procreation and long-existent social conditions, ideas of subjection are, in woman, normally connected with the idea of sexual relations. They form, so to speak, the harmonics which determine the tone-quality of feminine feeling. . . . an attentive observer of life may still easily recognize how the custom of unnumbered generations, in connection with the passive role with which woman has been endowed by Nature, has given her an instinctive inclina-tion to voluntary subordination to man; he will notice that exaggeration of custom-ary gallantry is very distasteful to women, and that a deviation from it in the direction of masterful behaviour, though loudly reprehended, is often accepted with secret satisfaction. Under the veneer of polite society the instinct of feminine servitude is everywhere discernible. (pp. 195–96)

Bonaparte, a disciple of Freud, produced what may be the most exten-sive invocation of biological factors in explaining women's alleged mas-ochism: "In coitus, the woman, in effect, is subjected to a sort of beating by the man's penis. She receives its blows and often, even, loves their violence" (cited in Hyde & Rosenberg, 1980, p. 87). Bonaparte interpreted the moment of conception as embodying the foundation of women's natural masochism, saying that "the fecundation of the female cell is initiated by a kind of wound; in its way, the female cell is primordially 'masochistic'" (p. 79). She went on to say that "all forms of masochism are related, and in essence, more or less female, from the wish to be eaten by the father in the cannibalistic oral phase, through that of being whipped or beaten by him in the sadistic-anal stage, to the wish, in the adult feminine stage, to be pierced" (p. 83). Moulton (1978) pointed out that Bonaparte seemed "eager to agree that women had no libido of their own, and referred to the female's 'belated and debilitated orgasm' as giving her no choice but to surrender to the superior power of the opposite sex and the masochistic enjoyment of pain" (p. 240).

The influence of the early psychoanalytic writers in focusing on a biological basis for female masochism is not peculiar either to their era or to psychoanalysts. Bardwick (1971) claimed a biological basis for female masochism:

> As to masochism as a feminine quality, we know that many female biological functions involve some physical discomfort and sometimes significant levels of pain. Before anesthesias and pain-reducing drugs were available, masochism would have been a very functional part of the woman's psychic equipment. In the face of inevitable pain, a little enjoyment would have gone a long way. . . . When pain is liable to be very severe, as in childbirth, most American women opt for anesthesia. But I also find that many women do not seek relief from the less extreme discomforts they experience when they menstruate, and occasionally I am told that they are glad to experience the symptoms as a monthly affirmation of their womanhood. It is also possible that during coitus women find moderate amounts of pain erotic, perhaps because the vagina is not very sensitive. In that case pain would heighten the sensation of genital fusion. (p. 14)

It is worth noting that, although the above paragraph seems to be a description of the biological basis of women's enjoyment of pain, it is for the most part a description of the fact that women have often been able to learn to endure pain, and Bardwick's last statement is in fact an implicit suggestion that one aspect of this "pain" is in fact not pain at all but rather is pleasure.

Horney (1967) noted that, according to the psychoanalytic view of masochism, satisfaction sought by women in sex and in motherhood is masochistic, and the content of the girl's early sexual wishes and fantasies concerning the father is the desire to be mutilated and castrated by him. Menstruation, according to the psychoanalysts, has hidden connotations of masochism, and intercourse and childbirth are thought to provide masochistic satisfaction. They further suggest that the mother's relationship to her children is masochistic, because she has to give to the child to meet the child's needs. Insofar as men indulge in masochistic fantasies, according to psychoanalytic theory, it is out of their desire or need to play "the female role." To summarize the psychoanalytic position briefly, one observes many of the things that happen to women (intercourse, childbirth, menstruation), which are interpreted as painful or masochistic, and then one assumes that whatever happens in relation to biology must be necessary for the survival of the species. It is therefore easy to reach the standard, sociobiological conclusion that whatever is happening *must* happen that way because it has survival value. There are substantial problems with such

90 reasoning, of course. These include the fact that not all of these things that happen to women are always painful for all women. Furthermore, the assumption that all women—even the women of Freud's time—are always underneath men and in pain during intercourse, or that being underneath one's partner is necessarily painful or even passive, is mistaken.

What Horney suggested in contrast to the traditional psychoanalytic formulation is that several factors in women's lives prepare them for a masochistic conception of their role. She said these include men's greater physical strength, women's knowledge that they can be raped, biological differences in intercourse, and menstruation and childbirth, with their accompanying bloodiness and pain. These experiences, she suggested, make it easier for the rest of the forces in society to shape women into roles in which they are willing to suffer, to withstand mistreatment, and to deny their own feelings. She said in summary: "The problem of feminine masochism cannot be related to factors inherent in the anatomical-physiological-psychic characteristics of woman alone, but must be considered as importantly conditioned by the culture-complex or social organization in which the particular masochistic woman has developed" (Horney, 1967, pp. 232–33). That is, Horney did not endorse a pure "biological inevitability" explanation, but nevertheless suggested that these biological factors *prepare* woman to accept a masochistic role, with our culture then taking over.

Horney's use of the term *feminine masochism* will shortly be examined from the standpoint of whether it correctly describes what it is intended to describe. First, however, each of her biologically related points will be examined. The fact that men often have greater physical strength than women might well lead some women to feel physically inferior, but that is worlds away from leading women to *want* to suffer, which is masochism. Next, the possibility that women can be raped need not lead women to enjoy pain, any more than the possibility that men can be stabbed, murdered, or raped needs to lead men to enjoy pain. To suggest that biological differences in intercourse lead women to be masochistic reflects, first of all, a mistaken assumption that intercourse has to take place—for biological reasons—with the woman underneath the man, and it reflects furthermore a narrow focus on penile penetration as the essence and totality of sexuality, to the exclusion of other aspects of sexuality and sensuality. For many women the moment of penetration is not the crux of their experience of sexuality, and since there are various opportunities for pleasure, and specifically for sexual pleasure, in women's lives, the focus on penetration as the foundation of a woman's personality, thus supposedly leading her to become generally masochistic, seems curious. In this connection, Moulton

(1978) has said, "*Receptive aims do not imply inertness:* the truly receptive vagina is grasping, secreting, and pleasure-giving through its own functions rather than just through the erotization of pain" (p. 245). The fact that women experience menstruation and, often, childbirth may mean that they experience some pain and shedding of blood, but this does not need to lead one to conclude that women seek out pain but only that women may well learn to endure pain. Related to this is Blum's (1977) recent, strong repudiation of the psychoanalytic view that the existence of frustrations in the "mother" role is proof that women are naturally masochistic. Blum wrote that women's wish for motherhood is not a wish to suffer but is rather a wish for an experience that brings a great deal of fulfillment and gratification, or that they at the very least have reason to believe that it will be so. He wrote:

Commitment to children, despite frustration or deprivation, is not equivalent to masochism or self-punishment. Maternal devotion should not be confused with masochistic enslavement or preservation of the object from aggression. Masochism may actually interfere with feminine empathy. . . . It is impossible to derive maternal devotion and empathy from masochism, narcissism, and penis envy. (pp. 183–84)

Indeed, stepping back for a moment in considering the proposition that women's actual suffering is proof of their innate *need* to suffer, it is instructive to consider that the ability to endure pain is classically considered a masculine trait, despite evidence that women in fact have greater tolerance for pain.

Although Horney made a significant break from the focus on biological factors as "proof" of women's innate masochism, she remained part of the second stream of thought that perpetuated the view of women as masochistic. Examination of her use of the term *feminine masochism* reveals that she, too, followed this stream, which takes the following path: some of the behavior frequently shown by women is observed, it is interpreted as masochistic, and then theories must be developed to account for this. Horney, it appears, became caught up in the additional psychoanalytic practice of noticing that women are often willing to deny some of their own needs or put someone else's needs ahead of their own, and calling this masochism. There is, however, a crucial distinction between that kind of behavior and the enjoyment of pain, and whether this distinction is made has often depended on the sex of the actor. Here is one example:

If one were to apply the label of masochist to any individual—male or female—who pursues a painful and dangerous occupation that holds little in the way of secure future rewards, one might discover that professional football players (virtually all of whom are male) would fall within this diagnostic category. Picture the adolescent male athlete who . . . spends many hours being brutally assaulted in the cold, the mud and the rain. He can count on frequent and serious injuries to his body in exchange for admiration and applause for his physical strength and

92   willingness to experience pain and injury so that others may enjoy themselves. . .

We do not, however, focus on the pain and injury inherent in the footballer's occupation as the primary motivation in his choice of career and label him a masochist. . . .What is regarded as secondary to the motivation of males is focused on as primary and pathological in the motivation of females. This distorted thinking, then, permits society's critics to overlook the brutal consequences of certain activities to females—exploitation by pimps, assault by rapists, and wife-beaters—because these are considered to be simply what the woman wants. (Newman & Caplan, 1982, p. 134)

The same behavior has not only been called different things depending on the person's sex, but entire conceptual, theoretical structures to explain it differently depending on sex have been created. One might well ask why men who beat women or who want their own needs met have not come to be called "people who are covering up their masochism." This has been done with women who are assertive, aggressive, or achievement-oriented: it has been said that this is a "masculine protest"—the woman's wish to deny her innate, inevitable dependency and masochism—and thereby women have been damned for such behavior. Equivalent interpretations have not been made when men have behaved in these ways, because biological explanations cannot be resorted to: men do not menstruate, give birth, get penetrated by women during sex-for-purposes-of-producing-offspring. Masochism is thus still regarded as biologically based, whether people are aware of that or not.

Keeping this warning in mind, then, it is time to examine the aspects of women's behavior that have led to their being called masochistic. Much of the behavior that has been so used is in fact *learned* behavior. What has often been called masochistic has tended to be the very essence of trained femininity in Western culture. Daughters are supposed to be trained to be nurturant, selfless (even self-denying), endlessly patient (e.g., see Bernard, 1981; Caplan, 1981; Chodorow, 1978). What often goes hand in hand with this is low self-esteem, and this makes sense. If women are to behave in this self-denying way, then since no person with decent self-respect would be endlessly nurturant and consider herself unnatural when she wanted something for herself, society must also train women to believe that without their nurturant behavior, without what they can *give* to another person, they are nothing.

This leads back to the theory cited earlier (Newman & Caplan, 1982), but now it can be applied to the problem of masochism in women of many kinds, not just juvenile prostitutes. That is, the way daughters are socialized severely restricts their comparison level of alternatives (Thibaut & Kelley, 1978). Growing females come to feel that their value comes from the degree to which they can be self-denying. It would take exceptional young people indeed to find resources and coping mechanisms that were not wholly self-denying but which allowed them to continue to be considered feminine. The juvenile prostitutes represent the extreme of girls who have so few resources that they cannot otherwise cope.

Once females have been trained in this way and are being nurturant, charitable, and so on, this behavior is labeled masochistic. It is forgotten that they have been intensively rewarded for behaving in this way, and that thereby a strong association has been formed between such behavior and the pleasure of the reward (which is usually someone's approval). It is forgotten that women have been frightened by the threat of being considered unfeminine, ugly, and so on if they do not behave selflessly. It goes unnoticed that in developmental psychology textbooks it is taught that a sign of maturity is the ability to delay gratification for a greater good or a greater reward in the end—what women learn to do is to delay their own gratification now, hoping to be loved or appreciated later on (the Persephone complex, the proposed female counterpart of the Icarus complex described by Murray, 1955), or even to deny their own needs altogether for the sake of meeting the needs of others: the sick, the weak, the powerless, the lame, their children, their husbands. If most people were told simply that there is a person who behaves in the way just described, they would probably think, "What a fine person that is!" But if the person were then placed in a psychological clinic or on a psychoanalyst's couch and were female, the behavior would be interpreted as indubitably masochistic.

The word *masochism* initially meant something very specific. It meant the enjoyment of pain. (In my practice I have never seen directly or even heard about behavior that really indicated enjoyment of the pain itself.) This word with a highly specific meaning, however, has come to be used to apply to a host of other behavior—most often with respect to women—and although the category of behavior it is used to describe has broadened dramatically, the word has retained its connotations of psychopathology and extremity. It is probably fair to say that it is as though the word *murder* came to be used to include not only what it really means but also the spanking of one's children when they run heedlessly into the street. If one were told that such behavior on the part of a parent might not indicate a conscious desire to murder the child but surely indicated an unconscious one, one would probably ignore such an interpretation. But something similar is what has happened with the word masochism. Indeed, as Lenzer (1975) has written, "What [Freud] should have said was that it was surprising that the term masochism had spread so widely in so short a time, that it had been applied to different kinds of phenomena which were never before

94   thought to have any relation to what had come to be understood as masochism" (pp. 278–79).

An extremely intelligent, feminist graduate student who had read a great deal about the theories of masochism in women commented, "Well, but it is true—women *do* behave masochistically, and that behavior has to be explained." When asked to what behavior she was referring, she said, "Women are often very nurturant, self-denying, giving people" (Dennis, personal communication, 1982). Like many of the theorists, this student had applied the term masochism incorrectly to non-masochistic, even prosocial, mature, loving behavior. If that behavior is called masochistic, then indeed one must try to understand how women become so deeply disturbed and pathological. If, however, the term "masochistic" is not applied to such behavior but rather the behavior is described as it is (i.e., unselfish, nurturant, etc.), then the reasons women behave that way become clear: because they are nice people, because they have been told they are good girls for doing so, and because, at a more basic level, society wants females to behave that way and takes great pains to see that it happens. In fact, as Dennis (personal communication, 1982) has pointed out, because women are punished for behaving non-masochistically (by being told they are unfeminine, for example, or that this is their masculine protest), behaving in nurturant and selfless ways actually avoids the pain of such punishments. Indeed, Jean Baker Miller (1976), describing women as a subordinate group in our society, has written: "A subordinate group has to concentrate on basic survival. . . . Open, self-initiated action in its own self-interest must also be avoided. Such actions can, and still do, literally result in death for some subordinate groups. In our own society, a woman's direct action can result in a combination of economic hardship, social ostracism, and psychological isolation—even the diagnosis of a personality disorder" (p. 10). The explanation for women's altruistic behavior, then, does not lie in some strange, individual psychopathology of these women. The explanation is clear, and pains must be taken to see that women's behavior is not miscategorized and thereby used as yet another way to show disrespect for women's strengths.

Summary

One could, of course, take the position that, even if one accepts everything in the foregoing argument, women are also motivated by unconscious masochism. Part of the fascination of the attempt to understand the unconscious is that it is next to, if not totally, impossible to prove or disprove the

existence of particular bits of unconscious content or motives. However, it 95
is not my purpose to prove that there is no such thing as unconscious masochism. My purpose is to demonstrate that (1) the notion that women are unconsciously, naturally masochistic is entirely unnecessary because all of the phenomena that this theory has been proposed to explain can be explained satisfactorily and fully by other means, primarily by an understanding of healthy, human motivation; and that (2) the notion that women are naturally, unconsciously masochistic tends, by and large, to do women a profound disservice.

References

Bardwick, J. (1971). *Psychology of women: A study of bio-cultural conflicts*. New York: Harper & Row.

Bernard, J. (1981). *The female world*. New York: The Free Press.

Blum, H. P. (1977). Masochism, the ego ideal, and the psychology of women. In H. P. Blum (Ed.), *Female psychology: Contemporary psychoanalytic views* (pp. 157–91). New York: International Universities Press.

Caplan, P. J. (1981). *Between women: Lowering the barriers*. Toronto: Personal Library Publishers.

Cavell, M. (1974). Since 1924: Toward a new psychology of women. In J. Strouse (Ed.), *Women and analysis* (pp. 189–96). New York: Dell.

Chodoff, P. (1978). Feminine psychology and infantile sexuality. In J. B. Miller (Ed.), *Psychoanalysis and women* (pp. 184–200). New York: Penguin.

Chodorow, N. (1978). *The reproduction of mothering: Psychoanalysis and the sociology of gender*. Berkeley: University of California Press.

Cohen, M. B. (1978). Personal identity and sexual identity. In J. B. Miller (Ed.), *Psychoanalysis and women* (pp. 156–82). New York: Penguin.

Deutsch, H. (1944). *The psychology of women* (Vol. 1). New York: Grune & Stratton.

Deutsch, H. (1969). The significance of masochism in the mental life of women. In R. Fliess (Ed.), *The psychoanalytic reader: An anthology of essential papers with critical introductions* (pp. 195–207). New York: International Universities Press. (Originally published 1930).

Dutton, D., & Painter, S. L. (1981). Traumatic bonding: The development of emotional attachments in battered women and other relationships of intermittent abuse. *Victimology: An International Journal, 6,* 139–55.

Freud, S. (1959). *Beyond the pleasure principle* (J. Strachey, Trans.) New York: Bantam Books. (Originally published 1920).

Freud, S. (1961). The economic problem of masochism. In J. Strachey (Ed. and Trans.), *The standard edition of the complete psychological works of Sigmund Freud* (Vol. 19, pp. 159–70). London: Hogarth Press. (Originally published 1924).

Freud, S. (1961). Negation. In J. Strachey (Ed. and Trans.), *The standard edition of the complete psychological works of Sigmund Freud* (Vol. 19, pp. 235–39). London: Hogarth Press. (Originally published 1925).

Horney, K. (1967). *Feminine psychology* (H. Kelman, Ed.). New York: Norton.

Horney, K. (1978). The problem of feminine masochism. In J. B. Miller (Ed.), *Psychoanalysis and women* (pp. 21–38). New York: Penguin.

Hyde, J. S., & Rosenberg, B. G. (1980). *Half the human experience: The psychology of women*. 2d ed. Lexington, MA: Heath.

96   Krafft-Ebing, R. V. (1950). *Psychopathia sexualis: A medico-forensic study*. New York: Pioneer Publications. (Originally published 1901).

Kreps, B. (1982, June). The case against pornography. *Homemaker's Magazine*, pp. 7–22.

Lenzer, G. (1975). On masochism: A contribution to the history of a phantasy and its theory. *Signs, 1*, 277–324.

Miller, J. B. (1976). *Toward a new psychology of women*. Boston: Beacon Press.

Miller, J. B. (Ed.) (1978). *Psychoanalysis and women*. New York: Penguin.

Mitchell, J. (1975). *Psychoanalysis and feminism*. New York: Vintage Books.

Moulton, R. (1978). A survey and reevaluation of the concept of penis envy. In J. B. Miller (Ed.), *Psychoanalysis and women* (pp. 240–58). New York: Penguin.

Murray, H. A. (1955). American Icarus. In A. Burton & R. E. Harris (Eds.), *Clinical studies of personality* (Vol. 2, pp. 615–41). New York: Harper.

Newman, F., & Caplan, P. J. (1982). Juvenile female prostitution as gender-consistent response to early deprivation. *International Journal of Women's Studies, 5*, 128–37.

Parkin, A. (1980). On masochistic enthralment: A contribution to the study of moral masochism. *International Journal of Psychoanalysis, 61*, 307–14.

Random House dictionary of the English language: The unabridged edition. (1967). New York: Random House.

Reich, W. (1972). *Character analysis* (3rd ed.). New York: Simon & Schuster.

Sherfey, M. J. (1972). *The nature and evolution of female sexuality*. New York: Random House.

Thibaut, J. W., & Kelley, H. H. (1978). *Interpersonal relations: A theory of interdependence*. New York: Wiley.

Thompson, C. (1964). *On women*. New York: New American Library.

Thompson, C. (1978a). Cultural pressures in the psychology of women. In J. B. Miller (Ed.), *Psychoanalysis and women* (pp. 69–84). New York: Penguin.

Thompson, C. (1978b). Some effects of the derogatory attitude toward female sexuality. In J. B. Miller (Ed.), *Psychoanalysis and women* (pp. 58–68). New York: Penguin.

Wolowitz, H. M. (1972). Hysterical character and feminine identity. In J. Bardwick (Ed.), *Readings on the psychology of women* (pp. 307–14). New York: Harper & Row.

PART II

Femaleness and Psychological Health

Question 3

Are Women More Likely to Be Mentally Ill?

The question of whether women have a higher rate of mental illness than men has been a controversial topic since the early 1970s. Equally important is the issue of what type of therapy is best for those women who do need help. As the following pair of articles demonstrates, the answer to the first question depends on how we define mental illness. There is also the matter of how we interpret the available data. Does women's higher rate of mental illness, reported in a number of studies, merely reflect their greater willingness to admit their problems and seek help? Or do these figures say something about the role of women? Gove and Tudor (1973), for example, traced part of the problem to the low level of satisfaction attached to the role of the housewife.

Another possible explanation for the reported different rates of mental illness can be found in the classic study of Inge Broverman and her colleagues (1970), which suggested that therapists held different standards of mental health for men and women. The "healthy male" was defined as "active, independent, competitive, and logical" while the "healthy female" was defined as "dependent, passive, and illogical." In the words of one psychologist, the Broverman study demonstrates that "a normal, average, healthy woman is a crazy human being" (Hyde, 1985, p. 334).

The question of whether there is sex-role bias in psychotherapy is a highly emotional one (Stricker, 1977). More recent replications of the Broverman study have not found the same sex bias (Phillips & Gilroy, 1985). This may indicate that sexism has declined among mental health professionals. However, there is also the possibility that the type of instrument used in these empirical studies is not sensitive enough to detect the subtle sex biases of today's sophisticated therapists.

100   Not surprisingly, the related question of what type of therapy best meets the needs of women patients is also a highly charged issue. The decade of the 1970s witnessed the development of alternatives to traditional therapy. Feminist psychotherapists moved toward less patriarchal approaches, such as establishing egalitarian relationships with their patients and validating the woman's discontent and rage. Some therapists see these as healthy responses to an oppressive society. Other therapists, however, argue that feminist therapy does not work for everyone and that it may be "irresponsible for a therapist to return a changed woman to an unchanged world without the skills to negotiate within it or the resources to maintain herself in the face of it" (Pearlman, 1985, p. 10).

The arguments raised by Walter Gove and Marilyn Johnson remain major issues for professionals in the mental health field. Do women have higher rates of illness as Gove asserts? Or is Gove's thesis weakened, as Johnson suggests, because his definition of mental illness excludes certain categories that consist largely of males? The two authors also disagree over what constitutes a solution. Gove finds advantages and disadvantages in both traditional and nontraditional therapies for women while Johnson argues that feminist therapy offers unique opportunities for female growth.

References

Broverman, I., Broverman, D. M., Clarkson, F. E., Rosenkrantz, P. S., & Vogel, S. R. (1970). Sex role stereotypes and clinical judgments of mental health. *Journal of Consulting and Clinical Psychology, 34*, 1–7.

Gove, W. R. & Tudor, J. F. (1973). Adult sex roles and mental illness. *American Journal of Sociology, 78*, 812–35.

Hyde, J. (1985). *Half the human experience: The psychology of women* (3rd ed.). Lexington, Mass.: D. C. Heath.

Pearlman, S. F. (1985, December). The future of therapy. *The Women's Review of Books, 3* (3), 10.

Phillips, R. D. & Gilroy, F. D. (1985). Sex role stereotypes and clinical judgments of mental health: The Broverman findings re-examined. *Sex Roles, 12,* [1–2], 179–93.

Stricker, G. (1977). Implications of research for psychotherapeutic treatment of women. *American Psychologist, 32,* 14–22.

Additional Reading

Ballou, M. & Gabalac, N. (1985). *A feminist position on mental health.* Springfield, Ill.: Charles C. Thomas.

Brodsky, A. M. & Hare-Mustin, R. (1980). *Women and psychotherapy: An assessment of research and practice.* New York: Guilford.

Brody, C. (1984). *Women therapists working with women.* New York: Springer.

Gove, W. R. (1980). Mental illness and psychiatric treatment among women: A response. *Psychology of Women Quarterly, 4* (3), 372–76.

Howell, E. & Bayes, M. (1981). *Women and mental health.* New York: Basic Books.

Rieker, P. P. & Carmen, E. (1984). *The gender gap in psychotherapy: Social realities and psychological processes.* New York: Plenum.

Rosewater, L. B. & Walker, L. E. A. (1985). *Handbook of feminist therapy: Women's issues in psychotherapy.* New York: Springer Publishing.

Yes

Mental Illness and Psychiatric Treatment among Women

WALTER R. GOVE

In the feminist (e.g., Bernard, 1971a, 1971b; Chesler, 1971a, 1971b, 1972) as well as the more academic literature (e.g., Bagley, 1977; Gove, 1978, 1979a; Gove & Tudor, 1973, 1977; Pearlin, 1975), it is commonly asserted that women have higher rates of mental illness than men. This is a controversial position that can be challenged on many grounds. The first part of this paper examines issues that lead to the conclusion that women have higher rates of mental illness. How mental illness should be defined and possible biases that may be involved in determining its incidence are discussed. The second part of the paper looks at two possible explanations of the sex differential in rates of mental illness: (1) sex and marital roles of men and women; and (2) learned helplessness among women. The third part of the paper briefly explores some societal implications of the psychiatric treatment of women. Particular attention is paid to the therapist's role as an agent of social control or change.

Do Women Have Higher Rates of Mental Illness?

To a substantial extent, Chesler (1971a, 1972) drew her conclusion that women have higher rates of mental illness than men from National Institute for Mental Health (NIMH) reports concerning psychiatric treatment in mental hospitals, general hospitals, and outpatient psychiatric clinics. Earlier studies, most of which were based exclusively on data from mental hospitals, had consistently indicated that from at least 1910 to the early 1960s men had higher rates of psychiatric treatment (Bohn, Gardner,

"Mental Illness and Psychiatric Treatment among Women" by Walter R. Gove, *Psychology of Women Quarterly*, 1980, *4* (3), 345–362. Copyright © 1980 by Division 35, American Psychological Association. Reprinted by permission of Cambridge University Press.

Dr. Gove is a sociologist and Professor of Sociology and Anthropology, Vanderbilt University, Nashville, Tennessee.

Alltop, Knatterval, & Solomon, 1966; Dorn, 1938; Dunham, 1959; *103*
Kramer, Pollack, & Redick, 1961). Furthermore, if one were to limit
oneself to data from mental hospitals, one would necessarily conclude that
in recent years men were increasingly more likely than women to receive
psychiatric treatment. For example, for state and county mental hospitals
the ratio of male to female patients was 1.14 in 1946, 1.32 in 1955, and 2.27
in 1972 (Kramer, 1977).

Chesler (1972) contends that both absolute and relative increases in
rates of psychiatric treatment for women began around 1964. This period
was a time of expansion in the scope and availability of psychiatric services, and there was a substantial increase in the number of persons who
received these services. For example, the number of persons seen in
mental health facilities excluding private outpatient care was 1,673,352 in
1955; 2,636,525 in 1965; and 6,409,477 in 1975 (Taube & Redick, 1977).
The increase in the rate of persons receiving inpatient psychiatric care was
comparatively slight, however, and occurred solely in general hospitals,
federally assisted community mental health centers, and VA hospitals. At
the same time there was a very sharp decline in the rate of inpatient
treatment in state and county mental hospitals and no change in the rates
in private psychiatric hospitals (Taube & Redick, 1977). The vast increase in psychiatric treatment occurred in nonprivate outpatient psychiatric services (233 patients per 100,000 population in 1955; 2,185 per
100,000 in 1975; Taube & Redick, 1977).

Following Chesler (1972), this would imply that in recent years women
had much higher rates of treatment in settings other than mental hospitals
and particularly in outpatient facilities. The most recent data for all treatment settings to provide a breakdown by gender of the patient are for 1971
(Kramer, 1977). They show that women have slightly higher rates of inpatient treatment in private mental hospitals and general hospitals and
slightly higher rates of outpatient psychiatric treatment. Men, in contrast,
have much higher rates of treatment in state and mental hospitals and
particularly in VA hospitals. Overall, men have higher rates of psychiatric
treatment when all facilities are combined (2049.2 per 100,000 for men
versus 1863.5 per 100,000 for women). In short, the data on psychiatric
treatment, excluding private outpatient care, show that men have higher
rates of psychiatric treatment. Thus if we equate psychiatric treatment with
mental illness, these data indicate that women do not have higher rates of
mental illness than men.

Very serious questions can be raised about the appropriateness of equating being in psychiatric treatment with being mentally ill. Elsewhere I
(Clancy & Gove, 1974; Gove 1978, 1979a; Gove & Tudor, 1973, 1977) have

104 strongly argued that many persons in psychiatric treatment are not mentally ill, at least when mental illness is narrowly and precisely defined. Many disorders, such as alcoholism and drug abuse, appear to have fallen into the domain of psychiatry due to historical accident and the successful entrepreneurship of the psychiatric profession (Gove, 1976) and do not fit a precise definition of mental illness.

A Precise Definition of Mental Illness

The position taken in this paper is that mental illness is most appropriately treated as a specific phenomenon involving personal discomfort (as indicated by distress, anxiety, depression, etc.), or mental disorganization (as indicated by confusion, thought blockage, motor retardation, and, in the more extreme cases, hallucinations and delusions), or a combination of both conditions, that is not caused by an organic or toxic condition. The two major categories of psychiatric dysfunction that fit this definition are the neurotic disorders and the functional psychoses. The chief characteristic of the neurotic disorders is either anxiety or depression, or both, in the absence of psychotic disorganization. The functional psychoses are psychotic disorders with no established organic cause (APA, 1968).

The two other categories that fit this definition are not often used. Transient situational disorders are acute symptomatic responses to overwhelming situations in which there is no underlying personal disturbance. When the situational stress diminishes, so do the symptoms. This diagnosis is assigned mainly to children and adolescents and only occasionally to adults. The other category is comprised of the psychophysiological disorders. These are characterized by somatic symptoms that appear to be the consequence of emotional tension, although the person may sometimes be unaware of the tension. The psychophysiological disorders do not fit within the definition of mental illness being used here as clearly as do the other disorders. They are included, however, because they are functional disorders and they reflect a fair amount of distress, albeit in a somewhat masked form.

There are a number of reasons for treating these disorders as a distinct set which corresponds to a relatively narrow definition of mental illness. First, there is a similarity in symptomatology—persons in all these diagnostic categories are typically severely distressed. Second, these disorders respond to the same general forms of therapy, namely, drug therapy and psychotherapy (Gove, 1978; Gove & Tudor, 1973; Kazdin & Wilson, 1978; Kellner, 1975; Klein & Davis, 1969; Malan, 1973; Smith & Glass, 1977). Third, cross-cultural and historical evidence suggests that the concept of mental illness does not typically include the types of disorders we are excluding (Gove, 1978; Gove & Tudor, 1977; Murphy, 1976).

Two frequently used diagnostic categories do not fit this precise definition of mental illness—the acute and chronic brain syndromes and the personality disorders. The brain syndromes are caused by a physical condition, either brain damage or toxins, and are not functional disorders (APA, 1968). Most investigators clearly believe it is important to distinguish between the brain syndromes and the disorders we are classifying as mental illness. The fact that the brain syndromes make up approximately 25 percent of the first admissions to public mental hospitals emphasizes the need to distinguish between the incidence of psychiatric treatment and the incidence of mental illness as defined in this paper.

Persons with a personality disorder do not experience personal discomfort, being neither anxious nor distressed, nor do they suffer from any form of psychotic disorganization. They are viewed as mentally ill because they do not conform to social norms and they are usually forced into treatment because their behavior is disruptive to others. These persons are characterized by aggressive, impulsive, goal-directed behavior which is either antisocial or asocial in nature and creates serious problems with and for others (APA, 1968; Dohrenwend, 1975; Klein & Davis, 1969; Kolb, 1973). Not only are the symptoms associated with the personality disorders different from those associated with mental illness as we have defined it, but the forms of therapy effective in the treatment of mental illness are not effective in the treatment of the personality disorders (Gove, 1978; Gove & Tudor, 1977; Klein & Davis, 1969; Malan, 1973). Moreover, data from non-Western societies are consistent with the distinction between the personality disorder and what we are labeling mental illness. Persons in these societies who manifest the behavior that would lead to a diagnosis of a personality disorder in our society are viewed as deviants, but not as ill, and shamans and healers do not believe that such behavior can be cured or changed (Murphy, 1976). In fact, the personality disorders have only recently come to be considered within the domain of psychiatry (e.g., Robbins, 1966).

It is worth noting that labeling theory, which provides the most comprehensive alternative theoretical explanation of mental illness to the one provided by the psychiatric perspective, would also exclude these disorders from the definition of mental illness. For example, Scheff (1966), who presents by far the clearest and most elaborate labeling explanation of mental illness, treats mental illness as residual deviance—namely, deviance for which we have no name and for which there is no societal role. As alcoholism, drug addiction, mental retardation, and senility are socially

106 recognized categories with relatively clearly defined expectations for behavior, Scheff does not see them as residual rule-breaking (i.e., mental illness). Thus I, a proponent of the psychiatric perspective, and Scheff (1985), one of its leading critics, are in agreement that these four forms of behavior should not be treated as mental illness.

Sex Differences Using a Precise Definition of Mental Illness

Applying this precise definition of mental illness to national data for 1966, Gove and Tudor (1973) found that women uniformly had higher rates of psychiatric treatment in mental hospitals, inpatient psychiatric treatment in general hospitals, and outpatient care in psychiatric clinics. Similarly, comprehensive reviews of studies conducted in Western industrial nations after World War II of the practices of private psychiatrists, the psychiatric care provided by general physicians, and the results of the community surveys of mental illness showed, without exception, that women had higher rates of mental illness (Gove & Tudor, 1973). The studies themselves did not use a consistent definition of mental illness, although the vast majority of the cases considered would fit under the definition of mental illness used in this paper.

An update of these reviews (Gove, 1979a) showed that in all the studies of practices of general physicians and private psychiatrists, women had higher rates of psychiatric treatment. Of the thirty-five community studies covered in the second review, thirty-four showed women to have higher rates of mental illness. The one exception, a small study ($n = 683$) by Brunetti (1973), indicated that the rates of mental illness between the sexes are so similar that if one more woman had been mentally ill, women would have had higher rates. In short, the work using a precise definition of mental illness consistently shows women to have higher rates than men.

Data on patients in institutional settings have not been updated. As noted above, the most recent complete statistics on treatment in institutional settings are those for 1971 presented in Kramer (1977). Kramer uses diagnostic categories consistent with recent NIMH practices. Previously, persons with alcohol and drug abuse problems were categorized under the brain syndrome diagnoses if they entered treatment in a toxic state and usually categorized as having a personality disorder if they entered in a nontoxic state. Kramer, however, treats alcoholic and drug disorders as two separate diagnostic categories. This means that persons diagnosed in his study as having an organic brain syndrome almost all had some form of senile disorder. He also combined the neurotic and psychotic depressive disorders. Kramer's data show men to have higher rates of psychiatric treatment than women. If, however, consistent with our precise definition of mental illness, we eliminate from consideration alcoholics, drug addicts, persons with an organic brain syndrome, and the mentally retarded, then women emerge as having higher rates of treatment for mental illness in state and county mental hospitals, general hospitals, community mental health centers (inpatient and outpatient), and other outpatient psychiatric services, as well as for all settings combined. Thus the most recent data on treatment in institutional settings are consistent with the earlier data presented in Gove and Tudor (1973).

In summary, if one uses a precise and narrow definition of mental illness, then the data uniformly indicate that women have higher rates of mental illness. In contrast, if one uses an eclectic definition, which includes a much wider range of deviant behavior, then the evidence is mixed. With an eclectic definition, women have higher rates in community surveys, private practices of psychiatrists, and among persons receiving psychiatric treatment from general physicians, whereas men have slightly higher rates in institutionalized settings as a combined category, although this is not true of some specific institutional settings. It is critical to recognize that the eclectic definition of mental illness encompasses a variety of very different phenomena. Regardless of the reader's preference for the precise or eclectic definition, he or she should keep in mind that in the remainder of this paper the term *mental illness* will be used to refer to a functional disorder involving the overt manifestation of distress, or mental disorganization, or a combination of both.

Are the Higher Rates for Women an Artifact of Response Bias?

Phillips and Segal (1969) have argued that in our society women are expected to be more emotional than men and as a consequence it is less stigmatizing for women to verbalize emotional problems. Women are presumed to be aware of this fact and are thus more willing than men to discuss their emotional difficulties. Thus it is the position of Phillips and Segal that the apparent higher rates of mental illness among women that are found in community surveys are an artifact of societal norms which make women more willing than men to articulate their emotional problems. Unfortunately, they present no evidence bearing directly on their argument. Phillips and Segal limit their discussion to respondent behavior in community surveys. Their argument, however, has frequently been expanded by others who see the processes they describe as reflecting a generalized response set that would lead women to seek psychiatric treatment.

In a series of three studies (Clancy & Gove, 1974; Gove & Geerken, 1977a; Gove, McCorkel, Fain, & Hughes, 1976), my associates and I examined the possibility that the reports of more psychiatric symptoms by

108 women in community surveys are an artifact of response bias. We employed the same general techniques as Phillips (Phillips & Clancy, 1970, 1972) and measured three types of response bias: perceived desirability or undesirability of psychiatric symptoms, need for approval, and tendency to yeasay or naysay. In all, we have used seven mental health scales, slightly varied our indices of response bias, and used different interviewing techniques (telephone interviews once, direct interviews twice).

Perception that psychiatric symptoms were not particularly undesirable, a tendency to yeasay, and a lack of need for approval were all fairly consistently related to the reporting of high rates of psychiatric symptoms. In all of the studies, however, there were no sex differences in the perceived desirability of psychiatric symptoms or in the respondents' need for approval and in two studies there were no sex differences in the tendency to yeasay or naysay. In Clancy and Gove (1974), however, women were more likely than men to naysay. As a consequence, in all but one case we found that controlling for response bias had no effect on the reports of either men or women, and in the one exception (Clancy & Gove, 1974) the controls resulted in an increase in the mental illness rates of women. As this is the only evidence bearing on Phillips and Segal's position, and it is all negative, it is reasonable to conclude that the higher rates of reports of psychiatric symptoms among women are not an artifact of sex differences in response bias. These studies, of course, bear most directly on community surveys which consistently find women more likely to report that they experience psychiatric symptoms.

Are the Higher Mental Illness Rates for Women an Artifact of Clinician or Patient Behavior?

A frequently cited study of Broverman et al. (1970) indicates that clinicians tend to see the average man as more emotionally healthy than the average woman. This finding, which is consistent with data on sex-role stereotypes among the general population (McKee & Sherriffs 1957, 1959; Sherriffs & McKee, 1957), has often been interpreted as suggesting that clinicians are more likely to perceive women as mentally ill, regardless of actual level of disorder. This presumed bias on the part of clinicians might account for the higher rates of treated mental illness among women (e.g., Abernathy, 1976; Abramowitz & Dokecki, 1977; Chesler, 1971b, 1972).

By now there is a fairly extensive body of clinical judgment analogue studies in which the evidence of such sex bias has been examined. This literature clearly suggests that for comparable levels of psychiatric disorder, clinicians are not more likely to perceive mental illness in women than in men. For example, Abramowitz et al. (1976) found that "the impact [on

clinical judgments] of varying the patient's gender was surprisingly slight. *109*
The patient received a better prognosis ($p <.05$) and elicited slightly more
empathy ($p <.10$) when identified as a woman" (p. 708). Similarly, Gomes
and Abramowitz (1976) concluded that "the main outcome of this investigation was the absence of consistent effects due to any of the four variables—patient sex and role-appropriateness and therapist sex and sex-role
traditionalism—implied in the polemic literature as likely sources of
clinical bias. . . . To the extent that any sex bias was exposed, it tended to
favor the female-identified rather than the male-identified stimulus-per-
son" (pp. 10–11). In fact, they found that the sex-role deviant female was
perceived as especially mature, even by clinicians whose personal reaction
to her was largely negative. Systematic reviews of these experimental studies are presented in Abramowitz and Dokecki (1977) and Zeldow (1978).
These studies clearly suggest that the higher rates of treatment among
women are not due to discrimination against women by clinicians.

It might appear that the Broverman et al. (1970) finding that clinicians
tend to perceive men as being in better mental health than women contradicts the results of the clinical judgment analogue studies, which would
suggest that clinicians do not discriminate against women. This is the
position taken by Davidson and Abramowitz (1980), who caution that the
analogue studies are suspect because clinicians may have discerned the
issue being investigated and carefully tempered their response. It can easily
be argued, however, that the results of the two types of studies are entirely
consistent and there is no contradiction to be explained away. If the average
woman is in poorer mental health, as the community studies indicate, then
results like those of Broverman et al. (1970) would not reflect a bias on the
part of clinicians but, rather, an accurate perception of reality. In short,
given the other data available, it is quite reasonable to assume that the
perceptions by clinicians that women tend to be in poorer mental health
and the finding that most clinicians are not biased against women "patients" in analogue studies are both valid and in no way contradictory.

The data reported by Broverman et al. (1970), Abramowitz et al. (1976),
Gomes and Abramowitz (1976), McKee and Sherriffs (1957, 1959), and
Sheriffs and McKee (1957) in fact suggest that expectations regarding
appropriate behavior are probably more stringent for males than for
females. It appears that both clinicians and members of the general community expect women to manifest poorer mental health. If this is true,
males may be more likely than females to experience a negative societal
reaction for comparable levels of mental illness. Tudor, Tudor, and Gove
(1977) found that both the literature and the national data on the treatment
for mental illness support such an interpretation. Furthermore, males are

110 much more likely than females to be institutionalized for other forms of mental impairment (Tudor, Tudor, & Gove, 1979).

To my knowledge, there are only three community studies that allow one to look at the help-seeking behavior of men and women controlling for level of impairment or perceived need for help. Two national studies (Gove, 1978; Gurin, Veroff, & Feld, 1960) demonstrate, controlling for level of self-defined impairment, that women are no more likely than men to seek professional help. In fact the very slight differences suggest men are more likely to seek help. Using a strategically drawn sample and controlling for the level of self-defined disorder, Blumenthal (1967) found that men were more likely to seek help than women ($p <.01$). In summary, the existing data indicate that women are no more likely than men to seek professional help for comparable levels of mental illness.

Some of the best data on the path into psychiatric treatment are those provided by Fink, Shapiro, Goldensohn, and Daily (1969), who studied an insured group of thirty thousand persons in New York City. In terms of visits to family physicians, "men were slightly below the medical group average with an index of 0.93 while women were slightly above with an index of 1.07" (a value of 1.0 indicates a rate equivalent to the medical group average). However, the index of psychiatric diagnosis by general physicians was 0.63 for men and 1.37 for women, indicating women were much more likely to receive a psychiatric diagnosis. Furthermore, the data showed that among persons receiving a psychiatric diagnosis, men and women were equally likely to receive a screening interview by a psychiatrist and were also equally likely subsequently to enter psychiatric treatment.

In conclusion, the evidence strongly suggests that the higher rates of mental illness among women in our society reflect real differences and are not artifactual.

Explanations of the Higher Rate of Mental Illness among Women

Sex and Marital Roles of Men and Women

Given that women do have higher rates of mental illness, this could plausibly be due to characteristics of their societal roles and life experiences or to biological factors. Elsewhere (Gove, 1978; Gove & Tudor, 1977) I have discussed in detail the evidence which suggests that the differences are not due to innate biological differences. My major reason for believing that the higher rates of mental illness among women are largely due to societal and not to biological factors is that they generally appear to be specific to particular societies at particular times (although the evidence is not conclusive) and, more important, women have higher rates only within specific roles. In particular, higher rates of mental illness appear to be limited to married women, with never-married, widowed, and divorced women having comparable, if not lower, rates than their male counterparts (e.g., Gove, 1972a, 1972b, 1973, 1979c).

In a recent overview of the literature on depression, Weissman and Klerman (1977) concluded that women had higher rates of depression than men and that these differences were not artifactual. They reviewed evidence bearing on the possibility that the higher rates of depression among women could be due to genetic factors, women's social status, the experience of more severe life events, or various endocrinological factors including premenstrual tension, oral contraceptives, and postpartum depression. They concluded that the higher rate of depression among women was primarily due to their disadvantaged social status and emphasized the link between marriage and depression.

There are a number of reasons for assuming that married women find their roles to be more frustrating and less rewarding than married men. In recent times the role of housewife has lost many of its societal functions; consequently, the wife contributes relatively less instrumentally to the household than she did in the past. The majority of wives still do not hold jobs and are restricted to one major societal role, that of housewife, whereas men occupy two such roles, that of household head and worker. A man typically has two sources of gratification, his family and his work, whereas a woman has only one, her family. Children, particularly when they are very young, channel women into situations in which the women are isolated from adult interaction yet confront seemingly incessant demands (Gove & Geerken, 1977b).

Even when a woman works, she typically occupies a less satisfying position than the married man. Women are discriminated against in the job market and they frequently hold positions that are not commensurate with their education. Furthermore, women are much less likely to have a career orientation. Perhaps more important, working wives are under a greater strain than their husbands. In addition to their jobs, they almost invariably perform most of the household chores, which means that they work considerably more hours per day than their husbands (Geerken & Gove, 1978; Gove & Tudor, 1973; Szalai, 1972, 1975). The literature also suggests that they find many of their instrumental activities frustrating, for these are of low status, routine, boring, and they require little skill. These factors suggest that the higher rates of mental illness among women can largely be attributed to the societal roles women occupy and particularly to the constraints associated with their marital roles.

112   *Learned Helplessness among Women*

It has been widely noted that the role expectations that confront women are more diffuse than those that confront men and, perhaps more important, that the feminine role is characterized by preparing for and adjusting to contingencies (e.g., Angrist, 1969; Gove & Tudor, 1973; Rose, 1951). It certainly seems to be the case that, because of interaction of marriage, children, and work, women experience a much less structured career path than men. Gove and Tudor (1973) have suggested that this characteristic of the feminine role probably creates problems for some women and may increase the likelihood that they will experience emotional difficulties; however, they see the nature of this interaction as very complex.

It has become popular to assume that the contingent nature and subordinate status of the feminine role result in many women having very little control over their lives and that this, in turn, may explain the higher rate of mental illness among women, particularly depression (e.g., Bagley, 1977; Radloff, 1975; Weissman & Klerman, 1977). This formulation has become known as the "learned helplessness hypothesis." To support this hypothesis, investigators have drawn almost exclusively on an article by Seligman (1974), which reviews evidence that animals in laboratory experiments who have absolutely no control over frequently occurring physical trauma appear to become depressed. The Seligman article is intriguing; however, no evidence has been presented that the total lack of control and the severity of trauma experienced by animals in these experiments have much in common with the role of women in our society. Furthermore, one should be very cautious in extrapolating behavior data from animals in laboratory experiments to the everyday life situation of humans.

Although further research is certainly required, the available evidence suggests that the learned helplessness hypothesis, at least in the rather simplistic form in which it has been presented, does not explain the higher rates of mental illness among women. A key component of the hypothesis is that girls learn in childhood to be helpless (Weissman & Klerman, 1977). However, girls outperform boys academically (e.g., Northby, 1958), and young boys have higher rates of mental illness than young girls, apparently because they are less capable than girls of meeting the expectations that confront them (Gove & Herb, 1974). Another core premise of the learned helplessness hypothesis is that women are more likely than men to feel that they lack control over their lives and are trapped by their life circumstances. Data from a national probability sample, however, indicate that there is no difference between men and women in the extent to which they (a) experience powerlessness or normlessness; (b) feel they have control over and

experience satisfaction with their daily activities; and (c) feel trapped by   *113*
their life circumstances (Gove, 1979b).

In conclusion, the evidence that exists runs counter to the learned helplessness hypothesis. This indirectly lends credence to the premise that the higher rates of mental illness among women largely reflect aspects of their marital role.

The Therapist as an Agent of Social Control or Societal Change

Now let us turn to some of the implicit political issues that follow from the premise that the higher rates of mental illness among women are primarily a product of their sex and marital roles. When an individual is so distressed or disorganized that his or her functioning is impaired, both society and the people directly involved with that individual have an interest in seeing that he or she is restored to a state in which he or she can function effectively. If the individual's emotional disturbance is in part a reaction to aspects of the social system, then society has a particular concern with the way in which the therapist goes about alleviating the person's disturbance. The therapist who uses procedures that alleviate the disturbance by helping the person to adjust to characteristics of the social structure as it exists is correctly seen as an agent who helps maintain the status quo. In contrast, the therapist who uses procedures that lead to a change in aspects of the person's environment that are reflective of the basic social structure is correctly seen as an agent of social change.

Obviously the emotional disturbances of many persons reflect idiosyncratic life experiences and personality traits that have very little to do with general characteristics of the social structure. In such cases, the therapist is concerned with dealing with those idiosyncratic conditions and, presumably, the goals of the patient, therapist, and society are in concordance. In those cases, however, in which the mental illness of a woman reflects societal conditions, the way the woman is treated inevitably has consequences for the maintenance or change of the societal structure, and her therapist is then, in the broadest sense of the word, a political agent.

Feminists are very aware that the therapists may be viewed as political agents. Levin, Kamin, and Levine (1974) refer to therapists as the "mediopsychological correlates to the gendarme" (p. 327). Moss and Sachs (1975) state that "what distinguishes feminist therapy from other therapies is that we make our values explicit, and incorporate them into the therapy process to promote changes in women that we believe will lead to changes in the

114   world and its ways" (p. 1). These authors indicate that feminist therapy encourages women to locate the source of their problem in society and that feminist therapists seek an entirely different world, and their therapy and life-styles reflect this vision. Chesler (1971a) claims that it is impossible for a man to treat a woman effectively. "Male psychologists, psychiatrists, and social workers must realize that as scientists they know nothing about women; their diagnosis, even their sympathy, is damaging and oppressive to women. Male clinicians should stop treating women altogether, however much this may hurt their wallets and/or sense of benevolent authority" (p. 384). Radical feminists view feminism itself as therapy (Mander & Rush, 1974).

Most clinicians do not construe feminism, by itself, as a form of therapy. There are numerous reasons for this, and here we will touch on only the most obvious. First, most therapists are not feminists, particularly in the pure sense of the term. Among other things, the vast majority of therapists are male. Second, therapists are concerned with treating the emotional problems of the individual, and these problems almost invariably reflect a number of factors that are idiosyncratic to that individual. It is almost invariably the case that even when some of the factors reflect problems associated with the societal conditions of women, numerous other factors will also be involved. The therapist who focused only on feminist issues would be ignoring the array of other factors that are components of the individual's problem. Third, feminism is essentially a political ideology and social movement aimed at changing pervasive social conditions; therapy is aimed at getting the individual to function effectively and happily in a niche carved out of the existing world. Thus, although it is possible for feminism and therapy to interact, they largely involve separate realms of social discourse. Fourth, a substantial number of women do not see their problems in feminist terms and thus will not be receptive to feminist therapy as such. With regard to this latter point, not only do both men and women tend to prefer a male therapist, but the proportion preferring a male therapist is higher among women than men (Chesler, 1971a, 1971b).

Most therapists who treat women whose problems in part reflect the societal role of women are essentially faced with a choice between two strategies, neither of which is particularly satisfactory. The therapist can work to change the individual's perspective and reactions so that she can accept and function in the world as it exists. In this case, the therapist is essentially reinforcing the status quo and should be very sensitive to the fact that this is so. This approach has the advantage that the therapist has direct contact with and thus presumably some control over the person whose behavior and perspective is to be dealt with. This approach is particularly compatible with a heavy reliance on drug therapy. It has the clear disadvantage, however, of attempting to get the individual to accept and adjust to what probably is most appropriately perceived as an unfair and unjust, but perhaps unchangeable, situation, and many patients may be unwilling or unable to make such an adjustment.

The other alternative is for the therapist to work to change the woman's microenvironment so that she no longer confronts inequalities in her daily life. This will almost always involve changing the behavior and attitudes of others, typically the husband and often children, as well as changing some of the life goals and activities of the woman. One of the consequences of this approach is that the woman's "consciousness" will probably be raised. The clear advantage to such an approach is that an effort is made to change the particular situation that is at least partially responsible for the woman's emotional difficulties. The disadvantage is that the therapist often will not have contact with all persons whose behavior and attitudes need to change and, regardless of contact, some of these persons may not desire to change. As the woman's "consciousness" will often be raised by such an approach and existing inequities brought out into the open, unless accompanying environmental change occurs, the person's immediate situation may deteriorate. This, of course, may lead to fairly drastic action, such as divorce. Since the divorced are by far in the poorest mental health of any marital category (Gove, 1972a, 1973, 1979c), there are obviously risks and limitations involved in this strategy. The therapist who elects this type of approach may take comfort from the belief that drastic changes in one's life situation *may* lead to long-term improvement. Furthermore, they may also take comfort from the fact that the very unhappily married are in even poorer mental health than the divorced (Gove & Style, 1977).

References

Abernathy, V. Cultural perspectives on the impact of women's changing roles in psychiatry. *American Journal of Psychiatry*, 1976, *133*, 657–61.

Abramowitz, C. V., & Dokecki, P. The politics of clinical judgment: Early empirical returns. *Psychological Bulletin*, 1977, *84*, 460–76.

Abramowitz, S. I., Roback, H., Schwartz, J., Yasuna, A., Abramowitz, C. V., & Gomes, B. Sex bias in psychotherapy: A failure to confirm. *American Journal of Psychiatry*, 1976, *133*, 706–09.

American Psychiatric Association. *Annual Report, 1967.* Washington, D.C.: U.S. Government Printing Office, 1968.

Angrist, S. The study of sex roles. *Journal of Social Issues*, 1969, *25*, 215–32.

Bagley, M. A preliminary look at female sex role learning and mental illness. Presented at the Annual Meeting of the Southern Sociological Society, Atlanta, Georgia, 1977.

116   Bernard, J. The paradox of the happy marriage. In V. Gornick & B. Moran (Eds.), *Women in sexist society: Studies in power and powerlessness.* New York: Basic Books, 1971. (a)

Bernard, J. *Women and the public interest.* Chicago: Aldine, 1971. (b)

Blumenthal, M. Sex as a source of heterogeneity in a mental health survey. *Journal of Psychiatric Research,* 1967, *5,* 75–87.

Bohn, A., Gardner, E., Alltop, L., Knatterval, G., & Solomon, M. Admission and prevalence rates for psychiatric facilities in four register areas. *American Journal of Public Health,* 1966, *56,* 2033–51.

Broverman, I., Broverman, D. M., Clarkson, I. E., Rosenkrantz, P. S., & Vogel, S. R. Sex role stereotypes and clinical judgments of mental health. *Journal of Consulting and Clinical Psychology,* 1970, *34,* 1–7.

Brunetti, P. M. Prévalence des troubles mentaux dans une population rurale du Vaucluse: Données nouvelles et recapitulatives. *L'Hygiène Mentale,* 1973, *62,* 1–5.

Chesler, P. Women as psychiatric and psychotherapeutic patients. *Journal of Marriage and the Family,* 1971, *33,* 746–59. (a)

Chesler, P. Patient and patriarch: Women in the psychotherapeutic relationship. In V. Gornick & B. Moran (Eds.), *Women in sexist society: Studies in Power and Powerlessness.* New York: Basic Books, 1971. (b)

Chesler, P. *Women and madness.* New York: Doubleday, 1972.

Clancy, K., & Gove, W. R. Sex differences in respondents' reports of psychiatric symptoms: An analysis of response bias. *American Journal of Sociology,* 1974, *78,* 205–44.

Davidson, C. V., & Abramowitz, S. I. Sex bias in clinical judgment: Later empirical returns. *Psychology of Women Quarterly,* 1980, *4,* 377–95.

Dohrenwend, B. The problem of validity in field studies of psychological disorder. *Journal of Health and Social Behavior,* 1975, *16,* 365–92.

Dorn, H. The incidence and future expectancy of mental disease. *Public Health Reports,* 1938, *53,* 1991–2004.

Dunham, W. *Social theory and mental disease.* Detroit, Mich.: Wayne State University Press, 1959.

Fink, R., Shapiro, S., Goldensohn, S., & Daily, E. The "filter-down" process in psychotherapy in a group medical care program. *Journal of Public Health,* 1969, *59,* 245–57.

Geerken, M., & Gove, W. R. Instrumental activities and family functioning. Mimeographed, 1978.

Gomes, B., & Abramowitz, S. I. Sex-related patient and therapist effects on clinical judgment. *Sex Roles,* 1976, *2,* 1–13.

Gove, W. Sex roles, marital roles, and mental illness. *Social Forces,* 1972, *51,* 34–44. (a)

Gove, W. Sex, marital status, and suicide. *Journal of Health and Social Behavior,* 1972, *13,* 204–13. (b)

Gove, W. Sex, marital status, and mortality. *American Journal of Sociology,* 1973, *79,* 45–67.

Gove, W. R. Deviant behavior, social intervention, and labelling theory. In L. Coser & O. Larsen (Eds.), *The uses of controversy in sociology.* New York: Free Press, 1976.

Gove, W. R. Sex differences in mental illness among adult men and women: An evaluation of four questions raised regarding the evidence of the higher rates of women. *Social Science and Medicine,* 12, 179–86.

Gove, W. R. Sex differences in the epidemiology of mental disorder. In E. Gomberg & D. Franks (Eds.), *Gender and psychopathology: Sex differences in disordered behavior.* Brunner/Mazel, 1979. (a)

Gove, W. R. Sex differences in mental illness: Some evidence on the learned helplessness hypothesis. Mimeographed, 1979. (b)

Gove, W. R. Sex, marital status, and psychiatric treatment: A research note. *Social Forces,* 1979, *58,* 89–93. (c)

Gove, W. R., & Geerken, M. Response bias in surveys of mental health: An empirical investigation. *American Journal of Sociology,* 1977, *82,* 1289–1317. (a)

Gove, W. R., & Geerken, M. The effect of children and employment on the mental health of 117 married men and women. *Social Forces*, 1977, *5*, 66–75. (b)

Gove, W. R., & Herb, T. Stress and mental illness among the young: A comparison of the sexes. *Social Forces*, 1974, *54*, 256–65.

Gove, W., McCorkel, J., Fain, T., & Hughes, M. Response bias in community surveys of mental health: Systematic bias or random noise? *Social Science and Medicine*, 1976, *10*, 497–502.

Gove, W., & Style, C. The role of marriage in American society. Paper presented at the meeting of the National Council on Family Relations, San Diego, Calif., 1977.

Gove, W., & Tudor, J. Adult sex roles and mental illness. *American Journal of Sociology*, 1973, *77*, 812–35.

Gove, W., & Tudor, J. Sex differences in mental illness: A comment on Dohrenwend and Dohrenwend. *American Journal of Sociology*, 1977, *82*, 1327–36.

Gurin, G., Veroff, J., & Feld, S. *Americans view their mental health.* New York: Basic Books, 1960.

Kazdin, A., & Wilson, G. T. Criteria for evaluating psychotherapy. *Archives of General Psychiatry*, 1978, *35*, 407–16.

Kellner, R. Psychotherapy in psychosomatic disorders. *Archives of General Psychiatry*, 1975, *32*, 1021–28.

Klein, D., & Davis, J. *Diagnosis and drug treatment of psychiatric disorders.* Baltimore: Williams & Wilkins, 1969.

Kolb, L. *Modern clinical psychiatry* (8th ed.). Philadelphia: Saunders, 1973.

Kramer, M. Psychiatric services and the changing institutional scene, 1950–1985. (Series B, No. 12.) Washington, D.C.: National Institute of Mental Health, 1977.

Kramer, M., Pollack, E., & Redick, R. Studies of the incidence and prevalence of hospitalized mental disorders in the United States: Current status and future goals. In P. Hock & J. Zubin (Eds.), *Comparative epidemiology of the mental disorders.* New York: Grune & Stratton, 1961.

Levin, S., Kamin, L., & Levine, E. Sexism and psychiatry. *American Journal of Orthopsychiatry*, 1974, *44*, 327–36.

Malan, D. The outcome of psychotherapy research: A historical review. *Archives of General Psychiatry*, 1973, *29*, 719–29.

Mander, A., & Rush, A. *Feminism as therapy.* New York: Random House, 1974.

McKee, J., & Sherriffs, A. The differential evaluation of males and females. *Journal of Personality*, 1957, *25*, 356–71.

McKee, J., & Sherriffs, A. Men's and women's beliefs, ideals and self-conceptions. *American Journal of Sociology*, 1959, *64*, 356–63.

Moss, L., & Sachs, N. Feminist therapy. Paper presented at the Annual Meeting of the American Orthopsychiatric Association, Washington, D.C., 1975.

Murphy, J. Psychiatric labeling in cross-cultural perspective. *Science*, 1976, *191*, 1019–28.

Northby, A. Sex differences in high school scholarship. *School and Society*, 1958, *86*, 63–64.

Pearlin, L. Sex roles and depression. In N. Datan & L. H. Ginsberg (Eds.), *Life span developmental psychology: Normative life crisis.* New York: Academic Press, 1975.

Phillips, D., & Clancy, K. Response biases in field studies of mental illness. *American Sociological Review.* 1970, *35*, 503–15.

Phillips, D., & Clancy, K. Some effects of "social desirability in survey studies." *American Journal of Sociology*, 1972, *77*, 921–40.

Phillips, D., & Segal, B. Sexual status and psychiatric symptoms. *American Sociological Review*, 1969, *34*, 58–72.

Radloff, L. Sex differences in depression: The effects of occupation and marital status. *Sex Roles*, 1975, *1*, 249–65.

Robbins, L. A historical review of the classification of behavior disorders and one current perspective. In L. Eron (Ed.), *The classification of behavior disorders.* Chicago: Aldine, 1966.

118 Rose, A. The adequacy of women's expectations for adult roles. *Social Forces*, 1951, *30*, 69–77.

Scheff, T. *Being mentally ill: A sociological theory.* Chicago: Aldine, 1966.

Scheff, T. Reply to Clancy and Gove. *American Sociological Review*, 1975, *40*, 252–57.

Seligman, M. Depression and learned helplessness. In R. Friedman & M. Katz (Eds.), *The psychology of depression: Contemporary theory and research.* Washington, D.C.: Winston & Sons, 1974.

Sherriffs, A., & McKee, J. Qualitative aspects of beliefs about men and women. *Journal of Personality*, 1957, *25*, 450–64.

Smith, M., & Glass, V. Meta-analysis of psychotherapy outcome studies. *American Psychologist*, 1977, *32*, 752–60.

Szalai, A. *The use of time: Daily activities of urban and suburban populations in twelve counties.* The Hague: Houghton, 1972.

Szalai, A. Women's time: Women in light of contemporary time-budget research. *Future*, 1975, October, 385–99.

Taube, C., & Redick, R. Provisional data on patient care episodes in mental health facilities 1977 (Statistical Note #139). Washington, D.C.: National Institute of Mental Health, 1977.

Tudor, W., Tudor, J., & Gove, W. R. The effect of sex role differences on the social control of mental illness. *Journal of Health and Social Behavior*, 1977, *18*, 98–112.

Tudor, W., Tudor, J., & Gove, W. R. The effect of sex role differences on the societal reaction to mental retardation. *Social Forces*, 1979, *57*, 871–86.

Weissman, M., & Klerman, G. Sex differences in the epidemiology of depression. *Archives of General Psychiatry*, 1977, *34*, 98–111.

Zeldow, R. Sex differences in psychiatric education and treatment. *Archives of General Psychiatry*, 1978, *35*, 89–93.

Mental Illness and Psychiatric Treatment Among Women: A Response

MARILYN JOHNSON

Gove builds on ideas presented in a widely read paper (Gove & Tudor, 1973) and elaborated in his recent work (Tudor, Tudor, & Gove, 1977). He argues in an interesting and carefully considered way that women have more mental illness than men, and he attempts to explain the difference. His thesis seems quite plausible at first sight. Intuitively one would expect the mental health of women to be adversely affected by their disadvantaged position in society. The simplest point of view would be to regard mental illness as a unitary concept and to assume that women would have more of it. The simplest point of view may not be the most accurate, however.

To speak of the overall mental health of the two sexes is too sweeping a generalization. The reported difference in mental health of married and unmarried women is one example of how it may be misleading to generalize about the mental health status of all women (Bernard, 1972). What conditions are to be included under the heading of mental illness? How do we determine if a person has one of these conditions? As Tudor, Tudor, and Gove (1977) have acknowledged, diagnoses are frequently of questionable reliability. "More so than in most forms of physical illness, the diagnosis of mental illness is often based on ambiguous symptoms, subject to a variety of interpretation" (p. 100).

In trying to estimate the number of mentally ill, should we count only those in treatment, or should we rely on surveys of the general population? Survey results often consist of self-reports of symptoms, but perhaps these self-reports are determined by factors other than mental illness, such as greater or lesser self-disclosure (Brooks, 1974) or impression management (Sherman, Trief, & Sprafkin, 1975). Also, the measure most commonly

"Mental Illness and Psychiatric Treatment among Women: A Response" by Marilyn Johnson, *Psychology of Women Quarterly, 4* (3), 363–371. Copyright © 1980 by Division 35, American Psychological Association. Reprinted by permission of Cambridge University Press.

Dr. Johnson is a counseling psychologist and director of the Student Counseling Center and Assistant Professor of Psychology and Social Sciences, Rush-Presbyterian-St. Luke's Medical Center, Chicago, Illinois.

120 used in survey studies of symptom self-reports, the Langner Scale, has been criticized despite its wide use (Seiler, 1976). Furthermore, a report of symptoms is not synonymous with mental illness; a person can acknowledge symptoms, but be coping with them.

Therefore, I agree with Gove that the issue of which sex has more mental illness is a controversial one, but I disagree with his approach to the problem and with his solution. My response will address two major points: Gove's precise definition of mental illness and his discussion of strategies for therapy with women.

Mental Illness Defined

In brief, Gove classifies clients with neuroses, functional psychoses, transient situational reactions, and psychophysiological disorders as mentally ill; clients with diagnoses of brain syndromes or personality disorders are not so classified. Gove's precise definition of mental illness seems problematic, especially in the choice of diagnostic categories. The new *Diagnostic and Statistical Manual of Mental Disorders* of the American Psychiatric Association which represents a great deal of work and thought on the part of many experts, has not limited mental disorders to those Gove would accept.

According to Gove, a sociopath is not defined as mentally ill, whereas an individual experiencing a transient situational crisis *is* so defined. Also, by excluding personality disorders and cases of substance abuse, he has effectively excluded groups that consist, in large part, of males. Dohrenwend and Dohrenwend (1976) reported that more males than females were diagnosed as having personality disorders in 22 of 26 studies they surveyed. Personality disorders include problems with aggression, impulse control, and sociopathy (APA, 1968), and more men than women in our society experience these symptoms (Zigler & Phillips, 1960). Many of these men are institutionalized, but in prisons rather than in mental hospitals, and thus they would not be counted among the mentally ill as defined by Gove (Howard & Howard, 1974).

Although women are reporting greater problems with substance abuse than in the past (Gomberg, 1974), men still constitute the majority of cases in this category. Weissman and Klerman (1977) have hypothesized that men use alcohol to escape from feelings of depression. If this is true, then which diagnosis might be obtained in survey studies? Since alcohol abuse is often more visible than depression, one would expect the client to be defined as an alcoholic and thus absent from the mentally ill group. According to Miller (1976), men fight hard to avoid feeling or appearing weak or helpless; perhaps much destructive behavior in men (alcoholism and drug abuse, assaultive acts, etc.) arises from this struggle against weakness. Let me cite a clinical example to point up the inequities of Gove's precise definition of mental illness.

A battered woman and her husband come for therapy; they report that the battering has occurred over a five-year period. The woman expresses great distress, is depressed, feels worthless, is not functioning well, and so forth. The man has a severe problem with alcohol and periodically explodes violently at his wife. He rarely experiences discomfort over the battering. He has come to therapy with his wife only because she has threatened to leave him unless they enter therapy.

According to Gove's definition, the wife suffers from mental illness, but the husband does not. She would be diagnosed as neurotic depressive, whereas the husband would be considered alcoholic and personality disordered, thus not mentally ill in Gove's view.

Such cases of mental illness in women (according to Gove's definition) may be seen more frequently as more women and girls suffering from battering, rape, and incest come into treatment. Although these problems have always existed, there is now greater social support for acknowledging and resolving them (Hepper, 1978; Courtois, 1979). In legal terms these women are victims of crime who can prosecute their tormentors. In terms of Gove's definition, however, their positions are quite different. If women respond to being victimized with anxiety, depression, lowered self-esteem, or feelings of insecurity, should they be defined as mentally ill? Are these reactions not to be expected? Whether her reaction is relatively short-lived or long-lasting, the victim will still be included in the mentally ill group. What of the status of the men who commit these crimes? They will be diagnosed as personality disordered and so not counted in Gove's statistics. Naturally, not all depression in women results from such victimization, but the above examples are not rare, and they illustrate the limitation of Gove's definition. This is another case of "blaming the victim" (Ryan, 1971).

Women and Therapy

Gove describes two strategies for therapists of women: the traditional and the feminist. The traditionalist assumes that the prevailing social norms for women reflect mental health and helps the woman adjust to society and to these norms. The feminist introduces feminist ideology into therapy and encourages the client to develop herself fully, even if this development

122 might lead to the loss of important relationships. Rawlings and Carter (1977) have noted a third therapeutic approach, the nonsexist. The primary distinction between the nonsexist and feminist therapist is that the feminist incorporates feminist theory and practice into therapy and the nonsexist does not. Both believe in egalitarianism between the sexes; this belief springs from a humanist philosophy among nonsexists and from feminist ideology in feminists. Proponents of each approach offer their own messages to the client.

Traditional: That is the way the world is, so learn to live with it.
Nonsexist: Some of your problems arise from the way the world is. If you had been socialized differently, you would not have to work through many of these issues.
Feminist: Some of your problems arise from the way the world is. Remember that the power differential between women and men is an often ignored contributor to your problem. You can work to change your life and you will have the support of many others like yourself.

I cannot agree with Gove that traditional and feminist therapies offer equally advantageous forms of help. It is my belief that feminist therapy offers unique opportunities for growth in women. The goals of feminism and therapy are not really discrepant and, in fact, can be combined in a satisfactory manner (Johnson, 1976; Kronsky, 1971; Williams, 1976). Contrary to Gove's belief, some nonfeminists will accept feminist therapy. In our early experience at the Philadelphia Feminist Therapy Collective, only 20 percent of the clients were nonfeminists, yet they were nearly as responsive to therapy as were the feminist clients (Johnson, 1976). The proportion of nonfeminist to feminist clients at the collective has grown in recent years, and these nonfeminist women have therapy outcomes similar to feminists (Chambless, 1978).

Defining oneself as a feminist therapist is a clear expression of one's values. It can be argued that such a definition is advantageous to the client because it defines the therapist's therapeutic-political stance; in other words, the client knows what she is "buying." Usually in psychotherapy the therapist's values are covert, and this is justified by the principle that such values should be kept out of therapy. Feminist therapists believe that it is both impossible and unwise to strive for a totally value-free therapeutic experience.

A core principle of feminist therapy is that the therapist should eschew the superior position so common to this role and should work to reduce the power differential between client and therapist. The feminist therapist's role is not limited to dealing with a client's interpersonal environment, as Gove seems to suggest. It may also involve (a) interpretation of the client's problems in terms of the social-political context; (b) support for anger, *123* aggression, and initiative-taking, when indicated, even when their expression may cause problems with significant others; (c) encouragement of trust and respect for other women; and (d) careful attention to the shared nature of emotional problems—for example, orgastic dysfunction in women is often related to men's premature ejaculation (Holroyd, 1978). Many feminist therapists also feel a commitment to support women publicly through participation in women's rights organizations or in the women's caucus of professional societies.

A popular theme in the women's movement has been "the personal is political." That is, the limitation of women to a few roles has political implications; the diagnosis of mental illness in women has, in the broadest sense, certain political significance. One advantage of feminist therapy groups (and the consciousness-raising groups that preceded them) has been a recognition that problems felt by some women to be unique to them have plagued other women in their group (Brodsky, 1973; Johnson, 1976). Such revelations have resulted in relief ("If they feel this way too, then maybe I am not crazy"), and sometimes in rage ("Who has been brainwashing us into believing we are crazy?"). Such recognition is therapeutic, in the broadest sense. Feminist therapists believe that it is essential to strip away some of the more clearly socially determined causes of distress in women so that therapeutic work can be done on each individual's unique problem. Feminist therapists know it is essential to discourage clients from blaming society for *all* of their distress. This type of therapy offers a mixture of social support and emphasis on individual responsibility.

Gove rightly states that significant others in a client's environment may be unwilling to make changes necessary to facilitate the client's continued growth, and that the resulting conflict may lead to divorce or loss of other important relationships. Feminist therapists take divorce as seriously as do other therapists. Most would agree with Miller's (1976) statement about the difficulties occurring when women seek self-definition and self-determination: "That is, women are not *creating* conflict; they are exposing the fact that conflict exists" (p. 126). As Klein (1976) has pointed out, emotional pain is not always an indication of psychopathology; it may result from movement toward growth. Whether the therapist views such pain as reflecting growth or pathology will have a powerful effect on the client.

The effects of the women's movement continue to filter down to women (and men) of all kinds. Once raised, consciousness does not disappear. The same phenomenon occurs in the development of consciousness of women's role as in intellectual or moral development (Kohlberg, 1969; Piaget, 1963). After advancing to a higher stage of development of con-

124 sciousness, the individual cannot again conceptualize women's role as she or he did formerly. The individual's constructs have changed and will remain changed. What significance does this have for psychotherapy? It means that more and more women will seek a therapeutic approach that acknowledges the existence of conflict arising in part out of women's role but does not accuse them of *creating* that conflict. This translates, in my view, to a greater need for feminist, or at least nonsexist therapy.

Final Thoughts

Two other points made by Gove require brief attention. First, the argument that research has demonstrated that there is no clinician bias against women is not a satisfactory one. Davidson and Abramowitz's (1980) warning that such studies are highly reactive is important; it is difficult to find a clinician today who does not know the "nonsexist" response to make when queried. Also, in summarizing the clinician bias research, Abramowitz and Dokecki (1977) noted the preponderance of analogues rather than naturalistic clinical studies. Until a substantial number of such naturalistic studies are carried out, the question of clinician bias cannot be definitively answered.

Second, Gove may rule out the learned helplessness hypothesis of female mental illness too readily. Seligman has accumulated work on learned helplessness and depression (Seligman, Klein, & Miller, 1976), and he and his colleagues are elaborating the theory for application to humans in other contexts (Abramson & Seligman, 1977). Also, the two studies cited to buttress the point that girls appear more competent than boys during childhood do not refute the learned helplessness hypothesis; other studies could be offered as evidence that girls *do* feel incompetent in various areas. For example, elementary school girls may expect to do less well than boys on certain tasks (Crandall, 1969), and adolescent girls may be more likely than adolescent boys to blame themselves for academic failure (Crandall, Katkovsky, & Crandall, 1965). It may be that women must reach adulthood and assume the marital role in order to feel the full force of learned helplessness, or it may be that learned helplessness is a factor in *some* women and not in others. It seems too early in the history of this interesting construct to conclude that it is irrelevant to mental illness in women.

In conclusion, it seems more useful to examine the relationship between the roles of women and men and the barriers to growth caused by these roles than to try to establish that one sex has more barriers than the other.

This idea has been echoed elsewhere (Dohrenwend & Dohrenwend, 125
1976):

Instead, the findings suggest that we should discard undifferentiated, uni-
dimensional concepts of psychiatric disorder and with them false questions about
whether women or men are more prone to "mental illness." In their place we
would substitute an issue posed by the relatively high female rates of neurosis and
manic-depressive psychosis, with their possible common denominator of depressive symptomatology, and the relatively high male rates of personality disorders with their possible common denominator of irresponsible and antisocial
behavior. The important question then becomes, What is there in the endowments
and experiences of men and women that pushes them in these different deviant
directions? (p. 1453)

References

Abramowitz, C., & Dokecki, P. The politics of clinical judgment: Early empirical returns.
Psychological Bulletin, 1977, *84*, 460–76.

Abramson, L., & Seligman, M. *Learned helplessness in humans: Critique and reformulation.*
Paper presented at the meeting of the American Psychological Association, San Francisco, Calif., August, 1977.

American Psychiatric Association. *Diagnostic and statistical manual of mental disorders, II.*
Washington, D.C.: American Psychiatric Association, 1968.

American Psychiatric Association. *Diagnostic and statistical manual of mental disorders, III.*
1980.

Bernard, J. *The future of marriage.* New York: Bantam Books, 1972.

Brodsky, A. The consciousness-raising group as a model for therapy with women. *Psychotherapy: Theory, Research and Practice*, 1973, *10*, 24–29.

Brooks, L. Interactive effects of sex and status on self-disclosure. *Journal of Counseling
Psychology*, 1974, *21*, 469–74.

Chambless, D. *Personal communication*, 1978.

Courtois, C. Standards for counseling victims of rape and incest. *The Counseling Psychologist*, 1979, *8* (1), 38–40.

Crandall, V. Sex differences in expectancy of intellectual and academic reinforcement. In C.
Smith (Ed.), *Achievement-related motives in children*. New York: Russell Sage Foundation, 1969.

Crandall, V., Katkovsky, W., & Crandall, V. Children's belief in their own control of
reinforcement in intellectual-academic achievement situations. *Child Development*,
1965, *36*, 91–109.

Davidson, C. V., & Abramowitz, S. I. Sex bias in clinical judgment: Later empirical returns.
Psychology of Women Quarterly, 1980, *4*, 377–95.

Dohrenwend, B., & Dohrenwend, B. Sex differences and psychiatric disorders. *American
Journal of Sociology*, 1976, *81*, 1447–54.

Gomberg, E. Women and alcoholism. In V. Franks & V. Burtle (Eds.), *Women in therapy*.
New York: Brunner/Mazel, 1974.

Gove, W., & Tudor, J. Adult sex roles and mental illness. *American Journal of Sociology*,
1973, *77*, 812–35.

126 Hepper, M. Counseling the battered wife: Myths, facts, and decisions. *Personnel and Guidance Journal*, 1978, *56*, 522–25.

Holroyd, J. Psychotherapy and women's liberation. In L. Harmon, J. Birk, L. Fitzgerald, & M. Tanney (Eds.), *Counseling women*. Monterey, Calif.: Brooks/Cole, 1978.

Howard, E., & Howard, J. Women in institutions: Treatment in prisons and mental hospitals. In V. Franks & V. Burtle (Eds.), *Women in therapy*. New York: Brunner/Mazel, 1974.

Johnson, M. An approach to feminist therapy. *Psychotherapy: Theory, Research and Practice*, 1976, *13*, 72–76.

Klein, M. Feminist concepts of therapy outcome. *Psychotherapy: Theory, Research and Practice*, 1976, *13*, 89–95.

Kohlberg, L. Stage and sequence: The cognitive developmental approach to socialization. In D. Goslin (Ed.), *Handbook of socialization theory and research*. Chicago: Rand McNally, 1969.

Kronsky, B. Feminism and psychotherapy. *Journal of Contemporary Psychotherapy*, 1971, *3*, 89–98.

Miller, J. *Toward a new psychology of women*. Boston: Beacon Press, 1976.

Piaget, J. *The origins of intelligence in children*. New York: Norton, 1963.

Rawlings, E., & Carter, D. Feminist and nonsexist psychotherapy. In E. Rawlings & D. Carter (Eds.), *Psychotherapy for women: Treatment toward equality*. Springfield, Ill.: C. C. Thomas, 1977.

Ryan, W. *Blaming the victim*. New York: Pantheon Books, 1971.

Seiler, L. Sex differences in mental illness: Comment on Clancy and Gove's interpretation. *American Journal of Sociology*, 1976, *81*, 1458–63.

Seligman, M., Klein, D., & Miller, W. Depression. In H. Leitenberg (Ed.), *Handbook of behavior modification and behavior therapy*. Englewood Cliffs, N.J.: Prentice-Hall, 1976.

Sherman, M., Trief, P., & Sprafkin, R. Impression management in the psychiatric interview: Quality, style, and individual differences. *Journal of Consulting and Clinical Psychology*, 1975, *43*, 867–71.

Tudor, W., Tudor, J., & Gove, W. The effect of sex role differences on the social control of mental illness. *Journal of Health and Social Behavior*, 1977, *18*, 98–112.

Weissman, M., & Klerman, G. Sex differences and the epidemiology of depression. *Archives of General Psychiatry*, 1977, *34*, 98–111.

Williams, E. *Notes of a feminist therapist*. New York: Dell, 1976.

Ziegler, E., & Phillips, L. Social effectiveness and symptomatic behaviors. *Journal of Abnormal and Social Psychology*, 1960, *61*, 231–38.

Question 4

Are Menstruating Women at the Mercy of Raging Hormones?

In 1981, the *Journal of the American Medical Association* described premenstrual syndrome (PMS) as "the newest women's health issue in the United States" (Gonzalez, 1981, p. 1393). The journal could have added that PMS is also one of the nation's most controversial women's health issues. The debate ranges from questions of definition and etiology to whether the syndrome actually exists.

Premenstrual syndrome was brought to public attention largely through the work of Katharina Dalton, a British physician. Dalton is perhaps best known for her participation in two 1980 murder trials in England in which she testified that both of the women defendants had a history of committing uncontrollable acts of aggression because they suffered from a severe form of PMS. Her expert testimony that progesterone therapy had eliminated their aggressive impulses led to probation rather than prison sentences for the two women.

The view of dramatic and possibly violent shifts in mood and behavior posited by PMS proponents flies in the face of much research over the past two decades which has minimized both the physiological and the psychological effects of menstruation. For example, an extensive review of the literature indicates that among the general population of women, menstrual cycle variables do not interfere with cognitive abilities. There is evidence that there may be some changes in sensorimotor areas, but the data are neither clear nor consistent (Sommer, 1983).

There do appear to be some shifts in hormonal levels during the menstrual cycle, but the assertion that hormones have a solely negative impact on the emotions has met with much disagreement. A number of studies also suggest that in some instances, reported menstrual stress can be traced

128 to the woman's beliefs and expectation (Ruble, 1977; Parlee, 1982). In one study of tribal societies, the researchers found that the women in some cultures do not report any negative menstrual symptoms (Paige & Paige, 1981).

Nevertheless, PMS continues to attract considerable discussion in professional journals, in the popular press and in the women's health movement. Self-help groups have sprung up around the country; and, to support members of these groups as well as to educate the lay public, there are at least two nationally circulated newsletters, one of which is in its third year of publication (Amato, 1986). In all of these resources, it is generally acknowledged that the first difficulty in examining the PMS symdrome is the lack of clarity that characterizes problems related to menstruation. Does PMS encompass the wide range of symptoms connected with premenstrual tension, or should it be reserved for a specific cluster of severe symptoms? Assuming that the syndrome does exist, what should be the proper treatment?

The popularity of PMS has led to the establishment of a number of specialized clinics to treat the newly discovered "disease." However, critics have expressed concern that progesterone may become the 1980s equivalent of Lydia Pinkham's Vegetable Compound, the nineteenth century's cure for "female complaints" (Heneson, 1984). These critics argue that there is no evidence that progesterone treatment works (Rose & Abplanalp, 1983). Others charge that there is no justification for labeling the problems that some women experience during their cycle as an illness (Rome, 1986).

The debate surfaced in the American Psychiatric Association in 1985 when a committee recommended that "Periluteal Dysphoric Disorder," a psychiatric name for PMS, be added to the new edition of the Diagnostic and Statistical Manual of Mental Disorders (DSM-III). As was noted in the introduction to question 2 on masochism, feminist psychiatrists and psychologists, as well as other mental health professionals, protested the proposed change. The case was made that such a diagnosis would unfairly stigmatize women with menstrual difficulties and label them as psychiatrically disturbed.

In June 1986, these protests led the Board of Trustees of the American Psychiatric Association to include a recommendation that a premenstrual-related category should be moved to the appendix of the revised Diagnostic Manual (DSM-III-R). Feminist critics of the revision continue to protest the action, arguing that the decision to list PMS in the appendix of the manual lends legitimacy to the myth that it is a psychiatric disorder and overlooks the hormonal and societal factors that are involved (Ahmann, 1987).

Is Katharina Dalton correct when she argues that a menstrual syndrome **129** exists, that there are women in need of help, and that practitioners should treat them instead of waiting for more research studies? Or is Randi Koeske correct when she argues that treating a questionable "disease" with an unproven cure is dangerous medicine?

References

Ahmann, S. (1987, January). Battle-scarred Diagnostic Manual gets APA approval. *Clinical Psychiatry News*, 2, 22.

Amato, Beth C. (Ed.) (1986, Nov./Dec.). *Cycles: A PMS Support Newsletter, 3* (1). (Available from Cycles, P.O. Box 524, Sharon, Mass. 02067).

Gonzalez, E. (1981, April 10). Premenstrual syndrome: An ancient woe deserving of modern scrutiny. *Journal of the American Medical Association, 245* (14), 1393–96.

Heneson, N. (1984). The selling of PMS. *Science 84, 5* (4), 67–71.

Paige, K., & Paige, J. (1981). *Politics and reproduction rituals*. Berkeley: University of California Press.

Parlee, M. (1982). Changes in mood and activation levels during the menstrual cycle in experimentally naive subjects. *Psychology of Women Quarterly, 7* (2), 119–31.

Rome, E. (1986). Premenstrual syndrome (PMS) examined through a feminist lens. In V. Olesen & N. Fugate (Eds.), *Culture, society and menstruation* (pp. 145–51). Cambridge: Hemisphere and Harper & Row.

Rose, R. & Abplanalp, J. M. (1983). The premenstrual syndrome. *Hospital practice*, 129–41.

Ruble, D. (1977). Premenstrual symptoms: A reinterpretation. *Science, 197,* 291–92.

Sommer, B. (1983). How does menstruation affect cognitive competence and psychophysiological response? *Women and Health, 8* (2/3), 53–90.

Additional Reading

Abplanalp, J. M. (1983). Premenstrual syndrome: A selective review. *Women and Health, 8* (2/3), 107–23.

Alagna, S. W. & Hamilton, J. A. (1986, August). Science in the service of mythology: The psychopathologizing of menstruation. Paper presented at the American Psychological Association annual meeting, Washington, D.C.

Asso, D. (1983). *The real menstrual cycle*. New York: John Wiley.

Bell, S. E. (1986). Premenstrual syndrome and the medicalization of menopause: A sociological perspective. In B. E. Ginsburg & B. F. Carter (Eds.), *Premenstrual syndrome: Ethical implications in a biobehavioral perspective*. New York: Plenum.

Clare, A. W. (1983). The relationship between psychopathology and the menstrual cycle. *Women and Health, 8* (2/3), 125–36.

Harrison, W., Rabkin, J., & Endicott, J. (1985). Psychiatric evaluation of pre-menstrual changes. *Psychosomatics, 26* (10), 789–99.

Laws, S. (1983). The sexual politics of premenstrual tension. *International Journal of Women's Studies, 6* (1), 19–31.

Laws, S., Hey, V., & Eagan, A. (1985). *Seeing red: The politics of pre-menstrual tension*. Dover, N.H.: Hutchinson.

130 Rubinow, D. & Roy-Byrne, P. (1984). Premenstrual syndromes: Overview from a methodological perspective. *American Journal of Psychiatry, 141* (2), 163–72.

Ruble, D. N. & Brooks-Gunn, J. (1979). Menstrual symptoms: A social cognition analysis. *Journal of Behavioral Medicine, 2*, 171–94.

Ruble, D. (1982). A developmental analysis of menstrual distress in adolescence. In R. C. Friedman (Ed.), *Behavior and the menstrual cycle*, (pp. 177–97). New York: Marcel Dekker.

What Is This PMS?

KATHARINA DALTON

In 1980 the Sixth International Congress of Psychosomatic Obstetrics and Gynaecology concluded that "premenstrual syndrome (PMS) must be regarded as an endocrinopathy . . . deserving of a place in the future not only at psychosomatic meetings but also at scientific conventions" (Van Keep and Utian, 1981), thus recognizing the hormonal element in PMS. Nevertheless it is general practitioners, observing patients in health and sickness, who are the doctors most likely to recognize the changes in mood during the menstrual cycle so characteristic of PMS; only they know the impact it has on the patient's family, neighbours, and workmates. The general practitioner also has the clinical competence to make the diagnosis and supervise treatment. PMS is thus the specialty of general practice.

Frank first described premenstrual tension in 1931 as "a feeling of incredible tension from 10 to 7 days preceding menstruation, which in most instances continues until the time the menstrual flow occurs." Later it was appreciated that many other symptoms may be involved, such as headaches, nausea, vertigo, joint pains, skin and mucosal lesions, rhinorrhoea, asthma, epilepsy, and mastalgia. In 1953 the term *premenstrual syndrome* was introduced "to prevent missing the diagnosis when tension was absent or overshadowed by a more serious complaint" (Greene and Dalton, 1953). PMS was defined as "the presence of recurrent symptoms in the premenstruum or early menstruation with complete absence in the postmenstruum." It must be emphasized that Frank's definition and this one are the same, and that they depend on the timing of symptoms, not on their type. The symptoms themselves are commonplace and also occur with great frequency in men, children, and postmenopausal women. Greene and Dalton insisted on the minimum time of recurrences of symptoms as three

"What Is This PMS?" by Katharina Dalton, *Journal of the Royal College of General Practitioners*, 1982, *32*, 717–23. Copyright © 1982 by the Journal of the Royal College of General Practitioners. Reprinted by permission.

Dr. Dalton is a physician specializing in gynecology and endocrinology in London, England.

132 menstrual cycles, with their absence in each postmenstruum. Today some investigators consider self-rating questionnaires used by women in only one premenstrual week sufficient for a diagnosis (Clare, 1977). This is not good enough.

PMS covers a wide spectrum from normality to gross abnormality. It has been studied by sociologists, psychologists, psychiatrists, gynaecologists, endocrinologists, and physicians, and it is a popular subject in the medical and lay press, but too often definitions are absent or incorrect so that comparisons cannot be made. A recent review of PMS by Reid and Yen (1981) describes it on the basis of symptoms: "The patient with severe PMS develops breast swelling and tenderness, abdominal bloating and a variable degree of oedema in the extremities in the luteal phase," but fails to define PMS. This again is not enough; there must be evidence of timing of symptoms and a symptom-free phase in the postmenstruum or pre-ovulatory phase.

Earlier doctors limited "symptoms" to those complaints severe enough to require medical attention. Today's psychologists administer self-rating questionnaires to identify premenstrual complainers in a healthy population and, having divided them into psychiatrically healthy and ill premenstrual complainers, draw conclusions on the degree of neuroticism and personality traits of PMS sufferers (Clare, 1982). Surveys of this type are as irrelevant to the elucidation of the aetiology and treatment of PMS as a similar general population study of diarrhoea sufferers would be in investigating the aetiology and therapeutic factors involved in ulcerative colitis or Crohn's disease.

Women presenting with premenstrual symptoms need a full clinical examination, for it is not uncommon to find evidence of hypertension, hypothyroidism, galactorrhoea, ovarian cysts, salpingitis, or endometriosis, all conditions which require specific treatment. Women in whom no physical abnormalities are discovered should be given a menstrual chart on which to record, with any chosen symbol, the three worst symptoms on the days they occur and also the dates of menstruation (Dalton, 1977). Positive charts are those showing symptoms occurring at the same time in the luteal phase of each cycle and at least seven consecutive days free from symptoms at the same time in each postmenstruum. This recording does not entail a great intellectual demand and can be used equally well by those with a poor understanding of English. In a few cases it may be possible to obtain retrospective information from prison or police documents (Dalton, 1980), medical records or worksheets, from which it may be possible to make a positive diagnosis and institute immediate treatment.

Many studies have relied on the Moos Menstrual Distress Questionnaire

(MMDQ), which as its name suggests was designed to identify sufferers of 133 menstrual distress (Moos, 1968). In such a questionnaire a woman is asked to rate some forty-seven symptoms on a six-point scale. The success of the self-assessment questionnaire depends on the diligence of the woman completing it each night for a minimum of three months, including high days and holidays. The findings are relevant only in the highly motivated or the obsessional woman, and there is the ever-present danger that she will forget to complete it one night and fill it in some days later giving a false answer. Even using the shortened Form T with Sampson and Jenner's (1977) sine wave modification, it is of no value in the diagnosis of PMS. No questions are asked regarding the absence of symptoms in the postmenstruums or the recurrence of symptoms in successive premenstruums. Such criteria cannot produce the necessary evidence so essential to the diagnosis of PMS. Sampson's 1979 paper, "PMS—A Double Blind Controlled Trial of Progesterone and Placebo," relied on such evidence from the MMDQ and even showed in Figure 1 the results of the questionnaire demonstrating the presence of symptoms in the postmenstruum in both the cycle under observation and the cycle before treatment commenced. Such trials merely demonstrate that progesterone has no value in menstrual distress, a term covering dysmenorrhoea, endometriosis, and menstrual exacerbation of symptoms present throughout the cycle. It is recognized that progesterone is specific to PMS and is of no value in dysmenorrhoea or endometriosis, so it was not unexpected that the value of progesterone in the trials of menstrual distress was no better than placebo.

PMS occurs in both ovular and anovular cycles, so basal temperature charts are of no diagnostic value (Reid and Yen, 1981). Similarly, as weight swings are normal physiological happenings, a daily weight chart alone is not diagnostic. At present the only biochemical test of diagnostic value in PMS is the sex hormone binding globulin (SHBG) estimation, which in fifty women with well-diagnosed severe premenstrual syndrome was found to be below the normal level of 50–80 nmol/DHT/I, whereas fifty control women who denied having any premenstrual symptoms all had values in the normal range (Dalton, 1981). However, the use of SHBG is limited to those who are free from medication and who are not obese or hirsute, so the ethnically hirsute races cannot be included. Furthermore, at present SHBG estimations are available only at a few specialized laboratories.

Noting the following points when taking a history can alert the clinician to a positive diagnosis of PMS. PMS starts and also increases in severity at times of hormonal upheaval, such as puberty, after a pregnancy, during or after taking oral contraceptives, after a spell of amenorrhoea or after sterilization. PMS sufferers are usually symptom-free during pregnancy

134 (Greene and Dalton, 1953) and are unable to tolerate the Pill due to side-effects. Women who have suffered from pre-eclampsia show an 87 percent incidence of PMS afterwards (Dalton, 1954) and a 90 percent incidence after postnatal depression (Dalton, 1977). Women with PMS also tend to have food cravings and are unable to tolerate long intervals without food (Okey and Robb, 1925; Harris, 1944; Billig, 1947; Dalton, 1977). Their tolerance to alcohol also varies over the cycle, being worse premenstrually. Their libido is often highest in the premenstruum (Israel, 1938; Gray, 1941), in contrast to sufferers of depression, who have a loss of libido throughout the month.

The many difficulties encountered in studies of PMS include the individual variations in the length of cycle in the same woman and between women. There are variations in the duration of the menstrual flow, the effects of stress (Dalton, 1968), age and parity (Dalton, 1954), a past history of pre-eclampsia (Greene and Dalton, 1953) or postnatal depression (Dalton, 1977), variations in hormonal states due to oral contraceptives, the woman's attitude toward a possible pregnancy, and the selection of suitable controls. The literature on PMS includes many examples of biased selection of subjects or controls, for example the use of women attending an infertility clinic (Benedek-Jaszmann and Hearn-Sturtevant, 1976), and the use of lithium in nineteen hospitalized women, including five with schizophrenia, four neurotics and three psychotics (Singer et al., 1974). A study of minor psychiatric and physical symptoms selected seven control women who had undergone a hysterectomy (Beaumont et al., 1975). The absorption and metabolism of oral progesterone was studied in five postmenopausal women (Whitehead et al., 1980), and another studied the effects of progesterone and four synthetic progestogens using twenty male medical students (Oelkers et al., 1974). An appeal on commercial radio asked for volunteers for PMS trials: the authors stated that a telephone conversation had ensured that the volunteers all had premenstrual complaints, but after a month's charting of symptoms only three had premenstrual symptoms alone, and thirty-four women had premenstrual *and* menstrual symptoms (Wood and Jakubowicz, 1980). None of these trials is acceptable because of their biased selection.

Perhaps the greatest problem comes in the selection of subjects for double-blind controlled therapeutic trials; because it is ethically wrong to include those in danger to themselves or others: those at risk of epileptic fits, acute asthma attacks, suicide, homicide, baby batterers, criminal damage, and alcoholic bouts are automatically excluded. Those with moderate symptoms, having completed a three-month chart, are usually at the end of their tether and demand treatment; they are no longer ready to accept the possibility of receiving a placebo. This difficulty can be partially overcome by treating the patients first and, when they are completely symptom-free on medication, allowing them one month's trial of another drug (Dalton, 1959 and 1976). The women then know their suffering can be relieved and have permission to return to effective treatment should they consider it necessary. On the other hand, women with only mild symptoms do not really need treatment.

In PMS there are two areas demanding further study which should not be confused: a fuller understanding of how the hormonal changes of menstruation affect normal women, and the prevention of suffering for those who are in distress during each premenstruum. PMS does exist and has only one definition: it is a syndrome needing treatment. It is the general practitioner's responsibility to diagnose and treat this common problem which has innumerable manifestations and, all too often, dire consequences.

References

Beaumont, P. J. V., Richard, D. H. & Gelder, M. G. (1975). A study of minor psychiatric and physical symptoms during the menstrual cycle. *British Journal of Psychiatry, 126,* 431–34.

Benedek-Jaszmann, L. J. & Hearn-Sturtevant, M. D. (1976). Premenstrual tension and functional infertility—aetiology and treatment. *Lancet, 1,* 1095–98.

Billig, H. E., Jr. & Spaulding, G. A., Jr. (1947). Hyperinsulinism of menses. *Industrial Medicine, 16,* 336–39.

Clare, A. W. (1977). Psychological profiles of women complaining of premenstrual symptoms. *Current Medical Research and Opinion, 4,* 23–28.

Clare, A. W. (1982). *Journal of Psychosomatic Obstetrics and Gynaecology, 1,* 22–31.

Dalton, K. (1954). Similarity of symptomatology of premenstrual syndrome and toxaemia of pregnancy and their response to progesterone. *British Medical Journal, 2,* 1071–76.

Dalton, K. (1959). Comparative trials of new oral progestogenic compounds in treatment of premenstrual syndrome. *British Medical Journal, 2,* 1307–09.

Dalton, K. (1968). Menstruation and examinations. *Lancet, 2,* 1386–88.

Dalton, K. (1976). *Pharmacological and Clinical Aspects of Bromocriptine.* Ed. Baylis, R. I. S., Turner, P. & McClay, D. W. P. pp. 106–08. London: MSC Consultants.

Dalton, K. (1977). *The Premenstrual Syndrome and Progesterone Therapy.* London: Heinemann.

Dalton, K. (1980). Cyclical criminal acts in premenstrual syndrome. *Lancet, 2,* 1070–71.

Dalton, K. (1981). Premenstrual syndrome. *British Journal of Psychiatry, 137,* 199.

Dalton, M. E. (1981). Sex hormone binding globulin levels in women with severe premenstrual syndrome. *British Postgraduate Medical Journal, 57,* 560–61.

Frank, R. T. (1931). The hormonal causes of premenstrual tension. *Archives of Neurology and Psychology, 26,* 1053.

Gray, L. A. (1941). The use of progesterone in nervous tension states. *Southern Medical Journal, 34,* 1004–06.

Greene, R. & Dalton, K. (1953). The premenstrual syndrome. *British Medical Journal, 1,* 1007–14.

136 Harris, S. Jr. (1944). Hyperinsulinism. *Southern Medical Journal, 37,* 714–17.

Israel, S. L. (1938). Premenstrual tension. *Journal of the American Medical Association, 110,* 1721.

Moos, R. H. (1968). The development of a menstrual distress questionnaire. *Psychosomatic Medicine, 30,* 853–67.

Oelkers, W., Schönestiöfer, M. & Blümel, A. (1974). Effects of progesterone and four synthetic progestogens on sodium balance and the renin-aldosterone system in man. *Journal of Clinical Endocrinology and Metabolism, 39,* 882–90.

Okey, R. & Robb, E. I. (1925). Studies of metabolism of women. Variations in the fasting blood sugar level and sugar tolerance in relation to the menstrual cycle. *Journal of Biological Chemistry, 65,* 165.

Reid, R. L. & Yen, S. S. Premenstrual syndrome. *American Journal of Obstetrics and Gynecology, 39,* 85–104.

Sampson, G. A. (1979). Premenstrual syndrome: a double blind controlled trial of progesterone and placebo. *British Journal of Psychiatry, 135,* 209–15.

Sampson, G. A. & Jenner, F. A. (1977). Studies of daily recordings from the Moos Menstrual Distress Questionnaire. *British Journal of Psychiatry, 130,* 265–71.

Singer, K., Cheng, R. & Schou, M. (1974). A controlled experiment of lithium in the premenstrual tension syndrome. *British Journal of Psychiatry, 124,* 50–51.

Van Keep, P. A. & Utian, W. H. (1981). *The Premenstrual Syndrome.* Lancaster: MTP Press.

Whitehead, M. I., Townsend, P. T. & Gill, D. K. (1980). Absorption and metabolism of oral progesterone. *British Medical Journal, 280,* 825–28.

Wood, C. & Jakubowicz, D. (1980). The treatment of premenstrual symptoms with mefenamic acid. *British Journal of Obstetrics and Gynaecology, 87,* 627–30.

Premenstrual Emotionality: Is Biology Destiny?

RANDI DAIMON KOESKE

Premenstrual tension was identified as a clinical entity by Frank in 1931. Although definitions have varied, the term is most commonly used to refer to the physical and emotional changes experienced by many women during the week or ten days prior to the onset of menstrual flow. Most commonly mentioned as characteristic of the *premenstrual syndrome,* a term popularized by Katharina Dalton (1964), are irritability, depression, and anxiety accompanied by water retention, abdominal discomfort, and headache. These symptoms seem to dissipate with the onset of menstrual flow (most researchers categorize painful menstruation, or dysmenorrhea, as a different clinical entity), leading several observers to describe the premenstrual phase of the cycle as a build-up of tension that is released in menstruation.

The support for any biological explanation of premenstrual behavior, however, has been equivocal at best. The generally unsystematic and methodologically questionable research characteristic of the area (for reviews, see Parlee, 1973, and Koeske, 1973) has complicated the task of untangling cause and effect. In particular, it has been rare for researchers to incorporate explicitly both physiological and social-cognitive factors in the same study in a manner that allows their separate and combined effects to be gauged. Most often the influences of the two sets of variables are confounded, although observed covariations are implicitly interpreted as evidence for biological influence.

Interestingly, the range of premenstrual behaviors and physical changes for which biology is the assumed explanation has now grown so wide that the utility and plausibility of the "explanation" may be seriously questioned. Behaviors reportedly influenced by cycle phase include negative affect (Benedek, 1961; Ivey & Bardwick, 1968), alcoholism (Janowsky et

"Premenstrual Emotionality: Is Biology Destiny?" by Randi Daimon Koeske, *Women and Health,* 1976, *1* (3), 11–14. Copyright © 1976 by The Haworth Press. Reprinted by permission. This article was completely rewritten in 1986 and new references were added.

Dr. Koeske is a Research Psychologist in the Psychology Department at the University of Pittsburgh.   *137*

138 al., 1969), suicide and attempted suicide (Dalton, 1964; Tonks, Rack, & Rose, 1968), unpremeditated violent crime (Morton et al., 1933), accident proneness (Dalton, 1964) and impaired judgment (Dalton, 1966), perceptual (Lamb et al., 1953) and performance (Dalton, 1964) changes, and sexual arousal (Moos et al., 1969). Most of these, with the possible exception of sexual arousal, are thought of as negative and, implicitly, unusual for women.

Cyclic changes in almost every body system and function have also been reported (Southam & Gonzaga, 1965), as have less common medical complaints such as glaucoma, epilepsy, migraine, susceptibility to infection, and allergic sensitivity (Dalton, 1968; Greene & Dalton, 1953). A recent review by Rubinow and Roy-Byrne (1984), for example, classified common symptoms of PMS into nine distinct categories, which included central nervous system, autonomic, neurovegetative, dermatological, fluid/electrolyte, and pain, all highly complex in their physiological regulation and expression.

Unfortunately, such attempts to clarify the incredible scope of PMS also make it more problematic to identify a single-factor (biological) explanation capable of uniting so complex a set of phenomena. The herculean proportions of the task have caused some researchers to question the possibility that any explanation of PMS as currently understood can be found (Parlee, 1973; Koeske, 1980, 1981). But others have been inspired to subdivide the whole into a package of identifiable disorders, each presumed to have a specific manifestation, etiology, and treatment (Endicott et al., 1981; Halbreich et al., 1982). Recent efforts to come to agreement on a definition of PMS have resulted in heated discussion of whether it should be considered a specific psychiatric diagnosis (as opposed to a gynecological disorder) and whether it is most properly thought of as an affective disorder, a stress-related disorder, or a time-dependent (cyclic) disorder. These debates are not only academic in nature; they will determine who is judged to have PMS, who may appropriately treat PMS, and by what means.

Alternative Explanations

My research approach has differed considerably from that of most researchers in the area because I have tried to study directly some aspects of the PMS phenomenon that others have taken for granted. Rather than take as my task the explanation of "symptoms" (whether somatic, emotional, or behavioral) occurring in the premenstrual phase of the cycle, I have asked what it is that makes the premenstruum salient to women and then considered how the process of "symptom" perception and explanation occur. I *139* have also wondered why some changes in physical state, mood, or behavior are noticed and explained as due to cycle phase while others are either unnoticed or explained in other ways. And I have considered whether current biological explanations of PMS may be inadequate because they have focused on too small a portion of the full phenomenon to understand it properly. Underlying my attempts at reconceptualization are a strong suspicion of the normative assumptions plaguing past conceptualizations and a belief in the necessity of constructing an explanation that requires an interaction of physiological and social-cognitive factors. I have tried to assume a "grain of truth" in the cultural tendency to connect cycle phase with unwanted or unusual behaviors but have not been satisfied that the process operates so simply. I present here the outline of an alternative conceptualization I have been formulating for the past several years, which I offer as a sufficient, plausible, and parsimonious explanation of premenstrual behavior and emotionality with some interesting implications for women.

In my preliminary research, I have taken two different approaches to untangling the now ill-defined area of premenstrual emotionality, both derived from the social psychological literature on attributions (or how people interpret the causes of events and behaviors in their social environment). Two of these studies have investigated commonsense beliefs about the influence of the menstrual cycle on behavior and commonsense understandings of emotional behavior displayed by premenstrual women (Koeske & Koeske, 1975; Koeske, 1975). Both have used experimental "person perception" formats in which cues describing a target person were varied systematically in order to examine their influence on perceptions of the target person. Using such a format, it is possible, for example, to examine whether the perception of identical behavior changes in meaning when it is ascribed to a premenstrual female target as compared to a non-premenstrual female target or to a male target. It is also possible to vary the behavior and situation of the target person described.

The results of these studies, conducted on college students, demonstrate that only negative behaviors (such as depressed or hostile moods or outbursts of anger) are interpreted as due to biology. Premenstrual displays of positive behavior, on the other hand, are attributed to personality or situational factors. Interestingly, when premenstrual negative behavior is ascribed to the influence of biology, the situational factors simultaneously influencing it are discounted in importance and the behavior is judged more extreme. In addition, the behavior is likely to be judged more unreasonable and unjustifiable, and more indicative of a changeable (i.e., tem-

140 peramental, irrational, and immature) personality than identical behavior displayed by either a non-premenstrual female or a male. The designation of menstruation as "the curse" begins to take on new meaning in light of these findings: negative behavior exhibited premenstrually is perceived as evidence for the prevailing negative stereotype of female emotional behavior while positive behavior is ignored as something to which biology is irrelevant. The documentation of such an attribution pattern points to a mechanism assuring the persistence of a negative stereotype in the face of disconfirming evidence and it isolates a belief system capable of construing not-so-uncommon behavior as unusual, inexplicable, and somehow less tied to the situation at hand.

What factors might underlie people's tendency to interpret only negative behavior as due to biology? An interesting possibility suggested by the second of these person perception studies is that negative behaviors like hostility are deemed unusual or "out-of-role" for women. As such, they may seem to require explanation by factors other than the situation. On the other hand, positive behaviors like pleasantness may be more readily assimilated to the female personality because they are considered characteristic. Thus, stereotypically unexpected behavior is noticed and attributed to biology, while positive behavior is viewed as characteristically "feminine" and ascribed to an interaction of personality and situational factors.

Another possibility, not specifically tested in these studies, is that women themselves may offer "premenstrual tension" as an explanation for negative behaviors—a sort of excuse or factor beyond their control. "I just wasn't myself" would be an example of such excuse behavior (which is common, by the way, among both men and women in explaining their own negative behavior). Unfortunately, attribution theory suggests that people tend to discount the influence of external or uncontrollable factors in explaining others' behavior and rely instead on personality and motivational explanations. Thus, behavior which is self-excused as due to the influence of biology may confirm a negative view of female personality for outside observers.

We can begin to understand why the interpretive bias documented in these studies may persist over time and confound our efforts to really understand premenstrual emotionality if we examine the process of "symptom" perception more closely. The medical model explanation postulates that a physiological "imbalance" associated with the premenstruum underlies the disturbing moods and behaviors experienced as PMS. In this model "symptoms" (bodily experiences, moods and behaviors indicative of an underlying disorder) seem to have a one-to-one relationship with underlying physiological processes: when one changes, so does the other.

The attributional model I have relied on, however, considers the process of noticing and making sense of self-changes to be a complex and problematic one (cf. Pennebaker, 1982). Some physiological processes take place without our awareness while others produce observable changes in the body. Body sensations, behavior, and mood can and do show comparable (i.e., PMS-like) changes in response to factors other than the menstrual cycle. How, then, do we know when we are changing in some way, and how do we decide that this change is due to the menstrual cycle?

Several lines of research suggest that menstruation itself (Campos & Thurow, 1978; Beaumont, Richards, Gelder, 1975) or a recurring pattern of symptoms (Rodin, 1976) provides women with the cue they need to decide when they are premenstrual. Thus, many women only *retrospectively* make sense of troublesome moods and behaviors or become aware of their cycle phase *after* emotional behaviors have already occurred. The process by which they make this decision is known to be a fallible one (Ruble, 1977; Ruble & Brooks-Gunn, 1979). Since menses can be either precipitated or delayed by concurrent life stress (Osofsky & Fisher, 1971; Arnold, 1978), and since stress is known to affect many aspects of the menstrual cycle (Ermini et al., 1978; Siegel, Johnson, & Sarason, 1979; Woods, Dery, & Most, 1982), relying on menstrual onset or specific somatic change to define cycle phase can result in misleading attributions: menstruation (and the premenstruum) may coincide with emotional and behavioral upheaval because both have been brought on by stress, not because the premenstruum "causes" emotional and behavioral upheaval. Is it any wonder, then, that a large percentage of women claiming to experience PMS fail to demonstrate a cyclic pattern of negative affect when asked to monitor themselves daily (Englander-Golden, 1977; Sommer, 1978; Hamilton et al., 1984)? Is it surprising that only a few PMS sufferers show unusual physiological patterns when assessed premenstrually (Bruce & Russell, 1962; Taylor, 1979; Andersen et al., 1977)? Is it any wonder that a variety of physiological interventions, many of which remove or significantly alter the pattern of perceivable body change experienced premenstrually, sometimes result in improved mood, even when no clearcut evidence of changes in underlying causal mechanism can be found (Green, 1982)? These findings, viewed as troubling in the medical model framework, become sensible when the cue value of cyclic somatic changes, not just the physiology underlying these changes, becomes the focus of attention.

The wider significance of the bias in interpreting premenstrual mood and behavior documented in my studies becomes especially apparent if the usual biological explanation of PMS represents an oversimplification of actual premenstrual emotionality. What if there is an increase in *both*

142 positive and negative emotional behaviors premenstrually and biology does not require a deterioration of mood and behavior premenstrually? Then the characteristic pattern for interpreting premenstrual emotional behavior would be reinforced, since negative emotions could increase premenstrually. The fact that positive emotions could also increase, however, would not undermine the credibility of the "premenstrual tension" explanation, since biology is judged irrelevant to positive behaviors.

In the second two studies I have conducted on this topic, I examined the plausibility of an explanation of premenstrual emotion which predicts just this pattern: that, potentially, both positive and negative emotions may be enhanced premenstrually and that it is the situational cues present at the time, not the pattern of physiological response, which determines whether positive or negative emotions (or any emotions at all) will be experienced. This hypothesis concerning premenstrual emotionality postulates a premenstrual increase in arousability or sensitivity, similar to the Schachter and Singer (1962) theory of emotion.

In researching their theory of emotion, Schachter and Singer gave injections of a placebo or epinephrine (an arousal-producing substance) to subjects under one of three interpretive sets. Subjects were either told that the injection would produce arousal symptoms, like sweating and rapid pulse (informed condition); or told that the injection would produce non-arousal symptoms, like itching and headache (misinformed condition); or were given no information about drug effects (uninformed condition). Subjects were then exposed to a social context which made salient one of two emotional labels, anger or euphoria.

Reasoning from an interactive theory of emotion, Schachter and Singer predicted that emotion would result only from the simultaneous presence of a state of physiological arousal and an emotional label to "explain" or interpret it. Results confirmed the hypothesis. Epinephrine-injected subjects were unaffected by the emotional cues if given an adequate explanation of their internal state (informed condition): they attributed their internal state to the injection. Uninformed or misinformed subjects injected with epinephrine, who could not explain their internal state by reference to the injection, experienced emotion (either anger or euphoria), depending on emotional cues. Placebo-injected subjects did not experience emotion even when emotional cues were provided. Thus both physiological and social-cognitive factors were necessary for the elicitation of emotion.

In my own research, I have attempted to demonstrate premenstrual arousability in two studies. In the first, I examined fluctuations on a variety of physiological and performance measures over the menstrual cycle, being careful to conceal the relevance of the menstrual cycle from my subjects.

Results showed a tendency for premenstrual arousability, as predicted. In *143* another study, I predicted and found preliminary suggestions that premenstrual mood (both positive and negative) was more strongly related to the situation than moods occurring at other cycle phases for women or for men, and that premenstrual negative moods occur only in stressful environments. The use of oral contraceptives did not appear to affect these relationships.

Is this premenstrual arousability-labeling hypothesis just another version of the biological explanation? I would argue emphatically no, because it suggests that negative moods and behaviors are not inevitable during the premenstruum. The specific emotions and behaviors that occur are instead due to the immediate situational cues and/or important cognitive elements of past experience. Moreover, the experience of emotion itself, whether positive or negative, is not in itself inevitable, according to the original theory. Schachter and Singer's informed subjects did not experience emotion when exposed to emotional cues because they had a neutral explanation for their internal sensations.

The arousability-labeling hypothesis also guides us to grant stress a central role in explaining PMS. It allows us to consider how ongoing stress can affect premenstrual mood either by altering arousability (through an increase in sympathetic reactivity) or by making negative emotional labels more salient and negative situations more likely. By directing our attention to the complex process of self-labeling, the hypothesis allows us to see how stress-*altered* cycles (in which the onset of menstrual flow or the severity of experienced body change has been affected) can reinforce a woman's sense of connection between the approach of menstruation and negative behavior change. We may then explore unrecognized contributory factors or prescribe lifestyle change treatments without claiming that PMS is only "in the head." The hypothesis allows us to use women's own experiences as a starting point but to go beyond them to a fuller understanding which complements, rather than denies or reifies, these experiences. Instead of a woman's body being a burden or a nuisance to her, it becomes, in this reconceptualization, a friend, more tuned in to the abuses heaped on it than her purely "mental" self is.

Challenging Negative Images

If it can be demonstrated that premenstruation, like epinephrine in Schachter and Singer's study, is not sufficient to produce emotion, it would do much to challenge the negative images of women implicit in the simple

144 biological explanation of premenstrual behavior. Currently, the attribution pattern linking negative premenstrual moods to biology supports women's tendency to discount the situational influences on their behavior, thus reinforcing passivity and focusing attention *away* from strategies which change the situation. The experience of guilt, anxiety, and self-doubt may instead result (Valins & Nisbett, 1971).

With a new perspective women might learn not to blame themselves and their biological state for their moods but to look to the situation for an explanation. Simultaneously learning to identify any premenstrual physical change as irrelevant to emotion (e.g., "water retention makes my tear ducts feel full" versus "I am depressed and about to cry"), like the epinephrine-informed condition in Schachter and Singer's study, could eliminate the experience of premenstrual emotion (without physiological intervention) and increase the likelihood of effective action to alter upsetting situations. An improved sense of self-control, self-understanding, and self-efficacy could result (Hamilton et al., 1984; Koeske, 1983; Heczey, 1978).

Thoughtful consideration and sound research is needed to avoid the pitfalls and hidden assumptions of the "biology is destiny" argument about women's behavior. To suggest that biology may, under certain conditions, have an influence on behavior is not identical to suggesting that behavior is reducible to biological variables. In fact, the arousability-labeling hypothesis ties the experience of emotion itself and the particular emotions experienced during the premenstruum more closely than before to the social-cognitive cues (labels) provided by the situation or past experience. Moreover, translating "overreaction" as "sensitivity" or "arousability" does much to convert an assumed liability into a potential asset. Future researchers may wish to document not only the increased premenstrual incidence of positive reactions to positive situations predicted by the hypothesis, but the similarly predicted ability to sense stress more acutely during the premenstruum. To turn the usual "biology is destiny" argument around, not altogether unseriously - it might be argued that such sensitivity to stress and the resultant experience in handling stress this sensitivity provides are valuable assets sorely needed by decisionmakers and political office holders.

References

Andersen, A. N., Larsen, J. F., Steenstrup, O. R., Svenstrup, B., & Nielsen, J. 1977. Effect of bromocriptine on the premenstrual syndrome. *Brit J Obstet Gynecol, 84:* 370–74.

Arnold, H. M. 1978. The interaction between neuroticism and perceived environmental stress in relation to menstrual cycle regularity. *Dissert Abstr Internat, 39, 4-B:* 1704.

Beaumont, P. J., Richards, D. H., & Gelder, M. G. 1975. A study of minor psychiatric and 145 physical symptoms during the menstrual cycle. *Brit J Psychiat, 126:* 431–34.

Benedek, T. F. 1961. Sexual functions in women and their disturbance. In S. Arieti, ed. *American Handbook of Psychiatry.* Vol. 1. New York: Basic Books.

Bruce, J., & Russell, G. F. M. 1962. Premenstrual tension: A study of weight changes and balances of water, sodium, and potassium. *Lancet, 2:* 267–71.

Campos, F., & Thurow, C. 1978. Attribution of moods and symptoms to the menstrual cycle. *Pers Soc Psychol Bull, 4:* 272–76.

Dalton, K. 1964. *The premenstrual syndrome.* Springfield, Ill.: Charles C. Thomas.

Dalton, K. 1966. The influence of mother's menstruation on her child. *Prod R Soc Med, 59:* 1014–16.

Endicott, J., Halbreich, U., Schact, S., & Nee, J. 1981. Premenstrual changes and affective disorders. *Psychosom Med, 43:* 519–30.

Englander-Golden, P., 1977. A longitudinal study of cyclical variations in moods and behaviors as a function of repression and the menstrual cycle. *Dissert Abstr Internat, 38, 5-B:* 2361–62.

Ermini, M., Maniglio, D., Zichella, L., Pancheri, P., Pancheri, L., & Bellaterra, M. 1978. Psychoneuroendocrine aspects of secondary amenorrhea. In L. Carenza, P. Pancheri, & L. Zichella, eds. *Clinical psychoneuroendocrinology in reproduction.* New York: Academic Press.

Frank, R. T. 1931. The hormonal causes of premenstrual tension. *Arch Neurol Psych, 26:* 1053–57.

Green, J. 1982. Recent trends in the treatment of premenstrual syndrome: A critical review. In R. C. Friedman, ed., *Behavior and the menstrual cycle.* New York: Marcel Dekker.

Greene, R., & Dalton, K. 1953. The premenstrual syndrome. *Brit Med J:* 1007–14.

Halbreich, U., Endicott, J., Schact, S., & Nee, J. 1982. The diversity of premenstrual changes as reflected in the Premenstrual Assessment Form. *Acta Psychiatr Scand, 65:* 46–65.

Hamilton, J. A., Parry, B. L., Blumenthal, S., Alagna, S., & Herz, E. 1984. Premenstrual mood changes: A guide to evaluation and treatment. *Psychiatr Annals, 14:* 426–35.

Heczey, M. D. 1978. Effects of biofeedback and autogenic training on menstrual experiences: Relationships among anxiety, locus of control, and dysmenorrhea. *Dissert Abstr Internat, 38, 11-B:* 5571.

Ivey, M. E., & Bardwick, J. M. 1968. Patterns of affective fluctuation in the menstrual cycle. *Psychosom Med, 30:* 336–45.

Janowsky, D. W., Gorney, R., Castelnuovo-Tedesco, P., & Stone, C. B. 1969. Premenstrual-menstrual increases in psychiatric admission rates. *Amer J Obstet Gynecol, 103:* 189–91.

Koeske, R. 1973. Physiological, social, and situational factors in the premenstrual syndrome. Unpublished MS.

Koeske, R. D. 1975. "Premenstrual tension" as an explanation of female hostility. Paper presented at the annual convention of the American Psychological Association.

Koeske, R. D. 1980. Theoretical perspectives on menstrual cycle research: The relevance of attributional approaches for the perception and explanation of premenstrual emotionality. In A. J. Dan, E. A. Graham, & C. P. Beecher, eds. *The menstrual cycle.* Vol. 1. New York: Springer.

Koeske, R. D. 1981. Theoretical and conceptual complexities in the design and analysis of menstrual cycle research. In P. Komnenich, M. McSweeney, J. A. Noack & N. Elder, eds. *The menstrual cycle.* Vol. 2. New York: Springer.

Koeske, R. D. 1983. "Curse" is foiled again: Thinking clearly about social and psychological factors in the premenstrual syndrome. Paper presented at the annual convention of the American Psychiatric Association.

Koeske, R. D., & Koeske, G. F. 1975. An attributional approach to moods and the menstrual cycle. *J Pers Soc Psychol, 3:* 473–78.

146 Lamb, W. M., Ulett, G. A., Masters, W. H., & Robinson, D. W. 1953. Premenstrual tension: EEG, hormonal, and psychiatric evaluation. *Amer J Psychiatry, 109:* 840–48.

Moos, R. H., Kopell, S. S., Melges, F. T., Yalom, I. D., Lunde, D. T., Clayton R. B., & Hamburg, D. A. 1969. Fluctuations in symptoms and moods during the menstrual cycle. *J Psychosom Res, 13:* 37–44.

Morton, J. H., Additon, R. G., Hunt, L., & Sullivan, J. J. 1933. A clinical study of premenstrual tension. *Amer J Obstet Gynecol, 65:* 1182–91.

Osofsky, H. J., & Fisher, S. 1971. Psychological correlates of the development of amenorrhea in a stress situation. *Psychosom Med, 33:* 515–37.

Parlee, M. B. 1973. The premenstrual syndrome. *Psychol Bull, 80:* 454–65.

Pennebaker, J. W. 1982. *The psychology of physical symptoms.* New York: Springer-Verlag.

Rodin, J., 1976. Menstruation, reattribution and competence. *J Pers Soc Psychol, 33:* 345–53.

Rubinow, D. R., & Roy-Byrne, P. 1984. Premenstrual syndromes: Overview from a methodologic perspective. *Am J Psychiatry, 141:* 163–71.

Ruble, D. N. 1977. Premenstrual symptoms: A reinterpretation. *Science, 197:* 291–92.

Ruble, D. N., & Brooks-Gunn, J. 1979. Menstrual symptoms: A social cognition analysis. *Behav Med, 2:* 171–94.

Schacter, S., & Singer, J. E. 1962. Cognitive, social, and physiological determinants of emotional state. *Psychol Rev, 69:* 379–99.

Siegel, J. M., Johnson, J. H., & Sarason, I. G. 1979. Life changes and menstrual discomfort. *J Hum Stress, 5:* 41–46.

Sommer, B. 1978. Stress and menstrual distress. *J Hum Stress, 4:* 5–10, 41–47.

Southam, A. L., & Gonzaga, F. P. 1965. Systemic changes during the menstrual cycle. *Am J Obstet Gynecol, 91:* 142–65.

Taylor, J. W. 1979. Plasma progesterone, oestradiol 17B, and premenstrual symptoms. *Acta Psychiatr Scand, 60:* 76–86.

Tonks, C. M., Rack, P. H., & Rose, M. J. 1968. Attempted suicide and the menstrual cycle. *J Psychosom Res, 11:* 319–23.

Valins, S., & Nisbett, R. E. 1971. *Attribution processes in the development and treatment of emotional disorders.* Morristown, N.J.: General Learning Corp.

Woods, N. F., Dery, G. K., & Most, A. 1982. Stressful life events and perimenstrual symptoms. *J Hum Stress, 8:* 23–31.

Question 5

Is the Menopause a Deficiency Disease?

The menopause has long been considered a significant turning point in a woman's life. It is surprising, therefore, that so little research of any value has been done on this topic until recently. As a result, the menopause, physiologically defined as a woman's last menstrual period, has been surrounded by myths and fears deeply entrenched in our culture.

Because of the tendency to see so much of feminine behavior as determined by biology, many of the early studies viewed the menopause as the single most important event of a woman's middle years. Classical Freudians, for example, defined the menopause in terms of a woman's obsolescence. As Helene Deutsch (1944) saw it, the end of monthly menstrual cycles was a "partial death" for the woman; "everything she acquired during puberty is now lost piece by piece; with the lapse of the reproductive service, her beauty vanishes, and usually the warm, vital flow of feminine emotional life as well" (pp. 459, 461).

Many researchers, even those who repudiate Freudian notions, still confound the problems of aging with menopause. For example, noting that many menopausal women in their mid-forties and early fifties experience a decline in their visual acuity, Winnifred Berg Cutler and her colleagues (1983) suggest that there is need for further research to determine if this visual phenomenon is related to hormone changes at menopause. Their recommendation comes in spite of the fact that it has been demonstrated that middle-aged men also experience a similar decline in visual acuity.

At present there are deep differences of opinion over both the nature of menopause and the question of treatment. When it became possible to synthesize artificial estrogen, physicians became interested in the possibilities of hormonal treatment of menopausal women. The notion of

148 menopause as a "deficiency disease" was first popularized by a gynecologist, Robert A. Wilson, in his book *Feminine Forever* (1966). Wilson advocated estrogen therapy for women from "puberty to grave" as a means of saving them from the death of their womanhood. By the early 1970s, estrogen replacement therapy (ERT) had become a widely prescribed treatment for menopause (McCrea, 1983).

But a series of studies between 1975 and 1980 indicated that women on ERT ran a much higher risk of developing endometrial cancer than non-users (Kaufert & McKinlay, 1985). The concept of menopause as a "deficiency disease" also came under attack from feminists who argued that menopause was a natural part of aging and therefore did not require medical treatment. In an interesting twist, Francis McCrea and Gerald Markle (1984) point out that the United States and England present mirror images of each other in respect to treatment of the menopause. In England, general practitioners have been reluctant to prescribe ERT, while health consumer groups, including feminists, have lobbied for increased use of the drug.

The following set of articles illustrate the continuing debate over the cause and treatment of menopausal problems. Penny Wise Budoff sees the problem of menopausal women as a physiological one. She argues that combined estrogen-progesterone therapy offers significant physical and psychological advantages for women who experience menopausal symptoms. John McKinlay and Sonja McKinlay, on the other hand, view the problem of menopause from a social circumstances perspective. They maintain that the symptoms of depression in the menopause years are probably caused by social and economic factors.

References

Cutler, W., Garcia, C. R. & Edwards, D. A. (1983). *Menopause: A guide for women and the men who love them.* New York: Norton.

Deutsch, H. (1944). *The psychology of women.* Vol. 2. New York: Grune and Stratton.

Kaufert, P. & McKinlay, S. (1985). Estrogen-replacement therapy: the production of medical knowledge and the emergence of policy. In E. Lewin and V. Olesen (Eds.), *Women, health and healing: Toward a new perspective* (pp. 114–38). Tavistock, England: Methuen.

McCrea, F. (1983). The politics of menopause: The "discovery" of a deficiency disease. *Social Problems, 31* (1), 111–23.

McCrea, F. B., & Markle, G. (1984). The estrogen replacement controversy in the USA and UK: Different answers to the same question? *Social Studies of Science, 14* (1), 1–26.

Wilson, R. (1966). *Feminine Forever.* New York: M. Evans.

Additional Reading

Asso, E. (1983). *The real menstrual cycle.* New York: John Wiley.

Ball, S. E. (In press). Changing ideas: The medicalization of menopause. *Social Science and Medicine.*

Bell, S. E. (1986). Premenstrual syndrome and the medicalization of menopause: A sociological perspective. In B. É. Ginsburg & B. F. Carter (Eds.), *Premenstrual syndrome: Ethical implications in a biobehavioral perspective.* New York: Plenum.

Dan, A. J., Graham, É. A., & Beecher, C. P. (1980). *The menstrual cycle: A synthesis of interdisciplinary research* (Vol. 1). New York: Springer.

Greenwood, S. (1984). *Menopause naturally: Preparing for the second half of life.* San Francisco: Volcano Press.

Kaufert, P. & Syrotuik, J. (1981). Symptom reporting at the menopause. *Social Science and Medicine, 151,* 173–84.

Kaufert, P. A. (1982). Myth and menopause. *Sociology of Health and Illness, 4* (2), 141–66.

Komnenich, P., McSweeney, M., Noack, J. A., & Elder, S. N. (Eds.) (1981). *The menstrual cycle: Research and implications for women's health* (Vol. 2). New York: Springer.

Lock, M. (1982). Models and practice in medicine. *Culture, Medicine, and Psychiatry, 6,* 261–80.

MacPherson, K. (1981). Menopause as disease: The social construction of a metaphor. *Advances in Nursing Science, 3,* (2), 95–113.

Nachtigall, L. & Heilman, J. R. (1986). *Estrogen: The facts can change your life.* New York: Harper & Row.

Notman, M. (1984). Psychiatric disorders of menopause. *Psychiatric Annals, 14,* (6), 448–53.

Parlee, M. B. (1984). Reproductive issues, including menopause. In G. Baruch & J. Brooks-Gunn (Eds.), *Women in mid-life* (pp. 303–13). New York: Plenum.

Voda, A. M. & Eliasson, M. (1983). Menopause: The closure of menstrual life. *Women and Health, 8* (2/3), 137–56.

Voda, A. M., Dinnerstein, M., & O'Donnell, S. R. (1982). *Changing perspectives on menopause.* Austin: University of Texas Press.

Yes

Cyclic Estrogen-Progesterone Therapy

PENNY WISE BUDOFF

The menopausal woman is a twentieth-century phenomenon. In the fourteenth-century, a woman's average life expectancy was thirty-three years. Although it had increased to forty-eight years by the turn of this century, older women were not yet a "problem," as they still did not exist in significant numbers. The life expectancy of a woman born today, however, is 77.5 years. Menopause now marks the midpoint of a woman's life, not the impending end. Today, women can count on living one-third of their lives postmenopausally. Thus the quality of that life becomes as important as the quantity of the years.

The intensity of menopausal symptoms a woman suffers depends on several factors. At menopause, a woman does not suddenly lose 100 percent of her estrogen; rather, the ovaries produce estrogen in ever decreasing amounts. The adrenal and ovary also produce a weak male hormone, androstenedione, part of which is converted into estrogen by the body's fat. As the ovary decreases its output of estrogen, production of androstenedione remains relatively static. This creates a change in the relative proportions of male and female hormones, and, in turn, may cause the appearance of dark, coarse facial hairs on the chin as well as arteriosclerotic problems.

There is marked individual variation in the amount and proportion of the remaining hormones the ovaries produce, and in the total length of time that this occurs. This is why some women have severe symptoms while others have few complaints. Women with more fat tend to be able to convert more androstenedione into estrogen and have fewer symptoms.

The worst suffering usually occurs after surgery or radiation. Because of the abruptness of the estrogen loss, the hot flashes, irritability, and anxiety that ensue are often intolerable. For most women, however, the estrogen

"Cyclic Estrogen-Progesterone Therapy" by Penny Wise Budoff, *Journal of the American Medical Women's Association*, 1984, *39* (1), 20–22; 30. Copyright © 1984 by the Journal of the American Medical Women's Association. Reprinted by permission.

Dr. Budoff is a physician and Medical Director of the Women's Medical Center in Bethpage, New York.

loss occurs at a moderate rate. The symptoms these women experience are milder. The total effect of the loss of estrogen depends in large measure on genetic resistance to aging, overall health, quality of diet, and activity.

During the 1950s women were treated for these symptoms with vitamin and exercise programs and tranquilizers, but by the 1960s doctors were attributing all menopausal symptoms to lost estrogen and enthusiastically offering to put it back. Estrogen replacement therapy (ERT) became the standard treatment of menopausal symptoms.

Then, in the mid-seventies, the media began to report higher than normal rates of endometrial cancer in women who had been on ERT. Everywhere, frightened women stopped their therapy. Among my own patients, many decided to grit their teeth and endure hot flashes rather than risk the hypothetical development of uterine cancer. (Of course, many women in this age group have had hysterectomies, and if you have no uterus, you don't have to worry about uterine cancer.)

But my patients had been treated differently. The ovaries produced two female hormones—estrogen *and* progesterone—so it made sense to me to replace both. If mother nature had found it necessary to provide both, I, a mere physician, was not going to presume to improve upon that. It seemed to me that, even in the cycles of posthysterectomy patients, the progesterone was essential to counteract the effects of the estrogen on the breasts. Therefore, each of my patients recieved estrogen plus progesterone.

When a woman is cycling monthly, her ovaries produce estrogen in the beginning of the cycle; after she ovulates, they also produce progesterone. At the end of the cycle, both hormone levels fall, bringing about a complete shedding of the endometrial lining (menstruation). The woman who does not ovulate does not produce progesterone, although she does produce estrogen. Without progesterone, the endometrial lining of the uterus is constantly stimulated by estrogen. The lining grows and grows, and finally the thickened lining outgrows its blood supply. Then it begins to disintegrate haphazardly, a little from one spot, then a little from another. Because the lining is too thick to begin with, the flow is heavy. The flow is sporadic, too, and may continue for a long time as one section after another sloughs off. This overgrowth of the lining, stimulated by estrogen, is similar to hyperplasia, which is thought to be a precursor of endometrial cancer.

When ovulation occurs, on the other hand, the endometrial lining is better differentiated and not crowded. When menstruation begins in an ovulatory cycle (or with progesterone added), the lining cleanly and precisely sloughs off down to the normal base. There is no prolonged heavy flow with days of irregular bleeding. Progesterone is a good housekeeper. It

152 efficiently gets rid of all the old, useless cells and prepares for the new month.

On the whole, my patients didn't mind having their periods back; they understood that this was a safer way to replace their hormones. Since it was nature's way, they accepted it. Their menses were pain-free and for most, lasted only two to four days; some had no more than a day of spotting. Many older patients, who received smaller doses of estrogen, experienced no flow.

Most physicians, recognizing the danger of too much estrogen stimulation, tell their patients to take estrogen for only three weeks of each month. But studies show that body fat releases the estrogen it has stored, so the effect of the estrogen continues even when the patient is not taking estrogen. It's not just the periodic break from added estrogen that women need; they also need progesterone.

In 1976, I made the following statement to a conference on women in industry:

I feel that it is the misuse of estrogen, and not the estrogen per se, that is the culprit and the cause of the prevailing controversy. If the basis of endometrial carcinoma lies in the progression from endometrial hyperplasia to cystic hyperplasia to adenomatous hyperplasia to adenocarcinoma, then the physician who misuses estrogen is at fault. He is not providing natural ovarian replacement because he is leaving out progesterone, which would not permit even the first step in the sequence (i.e., hyperplasia) to occur.

In 1976 I had 74 women in my practice who had been on combined estrogen-progesterone therapy (HRT) for years. I did a retrospective study of those patients, comparing them to 473 women in my practice who were not on HRT. The study was published in the *Journal of Reproductive Medicine* in May 1979. Blood pressure, blood sugars, and cholesterol levels remained unchanged in the women on HRT. Pap smears, however, tended to improve (Budoff & Sommers, 1979).

The most exciting part of the study was determining what changes had taken place within the uteri of the women who had been on therapy for a mean of five continuous years. Interestingly, the most common finding was a normal secretory endometrium resulting from progesterone. This indicates the important conclusion that progesterone, in sufficient quantity, counteracts, supersedes, and modifies the estrogen effect even when estrogen is given on a continual daily basis over long periods of time.

The next most common finding was an inactive endometrium. These uterine linings showed no indication that they had responded either to estrogen or to progesterone; the uterine linings simply had lost all function

and could not be rejuvenated. Others showed normal early cycle endometrium (proliferative endometrium). There were also two cases of hyperplasia, one slight and one adenomatous. After studying the data from this
tiny sample, I concluded my report by saying that "the use of long-term
estrogen does not inevitably lead to hyperplasia or adenocarcinoma."

These same trends were confirmed by another, larger retrospective
study published by Dr. Charles Hammond, in which 301 women were
treated with estrogen and a second group of 309 were not. Long-term
estrogen therapy (for more than five years) resulted in "significantly lower
rates of development of cardiovascular disease, hypertension, osteoporosis,
and fractures." It was also noted that the women on estrogen took fewer
tranquilizers and sedatives. There was a significant reduction in new occurrences of strokes, coronary artery disease, congestive heart failure, and
arteriosclerotic cerebral vascular disease, and a "lower incidence of weight
gain" (Hammond & Maxson, 1982).

Hammond showed, however, that the women who were cycled on estrogen alone had an increased incidence of endometrial cancer. There were
only three cases of endometrial cancer among the women in the control
group, as opposed to eleven cases in the group treated with estrogen only.
Among the women who received estrogen and progesterone, there were no
endometrial cancers at all. The women who took progesterone along with
estrogen experienced a lower incidence of malignancy than they would
have with no treatment at all.

Similar results were reported in a 1978 study conducted by Dr. R. D.
Gambrell. Among 1,694 patients receiving estrogen alone, the incidence of
endometrial cancer was 3.5 per 1,000. For the estrogen-progesterone users,
the incidence was 0.4 per 1,000, a rate lower than the spontaneous occurrence of endometrial malignancy in untreated post-menopausal women.

But what about the other benefits of HRT? Most women begin HRT
treatment to alleviate symptoms such as hot flashes and night sweats (which
are simply episodes of hot flashes that occur during the sleeping hours).
Hot flashes are uncomfortable enough during the waking hours, but night
sweats can cause additional problems by interfering with sleep. Women
complain that they either can't fall asleep or can't sleep through the night.
Women who suffer night sweats feel tired, weak, and unable to function.
Sleep deprivation can make anyone feel depressed and chronically out of
sorts.

Recent studies have shown that women on HRT sleep better and fall
asleep faster. Night sweats and hot flashes are real. Many women have been
told that these symptoms are imagined or made worse by their state of
mind, but recordings of skin temperature in the fingers show that there are

154 increases in skin temperature that correlate closely with the complaints of hot flashes. There is also evidence that the hot flashes are accompanied by dramatic increases in luteinizing hormone, produced by the pituitary. Hot flashes, however, are now thought to be associated with disturbances in the hypothalamus, the heat regulatory center of the brain. They are not symptoms dreamed up by women who have nothing better to do than complain.

Women who hope to continue an active sex life into their late fifties, sixties, and seventies may want to consider HRT. Estrogen will not make them young again, but it can have a profound effect on the vagina, which returns to its youthful state very quickly after estrogen replacement therapy has begun and will maintain itself as long as therapy continues.

Urologic problems also occur in menopause because the urinary tract, especially the lower portion, is situated close to the vagina, and its tissues are also dependent upon estrogen for their support. Some older women experience recurring bladder infections as these tissues become more fragile. Estrogen may help build up the defenses of the bladder and urinary tract against bacteria.

Although HRT can bring relief from these common menopausal complaints, there are other reasons for HRT that are perhaps more important. Loss of bone density in the spine leads to backache. Loss of height is caused by the vertebrae crushing and collapsing. It is a common symptom among elderly women and accounts for the stereotyped image of the "little old lady." Most women over the age of 65 shrink in height by some two inches and develop other symptoms of osteoporosis, including lumbar back pain, round of the upper back, and periodontal disease.

Perhaps the most important reason to consider HRT is the prevention of osteoporosis, one of the most neglected diseases of women. The disease affects women nine times more often than men, and white women are more likely to develop the problem than black women. Thin, delicate white women need to be the most concerned with osteoporosis. In youth and middle age women and men suffer approximately the same number of fractures, but after menopause the loss of the female hormone makes women more subject to osteoporosis and much more likely to suffer broken bones.

Hip fractures are a major cause of death among older women. The National Center for Health Statistics estimated that of 184,000 hip fractures in the United States in 1975, more than 132,000 occurred in women. Furthermore, one-third of osteoporotic women who suffer hip fractures die within six months. Hip fracture is the cause of death in nearly 58,000 women each year (compared with about 2,300 endometrial cancer deaths annually). These facts must make us reconsider the advice that women are currently getting about the dangers of estrogen. Estrogen replacement therapy for bone preservation can be accomplished with as little as 0.45 mg of conjugated estrogen daily (halfway between the usual 0.3 and 0.625 mg doses), combined with progesterone.

(Other factors can help reduce bone loss and should be part of a re-vitalizing regimen. Exercise helps maintain bones. So, if it is at all possible, patients should get up and get out, walk or exercise. Adding calcium and vitamin D to the daily vitamins is also essential to help retard bone loss.)

There is evidence that estrogen may have a protective effect against the occurrence of coronary artery disease. Some studies have shown that postmenopausal women have a decrease in their cholesterol levels after being treated with estrogen. A 1979 study by Dr. Barrett-Connor followed 1,496 women, of whom 39 percent were on ERT. The report states that lower cholesterol values were the most striking feature associated with estrogen. Other studies have shown that women on estrogen experience a decline in the total cholesterol level and an increase in the level of high density lipoproteins (HDLs). If replacement doses of estrogen can keep the HDL levels up, this should be another indication in its favor. And, as in the case of osteoporosis, the risk of death from cardiovascular disorder is greater than the risk of estrogen-induced endometrial cancer. The annual risk of estrogen-associated endometrial cancer deaths is less than 1 per 1,000, while the risk of cardiovascular death after age 55 exceeds 10 per 1,000.

I have also seen profound personality changes in some patients on ERT. Women who were crying and depressed, although previously they had been the backbone and strength of the family, suddenly rebounded on estrogen replacement therapy.

Should you consider HRT for yourself or your patients? That depends. If you are still fearful, don't. If you want estrogen forever because you are sedentary, thin, white, and fear for your bones, that's fine, too. You or your patient must make these decisions. You must guide your patient if there are contraindications to therapy. All your patients should be carefully screened before they are given estrogen. A Pap smear, mammography, blood work, and an endometrial biopsy should be done before initiating estrogen thera-py. If you do prescribe HRT, you must carefully monitor your patients. Any woman who goes on HRT should be seen by her physician every six months—before getting each new supply of hormones.

As for its risks, because of our ability to easily monitor patients for uterine cancer, I have less fear of it than I have of broken bones and coronary disease. Uterine cancer does not just sneak up and suddenly appear. It results from a process that can be watched over months and

156 years. A three- to four-minute aspiration every 12 to 24 months provides complete information on the status of the uterine lining. The endometrial biopsy, like the Pap smear, will give plenty of warning if something needs attention.

Whatever you do, make sure you consider all the available facts. You know your mind and body better than anyone else. If you try estrogen replacement therapy plus progesterone and it's good for you, continue. If it's not, stop. This decision, like any other, can be changed at any time. But remember, you may be spending a large part of your life as a postmenopausal woman. It is important that you make an informed, well-considered choice about what is best for your body and the quality of your life.

An expanded version of this essay appears in *No More Hot Flashes and Other Good News* by Penny Wise Budoff (New York: Warner Books, 1984).

References

Budoff, P. W. & Sommers, S. C. (1979, May). Estrogen-progesterone therapy in peri-menopausal women. *Journal of Reproductive Medicine, 22,* 241–47.

Hammond, C. B. & Maxson, W. S. (1982, January). Current status of estrogen therapy for the menopause. *Fertility and Sterility, 37,* 15.

Gambrell, R. D. (1982, April). The menopause: Benefits and risks of estrogen-progestogen replacement therapy. *Fertility and Sterility, 37,* 457–74.

Barrett-Connor, E., Brown, W. V., Turner, J., Austin, M., Criqui, M. H. (1979, May 18). Heart disease risk factors and hormone use in postmenopausal women. *Journal of American Medical Association, 241* (20): 2167–69.

Depression in Middle-Aged Women: Social Circumstances versus Estrogen Deficiency

JOHN B. McKINLAY AND SONJA M. McKINLAY

Many health professionals and members of the public believe that depression in middle-aged women is caused by endocrine changes associated with menopause and therefore can be treated with estrogens. Since all women around the age of fifty experience menopause, this belief has far-reaching consequences—it promotes a stereotype of middle-aged women as naturally depressed, anxious, or otherwise emotionally unstable. It is necessary to explain why menopause should be considered a "syndrome," although the onset of menstruation during puberty, which also occurs in all women and produces just as many physical and psychological symptoms, is regarded as healthy and normal.

Studies in many different nations and in both urban and rural areas have shown that depression affects more women than men. This higher rate of depression among women is a major challenge to public health, not only because of its magnitude but because it plays a key role in the explanation of other somatic and psychological problems. As a result of its growing importance, depression in middle-aged women has been widely and increasingly researched and written about. This extensive research can be divided into two schools of thought with profoundly different implications for both research and clinical practice. Advocates of one viewpoint, which might be called the estrogen deficiency perspective, claim that depression is triggered by endocrine changes during menopause. Supporters of the other view, which can be called the social circumstances perspective, dismiss that association as coincidental and instead argue that depression is related to social circumstances. Before trying to disentangle the relative contributions

"Depression in Middle-Aged Women: Social Circumstances Versus Estrogen Deficiency" by John B. McKinlay and Sonja M. McKinlay, *The Harvard Medical School Mental Health Letter*, 1986, 2 (10), 1–2. Copyright © 1986 by The Harvard Medical School Health Letter. Reprinted by permission.

Dr. John B. McKinlay is a medical sociologist and Professor, Department of Sociology, Boston University; Dr. Sonja M. McKinlay is an epidemiologist and Associate Professor (Research), Department of Community Health, Brown University, Providence, Rhode Island.

158 of endocrines and circumstances, we need to take a historical look at these opposing perspectives.

Estrogen Deficiency Perspective

Forty percent of first episodes of depression in women coincide with the menopausal years (45–55). But clearly not all women going through menopause are depressed. The estrogen deficiency perspective assumes that regardless of chronological age, a woman experiencing depression during menopause will be "cured" if her hormonal balance is reestablished. More than twenty years ago, medical advocates of this school made a plea for "the maintenance of adequate estrogen from puberty to the grave." Such radical statements were often based on scant and impressionistic data from self-selecting women. However, once it was "established" that depression during the middle years was "caused by" estrogen deficiency, an armamentarium of drugs and surgical procedures could be developed. Most of the enthusiasm for this type of treatment has been dampened by evidence that exogenous estrogen can contribute to cancer. The association of menopause with depression eventually became embodied in the diagnostic label "involutional melancholia," which was never shown to be valid and is now going out of use.

Social Circumstances Perspective

Women probably experience more personal change during the menopausal years than at any other time in their lives. Middle-aged women are at risk for illness or death of a husband, divorce, separation, midlife crisis of a husband, unemployment, death of parents, caring for frail elders, children leaving home, a move to a new neighborhood, and loss of social support. The effects of such changes clearly might lead to depression. Of course, not all changes affecting women during the menopausal years are for the worse. They may benefit from the relief of no longer worrying about conception, the joy of being a grandmother, freedom when children leave home, improvements in the quality of marriage, and opportunities to realize aspirations outside the home.

Whether life becomes better or worse for women during the middle years most likely depends on their social and economic status; that may explain the differences found in different studies. The experience of menopause is filtered through cultural experiences, expectations, and attitudes.

For example, in a Canadian study, 82 percent of women agreed that *159* "women become depressed and irritable at menopause." An anthropological study of 150 cultures found that whatever the status and activities of women during the fertile years, this role was reversed at menopause. Indian women of the Rajput caste, for example, report little depression or other psychological symptoms at menopause, a time when they may freely leave their veiled seclusion, visit and joke with men, and participate in other social activities once denied to them. Similarly, in China, menopausal symptoms are rare, perhaps because of the respect associated with age there.

A study of five different subcultures in Israel classified women on a continuum of modernization: traditional Arab women at one end, European-born Israelis at the other, and Jews from Turkey, Persia, and North Africa in the middle. The women in transition between traditional and modern lifestyles suffered the most difficulties during the menopausal years. Ethnic differences also occur in the United States: Jewish women have the highest rate of depression during menopause, other white women have intermediate rates, and black women the lowest rates.

The Massachusetts Study of Middle-Aged Women

Earlier research had limitations that we tried to overcome in our study of 2,500 middle-aged women in Massachusetts. We chose a random, community-based sample of women 45 to 55 years old, including inhabitants of urban, suburban, and rural areas. We used the most valid and reliable research instruments; and, most importantly, we distinguished between women who had a natural menopause and those who had undergone hysterectomies. Our aim was to discover the relationship of depression to menstrual status, attitudes towards menopause, general health, and social circumstances.

We used The Center for Epidemiologic Studies (CES-D) Scale, which required the women to report feelings of worthlessness and hopelessness, loss of appetite, sleep disturbance, and other depressive symptoms they had noticed in the past week. Each woman was also determined to be still menstruating, going through menopause, or past menopause; and we identified those who had undergone a hysterectomy or a bilateral oophorectomy (removal of both ovaries). We used educational status as an indicator of social and economic status. Our measures of health were the women's own judgment, physical symptoms, days of restricted activity, and chronic conditions (diabetes, high blood pressure, asthma, allergies, and so on).

160 Use of health care resources was measured by their consultation of health professionals, consultation of lay persons, use of prescription and over-the-counter medications, and surgery. For information about sources of stress, we asked how many people close to them had been ill, had died, had caused them worry, or had been particularly demanding in the previous nine months.

The only group of women in our study reporting an increase in depression were those who had recently had a hysterectomy, with or without a bilateral oophorectomy. They had twice as much depression as other menstrual status groups. This finding is important, because hysterectomy is one of the most common operations in the United States. Nearly 30 percent of women undergo hysterectomies—about 650,000 each year.

In recording attitudes toward menopause, we found that most women anticipated relief or reported no particular feelings. Less than 3 percent felt regret. Women with positive attitudes were less likely to be depressed, whether they had completed menopause or not. The health condition most strongly associated with depression was the number of physical ailments unrelated to menopause. The rate of depression also depended on marital status and education. Widowed, divorced, and separated women with less than twelve years of education were the most depressed. Never-married women had low rates of depression, and married women were intermediate. The only other social circumstance strongly and independently associated with depression was worry caused by a husband or by several family members (including husband or offspring).

Women who undergo a surgical menopause are quite distinctive. We showed in a previous study that they have poorer health and use more medical care than average before their surgery. Since depression is associated with physical symptoms, women who undergo a surgical menopause are more likely to be depressed. It is also possible that women with psychiatric illnesses are more likely to undergo hysterectomies. According to recent British findings, clinically depressed people are more likely to have surgery.

Our study suggests that depression in middle-aged women is associated mainly with events and circumstances unrelated to the hormonal changes that occur at menopause. Most hormone studies have been restricted to patient volunteers, a disproportionately large number of whom have had hysterectomies. There is little reliable information about hormonal changes and levels of circulating estrogen in a general population of middle-aged women. Without such reliable information, it is hard to study related emotional changes. It is possible that whenever psychological changes occur they are transitory and not necessarily depressive. The *161* general social environment of middle-aged women, as well as worries associated with caring for adolescent children, husbands, and elderly parents or in-laws, create a situation conducive to depression whether a woman is experiencing menopause or not.

This is a preliminary version of a much longer article with 131 references by John B. McKinlay, Sonja M. McKinlay and Donald Brambilla: "The relative contributions of endocrine changes and social circumstances to depression in mid-aged women," *Journal of Health and Social Behavior,* in press.

PART III

New Theories and Evidence in the Psychology of Women

Question 6

Do Women Fear Success?

When one looks at psychological research prior to the 1970s, one is struck by the fact that theories based on the study of male subjects and that worked to explain male behavior were assumed to apply to both sexes. John Atkinson's (1958) study of achievement motivation is a case in point. Although Atkinson devoted more than eight hundred pages to this topic, all of the research on sex differences can be found in one footnote (Horner, 1970). Similarly, there is a striking absence of any mention of female achievement in David McClelland's *The Achieving Society* (1961).

These early motivation researchers developed projective tests involving a work or achievement situation and then scored the responses in terms of the subjects' need for achievement. These tests proved to be a good predictor of male behavior, but were markedly less effective with female subjects. Interestingly, few researchers paid attention to the fact that they were ignoring half the human experience by excluding women and girls from their studies. One notable exception to this pattern is the work of Matina Horner. In the early 1960s she became interested in why female subjects did not express the type of achievement imagery found in the responses of male subjects. On the basis of her findings, she theorized that women have a motive to avoid success in achievement-related situations because they expect negative consequences such as social rejection (1968). Horner made it clear that she was not saying that women wanted to fail but rather that, in achievement situations, they were caught in a double bind, having to worry not only about failure but also about success (Horner, 1972).

Horner's work on female motivation, usually referred to as "fear of success," became one of the most extensively studied psychological theories involving women's behavior (Tresemer, 1976, 1977; Canavan-Gum-   *165*

166 pert, Garner & Gumpert, 1978; Paludi, Hruska, Guda & Bowman, 1986). In addition to the traditional attempts to replicate and challenge Horner's original research design, psychologists have related the concept of fear of success to the menstrual cycle (Patty & Ferrell, 1974), fertility (Hoffman, 1977), high school curriculum elected by students (Kimball & Leary, 1976), psychoanalytic theory (Kanefield, 1985), and female masochism (Greenbaum, 1981). Clinical and counseling psychologists now offer a wide variety of popular workshops and seminars on the fear of success. There are also a number of audio tapes on the subject, including one entitled "Overcoming the Fear of Success," narrated by Martha Friedman, a psychotherapist who has also written a book on this topic (1980, 1985).

In addition to Friedman's book, a number of other popular books on women's achievement conflicts also build on the idea of female fear of success. Sarah Hardesty and Nehama Jacobs, for example, in their book *Success and Betrayal: The Crisis of Women in Corporate America,* declare that in the twenty years since Horner first published her doctoral dissertation, "reality has borne out her theoretical supposition" (1986, p. 252). Colette Dowling's (1981) best-selling book, *The Cinderella Complex,* uses the idea of female fear of success to support the thesis that women have a hidden fear of independence. Pauline Rose Clance and Susan Ament Imes (1978) developed a related idea they call "the imposter phenomenon," which they claim characterizes many intelligent and otherwise competent women and prevents them from enjoying their achievements. Clance (1985) connects women's feelings of fraudulence to their fear of success and she describes various treatment strategies and self-help programs to aid victims of the disorder.

Although overall the concept of the fear of success has stimulated an enormous amount of research, both directly and indirectly, it has also been criticized on a number of grounds. Some feminist psychologists became concerned that popularized versions of Horner's work took a blaming-the-victim approach to women's problems, diverting attention from larger social issues that blocked female achievement (Henley, 1985). Furthermore, a number of the original conceptions of fear of success have not held up under scientific replication (Tresemer, 1977). Jacqueline Fleming goes so far as to conclude that "the concept has reached a methodological impasse" (1982, p. 64).

Despite this controversy, or perhaps because of it, fear of success continues to intrigue researchers at every level. Part of its appeal may be based on an intuitive feeling on the part of some psychologists that, despite the lack of scientific evidence, the motive to avoid success probably exists (Hyde, 1985). Support for this view can be found in the claim that the fear of success is quite prevalent among women who enter psychotherapy (Krueger, 1984). In addition, psychoanalysts have also shown renewed interest in fear of success (Person, 1982; Kanefield, 1985; Moulton, 1986).

It appears that, although empirical proof for the fear of success is lacking, psychologists have been reluctant to drop the concept entirely. Is it time, as Michele Paludi suggests, to abandon the notion of a fear of success? Or have psychologists simply been unable to design research studies to demonstrate that the phenomenon exists?

References

Atkinson, J. W. (Ed.) (1958). *Motives in fantasy, action and society: A method of assessment and study.* New York: Van Nostrand.

Canavan-Gumpert, D., Garner, K. & Gumpert, P. (1978). *The success-fearing personality: Theory and research with implications for the social psychology of achievement.* Lexington, Mass.: D. C. Heath.

Clance, P. R. & Imes, S. (1978). The impostor phenomenon in high-achieving women: Dynamics and therapeutic intervention. *Psychotherapy: Theory, Research and Practice, 15,* 241–47.

Clance, P. R. (1985). *The impostor phenomenon: When success makes you feel like a fake.* New York: Bantam.

Dowling, C. (1981). *The Cinderella complex: Women's hidden fear of independence.* New York: Summit.

Fleming, J. (1982). Projective and Psychometric approaches to measurement: The case of fear of success. In A. J. Stewart (Ed.), *Motivation and society: A volume in honor of David C. McClelland.* San Francisco: Jossey-Bass.

Friedman, M. (1980). *Overcoming the fear of success.* New York: Seaview.

Friedman, M. (1985). *Overcoming the fear of success.* Tape no. 20284. Brooklyn, N.Y.: Psychology Today Tapes.

Greenbaum, E. (1981). An aspect of masochism in women—fear of success: Some intrapsychic dimensions and therapeutic dimensions. In S. Klebanow (Ed.), *Changing concepts in psychoanalysis.* New York: Gardner Press.

Hardesty, S. & Jacobs, N. (1986). *Success and betrayal: The crisis of women in corporate America.* New York: Franklin Watts.

Henley, N. (1985). Psychology and gender. *Signs: Journal of Women in Culture and Society, 11,* 101–19.

Hoffman, L. W. (1977). Fear of success in males and females: 1965 and 1972. *Journal of Consulting and Clinical Psychology, 45,* 310–11.

Horner, M. S. (1968). Sex differences in achievement motivation and performance in competitive and noncompetitive situations. *Dissertation Abstracts International, 30,* 407B. (University Microfilms No. 69-12, 135)

Horner, M. S. (1970). Femininity and successful achievement: A basic inconsistency. In J. Bardwick, E. Douvan, M. S. Horner & D. Gutman, *Feminine personality and conflict* (pp. 45–74). Belmont, Calif.: Brooks/Cole.

Horner, M. S. (1972). Toward an understanding of achievement-related conflicts in women. *Journal of Social Issues, 28,* 157–75.

Hyde, J. (1985). *Half the human experience: The psychology of women.* Lexington, Mass.: D. C. Heath.

168   Kanefield, L. A. (1985). Psychoanalytic constructions of female development and women's conflicts about achievement, pts. 1–2. *Journal of the American Academy of Psychoanalysis, 13* (2/3): 229–46, 347–66.

Kimball, B. & Leary, R. L. (1976). Fear of success in males and females: Effects of developmental level and sex-linked course of study. *Sex Roles, 2,* 272–281.

Krueger, D. (1984). *Success and the fear of success in women.* New York: Free Press.

McClelland, D. C., Atkinson, J. W., Clark, R. A., & Lowell, E. L. (1953). *The Achievement Motive.* New York: Appleton-Century-Crofts.

McClelland, D. C. (1961). *The achieving society.* New York: Free Press.

Moulton, R. (1986). Professional success: A conflict for women. In J. L. Alpert (Ed.), *Psychoanalysis and women: Contemporary reappraisals.* (pp. 161–81). New York: Erlbaum, Analytic Press.

Paludi, M. A., Hruska, D., Guda, B., & Bowman, L. (1986, April). Fear of success: An updated review. Paper presented at the meeting of the Eastern Psychological Association, New York, N.Y.

Patty, R., & Ferrell, M. M. (1974). A preliminary note on the motive to avoid success and the menstrual cycle. *Journal of Psychology, 86,* 173–77.

Person, E. S. (1982). Women working: Fears of failure, deviance, and success. *Journal of the American Academy of Psychoanalysis, 10* (1), 67–84.

Tresemer, D. W. (1976). Research on fear of success: Full annotated bibliography. *Social and Behavioral Sciences Documents,* 1976, 6(2), 38, Ms. 1237. (Available in photocopy or microfiche from Select Press, P. O. Box 9838, San Rafael, Calif. 94912.)

Tresemer, D. W. (1977). *Fear of success.* New York: Plenum Press.

Additional Reading

Gravenkemper, S., & Paludi, M. A. (1983). Fear of success revisited: Introducing an ambiguous cue. *Sex Roles, 9,* 897–900.

Harvey, J. C. (1985). *If I'm so successful, why do I feel like a fake? The imposter phenomenon.* New York: Bantam.

Hyland, M. E., Curtis, C., & Mason, D. (1985). Fear of success: Motive and cognition. *Journal of Personality and Social Psychology, 49,* 1669–77.

Paludi, M. A. & Fankell-Hauser, J. (1982). An idiographic approach to the study of women's achievement striving. *Psychology of Women Quarterly, 10,* 89–100.

Sherif, C. W. (1979). What every intelligent person should know about psychology and women. In E. C. Synder (Ed.), *The study of women: Enlarging perspectives of social reality* (pp. 143–183). New York: Harper & Row.

Toward an Understanding of Achievement-related Conflicts in Women

MATINA S. HORNER

The prevalent image of women found throughout history, in both scholarly and popular circles, has converged on the idea that femininity and individual achievements which reflect intellectual competence or leadership potential are desirable but mutually exclusive goals. The aggressive and, by implication, masculine qualities inherent in a capacity for mastering intellectual problems, attacking difficulties, and making final decisions are considered fundamentally antagonistic to or incompatible with femininity. Since the time of Freud's treatise on the "Psychology of Women," the essence of femininity has been equated with the absence or "the repression of aggressiveness, which is imposed upon women by their constitutions and by society" (Freud, 1933, p. 158). For instance:

... it is highly probable that the undoubted superiority of the male sex in intellectual and creative achievement is related to their greater endowment of aggression. . . . The hypothesis that women, if only given the opportunity and encouragement, would equal or surpass the creative achievements of men is hardly defensible. [Storr, 1970, p. 68]

Each step forward as a successful American regardless of sex means a step back as a woman. [Mead, 1949]

It has taken us a long time to become aware of the extent to which this image of woman has actually been internalized, thus acquiring the capacity to exert psychological pressures on our behavior of which we are frequently unaware.

It is clear in our data, just as in Broverman, Vogel, Broverman, Clark-

"Toward an Understanding of Achievement-Related Conflicts in Women" by Matina S. Horner, *Journal of Social Issues*, 28 (2), 157–176. Copyright © 1972 by the Society for the Psychological Study of Social Issues. Reprinted by permission.

Dr. Horner is President of Radcliffe College and Associate Professor, Department of Psychology, Harvard University.

170   son, and Rosenkrantz (1970), that the young men and women tested over the past seven years still tend to evaluate themselves and to behave in ways consistent with the dominant stereotype that says competition, independence, competence, intellectual achievement, and leadership reflect positively on mental health and masculinity but are basically inconsistent or in conflict with femininity.

Thus, despite the fact that we have a culture and an educational system that ostensibly encourage and prepare men and women identically for careers, the data indicate that social and, even more importantly, internal psychological barriers rooted in this image really limit the opportunities to men.

A Psychological Barrier to Achievement in Women

Maccoby (1963) has pointed out that a girl who maintains the qualities of independence and active striving which are necessary for intellectual mastery defies the conventions of sex-appropriate behavior and must pay a price in anxiety. This idea is encompassed in the conceptualization (Horner, 1968) of the Motive to Avoid Success (M_s), which was developed in an attempt to understand or explain the major unresolved sex differences detected in previous research on achievement motivation (Atkinson, 1958; McClelland, Atkinson, Clark, & Lowell, 1953). When it was first introduced as a psychological barrier to achievement in women, the Motive to Avoid Success was conceptualized within the framework of an expectancy-value theory of motivation as a latent, stable personality disposition acquired early in life in conjunction with standards of sex-role-identity. In expectancy-value theories of motivation, the most important factors in determining the arousal of these dispositions or motives and thereby the ultimate strength of motivation and direction of one's behavior are: (1) the expectations or beliefs the individual has about the nature and likelihood of the consequences of his/her actions, and (2) the value of these consequences to the individual in light of his/her particular motives. Anxiety is aroused, according to the theory, when one expects that the consequences of action will be negative. The anxiety then functions to inhibit the action expected to have the negative consequences; it does not, however, determine which action will then be undertaken. In other words, within this framework, avoidance motives inhibit actions expected to have unattractive consequences. They can tell us what someone will *not do*, but not what he or she *will* do. The latter is a function of which positive-approach motives and tendencies are characteristic of the individual (Atkinson & **171** Feather, 1966; Horner, 1970a).

With this in mind, I argued that most women have a motive to avoid success—that is, a disposition to become anxious about achieving success because they expect negative consequences (such as social rejection and/or feelings of being unfeminine) as a result of succeeding. Note that this is not to say that most women "want to fail" or have a "motive to approach failure." The presence of a "will to fail" would, in accordance with the theory, imply that they actively seek out failure because they anticipate or expect positive consequences from failing. The presence of a motive to avoid success, on the other hand, implies that the expression of the achievement-directed tendencies of most otherwise positively motivated young women is inhibited by the arousal of a thwarting disposition to be anxious about the negative consequences they expect will follow the desired success.

A review of the results of the several studies carried out over the past few years, summarized in table 6.1, substantiates the idea that despite the emphasis on a new freedom for women, particularly since the mid-sixties, negative attitudes expressed toward and about successful women have

Table 6.1: Incidence of Fear of Success Imagery in Samples Tested, 1964–1970

Study	Year Data Gathered	Nature of the Sample	N	Subjects Showing the Response TAT Format (Standard Verbal Cue)	
				N	%
Horner, 1968	1964	*College Freshmen & Sophomores*	178		
		Males	88	8	9.1
		Females	90	59	65.5
Horner & Rhoem, 1968	1967	*All Female*			
		Junior High (7th grade)	19	9	47.0
		Senior High (11th grade)	15	9	60.0
		College Undergraduates	27	22	81.0
		Secretaries	15	13	86.6
		Students at an Eastern University			
Schwenn, 1970	1969	Female Juniors*	16	12	75.0
Horner, 1970b	1969	Female Juniors/Seniors	45	38	84.4
		Same Subjects*	45	34	75.5
		Female Law School Students	15	13	86.6
Watson, 1970	1970	Female Summer School Students	37	24	65.0
Prescott, 1971	1970	Male Freshmen	36	17	47.2
		Female Freshmen	34	30	88.2
		Same Females 3 months later	34	29	85.3

*Questionnaire format employed.

172 remained high and perhaps have even increased and intensified among both male and female subjects.

Individual Differences in the Strength of the Motive to Avoid Success: Its Assessment and Functional Significance

It was hypothesized (Horner, 1968) that the motive to avoid success would be significantly more characteristic of women than of men, and also more characteristic of high-achievement-oriented, high-ability women who aspire to and/or are capable of achieving success than of low-achievement-oriented, low-ability women who neither aspire to nor can achieve success. After all, if one neither wants nor can achieve success, the expectancy of negative consequences because of success would be rather meaningless. It was assumed that individual differences in the strength of the motive to avoid success would not be manifested in behavior unless aroused by the expectancy that negative consequences would follow success. This is most likely to occur in competitive achievement situations in which performance reflecting intellectual and leadership ability is to be evaluated against a standard of excellence and *also* against a competitor's performance. Once aroused, the tendency or motivation to avoid success would inhibit the expression of all positive motivation or tendencies to do well and thus should have an adverse effect on performance in these situations. It was assumed, furthermore, that the negative incentive value or repulsive aspects of success should be greater for women in interpersonal competition than in noncompetitive achievement situations, especially against male competitors.

In order to test our hypotheses about the presence and impact of the motive to avoid success, it was necessary to develop a measure of individual differences in the motive. At the end of the Standard Thematic Apperceptive Test (TAT) for measuring the achievement motive, in which verbal leads rather than pictures were used, an additional verbal lead connoting a high level of accomplishment in a mixed-sex competitive achievement situation was included. The 90 females in the initial study responded to the lead "After first term finals, Anne finds herself at the top of her medical school class." For the 88 males in the sample, the lead was "After first term finals, John finds himself at the top of his medical school class." The subjects were predominantly freshmen and sophomore undergraduate students at a large midwestern university.

A very simple present-absent system was adopted for scoring fear of

success imagery. The specific criteria used as an indication of the motive to *173*
avoid success were developed in accordance with Scott's (1958) results. His
data show what happens in a TAT when a person is confronted with a cue
or situation that represents a threat rather than a goal, or simultaneously
represents a goal and a threat. These can be found in Horner (1968,
1970b). Briefly, the Motive to Avoid Success is scored as present if the
subjects, in response to a thematic lead about a successful figure *of their own
sex,* made statements in their stories showing conflict about the success, the
presence or anticipation of negative consequences because of the success,
denial of effort or responsibility for attaining the success, denial of the cue
itself, or some other bizarre or inappropriate response to the cue. In
accordance with our hypothesis, fear of success imagery dominated the
female responses and was relatively absent in the male responses.

In response to the successful male cue, more than 90 percent of the men
in the study showed strong positive feelings and indicated increased striving, confidence in the future, and a belief that this success would be
instrumental to fulfilling other goals—such as providing a secure and
happy home for some girl. For example, there was the story in which John
is thinking about his girl, Cheri, whom he will marry at the end of medical
school and to whom he can give all the things she desires after he becomes
established. He decides he must not let up but must work even harder than
he did before so as to be able to go into research. Fewer than 10 percent of
the men responded at all negatively, and these focused primarily on the
young man's rather dull personality.

On the other hand, in response to the successful female cue 65 percent of
the girls were disconcerted, troubled, or confused. Unusual excellence in
women was clearly associated for them with the loss of femininity, social
rejection, personal or societal destruction, or some combination of the
above. Their responses were filled with negative consequences and affect,
righteous indignation, withdrawal rather than enhanced striving, concern,
even an inability to accept the information presented in the cue. In a typical
story, for example, Anne deliberately lowers her academic standing the
next term and does all she subtly can to help Carl, whose grades come up.
She soon drops out of med school, they marry, and Carl goes on in school
while she raises their family.

Some girls stressed that Anne is unhappy, aggressive, unmarried, or so
ambitious that she uses her family, husband, and friends as tools in the
advancement of her career. Others argued that Anne is a code name for a
nonexistent person created by a group of med students who take turns
taking exams and writing papers for Anne. In other words, women showed

174 significantly more evidence of the motive to avoid success than did the men, with 59 of the 90 women scoring high and only 8 of the 88 men doing so. (The chi square difference of 58.05 was significant at $p < .0005$.)

The pattern of sex differences in the production of fear of success imagery found in the first study has been maintained in the subsequent samples of (white) men and women tested since that time (see table 6.1). The major difference has been an increase, noted over the past two years, in the extent to which fear of success imagery or negative consequences are expressed by male subjects in response to cues about successful male figures, who have come increasingly to be viewed as lacking a social consciousness and having "Waspish" or selfish personalities; for example, "John will finish med school with very high honors—marry the fattest woman in town and become an extremely rich and self-centered doctor."

The fact that college students of both sexes, but especially the men, began to take an increasingly negative view of success as it has been traditionally defined is reflected in another set of recent data collected in the winter of 1970 (Prescott, 1971). Forty-seven percent of the 36 male freshmen undergraduates in this sample responded with negative imagery to the cue. This was a significant increase with respect to previous male samples. Even in this sample, however, significant sex differences in the presence of fear of success imagery were maintained. Thirty, or 88 percent, of the 34 women tested scored high in fear of success compared with 17, or 47 percent, of the 36 men tested ($x^2 = 13.43$, $p < .01$). Furthermore, the content of the stories differed significantly between the sexes. Most of the men who responded with the expectation of negative consequences because of success were not concerned about their masculinity but were instead likely to have expressed existential concerns about finding "non-materialistic happiness and satisfaction in life." These concerns, which reflect changing attitudes toward traditional kinds of success or achievement in our society, played little, if any, part in the female stories. Most of the women who were high in fear of success imagery continued to be concerned about the discrepancy between success in the situation described and feminine identity. In the past two years, the manifest content of this concern has been demonstrated in several new themes that were not evident in previous work. Take, for example, the story in which Anne feels out of place and has *"a fear of becoming a lesbian . . . maybe she shouldn't have cheated* on the exam, then the other men would have felt better about her being stupid"; or that in which she wants to go on to a career in law and doesn't particularly want children: "Her husband wants to do as well as she is, but feels unable to. She will go on in law school. *He will substitute sugar for her pills so she gets knocked up.* She has the baby—in between lectures— *175* and an hour later is back at the books. He hits his head against the wall."

One of the objectives of several studies done was simply to observe the incidence of fear of success imagery in female subjects at different ages and at different educational, occupational, and ability levels. The specific content of the verbal lead used in each sample was altered so as to make the situation described more consistent and meaningful with respect to the age, educational level, and occupation of the subjects being tested. For instance, at the junior high and high school levels the cue used was "Sue has just found out that she has been made valedictorian of her class." The results summarized in table 6.1 show that the incidence of M_{-s} in the samples we tested ranged from a low of 47 percent in a seventh-grade sample to a high of 88 percent in a sample of high-ability undergraduate students at a high-ranking Eastern school. The incidence of fear of success found in a sample of administrative secretaries in a large corporation, all of whom were able high school graduates, was also high (86.6 percent). In each of the female *college* samples tested so far, fear of success imagery has ranged from 60 percent to 88 percent.

The Impact of M_{-s} on Levels of Aspiration and Performance in Achievement-Oriented Situations

In light of the vast sex differences found in the presence of fear of success imagery, it seemed very important to study the differential impact of individual differences in the motive to avoid success on performance and levels of aspiration in achievement-oriented situations and, furthermore, to understand what personal and situational factors are most effective in arousing the motive or in keeping it in check.

In accordance with the theory, the motive to avoid success is believed to affect performance only in situations in which it is aroused. The assumption that fear of success is aroused in situations in which there is concern over or anxiety about competitiveness and its aggressive overtones was tested and received support in the first study (Horner, 1968). For thirty male and thirty female subjects it was possible to compare the level of their performance on a number of achievement tasks in a large mixed-sex competitive situation with their own subsequent performance in a strictly noncompetitive but achievement-oriented situation in which the only competition involved was with the task and one's internal standards of excellence. This was the best group on which to test the hypothesis because each

176 subject acted as his or her own control for ability effects. Thirteen of the seventeen girls in this group who had scored high in the M_{-s} performed at a significantly lower level in the mixed-sex competitive condition than they subsequently did in the noncompetitive condition. Twelve of the thirteen girls in the group who had scored low in fear of success on the other hand did better under the competitive condition, as did most of the male (2/3) subjects in this group (Horner, 1968). In other words, in accordance with the hypothesis only one of the thirteen girls low in fear of success showed the performance decrement under competition which was characteristic of the girls high in fear of success. (The chi square difference between the groups was 11.37, $p < .01$.)

Anxiety about success was the only one of the four other psychological variables for which individual differences were assessed in the study that predicted female performance. It is important to note that the motive to avoid success showed no relationship with the strength of the affiliation motive, nor did the latter predict the performance of the female subjects. The results of this part of the study clearly indicated that young women, especially those high in the motive to avoid success, would be least likely to develop their interests and explore their intellectual potential when competing against others, especially against men.

These conclusions, drawn from the preceding *within*-subject analysis, were supported by comparing the questionnaire responses of all ninety female subjects who had been randomly assigned to one of three experimental conditions, two competitive and one noncompetitive. Following her performance in one of the achievement-oriented conditions, each subject was asked to indicate on a scale, "How important was it for you to do well in this situation?" In both competitive conditions the mean level of importance reported by subjects high in anxiety about success was significantly lower than for subjects low in anxiety about success ($p < .05$). In the noncompetitive condition the difference, although short of the conventionally accepted level of significance ($p < .10$), was in the same direction. For subjects high in motive to avoid success, differences in mean level of importance between the noncompetitive condition and each of the competitive conditions were significant ($p < .05$); but no significant differences were found between the conditions for the subjects low in motive to avoid success. A more complete discussion of these results can be found in Horner (1968).

Arousing or Minimizing M_{-s}

Schwenn's (1970) results in a small pilot study of sixteen women at an outstanding Eastern women's college began our exploration of the personal

and situational elements present during the college experience which
arouse the motive to avoid success. Most of the students arrive at the highly
select school dedicated to the idea of distinguishing themselves in a future
career, even if they are not sure what it will be. According to Schwenn's
data, by the time these women are juniors most have changed their plans
and aspirations in a less ambitious, more traditionally feminine direction.
This is similar to Tangri's (1969) findings at a large Midwestern university.
Although Schwenn's sample was small, approximating a case-study approach, the findings were useful in raising a number of important questions for further exploration.

Schwenn used a questionnaire and intensive interviews to explore the
impact on behavior of the motive to avoid success. Particular attention was
paid to how this motive influences the educational and career aspirations of
these very bright and highly motivated young women, especially at a time in
our society when self-actualization and the equality of women are drawing
much public attention. All the girls in the sample were doing well and had
grade-point averages of B or better. Nevertheless, twelve of the sixteen girls
showed evidence of fear of success on a modified questionnaire version of
the TAT cue. In this version subjects are not asked to write a thematic story
but are asked instead simply to describe the person represented in the cue.
The same scoring criteria are used for both forms, and evidence of fear of
success from both is highly correlated (Horner, 1970b). Subjects whose
descriptions indicated the possible presence of a motive to avoid success
manifested their anxiety in several ways. To begin with, they prefer not to
divulge the fact that they are doing well to male peers, preferring instead to
make their failures known. The more successful they were, the less likely
they were to want to say so. All three of the girls who had straight A averages
would prefer to tell a boy that they have gotten a "C". Most of the girls with
B's preferred to report an "A." Whereas all four of the girls whose descriptions manifested low fear of success said they were more likely to report an
"A" to a male friend (sometimes coupled with an explanation), only one-
third of the twelve girls indicating high fear of success were likely to do so.

Even more important perhaps is the fact that only two of the sixteen girls
in the sample had in fact after three years of college changed their plans
toward a more ambitious or more traditionally masculine direction. The
rest report changes in their majors and future career plans toward what *each
of them considered to be a more traditional, appropriately feminine, and less
ambitious one*—for example, to work for a politician instead of being a
politician, to teach instead of going to law school, to become a housewife
instead of any number of things.

Individual differences in evidence of M_{-s} were very effective in predict-

178 ing these patterns of behavior. Eleven of the twelve girls in the study whose descriptions suggested the presence of high fear of success had actually changed their aspirations toward a more traditional direction. Only one of the four evidencing low fear of success did so. A Fisher test showed this difference to be significant at better than the .05 level.

Just how important it is to attend to an individual's subjective expectations and evaluation of certain careers was clearly emphasized by the subject who changed her career goals from medicine to law because "Law School is less ambitious, it doesn't take as long . . . is more flexible in terms of marriage and children. It is *less masculine* in that it is more accepted now for girls to go to law school." The others who changed their aspirations from law school to "teaching" or "housewife" apparently did not hold the same expectations about a law career.

Although several of the girls had started out majoring in the natural sciences with the intent of pursuing a medical career, all were now, as juniors, majoring in traditionally female areas like English, fine arts, French, and history. These findings reflect the idea that no one seriously objects to higher education in a woman provided the objective is to make her a generally educated and thus a more interesting and enlightened companion, wife, and/or mother. The objections arise only when the individual's objectives become more personal and career-oriented, especially in nontraditional areas. These findings are, furthermore, consistent with a subsequent analysis of data gathered from the 90 female subjects in the initial study (Horner, 1968). This analysis showed that 88.9 percent of the 59 girls high in fear of success were majoring in the humanities and 56 percent of the 31 low in anxiety about success were concentrating in the less traditional natural sciences like math and chemistry.

Two factors explored by Schwenn in her study as the ones most likely to arouse the motive to avoid success and thus to negatively influence the achievement strivings of these girls were the parental attitudes and those of the male peers toward appropriate sex role behavior.

The 16 girls in this sample lend support to Komarovsky's (1959) argument that in the later college years girls experience a sudden reversal in what parents applaud for them; that is, whereas they have previously been applauded for academic success these girls now find themselves being evaluated "in terms of some abstract standard of femininity with an emphasis on marriage as the appropriate goal for girls of this age."

This is again consistent with the results of a follow-up analysis of data gathered in the initial study which showed that 78 percent of the 59 girls who scored high in fear of success came from predominantly upper-middle and middle-class homes, with fathers who were successful business or professional men. Their families placed a premium value on competence and independence, and this is just the kind of background that McClelland and others (see McClelland, 1961) have shown to be conducive to the development of high achievement motivation, the expression of which is subsequently viewed as inconsistent with a feminine sex-role stereotype. This provides the basis for the conflict manifested in the motive to avoid success. Only 33 percent of the 31 subjects who had scored low in fear of success, on the other hand, had backgrounds of this type; the rest of the girls low in fear of success came from primarily lower-middle-class homes.

There was apparently no relationship in the Schwenn study between shifts in the attitudes of the parents and fear of success in the girls, nor did there appear to be any direct indication that parents had influenced anyone to turn away from a role-innovative type of career. If anything, the unintended effect appears to be in the opposite direction—as in the case of the girl who said, "There is a lot of pressure from my mother to get married and not have a career. This *is one reason I am going to have a career* and wait to get married."

Some girls even report being motivated for careers by the negative examples set by their mothers:

My mother is now working as a secretary, but she didn't work until now. I don't want to end up like that.

Another reason I am going to have a career and wait to get married is a reaction to my mother's empty life.

How much of this is a pattern really restricted to this sample or one that can be generalized is an important question which remains to be seen in later studies.

Attitudes of Male Peers

The attitude of male peers toward the appropriate role of women, which they apparently do not hesitate to express, appears to be a most significant factor in arousing the motive to avoid success. In the Schwenn study (1970), the girls who showed evidence of anxiety about success and social rejection and who had altered their career aspirations toward a more traditional direction were either not dating at all (those with the all A averages) or were dating men who do not approve of "career women." When asked, for instance, how the boys in their lives feel about their aspirations, frequent responses were "they laugh," "think it's ridiculous for me to go to graduate school or law school," or "say I can be happy as a housewife and I just need to get a liberal arts education." Several indicated they were "turning more and more to the traditional role" because of the attitudes of

180 male friends whose opinions were important: "I need someone [a man] to respect me and what I want to do, to lend importance to what I sense is important." This is consistent with the idea, frequently reported in the literature, that women are dependent on others for their self-esteem and have difficulty believing they can function well autonomously.

Those girls on the other hand who had scored low in fear of success or those who had scored high in fear of success but were continuing to strive for innovative careers were either engaged to or seriously dating men who were not against nor threatened by their success. In fact, they expected it of their girls and provided much encouragement for them: "I would have to explain myself if I got a C."

One of the factors distinguishing the couples in this second group from those in the first is a mutual understanding, either overt or covert, that the boy is the more intelligent of the two: "He's so much smarter . . . competition with him would be hopeless." This fact or belief seems to be sufficient to keep the motive from being aroused and affecting the behavior of the girls in this second group. Tension exists between the couples in the first group rooted in the fear that she is the more intelligent one.

The importance of male attitudes is being further tested in a current study which looks at how fear of success influences the expectations and performance of young (college) girls when competing against their own boyfriends, as compared to how well they have done in a previous noncompetitive setting. The attitudes of the boyfriends toward achievement in women are assessed prior to performance in this situation. It is hypothesized that negative attitudes on the part of the men will be significantly correlated with arousal of fear of success in their girlfriends, which will be manifested in performance decrements by the girls when competing against their boyfriends.

As our work has progressed it has become increasingly clear that the problems of achievement motivation in women are more complex than simply the matter of whether or not women have internalized a more or less traditional view of the female role. A complex relationship or interaction appears to exist between the girl's internal personality dispositions or motives and certain situational factors which determine the nature of the expectancy a girl has about the consequences of her actions and the value of these consequences to her in that situation. It is these latter factors which determine whether or not internalized dispositions will be aroused and therefore influence behavior. Does, for instance, the girl care about the male competitor and the possible rejection that may ensue if she does better than he does?

Consequences of the Motive to Avoid Success

As indicated, our data argue that unfortunately femininity and competitive achievement continue in American society to be viewed as two desirable but mutually exclusive ends. As a result, the recent emphasis on the new freedom for women has not been effective in removing the psychological barrier in many otherwise achievement-motivated and able young women that prevents them from actively seeking success or making obvious their abilities and potential. There is mounting evidence in our data suggesting that many achievement-oriented American women, especially those high in the motive to avoid success, when faced with the conflict between their feminine image and developing their abilities and interests, disguise their ability and abdicate from competition in the outside world—just like Sally in the Peanuts cartoon who at the tender age of five says: "I never said I wanted to *be* someone. All I want to do when I grow up is be a good wife and mother. So . . . why should I have to go to kindergarten?" When success is likely or possible, threatened by the negative consequences they expect to follow success, young women become anxious and thwart their positive achievement strivings. In this way, their abilities, interests, and intellectual potentials remain inhibited and unfulfilled.

A subsequent analysis of the data in the initial study (Horner, 1968), together with that of our most recent studies, shows however that these processes do not occur without a price, a price paid in feelings of frustration, hostility, aggression, bitterness, and confusion which are plainly manifested in the fantasy productions of young women. This was made clear by a comparison of the thematic apperceptive imagery written in response to the cue "Anne is sitting in a chair with a smile on her face" by women who had scored high in fear of success with that by those who had scored low. In response to the "smile cue," more than 90 percent of those low in fear of success imagery wrote positive, primarily affiliative stories centering on such things as dates, engagements, and forthcoming marriages, as well as a few on successful achievements. On the other hand, less than 20 percent of the 59 women who scored high in fear of success responded in this way. The rest of the responses, if not bizarre, were replete with negative imagery centering on hostility toward or manipulation of others.

Stories characteristic of the girls low in fear of success are exemplified by the following:

182 Her boyfriend has just called her . . . Oh boy. I'm so excited what shall I wear . . . Will he like me? I am so excited. Ann is very happy. Ann will have a marvelous time.

Anne is happy—she's happy with the world because it is so beautiful. It's snowing, and nice outside—she's happy to be alive and this gives her a good warm feeling. Well, Anne did well on one of her tests.

In comparison, the stories written by girls high in fear of success were dramatically different and distressing. Consider these examples:

Anne is recollecting her conquest of the day. She has just stolen her ex-friend's boyfriend away, right before the High School Senior Prom because she wanted to get back at her friend.

She is sitting in a chair smiling smugly because she has just achieved great satisfaction from the fact that she hurt somebody's feelings.

Gun in hand she is waiting for her stepmother to return home.

Anne is at her father's funeral. There are over 200 people there. She knows it is unseemly to smile but cannot help it . . . Her brother Ralph pokes her in fury but she is uncontrollable . . . Anne rises dramatically and leaves the room, stopping first to pluck a carnation from the blanket of flowers on the coffin.

At this point we can only speculate about how much of what was expressed in the fantasy productions of these girls was a true reflection of their actual behavior or intents, and secondly, if it was, what repercussions there might be. The psychodynamic causes and consequences of these differences are among a number of yet unanswered questions.

The results from data gathered by Watson (1970) as part of a larger study show a significant relationship between presence of the motive to avoid success and self-reported drug-taking which is relevant to the psychodynamic issues raised. The drug-taking measure involved a questionnaire estimate by the subjects of their frequency of use of drugs such as marijuana, LSD, and speed. Of the 37 college women in Watson's study, 24 (65 percent) scored high in fear of success. Of these, 13 described themselves as using drugs frequently, 6 moderately, and 5 never. Of the 13 girls low in fear of success, only 1 was a heavy drug user, 5 were moderate, and 7 never used them. The chi square difference between the groups was 8.12, with $df = 2, p < .05$. Whereas 54 percent of the high fear of success girls reported heavy drug usage, only 7.7 percent of the low fear of success girls did so.

The causal direction of this observed relationship can only be a matter of speculation at this point. Just what the functional significance of heavy drug use is for high fear of success women remains a question that must be considered along with the rest of the data showing that negative conse- *183* quences for women ensue when the expression of their achievement needs or efficacious behavior is blocked by the presence of the motive to avoid success.

Conclusions

It is not unreasonable now to speculate that what we have observed in the laboratory does in fact extend into and influence the intellectual, professional, and personal lives of men and women in our society.

In light of the high and, if anything, increasing incidence of the motive to avoid success found among women in our studies (see table 6.1), the predominant message seems to be that most highly competent and otherwise achievement-motivated young women, when faced with a conflict between their feminine image and expressing their competencies or developing their abilities and interests, adjust their behaviors to their internalized sex-role sterotypes. We have seen that even within our basically achievement-oriented society the anticipation of success, especially in interpersonal competitive situations, can be regarded as a mixed blessing if not an outright threat. Among women, the anticipation of success especially against a male competitor poses a threat to the sense of femininity and self-esteem and serves as a potential basis for becoming socially rejected—in other words, the anticipation of success is anxiety-provoking and as such inhibits otherwise positive achievement-directed motivation and behavior. In order to feel or appear more feminine, women, especially those high in fear of success, disguise their abilities and withdraw from the mainstream of thought, activism, and achievement in our society. This does not occur, however, without a high price, a price paid by the individual in negative emotional and interpersonal consequences and by the society in a loss of valuable human and economic resources.

The issues addressed here are particularly important in light of the population problems now facing society and the appeals being made to women to have fewer children. Inasmuch as having children is one of the major sources of self-esteem for women, it becomes necessary to have other options for enhancing self-esteem available to those who will respond to appeals to avoid overpopulation. Achievement in the outside world is one such possibility, but one which we have found is not at present a viable option because of the presence of psychological barriers like the motive to avoid success. It is clear that much remains to be done to respond fully to

184 the issues raised and to understand the factors involved in the development and subsequent arousal of a motive to avoid success.

References

Atkinson, J. W. (Ed.) *Motives in fantasy, action, and society.* Princeton, N.J.: Van Nostrand, 1958.

Atkinson, J. W., & Feather, N. T. *A theory of achievement motivation.* New York: Wiley, 1966.

Broverman, I. K., Vogel, S. R., Broverman, D. M., Clarkson, F. E., & Rosenkrantz, P. S. Sex role stereotypes and clinical judgments of mental health. *Journal of Consulting and Clinical Psychology,* 1970, *34* (1), 1–7.

Freud, S. The psychology of women. In *New introductory lectures on psychoanalysis.* New York: Norton, 1933. (Republished 1965.)

Horner, M. Sex differences in achievement motivation and performance in competitive and non-competitive situations. Unpublished doctoral dissertation, University of Michigan, 1968.

Horner, M. Femininity and successful achievement: A basic inconsistency. In J. Bardwick, E. M. Douvan, M. S. Horner, & D. Gutmann (Eds.), *Feminine personality and conflict.* Belmont, Calif.: Brooks-Cole, 1970 (a).

Horner, M. The motive to avoid success and changing aspirations of college women. Unpublished manuscript, Harvard University, 1970 (b).

Horner, M., & Rhoem, W. The motive to avoid success as a function of age, occupation and progress at school. Unpublished manuscript, University of Michigan, 1968.

Komarovsky, M. Functional analysis of sex roles. *American Sociological Review,* 1959, *15,* 508–16.

Maccoby, E. Women's intellect. In S. M. Farber and R. H. L. Wilson (Eds.), *The potential of women.* New York: McGraw-Hill, 1963.

McClelland, D. C., Atkinson, J. W., Clark, R. A., & Lowell, E. L. *The achievement motive.* New York: Appleton-Century-Crofts, 1953.

McClelland, D. C. *The achieving society.* New York: Van Nostrand, 1961.

Mead, M. *Male and female.* New York: Morrow, 1949. (Republished New York: Dell, 1968.)

Prescott, D. Efficacy-related imagery, education and politics. Unpublished honors thesis, Harvard University, 1971.

Schwenn, M. Arousal of the motive to avoid success. Unpublished junior honors thesis, Harvard University, 1970.

Scott, W. A. The avoidance of threatening material in imaginative behavior. In Atkinson, J. W. (Ed.), *Motives in fantasy, action and society.* Princeton, N.J.: Van Nostrand, 1958.

Storr, A. *Human aggression.* New York: Bantam, 1970.

Tangri, S. Role innovation in occupational choice. Unpublished doctoral dissertation, University of Michigan, 1969.

Watson, R. Female and male responses to the succeeding female cue. Unpublished manuscript, Harvard University, 1970.

Psychometric Properties and Underlying Assumptions of Four Objective Measures of Fear of Success

MICHELE A. PALUDI

More than thirty years have passed since McClelland, Atkinson, Clark, and Lowell published *The Achievement Motive* (1953), and the research on need for achievement is still proceeding along several dimensions. One popular component of achievement motivation is the motive-to-avoid-success or fear-of-success (FOS) construct, introduced by Horner (1968) in order to "fill a gap" in the understanding of achievement motivation, particularly among women (see also Midgley & Abrams, 1974; Patty & Ferrell, 1974; Schwenn[1]). Horner argued that in competitive achievement situations, especially those in which important men (i.e., prospective dates, boy-friends) are present, success-seeking women of high ability have not only a motive to approach success and a motive to avoid failure but also a motive to become anxious about being successful: a motive to avoid success. Such a motive is present because of the expectation of negative consequences as a result of succeeding (loss of femininity, social rejection, and disapproval). As Horner (1969) pointed out: "A bright woman is caught in a double bind. In testing and other achievement-oriented situations, she worries not only about failure but also about success. If she fails, she is not living up to her own standards of performance, if she succeeds, she is not living up to societal expectations about the female role" (p. 38).

Fear of success has been accepted as a proven personality trait and has worked its way into standard sources of gospel. However, Horner's findings are not as robust as originally assumed.[2] Several of the original conceptions

"Psychometric Properties and Underlying Assumptions of Four Objective Measures of Fear of Success," *Sex Roles*, 1984, *10* (9/10), 765–81. Copyright © 1984 by Plenum Publishing Corporation. Reprinted by permission.

Dr. Paludi is Associate Professor, Department of Psychology, Kent State University, Kent, Ohio.
1. Schwenn, M. *Arousal of the motive to avoid success.* Unpublished junior honors thesis. Harvard University, 1970.
2. Zanna, M. P. *Intellectual competition and the female student* (Report to the U.S. Department of Health, Education and Welfare). Princeton University, 1973.

186 of FOS have not been supported by empirical data. As Tresemer's review (1974) of Horner's study pointed out, the intuitive appeal of FOS has resulted in a tendency to regard the concept as proven and to overlook its many complexities. Zuckerman and Wheeler's (1975) critical review of FOS concluded that a good poker player would not call a bet concerning the construct. Indeed, Helen Thompson Woolley's (1910) appraisal of the quality of the research on sex differences applies to today's treatment of FOS: "There is perhaps no field aspiring to be scientific where flagrant personal bias, logic martyred in the cause of supporting a prejudice, unfounded in assertions, and even sentimental rot and drivel, have run riot to such an extent as here."

Since the numerous reviews of the methodological, statistical, and conceptual problems with Horner's study (e.g., Tresemer, 1974, 1977; Zuckerman & Wheeler, 1975), researchers have taken several new directions in studying the FOS construct. This state of affairs calls for a critical appraisal of the current state of the art. This article reviews the problems and proposed solutions to the problems raised by Horner's and subsequent studies concerning FOS in terms of measurement reliability, measurement validity, and the validity of the FOS construct.

Measurement of FOS

In order to exhibit the FOS motive as operating in women and not in men, Horner gave undergraduate students the opening sentence of a story to complete. Women were administered the following cue: "After first term finals, Anne finds herself at the top of her medical school class." For the men, the verbal lead was the same except that the cue character's name was given as "John" and "her" was changed to "his." Horner (1968, p. 105) wrote:

Any of the following types of imagery was scored as fear of success:

    a. negative consequences because of the success;
    b. anticipation of negative consequences because of the success;
    c. negative affect because of the success;
    d. instrumental activity away from present or future success, including leaving the field for more traditional female work such as nursing, school teaching, or social work;
    e. any direct expression of conflict about success.

Also scored was evidence of:

f. denial of the situation described by the cue,

g. bizarre, inappropriate, unrealistic or non-adaptive responses to the situation described by the cue.

Employing this scoring system, Horner observed differences between men and women in the kinds of responses they made to the projective cue. Women projected signifcantly more evidence of FOS than did men: 65 percent versus 9 percent.

Horner reasoned that sensitivity to the sex of the cue character served to distort judgment and prejudice women against the success of another woman. By relying on McClelland et al.'s (1953) approach to motivation, Horner accepted the view, advanced in psychoanalytic writings, that motives are developed early in childhood and become relatively stable attributes of personality, highly resistant to change. Monahan, Kuhn, and Shaver's (1974) and Solomon's (1975) research, on the other hand, demonstrated that a cultural interpretation is preferable to an intrapsychic one. Their research designs crossed subject and task factors: half of the men and half of the women subjects wrote stories to a cue depicting a successful woman; the other half of both sexes wrote stories to a cue involving a successful man. Results from both of these studies indicated that both men and women projected more FOS imagery onto the successful woman than to the man, suggesting a cultural explanation: "the stereotypes surrounding women's achievements are negative ones, learned and accepted by both sexes" (Monahan et al., 1974, p. 61).

Additional Features Present in Cue

Level of Success Achieved. Once again, the sex of the character in the cue was believed to be the most critical variable. Amid the proliferation of studies, relatively few researchers have explored Horner's storytelling method in order to identify factors other than the cue character's gender that could contribute to the amount of projected FOS imagery. For example, the verbal lead or cue employed in much of the research on FOS depicted Anne and John at the top of the medical school class and, by implication, ranking first. Anne's and John's position in medical school, not their gender, may be a salient feature of the cue. It is possible that subjects' responses reflect anxiety about the level of success achieved, rather than anxiety about success in general. If this interpretation is correct, responses to the Anne and John cue will be related only in situations where their success is defined as "number one."

Paludi (1979) provided some clarification of this issue. She asked intro-

188 ductory psychology students to tell a story about Anne or John, who ranked either at the top, in the top 5 percent, top 15 percent, top 25 percent, or top half of their medical school class. Analyses indicated that more negative imagery was projected onto Anne by both men and women if she ranked very highly than if she did not. Anne was depicted as being concerned, as Horner had argued, with social rejection and ostracism as a consequence of succeeding. In contrast to the results reported for the Anne stimulus, more negative imagery was projected onto John by subjects of both sexes if he ranked toward the middle of his class than if he did not. The "not too successful" John was characterized as unhappy and depressed over his inability to do well in medical school.

An important question in regard to Paludi's study centers on the conditions defining varying positions for Anne and John in the *bottom* portion of the distribution of class ranks. Recently, Fogel and Paludi[3] asked male and female introductory psychology students to tell a story about Anne or John, who ranked in the bottom half, bottom 25 percent, bottom 15 percent, bottom 5 percent, or bottom of their medical school class. More negative imagery was projected onto Anne by both sexes when she was at the bottom of her class than when she ranked in the bottom half. A similar pattern was noted for men and women who responded to the John cue, although a greater amount of negative imagery was present in protocols about John when he ranked at the bottom of his class than about Anne in this position.

If we were to extend the graph Paludi (1979) presented of her data to include the results of the Fogel and Paludi study, we would find that John's curve remained high (i.e., high frequency of negative imagery from the top 50 percent to bottom of the class), but Anne's followed a U-shaped function of degree of "nonsuccess" (with high frequency of negative imagery at the top of the class and again at the bottom of the class), not converging with John's at the point where both were depicted at the very bottom of the class.

It should be emphasized that the content of negative imagery in the protocols written about Anne and John in the latter study was different from what Paludi (1979) observed. While FOS may describe the negative imagery present in the protocols written about Anne at the top of her medical school class, fear of failure (Anderson, 1962) more adequately describes the imagery present in the protocols written about Anne at the bottom of her class—negative affect, discouragement, anticipation of future failure, and desire to leave the situation. Fear of failure also illustrates

---

3. Fogel, R., & Paludi, M. A. *Fear of success and failure or norms for achievement?* Paper presented at the 6th annual Conference on Research on Women and Education, Pacific Grove, Calif., December 1980.

the content of the protocols written about John when he is ranked in the *189* middle to bottom of his class.

The results of these studies constitute compelling evidence that success and also failure in competitive achievement situations is differentially perceived and evaluated according not only to sex of the cue character but also to the degree of success or failure obtained. These results also support Feather and Simon's (1975) finding of a pervasive tendency to upgrade successful males in relation to unsuccessful males and downgrade unsuccessful males in relation to unsuccessful females.

Occupation in Which Success Was Achieved.   A second salient feature of Horner's (1968) FOS verbal cue may be the occupation in which Anne and John were successful. Feather and Simon (1975) observed that part of the definition of sex roles in society involves assumptions about the types of occupations held to be appropriate for men and women. Success at an occupation is more highly valued when the success is consistent with societal conceptions about the sex role than when it is inconsistent. Thus, as Feather and Simon (1975) point out, "the consequences of succeeding at medical school are more positive for males (success is consistent with masculine image) than for females (success is inconsistent with the feminine image)" (p. 21). Therefore, because Horner's cue depicted Anne at the top of her medical school class, it can be hypothesized that protocols written by women reflected anxiety about success that is "out of place" for women.[4]

Intuitively, this "sex-role inappropriateness" hypothesis would suggest that men, too, project negative imagery onto a successful male cue character when the latter's success occurs in a nontraditional setting such as nursing. Such a result was obtained by Cherry and Deaux,[5] Feather and Simon (1975); Janda, O'Grady, and Capps (1978); and Tresemer and Pleck. Therefore, in addition to the sex of the subject or protagonist being an important factor in Horner's study, "medical school"—with its numerous connotations—may have been salient.

Ambiguous Cue.   Another way to examine the sex-role inappropriateness explanation is to examine the effects of an ambiguous cue on the incidence

4. Tresemer, D. W., & Pleck, J. *Maintaining and changing sex-role boundaries in men (and women).* Paper presented at the Women: Resource for a Changing World Conference, Radcliffe Institute, Cambridge, Mass., April 1972.
5. Cherry, F., & Deaux, K. *Fear of success versus fear of gender-inconsistent behavior: A sex similarity.* Paper presented at the annual meeting of the Midwestern Psychological Association, Chicago, 1975.

190 of projected FOS imagery. Tresemer (1974) suggested that Horner's cue was too limiting and specific: "Horner forced subjects to react to a narrow, focused concrete situation: a person is number one in a male-dominated field" (p. 85). Tresemer advocated a return to the traditional ambiguity characteristic of projective tests. The use of ambiguous cues would allow researchers, he argued, to observe subjects' personal perceptions of success. In this way, external factors, such as the specific connotations of externally imposed verbal cues, would not bias the subjects' protocols. To test this hypothesis, Tresemer administered the following cues: "After much work, Joe (Judy) has finally gotten what he (she) wanted." Twenty-three percent of the 110 male subjects and 22 percent of the 111 females projected FOS imagery onto the cue character. For women, this percentage represented significantly less FOS imagery than was reported in Horner's (1968) study. Perhaps FOS is not nearly as prevalent among women as Horner suggested.

Causal Attribution.   However, the causal attribution of ability and effort ("after much work") is implied in Tresemer's cue. Horner's Anne and John cue implied external attributional process: "finds her(him)self," as if it came as an unexpected surprise, from luck. The main objective of a recent study by Gravenkemper[6] was to investigate the incidence of FOS imagery in men and women who were administered an ambiguous projective verbal cue free from the effort, ability, and luck implication: "John (Anne) has succeeded." In allowing subjects to define success for themselves, Gravenkemper hypothesized that subjects would exhibit relatively little FOS imagery and there would not be a significant difference in the amount of FOS projected by men and women. Gravenkemper's hypotheses were confirmed with 79 female and 64 male introductory psychology students. Results indicated that only 14.1 percent of the men and 7.6 percent of the women projected FOS imagery. It appears that when subjects are given the opportunity to define success for themselves, they project relatively little FOS imagery onto a cue character. It is interesting that Gravenkemper's subjects' stories centered on success in the areas of school, job, and athletics.

On the basis of the studies reported above, Horner's (1968) conclusions are not warranted. Sex of subjects is only one possible explanation for the results obtained. Of course, it is still too early to state which of the other identified factors or combinations are responsible for increased projected

6. Gravenkemper, S. A. *Fear of success revisited: Introducing an ambiguous cue.* Paper presented at the Fifth Annual Conference on Research on Women and Education, Cleveland, 1979.

FOS imagery, since no attempt has been made to examine them simultaneously, and researchers have not all employed the same scoring technique in analyzing protocols. Some have used Horner's (1968) simple present-absent scoring system (Hoffman, 1974, 1977; Monahan et al., 1974), while others have employed Horner's modified scoring system.[7] A third fantasy-based measure, designed by Paludi[8] has also been used (e.g., Fogel & Paludi, n. 3; Gravenkemper, n. 6). Therefore, whether or not the results obtained in studies of FOS are due to variations in the cue presentation or to differences in scoring systems, remains an open question.

Alternative Measurement Techniques

A considerable amount of evaluation and controversy has been devoted to the interpretation of protocols written to projective verbal cues in FOS research.[9] Because the projective verbal lead may be eliciting a reaction to its own superficial content rather than a direct expression of motive strength, several "objective" instruments designed to tap FOS have been developed. Most of the current tests of FOS use true-false questions; semantic differential items; interview questions; and situation-specific items.

True-False (Yes-No) Measures

Good and Good (1973) developed a twenty-nine-item dichotomously scored self-report measure of FOS. Their scale reflects the belief that FOS is experienced by people who worry about antagonizing others as a result of succeeding. For example, "I sometimes do less than my very best so that no

7. Horner, M. S., Tresemer, D. W., Berens, A. E., & Watson, R. I. Jr. *Scoring manual for an empirically derived scoring system for motive to avoid success.* Unpublished manuscript, Harvard University, 1973. Each protocol is judged on six categories, with numerical weights assigned to each category: (a) contingent negative consequences (+2); (b) noncontingent negative consequences (+2); (c) interpersonal engagement (+2); (d) relief (+1); (3) absence of instrumental activity (+1); (f) absence of mentions of other people (−2).
8. The scoring manual (Paludi, M. A., *Scoring manual for fear of success imagery,* Unpublished manuscript, University of Cincinnati, 1978) is modeled after the McClelland et al. (1953) manual for scoring achievement motivation. It describes in detail what is meant by fear of success by specifying which kinds of projective imagery should be taken as illustrative of fear of success and which kinds of imagery should not. Included are sample protocols written to various cues—both ambiguous and situation specific— and an accompanying discussion of why they were scored as they were. Proper use of the training manual should allow the novice scorer to become an expert with good reliability. The training materials include (a) sample stories written to a variety of cues, (b) detailed scoring of the protocols, (c) explanations of details of scoring, (d) instructions for computing the reliability of the novice scorer to that of the author. The scoring criteria for fear-of-success imagery were derived from the literature and represent extensions of the categories developed by Horner.
9. Moore, K. A. *Fear of success: The distribution, correlates, reliability and consequences for fertility of fear of success among respondents in a metropolitan survey population.* Paper presented at the meeting of the American Psychological Association, New Orleans, August 1974.

one will be threatened"; "I often worry about the possibility that others will think I am a 'show off' "; "I worry that I may become so knowledgeable that others will not like me"; and "If I were to do well at something, I would worry that someone might try to undermine my success." Good and Good reported an internal consistency reliability estimate (KR-20) of .81 for 103 male and 125 female undergraduate students. The authors also reported a significantly higher FOS score for females. They have not limited their items to FOS in academic situations, thus avoiding one of the pitfalls of Horner's approach. Good and Good's questionnaire was not, however, correlated with Horner's (1968) fantasy-based measure of FOS or related to performance behavior. These two points will be subsequently discussed further.

Pappo,[10] incorporating the perspective of Henry Stack Sullivan, developed a yes-no measure that purports to tap the following aspects of FOS: (1) negative affective reaction, "If someone calls attention to me when I'm doing well, I often feel awkward"; (2) repudiation of competence or motivation, "Persuasive people can influence my ideas"; (3) sabotage of success, "As a game [card game, word game, chess, competitive sports, etc.] reaches the winning point, I start thinking about other things"; (4) preoccupation with evaluation and competition, "I try the hardest when my work is being evaluated"; (5) self-doubt and negative self-evaluation, "There are times when I don't think I have what it takes to be a success in the area I am interested in"; (6) distractibility and impairment of concentration, "Frequently at crucial points in intellectual discussions, my mind goes blank." Pappo reported a KR-20 of .89 using a sample of 115 male and 170 female undergraduate students. No significant sex difference in the way men and women answer the questionnaire was found. Concurrent validity was assessed for the Pappo scale by correlating it with three personality tests relevant to the characteristics of success-fearers: Rotter's (1966) Internal-External Scale, the Rosenberg Self-Esteem Scale (Rosenberg, 1965), and the Debilitating Anxiety Scale (Alpert & Haber, 1960). As hypothesized, Canavan-Gumpert, Garner, and Gumpert (1978) found people who fear success to be externals, to have more negative self-esteem, and to express anxiety in academic testing situations.

Pappo reported that her male and female subjects who had high FOS scores significantly lowered their performance on a digit-symbol task after they were debriefed about their performance on a previous task. Subsequent use of Pappo's questionnaire with law students by Curtis, Zanna,

10. Pappo, M. *Fear of success: An empirical and theoretical analysis.* Unpublished doctoral dissertation, Teachers College, Columbia University, 1972.

and Campbell[11] indicated that men and women who scored high in FOS were more likely to indicate the desire to volunteer answers in their classes, but not actually to do so; they performed less well on their law school admissions exam and believed they were poor at logical reasoning and hypothesis testing. On the other hand, high FOS scorers did not perform poorly in their law courses, nor did they anticipate doing less well than low FOS scorers.

Pappo's questionnaire, like Good and Good's, has not been correlated with Horner's (1968) nor with any other FOS measure. Unlike the Good and Good (1973) measure, however, Pappo's scale is limited to fear of success in academic situations. Cohen[12] sought to improve Pappo's FOS scale by measuring anxiety about success in general, not solely academic achievement. Cohen tests "the equation of accomplishment with competitive defeat of another," which leads to fantasy retaliation by the defeated competitor. Cohen conceives of FOS as a defense against letting go, espousing a neo-Freudian orientation to psychodynamic phenomena. To her, FOS is based in the anal stage of development, emphasizing concerns of control and fear of loss of control, shame, humiliation, and self-assertion versus submission.

On the basis of a factor analysis of her sixty-four-item, true-false scale, Cohen identified nine factors that were characteristic of high FOS scorers: (1) anxiety over the expression of needs and preferences, "It makes me feel uneasy to have to ask other people for things"; (2) reluctance to acknowledge personal competence, "I generally feel uptight about telling a boss or professor that I think I'm entitled to a better deal"; (3) impaired concentration and distractability, "I have often 'woken up' during a lecture or a meeting and realized that I haven't heard a word that was said"; (4) indecisiveness, "It pays to check out your ideas with other people before making a final decision"; (5) safety value syndrome—fear of loss of control, "It's important not to get too excited about things one really desires"; (6) illegitimacy of self-promotive behavior, "I sometimes have trouble acting like myself when I'm with people I don't know"; (7) anxiety over being the focus of attention, "I hate having a fuss made over me"; (8) preoccupation with competition and evaluation, "When someone I know well succeeds at something, I usually feel that I've lost out in comparison"; (9) preoccupation with the underplaying of effectiveness, "I sometimes 'play down' my competence in front of others so they won't think I'm bragging."

11. Curtis, R., Zanna, M. P., & Campbell, W. W. *Sex, fear of success, and the perceptions and performance of law school students.* Unpublished manuscript, Adelphi University, 1973.
12. Cohen, N. E. *Explorations in the fear of success.* Unpublished doctoral dissertation, Columbia University, 1974.

194   Cohen reported an insignificant difference between the mean FOS scores for her 88 male and 150 female undergraduate students. She also reported (a) a KR-20 split-half reliability coefficient of .90; (b) a correlation between her scale and Pappo's of .74; (c) high FOS scorers in a validation experiment (241 high school juniors and seniors) more often devalued their performance, attributed effective performance to luck, and performed worse when paired with a same-sex opponent on a memory task. This last result supported Cohen's theoretical prediction that FOS would be linked with recurrent Oedipal conflict and symbolically associated with a same-sex peer.

Both Pappo and Cohen conceived of FOS in a different way than did Horner (1968). Zuckerman and Allison (1976), however, accept much of Horner's conceptual foundation for FOS. Zuckerman and Allison developed a twenty-seven-item agree-disagree Fear of Success Scale (FOSS) and found significantly more responses indicative of FOS in women than in men. Items dealt with only one aspect of success: success in competition. For example, "The rewards of a successful competition are greater than those received from cooperation"; "I am happy only when I am doing better than others"; "Often, the cost of success is greater than the reward"; "I believe that successful people are often sad and lonely." Zuckerman and Allison reported significant but low correlations between their scale and Horner's, both for the 174 male (.16) and 170 female subjects (.18). In addition, subjects who scored high FOS performed significantly lower on an anagram task and attributed their success to external causes and their failure to internal causes.

Semantic Differential Items

Feather and Simon (1975) asked 48 female subjects to use semantic scales to rate males and females who succeeded (or failed) at different occupations (medicine or nursing) on three matters of concern: (1) personality—for example, pleasant/unpleasant, logical/intuitive, tough/tender; (2) causal attribution of the success or failure—for example, ability, examiner's error, luck; and (3) perceived likelihood of various consequences—for example, Anne (John) feels thoroughly contented, wonders if it is all worthwhile, continues to top the class. Feather and Simon's subjects upgraded successful males in relation to unsuccessful males and devalued successful females in relation to unsuccessful females. Their semantic differential scales were not correlated with Horner's (1968) measure and their items were based on a cue limited to fear of success in academic settings. The first problem was attacked experimentally by Paludi.[13] She

13. Paludi, M. A. *Impact of androgynous and traditional sex-role orientations on reactions to successful men and women in sex-linked occupations.* Unpublished master's thesis, University of Cincinnati, 1978.

extended Feather and Simon's design by also administering Horner's storytelling method in conjunction with the semantic differential scales and
found no correlation between the two measurement techniques.

A ten-item questionnaire with similar questions to Feather and Simon's
has been developed by Spence (1974), who asked her subjects to answer the
items following completion of their storytelling task. Questions run the
gamut from "How likeable do Anne's classmates consider her?" (answered
on a 5-point scale) to "How physically attractive is she?" and "If she doesn't
complete her degree, what is the most likely reason?" (answered from
responses provided from protocols written to the projective cue). Knapp[14]
designed a similar questionnaire to be used in conjunction with Horner's
medical school cue with items as follows:

Anne is:
   abnormal—probably not very feminine
      YES! yes—?—no NO!
   happy but surprised she did so well (feels luck played a part)
      YES! yes—?—no NO!

An Interview Measure of FOS

One part of Horner's results which merits consideration is the assumption
of the acquisition of FOS, its origins, or even how it may be eliminated.
Thus, the main objective of a series of studies by Paludi[15] concerns the
development of an interview measure designed to elicit success and FOS
themes and to identify personal, peer, and parental influences on these
themes. The interview items Paludi has been using with women aged 20 to
63 are adapted from McClelland and Winter's (1971) research on motivating economic achievement:

What, specifically, do you want to accomplish in the next two years?
What specific steps do you plan to take to achieve these goals?
What blocks in yourself will you have to overcome to achieve these goals?
What blocks in the world will you have to overcome in order to achieve these goals?
How do you feel about the possibility of achieving these goals?
How do your parents feel about you achieving these goals?
How do your men acquaintances feel about you achieving these goals?
How do your women acquaintances feel about you achieving these goals?
How does your spouse feel about you achieving these goals?
Have you ever been in a situation where you were about to succeed at something,
and wondered if it was worth it or got afraid of your success or something it might
produce?

14. Knapp, J. J. *Fear of academic success: A comparison of academically above-average, single, male and female college students*. Unpublished master's thesis, University of Florida, 1972.
15. Paludi, M. A. *On the measurement of success and fear of success*. Paper presented at the Fifth Annual Conference on Research on Women and Education, Cleveland, 1979.

196   Paludi has reported that the interview items have elicited information readily attainable from Horner's fantasy-based measure. Her interview responses are inconsistent with her female subjects' rejection of Anne at the top of her medical school class. A major theme that has resulted from this technique is a reformulation of Horner's theory: FOS is not deep-seated in women's personality, but situationally determined. Women may not internalize the motive at a very early age. On the contrary, women may evaluate their behaviors in the light of the specific situation, sometimes acting in accord with sex-role norms, sometimes not. Women may consciously sum up each situation as it presents itself and either engage in sex-appropriate "failure" behaviors or demonstrate achievement-oriented skills. Women's behavior may also be fundamentally influenced by social aspects of the situation. Women may be role-calculating, making the most of their rewards (Kaufman & Richardson, 1982). Some excerpts of the women's interviews follow.

The more I've achieved, the more I've been isolated, the more I've been perceived as different. The more I've been perceived as different, the more I perceive myself as different.

Many women are jealous of me because I am going to school. They laugh at me. They are probably afraid of changing their lives. I can't talk about anything important because they are not interested in the same things I am. Most men think it's terrific. They understand why I'm going to college but they don't understand why I don't have time to date them.

I've never been afraid of my successes, although I have succeeded at something and wondered if it was worth it. I can work toward success and/or a goal and achieve it and then it's done and I'm proud, but something is always missing. I guess I expect fireworks to go off. I like to succeed at something, but then, on the other hand, it seems like after it's done, it was no big deal after all.

Paludi's interview measure[16] is currently undergoing technical psychometric work to refine it and make it more efficient by eliminating spurious questions and including questions that increase its accuracy. An advantage of such a measure is that information can be elicited on all the issues of concern by devising appropriate interview items, a kind of control not afforded by Horner's storytelling method.

Situation-Specific Items

Amid the measurement proliferation, relatively few experimenters have explored the relationship of FOS to performance behavior: Do those who

---

16. Paludi, M. A. Unpublished data, Franklin and Marshall College, 1980.

fear success on a projective or objective test avoid success in achievement situations?

Makosky[17] has provided some clarification of this issue. She observed that women who score high on FOS do not fear to compete in general, only in instances where the task is considered "masculine" or where competition is against a man. "High" FOS women were so classified on the basis of their responses to the storytelling cue used initially by Horner (1968). Makosky's results are limited by the measurement technique, considering the criticisms of the projective cue discussed earlier. In addition, the FOS measure used in her studies was unrelated to the performance task of solving anagrams. There is, therefore, a need for a situation-based paper-and-pencil measure of FOS to be used in predictive validity research (which will be discussed further in a subsequent section).

The main objective of an initial study in a series of experiments designed by Schulenberg[18] concerned the development of a situationally based measure of FOS. He wrote eleven scenarios to comprise a situation-specific inventory assessing FOS and then administered the instrument in conjunction with the projective verbal cue to 50 male and 50 female introductory psychology students. In writing the scenarios, Schulenberg assumed (as did Horner) that the feared negative consequences for success are deviation from social norms and stereotypes (for example, loss of femininity). Examples of scenarios employed by Schulenberg follow:

You and your boyfriend (girlfriend) are taking freshman English together. As the professor passes back the midterm exams, you notice that your boyfriend (girlfriend) got a B. You, however, got an A. When your boyfriend (girlfriend) asks what you got on the exam, you say:

a. I got an A!!
b. I did O.K.
c. I got a C.

Recently, you've met a young man (lady). You like him (her) and would like to get to know him (her) better. One day, you both decide to go play some racquetball. As you warm up, it becomes obvious that he (she) is not real good. You feel that you could beat him (her) quite easily. Since you just met him (her), you're not sure how he (she) would react to losing. You play one game and win 21 to 4. He (she)

17. Makosky, V. P. *Fear of success, sex-role orientation of the task, and competitive condition as variables affecting women's performance in achievement-oriented situations.* Paper presented at the annual meeting of the Midwestern Psychological Association, Cleveland, May 1972.
18. Schulenberg, J. E. *Toward the development of a situationally based measure of fear of success: Initial findings.* Paper presented at the Sixth Annual Conference on Research on Women and Education, Pacific Grove, Calif., December 1980.

198 wants to play some more and suggests a little tournament in which the winner of two out of three games would be the champion. You would:

a. let him (her) win the next two games
b. win the second game to end the tournament
c. let him (her) win the second game, but you would win the third game

Coding of the scenarios was accomplished using the following scale: An alternative indicative of a FOS response (determined by Paludi's scoring system [n. 8]) received a score of 3; a neutral score received a score of 2; a non-FOS response received a score of 1. Schulenberg reported a significantly higher mean score for the females than for the males. It should be pointed out, however, that both men's and women's scores were closer to 2, the neutral response, than to 1 or 3.

A Pearson product-moment correlation coefficient performed on the scores from the projective FOS measure and from Schulenberg's test revealed virtually no relationship for men or for women. To date, the Schulenberg scale has not been validated with any performance measure.

Reliability, Validity, and the Reality Status of the Fear-of-Success Construct

The wide differences in how FOS has been measured has resulted in a "now-you-see-it-now-you-don't" phenomenon (Alper, 1974). A review of 64 studies (Paludi)[19] revealed that the percentage of subjects exhibiting FOS has ranged from 6 percent to 93 percent in females, with a median of 49 percent; from 7 percent to 95 percent in males, with a median of 45 percent. In addition, measure reliability of both the fantasy-based and objective techniques has been inconsistent.

Test-retest reliability for the fantasy-based FOS measure has been low (Moore, n. 9; Paludi, n. 19). In addition, the majority of studies employing Horner's storytelling method have only administered the single medical school cue. Experimenters who did administer several cues to the same subjects either failed to report the homogeneity reliability (e.g., Karabenick & Marshall, 1974; Weston & Mednick, 1970) or reported low correlation coefficients (e.g., Morgan & Mausner, 1973).

Interrater reliability for the storytelling techniques has ranged between 80 and 96 percent. However, not all investigators using the fantasy-based method have used the same scoring system. In addition, FOS scores are likely to reflect the judges' gender (Robbins & Robbins, 1973), and their expectancies.[20] Finally, Tresemer (1974, 1977) suggested that judges have

---

19. Paludi, M. A. Unpublished data, University of Cincinnati, 1979.
20. Levine, A., & Crumrine, J. *Women and the fear of success: A problem in replication.* Paper presented

incorrectly rated all negative themes in a subject's protocol as evidence of *199*
FOS: thus, failing to take into account the theoretical basis of FOS: that
success will bring negative consequences. Therefore, serious methodological flaws exist in the scoring of FOS protocols.

Measure reliability for the newer FOS measurement techniques has
either usually not been analyzed and/or reported (e.g., Feather & Simon,
1975; Gravenkemper, n. 6; Schulenberg, n. 18) or has been reported in
terms of a split-half coefficient (e.g., Cohen, n. 12).

Likewise, the fantasy-based and objective FOS measures have not been
properly validated. Neither Horner (1968) nor other users of the storytelling method (e.g., Hoffman, 1974; Monahan et al., 1974) have compared
FOS themes of an aroused and nonaroused group of subjects. Concurrent
validity has been assessed by Pappo (n. 10); construct validity by Paludi[21]
and Schulenberg (n. 18); predictive validity by Cohen (n. 12), Makosky (n.
17), Pappo (n. 10), and Zuckerman and Allison (1976). Overall, it may be
concluded that various validity experiments have not shown consistent
interactions with FOS. This is, perhaps, a result of the fact that not all
researchers have conceptualized FOS similarly.

According to Horner (1968), the feared negative consequences for success are deviation from social norms and stereotypes. This is the same
theoretical basis underlying Schulenberg's (n. 18) situation-specific technique and Zuckerman and Allison's (1976) FOS. Pappo's (n. 10) and
Cohen's (n. 12) questionnaires are couched in the psychoanalytic approach
to FOS: the feared negative consequences are the defeat of one's defenses
against murderous rage or Oedipal success. This is similar to an approach
recently espoused by Friedman (1980). Since the new FOS measures deal
with either academic, competitive success (e.g., Pappo, n. 10) or success in
general (e.g., Good & Good, 1973; Paludi, n. 15; Schulenberg, n. 18), it
should come as no surprise that they have not been found to be related to
Horner's projective FOS measure.

The new FOS scales are very appealing because they appear to resolve
many of the problems reported in past studies with Horner's measure.
However, it would be premature to switch to any of the new FOS measures.
Each has its own limitations, as Tresemer (1977) pointed out: "In embrac-
ing any of these new measures, there is a danger of repeating the misunder-
standings about Horner's measure with a new instrument. It has been
clearly demonstrated that the phrase 'fear of success' attracts attention, but
that any one scale 'measures' a person's individual fear any better than
another cannot, at this point, be known" (p. 171).

at the meeting of the American Sociological Association, New York, August 1973.
21. Paludi, M. A. Unpublished data, University of Cincinnati, 1980.

200 *Construct Validity of FOS*

Is there a fear of success? Do women fear success? The popularity of the construct is based partially on the belief that FOS has a substantial impact on women's lives and professional careers. There is little evidence to support this assertion. Even if FOS were a valid motive, it does not appear to be a motive experienced uniquely by women. Fear of success cannot, therefore, be easily used as an explanation for men and women's differential achievements. One cannot conclude from the research to date that FOS acts as a counterforce against women's or men's tendency to achieve. Too many inherent methodological, conceptual, and statistical flaws in FOS research preclude calling FOS a motive, a proven personality trait. In addition, experiencing anxiety over success may not be pathological, but a normative part of one's development (Sassen, 1980).

Based on a review of studies subsequent to Horner's original experiment, the following conclusions may be stated:

1. Fear of success and sex-role orientation appear to be unrelated.
2. No reliable age or sex differences in fear of success have been observed.
3. Whether fear of success taps a motive or cultural stereotype is not clear.
4. The reliability of the measures of fear of success is low.
5. There has been no consistent relationship between fear of success and any behavioral measure.
6. Fear of success has shown no relationship to ability (in the form of SAT scores, grade point average, IQ, career goals) in women.
7. Inconsistent data exist to support the assertions that fear of success is less likely among black women and more likely among black men.

It would, therefore, appear to be desirable to abandon the label "fear of success," since its continued use serves only to reinforce the popular and widespread, but scientifically unfounded, idea that sex differences in occupational or academic participation are attributable to an intrapsychic difference between men and women, an approach that blames the victim. To date, fear of success has failed. To the extent that new methodological advances can be empirically integrated with FOS, subsequent research and theory will increase in precision.

References

Alper, T. G. Achievement motivation in college women: A now-you-see-it-now-you-don't phenomenon. *American Psychologist,* 1974, *29,* 194–203.

Alpert, R., & Haber, R. N. Anxiety in academic achievement situations. *Journal of Abnormal and Social Psychology,* 1960, *61,* 207–15.

Anderson, R. C. Failure imagery in the fantasy of induced arousal. *Journal of Educational Psychology*, 1962, *53*, 293–98.

Canavan-Gumpert, D., Garner, K., & Gumpert, P. *The success-fearing personality*. Lexington, Mass.: D. C. Heath, 1978.

Feather, N. T., & Simon, J. G. Reactions to male and female success and failure in sex-linked occupations: Impressions of personality, causal attributions and perceived likelihood of different consequence. *Journal of Personality and Social Psychology*, 1975, *68*, 119–28.

Friedman, M. *Overcoming the fear of success*. New York: Seaview, 1980.

Good, L. R., & Good, K. C. An objective measure of the motive to avoid success. *Psychological Reports*, 1973, *33*, 1009–10.

Hoffman, L. W. Fear of success in males and females: 1965 and 1972. *Journal of Consulting and Clinical Psychology*, 1974, *42*, 353–58.

Hoffman, L. W. Fear of success in 1965 and 1974: A follow-up study. *Journal of Consulting and Clinical Psychology*, 1977, *45*, 310–21.

Horner, M. S. *Sex differences in achievement motivation and performance in competitive and noncompetitive situations*. Doctoral dissertation, University of Michigan, Ann Arbor, 1968.

Horner, M. S. Fail: Bright women. *Psychology Today*, 1969, *3*, 36–38, 62.

Janda, L. H., O'Grady, K. E., & Capps, C. F. Fear of success in males and females in sex-linked occupations. *Sex Roles*, 1978, *4*, 43–50.

Karabenick, S. A., & Marshall, J. M. Performance of females as a function of fear of success, fear of failure, type of opponent, and performance-contingent feedback. *Journal of Personality*, 1974, *42*, 220–37.

Kaufman, D. R., & Richardson, B. L. *Achievement and women: Challenging the assumptions*. New York: Free Press, 1982.

McClelland, D. C., Atkinson, J. W., Clark, R. A., & Lowell, E. L. *The achievement motive*. New York: Appleton-Century-Crofts, 1953.

McClelland, D. C., & Winter, D. G. *Motivating economic achievement*. New York: Macmillan, 1971.

Midgley, N., & Abrams, M. S. Fear of success and locus of control in young women. *Journal of Consulting and Clinical Psychology*, 1974, *42*, 737.

Monahan, L., Kuhn, D., & Shaver, P. Intrapsychic vs. cultural explanations of the fear of success motive. *Journal of Personality and Social Psychology*, 1974, *29*, 60–64.

Morgan, S. W., & Mausner, B. Behavioral and fantasied indicators of avoidance of success in men and women. *Journal of Personality*, 1973, *41*, 457–469.

Paludi, M. A. Horner revisited: How successful must Anne and John be before FOS sets in? *Psychological Reports*, 1979, *44*, 1319–22.

Patty, R., & Ferrell, M. M. A preliminary note on the motive to avoid success and the menstrual cycle. *Journal of Psychology*, 1974, *86*, 173–77.

Robbins, L., & Robbins, E. Comment on "Toward an Understanding of Achievement-Related Conflicts in Women." *Journal of Social Issues*, 1973, *29*(1), 133–37.

Rosenberg, M. *Society and the adolescent self-image*. Princeton: Princeton University Press, 1965.

Rotter, J. B. Generalized expectancies for internal versus external control of reinforcement. *Psychological Monographs*, 1966, *80* (1, Whole No. 609).

Sassen, G. Success anxiety in women: A constructivist interpretation of its source and significance. *Harvard Educational Review*, 1980, *50*, 13–24.

Solomon, L. Z. Perception of a successful person of the same sex or the opposite sex. *Journal of Social Psychology*, 1975, *85*, 133–34.

Spence, J. T. The Thematic Apperception Test and attitudes toward achievement in women: A new look at the motive to avoid success and a new method of measurement. *Journal of Consulting and Clinical Psychology*, 1974, *42*, 427–37.

202   Tresemer, D. W. Fear of success: Popular but unproven. *Psychology Today*, 1974, *7*, 82–85.

Tresemer, D. W. *Fear of success*. New York: Plenum, 1977.

Weston, P. J., & Mednick, M. T. Race, social class, and the motive to avoid success in women. *Journal of Cross-Cultural Psychology*, 1970, *1*, 284–91.

Woolley, H. T. Psychological literature: A review of the recent literature on the psychology of sex. *Psychological Bulletin*, 1910, *7*, 335–42.

Zuckerman, M., & Allison, S. N. An objective measure of fear of success: Construction and validation. *Journal of Personality Assessment*, 1976, *40*, 424–27.

Zuckerman, M., & Wheeler, L. To dispel fantasies about the fantasy-based measure of fear of success. *Psychological Bulletin*, 1975, *82*, 932–46.

Is Androgyny a Solution?

A computer search of the psychological literature for the period 1967–86 indicates that Sandra Lipsitz Bem, who came to prominence as the result of her work on androgyny, has received more individual citations than any other theorist in the field of the psychology of women. Androgyny, a term which became popular in the 1970s, refers to people who are high in both feminine and masculine traits.

Although a few other early theorists, such as Carl Jung (1953), had discussed the masculine and feminine components inherent in every individual, the traditional psychological approach to mental health encouraged men to be masculine and women to be feminine. Bem pioneered in equating androgyny with mental health and created an instrument to measure androgynous traits: the Bem Sex Role Inventory (1974).

Noting that research appeared to indicate high masculinity and high femininity had negative consequences, Bem hypothesized that an individual with both masculine and feminine traits would be able to function more flexibly than sex-stereotyped individuals. Initially, androgyny attracted a great deal of favorable comment. Part of its appeal may have been the fact that the concept of androgyny emerged just as more and more women were beginning to associate traditional sex-role stereotypes with discrimination in the marketplace.

The popular interpretation of androgyny as synonymous with a gender-free world in which individuals could realize their potential without sex-role restrictions found a great deal of favor not only among feminists but also among psychologists and clinicians. Over one hundred studies were carried out between 1976 and 1984 relating various measures of mental health and androgyny (Bem, 1985). Androgyny at first glance appeared to

204 be so beneficial that some clinicians began to discuss how to "androgynize" exclusively masculine or feminine clients (Zeldow, 1982, p. 401).

Despite this early success, androgyny quickly fell from favor in the 1980s because of methodological and conceptual problems. In a comprehensive survey using meta-analysis, Marylee Taylor and Judith Hall (1982) found that certain "masculine" traits were a better predictor of psychological well-being than was androgyny. Morover, on reconsideration, some feminist scholars concluded that Bem's theory implied that women needed to become more like men in order to function better. Bernice Lott was one of those who rejected the notion that there are separate feminine and masculine ways of behaving. "To label some behaviors as feminine and some as masculine," she charged, "is to reinforce verbal habits which undermine the possibility of degenderizing behavior" (1981, p. 178).

Interestingly, Bem has begun to have second thoughts about her earlier research. In a revision of her theory, she agrees with many of her critics who pointed out that masculinity and femininity are not independent variables. In her new work on gender-schema theory, Bem now argues that these traits are the product of a belief system that organizes our world into masculine and feminine components (Bem, 1985).

The following two articles by Bem demonstrate how research in pursuit of one objective may be reshaped to serve the needs of a new theory. Is androgyny still a worthwhile goal or does Bem's new gender-schema theory better serve the goal articulated in her earlier article on androgyny: "to help free the human personality from the restricting prison of sex-role stereotyping"?

References

Bem, S. L. (1974). The measurement of psychological androgyny. *Journal of Consulting and Clinical Psychology, 42*, 155–62.

Bem, S. L. (1985). Androgyny and gender schema theory: A conceptual and empirical integration. In T. B. Sonderegger (Ed.), *Nebraska symposium on motivation, 1984: The psychology of gender, Current Theory and Research in Motivation, 32*, 179–226. Lincoln: University of Nebraska Press.

Jung, C. G. (1953). Anima and animus. In *Two essays on analytical psychology: Collected Works of C. G. Jung* (pp. 186–209). New York: Bollingen Foundation, Pantheon Books.

Lott, B. (1981). A feminist critique of androgyny: Towards the elimination of gender attributions for learned behavior. In C. Mayo & N. M. Henley (Eds.), *Gender and Nonverbal Behavior* (pp. 171–80). New York: Springer-Verlag.

Taylor, M. C. & Hall, J. A. (1982). Psychological androgyny: Theories, methods and conclusions. *Psychological Bullletin, 92* (2), 347–66.

Zeldow, P. B. (1982). The androgynous vision: A critical examination. *Bulletin of the Menninger Clinic, 46* (5), 401–13.

Additional Reading

Bem, S. L. (1984). Reply to Morgan and Ayim. *Signs: Journal of Women in Culture and Society, 10* (1), 197–99.

Bem, S. L. (1987). Gender schema theory and the romantic tradition. In P. Shaver and C. Hendrick (Eds.), Sex and Gender. *Review of Personality and Social Psychology, 7*, 25–71.

Condry, J. C. (1984). Gender identity and social competence. *Sex Roles, 11* (5/6), 485–511.

Cook, E. P. (1985). *Psychological Androgyny.* New York: Pergamon Press.

Kravetz, D., & Jones, L. E. (1981). Androgyny as a standard of mental health. *American Journal of Orthopsychiatry, 51* (3), 502–09.

Marsh, H. W., & Myers, M. (1986). Masculinity, femininity, and androgyny; A methodological and theoretical critique. *Sex Roles, 14* (7/8), 397–430.

Morawski, J. (1987). The troubled quest for masculinity, femininity, and androgyny. In P. Shaver and C. Hendrick (Eds.), Sex and Gender. *Review of Personality and Social Psychology, 7*, 44–69.

Morgan, K. P. & Ayim, M. (1984). Comments on Bem's 'gender schema theory' and its implications for child development: Raising gender-aschematic children in a gender-schematic society. *Signs: Journal of Women in Culture and Society, 10* (1), 188–96.

Ruble, T. L. (1983). Sex sterotypes: Issues of change in the 1970s. *Sex Roles, 9* (3), 397–402.

Tinsley, E. G., Sullivan-Guest, S., & McGuire, J. (1984). Feminine sex role and depression in middle-aged women. *Sex Roles, 11* (1/2), 25–32.

Werner, P. D., & LaRussa, G. W. (1985). Persistence and change in sex-role stereotypes. *Sex Roles, 12* (9/10), 1089–1100.

Yes

Probing the Promise of Androgyny

SANDRA LIPSITZ BEM

I consider myself an empirical scientist, and yet my interest in sex roles is and has always been frankly political. My hypotheses have derived from no formal theory but rather from a set of strong intuitions about the debilitating effects of sex-role stereotyping, and my major purpose has always been a feminist one: to help free the human personality from the restricting prison of sex-role stereotyping and to develop a conception of mental health which is free from culturally imposed definitions of masculinity and femininity.

But political passion does not persuade, and unless one is a novelist or a poet, one's intuitions are not typically compelling to others. Thus, because I *am* an empirical scientist, I have chosen to utilize the only legitimated medium of persuasion which is available to me: the medium of empirical data. What I should like to do in this paper is to summarize the data on psychological androgyny that we have collected over the last four years, and, in addition, to raise even deeper questions about the traditional conception of sexual identity and its centrality in the definition of the healthy personality, questions which go well beyond my current data.

The ideal or healthy personality has traditionally included a concept of sexual identity with three basic components: (1) a sexual preference for members of the opposite sex; (2) a sex-role identity as either masculine or feminine, depending upon one's gender; and (3) a gender identity, that is, a secure sense of one's maleness or femaleness (cf., Green, 1974). I should like to comment in this paper on each of these three components in turn.

"Probing the Promise of Androgyny" and "Beyond Androgyny: Some Presumptuous Prescriptions for a Liberated Sexual Identity" are two titles for the same article which was originally presented by Sandra Lipsitz Bem as the keynote address for an American Psychological Association–National Institute of Mental Health Conference on the Research Needs of Women, Madison, Wisconsin, May 31, 1975. Copyright © 1976 by Sandra L. Bem. Reprinted with permission of the author. The proceedings of the whole conference were published by J. Sherman and F. Denmark (Eds.), *The Psychology of Women: Future Directions in Research.* New York: Psychological Dimensions, Inc., 1978.
Dr. Bem is Professor of Psychology and Women's Studies, Cornell University, Ithaca, New York.

Sexual Preference

With respect to the first component, that of sexual preference, my remarks can be brief. Let me simply assert, along with the proponents of gay liberation and the recently enlightened American Psychiatric Association, that one's sexual preferences ought ultimately to be considered orthogonal to any concept of mental health or ideal personality. Let us begin to use the terms *homosexual* and *heterosexual* to describe acts rather than persons and to entertain the possibility that compulsive exclusivity in one's sexual responsiveness, whether homosexual or heterosexual, may be the product of a repressive society which forces us to label ourselves as one or the other.

Sex-Role Identity

I turn now to the concept of sex-role identity, a concept which has traditionally been conceptualized in terms of masculinity and femininity. Both historically and cross-culturally, masculinity and femininity have represented complementary domains of positive traits and behaviors. Different theorists have different labels for these domains. According to Parsons (Parsons & Bales, 1955), masculinity has been associated with an instrumental orientation, a cognitive focus on getting the job done or the problem solved, whereas femininity has been associated with an expressive orientation, an affective concern for the welfare of others and the harmony of the group. Similarly, Bakan (1966) has suggested that masculinity is associated with an "agentic" orientation, a concern for oneself as an individual, whereas femininity is associated with a "communal" orientation, a concern for the relationship between oneself and others. Finally, Erikson's (1964) anatomical distinction between "inner" (female) and "outer" (male) space represents an analogue to a quite similar psychological distinction between a masculine "fondness for what works and for what man can make, whether it helps to build or to destroy" and a more "ethical" feminine commitment to "resourcefulness in peacekeeping and devotion in healing."

My own research has focused on the concept of psychological androgyny. As such, it has been predicated on the assumption that it is possible, in principle, for an individual to be both masculine and feminine, both instrumental and expressive, both agentic and communal, depending upon the situational appropriateness of these various modalities; and even

208   that it is possible for an individual to blend these complementary modalities in a single act, being able, for example, to fire an employee if the circumstances warrant it, but to do so with sensitivity for the human emotion that such an act inevitably produces.

The possibility that a single individual can embody both masculinity and femininity has, of course, been expressed by others as well. Jung (1953) described the *anima* and *animus* which he believed to be present in us all, and more recently, Bakan (1966) has argued that viability—both for the individual and for society—depends on the successful integration of both agency and communion. Moreover, the concept of androgyny itself can now be found not only in the psychological literature (e.g., Berzins & Welling, 1974; Block, 1973; Pleck, 1975; Spence, Helmreich, & Stapp, 1975), but in the literature of other disciplines as well (e.g., Bazin & Freeman, 1974; Gelpi, 1974; Harris, 1974; Heilbrun, 1973; Secor, 1974; Stimpson, 1974).

And yet, although I believe that it is *possible* for people to be both masculine and feminine, I also believe that traditional sex roles prevent this possibility from ever becoming a reality for many individuals. Over the last few years, the Women's Liberation Movement has made us all aware of the many ways that we, both men and women, have become locked into our respective sex roles. As women, we have become aware of the fact that we are afraid to express our anger, to assert our preferences, to trust our own judgment, to take control of situations. As men, we have become aware of the fact that we are afraid to cry, to touch one another, to own up to our fears and weaknesses.

But there have been very little data within psychology to give legitimacy to these experiential truths. In many ways, my goal over the last few years has been to gather some of that legitimizing data, to try to demonstrate that traditional sex roles do restrict behavior in important human ways.

Although no previous research bears on this hypothesis directly, a review of the relevant literature nevertheless corroborates our underlying assumption that a high level of sex-typing may not be desirable. For example, high femininity in females has consistently been correlated with high anxiety, low self-esteem, and low social acceptance (e.g., Cosentino & Heilbrun, 1964; Gall, 1969; Gray, 1957; Sears, 1970; Webb, 1963); and, although high maculinity in males has been correlated during adolescence with better psychological adjustment (Mussen, 1961), it has been correlated during adulthood with high anxiety, high neuroticism, and low self-acceptance (Harford et al., 1967; Mussen, 1962). In addition, greater intellectual development has been correlated quite consistently with cross sex-typing, i.e., with masculinity in girls and with femininity in boys. Boys and girls who are more sex-typed have been found to have lower overall intelligence, *209* lower spatial ability, and lower creativity (Maccoby, 1966).

The point, of course, is that the two domains of masculinity and femininity are both fundamental. In a modern complex society like ours, an adult clearly has to be able to look out for himself and to get things done. But an adult also has to be able to relate to other human beings as people, to be sensitive to their needs and to be concerned about their welfare, as well as to be able to depend on them for emotional support. Limiting a person's ability to respond in one or the other of these two complementary domains thus seems tragically and unnecessarily destructive of human potential.

In addition, it would also seem to be the case that masculinity and femininity may each become negative and even destructive when they are represented in extreme and unadulterated form. Thus, extreme femininity, untempered by a sufficient concern for one's own needs as an individual, may produce dependency and self-denial, just as extreme masculinity, untempered by a sufficient concern for the needs of others, may produce arrogance and exploitation. As Bakan (1966) has put it, the fundamental task of every organism is to "try to mitigate agency with communion." Thus, for fully effective and healthy human functioning, both masculinity and femininity must each be tempered by the other, and the two must be integrated into a more balanced, a more fully human, a truly androgynous personality. An androgynous personality would thus represent the very best of what masculinity and femininity have each come to represent, and the more negative exaggerations of masculinity and femininity would tend to be cancelled out.

The Bem Sex-Role Inventory

With this model of perfection in mind, I then moved to the more mundane task of trying to bring the concept of androgyny down to empirical reality. I began by constructing the Bem Sex-Role Inventory (or BSRI), a paper-and-pencil instrument which permits us to distinguish androgynous individuals from those with more sex-typed self concepts.

Unlike most previous masculinity-femininity scales, the BSRI treats masculinity and femininity as two orthogonal dimensions rather than as two ends of a single dimension (see Constantinople, 1974, for a critique of previous sex-role inventories). Moreover, masculinity and femininity each represent *positive* domains of behavior. Too often femininity has been defined simply as the absence of masculinity rather than as a positive dimension in its own right, a practice which may itself be partially respon-

210 sible for the negative picture of the feminine woman that emerges in the psychological literature. For once, I wanted to give the feminine woman an equal chance to be no "sicker" than anyone else.

Specifically, the BSRI consists of twenty masculine personality characteristics (e.g., ambitious, self-reliant, independent, assertive) and twenty feminine personality characteristics (e.g., affectionate, gentle, understanding, sensitive to the needs of others). I chose the particular characteristics that I did because they were all rated by both males and females as being significantly more desirable in American society for one sex than for the other. The BSRI also contains twenty neutral characteristics (e.g., truthful, happy, conceited, unsystematic) which serve as filler items. All sixty characteristics are shown in table 7.1.[1]

When taking the BSRI, a person is asked to indicate on a scale from 1 ("Never or almost never true") to 7 ("Always or almost always true") how well each characteristic describes himself or herself. The degree of sex-role stereotyping in the person's self concept is then defined as Student's t-ratio for the difference between the total points assigned to the feminine and masculine attributes, respectively. We use the t-ratio rather than a simple difference score primarily because it allows us to ask whether a person's masculinity and femininity scores differ significantly from one another, and if they do ($t \geq 2.025, p < .05$), to characterize that person as significantly sex-typed or sex-reversed. Thus, if a person's masculinity score is significantly higher than his or her femininity score, that person is said to have a masculine sex role, and if a person's femininity score is significantly higher than his or her masculinity score, that person is said to have a feminine sex role. In contrast, if a person's masculinity and femininity scores are approximately equal ($t \leq 1$, n.s.), that person is said to have an androgynous sex role. An androgynous sex role thus represents the equal endorsement of both masculine and feminine personality characteristics, a balance, as it were, between masculinity and femininity. Normative data on a sample of over two thousand undergraduates from both a university and a community college indicate that approximately one-third of both popula-

---

1. In attempting to balance the overall social desirability of the masculine and feminine adjectives, I was surprised to discover that many feminine adjectives were judged to be more socially desirable "for a woman" than were any masculine adjectives "for a man." This would seem to contradict the frequently reported finding in the literature that masculine attributes are more socially desirable than feminine ones. It should be noted, however, that my judges rated the social desirability of each adjective as it applied to a particular sex. In the absence of such specification, perhaps judges implicitly picture a male and make their judgments accordingly, thereby lowering the desirability of all feminine attributes. In order to equate the overall social desirability of the feminine and masculine adjectives, I was therefore forced to include a few feminine adjectives which were somewhat lower in social desirability (e.g., gullible), and thereby to increase somewhat the variance of the social desirability ratings within the set of feminine adjectives.

Table 7.1: The Masculine, Feminine, and Neutral Items on the BSRI

Masculine items	Feminine items	Neutral items
49. Acts as a leader	11. Affectionate	51. Adaptable
46. Aggressive	5. Cheerful	36. Conceited
58. Ambitious	50. Childlike	9. Conscientious
22. Analytical	32. Compassionate	60. Conventional
13. Assertive	53. Does not use harsh language	45. Friendly
10. Athletic	35. Eager to soothe hurt feelings	15. Happy
55. Competitive	20. Feminine	3. Helpful
4. Defends own beliefs	14. Flatterable	48. Inefficient
37. Dominant	59. Gentle	24. Jealous
19. Forceful	47. Gullible	39. Likable
25. Has leadership abilities	56. Loves children	6. Moody
7. Independent	17. Loyal	21. Reliable
52. Individualistic	26. Sensitive to the needs of others	30. Secretive
31. Makes decisions easily	8. Shy	33. Sincere
40. Masculine	38. Soft spoken	42. Solemn
1. Self-reliant	23. Sympathetic	57. Tactful
34. Self-sufficient	44. Tender	12. Theatrical
16. Strong personality	29. Understanding	27. Truthful
43. Willing to take a stand	41. Warm	18. Unpredictable
28. Willing to take risks	2. Yielding	54. Unsystematic

Note: The number preceding each item reflects the position of each adjective as it actually appears on the Inventory. A subject indicates how well each item describes himself or herself on the following scale: (1) Never or almost never true; (2) Usually not true; (3) Sometimes but infrequently true; (4) Occasionally true; (5) Often true; (6) Usually true; (7) Always true or almost always true.

tions can be classified as significantly sex-typed, and another third as androgynous. Fewer than 10 percent can be classified as sex-reversed.[2]

Psychometric analyses on the BSRI indicate that it is quite satisfactory as a measuring instrument (Bem, 1974). As anticipated, the masculinity and femininity scores turned out to be empirically as well as conceptually independent (average $r = -.03$), thereby vindicating our decision to design an inventory that would not treat masculinity and femininity as two

2. A number of alternative methods for scoring androgyny have been suggested by other investigators (e.g., Spence, Helmreich, and Stapp, 1975; Strahan, 1975). The major question seems to involve whether it is appropriate to characterize as androgynous only those individuals who score high on both masculinity and femininity, or whether those who score low on both should be so characterized as well. We are currently in the process of reanalyzing our behavioral data in an attempt to answer this question empirically, but it is worth noting that only 1 percent of the undergraduates we have tested fall below the midpoint on both the 7-point masculinity and femininity scales. Thus, on the two college campuses we have tested, there are very few low-low scorers in any *absolute* sense of that term.

212 ends of a single dimension. Moreover, the *t*-ratio itself is internally consistent (average $\alpha = .86$), reliable over a four-week interval (average $r = .93$), and uncorrelated with the tendency to describe oneself in a socially desirable direction (average $r = -.06$).

The Avoidance of Cross-Sex Behavior

Once the BSRI was in hand, we were then in a position to ask whether traditional sex roles actually do lead some people to restrict their behavior in accordance with sex-role stereotypes. Specifically, do masculine men and feminine women actively avoid activities just because those activities happen to be stereotyped as more appropriate for the other sex; and, if they have to perform cross-sex activity for some reason, does it cause them discomfort to do so? In other words, is cross-sex behavior motivationally problematic for the sex-typed individual, or would he or she be perfectly willing to engage in such behavior if the situation were structured to encourage it?

In order to find out, Ellen Lenney and I designed a study in which many of the more obvious external barriers to cross-sex behavior had been removed (Bem & Lenney, 1976). Thus, both masculine and feminine activities were explicitly available to all the subjects; it was made clear that we did not care how well they could do each activity or, indeed, if they had ever done the activity before; and the less sex-appropriate activities were always the more highly rewarded.

Subjects were told that we were preparing to do a study to find out whether people make different personality judgments about an individual as a function of the particular activity that he or she happens to be seen performing, and that we therefore needed pictures of the same person performing many different activities. The activities were arranged in pairs, and subjects were asked to select the one activity from each pair that they would prefer to perform during the photography session which was to follow. For example, one pair asked female subjects whether they would rather "prepare a baby bottle by mixing powdered formula with milk" for 2¢ or "oil squeaky hinges on a metal box" for 4¢. Although it was not made explicit, twenty of the activities were stereotypically masculine (e.g., "Nail two boards together"; "Attach artificial bait to a fishing hook"), twenty were stereotypically feminine (e.g., "Iron cloth napkins"; "Wind a package of yarn into a ball"), and twenty were stereotypically neutral (e.g., "Play with a yo-yo"; "Peel oranges").

Of the thirty pairs, fifteen required the subject to choose between activities which differed in their sex-role connotations. Of these, five pitted neutral activities against masculine ones, five pitted neutral activities against feminine ones, and five pitted masculine and feminine activities against each other. In all of the sex-role conflict pairs, however, it was the less sex-appropriate activity which always paid more. In the remaining fifteen pairs, both activities were either masculine, feminine, or neutral, and one activity was arbitrarily assigned to be the higher paying. These control pairs served primarily as a baseline measure of each subject's responsiveness to the differences in payment, and they also guaranteed that a minimum number of masculine, feminine, and neutral activities would be chosen by every subject.

In an attempt to get the purest possible measure of preference, unconfounded by the effects of competence at or familiarity with the various activities, great care was taken to assure the subjects that we were not at all interested in how well they could perform each activity or, indeed, if they had ever done the activity before. For example, they were explicitly told that they would be given only one or two minutes for each activity, not necessarily enough time for the activity to be completed, and that all we really wanted was for them to become sufficiently involved in each activity for a convincing photograph to be taken. They were also assured that simple written instructions would be available for each of the activities that they selected. In addition, in order to prevent subjects from becoming overly self-conscious about how their pictures would look, they were also assured that the later study would be done at a different university and that no one they knew would ever be likely to see their pictures. Finally, no emphasis whatever was placed on having the pictures reflect the "true" personality of the individual subject. If anything, what was implied was that we needed each subject to perform as wide a variety of different kinds of activities as possible.

As anticipated, the results indicated that sex-typed subjects were significantly more stereotyped in their choices than androgynous or sex-reversed subjects, who did not differ significantly from one another. In other words, the masculine man and the feminine woman were significantly more likely to select their own sex's activities and to reject the other sex's activities, even though such choices cost them money and even though we tried to make it as easy as we could for the subject to select cross-sex activity.

In order to find out whether sex-typed subjects would also experience greater discomfort if they had no choice but to perform cross-sex activity, the subjects then proceeded to perform three masculine, three feminine, and three neutral activities while the experimenter pretended to photograph them, and then indicated how they felt after each activity on a series of rating scales. Specifically, subjects indicated on a seven-point scale how "masculine" (for males) or "feminine" (for females), how "attractive,"

214 how "likeable," how "nervous," and how "peculiar" they had felt while performing each activity. They also indicated how much they had enjoyed each activity.

The results indicated that sex-typed subjects felt significantly worse than androgynous or sex-reversed subjects, who, again, did not differ significantly from one another. That is, it was the masculine men and the feminine women who experienced the most discomfort and who felt the worst about themselves after performing cross-sex activities. Thus, it would appear that cross-sex activity is problematic for sex-typed individuals, and that traditional sex roles do produce an unnecessary and perhaps even dysfunctional pattern of avoidance for many people.

Armed with this demonstration that sex-role stereotyping restricts simple, everyday behaviors, we can now inquire into whether such stereotyping also constricts the individual's ability to function effectively in more profound domains as well. Is the masculine male deficient in the domains of expressiveness and communion? Does the feminine female have but limited access to the domains of instrumentality and agency? It is to these broader questions that the bulk of my research has been addressed, and it is to these that we now turn.

Independence and Nurturance

We began by designing a pair of studies on independence and nurturance (Bem, 1975). The first was designed to tap the "masculine" domain of independence. It utilized a standard conformity paradigm to test the hypothesis that masculine and androgynous subjects would both remain more independent from social pressure than feminine subjects. The second study was designed to tap the "feminine" domain of nurturance. By offering subjects the opportunity to interact with a tiny kitten, it tested the hypothesis that feminine and androgyonous subjects would both be more nurturant or playful than masculine subjects. Taken together, these two studies offer one test of the hypothesis that nonandrogynous subjects would do well only when the situation calls for behavior which is congruent with their self-definition as masculine or feminine, whereas androgynous subjects would do well regardless of the sex-role stereotype of the particular behavior in question. That is, they would perform as well as masculine subjects on the masculine task, and they would perform as well as feminine subjects on the feminine task.

In the study of independence, which Karen Rook and Robyn Stickney helped to design, we brought four males or four females into the laboratory for what they thought was an experiment on humor. We placed the subjects in individual booths equipped with microphones and earphones and showed them a series of cartoons which we asked them to rate for funniness. The cartoons used in this study had been previously rated by a set of independent judges, with half of them judged to be very funny and half judged to be very unfunny.

As each new cartoon appeared on the screen, the subjects heard the experimenter call on each person in turn for his or her rating. Although the subjects believed that they were hearing each others' voices, in fact, what they were actually hearing was a tape recording. In order to induce conformity, the tape included thirty-six trials during which all three taped voices gave false responses, agreeing that a particular cartoon was funny when it wasn't, and vice versa. We gave subjects this somewhat subjective task of judging cartoons for funniness—rather than length of lines or the like—so that false norms might impose pressure to conform without appearing to be bizarre.

As expected, the masculine and androgynous subjects did not differ significantly from one another, and both were significantly more independent than the feminine subjects. This was true for both males and females.

In the study of nurturance, which Jenny Jacobs helped me to design, subjects came to the laboratory individually for an experiment described as a study of mood. The subjects were informed that we wanted to know how different activities would affect their moods and that we would ask them to perform a number of different activities and to rate their moods after each.

For one of the activities, we brought a kitten into the room and asked the subjects to interact with it in any way that they wished. We placed the kitten into a child's playpen which had been completely enclosed by chicken wire, and we showed the subjects how to open the playpen so that they could take the kitten out if they wanted to. The room also contained various toys that a kitten might enjoy, for example, a pencil, a ball of yarn, etc. The subject was left alone in the room with the kitten for five minutes while we observed from behind a one-way mirror. The main behavior that we measured in this situation was how much the subject *touched* the kitten. At the end of the five-minute period, we also asked the subject to indicate how much he or she had enjoyed playing with the kitten.

Later in the experiment, we again placed the kitten into its playpen, and we gave subjects ten minutes to do anything in the room that they wished. They could play with the kitten, or they could read magazines, work puzzles, play with a three-dimensional tilting maze, or whatever. Once again, we observed them from behind the one-way mirror to see how much they played with the kitten when they didn't have to.

As expected, the feminine and androgynous men did not differ significantly from one another, and both were significantly more responsive to the

216 kitten than the masculine men. Thus, the male data confirmed our hypothesis. But the female data did not. As expected, the androgynous women, like the androgynous men, were quite responsive to the kitten, but the feminine women were significantly less responsive, and the masculine women fell ambiguously in between.

Considering these two studies together, we see that, as predicted, only the androgynous subjects, both male and female, displayed a high level of masculine independence when under pressure to conform as well as a high level of feminine playfulness or nurturance when given the opportunity to interact with a tiny kitten. Thus, only the androgynous subjects were *both* masculine and feminine.

In contrast, the nonandrogynous subjects all seemed to show a behavioral deficit of one sort or another. For example, nonandrogynous males did well only when the behavior was congruent with their self-definition as masculine or feminine. Thus, the masculine males were low in feminine nurturance, and the feminine males were low in masculine independence.

Interestingly, the results for the nonandrogynous females were more complex. As we had anticipated, the masculine women were quite independent, but they were not significantly less responsive to the kitten than the androgynous women. Hence, we cannot conclude that the masculine woman has necessarily been impaired in her expressive functioning. Rather, it is the feminine woman who, at this juncture, appears to be the most restricted. Thus, not only was she low in independence but she was also low in her nurturance toward the kitten. Of course, it is possible that feminine women might simply find animals unappealing for some reason, and that they could therefore be expected to display much greater nurturance if they were given the opportunity to interact with another human being rather than with a kitten. But the possibility must also be considered that feminine women may simply be more inhibited than we had initially anticipated, and that their inhibition may extend beyond the instrumental domain.

This asymmetry between the males and the females was not anticipated in our initial hypotheses, which were, of course, completely symmetric with respect to gender. But as we shall see below, further research has only served to confirm the asymmetry and to suggest that traditional sex roles are constricting the two sexes in fundamentally different ways.

Further Explorations of the Expressive Domain

Why were the feminine women so unresponsive to the kitten? Do they simply find animals unappealing for some reason? Was there some other feature of the situation which inhibited them? Or, contrary to conventional wisdom, are they simply not competent in the expressive domain?

In order to give the feminine women a fairer test of their expressive functioning, we carried out two additional studies. Because we wished to clarify whether the initial failure of the feminine women to respond nurturantly was unique to animals, both of these studies were designed to be genuinely interpersonal situations where the subject's nurturant sympathies would be more likely to be aroused. In addition, because it also seemed possible that feminine women might be insufficiently assertive to act out their nurturant feelings if the situation required that they take responsibility for initiating the interaction with their partner, the second study was designed not only to be genuinely interpersonal, but also to place the subject into a more passive role which would require very little initiative or improvisation and where there would be virtually no ambiguity about what a subject *ought* to do if he or she wished to be nurturant. Accordingly, the first study gave the subject the opportunity to interact with a human baby, and the second required the subject to listen to a fellow student who openly shared some of his or her unhappy emotions (Bem, Martyna, and Watson, 1976).

In the baby study, which Carol Watson and Bart Astor helped me to design, each subject was left alone with a five-month-old baby for a period of ten minutes with the understanding that we would be observing the infant's reactions to a stranger through the one-way mirror. In fact, we were measuring the subject's responsiveness to the baby. Using time-sampling procedures, we measured such things as how much the subject smiled at the baby, talked to the baby, touched the baby, etc., and then we derived a global measure of the subject's responsiveness by adding together various combinations of these behaviors.

Parenthetically, I would like to note that the study involved fifteen different babies, each of whom got to play with one representative of each of the six different sex roles. That way, no baby was required to be "mauled" by more than six undergraduates, and most parents were eager to have their children participate and to join us behind the one-way mirror to watch the interaction. Each baby was dressed in sex-neutral clothing and was introduced to half of the subjects as "David" and to a counterbalanced half as "Lisa." Naturally, great care was taken to protect the health and well-being of the babies who participated. For example, all subjects were urged to cancel their appointments if they felt the slightest bit ill; all of the toys and lab coats were thoroughly washed before every session; and the baby's mother or father was explicitly instructed to ask that the session be terminated if the baby ever seemed to be particularly distressed. In addition, each baby was "interviewed" before the study began to make certain that he or she was not yet afraid of strangers.

Once again, the results for men were exactly as we had predicted.

218 Feminine and androgynous men did not differ significantly from one another, and both were significantly more responsive to the baby than the masculine men. But alas, there were simply no significant behavioral differences which emerged among the women. Interestingly, the feminine women did indicate on a questionnaire that they were significantly more interested in having an affectionate relationship with the baby than any of the other women, but as noted above, there was no evidence that the feminine women actually behaved any more affectionately toward the baby than anyone else. Thus, the feminine women did not display any particular deficiency in the expressive domain, but neither did they distinguish themselves by being particularly nurturant or responsive.

In surveying the pattern of data yielded by the feminine women, it occurred to me that both the kitten and the baby can be thought of as relatively passive stimuli, stimuli that required the subject to initiate and sustain the interaction. It therefore seemed possible that feminine women might simply be insufficiently assertive to act out their nurturant feelings in a situation where they must take responsibility for initiating and sustaining the interaction, and that they might display much greater nurturance if they were permitted to play a more passive or responsive role in the interaction. Accordingly, the final study that I shall describe was designed to evoke sympathetic and supportive listening on the part of the subject, but without at the same time requiring the subject to play an active or initiating role in the interaction.

In this study, which Wendy Martyna and Dorothy Ginsberg helped to design, two same-sex subjects (one of whom was actually an experimental assistant) participated in a study of "the acquaintance process." They appeared to draw lots to determine which of the two would take the role of "talker" and which the role of "listener," but in fact, the experimental assistant always served as the talker and the subject always served as the listener.

The talker began with some relatively impersonal background information, e.g., hometown, number of siblings, etc. But he or she soon became more personal. In general, the talker described himself or herself as a recent and rather lonely transfer student to Stanford. He or she talked about missing old friends, about how difficult it was to make new friends now that cliques had already become established, and about spending much more time alone than he or she really wanted to. In short, the talker described feelings common to many new transfer students. The talker did not seem neurotic, just somewhat isolated, and rather pleased to have this opportunity to share some of his or her feelings with another person. In contrast, the subject—as listener—was allowed to ask questions and to make comments, but was instructed never to shift the focus of the conversation to himself or herself.

We observed the conversation from behind a one-way mirror and recorded a number of the subjects' behaviors, such as how much responsiveness they showed in their facial expression, how many times they nodded, how many comments they made, and how positively they reacted to the talker's implicit request for further contact. After the conversation, we also asked subjects to indicate how concerned they felt about the talker as a person, and we asked both the talker and the experimenter to rate how nurturant the subject had seemed to them. We then derived a global responsiveness score for each subject by averaging together these various measures.

Once again, the male data confirmed our hypotheses. For the third time in our research on the expressive domain, feminine and androgynous males did not differ significantly from one another, and both were significantly more responsive than masculine males. And for the first time in our entire research program, the feminine females apparently found a situation tailored for their talents, for they were the most responsive listeners of all. Specifically, the feminine females were significantly more responsive than anyone else, the masculine males were significantly less responsive than anyone else, and the remaining four groups all clustered together at about the same level.

Summing Up

I believe that we are now in a position to state some of the things we have learned about androgyny and sex-typing. I shall begin with the men because they're easy. Consider, first, the androgynous male. He performs spectacularly. He shuns no behavior just because our culture happens to label it as female, and his competence crosses both the instrumental and the expressive domains. Thus, he stands firm in his opinions, he cuddles kittens and bounces babies, and he has a sympathetic ear for someone in distress. Clearly, he is a liberated companion for the most feminist among us.

In contrast, the feminine male does well only in the expressive domain, and the masculine male does well only in the instrumental domain. Because at least one-third of college-age males would be classified as masculine under our definition, it is particularly distressing that the masculine males were less responsive in all of the diverse situations that we designed to evoke their more tender emotions, to tug, if only a little, on their heartstrings. I do not know, of course, whether the masculine men were simply unwilling to act out any tender emotions that they might have been experiencing, or whether their emotionality was sufficiently inhibited so that they did not readily experience the emotions we sought to tap. But in either case, their partners in the interaction received less emotional sustenance than they would have otherwise.

We cannot conclude, of course, that masculinity inhibits all tender emotionality in the masculine male. Obviously, none of the laboratory situations that we devised was as powerful as, say, having a child who becomes ill or a friend who seems about to have a nervous breakdown. We can conclude, however, that their thresholds for tender emotionality are higher than all the other men and women we have observed. And that, I believe, is sufficient cause for concern.

Let us turn now to the more complex pattern of results shown by the women. Like their male counterparts, androgynous women also fare well in our studies. They, too, willingly perform behaviors that our culture has labeled as unsuitable for their sex, and they, too, function effectively in both the instrumental and the expressive domains.

Pleasantly enough, the masculine women appear to join their an-drogynous sisters in functioning effectively, for they show no particular deficiency in either domain. As anticipated, the masculine women did not shun cross-sex activity, and they maintained their independence under pressure to conform. But, contrary to our initial hypotheses, they also showed no striking deficits in their ability to relate to the kitten or to the baby or to the lonely student. It is true, of course, that both the masculine and the androgynous women were significantly less responsive to the lonely student than the feminine women, but as we shall see below, it may be the extreme responsiveness of the feminine women, like the extreme unrespon-siveness of the masculine men, which requires explanation. This similarity of response between the sex-reversed and androgynous women is in sharp contrast to the results for men, and it suggests to us that growing up female in our society may be sufficient to give virtually all women at least an adequate threshold of emotional responsiveness. It further suggests that what differentiates women from one another is not the domain of ex-pressiveness or communion, but whether their sense of instrumentality or agency has been sufficiently nourished as well.

And it is this thought that brings us finally to the feminine woman. She does not willingly perform cross-sex behaviors; she reports discomfort when required to do so; she yields to pressures for conformity; she does not initiate play with a kitten; and she does not distinguish herself in that most traditional of all female behaviors, the nurturance of a human infant. But she does give extraordinary support to a lonely sister who asks for nothing more than a sympathetic ear.

What this pattern suggests to me is that the major effect of femininity in women—untempered by a sufficient level of masculinity—may not be to inhibit instrumental or masculine behaviors per se, but to inhibit any behavior at all in a situation where the "appropriate" behavior is left ambiguous or unspecified.

Thus, although it is possible that the feminine women were particularly responsive to the lonely student because she alone was uniquely able to arouse their nurturant sympathies, it is striking to me that the feminine women distinguished themselves in the one situation where their behavior was sufficiently constrained by the experimenter's instruction that there was little initiative or improvisation possible and virtually no ambiguity about what a subject *ought* to do if he or she wished to be responsive. In contrast, all of our other studies have left the subjects much more to their own devices with regard to the particular behavior that they were "supposed" to initiate.

This leads me to speculate that the feminine woman may be overly concerned about the possible negative consequences of her behavior, regardless of whether that behavior is masculine-instrumental or feminine-expressive. Hence, when it is unclear whether a particular behavior will yield a positive evaluation or a positive outcome, feminine women become inhibited. Either they withdraw from the situation or, if withdrawal is not feasible, they engage in the "safest" behavior or as little behavior as possible. Their goal in such a situation is to avoid doing anything that might get them into trouble, embarrass them or bring any kind of negative evaluation upon themselves. In other words, they take no risks; they play it safe. Conversely, when it is quite clear what behavior or behaviors will produce a positive outcome or a positive evaluation—as in the interaction with the lonely student—then feminine women become very active and do very well. This interpretation is not inconsistent with previous findings noted earlier that femininity in females is typically associated with high anxiety and poor social adjustment.

These speculations about the feminine woman conclude what I think I have learned up to this point about the evils of sex-typing and the potential promise of androgyny. As I stated earlier, however, the major purpose of my research has always been a political one: to help free the human personality from the restricting prison of sex-role stereotyping and to develop a conception of mental health that is free from culturally imposed definitions of masculinity and femininity.

Certainly, androgyny seems to represent the fulfillment of this goal. For if there is a moral to the concept of psychological androgyny, it is that *behavior* should have no gender. But there is an irony here, for the concept

222   of androgyny contains an inner contradiction and hence the seeds of its own destruction. Thus, as the etymology of the word implies, the concept of androgyny necessarily presupposes that the concepts of masculinity and femininity themselves have distinct and substantive content. But to the extent that the androgynous message is absorbed by the culture, the concepts of masculinity and femininity will cease to have such content, and the distinctions to which they refer will blur into invisibility. Thus, when androgyny becomes a reality, the *concept* of androgyny will have been transcended. (See Rebecca, Hefner, & Oleshansky, 1976, and Hefner, Rebecca, & Oleshansky, 1975, for a discussion of the concept of sex-role transcendence.)

Gender Identity

As I noted in the introduction to this paper, the ideal or healthy personality has traditionally included a concept of sexual identity with three basic components: (1) a sexual preference for members of the opposite sex; (2) a sex-role identity as either masculine or feminine, depending upon one's gender; and (3) a gender identity, i.e., a secure sense of one's maleness or femaleness.

In discussing the first two of these components, it is clear that my contribution has been largely iconoclastic. Thus, I have proposed that we reject sexual preference as relevant to anything other than the individual's own love or pleasure. And I have all but said that the best sex-role identity is no sex-role identity. I think I am prepared to be somewhat less cavalier with the concept of gender identity.

For even if people were all to become psychologically androgynous, the world would continue to consist of two sexes, male and female would continue to be one of the first and most basic dichotomies that young children would learn, and no one would grow up ignorant of or even indifferent to his or her gender. After all, even if one is psychologically androgynous, one's gender continues to have certain profound physical implications.

Thus, being a female typically means that you have a female body build; that you have female genitalia; that you have breasts; that you menstruate; that you can become pregnant and give birth; and that you can nurse a child. Similarly, being a male typically means that you have a male body build; that you have male genitalia; that you have beard growth; that you have erections; that you ejaculate; and that you can impregnate a woman and thereby father a child. No matter how psychologically androgynous you may be, you typically "inherit" one or the other of these two sets of biological givens, and you do not get to choose which of the two sets you would prefer.

Precisely because these are biological givens which cannot be avoided or escaped, except perhaps by means of a very radical and mutilating surgery, it seems to me that psychological health must necessarily include having a healthy sense of one's maleness or femaleness, a "gender identity" if you like. But I would argue that a healthy sense of maleness or femaleness involves little more than being able to look into the mirror and to be perfectly comfortable with the body that one sees there. One's gender does dictate the nature of one's body, after all, and hence one ought to be able to take one's body very much for granted, to feel comfortable with it, and perhaps even to like it.

But beyond being comfortable with one's body, one's gender need have no other influence on one's behavior or on one's life style. Thus, although I would suggest that a woman ought to feel comfortable about the fact that she can bear children if she wants to, this does not imply that she ought to want to bear children, nor that she ought to stay home with any children that she does bear. Similarly, although I would suggest that a man ought to feel perfectly comfortable about the fact that he has a penis which can become erect, this in no way implies that a man ought to take the more active role during sexual intercourse, nor even that his sexual partners ought all to be female.

Finally, I would argue that a healthy sense of one's maleness or femaleness becomes all the more possible precisely when the artificial constraints of gender are eliminated and when one is finally free to be one's own unique blend of temperament and behavior. When gender no longer functions as a prison, then and only then will we be able to accept as given the fact that we are male or female in exactly the same sense that we accept as given the fact that we are human. Then and only then will we be able to consider the fact of our maleness or femaleness to be so self-evident and non-problematic that it rarely ever occurs to us to think about it, to assert that it is true, to fear that it might be in jeopardy, or to wish that it were otherwise.

Let me conclude, then, with my personal set of prescriptions for a liberated sexual identity:

Let sexual preference be ignored;
Let sex roles be abolished; and
Let gender move from figure to ground.

References

Bakan, D. *The duality of human existence.* Chicago: Rand McNally, 1966.

Bazin, N. T., & Freeman, A. The androgynous vision. *Women's Studies,* 1974, *2,* 185–215.

Bem, S. L. The measurement of psychological androgyny. *Journal of Consulting and Clinical Psychology,* 1974, *42,* 155–62.

Bem, S. L. Sex-role adaptability: One consequence of psychological androgyny. *Journal of Personality and Social Psychology,* 1975, *31,* 634–43.

Bem, S. L., & Lenney, E. Sex-typing and the avoidance of cross-sex behavior. *Journal of Personality and Social Psychology,* 1976, *33,* 48–54.

Bem, S. L., Martyna, W., & Watson, C. Sex-typing and androgyny: Further explorations of the expressive domain. *Journal of Personality and Social Psychology,* 1976, *34,* 1016–23.

Berzins, J. I., & Welling, M. A. The PRF ANDRO Scale: A measure of psychological androgyny derived from the Personality Research Form. Unpublished manuscript, University of Kentucky, 1974.

Block, J. H. Conceptions of sex role: Some cross-cultural and longitudinal perspectives. *American Psychologist.* 1973, *28,* 512–26.

Constantinople, A. Masculinity-femininity: An exception to a famous dictum. *Psychological Bulletin,* 1974, *80,* 389–407.

Cosentino, F., & Heilbrun, A. B. Anxiety correlates of sex-role identity in college students. *Psychological Reports,* 1964, *14,* 729–30.

Erikson, E. Inner and outer space: Reflections on womanhood. In R. J. Lifton (Ed.), *The woman in America.* New York: Houghton Mifflin, 1964.

Gall, M. D. The relationship between masculinity-femininity and manifest anxiety. *Journal of Clinical Psychology,* 1969, *25,* 294–95.

Gelpi, B. C. The politics of androgyny. *Women's Studies,* 1974, *2,* 151–60.

Gray, S. W. Masculinity-femininity in relation to anxiety and social acceptance. *Child Development,* 1957, *28,* 203–14.

Green, R. *Sexual identity conflict in children and adults.* New York: Basic Books, 1974.

Harford, T. C., Willis, C. H., & Deabler, H. L. Personality correlates of masculinity-femininity. *Psychological Reports,* 1967, *21,* 881–84.

Harris, D. A. Androgyny: The sexist myth in disguise. *Women's Studies,* 1974, *2,* 171–84.

Hefner, R., Rebecca, M., & Oleshansky, B. Development of sex role transcendence. *Human Development,* 1975, *18* (3), 143–158.

Heilbrun, C. G. *Toward a recognition of androgyny.* New York: Alfred A. Knopf, 1973.

Jung, C. G. Anima and animus. In *Two essays on analytical psychology: Collected works of C. G. Jung.* Vol. 7. Bollinger Foundation, 1953. Pp. 186–209.

Maccoby, E. E. Sex differences in intellectual functioning. In E. E. Maccoby (Ed.), *The development of sex differences.* Stanford, Ca.: Stanford University Press, 1966. Pp. 25–55.

Mussen, P. H. Some antecedents and consequents of masculine sex-typing in adolescent boys. *Psychological Monographs,* 1961, *75,* No. 506.

Mussen, P. H. Long-term consequents of masculinity of interests in adolescence. *Journal of Consulting Psychology,* 1962, *26,* 435–40.

Parsons, T., & Bales, R. F. *Family, socialization and interaction process.* New York: Free Press, 1955.

Pleck, J. H. Masculinity-femininity: Current and alternative paradigms. *Sex Roles,* 1975, *1,* 161–78.

Rebecca, M., Hefner, R., & Oleshansky, B. A model of sex-role transcendence. *Journal of Social Issues,* 1976, *32* (3), 197–206.

Sears, R. R. Relation of early socialization experiences to self-concepts and gender role in middle childhood. *Child Development,* 1970, *41,* 267–89.

Secor, C. Androgyny: An early reappraisal. *Women's Studies,* 1974, *2,* 161–69.

Spence, J. T., Helmreich, R., & Stapp, J. Ratings of self and peers on sex-role attributes and their relation to self-esteem and conceptions of masculinity and femininity. *Journal of Personality and Social Psychology,* 1975, *32,* 29–39.

Stimpson, C. R. The androgyne and the homosexual. *Women's Studies,* 1974, *2,* 237–48.

Strahan, F. Remarks on Bem's measurement of psychological androgyny: Alternatives, methods and a supplementary analysis. *Journal of Consulting and Clinical Psychology,* 1975, *43,* 568–71.

Webb, A. P. Sex-role preferences and adjustment in early adolescents. *Child Development,* 1963, *34,* 609–18.

Gender Schema Theory and Its Implications for Child Development: Raising Gender-aschematic Children in a Gender-schematic Society

SANDRA LIPSITZ BEM

As every parent, teacher, and developmental psychologist knows, male and female children become "masculine" and "feminine," respectively, at a very early age. By the time they are four or five, for example, girls and boys have typically come to prefer activities defined by the culture as appropriate for their sex and also to prefer same-sex peers. The acquisition of sex-appropriate preferences, skills, personality attributes, behaviors, and self-concepts is typically referred to within psychology as the process of sex typing.

The universality and importance of this process is reflected in the prominence it has received in psychological theories of development, which seek to elucidate how the developing child comes to match the template defined as sex-appropriate by his or her culture. Three theories of sex typing have been especially influential: psychoanalytic theory, social learning theory, and cognitive-developmental theory. More recently, a fourth theory of sex typing has been introduced into the psychological literature—gender schema theory.

This article is designed to introduce gender schema theory to feminist scholars outside the discipline of psychology. In order to provide a background for the conceptual issues that have given rise to gender schema theory, I will begin with a discussion of the three theories of sex typing that have been dominant within psychology to date.

Dr. Bem is Professor of Psychology and Women's Studies, Cornell University, Ithaca, New York.

Psychoanalytic Theory

The first psychologist to ask how male and female are transmuted into masculine and feminine was Freud. Accordingly, in the past virtually every major source book in developmental psychology began its discussion of sex typing with a review of psychoanalytic theory.[1]

Psychoanalytic theory emphasizes the child's identification with the same-sex parent as the primary mechanism whereby children become sex typed, an identification that results from the child's discovery of genital sex differences, from the penis envy and castration anxiety that this discovery produces in females and males, respectively, and from the successful resolution of the Oedipus conflict.[2] Although a number of feminist scholars have found it fruitful in recent years to work within a psychoanalytic framework,[3] the theory's "anatomy is destiny" view has been associated historically with quite conservative conclusions regarding the inevitability of sex typing.

Of the three dominant theories of sex typing, psychoanalytic theory is almost certainly the best known outside the discipline of psychology, although it is no longer especially popular among research psychologists. In part, this is because the theory is difficult to test empirically. An even more important reason, however, is that the empirical evidence simply does not justify emphasizing either the child's discovery of genital sex differences in particular[4] or the child's identification with his or her same-sex parent[5] as a crucial determinant of sex typing.

1. See, e.g., Paul H. Mussen, "Early Sex-Role Development," in *Handbook of Socialization Theory and Research*, ed. David A. Goslin (Chicago: Rand McNally & Co., 1969), pp. 707–31. For a more recent review that does not even mention psychoanalytic theory, see Aletha C. Huston, "Sex-Typing," *Handbook of Child Psychology*, ed. Paul Mussen, 4th ed. (New York: John Wiley & Sons, 1983).
2. Urie Bronfenbrenner, "Freudian Theories of Identification with Their Derivatives," *Child Development* 31, no. 1 (March 1960): 15–40; Sigmund Freud, "Some Psychological Consequences of the Anatomical Distinction between the Sexes (1925)," in *Collected Papers of Sigmund Freud*, ed. Ernest Jones, 5 vols. (New York: Basic Books, 1959), 5:186–97; Sigmund Freud, "The Passing of the Oedipus Complex (1924)," ibid., 2:269–76.
3. E.g., Nancy Chodorow, *The Reproduction of Mothering: Psychoanalysis and the Sociology of Gender* (Berkeley: University of California Press, 1978); Gayle Rubin, "The Traffic in Women: Notes on the 'Political Economy' of Sex," in *Toward an Anthropology of Women*, ed. Rayna Reiter (New York: Monthly Review Press, 1975), pp. 157–210.
4. Lawrence Kohlberg, " A Cognitive-Developmental Analysis of Children's Sex-Role Concepts and Attitudes," in *The Development of Sex Differences*, ed. Eleanor E. Maccoby (Stanford, Calif.: Stanford University Press, 1966), pp. 82–173; Maureen J. McConaghy, "Gender permanence and the Genital Basis of Gender: Stages in the Development of Constancy of Gender Identity," *Child Development* 50, no. 4 (December 1979): 1223–26.
5. Eleanor E. Maccoby and Carol N. Jacklin, *The Psychology of Sex Differences* (Stanford, Calif.: Stanford University Press, 1974).

Social Learning Theory

In contrast to psychoanalytic theory, social learning theory emphasizes the rewards and punishments that children receive for sex-appropriate and sex-inappropriate behaviors, as well as the vicarious learning that observation and modeling can provide.[6] Social learning theory thus locates the source of sex typing in the sex-differentiated practices of the socializing community.

Perhaps the major virtue of social learning theory for psychologists is that it applies to the development of psychological femaleness and maleness the very same general principles of learning that are already known to account for the development of a multitude of other behaviors. Thus, as far as the formal theory is concerned, gender does not demand special consideration; that is, no special psychological mechanisms or processes must be postulated in order to explain how children become sex typed beyond those already used to explain how children learn other socialized behaviors.

Interestingly, the theory's generality also constitutes the basis of its appeal to feminist psychologists in particular. If there is nothing special about gender, then the phenomenon of sex typing itself is neither inevitable nor unmodifiable. Children become sex typed because sex happens to be the basis of differential socialization in their culture. In principle, however, any category could be made the basis for differential socialization.

Although social learning theory can account for the young child's acquiring a number of particular behaviors that are stereotyped by the culture as sex appropriate, it treats the child as the relatively passive recipient of environmental forces rather than as an active agent striving to organize and thereby to comprehend the social world. This view of the passive child is inconsistent with the common observation that children themselves frequently construct and enforce their own version of society's gender rules. It is also inconsistent with the fact that the flexibility with which children interpret society's gender rules varies predictably with age. In one study, for example, 73 percent of the four-year-olds and 80 percent of the nine-year-olds believed—quite flexibly—that there should be no sexual restrictions on one's choice of occupation. Between those ages, however, children held more rigid opinions, with the middle children being the least flexible of all. Thus, only 33 percent of the five-year-olds, 10 percent of the

6. Walter Mischel, "Sex-Typing and Socialization," in *Carmichael's Manual of Child Psychology*, ed. Paul H. Mussen, 2 vols. (New York: John Wiley & Sons, 1970), 2:3–72.

six-year-olds, 11 percent of the seven-year-olds, and 44 percent of the eight- *229*
year-olds believed there should be no sexual restrictions on one's choice of
occupation.[7]

This particular developmental pattern is not unique to the child's interpretation of gender rules. Even in a domain as far removed from gender
as syntax, children first learn certain correct grammatical forms through
reinforcement and modeling. As they get a bit older, however, they begin to
construct their own grammatical rules on the basis of what they hear
spoken around them, and they are able only later still to allow for exceptions to those rules. Thus, only the youngest and the oldest children say
"ran"; children in between say "runned."[8] What all of this implies, of
course, is that the child is passive in neither domain. Rather, she or he is
actively constructing rules to organize—and thereby to comprehend—the
vast array of information in his or her world.

Cognitive-Developmental Theory

Unlike social learning theory, cognitive-developmental theory focuses almost exclusively on the child as the primary agent of his or her own sex-role
socialization, a focus reflecting the theory's basic assumption that sex typing follows naturally and inevitably from universal principles of cognitive
development. As children work actively to comprehend their social world,
they inevitably "label themselves—call it alpha—and determine that there
are alphas and betas in the environment. Given the cognitive-motivational
properties of the self, . . . the child moves toward other alphas and away
from betas. That is, it is the child who realizes what gender he or she is, and
in what behaviors he or she should engage."[9] In essence, then, cognitive-
developmental theory postulates that, because of the child's need for cognitive consistency, self-categorization as female or male motivates her or
him to value that which is seen as similar to the self in terms of gender. This
gender-based value system, in turn, motivates the child to engage in gender-congruent activites, to strive for gender-congruent attributes, and to
prefer gender-congruent peers. "Basic self-categorizations determine basic
valuings. Once the boy has stably identified himself as male, he then values

---

7. William Damon, *The Social World of the Child* (San Francisco: Jossey-Bass, 1977).
8. Courtney B. Cazden, "The Acquisition of Noun and Verb Inflections," *Child Development* 39, no. 2
(June 1968): 433–48; Herbert H. Clark and Eve V. Clark, *Psychology and Language: An Introduction to
Psycholinguistics* (New York: Harcourt Brace Jovanovich, 1977).
9. Michael Lewis and Jeanne Brooks-Gunn, *Social Cognition and the Acquisition of Self* (New York:
Plenum Publishing Corp., 1979), p. 270.

230 positively those objects and acts consistent with his gender identity."[10]

The cognitive-developmental account of sex typing has been so influential since its introduction into the literature in 1966 that many psychologists now seem to accept almost as a given that the young child will spontaneously develop both a gender-based self-concept and a gender-based value system even in the absence of external pressure to behave in a sex-stereotyped manner. Despite its popularity, however, the theory fails to explicate why sex will have primacy over other potential categories of the self such as race, religion, or even eye color. Interestingly, the formal theory itself does not dictate that any particular category should have such primacy. Moreover, most cognitive-developmental theorists do not explicitly ponder the "why sex" question nor do they even raise the possibility that other categories could fit the general theory just as well. To the extent that cognitive-developmental psychologists address this question at all, they seem to emphasize the perceptual salience to the child of the observable differences between the sexes, particularly biologically produced differences such as size and strength.[11]

The implicit assumption here that sex differences are naturally and inevitably more perceptually salient to children than other differences may not have cross-cultural validity. Although it may be true that our culture does not construct any distinctions between people that we perceive to be as compelling as sex, other cultures do construct such distinctions, for example, distinctions between those who are high caste and those who are low caste, between those who are inhabited by spirits and those who are not, between those who are divine and those who are mortal, between those who are wet and those who are dry, or between those who are open and those who are closed.[12] Given such cross-cultural diversity, it is ironic that a theory emphasizing the child's active striving to comprehend the social world should not be more open to the possibility that a distinction other than sex might be more perceptually salient in another cultural context. What appears to have happened is that the universality and inevitability that the theory claims for the child's cognitive processes have been implicitly and gratuitously transferred to one of the many substantive domains upon which those processes operate: the domain of gender.

10. Kohlberg, p. 89.
11. Kohlberg; Lewis and Brooks-Gunn; Dorothy Z. Ullian, "The Child's Construction of Gender: Anatomy as Destiny," in *Cognitive and Affective Growth: Developmental Interaction*, ed. Edna K. Shapiro and Evelyn Weber (Hillsdale, N.J.: Lawrence Erlbaum Associates, 1981), pp. 171–85.
12. For a discussion of the wet-dry distinction, see Anna S. Meigs, "Male Pregnancy and the Reduction of Sexual Opposition in a New Guinea Highlands Society," *Ethnology* 15, no. 4 (1976): 393–407; for a discussion of the open-closed distinction, see Sally Falk Moore, "The Secret of the Men: A Fiction of Chagga Initiation and Its Relation to the Logic of Chagga Symbolism," *Africa* 46, no. 4 (1976): 357–70.

This is not to say, of course, that cognitive-developmental theory is *231* necessarily wrong in its implicit assumption that all children have a built-in readiness to organize their perceptions of the social world on the basis of sex. Perhaps evolution has given sex a biologically based priority over many other categories. The important point, however, is that the question of whether and why sex has cognitive primacy is not included within the bounds of cognitive-developmental theory. To understand why children become *sex* typed rather than say, race or caste typed, we still need a theory that explicitly addresses the question of how and why children come to utilize sex in particular as a cognitive organizing principle.

Gender Schema Theory

Gender schema theory[13] contains features of both the cognitive-developmental and the social learning accounts of sex typing. In particular, gender schema theory proposes that sex typing derives in large measure from gender-schematic processing, from a generalized readiness on the part of the child to encode and to organize information—including information about the self—according to the culture's definitions of maleness and femaleness. Like cognitive-developmental theory, then, gender schema theory proposes that sex typing is mediated by the child's own cognitive processing. However, gender schema theory further proposes that gender-schematic processing is itself derived from the sex-differentiated practices of the social community. Thus, like social learning theory, gender schema theory assumes that sex typing is a learned phenomenon and, hence, that it is neither inevitable nor unmodifiable. In this discussion, I shall first consider in some detail what gender-schematic processing is and how it mediates sex typing; I shall then explore the conditions that produce gender-schematic processing, thereby providing an explicit account of why sex comes to have cognitive primacy over other social categories.

Gender-schematic Processing

Gender schema theory begins with the observation that the developing child invariably learns his or her society's cultural definitions of femaleness

13. Sandra L. Bem, "Gender Schema Theory: A Cognitive Account of Sex Typing," *Psychological Review* 88, no. 4 (July 1981): 354–64; and "Gender Schema Theory and Self-Schema Theory Compared: A Comment on Markus, Crane, Bernstein, and Siladi's 'Self-Schemas and Gender,'" *Journal of Personality and Social Psychology* 43, no. 6 (December 1982): 1192–94.

232 and maleness. In most societies, these definitions comprise a diverse and sprawling network of sex-linked associations encompassing not only those features directly related to female and male persons—such as anatomy, reproductive function, division of labor, and personality attributes—but also features more remotely or metaphorically related to sex, such as the angularity or roundedness of an abstract shape and the periodicity of the moon. Indeed, no other dichotomy in human experience appears to have as many entities linked to it as does the distinction between female and male.

But there is more. Gender schema theory proposes that, in addition to learning such content-specific information about gender, the child also learns to invoke this heterogeneous network of sex-related associations in order to evaluate and assimilate new information. The child, in short, learns to encode and to organize information in terms of an evolving gender schema.

A schema is a cognitive structure, a network of associations that organizes and guides an individual's perception. A schema functions as an anticipatory structure, a readiness to search for and to assimilate incoming information in schema-relevant terms. Schematic information processing is thus highly selective and enables the individual to impose structure and meaning onto a vast array of incoming stimuli. More specifically, schematic information processing entails a readiness to sort information into categories on the basis of some particular dimension, despite the existence of other dimensions that could serve equally well in this regard. Gender-schematic processing in particular thus involves spontaneously sorting attributes and behaviors into masculine and feminine categories or "equivalence classes," regardless of their differences on a variety of dimensions unrelated to gender, for example, spontaneously placing items like "tender" and "nightingale" into a feminine category and items like "assertive" and "eagle" into a masculine category. Like schema theories generally,[14] gender schema theory thus construes perception as a constructive process in which the interaction between incoming information and an individual's preexisting schema determines what is perceived.

What gender schema theory proposes, then, is that the phenomenon of sex typing derives, in part, from gender-schematic processing, from an individual's generalized readiness to process information on the basis of the sex-linked associations that constitute the gender schema. Specifically, the theory proposes that sex typing results, in part, from the assimilation of the

14. Ulric Neisser, *Cognition and Reality* (San Francisco: W. H. Freeman & Co., 1976); Shelley E. Taylor and Jennifer Crocker, "Schematic Bases of Social Information Processing," in *Social Cognition, the Ontario Symposium,* ed. E. Tory Higgins, C. Peter Herman, and Mark P. Zanna (Hillsdale, N.J.: Lawrence Erlbaum Associates, 1981), 1:89–135.

self-concept itself to the gender schema. As children learn the contents of 233
their society's gender schema, they learn which attributes are to be linked
with their own sex and, hence, with themselves. This does not simply entail
learning the defined relationship between each sex and each dimension or
attribute—that boys are to be strong and girls weak, for example—but
involves the deeper lesson that the dimensions themselves are differentially
applicable to the two sexes. Thus the strong-weak dimension itself is absent
from the schema to be applied to girls just as the dimension of nurturance is
implicitly omitted from the schema to be applied to boys. Adults in the
child's world rarely notice or remark upon how strong a little girl is
becoming or how nurturant a little boy is becoming, despite their readiness
to note precisely these attributes in the "appropriate" sex. The child learns
to apply this same schematic selectivity to the self, to choose from among
the many possible dimensions of human personality only that subset defined as applicable to his or her own sex and thereby eligible for organizing
the diverse contents of the self-concept. Thus do children's self concepts
become sex typed, and thus do the two sexes become, in their own eyes, not
only different in degree, but different in kind.

Simultaneously, the child also learns to evaluate his or her adequacy as a
person according to the gender schema, to match his or her preferences,
attitudes, behaviors, and personal attributes against the prototypes stored
within it. The gender schema becomes a prescriptive standard or guide,[15]
and self-esteem becomes its hostage. Here, then, enters an internalized
motivational factor that prompts an individual to regulate his or her behavior so that it conforms to cultural definitions of femaleness and maleness.
Thus do cultural myths become self-fulfilling prophecies, and thus, according to gender schema theory, do we arrive at the phenomenon known
as sex typing.

It is important to note that gender schema theory is a theory of process,
not content. Because sex-typed individuals are seen as processing information and regulating their behavior according to whatever definitions of
femininity and masculinity their culture happens to provide, the process of
dividing the world into feminine and masculine categories—and not the
contents of the categories—is central to the theory. Accordingly, sex-typed
individuals are seen to differ from other individuals not primarily in the
degree of femininity or masculinity they possess, but in the extent to which
their self-concepts and behaviors are organized on the basis of gender

15. Jerome Kagan, "Acquisition and Significance of Sex Typing and Sex Role Identity," in *Review of Child Development Research*, ed. Martin L. Hoffman and Lois W. Hoffman (New York: Russell Sage Foundation, 1964), 1:137–67.

234 rather than on the basis of some other dimension. Many non-sex-typed individuals may describe themselves as, say, nurturant or dominant without implicating the concepts of femininity or masculinity. When sex-typed individuals so describe themselves, however, it is precisely the gender connotations of the attributes or behaviors that are presumed to be salient for them.

Empirical Research on Gender-schematic Processing

Recent empirical research supports gender schema theory's basic contention that sex typing is derived from gender-schematic processing. In a variety of studies using different subject populations and different paradigms, female and male sex-typed individuals have been found to be significantly more likely than non-sex-typed individuals to process information—including information about the self—in terms of gender.[16]

One study, for example, used a memory task to determine whether gender connotations are, in fact, more "cognitively available" to sex-typed individuals than to non-sex-typed individuals, as gender schema theory claims.[17] The subjects in this study were forty-eight male and forty-eight female undergraduates who had described themselves as either sex typed or non–sex typed on the Bem Sex Role Inventory (BSRI).[18]

16. Susan M. Andersen and Sandra L. Bem, "Sex Typing and Androgyny in Dyadic Interaction: Individual Differences in Responsiveness to Physical Atractiveness," *Journal of Personality and Social Psychology* 41, no. 1 (July 1981): 74–86; Bem, "Gender Schema Theory"; Kay Deaux and Brenda Major, "Sex-related Patterns in the Unit of Perception," *Personality and Social Psychology Bulletin* 3, no. 2 (Spring 1977): 297–300; Brenda Girvin, "The Nature of Being Schematic: Sex-Role Self-Schemas and Differential Processing of Masculine and Feminine Information" (Ph.D. diss., Stanford University, 1978); Robert V. Kail and Laura E. Levine, "Encoding Processes and Sex-Role Preferences," *Journal of Experimental Child Psychology* 21, no. 2 (April 1976): 256–63; Lynn S. Liben and Margaret L. Signorella, "Gender-related Schemata and Constructive Memory in Children," *Child Development* 51, no. 1 (March 1980): 11–18; Richard Lippa, "Androgyny, Sex Typing, and the Perception of Masculinity-Femininity in Handwriting," *Journal of Research in Personality* 11, no. 1 (March 1977): 21–37; Hazel Markus et al., "Self-Schemas and Gender," *Journal of Personality and Social Psychology* 42, no. 1 (January 1982): 38–50; Shelley E. Taylor and Hsiao-Ti Falcone, "Cognitive Bases of Stereotyping: The Relationship between Categorization and Prejudice," *Personality and Social Psychology Bulletin* 8, no. 3 (September 1982): 426–32.

17. Bem, "Gender Schema Theory," pp. 356–58.

18. The Bem Sex Role Inventory, or BSRI, is an instrument that identifies sex-typed individuals on the basis of their self-concepts or self-ratings of their personal attributes. The BSRI asks the respondent to indicate on a seven-point scale how well each of sixty attributes describes himself or herself. Although it is not apparent to the respondent, twenty of the attributes reflect the culture's definition of masculinity (e.g., assertive), and twenty reflect its definition of femininity (e.g., tender), with the remaining attributes serving as filler. Each respondent receives both a masculinity and a femininity score, and those who score above the median on the sex-congruent scale and below the median on the sex-incongruent scale are defined as sex typed. That is, men who score high in masculinity and low in femininity are defined as sex typed, as are women who score high in femininity and low in masculinity.

During the experimental session, subjects were presented with a randomly ordered sequence of sixty-one words that included proper names, animal names, verbs, and articles of clothing. Half of the proper names were female, half were male; one-third of the items within each of the other semantic categories had been consistently rated by undergraduate judges as feminine (e.g., butterfly, blushing, bikini), one-third as masculine (e.g., gorilla, hurling, trousers), and one-third as neutral (e.g., ant, stepping, sweater). The words were presented on slides at three-second intervals, and subjects were told that their recall would later be tested. Three seconds after the presentation of the last word, they were given a period of eight minutes to write down as many words as they could, in whatever order they happened to come to mind.

As expected, the results indicated that although sex-typed and non-sex-typed individuals recalled equal numbers of items overall, the order in which they recalled the items was different. Once having recalled a feminine item, sex-typed individuals were more likely than non-sex-typed individuals to recall another feminine item next rather than a masculine or a neutral item. The same was true for masculine items. In other words, the sequence of recall for sex-typed individuals revealed significantly more runs or clusters of feminine items and of masculine items than the sequence of recall for non-sex-typed individuals. Thinking of one feminine (or masculine) item could enhance the probability of thinking of another feminine (or masculine) item in this way only if the individual spontaneously encodes both items as feminine (or masculine), and the gender schema thereby links the two items in memory. These results thus confirm gender schema theory's claim that sex-typed individuals have a greater readiness than do non-sex-typed individuals to encode information in terms of the sex-linked associations that constitute the gender schema.

A second study tested the hypothesis that sex-typed individuals have a readiness to decide on the basis of gender which personal attributes are to be associated with their self-concepts and which are to be dissociated from their self-concepts.[19] The subjects in this second study were another set of forty-eight male and forty-eight female undergraduates who had also de-

---

The BSRI is described in detail in the following articles: Sandra L. Bem, "The Measurement of Psychological Androgyny," *Journal of Consulting and Clinical Psychology* 42, no. 2 (April 1974): 155–62; "On the Utility of Alternative Procedures for Assessing Psychological Androgyny," *Journal of Clinical and Consulting Psychology* 45, no. 2 (April 1977): 196–205; "The Theory and Measurement of Androgyny: A Reply to the Pedhazur-Tetenbaum and Locksley-Colten Critiques," *Journal of Personality and Social Psychology* 37, no. 6 (June 1979): 1047–54; and *A Manual for the Bem Sex Role Inventory* (Palo Alto, Calif.: Consulting Psychologists Press, 1981).
19. Bem, "Gender Schema Theory," pp. 358–61.

236 scribed themselves as sex typed or non–sex typed on the Bem Sex Role Inventory. During each of the individual experimental sessions, the sixty attributes from the BSRI were projected on a screen one at time, and the subject was requested to push one of two buttons, "Me" or "Not Me," to indicate whether the attribute was or was not self-descriptive. Of interest in this study was the subject's response latency, that is, how long it took the subject to make a decision about each attribute.

Gender schema theory predicts and the results of this study confirm that sex-typed subjects are significantly faster than non-sex-typed subjects when endorsing sex-appropriate attributes and when rejecting sex-inappropriate attributes. These results suggest that when deciding whether a particular attribute is or is not self-descriptive, sex-typed individuals do not bother to go through a time-consuming process of recruiting behavioral evidence from memory and judging whether the evidence warrants an affirmative answer—which is presumably what non-sex-typed individuals do. Rather, sex-typed individuals "look up" the attribute in the gender schema. If the attribute is sex appropriate, they quickly say yes; if the attribute is sex inappropriate, they quickly say no. Occasionally, of course, even sex-typed individuals must admit to possessing an attribute that is sex inappropriate or to lacking an attribute that is sex appropriate. On these occasions, they are significantly slower than non-sex-typed individuals. This pattern of rapid delivery of gender-consistent self-descriptions and slow delivery of gender-inconsistent self-descriptions confirms gender schema theory's contention that sex-typed individuals spontaneously sort information into categories on the basis of gender, despite the existence of other dimensions that could serve equally well as a basis for categorization.

Antecedents of Gender-schematic Processing

But how and why do sex-typed individuals develop a readiness to organize information in general, and their self-concepts in particular, in terms of gender? Because gender-schematic processing is considered a special case of schematic processing, this specific question is superseded by the more general question of how and why individuals come to organize information in terms of any social category, that is, how and why a social category becomes transformed into a cognitive schema.

Gender schema theory proposes that the transformation of a given social category into the nucleus of a highly available cognitive schema depends on the nature of the social context within which the category is embedded, not on the intrinsic nature of the category itself. Given the proper social con-

text, then, even a category like eye color could become a cognitive schema.
More specifically, gender schema theory proposes that a category will become a schema if: (1) the social context makes it the nucleus of a large associative network, that is, if the ideology and/or the practices of the culture construct an association between that category and a wide range of other attributes, behaviors, concepts, and categories; and (2) the social context assigns the category broad functional significance, that is, if a broad array of social institutions, norms, and taboos distinguishes between persons, behaviors, and attributes on the basis of this category.

This latter condition is most critical, for gender schema theory presumes that the culture's insistence on the functional importance of the social category is what transforms a passive network of associations into an active and readily available schema for interpreting reality. We all learn many associative networks of concepts throughout life, many potential cognitive schemata, but the centrality or functional importance assigned by society to particular categories and distinctions animates their associated networks and gives these schemata priority and availability over others.

From the perspective of gender schema theory, then, gender has come to have cognitive primacy over many other social categories because the culture has made it so. Nearly all societies teach the developing child two crucial things about gender: first, as noted earlier, they teach the substantive network of sex-related associations that can come to serve as a cognitive schema; second, they teach that the dichotomy between male and female has intensive and extensive relevance to virtually every domain of human experience. The typical American child cannot help observing, for example, that what parents, teachers, and peers consider to be appropriate behavior varies as a function of sex; that toys, clothing, occupations, hobbies, the domestic division of labor—even pronouns—all vary as a function of sex.

Gender schema theory thus implies that children would be far less likely to become gender schematic and hence sex typed if the society were to limit the associative network linked to sex and to temper its insistence on the functional importance of the gender dichotomy. Ironically, even though our society has become sensitive to negative sex stereotypes and has begun to expunge them from the media and from children's literature, it remains blind to its gratuitous emphasis on the gender dichotomy itself. In elementary schools, for example, boys and girls line up separately or alternately; they learn songs in which the fingers are "ladies" and the thumbs are "men"; they see boy and girl paper-doll silhouettes alternately placed on the days of the month in order to learn about the calendar. Children, it will be noted, are not lined up separately or alternately as blacks and whites;

238 fingers are not "whites" and thumbs "blacks"; black and white dolls do not alternately mark the days of the calendar. Our society seeks to deemphasize racial distinctions but continues to exaggerate sexual distinctions.

Because of the role that sex plays in reproduction, perhaps no society could ever be as indifferent to sex in its cultural arrangements as it could be to, say, eye color, thereby giving the gender schema a sociologically based priority over many other categories. For the same reason, it may even be, as noted earlier, that sex has evolved to be a basic category of perception for our species, thereby giving the gender schema a biologically based priority as well. Be that as it may, however, gender schema theory claims that society's ubiquitous insistence on the functional importance of the gender dichotomy must necessarily render it even more cognitively available—and available in more remotely relevant contexts—than it would be otherwise.

It should be noted that gender schema theory's claims about the antecedents of gender-schematic processing have not yet been tested empirically. Hence it is not possible at this point to state whether individual differences in gender-schematic processing do, in fact, derive from differences in the emphasis placed on gender dichotomy in individuals' socialization histories, or to describe concretely the particular kinds of socialization histories that enhance or diminish gender-schematic processing. Nevertheless, I should like to set forth a number of plausible strategies that are consistent with gender schema theory for raising a gender-aschematic child in the midst of a gender-schematic society.

This discussion will, by necessity, be highly speculative. Even so, it will serve to clarify gender schema theory's view of exactly how gender-schematic processing is learned and how something else might be learned in its place. As we shall see, many of the particular strategies recommended for raising gender-aschematic children are strategies that have already been adopted by feminist parents trying to create what is typically called a nonsexist or a gender-liberated form of childrearing. In these cases, what gender schema theory provides is a new theoretical framework for thinking about the psychological impact of various childrearing practices. Sprinkled throughout the discussion will be examples taken from my own home. These are meant to be illustrations and not systematic evidence that such strategies actually decrease gender-schematic processing.

Raising Gender-aschematic Children

Feminist parents who wish to raise gender-aschematic children in a gender-schematic world are like any parents who wish to inculcate their children with beliefs and values that deviate from those of the dominant culture. Their major option is to try to undermine the dominant ideology *239* before it can undermine theirs. Feminist parents are thus in a difficult situation. They cannot simply ignore gender in their childrearing as they might prefer to do, because the society will then have free rein to teach their children the lessons about gender that it teaches all other children. Rather, they must manage somehow to inoculate their children against gender-schematic processing.

Two strategies are suggested here. First, parents can enable their children to learn about sex differences initially without their also learning the culture's sex-linked associative network by simultaneously retarding their children's knowledge of sex's cultural correlates and advancing their children's knowledge of sex's biological correlates. Second, parents can provide alternative or "subversive" schemata that their children can use to interpret the culture's sex-linked associative network when they do learn it. This step is essential if children are not simply to learn gender-schematic processing somewhat later than their counterparts from more traditional homes. Whether one is a child or an adult, such alternative schemata "build up one's resistance" to the lessons of the dominant culture and thereby enable one to remain gender-aschematic even while living in a gender-schematic society.

Teaching Children about Sex Differences

Cultural Correlates of Sex. Children typically learn that gender is a sprawling associative network with ubiquitous functional importance through their observation of the many cultural correlates of sex existing in their society. Accordingly, the first step parents can take to retard the development of gender-schematic processing is to retard the child's knowledge of these cultural messages about gender. Less crudely put, parents can attempt to attenuate sex-linked correlations within the child's social environment, thereby altering the basic data upon which the child will construct his or her own concepts of maleness and femaleness.

In part, parents can do this by eliminating sex stereotyping from their own behavior and from the alternatives that they provide for their children, just as many feminist parents are already doing. Among other things, for example, they can take turns making dinner, bathing the children, and driving the car; they can ensure that all their children—regardless of sex— have both trucks and dolls, both pink and blue clothing, and both male and female playmates; and they can arrange for their children to see women and men in nontraditional occupations.

When children are quite young, parents can further inhibit cultural

240 messages about gender by actually censoring books and television programs whose explicit or implicit message is that the sexes differ on nonbiological dimensions. At present, this tactic will eliminate many children's
books and most television programming. Ironically, it will also temporarily
eliminate a number of feminist books designed to overcome sex stereotypes; even a book which insists that it is wrong for William not to be
allowed to have a doll by implication teaches a child who has not yet learned
the associative network that boys and dolls do not normally go together.

To compensate for this censorship, parents will need to seek out—and
to create—materials that do not teach sex stereotypes. With our own
children, my husband and I got into the habit of doctoring books whenever
possible so as to remove all sex-linked correlations. We did this, among
other ways, by changing the sex of the main character; by drawing longer
hair and the outline of breasts onto illustrations of previously male truck
drivers, physicians, pilots, and the like; and by deleting or altering sections
of the text that described females or males in a sex-stereotyped manner.
When reading children's picture books aloud, we also chose pronouns that
avoided the ubiquitous implication that all characters without dresses or
pink bows must necessarily be male: "And what is this little piggy doing?
Why, he or she seems to be building a bridge."

All of these practices are designed to permit very young children to dwell
temporarily in a social environment where, if the parents are lucky, the
cultural correlations with sex will be attenuated from, say, .96 to .43.
According to gender schema theory, this attenuation should retard the
formation of the sex-linked associative network that will itself form the basis
of the gender schema. By themselves, however, these practices teach children only what sex is not. But children must also be taught what sex is.

Biological Correlates of Sex. What remains when all of the cultural correlates of sex are attenuated or eliminated, of course, are two of the un-
disputed biological correlates of sex: anatomy and reproduction. Accordingly, parents can make these the definitional attributes of femaleness and
maleness. By teaching their children that the genitalia constitute the definitive attributes of females and males, parents help them to apprehend the
merely probabilistic nature of sex's cultural correlates and thereby restrict
sex's associative sprawl. By teaching their children that whether one is
female or male makes a difference only in the context of reproduction,
parents limit sex's functional significance and thereby retard gender-schematic processing. Because children taught these lessons have been provided with an explicit and clear-cut rule about what sex is and when sex
matters, they should be predisposed to construct their own concepts of

femaleness and maleness based on biology, rather than on the cultural correlates to which they have been exposed. And to the extent that young children tend to interpret rules and categories rigidly rather than flexibly, this tendency will serve to enhance their belief that sex is to be narrowly defined in terms of anatomy and reproduction rather than to enhance a traditional belief that every arbitrary gender rule must be strictly obeyed and enforced. Thus there may be an irony, but there is no inconsistency in the fact that an emphasis on the biological differences between the sexes should here be advocated as the basis for feminist child rearing.

The liberation that comes from having an unambiguous genital definition of sex and the imprisonment that comes from not having such a definition are nicely illustrated by the story of what happened to our son Jeremy, then age four, the day he decided to wear barrettes to nursery school. Several times that day, another little boy told Jeremy that he, Jeremy, must be a girl because "only girls wear barrettes." After trying to explain to this child that "wearing barrettes doesn't matter" and that "being a boy means having a penis and testicles," Jeremy finally pulled down his pants as a way of making his point more convincingly. The other child was not impressed. He simply said, "Everybody has a penis; only girls wear barrettes."

In the American context, children do not typically learn to define sex in terms of anatomy and reproduction until quite late, and, as a result, they— like the child in the example above—mistakenly treat many of the cultural correlates of sex as definitional. This confusion is facilitated, of course, by the fact that the genitalia themselves are not usually visible and hence cannot be relied on as a way of identifying someone's sex.

Accordingly, when our children asked whether someone was male or female, we frequently denied certain knowledge of the person's sex, emphasizing that without being able to see whether there was a penis or a vagina under the person's clothes, we had no definitive information. Moreover, when our children themselves began to utilize nonbiological markers as a way of identifying sex, we gently teased them about that strategy to remind them that the genitalia—and only the genitalia—constitute the definition of sex: "What do you mean that you can tell Chris is a girl because Chris has long hair? Does Chris's hair have a vagina?"

We found Stephanie Waxman's picture book *What Is a Girl? What Is a Boy?* to be a superb teaching aid in this context.[20] Each page displays a vivid and attractive photograph of a boy or a girl engaged in some behavior stereotyped as more typical of or more appropriate for the other sex. The

20. Stephanie Waxman, *What Is a Girl? What Is a Boy?* (Culver City, Calif.: Peace Press, 1976).

242 accompanying text says such things as, "Some people say a girl is someone with jewelry, but Barry is wearing a necklace and he's a boy." The book ends with nude photographs of both children and adults, and it explicitly defines sex in terms of anatomy.

These particular lessons about what sex is, what sex is not, and when sex matters are designed to make young children far more naive than their peers about the cultural aspects of gender and far more sophisticated than their peers about the biological aspects of sex. Eventually, of course, their naiveté will begin to fade, and they too will begin to learn the culture's sprawling network of sex-linked associations. At that point, parents must take steps to prevent that associative network from itself becoming a cognitive schema.

Providing Alternative Schemata

Let us presume that the feminist parent has successfully produced a child who defines sex in terms of anatomy and reproduction. How is such a child to understand the many sex-linked correlations that will inevitably begin to intrude upon his or her awareness? What alternative schemata can substitute for the gender schema in helping the child to organize and to assimilate gender-related information?

Individual Differences Schema.   The first alternative schema is simply a child's version of the time-honored liberal truism used to counter stereotypic thinking in general, namely, that there is remarkable variability of individuals within groups as compared with the small mean differences between groups. To the child who says that girls do not like to play baseball, the feminist parent can thus point out that although it is true that some girls do not like to play baseball, it is also true that some girls do (e.g., your Aunt Beverly and Alissa who lives across the street) and that some boys do not (e.g., your dad and Alissa's brother Jimmy). It is, of course, useful for parents to supply themselves with a long list of counterexamples well in advance of such occasions.

This individual differences schema is designed to prevent children from interpreting individual differences as sex differences, from assimilating perceived differences among people to a gender schema. Simultaneously, it should also encourage children to treat as a given that the sexes are basically similar to one another and, hence, to view all glib assertions about sex differences as inherently suspect. And it is with this skepticism that feminist consciousness begins.

Cultural Relativism Schema.   As the child's knowledge and awareness grow, he or she will gradually begin to realize that his or her family's beliefs and attitudes about gender are at variance with those of the dominant culture. Accordingly, the child needs some rationale for not simply accepting the majority view as the more valid. One possible rationale is cultural relativism, the notion that "different people believe different things" and that the coexistence of even contradictory beliefs is the rule in society rather than the exception.

Children can (and should) be introduced to the schema of cultural relativism long before it is pertinent to the domain of gender. For example, our children needed the rationale that "different people believe different things" in order to understand why they, but not the children next door, had to wear seat belts; why our family, but not the family next door, was casual about nudity in the home. The general principle that contradictory beliefs frequently coexist seems now to have become a readily available schema for our children, a schema that permits them to accept with relative equanimity that they have different beliefs from many of their peers with respect to gender.

Finally, the cultural relativism schema can solve one of the primary dilemmas of the liberal feminist parent: how to give one's children access to the riches of classical literature—as well as to the lesser riches of the mass media—without abandoning them to the forces that promote gender-schematic processing. Happily, the censorship of sex-stereotyped materials that is necessary to retard the initial growth of the sex-linked associative network when children are young can end once children have learned the critical lesson that cultural messages reflect the beliefs and attitudes of the person or persons who created those messages.

Accordingly, before we read our daughter her first volume of fairy tales, we discussed with her the cultural beliefs and attitudes about men and women that the tales would reflect, and while reading the tales, we frequently made such comments as, "Isn't it interesting that the person who wrote this story seems to think girls always need to be rescued?" If such discussions are not too heavy-handed, they can provide a background of understanding against which the child can thoroughly enjoy the stories themselves, while still learning to discount the sex stereotypes within them as irrelevant both to their own beliefs and to truth. The cultural relativism schema thus brings children an awareness that fairy tales are fairy tales in more than one sense.

Sexism Schema.   Cultural relativism is fine in its place, but feminist parents will not and should not be satisfied to pretend that they think all

244 ideas—particularly those about gender—are equally valid. At some point, they will feel compelled to declare that the view of women and men conveyed by fairy tales, by the mass media—and by the next-door neighbors—is not only different, but wrong. It is time to teach one's children about sexism.

Moreover, it is only by giving children a sexism schema, a coherent and organized understanding of the historical roots and the contemporaneous consequences of sex discrimination, that they will truly be able to comprehend why the sexes appear to be so different in our society: why, for example, there has never been a female president of the United States; why fathers do not stay home with their children; and why so many people believe these sex differences to be the natural consequence of biology. The child who has developed a readiness to encode and to organize information in terms of an evolving sexism schema is a child who is prepared to oppose actively the gender-related constraints that those with a gender schema will inevitably seek to impose.

The development of a sexism schema is nicely illustrated by our daughter Emily's response to Norma Klein's book *Girls Can Be Anything*.[21] One of the characters is Adam Sobel, who insists that "girls are always nurses and boys are always doctors" and that "girls can't be pilots, . . . they have to be stewardesses." After reading this book, our daughter, then age four, spontaneously began to label with contempt anyone who voiced stereotyped beliefs about gender an "Adam Sobel." Adam Sobel thus became for her the nucleus of an envolving sexism schema, a schema that enables her now to perceive—and also to become morally outraged by and to oppose—whatever sex discrimination she meets in daily life.

As feminist parents, we wish it could have been possible to raise our children with neither a gender schema nor a sexism schema. At this historical moment, however, that is not an option. Rather we must choose either to have our children become gender schematic and hence sex typed, or to have our children become sexism schematic and hence feminists. We have chosen the latter.

A Comment on Psychological Androgyny

The central figure in gender schema theory is the sex-typed individual, a shift in focus from my earlier work in which the non-sex-typed individual—the androgynous individual in particular—commanded center

21. Norma Klein, *Girls Can Be Anything* (New York: E. P. Dutton, 1973).

stage.[22] In the early 1970s, androgyny seemed to me and to many others a 245 liberated and more humane alternative to the traditional, sex-biased standards of mental health. And it is true that this concept can be applied equally to both women and men, and that it encourages individuals to embrace both the feminine and the masculine within themselves. But advocating the concept of androgyny can also be seen as replacing a prescription to be masculine *or* feminine with the doubly incarcerating prescription to be masculine *and* feminine. The individual now has not one but two potential sources of inadequacy with which to contend. Even more important, however, the concept of androgyny is problematic from the perspective of gender schema theory because it is based on the presupposition that there is a feminine and a masculine within us all, that is, that "femininity" and "masculinity" have an independent and palpable reality and are not cognitive constructs derived from gender-schematic processing. Focusing on androgyny thus fails to prompt serious examination of the extent to which gender organizes both our perceptions and our social world.

In contrast, the concept of gender-schematic processing directs our attention to the promiscuous availability of the gender schema in contexts where other schemata ought to have priority. Thus, if gender schema theory has a political message, it is not that the individual should be androgynous. Rather, it is that the network of associations constituting the gender schema ought to become more limited in scope and that society ought to temper its insistence on the ubiquitous functional importance of the gender dichotomy. In short, human behaviors and personality attributes should no longer be linked with gender, and society should stop projecting gender into situations irrelevant to genitalia.

22. Sandra L. Bem, "Sex-Role Adaptability: One Consequence of Psychological Androgyny," *Journal of Personality and Social Psychology* 31, no. 4 (April 1975): 634–43; Sandra L. Bem, Wendy Martyna, and Carol Watson, "Sex-Typing and Androgyny: Further Explorations of the Expressive Domain." *Journal of Personality and Social Psychology* 34, no. 5 (November 1976): 1016–23; Sandra L. Bem, "Beyond Androgyny: Some Presumptuous Prescriptions for a Liberated Sexual Identity," in *The Future of Women, Issues in Psychology*, ed. Julia Sherman and Florence Denmark (New York: Psychological Dimensions, Inc., 1978), pp. 1–23; Sandra L. Bem and Ellen Lenney, "Sex-Typing and the Avoidance of Cross-Sex Behavior," *Journal of Personality and Social Psychology* 33, no. 1 (January 1976): 48–54.

Question 8

Does Mothering Behavior Contribute to the Devaluation of Women?

In 1978, Nancy Chodorow published *The Reproduction of Mothering*, a widely discussed book which sought to answer the question "why do women mother?" That is, why is it that in the face of the political, social, economic, and demographic changes over the past two centuries, mothers remain primarily responsible for childrearing?

The more traditional answers to this question tend to rely on biology or sex-role socialization. For example, Alice Rossi (1977, 1978, 1984) suggests that there is a biologically based potential for a greater investment in the child by the mother than by the father, at least during the first months of life. Other social scientists trace the role of the mother as the primary caretaker to role training and identification. According to this theory, girls learn to be mothers just as they learn other sex-appropriate behavior.

Rejecting biological explanations and finding role-socialization theory inadequate, Chodorow argues that the process of childcare done by mothers produces daughters who wish to be mothers. She then discusses the implications of the cycle, one of which is that girls emerge from childhood with a capacity for empathy and relationship built into their self-definition in a way that boys do not. This process also tends to produce men who denigrate women and women who may lack a sense of autonomy and self-confidence. The way out, according to Chodorow, would be equal parenting by the father and the mother.

While Chodorow's work has received much praise, it has also been severely criticized. One problem is that much of her evidence is drawn from clinical cases of individuals seeking treatment; therefore, her sample is not representative of the larger population. Others have faulted her for failing to examine the many structural factors in the larger society, such as inequitable salary scales, which make it in the family's interest to have the man devote his time to paid work while the woman takes care of the children (Bart, 1984). Joseph Pleck (1981) questions the need for a psychodynamic theory such as Chodorow's to account for man's negative attitude toward women. He points out that the simplest explanation is that men's views allow them to justify their relatively privileged position.

Alice Rossi challenges both Chodorow's methodology and her solutions. Do women mother for psychic reasons, or can we, as Rossi argues, find a more satisfactory explanation in the biological sciences? She also raises the question of how fathers will be able to participate equally in childcare if, as Chodorow seems to suggest, they are incapacitated by their own negative developmental experience.

References

Bart, P. (1984). Review of Chodorow's *The Reproduction of Mothering*. In J. Treblicot (Ed.), *Mothering Essays in Feminist Theory* (pp. 147–52). Totawa, N.J.: Rowman & Allanheld.

Chodorow, N. (1978). *The reproduction of mothering: Psychoanalysis and the sociology of gender*. Berkeley: University of California Press.

Pleck, J. (1981). *The myth of masculinity*. Cambridge: MIT Press.

Rossi, A. S. (1977). A biosocial perspective on parenting. *Daedalus, 106* (2), 1–31.

Rossi, A. S. (1978). The biosocial side of parenting. *Human Nature, 1* (6), 72–79.

Rossi, A. S. (1984). Gender and parenthood, American Sociological Association, 1983 presidential address. *American Sociological Review, 49* (2), 1–19.

Additional Reading

Badinter, E. (1980). *Mother love: Myth and reality: Motherhood in modern history*. New York: Macmillan.

Chodorow, N. (1981). Reply by Nancy Chodorow. *Signs: Journal of Women in Culture and Society, 6* (3), 500–14.

Chodorow, N., Dinnerstein, D., & Gottlieb, R. (1984). Mothering and the reproduction of power: An exchange. *Socialist Review, 14* (6), 121–30.

Dinnerstein, D. (1976). *The mermaid and the minotaur: Sexual arrangements and human malaise*. New York: Harper & Row.

Gerson, M. J., Alpert, J. L., & Richardson, M. W. (1984). Mothering: The view from psychological research. *Signs: Journal of Women in Culture and Society, 9* (3), 434–53.

Gottlieb, R. (1984). Mothering and the reproduction of power: Chodorow, Dinnerstein and social theory. *Socialist Review 14* (5), 93–119.

Gross, H. E., Bernard, J., Dan, A. J., Glazer, N., Lorber, J., McClintock, M., Newton, N., & Rossi, A. (1979). Viewpoint: Considering "A biosocial perspective on parenting." *Signs: Journal of Women in Culture and Society, 4* (4), 695–717.

Lerner, L., Parlee, M. B., Nadelson, C., & Benjamin, J. (1982). Special book review.

248   Chodorow's *Reproduction of mothering:* an appraisal. *The Psychoanalytic Review,* 69 (1), 151–62.

Lorber, J., Coser, R. L., Rossi, A. S. (1981). On *The Reproduction of Mothering:* A methodological debate. *Signs: Journal of Women in Culture and Society,* 6 (3), 482–514.

Trebilcot, J. (1983). *Mothering: Essays in feminist theory.* Totowa, N.J.: Rowman & Allanheld.

Feminism and Difference: Gender, Relation, and Difference in Psychoanalytic Perspective

NANCY CHODOROW

I would go so far as to say that even before slavery or class domination existed, men built an approach to women that would serve one day to introduce differences among us all.

—*Claude Lévi-Strauss*[1]

In both the nineteenth- and twentieth-century women's movements, it has often been argued that the degendering of society would eliminate male dominance, so that gender and sex would not determine social existence. One approach has sometimes held that "female" virtues or qualities— nurturance, for instance—should be spread throughout society and re- place aggression, competitiveness, and so forth; but these virtues are seen as acquired, a product of women's development or social location, and acquirable by men, given appropriate development, experience, and social reorganization. (This approach has at times held that women need to acquire certain "male" characteristics and modes of action—autonomy, independence, assertiveness—again, assuming that such characteristics are acquired.)

Another approach has tended toward an essentialist position, posing male-female differences as innate. Not the degendering of society, but its appropriation by women, with their virtues, is seen as the solution to male dominance. These virtues are uniquely feminine and usually thought to emerge from women's biology, which is then seen as intrinsically con- nected to or entailing a particular psyche; or a particular social role, such as mothering; or a particular body image (more diffuse, holistic, nonphallo- centric); or a particular sexuality (not centered on a particular organ and its

1. Quoted in Adrienne Rich, *On Lies, Secrets, and Silence* (New York: W. W. Norton, 1979), p. 84.

"Feminism and Difference: Gender Relation, and Difference in Psychoanalytic Perspective" by Nancy Chodorow, *Socialist Review*, 1979, *46*, 42–64. Copyright © 1979 by the Socialist Review. Reprinted by permission.

Dr. Chodorow is Associate Professor, Department of Sociology, University of California, Berkeley. *249*

250 goals; at times, lesbianism). In this view, women are intrinsically better than men and their virtues are not available to men.

In the beginning of the contemporary women's movement, the former view tended to predominate. More recently, versions of the second view have become much more prevalent and attractive to many feminists (and often to antifeminists as well). The liberal women's movement continues to hold the first view, as do socialist-feminists. The latter view, in various forms, is held by some radical feminists and lesbian feminists in the United States and is also prevalent among certain segments of the French women's movement.

This paper focuses on the question of gender or sex difference, particularly on thoughts about difference among French theorists. It argues against the essentialist view of difference and examines the contribution that psychoanalytic theory can make to understanding the question of sex or gender difference. The argument here contrasts with certain readings of psychoanalysis. It criticizes the (Lacan-influenced) views advanced by French theorists of difference like Luce Irigaray, and it contests the claims for Freudian orthodoxy made by most Marxist appropriators of psychoanalysis, such as the Frankfurt School and their followers, or Juliet Mitchell. I argue for another Marxist and feminist appropriation of psychoanalysis, one that stresses the relational ego rather than the instincts and autonomous ego.

Is gender best understood by focusing on differences between women and men, on women's and men's uniqueness? Should gender difference be a central organizing concept for feminism? My understanding is that "difference" as posed by "The Future of Difference" is absolute, abstract, and irreducible.[2] It is assumed to involve questions of the essence of gender, differences between women and men, each seen as an absolute category.

Gender difference is not absolute, abstract, or irreducible; it does not involve an essence of gender. Gender differences, and the experience of difference, are socially and psychologically created and situated just as are differences among women. Difference and gender difference do not exist as things in themselves: they are created relationally, and we cannot understand difference apart from this relational construction.

2. I will not discuss differences among women. Differences among women (of class, race, sexual preference, nationality, ethnicity, mothers and non-mothers) are all significant for feminist theory and practice, but these remain concrete differences. We can see how differences among women are socially situated, how they grow from particular social relations (the meaning and experience of race, or of sexual preference, for example), how they may contain physiological elements, yet only gain specific meaning in particular historical contexts and social formations. See, for example, "Women's Exile: Interview with Luce Irigaray," *Ideology and Consciousness* 1 (1977), pp. 57–76; and Monique Plaza, "'Phallomorphic Power' and the Psychology of 'Woman,'" *Ideology and Consciousness* 4 (1978), pp. 4–36.

Psychoanalysis, by providing a history of the emergence of separateness, differentiation, and perceptions of difference in early childhood, clarifies many of the issues involved in questions of difference. It provides a particularly useful means to see the relational and situated construction of difference and gender difference. Moreover, psychoanalysis provides an account of these issues as general psychological issues, as well as issues specific to the question of gender. I will discuss two aspects of the general subject of separateness, differentiation, and perceptions of difference and their emergence. First, I will consider how separation-individuation occurs relationally in the first "me"–"not-me" division, in the development of the "I," or self: I will suggest that we have to understand this separation-individuation in relation to other aspects of development, that it has particular implications for women, and that differentiation is not synonymous with difference or separateness. Second, I will talk about the ways that difference and gender difference are created distinctly, in different relational contexts, for girls and boys, and, hence, for women and men.

My goal is to reflect upon and help clarify a number of issues relevant to feminist theory and to particular strands of feminist politics. There is now a preoccupation with psychological separateness and autonomy, with individuality, as a necessary women's goal, a preoccupation growing out of many women's feelings of not having distinct autonomy as separate selves in comparison, say, to men. This may find a political counterpart in equal rights arguments based on notions of women as individuals rather than part of a collectivity or social group. And there is also a widespread view that gender differences are essential, that women are fundamentally different from men, and that these differences must be recognized, theorized, and maintained. (This may find a political counterpart in notions that women's special nature will guarantee a good society if we have a feminist revolution.)

Differentiation

Psychoanalysis talks of the process of "differentiation" or "separation-individuation."[3] A child of either gender is born originally with what is called a "narcissistic relation to reality"; cognitively and libidinally it experiences itself as merged and continuous with the world in general, and with its mother or caretaker in particular.

3. The work of Margaret S. Mahler, *On Human Symbiosis and the Vicissitudes of Individuation* (New York: International Universities Press, 1968), is paradigmatic here. For a more extended discussion of the earliest development of the self along lines suggested here, see Nancy Chodorow, *The Reproduction of Mothering: Psychoanalysis and the Sociology of Gender* (Berkeley: University of California Press, 1978), chs. 4 and 5.

252   Differentiation, or separation-individuation, means coming to perceive a demarcation between the self and the object world, coming to perceive the subject/self as distinct or separate from the object/other. An essential early task of infantile development, it involves the development of ego boundaries (a sense of personal psychological division from the rest of the world) and of a body ego (a sense of the permanence of one's physical separateness and the predictable boundedness of one's own body, of distinction between inside and outside).

This differentiation requires physiological maturation (for instance, the ability to perceive object constancy), but such maturation is not enough. Differentiation happens *in relation to* the mother or whomever is the child's primary caretaker. It develops through experiences of the mother's departure and return and through frustration, which emphasizes the child's separateness and the fact that it doesn't control all its own experiences and gratifications. Some of these experiences and gratifications come from within, some from without. If it were not for these frustrations, these disruptions of primary oneness, total holding and gratification, the child would not need to begin to perceive the other, the "outer world," as separate and not an extension of itself. Developing separateness thus involves, in particular, perceiving the mother or primary caretaker as separate and "not-me," where once we were an undifferentiated symbiotic unity.

Separateness, then, is not simply given from birth, nor does it emerge from the individual alone. Differentiation occurs in relationship, separateness is defined relationally: "I" am *"not-you."* Moreover, "you," or the other, is differentiated. Differentiation involves perceiving the *particularity* of the mother or primary caretaker in contrast to the rest of the world. As the self is differentiated from the object world, the object world is itself differentiated.

From a psychoanalytic perspective, learning to distinguish me and not-me is necessary for a person to grow into a functioning human being. It is also inevitable, since experiences of departure, of discontinuity in handling, feeding, where one sleeps, how one is picked up and by whom, of lack of total relational and physical gratification, are unavoidable. But for our understanding of "difference" in this connection, the concept of differentiation and the processes that characterize it need elaboration.

First, in most psychoanalytic formulations, and in the prevalent understandings of development, the mother, or the outside world, is simply the other, not-me, one who does or does not fulfill an expectation. This perception arises originally from the infant's cognitive inability to differentiate self and world; the infant does not distinguish between its desires for love and satisfaction and those of its primary love object and object of identification. The self here is the infant or growing child, and psychoanalytic accounts take the viewpoint of this child.

However, adequate separation, or differentiation, involves not simply perceiving the separateness, or otherness, of the other. It involves perceiving their subjectivity and selfhood as well. Differentiation, separation, disruption of the narcissistic relation to reality, are developed through learning that the mother is a separate being with separate interests, interests and activities that do not always coincide with just what the infants wants at the time. They involve the ability to experience and perceive the object/other (the mother) in aspects apart from its sole relation to the ability to gratify the infant's/subject's needs and wants; they involve seeing the object as separate from the self *and* from the self's needs.[4] The infant must change here from a "relationship to a subjectively conceived object to a relationship to an object objectively perceived."[5]

In infantile development, this change requires cognitive sophistication and the growing ability to integrate various images and experiences of the mother that come with the development of ego capacities. But these capacities are not enough. The ability to perceive the other as a self, finally, requires an emotional shift and a form of emotional growth. The adult self not only experiences the other as distinct and separate; it also does not experience the other solely in terms of its own needs for gratification and its own desires.

This interpretation implies that true differentiation, true separateness, cannot be simply a perception and experience of self-other, of presence-absence. It must involve two selves, two presences, two subjects. Recognizing the other as a subject is possible only to the extent that one is not dominated by felt need and one's own exclusive subjectivity. Such recognition enables appreciation and perception of many aspects of the other person. Whether we understand differentiation only from the viewpoint of the infant as a self or from the viewpoint of two interacting selves thus has consequences for what we think of as a mature self. If the mature self grows only out of the infant as a self, the other need never be accorded their own selfhood.

The fact that separation-individuation, or differentiation, involves not simply perceiving the otherness of the other, but their selfhood/subjectivity as well, is consequential not only for the development of one's own self-

---

4. Ernest G. Schachtel, "The Development of Focal Attention and the Emergence of Reality" (1954), in *Metamorphosis* (New York: Basic Books, 1959), provides the best discussion I know of this process.
5. D. W. Winnicott, "The Theory of the Parent-Infant Relationship" (1960), in *The Maturational Processes and the Facilitating Environment* (New York: International Universities Press, 1965).

254 hood, but also for perceptions of women. Hence, it seems to me essential to a feminist appropriation of psychoanalytic conceptions of differentiation. Since women, as mothers, are the primary caretakers of infants, if the child (or the psychoanalytic account) only takes the viewpoint of the infant as a (developing) self, then you get the *mother* only as an object. But from a feminist perspective, perceiving the particularity of the mother must involve according the mother her own selfhood. This is a necessary part of the development process, though it is also often resisted and experienced only conflictually and partially. Throughout life, perceptions of the mother move between perceiving her particularity and selfhood, and perceiving her as a narcissistic extension, a not-separate other whose sole reason for existence is to gratify wants and needs.

Few accounts recognize the import of this particular stance toward the mother. Alice Balint's proto-feminist account is the best I know of the infantile origins of adult perceptions of mother as object:

> Most men (and women)—even when otherwise quite normal and capable of an "adult," altruistic form of love which acknowledges the interests of the partner— retain towards their mothers this naive egoistic attitude throughout their lives. For all of us it remains self-evident that the interests of mother and child are identical, and it is the generally acknowledged measure of the goodness or badness of the mother how far she really feels this identity of interests.[6]

These perceptions, as a product of infantile development, will persist as long as (only) women mother, and they are one major reason why equal parenting is a necessary component of sexual equality. But I think that women, even within the ongoing context of women's mothering, can and must liberate ourselves from such perceptions in our personal emotional lives as much as possible, and certainly in our theorizing and politics.[7]

A second elaboration of psychoanalytic accounts of differentiation concerns the affective or emotional distinction between differentiation or separation-individuation and *difference*. Difference and differentiation are, of course, related to and feed into one another; it is in some sense true that cognitive or linguistic distinction, or division, must imply difference. However, it is possible to be separate, to be differentiated, without caring about or emphasizing difference, without turning the cognitive fact into an emotional, moral, or political one. In fact, assimilating difference to differentia-

---

6. Alice Balint, "Love for the Mother and Mother Love" (1939), in Michael Balint, *Primary Love and Psycho-Analytic Technique* (New York: Liveright, 1965), p. 97.
7. The new feminist/feminine blame-the-mother literature is one contemporary manifestation of failure in such a task. See especially Nancy Friday, *My Mother, My Self* (New York: Dell, 1977). Of course, this is not to ignore or pass over the fact that men have been past masters of such perceptions of women.

tion is defensive and reactive, a reaction to not feeling separate enough. Such assimilation involves arbitrary boundary creation and an assertion of hyper-separateness to reinforce a lack of security in a person's sense of their self as a separate person. But you can be separate from and similar to someone at the same time. For example, you can recognize their subjectivity and humanity as you recognize your own, your *commonality* as active subjects. Or, a woman can recognize her similarity, commonality, even continuity, with her mother, because she has developed enough of an unproblematic sense of separate self. The other side of being able to experience separateness and commonality, however, of recognizing the other's subjectivity, is the ability to recognize difference with a small *d*, differences that are produced and situated historically—for instance, the kinds of meaningful differences among women that I mentioned earlier.

The distinction between differentiation/separateness and difference relates to a third consideration, even more significant for difference and gender difference. Much psychoanalytic theory has centered its account of early infant development on separation-individuation, on the creation of the separate self, on the "me"–"not-me" distinction. There are other ways of looking at the development of self, other important and fundamental aspects to the self. Separation, the "me"–"not me" division, looms larger, both in our psychological life and theoretically, to the extent that these other aspects of the self are not developed (or theoretically stressed).

Object-relations theory shows that the development of self is not primarily the development of ego boundaries and a body ego.[8] Concomitant with the earliest development of its sense of separate self, the infant constructs an internal set of unconscious, affectively loaded representations of others in relation to its self, and an internal sense of self in relationship emerges. Images of felt good and bad aspects of the mother or primary caretaker, caretaking experiences, and the mothering relationship become part of the self, of a relational ego structure, through unconscious mental processes that appropriate and incorporate these images. With maturation, these early images and fragments of perceived experience become put together into a self. As externality and internality are established, therefore, what comes to be internal includes what originally were aspects of the other

8. I am drawing in what follows particularly on the work of D. W. Winnicott and Michael Balint. See Winnicott, *The Maturational Processes,* and *Playing and Reality* (New York: Basic Books, 1971); and Balint, *Primary Love,* and *The Basic Fault: Therapeutic Aspects of Regression* (London: Tavistock, 1968). See also W. R. D. Fairbairn, *An Object Relations Theory of the Personality* (New York: Basic Books, 1952), and Hans Loewald, "Internalization, Separation, Mourning, and the Superego," *Psychoanalytic Quarterly* 31 (1962), pp. 483–504.

256 and the relation to the other. (Similarly, what is experienced as external may include what was originally part of the developing self's experience.) Externality and internality, then, do not follow easily observable physiological boundaries but are constituted by psychological and emotional processes as well.

These unconscious early internalizations (that affect and constitute the internal quality of selfhood) may remain more or less fragmented, or they may develop a quality of wholeness. A sense of continuity of experience and opportunity to integrate a complex of (at least somewhat) complementary and consistent images enables the emergence of the "I" as a continous being with an identity. This more internal sense of self, or of "I," is not dependent on separateness or difference from an other. A "true self," or "central self," emerges through the experience of continuity, which the mother or caretaker helps to provide, through not having continually to react to and ward off environmental intrusions and not being continually in need.

The integration of a "true self" that feels alive and whole involves a particular set of internalized feelings about others in relation to the self. These include developing a sense that one is able to affect others and one's environment (a sense that one has not been inhibited by overanticipation of all one's needs), a sense that one has been accorded one's own feelings and a spontaneity about these feelings (a sense that one's feelings or needs have not been projected onto one), and a sense that there is a fit between one's feelings and needs and the mother or caretaker. These feelings all give the self a sense of agency and authenticity.

This sense of agency, then, results from caretakers who do not project experiences or feelings onto the child and who do not let the environment impinge indiscriminately. It results from empathic caretakers who understand and validate the infant's experience as that of a real self. Thus, the sense of agency, which is one basis of the inner sense of continuity and wholeness, grows out of the nature of the parent-infant relationship.

Another important aspect of internalized feelings about others in relation to the self concerns a capacity (or sense of wholeness) that develops through an internal sense of relationship with another.[9] The presence of the primary parent becomes an internal sense of the presence of another who is caring and affirming. The self comes into being here through first feeling confidently alone in the presence of its mother, then through this presence becoming internal. Part of its self becomes a good internal mother. This suggests that the central core of self is, internally, a relational ego, a

9. See Winnicott, "The Capacity to Be Alone" (1958), in *The Maturational Processes.*

sense of self-in-good-relationship. The presence or absence of others, their sameness or difference, then becomes something that is not a question of the infant's existing or not. A "capacity to be alone," a relational rather than reactive autonomy, develops because of a sense of the ongoing presence of another.

The senses of agency, of a true self that does not develop reactively, of a relational self or ego core, and of an internal continuity of being, are fundamental to an unproblematic sense of self, and provide the basis of both autonomy and spontaneity. The strength, or wholeness, of the self, in this view, does not depend only or even centrally on its degree of separateness (although the extent of confident distinctness certainly affects and is part of the sense of self). The more secure the central self, or ego core, the less one has to define one's self through separateness from others. Separateness becomes, then, a more rigid, defensive, rather fragile, secondary criterion of the strength of the self and of the "success" of individuation.

This view suggests that no one has a separateness consisting in me—not-me distinctions. Part of myself is always that which I have taken in; we are all to some degree incorporations and extensions of others. Separateness from the mother, defining oneself apart from her (and from other women), is not the only or final goal for women's ego strength and autonomy. In the process of differentiation, leading to a genuine autonomy, people maintain contact with those with whom they had their earliest relationships, where this contact is part of who we are. "I am" is not definition through negation, is not "who I am not." Developing a sense of confident separateness must be a part of all children's development. But once this confident separateness is established, one's relational self can become more central to one's life. *Differentiation is not distinctness and separateness, but a particular way of being connected to others.* This connection to others, based on early incorporations, in turn enables that empathy and confidence that is basic to the recognition of the other as a self.

What does all this have to do with male-female difference, with gender difference? What we learn from the more general inquiry is that we can only think of differentiation and the emergence of the self relationally. Differentiation occurs, and separation emerges, in relationship; they are not givens. Second, to single out separation as the core of a notion of self and of the process of differentiation may well be inadequate, and it is certainly not the only way to discuss the emergence of self or what constitutes a strong self. Differentiation includes internalization of aspects of the primary caretaker and caretaking relationship.

Finally, we learn that essential attitudes toward mothers and expecta-

258 tions of mothers—attitudes and expectations that enter into experiences of women more generally—emerge in the earliest differentiation of self. These attitudes and expectations arise during the emergence of separateness: given that differentiation and separation are developmentally problematic, and given that women are primary caretakers, the mother, who is a woman, becomes and remains for children of both genders the other, or object. She is not accorded autonomy or selfness. Such attitudes arise also from the gender-specific character of the early, emotionally charged, self and object images that affect the development of self and the sense of autonomy and spontaneity. They are internalizations of feelings about the self in relation to the *mother*, who is then often experienced as either overwhelming or overdenying. These attitudes, often unconscious, always with a basis in unconscious, emotionally charged feelings and conflicts, a precipitate of the early relationship to the mother and of an unconscious sense of self, may be more fundamental and determining of psychic life than more conscious and explicit attitudes to "sex differences" or "gender differences" themselves.

This inquiry suggests a psychoanalytic grounding for goals of emotional and psychic life other than separateness and autonomy, for notions that stress our connectedness rather than our separation one from another. Feelings of adequate separateness, fear of merger, are indeed issues for women, because of the ongoing sense of oneness and primary identification with our mothers (and children). A transformed organization of parenting would help women to resolve these issues. However, autonomy, spontaneity, and a sense of agency need not be based on self-other distinctions, on the individual as individual, but can be based on the fundamental interconnectedness, not synonymous with merger, that grows out of our earliest unconscious developmental experience and that enables a nonreactive separateness.[10]

Gender Differences in the Creation of Difference

We are not born with perceptions of gender difference; these emerge developmentally. In the traditional psychoanalytic view, however, when sexual difference is first seen, it has self-evident value: a girl perceives her lack of a penis, knows instantly that she wants one, and subsequently

10. My interpretation here of differentiation, the self, and the goals of psychic life contrasts with the traditional Freudian view which stresses ego and superego autonomy. For an excellent discussion of questions of ego autonomy and psychic structure, see Jessica Benjamin, "The Ends of Internalization: Adorno's Social Psychology," *Telos* 32 (1977), pp. 42–64.

defines herself and her mother as lacking, inadequate, castrated; a boy instantly knows having a penis is better, and fears the loss of his own.[11] This traditional account violates a fundamental rule of psychoanalytic interpretation. When the analyst finds trauma, shock, strong fears, or conflict, it is a sign to look for the roots of such feelings.[12] Freud, because of his inability to focus on the pre-oedipal years and the relationship of mother to child, could not follow his own rule here.

Clinical and theoretical writings since Freud suggest another interpretation of the emergence of perceptions of gender difference, one that reverses the perception of who experiences the greater trauma and retains only the claim that gender identity and the sense of masculinity and femininity develop differently for men and women.[13] These accounts suggest that for men core gender identity and masculinity are issues in a way that core gender identity and femininity are not for women. Core gender identity here is a cognitive sense of gendered self, that one is male or female. It is established in the first two years, concomitantly with the establishment of the sense of self. Later evaluations of the desirability of one's gender and of the activities and modes of behaving associated with it, or of one's own sense of adequacy at fulfilling gender-role expectation, are built upon this fundamental gender identity. They do not create or change it.

Most people develop an unambiguous core gender identity, a sense that they are female or male. But because women mother, the sense of maleness in men differs from the sense of femaleness in women. Maleness is more conflictual and more problematic. Underlying, or built into, core male gender identity is an early, nonverbal, unconscious, almost somatic sense of primary oneness with the mother, an underlying sense of femaleness that continually, usually unnoticeably, but sometimes insistently, challenges and undermines the sense of maleness.

Thus, because of a primary oneness and identification with his mother, a primary femaleness, a boy's and a man's core gender identity itself—the seemingly unproblematic cognitive sense of being male—is an issue. A boy must learn his gender identity as being not-female, or not-mother. Subsequently, again because of the primacy of the mother in early life and because of the absence of concrete, real, available male figures of identifica-

---

11. See Freud, "The Dissolution of the Oedipus Complex" (1924), *Standard Edition of the Complete Psychological Works* (SE), vol. 19, pp. 172–97; "Some Psychical Consequences of the Anatomical Distinction between the Sexes" (1925), SE, vol. 19, pp. 243–58; and "Femininity" (1933), in *New Introductory Lectures on Psychoanalysis*, SE, vol. 22, pp. 112–35.
12. See Roy Schafer, "Problems in Freud's Psychology of Women," *Journal of the American Psychoanalytic Association*, vol. 22, no. 3 (1974), pp. 459–85.
13. See Robert Stoller, "Facts and Fancies: An Examination of Freud's Concept of Bisexuality," in Jean Strouse, ed., *Women and Analysis* (New York: Grossman Publishers, 1974), and other Stoller writings.

260 tion and love who are as salient for him as female figures, learning what it is to be masculine is also defined as not-feminine, or not-womanly. Because of early-developed, conflictual core gender identity problems and later problems of adequate masculinity, it becomes important to men to have a clear sense of gender difference, of what is masculine and what is feminine, and to maintain rigid boundaries between these. (Researchers find, for example, that fathers sex-type children more than mothers. They treat sons and daughters more differently and enforce gender role expectations more vigorously.)[14] Boys and men come to deny the feminine identification within themselves and those feelings they experience as feminine: feelings of dependence, relational needs, emotions generally. They come to emphasize differences, not commonalities or continuities, between themselves and women, especially in situations that evoke anxiety because they threaten to challenge gender difference or to remind boys and men of their potentially feminine attributes.

Conflicts concerning core gender identity interact with and build upon particular ways that boys experience processes of differentiation and the formation of the self.[15] Both sexes establish separateness in relation to their mother, and internalizations in the development of self are internalizations of aspects of the mother as well. But because the mother is a woman, these experiences differ. Even as children of both sexes are originally part of herself, a mother unconsciously and often consciously experiences her son as more of an other than her daughter and, reciprocally, a son's male core gender identity develops away from his mother. The male's self, as a result, becomes based on a more fixed "me"–"not-me" distinction; separateness and difference as a component of differentiation becomes more salient. The female's self, by contrast, is less separate, involving a less fixed "me"–"not-me" distinction, creating the problems of sense of separateness and autonomy that I mention above.

At the same time, core gender identity for a girl is not problematic in the sense that it is for boys. It is built upon, and does not contradict, her primary sense of oneness and identification with her mother and is assumed easily along with her developing sense of self. Girls grow up with a sense of continuity and similarity to their mother, a relational connection to the world. For them, difference is not originally problematic nor funda-

---

14. For reviews of the social psychological literature on this, see Miriam Johnson, "Sex Role Learning in the Nuclear Family," *Child Development* 34 (1963), pp. 319–34, and "Fathers, Mothers, and Sex-Typing," *Sociological Inquiry*, vol. 45, no. 1 (1975), pp. 15–26; and Eleanor Maccoby and Carol Jacklin, *The Psychology of Sex Differences* (Stanford, Calif.: Stanford University Press, 1974).
15. For further discussion see Chodorow, *Reproduction*, ch. 5.

mental to their psychological being or identity. They do not define them-selves as not-men, or not-male, but as "I, who is female." Girls and women may have problems with their sense of continuity and similarity, if this sense is too strong and they have no sense of a separate self. However, these problems are not inevitable products of having a sense of continuity and similarity, since selfhood does not depend only on the strength and imper-meability of ego boundaries. Nor are these problems bound up with ques-tions of gender; rather, they are bound up with questions of self.

What may be problematic in the development of gender identification for girls concerns not the existence of core gender identity (the unques-tioned knowledge that one is female) but later-developed conflicts around such an identity, and the identifications, learning, and cognitive choices that this implies. Girls' difficulties in establishing a feminine identity have to do not with the inaccessibility and negative definition of this identity or its assumption by denial, but with the problems that may arise from identification with a negatively valued gender category and with an am-bivalent maternal figure, whose mothering and femininity are accessible but devalued, and often conflictual for the mother herself. Conflicts here are conflicts of power and cultural and social value, even as identification and the assumption of core gender identity are straightforward. Such conflicts, I would suggest, arise later in development and are less pervasively deter-mining of psychological life for women than are masculine conflicts around core gender identity and gender difference.

Men's and women's understanding of difference, and gender difference, must thus be understood in the relational context in which these are created, in their respective relation to their mother, who is their primary caretaker, love object, and object of identification, and who is a woman in a gender-organized world. This relational context means that difference, and gender difference, are central for males—one of the earliest, most basic male developmental issues—and not central for females. It gives men a psychological investment in difference that women do not have.

In earliest development, according to psychoanalytic accounts since Freud, it is very clear that males are "not-females"; core gender identity and the sense of masculinity are defined more negatively, in terms of that which is not female, or not-mother, than they are in positive terms. By contrast, it is not the case that females develop as "not-males"; female core gender identity and the sense of femininity are defined positively, as that which is female, or like mother. Difference from males is not so salient. An alternative way to put this is to suggest that developmentally, the maternal

262 identification represents and is experienced as generically human for children of both genders.[16]

Because men have power and cultural hegemony in our society, however, a notable thing happens. Men use and have used this hegemony to appropriate and transform these experiences: both in everyday life and in theoretical and intellectual formulations, men have come to define maleness as that which is basically human, and to define women as not-men. This transformation is first learned in, and helps to constitute, the oedipal transition—the cultural, affective, and sexual learnings of the meaning and valuation of sex differences.[17] Because Freud was not attentive to pre-oedipal development (and because of his sexism), he took this meaning and valuation as a self-evident given rather than a developmental and cultural product.

This transformed interpretation of difference, an interpretation learned in the oedipal transition, is produced by means of masculine cultural hegemony and power. Men are able to institutionalize their unconscious defenses against developmental conflicts that are repressed from consciousness but strongly experienced. This interpretation of difference is imposed on earlier developmental processes and is not the deepest, unconscious root of either the female or the male sense of gendered self. In fact, the primary sense of gendered self that emerges in earliest development constantly challenges and threatens men and gives a certain potential psychological security, even liberation, to women. The transformed interpretation of difference is not inevitable, given other parenting arrangements and other arrangements of power between the sexes. (It is especially insofar as women's lives and self-conception are male-defined that difference becomes more salient for us, as does differential evaluation of the sexes. Insofar as women's lives and self-conception become less male-defined, differences from men become less salient.)[18]

16. Johnson, "Fathers, Mothers," makes this suggestion, and suggests further that the father's masculinity introduces gender difference.

17. See Juliet Mitchell, *Psychoanalysis and Feminism* (New York: Pantheon Books, 1974).

18. The male and female bodies clearly have relevance for the question of gender difference. We live an embodied life: we live with those genital and reproductive organs and capacities, those hormones and chromosomes, that locate us physiologically as male or female. But, to turn to psychoanalysis once again, Freud's earliest discovery showed that there is nothing self-evident about this biology. How anyone understands, fantasizes about, symbolizes, internally represents, or feels about their physiology is a product of developmental experience in their family and not a direct product of this biology itself. These feelings, moreover, may be shaped by considerations completely apart from that biology. Considerations apart from biology also shape perceptions of anatomical "sex differences" and the psychological development of these sex differences into forms of sexual object choice, mode, or aim, into femininity or masculinity as psychoanalysis defines these, into activity or passivity, into one's choice of organ of erotic pleasure, and so forth.

We cannot know what children would make of their bodies in a nongender or nonsexually organized social world, what kind of sexual structuration or gender identities would develop. But it is not obvious

Evaluating Difference

What are the implications of this inquiry into psychoanalytic understandings of differentiation and gender difference for our understanding of difference and for our evaluation of the view that difference is central to feminist theory?

My inquiry suggests that our own sense of differentiation, of separateness from others, as well as our psychological and cultural experience and interpretation of gender or sexual difference, are created through psychological, social, and cultural processes, and through relational experiences. We can only understand gender difference, and human distinctness and separation, relationally and situationally,[19] as part of a system of asymmetrical social relationships embedded in inequalities of power, in which we grow up as selves, and as women and men. Our experience and perception of gender are processual; they are produced developmentally and in our daily social and cultural lives.

Difference is psychologically salient for men in a way that it is not for women, because of gender differences in early formative developmental processes and the particular unconscious conflicts and defenses these produce. This salience in turn has been transferred into a conscious cultural preoccupation with gender difference. It has also become intertwined with and helped to produce more general cultural notions that individualism, separateness, and distance from others are desirable and requisite to autonomy and human fulfillment.[20] Throughout these processes, it is women, as mothers, who become the objects apart from which separateness, difference, and autonomy are defined.

Ideologies of difference, ideologies that define us as women and as men—and inequality itself—are produced, socially, psychologically, and culturally, by people living in and creating their social, psychological, and cultural worlds. Women participate in the creation of these worlds and ideologies, even if our ultimate power and cultural hegemony are less than

that there would be major significance to biological sex differences, to gender difference, or to different sexualities. There might be a multiplicity of sexual organizations, identities, practices, perhaps even of genders themselves. Particular bodily attributes would not necessarily be so determining of who we are, what we do, how we are perceived, who are our sexual partners.

19. See Barrie Thorne, "Gender . . . How Is It Best Conceptualized?" paper presented to the Meetings of the American Sociological Association, San Francisco, August 1978.

20. For a discussion of these general cultural preoccupations and their psychological origins, see Evelyn Fox Keller, "Gender and Science," *Psychoanalysis and Contemporary Thought*, vol. 1, no. 3 (1978), pp. 409–33.

264 those of men. To speak of difference as a final, irreducible concept and to focus on gender differences as central is to reify and deny the *processes* that create the meaning and significance of gender. To see men and women as qualitatively different kinds of people, rather than seeing gender as processual, reflexive, and constructed, is to reify and deny *relations* of gender, to see gender differences as permanent rather than created and situated.

We certainly need to understand how difference comes to be important, how it is produced, and how it reproduces sexual inequality. But we should not appropriate differentiation and separateness, or difference, for ourselves and take it as given. Feminist theories and feminist inquiry based on the notion of essential difference, or focused on demonstrating difference, ultimately rely on the defensively constructed masculine models of gender that are presented to us as our cultural heritage, rather than creating new understandings of gender and difference that grow from our own politics, theorizing, and experience.

On *The Reproduction of Mothering:*
A Methodological Debate

ALICE S. ROSSI

I have read Nancy Chodorow's book three times, surely a measure of both its difficulty and its challenge. Each time I experienced the same sharp polarity of response, awe, and admiration on the one side, disappointment and disagreement on the other. I had been much impressed by Chodorow's essay in *Woman, Culture, and Society,* in which she first developed her core insight: because they are the same gender as their daughters and have themselves been girls, mothers of daughters tend to experience their infant daughters as less separate from themselves than they do their infant sons.[1] That insight was a brilliant one that contributes to an understanding of results in personality research. Many findings on gender differences are consistent with Chodorow's thesis of mothers' closer bond to daughters than to sons, and the closer identification of daughters than of sons to their mothers. The consequence of this pattern of early socialization is a less sharply differentiated self in girls than boys, and hence in women a greater sensitivity to others, greater capacity for empathy, and greater field dependency than in men. Since her theory implies that there is more than sex-role socialization at work in this process, I had expected the book to amplify this basic insight. I was not prepared for so extended an exegesis of psychoanalytic theory, past and present, or for the nearly total embeddedness of her theory in psychodynamic terms.

Such dependence on one particular theoretical perspective raises in my mind three main questions: (1) What constitutes "evidence" in Chodorow's book? (2) Does her central insight require the burden of so much

---

1. Chodorow, N. (1974). Family Structure and feminine personality. In *Woman, Culture, and Society,* ed. Michelle Zimbalist Rosaldo and Louise Lamphere (Stanford, Calif.: Stanford University Press).

"On the Reproduction of Mothering: A Methodological Debate" by Alice S. Rossi, *Signs: Journal of Women in Culture and Society,* 1981, 6 (3), 492–500. Copyright © 1981 by University of Chicago Press. Reprinted by permission.

Dr. Rossi is Professor, Department of Sociology, University of Massachusetts.

266 psychoanalytic theory and so harsh a rejection of theories in biology and developmental psychology? (3) Can (or should) significant institutional change effect a change in mother-infant dynamics? Can any amount of equal parenting or supplemental parenting by nonparents go very far in blurring the tendency for greater separation of sons from mothers than daughters from mothers?

Nature of the Evidence

I currently define myself as a developmental biosocial scientist, with strong research inclinations to behavioral science. As a consequence I found it took a good deal of time and patience to translate some of Chodorow's terms and concepts. Until one does, or unless one does, a reader like myself can be irked, misled, or otherwise bothered by her analysis. Thus, for example, when Chodorow says "investigate" she does not mean to engage in social research but to "speculate" or to "theorize." When she says "demonstrate" she means to cite illustrations consistent with a theory.[2] When she uses the term "methodological" she means to be consistent and logical in terms of a particular theory. Only if one has learned to translate her terminology can a reader understand her meaning when she refers to Talcott Parsons's work on family structure as "empirical investigations of parenting," which is the very last way I would ever describe Parsons's contribution to family sociology.[3]

Chodorow writes, "For me, the strength of psychoanalysis is as an interpretive theory and not as a behavioral science" (p. 41n), and she has little trouble in using clinical cases as evidence. I, on the contrary, do not easily accept clinical cases as adequate evidence in any area of theory or research, for the following reason: I cannot accept, as Chodorow does, the view that "pathology reflects in exaggerated form, differences in what are in fact normal tendencies" (p. 109). Pathology can involve not simply exaggeration of normal tendencies but actual reversals from normal tendencies. To determine which possibility applies in a particular instance requires

2. Thus she writes, in an introduction to the preoedipal mother-daughter relationships, "In what follows, I rely on extensive accounting and quoting. This is necessary because a simple assertion of the distinctions that I wish to demonstrate would not be persuasive without the clinical illustrations" (p. 99n.).

3. A typical summary statement following a description of clinical cases and theory is: "I conclude, from the evidence in Bibring's, Slater's, and Whiting's accounts . . ." (p. 107). I translate this to mean: "I suggest, from the speculations of Bibring, Slater, Whiting. . . ."

that clinical evidence be compared with evidence from "normal cases." But if you have access to such "normal" cases, you do not need clinical cases to begin with. At least not if your object is a theory that applies to basically healthy adults; obviously clinical cases are informative if you are developing a theory to explain pathology. Since Chodorow is clearly concerned with development in healthy adults and not with psychiatric patients, I cannot accept her mode of using clinical illustrations. While I understand her attraction to clinical cases because of the depth of insight they provide, I remain skeptical about their adequacy for or relevance to an understanding of normal developmental processes.

The purpose of my caveat is not to lessen the book's importance but to clarify the way in which it should be read: as a source of insights and as an effort to develop a plausible theory checked against clinical case illustrations. This means a reader should be forewarned that the book cannot be viewed as the expression of substantiated, tested theory. The further implication is that those of us with research inclinations carry some responsibility for translating Chodorow's theories into testable hypotheses and doing the research to confirm or disprove them.

Focus on Psychoanalysis and Rejection of Biology and Developmental Psychology

Chodorow's book sifts psychoanalytic theory and combines it with a critical sociological perspective. Along the way she attempts to deny the relevance of either theory or research findings from biology and developmental psychology.

That Chodorow leans so heavily on psychoanalysis is, of course, her privilege. She does well with it. There is a good review of Freudian and ego psychology theory and a careful critique of both. Where object-relations theory is concerned, however, she does not really use her sociological perspective to show its limitations. Nowhere in the book does Chodorow offer the smallest critical comment on the work of object-relations theorists like Alice and Michael Balint, Harry Guntrip, or W. R. D. Fairbairn. I have difficulty with all three variants of psychoanalytic theory where infant development is concerned. In the Freudian school, the infant is "all id," all quasi-biological drives, and the ego arises out of the id. In the hands of ego psychologists, the infant is an "undifferentiated ego-id matrix" or a "primal psychophysical self." In object-relations theory, the infant is a "unitary ego."

268   I do not see that any of the three views of the human infant are as useful or as illuminating as the understanding made possible by knowledge of the physiological capacities of the human infant, as found in research on either brain anatomy and development or the behavioral repertoire of the infant at various stages during the first year of life. I believe it is precisely because psychoanalytic theory is rooted in clinical practice that it can never be adequate as an approach to understanding infant development. Clinical practice relies on verbal recall and hence can reach back only to the third, or at most the second, year of life. It cannot tap preverbal stages of infant development in the first year. Yet these early months are critical to Chodorow's theories concerning the etiology of differential attachment by mothers to daughters compared with sons, and the corresponding closer identification of girls than of boys with their mothers.

There is one important characteristic of the human species that reflects the evolutionary price that was paid for the development of large cranial capacity. All human infants are born *premature* as a consequence of the competition between bipedal gait and skull size. For a human to be as mature at birth as our closest genetic relative, the chimpanzee, would require a pelvic opening so large that the bipedal gait would be clumsy and inefficient for human labor or flight from predators. Hence a human infant must reach the age of nine months before it is at the developmental stage of the chimpanzee at birth. This fact of prematurity is critical to an understanding of the preverbal young infant. At birth the infant brain is dominated by the limbic system, which is quite well developed, and by a rudimentary visual-motor-auditory system. There is little myelinization of brain matter in the cortex or the association areas of the brain in the first several months of life.[4] There cannot be any "ego" in the absence of a functioning cortex and association areas of the brain. The infant may develop sensory differentiation where taste, touch, smell, and sight are concerned, but not a sense of self. At only a few weeks of age, infants can differentiate the smell of their own mothers' milk from that of other mothers. It is likely that the infant is also differentiating touch and sound cues from the primary caretakers, but it is impossible for an infant to feel such emotions as envy, as many psychoanalysts claim. No therapist can retrieve

4. See K. Gibson, "Brain Structure and Intelligence in Macaques and Human Infants from a Piagetian Perspective," in *Primate Bio-social Development: Biological Social and Ecological Determinants,* ed. S. Kolinkoff and F. E. Poirer (New York: Garland Publishing Inc., 1977); E. Tronick and H. Adamson, "Structure of Early Face-to-Face Communicative Interactions," in *Before Speech: The Beginnings of Human Communication,* ed. M. Bullowa (New York: Cambridge University Press, 1979); C. M. Super, "Behavioral Development in Infancy," in *Handbook of Cross-cultural Human Development,* ed. R. L. Munroe, R. H. Munroe, and B. Whiting (New York: Garland Publishing, Inc., 1980); and A. Montague, *Touching: The Human Significance of Skin* (New York: Columbia University Press, 1971).

in verbal interaction with a patient anything from the sensory memory of the first year of life. Whatever those memories are, they remain in the sensory mode in which they were first experienced—smell, sound, taste, and touch.

My point in these examples is that findings from research in brain anatomy, biochemistry, and cross-species comparisons contribute as much if not more than the theoretical concepts of psychoanalysis to understanding the young human infant and its relation to the mothering adult. Such fields also alert us to the importance of being precise about the age of the child even in theoretical or speculative writing. But the ages of the children discussed in Chodorow's book are for the most part unspecified. One rarely knows if she is talking about an infant of two weeks, three months, or twelve months.[5] This confusion is serious since age is critical to infants' physiological capacities and hence to their social and psychological developmental capacities.

Chodorow is opposed to the incorporation of physiological factors into her theoretical perspective, just as object-relations and ego psychology theorists have been. She urges sociologists to be sensitive to the independent play of psychic phenomena, but I would urge her, by the same token, to be more sensitive and less closed to the independent and interdependent play of biological phenomena. I found the political stance that she, like many other feminists, takes toward the significance of biological factors a disturbing and limiting one. Hers is not an open and intellectual perspective that takes evidence from any quarter. She seems to reject any theory of physiological factors as a major influence on development, even though her own theory is itself rooted in the biology of sex. A few examples of her general "tone" in this area will communicate what it is I found troubling.

She argues at one point that "it is important to explore intragender

5. Even in Chodorow's assessment of reviews on gender differences, she ignores the age of the children involved in the research. E.g., she comments concerning the Maccoby and Jacklin (Eleanor Emmons Maccoby and Carol Nagy Jacklin, *The Psychology of Sex Differences* [Stanford, Calif.: Stanford University Press, 1974]) review: "I was left feeling a little as if a magic disappearing trick had been performed. All the experiences of being manipulated, channeled, and restricted which women and men have been commenting on, and which they have felt deeply and continuously, were suddenly figments of our imagination" (p. 98n.). The experience of such pressures and constraints are real, but they are irrelevant here because they involve adolescents and adults, while the Maccoby and Jacklin review deals largely with children under six years of age. Psychoanalytically inclined theorists do not like to come to grips with the growing evidence that very little of what occurs under six years of age predicts characteristics in adolescence and adulthood, or that hormonal events and physical changes in puberty can extinguish all but minor trace effects of early experiences and substitute a whole new set of characteristics predictive of adult personality. Thus whether a person was early or late in sexual maturation bears a stronger relation to adult personality and social role than the child-rearing practices of parents with prepubescent children. See O. Brim, Jr., and J. Kagan, eds., *Constancy and Change in Human Development* (Cambridge, Mass.: Harvard University Press, 1980) for a good recent review of the state of knowledge on the consequences of early experience on characteristics at later stages of the life span.

270 differences and intergender similarities *in order to argue against views of natural or biological gender differences*" (p. 215, my emphasis). One might express a hope of *not* finding strong evidence for exclusively or largely biological explanations, but it seems more appropriate for a social scientist to leave this possibility open rather than to encourage research in order to defend an already formed position. New knowledge ought to be input to the position one holds, or if the new evidence demands it, one should revise that position.

At another point, in describing the fact that Maccoby and Jacklin found very few consistent differences between boys and girls in their review of empirical research on sex differences, Chodorow comments, "As support against biological arguments for gender differences, these findings *may do the trick*" (p. 98, my emphasis). Such a statement shows a surprising lack of scientific objectivity. It is all the more noteworthy in light of Chodorow's later claim that Maccoby and Jacklin did not find many gender differences because the studies they reviewed were not subtle enough, did not probe unconscious structures, and hence missed important psychological differences between girls and boys that flow from different relations to the mother. You cannot have it both ways. You cannot reject a body of evidence because it excludes your favorite variables and accept that same body of evidence because it supports your prejudice. At least you cannot do this and claim a scientific approach to a problem. The book would have been enriched by a little *more* criticism of psychoanalytic theory and evidence, and a little *less* criticism of biological and psychological theory and evidence.

Coparenting as a Goal in Social Change

I find it difficult to accept Chodorow's belief that it is feasible and possible to effect so fundamental a change in parenting practices that sons and daughters would grow up with similar psychological characteristics. If Chodorow is right that the process described by her theory represents a fundamental building block for many subsequent gender differences and is deeply embedded in the unconscious, then a social goal of shared parenting and equal outcomes in the characteristics of sons and daughters will not be as easy to attain as the last part of Chodorow's book suggests. The implication of her analysis is that the arena for social and personality change must be in the very early months and years of the child's life and through the medium of identical patterns of relating to same-sex and to opposite-sex children. No amount of parent education or revisions of school curricula for children could effect the fundamental changes she seems to think attainable.

In my judgment, the book does not give this important point sufficiently sustained attention. Chodorow does not seem to want to accept the implications of her own analysis of mothering. She argues that it is not who does the caring but how they do it that matters; that physical care is not enough to enable physical and psychological growth in the infant; and that an infant needs not simply food and clean clothes but also physical contact with a person who is "emotionally there." Yet on another page she claims that "people other than biological mothers can provide adequate care" (p. 217).

What confidence do we have that any other adults than those who devote hours each day, every day, with special motivation of their own to bond and care for an infant, while holding expectations for the child's future self, can do this "adequate job" of being "psychologically there"? Besides, I myself do not want to hold to a criterion of merely "adequate" care but to one of "optimal" care, and I have grave doubts that it is possible to institutionalize early childcare in a way that provides both the quality and the continuity necessary for optimal infant development in the first two years of life.

Note, I am *not* talking about supplemental childcare for children who have reached nursery school age but about the primary care of infants and toddlers. Continuity and quality in caretakers are hard to come by. Here again, it is not the psychoanalytic theorist or feminist theorist but the researcher in infant development who furnishes the kind of evidence that gives one pause about any ready substitute for the parent's provision of this quality and continuity. Researchers like Daniel Stern and Edward Tronick have been investigating the emergence of parent-infant interaction, noting the subtle process whereby infants inform their mothers and mothers learn to be alert to cues from the infant on the timing, intensity, and termination of interaction between them.[6] If the interaction becomes overstimulating to infants, they terminate exchange by breaking eye contact or averting their heads, and because mothers as primary caretakers have watched this process frequently, they learn the cues that are difficult for others to sense in relating to the infant. Experimental research that gets the biological mother to change the script, or to feign lack of interest when the baby initiates the interaction, shows a profile of partial regression and withdrawal in the infant, for all the world like the physical reactions of infant rhesus monkeys and chimpanzees deprived of maternal care. Like the chimp infant, the

6. See, e.g., Daniel Stern and J. Gibbon, "Temporal Expectancies of Social Behaviors in Mother-Infant Play," in *Origins of the Infant's Social Responsiveness*, ed. Evelyn B. Thoman (New York: Halsted Press, 1979).

272 human infant withdraws: curled up, head averted, slump-shouldered, eyes closed, smile vanished—a profile of anxiety turned into regressive depression. That fathers overstimulate their infants by not learning the cues that tell when to stop may be because men spend less time with their infants than mothers do. On the other hand, this may not be the whole explanation, since other studies suggest that women observe more closely, make more frequent eye contact, even show more pupil dilation when exposed to young infants than men do. To what extent this gender difference could be removed by adequate socialization of males in infant care is an open question. It is not very likely that other adults will spend the number of hours with the same motivation in observing an infant that the parents themselves do. Infants vary, and it takes time to absorb the subtle knowledge of individual infants and to substitute for the child's own parent. Whether trained infant caretakers could acquire and apply such knowledge to several infants simultaneously is something we do not yet know.

It is not clear to me whether Chodorow believes that in time, fathers could acquire the level of skills, the responsiveness to infants, and the amount of time and energy to invest in parenting that is necessary for them to do for sons what mothers do for daughters. It is not even clear whether she views this as a desirable outcome. Should women be resocialized to curb the tendency to bond with their daughters more closely than with their sons? On such a question hinges whether our goal is to encourage men to be more like women or women more like men in parenting styles. With either choice, there is no easy blueprint for how to achieve such a goal, and the chances thus remain great that the developmental process Chodorow has described may contribute to gender differences for many generations to come.

I emphasize again that I am talking about the very young child. There is no question from the evidence that has now accumulated that children can sustain and indeed benefit from multiple supplementary caretakers once they have passed their third or fourth birthday. From the evidence of child development research, we have reason to believe that, by the third year, there is a deeply embedded mental representation of self as male or female which can take a good deal of challenging experience without becoming disturbed. It is all to the good to encourage more intimacy between men and children from an early age, and for this reason parental leave before and/or after birth is an effective policy to espouse for both men and women workers. But I do not expect gender differences to dissipate as a consequence of shared parenting patterns. I believe that the mother-daughter relationship will continue to be more intense than and qualitatively different from mother-son relationships, and father-son relationships from father-daughter relationships. The woman's physical experience of menstruation, pregnancy, and birthing remains to differentiate the parents. A young boy is not merely distancing himself from his opposite-sex mother but acting out a maleness rooted in his internal biochemical functioning that is different from a girl's, and his external motor and sensual responses will accordingly differ from his sister's. That few gender differences are found in early childhood is not a demonstration that biology does not matter, since the critical stages of sex dimorphism occur in puberty and adolescence.

Indeed, exposure to the relevant biological sciences, now coupled with Chodorow's powerful argument about same-sex mothering and its developmental consequences, leads me to find less and less adequate the proposals feminists have urged as solutions to sex inequality. But then, I have never been persuaded that sex equality means an identical profile of characteristics between men and women. Chodorow has given us a challenging book that repeatedly suggests the complexities that confront feminist theory as well as proposals for action. The charge to us as researchers is to test some of her complex ideas, and the challenge to us as activists is to reassess our simplistic solutions in light of these research results.

Question 9

Do Women Speak in a Different Moral Voice?

Carol Gilligan's *In a Different Voice* (1982) is one of those rare books that has attracted considerable attention not only in academic circles but in popular ones as well. *Ms.* magazine, for example, selected Gilligan as "Woman of the Year, 1984" because, in the words of the award, "her work has created a new appreciation for a previously uncatalogued female sensibility, as well as possibilities for new understanding between the genders" (Van Gelder, 1984, p. 38).

Gilligan is by no means the first psychologist to discuss differences in moral reasoning between men and women. Sigmund Freud, Jean Piaget, Erik Erikson, and Lawrence Kohlberg all depicted women as following a different line of moral development than men, one based on a concern with human relationships. Where Gilligan departs from these other theorists is in placing a higher value on women's differences.

Gilligan focuses on Kohlberg's stage theory of moral development, which she claims tends to locate women at level 3, characterized by a regard for "what pleases or helps others," while placing men at the more mature level 4, which focuses on a concern with law and justice. As Gilligan points out in the following pages, Kohlberg and other psychologists have erred in adopting male behavior as the norm. She notes the paradox that the traits traditionally associated with the "goodness" of women—caring and sensitivity to others—are the very same characteristics that render them relatively inferior on moral-judgment scales.

Building on Chodorow, Gilligan notes that women are oriented toward attachment and "connectedness" to others while men are inclined toward individuation and "separateness" from others. The result, she argues, is not that women's moral development is less mature than men's but rather that it is different. In her work, women's "ethic of care" becomes the 275 equivalent of men's "ethic of justice."

Gilligan has been praised for challenging the male bias in previous theories on moral development. However, her work has also stimulated considerable disagreement. For example, Catherine G. Greeno and Eleanor Maccoby (1986) argue that because Gilligan ignores more recent work which does not show men scoring at higher levels, she is attacking a straw person. There is also the question of whether Gilligan, by basing a theory of moral development in part on the responses of women to abortion, has built sex bias into her work (Wallston, in press). Others have criticized her abortion research from a different perspective, noting that in failing to consider the race, religion, class, or ethnicity of her subjects, Gilligan ignores variables that may be more influential than gender in determining moral decision making (Auerbach, Blum, Smith, & Williams, 1985).

Feminists have also voiced concern over what effect studies like Gilligan's, which focus on sex differences, will have on the political advancement of women. Whether or not Gilligan's conclusions can be used to support traditional sex-role stereotypes, it is clear that her work contrasts sharply with that of feminist psychologists of the 1970s who developed concepts such as androgyny to minimize the significance of sex differences. Do women speak in a different voice, as Gilligan maintains, or is her thesis undermined by serious methodological flaws, as Colby and Damon argue in their essay?

References

Auerbach, J., Blum, L. Smith, V., & Williams, C. (1985). *Feminist Studies, 11* (1), pp. 149–61.

Gilligan, C. (1982). *In a different voice: Psychological theory and women's development.* Cambridge: Harvard University Press.

Greeno, C. G., & Maccoby, E. E. (1986). How different is the "different voice?" *Signs: Journal of Women in Culture and Society, 11* (2), 310–16.

Van Gelder, L. (1984). Carol Gilligan: Leader for a different kind of future. *Ms. XII* (7), 37–40; 101.

Wallston, B. S. (in press). Social psychology of women and gender. *Journal of Applied Social Psychology.*

Additional Reading

Baumrind, D. (1986). Sex differences in moral reasoning: Response to Walker's (1984) conclusions that there are none. *Child Development,* 57 (2), 511–21.

276 Benjamin, J. (1983). Review of *In a Different Voice*, *Signs: Journal of Women in Culture and Society*, 9 (2), 297–98.

Benton, C. J., Hernandez, A. C. R., Schmidt, A., Schmitz, M. D., Stone, A. J. & Weiner, B. (1983). Is hostility linked with affiliation among males and with achievement among females? A critique of Pollak and Gilligan. *Journal of Personality and Social Psychology*, 45, 1167–71.

Boyd, D. R. (1983). Careful justice or just caring: A response to Gilligan. *Proceedings of the Philosophy of Education Society*, 38, 63–69.

Brabeck, M. (1983). Moral judgment: Theory and research on differences between males and females. *Developmental Review*, 3, 274–91.

Bussey, K., & Maughan, B. (1982). Gender differences in moral reasoning. *Journal of Personality and Social Psychology*, 42, 701–06.

Douvan, E. (1983). Learning to listen to a different drummer. *Contemporary Psychology*, 28, 261–62.

Ford, M. R. & Lowery, C. R. (1986). Gender differences in moral reasoning: A comparison of the use of justice and care orientations. *Journal of Personality and Social Psychology*, 50 (4), 777–83.

Gibbs, J. C., Arnold, K. D., & Burkhart, J. E. (1984). Sex differences in expression of moral judgment. *Child Development*, 55 (3), 1040–43.

Gilligan, C. & Belenky, M., (1980). A naturalistic study of abortion decisions. In R. L. Selman and R. Yando (Eds.), *Clinical-Developmental Psychology* (pp. 69–90). San Francisco: Jossey Bass.

Gilligan, C. (1986). Remapping development: The power of divergent data. In Cirillo, L., & Wapner, S. (Eds.), *Value Presuppositions in Theories of Human Development*. Hillside, N.J.: Lawrence Erlbaum.

Gottlieb, D., Taylor, S., & Ruderman, A. (1977). Cognitive bases of children's moral judgments. *Developmental Psychology*, 13, 547–56.

Greeno, C. G., & Maccoby, E. E. (1986). How different is the "different voice"? *Signs: Journal of Women in Culture and Society*, 11 (2), 310–16.

Hayles, N. K. (1986). Carol Gilligan and "The Mill on the Floss." *Signs: Journal of Women in Culture and Society*, 12 (1), 23–39.

Kerber, L., Greeno, C., Maccoby, E., Luria, Z., Stack, C. & Gilligan, C. (1986). On a different voice: An interdisciplinary forum. *Signs: Journal of Women in Culture and Society*, 11 (2), 304–33.

Kohlberg, L. (1984). *The psychology of moral development: Essays on moral development* (Vol. 2). San Francisco: Harper & Row.

Lifton, P. D. (1982). Should Heinz's wife read this book? *Journal of Personality Assessment*, 46, 550–51.

Lifton, P. (1985). Individual differences in moral development. *Journal of Personality*, 53 (2), 306–34.

Lyons, N. (1983). Two perspectives: On self, relationships and morality. *Harvard Educational Review*, 53 (2), 125–45.

Moessinger, P., Kitchener, R., & Broughton, J. M. (Eds.) (In press). Women and moral development. *New Ideas in Psychology*.

Murphy, J., & Gilligan, C. (1980). Moral development in late adolescence and adulthood: A critique and reconstruction of Kohlberg's theory. *Human Development*, 23, 77–104.

Nunner-Winkler, G. (1984). Two moralities? A critical discussion of an ethic of care and responsibility versus an ethic of rights and justice. In W. Kurtines & J. Gewirtz (Eds.), *Morality, moral behavior and moral development* (pp. 348–61). New York: Wiley.

Pollak, S., & Gilligan, C. (1985). Killing the messenger. *Journal of Personality and Social Psychology*, 48 (2), 374–75.

Reimer, M. (1983). Gender difference in moral judgment. *Smith College Studies in Social Work*, 54 (1), 1–12.

Snarey, J. (1985). Cross-cultural universability of social moral development: A critical 277
review of Kohlbergian research. *Psychological Bulletin, 97* (2), 202–32.

Walker, L. (1984). Sex differences in development of moral reasoning: A critical review.
Child Development, 55 (3), 677–91.

Walker, L. (1986). Experiential and cognitive sources of moral development. *Human
Development, 29* (2), 113–24.

Walker, L. (1986). Sex differences in the development of moral reasoning: A rejoinder to
Baumrind. *Child Development, 57* (2), 522–26.

West, J. D., & Bursor, D. E. (1984). Gilligan and Kohlberg: Gender issue in moral
development. *Journal of Humanistics Education and Development, 22* (4), 134–42.

Yes

In a Different Voice: Women's Conceptions of Self and of Morality

CAROL GILLIGAN

The arc of developmental theory leads from infantile dependence to adult autonomy, tracing a path characterized by an increasing differentiation of self from other and a progressive freeing of thought from contextual constraints. The vision of Luther, journeying from the rejection of a self defined by others to the assertive boldness of "Here I stand" and the image of Plato's allegorical man in the cave, separating at last the shadows from the sun, has taken powerful hold on the psychological understanding of what constitutes development. Thus, the individual, meeting fully the developmental challenges of adolescence as set for him by Piaget, Erikson, and Kohlberg, thinks formally, proceeding from theory to fact, and defines both the self and the moral autonomously, that is, apart from the identification and conventions that had comprised the particulars of his childhood world. So equipped, he is presumed ready to live as an adult, to love and work in a way that is both intimate and generative, to develop an ethical sense of caring and a genital mode of relating in which giving and taking fuse in the ultimate reconciliation of the tension between self and other.

Yet the men whose theories have largely informed this understanding of development have all been plagued by the same problem, the problem of women, whose sexuality remains more diffuse, whose perception of self is so much more tenaciously embedded in relationships with others and whose moral dilemmas hold them in a mode of judgment that is insistently contextual. The solution has been to consider women as either deviant or deficient in their development.

That there is a discrepancy between concepts of womanhood and adulthood is nowhere more clearly evident than in the series of studies on sex-role stereotypes reported by Broverman, Vogel, Broverman, Clarkson,

Dr. Gilligan is Associate Professor, Harvard Graduate School of Education, Harvard University.

and Rosenkrantz (1972). The repeated finding of these studies is that the qualities deemed necessary for adulthood—the capacity for autonomous thinking, clear decision making, and responsible action—are those associated with masculinity but considered undesirable as attributes of the feminine self. The stereotypes suggest a splitting of love and work that relegates the expressive capacities requisite for the former to women while the instrumental abilities necessary for the latter reside in the masculine domain. Yet, looked at from a different perspective, these stereotypes reflect a conception of adulthood that is itself out of balance, favoring the separateness of the individual self over its connection to others and leaning more toward an autonomous life of work than toward the interdependence of love and care.

This difference in point of view is the subject of this essay, which seeks to identify in the feminine experience and construction of social reality a distinctive voice, recognizable in the different perspective it brings to bear on the construction and resolution of moral problems. The first section begins with the repeated observation of difference in women's concepts of self and of morality. This difference is identified in previous psychological descriptions of women's moral judgments and described as it again appears in current research data. Examples drawn from interviews with women in and around a university community are used to illustrate the characteristics of the feminine voice. The relational bias in women's thinking that has, in the past, been seen to compromise their moral judgment and impede their development now begins to emerge in a new developmental light. Instead of being seen as a developmental deficiency, this bias appears to reflect a different social and moral understanding.

This alternative conception is enlarged in the second section through consideration of research interviews with women facing the moral dilemma of whether to continue or abort a pregnancy. Since the research design allowed women to define as well as resolve the moral problem, developmental distinctions could be derived directly from the categories of women's thought. The responses of women to structured interview questions regarding the pregnancy decision formed the basis for describing a developmental sequence that traces progressive differentiations in their understanding and judgment of conflicts between self and other. While the sequence of women's moral development follows the three-level progression of all social developmental theory, from an egocentric through a societal to a universal perspective, this progression takes place within a distinct moral conception. This conception differs from that derived by Kohlberg from his all-male longitudinal research data.

This difference then becomes the basis in the third section for challeng-

280 ing the current assessment of women's moral judgment at the same time that it brings to bear a new perspective on developmental assessment in general. The inclusion in the overall conception of development of those categories derived from the study of women's moral judgment enlarges developmental understanding, enabling it to encompass better the thinking of both sexes. This is particularly true with respect to the construction and resolution of the dilemmas of adult life. Since the conception of adulthood retrospectively shapes the theoretical understanding of the development that precedes it, the changes in that conception that follow from the more central inclusion of women's judgments recast developmental understanding and lead to a reconsideration of the substance of social and moral development.

Characteristics of the Feminine Voice

The revolutionary contribution of Piaget's work is the experimental confirmation and refinement of Kant's assertion that knowledge is actively constructed rather than passively received. Time, space, self, and other, as well as the categories of developmental theory, all arise out of the active interchange between the individual and the physical and social world in which he lives and of which he strives to make sense. The development of cognition is the process of reappropriating reality at progressively more complex levels of apprehension, as the structures of thinking expand to encompass the increasing richness and intricacy of experience.

Moral development, in the work of Piaget and Kohlberg, refers specifically to the expanding conception of the social world as it is reflected in the understanding and resolution of the inevitable conflicts that arise in the relations between self and others. The moral judgment is a statement of priority, an attempt at rational resolution in a situation where, from a different point of view, the choice itself seems to do violence to justice.

Kohlberg (1969), in his extension of the early work of Piaget, discovered six stages of moral judgment, which he claimed formed an invariant sequence, each successive stage representing a more adequate construction of the moral problem, which in turn provides the basis for its more just resolution. The stages divide into three levels, each of which denotes a significant expansion of the moral point of view from an egocentric through a societal to a universal ethical conception. With this expansion in perspective comes the capacity to free moral judgment from the individual needs and social conventions with which it had earlier been confused and anchor it instead in principles of justice that are universal in application. These principles provide criteria upon which both individual and societal claims can be impartially assessed. In Kohlberg's view, at the highest stages of development morality is freed from both psychological and historical constraints, and the individual can judge independently of his own particular needs and of the values of those around him.

That the moral sensibility of women differs from that of men was noted by Freud (1925/1961) in the following by now well-quoted statement:

I cannot evade the notion (though I hesitate to give it expression) that for women the level of what is ethically normal is different from what it is in man. Their superego is never so inexorable, so impersonal, so independent of its emotional origins as we require it to be in men. Character-traits which critics of every epoch have brought up against women—that they show less sense of justice than men, that they are less ready to submit to the great exigencies of life, that they are more often influenced in their judgments by feelings of affection or hostility—all these would be amply accounted for by the modification in the formation of their superego which we have inferred above. (pp. 257 58)

While Freud's explanation lies in the deviation of female from male development around the construction and resolution of the Oedipal problem, the same observations about the nature of morality in women emerge from the work of Piaget and Kohlberg. Piaget (1932/1965), in his study of the rules of children's games, observed that, in the games they played, girls were "less explicit about agreement [than boys] and less concerned with legal elaboration" (p. 93). In contrast to the boys' interest in the codification of rules, the girls adopted a more pragmatic attitude, regarding "a rule as good so long as the game repays it" (p. 83). As a result, in comparison to boys, girls were found to be "more tolerant and more easily reconciled to innovations" (p. 52).

Kohlberg (1971) also identifies a strong interpersonal bias in the moral judgments of women, which leads them to be considered as typically at the third of his six-stage developmental sequence. At that stage, the good is identified with "what pleases or helps others and is approved of by them" (p. 164). This mode of judgment is conventional in its conformity to generally held notions of the good but also psychological in its concern with intention and consequences as the basis for judging the morality of action.

That women fall largely into this level of moral judgment is hardly surprising when we read from the Broverman et al. (1972) list that prominent among the twelve attributes considered to be desirable for women are tact, gentleness, awareness of the feelings of others, strong need for security, and easy expression of tender feelings. And yet, herein lies the paradox, for the very traits that have traditionally defined the "goodness" of

282 women, their care for and sensitivity to the needs of others, are those that mark them as deficient in moral development. The infusion of feeling into their judgments keeps them from developing a more independent and abstract ethical conception in which concern for others derives from principles of justice rather than from compassion and care. Kohlberg, however, is less pessimistic than Freud in his assessment, for he sees the development of women as extending beyond the interpersonal level, following the same path toward independent, principled judgment that he discovered in the research on men from which his stages were derived. In Kohlberg's view, women's development will proceed beyond Stage Three when they are challenged to solve moral problems that require them to see beyond the relationships that have in the past generally bound their moral experience.

What then do women say when asked to construct the moral domain; how do we identify the characteristically "feminine" voice? A Radcliffe undergraduate, responding to the question, "If you had to say what morality meant to you, how would you sum it up?," replies:

When I think of the word morality, I think of obligations, I usually think of it as conflicts between personal desires and social things, social considerations, or personal desires of yourself versus personal desires of another person or people or whatever. Morality is that whole realm of how you decide these conflicts. A moral person is one who would decide, like by placing themselves more often than not as equals, a truly moral person would always consider another person as their equal . . . in a situation of social interaction, something is morally wrong where the individual ends up screwing a lot of people. And it is morally right when everyone comes out better off.[1]

Yet when asked if she can think of someone whom she would consider a genuinely moral person, she replies, "Well, immediately I think of Albert Schweitzer because he has obviously given his life to help others." Obligation and sacrifice override the ideal of equality, setting up a basic contradiction in her thinking.

Another undergraduate responds to the question, "What does it mean to say something is morally right or wrong?," by also speaking first of responsibilities and obligations:

Just that it has to do with responsibilities and obligations and values, mainly values. . . . In my life situation I relate morality with interpersonal relationships that have to do with respect for the other person and myself. [Why respect other people?] Because they have a consciousness or feelings that can be hurt, an awareness that can be hurt.

1. The Radcliffe women whose responses are cited were interviewed as part of a pilot study on undergraduate moral development conducted by the author in 1970.

The concern about hurting others persists as a major theme in the responses of two other Radcliffe students:

[Why be moral?] Millions of people have to live together peacefully. I personally don't want to hurt other people. That's a real criterion, a main criterion for me. It underlies my sense of justice. It isn't nice to inflict pain. I empathize with anyone in pain. Not hurting others is important in my own private morals. Years ago, I would have jumped out of a window not to hurt my boyfriend. That was pathological. Even today though, I want approval and love and I don't want enemies. Maybe that's why there is morality—so people can win approval, love and friendship.

My main moral principle is not hurting other people as long as you aren't going against your own conscience and as long as you remain true to yourself. . . . There are many moral issues such as abortion, the draft, killing, stealing, monogamy, etc. If something is a controversial issue like these, then I always say it is up to the individual. The individual has to decide and then follow his own conscience. There are no moral absolutes. . . . Laws are pragmatic instruments, but they are not absolutes. A viable society can't make exceptions all the time, but I would personally. . . . I'm afraid I'm heading for some big crisis with my boyfriend someday, and someone will get hurt, and he'll get more hurt than I will. I feel an obligation to not hurt him, but also an obligation to not lie. I don't know if it is possible to not lie and not hurt.

The common thread that runs through these statements, the wish not to hurt others and the hope that in morality lies a way of solving conflicts so that no one will get hurt, is striking in that it is independently introduced by each of the four women as the most specific item in their response to a most general question. The moral person is one who helps others; goodness is service, meeting one's obligations and responsibilities to others, if possible, without sacrificing oneself. While the first of the four women ends by denying the conflict she initially introduced, the last woman anticipates a conflict between remaining true to herself and adhering to her principle of not hurting others. The dilemma that would test the limits of this judgment would be one where helping others is seen to be at the price of hurting the self.

The reticence about taking stands on "controversial issues," the willingness to "make exceptions all the time" expressed in the final example above, is echoed repeatedly by other Radcliffe students, as in the following two examples:

I never feel that I can condemn anyone else. I have a very relativistic position. The basic idea that I cling to is the sanctity of human life. I am inhibited about impressing my beliefs on others.

I could never argue that my belief on a moral question is anything that another

284 person should accept. I don't believe in absolutes. . . . If there is an absolute for moral decisions, it is human life.

Or as a thirty-one-year-old Wellesley graduate says, in explaining why she would find it difficult to steal a drug to save her own life despite her belief that it would be right to steal for another: "It's just very hard to defend yourself against the rules. I mean, we live by consensus, and you take an action simply for yourself, by yourself, there's no consensus there, and that is relatively indefensible in this society now."

What begins to emerge is a sense of vulnerability that impedes these women from taking a stand, what George Eliot (1860/1965) regards as the girl's "susceptibility" to adverse judgments of others, which stems from her lack of power and consequent inability to do something in the world. While relativism in men, the unwillingness to make moral judgments that Kohlberg and Kramer (1969) and Kohlberg and Gilligan (1971) have associated with the adolescent crisis of identity and belief, takes the form of calling into question the concept of morality itself, the women's reluctance to judge stems rather from their uncertainty about their right to make moral statements or, perhaps, the price for them that such judgment seems to entail. This contrast echoes that made by Matina Horner (1972), who differentiated the ideological fear of success expressed by men from the personal conflicts about succeeding that riddled the women's responses to stories of competitive achievement.

Most of the men who responded with the expectation of negative consequences because of success were not concerned about their masculinity but were instead likely to have expressed existential concerns about finding a "non-materialistic happiness and satisfaction in life." These concerns, which reflect changing attitudes toward traditional kinds of success or achievement in our society, played little, if any, part in the female stories. Most of the women who were high in fear of success imagery continued to be concerned about the discrepancy between success in the situation described and feminine identity. (pp. 163–64)

When women feel excluded from direct participation in society, they see themselves as subject to a consensus or judgment made and enforced by the men on whose protection and support they depend and by whose names they are known. A divorced middle-aged woman, mother of adolescent daughters, resident of a sophisticated university community, tells the story as follows:

As a woman, I feel I never understood that I was a person, that I can make decisions and I have a right to make decisions. I always felt that that belonged to my father or my husband in some way or church which was always represented by a male clergyman. They were the three men in my life: father, husband, and clergyman, and they had much more to say about what I should or shouldn't do. They were really authority figures which I accepted. I didn't rebel against that. It only has lately occurred to me that I never even rebelled against it, and my girls are much more conscious of this, not in the militant sense, but just in the recognizing sense. . . . I still let things happen to me rather than make them happen, than to make choices, although I know all about choices. I know the procedures and the steps and all. [Do you have any clues about why this might be true?] Well, I think in one sense, there is less responsibility involved. Because if you make a dumb decision, you have to take the rap. If it happens to you, well, you can complain about it. I think that if you don't grow up feeling that you ever had any choices, you don't either have the sense that you have emotional responsibility. With this sense of choice comes this sense of responsibility.

The essence of the moral decision is the exercise of choice and the willingness to accept responsibility for that choice. To the extent that women perceive themselves as having no choice, they correspondingly excuse themselves from the responsiblity that decision entails. Childlike in the vulnerability of their dependence and consequent fear of abandonment, they claim to wish only to please but in return for their goodness they expect to be loved and cared for. This, then, is an "altruism" always at risk, for it presupposes an innocence constantly in danger of being compromised by an awareness of the trade-off that has been made. Asked to describe herself, a Radcliffe senior responds:

I have heard of the onion skin theory. I see myself as an onion, as a block of different layers, the external layers for people that I don't know that well, the agreeable, the social, and as you go inward there are more sides for people I know that I show. I am not sure about the innermost, whether there is a core, or whether I have just picked up everything as I was growing up, these different influences. I think I have a neutral attitude towards myself, but I do think in terms of good and bad. . . . Good—I try to be considerate and thoughtful to other people and I try to be fair in situations and be tolerant. I use the words but I try and work them out practically. . . . Bad things—I am not sure if they are bad, if they are altruistic or I am doing them basically for approval of other people. [Which things are these?] The values I have when I try to act them out. They deal mostly with interpersonal type relations. . . . If I were doing it for approval, it would be a very tenuous thing. If I didn't get the right feedback, there might go all my values.

Ibsen's play *A Doll's House* (1879/1965), depicts the explosion of just such a world through the eruption of a moral dilemma that calls into question the notion of goodness that lies at its center. Nora, the "squirrel wife," living with her husband as she had lived with her father, puts into action this conception of goodness as sacrifice and, with the best of intentions, takes the law into her own hands. The crisis that ensues, most

286 painfully for her in the repudiation of that goodness by the very person who was its recipient and beneficiary, causes her to reject the suicide that she had initially seen as its ultimate expression and choose instead to seek new and firmer answers to the adolescent questions of identity and belief.

The availability of choice and with it the onus of responsibility has now invaded the most private sector of the woman's domain and threatens a similar explosion. For centuries, women's sexuality anchored them in passivity, in a receptive rather than active stance, where the events of conception and childbirth could be controlled only by a withholding in which their own sexual needs were either denied or sacrificed. That such a sacrifice entailed a cost to their intelligence as well was seen by Freud (1908/1959) when he tied the "undoubted intellectual inferiority of so many women" to "the inhibition of thought necessitated by sexual suppression" (p. 199). The strategies of withholding and denial that women have employed in the politics of sexual relations appear similar to their evasion or withholding of judgment in the moral realm. The hesitance expressed in the previous examples to impose even a belief in the value of human life on others, like the reluctance to claim one's sexuality, bespeaks a self uncertain of its strength, unwilling to deal with consequence, and thus avoiding confrontation.

Thus women have traditionally deferred to the judgment of men, although often while intimating a sensibility of their own which is at variance with that judgment. Maggie Tulliver, in *The Mill on the Floss* (Eliot, 1860/1965), responds to the accusations that ensue from the discovery of her secretly continued relationship with Phillip Wakeham by acceding to her brother's moral judgment while at the same time asserting a different set of standards by which she attests her own superiority:

I don't want to defend myself. . . . I know I've been wrong—often continually. But yet, sometimes when I have done wrong, it has been because I have feelings that you would be the better for if you had them. If *you* were in fault ever, if you had done anything very wrong, I should be sorry for the pain it brought you; I should not want punishment to be heaped on you. (p. 188)

An eloquent defense, Kohlberg would argue, of a Stage Three moral position, an assertion of the age-old split between thinking and feeling, justice and mercy, that underlies many of the clichés and stereotypes concerning the difference between the sexes. But considered from another point of view, it is a moment of confrontation, replacing a former evasion, between two modes of judging, two differing constructions of the moral domain—one traditionally associated with masculinity and the public world of social power, the other with femininity and the privacy of domestic interchange. While the developmental ordering of these two points of view has been to consider the masculine as the more adequate and thus as replacing the feminine as the individual moves toward higher stages, their reconciliation remains unclear.

The Development of Women's Moral Judgement

Recent evidence for a divergence in moral development between men and women comes from the research of Haan[2] and Holstein (1976), whose findings lead them to question the possibility of a "sex-related bias" in Kohlberg's scoring system. This system is based on Kohlberg's six-stage description of moral development. Kohlberg's stages divide into three levels, which he designates as preconventional, conventional, and postconventional, thus denoting the major shifts in moral perspective around a center of moral understanding that equates justice with the maintenance of existing social systems. While the preconventional conception of justice is based on the needs of the self, the conventional judgment derives from an understanding of society. This understanding is in turn superseded by a postconventional or principled conception of justice where the good is formulated in universal terms. The quarrel with Kohlberg's stage scoring does not pertain to the structural differentiation of his levels but rather to questions of stage and sequence. Kohlberg's stages begin with an obedience and punishment orientation (Stage One), and go from there in invariant order to instrumental hedonism (Stage Two), interpersonal concordance (Stage Three), law and order (Stage Four), social contract (Stage Five), and universal ethical principles (Stage Six).

The bias that Haan and Holstein question in this scoring system has to do with the subordination of the interpersonal to the societal definition of the good in the transition from Stage Three to Stage Four. This is the transition that has repeatedly been found to be problematic for women. In 1969, Kohlberg and Kramer identified Stage Three as the characteristic mode of women's moral judgments, claiming that, since women's lives were interpersonally based, this stage was not only "functional" for them but also adequate for resolving the moral conflicts that they faced. Turiel (1973) reported that while girls reached Stage Three sooner than did boys, their judgments tended to remain at that stage while the boys' development continued further along Kohlberg's scale.[3] Gilligan, Kohlberg, Lerner, and

---

2. Haan, N. *Activism as moral protest: Moral judgments of hypothetical dilemmas and an actual situation of civil disobedience.* Unpublished manuscript, University of California at Berkeley, 1971.
3. Turiel, E. *A comparative analysis of moral knowledge and moral judgment in males and females.* Unpublished manuscript, Harvard University, 1973.

288 Belenky (1971) found a similar association between sex and moral-judgment stage in a study of high-school students, with the girls' responses
being scored predominantly at Stage Three while the boys' responses were
more often scored at Stage Four.

This repeated finding of developmental inferiority in women may, however, have more to do with the standard by which development has been
measured than with the quality of women's thinking per se. Haan's data on
the Berkeley Free Speech Movement and Holstein's (1976) three-year longitudinal study of adolescents and their parents indicate that the moral
judgments of women differ from those of men in the greater extent to which
women's judgments are tied to feelings of empathy and compassion and are
concerned more with the resolution of "real-life" as opposed to hypothetical dilemmas (Haan, p. 34). However, as long as the categories by
which development is assessed are derived within a male perspective from
male research data, divergence from the masculine standard can be seen
only as a failure of development. As a result, the thinking of women is often
classified with that of children. The systematic exclusion from consideration of alternative criteria that might better encompass the development of
women indicates not only the limitations of a theory framed by men and
validated by research samples disproportionately male and adolescent but
also the effects of the diffidence prevalent among women, their reluctance
to speak publicly in their own voice, given the constraints imposed on them
by the politics of differential power between the sexes.

In order to go beyond the question, "How much like men do women
think, how capable are they of engaging in the abstract and hypothetical
construction of reality?" it is necessary to identify and define in formal
terms developmental criteria that encompass the categories of women's
thinking. Such criteria would include the progressive differentiations,
comprehensiveness, and adequacy that characterize higher-stage resolution of the "more frequently occurring, real-life moral dilemmas of
interpersonal, empathic, fellow-feeling concerns" (Haan, p. 34), which
have long been the center of women's moral judgments and experience. To
ascertain whether the feminine construction of the moral domain relies on
a language different from that of men, but one which deserves equal
credence in the definition of what constitutes development, it is necessary
first to find the places where women have the power to choose and thus are
willing to speak in their own voice.

When birth control and abortion provide women with effective means
for controlling their fertility, the dilemma of choice enters the center of
women's lives. Then the relationships that have traditionally defined wom-
en's identities and framed their moral judgments no longer flow inevitably

from their reproductive capacity but become matters of decision over which they have control. Released from the passivity and reticence of a sexuality that binds them in dependence, it becomes possible for women to question with Freud what it is that they want and to assert their own answers to that question. However, while society may affirm publicly the woman's right to choose for herself, the exercise of such choice brings her privately into conflict with the conventions of femininity, particularly the moral equation of goodness with self-sacrifice. While independent assertion in judgment and action is considered the hallmark of adulthood and constitutes as well the standard of masculine development, it is rather in their care and concern for others that women have both judged themselves and been judged.

The conflict between self and other thus constitutes the central moral problem for women, posing a dilemma whose resolution requires a reconciliation between feminity and adulthood. In the absence of such a reconciliation, the moral problem cannot be resolved. The "good woman" masks assertion in evasion, denying responsibility by claiming only to meet the needs of others, while the "bad woman" forgoes or renounces the commitments that bind her in self-deception and betrayal. It is precisely this dilemma—the conflict between compassion and autonomy, between virtue and power—which the feminine voice struggles to resolve in its effort to reclaim the self and to solve the moral problem in such a way that no one is hurt.

When a woman considers whether to continue or abort a pregnancy, she contemplates a decision that affects both self and others and engages directly the critical moral issue of hurting. Since the choice is ultimately hers and therefore one for which she is responsible, it raises precisely those questions of judgment that have been most problematic for women. Now she is asked whether she wishes to interrupt that stream of life which has for centuries immersed her in the passivity of dependence while at the same time imposing on her the responsibility for care. Thus the abortion decision brings to the core of feminine apprehension, to what Joan Didion (1972) calls "the irreconcilable difference of it—that sense of living one's deepest life underwater, that dark involvement with blood and birth and death" (p. 14), the adult questions of responsibility and choice.

How women deal with such choices has been the subject of my research, designed to clarify, through considering the ways in which women construct and resolve the abortion decision, the nature and development of women's moral judgment. Twenty-nine women, diverse in age, race, and social class, were referred by abortion and pregnancy counseling services and participated in the study for a variety of reasons. Some came to gain

290 further clarification with respect to a decision about which they were in conflict, some in response to a counselor's concern about repeated abortions, and others out of an interest in and/or willingness to contribute to ongoing research. Although the pregnancies occurred under a variety of circumstances in the lives of these women, certain commonalities could be discerned. The adolescents often failed to use birth control because they denied or discredited their capacity to bear children. Some of the older women attributed the pregnancy to the omission of contraceptive measures in circumstances where intercourse had not been anticipated. Since the pregnancies often coincided with efforts on the part of the women to end a relationship, they may be seen as a manifestation of ambivalence or as a way of putting the relationship to the ultimate test of commitment. For these women, the pregnancy appeared to be a way of testing truth, making the baby an ally in the search for male support and protection or, that failing, a companion victim of his rejection. There were, finally, some women who became pregnant either as a result of a failure of birth control or intentionally as part of a joint decision that later was reconsidered. Of the twenty-nine women, four decided to have the baby, one miscarried, twenty-one chose abortion, and three remained in doubt about the decision.

In the initial part of the interview, the women were asked to discuss the decision that confronted them, how they were dealing with it, the alternatives they were considering, their reasons for and against each option, the people involved, the conflicts entailed, and the ways in which making this decision affected their self-concepts and their relationships with others. Then, in the second part of the interview, moral judgment was assessed in the hypothetical mode by presenting for resolution three of Kohlberg's standard research dilemmas.

While the structural progression from a preconventional through a conventional to a postconventional moral perspective can readily be discerned in the women's responses to both actual and hypothetical dilemmas, the conventions that shape women's moral judgments differ from those that apply to men. The construction of the abortion dilemma, in particular, reveals the existence of a distinct moral language whose evolution informs the sequence of women's development. This is the language of selfishness and responsibility, which defines the moral problem as one of obligation to exercise care and avoid hurt. The infliction of hurt is considered selfish and immoral in its reflection of unconcern, while the expression of care is seen as the fulfillment of moral responsibility. The reiterative use of the language of selfishness and responsibility and the underlying moral orientation it reflects sets the women apart from the men whom Kohlberg studied and may be seen as the critical reason for their failure to develop within the constraints of his system.

In the developmental sequence that follows, women's moral judgments proceed from an initial focus on the self at the *first level* to the discovery, in the transition to the *second level*, of the concept of responsibility as the basis for a new equilibrium between self and others. The elaboration of this concept of responsibility and its fusion with a maternal concept of morality, which seeks to ensure protection for the dependent and unequal, characterizes the *second level* of judgment. At this level the good is equated with caring for others. However, when the conventions of feminine goodness legitimize only others as the recipients of moral care, the logical inequality between self and other and the psychological violence that it engenders create the disequilibrium that initiates the *second* transition. The relationship between self and others is then reconsidered in an effort to sort out the confusion between conformity and care inherent in the conventional definition of feminine goodness and to establish a new equilibrium, which dissipates the tension between selfishness and responsibility. At the *third level*, the self becomes the arbiter of an independent judgment that now subsumes both conventions and individual needs under the moral principle of nonviolence. Judgment remains psychological in its concern with the intention and consequences of action, but it now becomes universal in its condemnation of exploitation and hurt.

Level I: Orientation to Individual Survival

In its initial and simplest construction, the abortion decision centers on the self. The concern is pragmatic, and the issue is individual survival. At this level, "should" is undifferentiated from "would," and others influence the decision only through their power to affect its consequences. An eighteen-year-old, asked what she thought when she found herself pregnant, replies: "I really didn't think anything except that I didn't want it. [Why was that?] I didn't want it, I wasn't ready for it, and next year will be my last year and I want to go to school."

Asked if there was a right decision, she says, "There is no right decision. [Why?] I didn't want it." For her the question of right decision would emerge only if her own needs were in conflict: then she would have to decide which needs should take precedence. This was the dilemma of another eighteen-year-old, who saw having a baby as a way of increasing her freedom by providing "the perfect chance to get married and move away from home," but also as restricting her freedom "to do a lot of things."

292   At this first level, the self, which is the sole object of concern, is constrained by lack of power; the wish "to do a lot of things" is constantly belied by the limitations of what, in fact, is being done. Relationships are, for the most part, disappointing: "The only thing you are ever going to get out of going with a guy is to get hurt." As a result, women may in some instances deliberately choose isolation to protect themselves against hurt. When asked how she would describe herself to herself, a nineteen-year-old, who held herself responsible for the accidental death of a younger brother, answers as follows:

I really don't know. I never thought about it. I don't know. I know basically the outline of a character. I am very independent. I don't really want to have to ask anybody for anything and I am a loner in life. I prefer to be by myself than around anybody else. I manage to keep my friends at a limited number with the point that I have very few friends. I don't know what else there is. I am a loner and I enjoy it. Here today and gone tomorrow.

The primacy of the concern with survival is explicitly acknowledged by a sixteen-year-old delinquent in response to Kohlberg's Heinz dilemma, which asks if it is right for a desperate husband to steal an outrageously overpriced drug to save the life of his dying wife:

I think survival is one of the first things in life and that people fight for. I think it is the most important thing, more important than stealing. Stealing might be wrong, but if you have to steal to survive yourself or even kill, that is what you should do. . . . Preservation of oneself, I think, is the most important thing; it comes before anything in life.

The First Transition: From Selfishness to Responsibility

In the transition which follows and criticizes this level of judgment, the words selfishness and responsibility first appear. Their reference initially is to the self in a redefinition of the self-interest which has thus far served as the basis for judgment. The transitional issue is one of attachment or connection to others. The pregnancy catches up the issue not only by representing an immediate, literal connection, but also by affirming, in the most concrete and physical way, the capacity to assume adult feminine roles. However, while having a baby seems at first to offer respite from the loneliness of adolescence and to solve conflicts over dependence and independence, in reality the continuation of an adolescent pregnancy generally compounds these problems, increasing social isolation and precluding further steps toward independence.

To be a mother in the societal as well as the physical sense requires the assumption of parental responsibility for the care and protection of a child.

However, in order to be able to care for another, one must first be able to care responsibly for oneself. The growth from childhood to adulthood, conceived as a move from selfishness to responsibility, is articulated explicitly in these terms by a seventeen-year-old who describes her response to her pregnancy as follows:

I started feeling really good about being pregnant instead of feeling really bad, because I wasn't looking at the situation realistically. I was looking at it from my own sort of selfish needs because I was lonely and felt lonely and stuff. . . . Things weren't really going good for me, so I was looking at it that I could have a baby that I could take care of or something that was part of me, and that made me feel good . . . but I wasn't looking at the realistic side . . . about the responsibility I would have to take on . . . I came to this decision that I was going to have an abortion [because] I realized how much responsibility goes with having a child. Like you have to be there, you can't be out of the house all the time which is one thing I like to do . . . and I decided that I have to take on responsibility for myself and I have to work out a lot of things.

Stating her former mode of judgment, the wish to have a baby as a way of combating loneliness and feeling connected, she now criticizes that judgment as both "selfish" and "unrealistic." The contradiction between wishes for a baby and for the freedom to be "out of the house all the time"—that is, for connection and also for independence—is resolved in terms of a new priority, as the criterion for judgment changes. The dilemma now assumes moral definition as the emergent conflict between wish and necessity is seen as a disparity between "would" and "should." In this construction the "selfishness" of willful decision is counterposed to the "responsibility" of moral choice:

What I want to do is to have the baby, but what I feel I should do which is what I need to do, is have an abortion right now, because sometimes what you want isn't right. Sometimes what is necessary comes before what you want, because it might not always lead to the right thing.

While the pregnancy itself confirms femininity—"I started feeling really good; it sort of made me feel, like being pregnant, I started feeling like a woman"—the abortion decision becomes an opportunity for the adult exercise of responsible choice.

[How would you describe yourself to yourself?] I am looking at myself differently in the way that I have had a really heavy decision put upon me, and I have never really had too many hard decisions in my life, and I have made it. It has taken some responsibility to do this. I have changed in that way, that I have made a hard decision. And that has been good. Because before, I would not have looked at it realistically, in my opinion. I would have gone by what I wanted to do, and I

294 wanted it, and even if it wasn't right. So I see myself as I'm becoming more mature in ways of making decisions and taking care of myself, doing something for myself. I think it is going to help me in other ways, if I have other decisions to make put upon me, which would take some responsibility. And I would know that I could make them.

In the epiphany of this cognitive reconstruction, the old becomes transformed in terms of the new. The wish to "do something for myself" remains, but the terms of its fulfillment change as the decision affirms both femininity and adulthood in its integration of responsibility and care. Morality, says another adolescent, "is the way you think about yourself . . . sooner or later you have to make up your mind to start taking care of yourself. Abortion, if you do it for the right reasons, is helping yourself to start over and do different things."

Since this transition signals an enhancement in self-worth, it requires a conception of self which includes the possibility for doing "the right thing," the ability to see in oneself the potential for social acceptance. When such confidence is seriously in doubt, the transitional questions may be raised but development is impeded. The failure to make this first transition, despite an understanding of the issues involved, is illustrated by a woman in her late twenties. Her struggle with the conflict between selfishness and responsibility pervades but fails to resolve her dilemma of whether or not to have a third abortion.

I think you have to think about the people who are involved, including yourself. You have responsibilities to yourself . . . and to make a right, whatever that is, decision in this depends on your knowledge and awareness of the responsibilities that you have and whether you can survive with a child and what it will do to your relationship with the father or how it will affect him emotionally.

Rejecting the idea of selling the baby and making "a lot of money in a black market kind of thing . . . because mostly I operate on principles and it would just rub me the wrong way to think I would be selling my own child," she struggles with a concept of responsibility which repeatedly turns back on the question of her own survival. Transition seems blocked by a self-image which is insistently contradictory:

[How would you describe yourself to yourself?] I see myself as impulsive, practical—that is a contradiction—and moral and amoral, a contradiction. Actually the only thing that is consistent and not contradictory is the fact that I am very lazy which everyone has always told me is really a symptom of something else which I have never been able to put my finger on exactly. It has taken me a long time to like myself. In fact there are times when I don't, which I think is healthy to a point and sometimes I think I like myself too much and I probably evade myself too much, which avoids responsibility to myself and to other people who like me. I am pretty unfaithful to myself . . . I have a hard time even thinking that I am a human being, simply because so much rotten stuff goes on and people are so crummy and insensitive.

Seeing herself as avoiding responsibility, she can find no basis upon which to resolve the pregnancy dilemma. Instead, her inability to arrive at any clear sense of decision only contributes further to her overall sense of failure. Criticizing her parents for having betrayed her during adolescence by coercing her to have an abortion she did not want, she now betrays herself and criticizes that as well. In this light, it is less surprising that she considered selling her child, since she felt herself to have, in effect, been sold by her parents for the sake of maintaining their social status.

The Second Level: Goodness as Self-Sacrifice

The transition from selfishness to responsibility is a move toward social participation. Whereas at the first level, morality is seen as a matter of sanctions imposed by a society of which one is more subject than citizen, at the second level, moral judgment comes to rely on shared norms and expectations. The woman at this level validates her claim to social membership through the adoption of societal values. Consensual judgment becomes paramount and goodness the overriding concern as survival is now seen to depend on acceptance by others.

Here the conventional feminine voice emerges with great clarity, defining the self and proclaiming its worth on the basis of the ability to care for and protect others. The woman now constructs the world perfused with the assumptions about feminine goodness reflected in the stereotypes of the Broverman et al. (1972) studies. There the attributes considered desirable for women all presume an other, a recipient of the "tact, gentleness, and easy expression of feeling" which allow the woman to respond sensitively while evoking in return the care which meets her own "very strong need for security" (p. 63). The strength of this position lies in its capacity for caring; its limitation is the restriction it imposes on direct expression. Both qualities are elucidated by a nineteen-year-old who contrasts her reluctance to criticize with her boyfriend's straightforwardness:

I never want to hurt anyone, and I tell them in a very nice way, and I have respect for their own opinions, and they can do the things the way that they want, and he usually tells people right off the bat. . . . He does a lot of things out in public which I do in private. . . . it is better, the other [his way], but I just could never do it.

While her judgment clearly exists, it is not expressed, at least not in public.

296 Concern for the feelings of others imposes a deference which she nevertheless criticizes in an awareness that, under the name of consideration, a vulnerability and a duplicity are concealed.

At the second level of judgment, it is specifically over the issue of hurting that conflict arises with respect to the abortion decision. When no option exists that can be construed as being in the best interest of everyone, when responsibilities conflict and decision entails the sacrifice of somebody's needs, then the woman confronts the seemingly impossible task of choosing the victim. A nineteen-year-old, fearing the consequences for herself of a second abortion but facing the opposition of both her family and her lover to the continuation of the pregnancy, describes the dilemma as follows:

I don't know what choices are open to me; it is either to have it or the abortion; these are the choices open to me. It is just that either way I don't . . . I think what confuses me is it is a choice of either hurting myself or hurting other people around me. What is more important? If there could be a happy medium, it would be fine, but there isn't. It is either hurting someone on this side or hurting myself.

While the feminine identification of goodness with self-sacrifice seems clearly to dictate the "right" resolution of this dilemma, the stakes may be high for the woman herself, and the sacrifice of the fetus, in any event, compromises the altruism of an abortion motivated by a concern for others. Since femininity itself is in conflict in an abortion intended as an expression of love and care, this is a resolution which readily explodes in its own contradiction.

"I don't think anyone should have to choose between two things that they love," says a twenty-five-year-old woman who assumed responsibility not only for her lover but also for his wife and children in having an abortion she did not want:

I just wanted the child and I really don't believe in abortions. Who can say when life begins. I think that life begins at conception and . . . I felt like there were changes happening in my body and I felt very protective . . . [but] I felt a responsibility, my responsibility if anything ever happened to her [his wife]. He made me feel that I had to make a choice and there was only one choice to make and that was to have an abortion and I could always have children another time and he made me feel if I didn't have it that it would drive us apart.

The abortion decision was, in her mind, a choice not to choose with respect to the pregnancy—"That was my choice, I had to do it." Instead, it was a decision to subordinate the pregnancy to the continuation of a relationship that she saw as encompassing her life—"Since I met him, he has been my life. I do everything for him; my life sort of revolves around him." Since she wanted to have the baby and also to continue the relationship, either choice could be construed as selfish. Furthermore, since both alternatives entailed hurting someone, neither could be considered moral. Faced with a decision which, in her own terms, was untenable, she sought to avoid responsibility for the choice she made, construing the decision as a sacrifice of her own needs to those of her lover. However, this public sacrifice in the name of responsibility engendered a private resentment that erupted in anger, compromising the very relationship that it had been intended to sustain.

Afterwards we went through a bad time because I hate to say it and I was wrong, but I blamed him. I gave in to him. But when it came down to it, I made the decision. I could have said, "I am going to have this child whether you want me to or not," and I just didn't do it.

Pregnant again by the same man, she recognizes in retrospect that the choice in fact had been hers, as she returns once again to what now appears to have been missed opportunity for growth. Seeking, this time, to make rather than abdicate the decision, she sees the issue as one of "strength" as she struggles to free herself from the powerlessness of her own dependence:

I think that right now I think of myself as someone who can become a lot stronger. Because of the circumstances, I just go along like with the tide. I never really had anything of my own before . . . [this time] I hope to come on strong and make a big decision, whether it is right or wrong.

Because the morality of self-sacrifice had justified the previous abortion, she now must suspend that judgment if she is to claim her own voice and accept responsibility for choice.

She thereby calls into question the underlying assumption of Level Two, which leads the woman to consider herself responsible for the actions of others, while holding others responsible for the choices she makes. This notion of reciprocity, backward in its assumptions about control, disguises assertion as response. By reversing responsibility, it generates a series of indirect actions which leave everyone feeling manipulated and betrayed. The logic of this position is confused in that the morality of mutual care is embedded in the psychology of dependence. Assertion becomes personally dangerous in its risk of criticism and abandonment, as well as potentially immoral in its power to hurt. This confusion is captured by Kohlberg's (1969) definition of Stage Three moral judgment, which joins the need for approval with the wish to care for and help others.

When thus caught between the passivity of dependence and the activity of care, the woman becomes suspended in an immobility of both judgment and action. "If I were drowning, I couldn't reach out a hand to save myself,"

298 so unwilling am I to set myself up against fate" (p. 7), begins the central character of Margaret Drabble's novel, *The Waterfall* (1971), in an effort to absolve herself of responsibility as she at the same time relinquishes control. Facing the same moral conflict which George Eliot depicted in *The Mill on the Floss*, Drabble's heroine proceeds to relive Maggie Tulliver's dilemma but turns inward in her search for the way in which to retell that story. What is initially suspended and then called into question is the judgment which "had in the past made it seem better to renounce myself than them" (Drabble, p. 50).

The Second Transition: From Goodness to Truth

The second transition begins with the reconsideration of the relationship between self and other, as the woman starts to scrutinize the logic of self-sacrifice in the service of a morality of care. In the interview data, this transition is announced by the reappearance of the word selfish. Retrieving the judgmental initiative, the woman begins to ask whether it is selfish or responsible, moral or immoral, to include her own needs within the compass of her care and concern. This question leads her to reexamine the concept of responsibility, juxtaposing the outward concern with what other people think with a new inner judgment.

In separating the voice of the self from those of others, the woman asks if it is possible to be responsible to herself as well as to others and thus to reconcile the disparity between hurt and care. The exercise of such responsibility, however, requires a new kind of judgment whose first demand is for honesty. To be responsible, it is necessary first to acknowledge what it is that one is doing. The criterion for judgment thus shifts from "goodness" to "truth" as the morality of action comes to be assessed not on the basis of its appearance in the eyes of others, but in terms of the realities of its intention and consequence.

A twenty-four-year-old married Catholic woman, pregnant again two months following the birth of her first child, identifies her dilemma as one of choice: "You have to now decide; because it is now available, you have to make a decision. And if it wasn't available, there was no choice open; you just do what you have to do." In the absence of legal abortion, a morality of self-sacrifice was necessary in order to insure protection and care for the dependent child. However, when such sacrifice becomes optional, the entire problem is recast.

The abortion decision is framed by this woman first in terms of her responsibilities to others: having a second child at this time would be contrary to medical advice and would strain both the emotional and financial resources of the family. However, there is, she says, a third reason for having an abortion, "sort of an emotional reason. I don't know if it is selfish or not, but it would really be tying myself down and right now I am not ready to be tied down with two."

Against this combination of selfish and responsible reasons for abortion is her Catholic belief that

. . . it is taking a life, and it is. Even though it is not formed, it is the potential, and to me it is still taking a life. But I have to think of mine, my son's and my husband's, to think about, and at first I think that I thought it was for selfish reasons, but it is not. I believe.that too, some of it is selfish. I don't want another one right now; I am not ready for it.

The dilemma arises over the issue of justification for taking a life: "I can't cover it over, because I believe this and if I do try to cover it over, I know that I am going to be in a mess. It will be denying what I am really doing." Asking "Am I doing the right thing; is it moral?," she counterposes to her belief against abortion her concern with the consequences of continuing the pregnancy. While concluding that "I can't be so morally strict as to hurt three other people with a decision just because of my moral beliefs," the issue of goodness still remains critical to her resolution of the dilemma:

The moral factor is there. To me it is taking a life, and I am going to take that upon myself, that decision upon myself and I have feelings about it, and talked to a priest . . . but he said it is there and it will be from now on, and it is up to the person if they can live with the idea and still believe they are good.

The criteria for goodness, however, move inward as the ability to have an abortion and still consider herself good comes to hinge on the issue of selfishness with which she struggles to come to terms. Asked if acting morally is acting according to what is best for the self or whether it is a matter of self-sacrifice, she replies:

I don't know if I really understand the question. . . . Like in my situation where I want to have the abortion and if I didn't it would be self-sacrificing, I am really in the middle of both those ways . . . but I think that my morality is strong and if these reasons—financial, physical reality and also for the whole family involved— were not here, that I wouldn't have to do it, and then it would be a self-sacrifice.

The importance of clarifying her own participation in the decision is evident in her attempt to ascertain her feelings in order to determine whether or not she was "putting them under" in deciding to end the pregnancy. Whereas in the first transition, from selfishness to responsibility, women made lists in order to bring to their consideration needs other than their own, now, in the second transition, it is the needs of the self which have to be deliberately uncovered. Confronting the reality of her own wish for an abortion, she now must deal with the problem of selfishness and the qualification that she feels it imposes on the "goodness" of her decision. The primacy of this concern is apparent in her description of herself:

> I think in a way I am selfish for one thing, and very emotional, very . . . and I think that I am a very real person and an understanding person and I can handle life situations fairly well, so I am basing a lot of it on my ability to do the things that I feel are right and best for me and whoever I am involved with. I think I was very fair to myself about the decision, and I really think that I have been truthful, not hiding anything, bringing out all the feelings involved. I feel it is a good decision and an honest one, a real decision.

Thus she strives to encompass the needs of both self and others, to be responsible to others and thus to be "good" but also to be responsible to herself and thus to be "honest" and "real."

While from one point of view, attention to one's own needs is considered selfish, when looked at from a different perspective, it is a matter of honesty and fairness. This is the essence of the transitional shift toward a new conception of goodness which turns inward in an acknowledgement of the self and an acceptance of responsibility for decision. While outward justification, the concern with "good reasons," remains critical for this particular woman: "I still think abortion is wrong, and it will be unless the situation can justify what you are doing." But the search for justification has produced a change in her thinking, "not drastically, but a little bit." She realizes that in continuing the pregnancy she would punish not only herself but also her husband, toward whom she had begun to feel "turned off and irritated." This leads her to consider the consequences self-sacrifice can have both for the self and for others. "God," she says, "can punish, but He can also forgive." What remains in question is whether her claim to forgiveness is compromised by a decision that not only meets the needs of others but that also is "right and best for me."

The concern with selfishness and its equation with immorality recur in an interview with another Catholic woman whose arrival for an abortion was punctuated by the statement, "I have always thought abortion was a fancy word for murder." Initially explaining this murder as one of lesser degree—"I am doing it because I have to do it. I am not doing it the least bit because I want to," she judges it "not quite as bad. You can rationalize that it is not quite the same." Since "keeping the child for lots and lots of reasons was just sort of impractical and out," she considers her options to be either abortion or adoption. However, having previously given up one child for adoption, she says, "I knew that psychologically there was no way that I could hack another adoption. It took me about four-and-a-half years to get my head on straight; there was just no way I was going to go through it again." The decision thus reduces in her eyes to a choice between murdering the fetus or damaging herself. The choice is further complicated by the fact that by continuing the pregnancy she would hurt not only herself but also her parents, with whom she lived. In the face of these manifold moral contradictions, the psychological demand for honesty that arises in counseling finally allows decision:

> On my own, I was doing it not so much for myself; I was doing it for my parents. I was doing it because the doctor told me to do it, but I had never resolved in my mind that I was doing it for me. Because it goes right back to the fact that I never believed in abortions. . . . Actually, I had to sit down and admit, no, I really don't want to go the mother route now. I honestly don't feel that I want to be a mother, and that is not really such a bad thing to say after all. But that is not how I felt up until talking to Maureen [her counselor]. It was just a horrible way to feel, so I just wasn't going to feel it, and I just blocked it right out.

As long as her consideration remains "moral," abortion can be justified only as an act of sacrifice, a submission to necessity where the absence of choice precludes responsibility. In this way, she can avoid self-condemnation, since, "When you get into moral stuff then you are getting into self-respect and that stuff, and at least if I do something that I feel is morally wrong, then I tend to lose some of my self-respect as a person." Her evasion of responsibility, critical to maintaining the innocence necessary for self-respect, contradicts the reality of her own participation in the abortion decision. The dishonesty in her plea of victimization creates the conflict that generates the need for a more inclusive understanding. She must now resolve the emerging contradiction in her thinking between two uses of the term right: "I am saying that abortion is morally wrong, but the situation is right, and I am going to do it. But the thing is that eventually they are going to have to go together, and I am going to have to put them together somehow." Asked how this could be done, she replies:

> I would have to change morally wrong to morally right. [How?] I have no idea. I don't think you can take something that you feel is morally wrong because the situation makes it right and put the two together. They are not together, they are opposite. They don't go together. Something is wrong, but all of a sudden because you are doing it, it is right.

This discrepancy recalls a similar conflict she faced over the question of euthanasia, also considered by her to be morally wrong until she "took care of a couple of patients who had flat EEGs and saw the job that it was doing on their families." Recalling that experience, she says:

302 You really don't know your blacks and whites until you really get into them and are being confronted with it. If you stop and think about my feelings on euthanasia until I got into it, and then my feelings about abortion until I got into it, I thought both of them were murder. Right and wrong and no middle but there is a gray.

In discovering the gray and questioning the moral judgments which formerly she considered to be absolute, she confronts the moral crisis of the second transition. Now the conventions which in the past had guided her moral judgment become subject to a new criticism, as she questions not only the justification for hurting others in the name of morality but also the "rightness" of hurting herself. However, to sustain such criticism in the face of conventions that equate goodness with self-sacrifice, the woman must verify her capacity for independent judgment and the legitimacy of her own point of view.

Once again transition hinges on self-concept. When uncertainty about her own worth prevents a woman from claiming equality, self-assertion falls prey to the old criticism of selfishness. Then the morality that condones self-destruction in the name of responsible care is not repudiated as inadequate but rather is abandoned in the face of its threat to survival. Moral obligation, rather than expanding to include the self, is rejected completely as the failure of conventional reciprocity leaves the woman unwilling any longer to protect others at what is now seen to be her own expense. In the absence of morality, survival, however "selfish" or "immoral," returns as the paramount concern.

A musician in her late twenties illustrates this transitional impasse. Having led an independent life which centered on her work, she considered herself "fairly strong-willed, fairly in control, fairly rational and objective" until she became involved in an intense love affair and discovered in her capacity to love "an entirely new dimension" in herself. Admitting in retrospect to "tremendous naiveté and idealism," she had entertained "some vague ideas that some day I would like a child to concretize our relationship . . . having always associated having a child with all the creative aspects of my life." Abjuring, with her lover, the use of contraceptives because, "as the relationship was sort of an ideal relationship in our minds, we liked the idea of not using foreign objects or anything artificial," she saw herself as having relinquished control, becoming instead "just simply vague and allowing events to just carry me along." Just as she began in her own thinking to confront "the realities of that situation"—the possibility of pregnancy and the fact that her lover was married—she found herself pregnant. "Caught" between her wish to end a relationship that "seemed more and more defeating" and her wish for a baby, which "would be a connection that would last a long time," she is paralyzed by her inability to resolve the dilemma which her ambivalence creates.

The pregnancy poses a conflict between her "moral" belief that "once a certain life has begun, it shouldn't be stopped artificially" and her "amazing" discovery that to have the baby she would "need much more [support] than I thought." Despite her moral conviction that she "should" have the child, she doubts that she could psychologically deal with "having the child alone and taking the responsibility for it." Thus a conflict erupts between what she considers to be her moral obligation to protect life and her inability to do so under the circumstances of this pregnancy. Seeing it as "my decision and my responsibility for making the decision whether to have or have not the child," she struggles to find a viable basis on which to resolve the dilemma.

Capable of arguing either for or against abortion "with a philosophical logic," she says, on the one hand, that in an overpopulated world one should have children only under ideal conditions for care but, on the other, that one should end a life only when it is impossible to sustain it. She describes her impasse in response to the question of whether there is a difference between what she wants to do and what she thinks she should do:

Yes, and there always has. I have always been confronted with that precise situation in a lot of my choices, and I have been trying to figure out what are the things that make me believe that these are things I should do as opposed to what I feel I want to do. [In this situation?] It is not that clear cut. I both want the child and feel I should have it, and I also think I should have the abortion and want it, but I would say it is my stronger feeling, and that I don't have enough confidence in my work yet and that is really where it is all hinged, I think . . . [the abortion] would solve the problem and I know I can't handle the pregnancy.

Characterizing this solution as "emotional and pragmatic" and attributing it to her lack of confidence in her work, she contrasts it with the "better thought out and more logical and more correct" resolution of her lover who thinks that she should have the child and raise it without either his presence or financial support. Confronted with this reflected image of herself as ultimately giving and good, as self-sustaining in her own creativity and thus able to meet the needs of others while imposing no demands of her own in return, she questions not the image itself but her own adequacy in filling it. Concluding that she is not yet capable of doing so, she is reduced in her own eyes to what she sees as a selfish and highly compromised fight

for my survival. But in one way or another. I am going to suffer. Maybe I am going to suffer mentally and emotionally having the abortion, or I would suffer what I

304 think is possibly something worse. So I suppose it is the lesser of two evils. I think it is a matter of choosing which one I know that I can survive through. It is really. I think it is selfish, I suppose, because it does have to do with that. I just realized that. I guess it does have to do with whether I would survive or not. [Why is this selfish?] Well, you know, it is. Because I am concerned with my survival first, as opposed to the survival of the relationship or the survival of the child, another human being . . . I guess I am setting priorities, and I guess I am setting my needs to survive first. . . . I guess I see it in negative terms a lot . . . but I do think of other positive things; that I am still going to have some life left, maybe. I don't know.

In the face of this failure of reciprocity of care, in the disappointment of abandonment where connection was sought, survival is seen to hinge on her work which is "where I derive the meaning of what I am. That's the known factor." While uncertainty about her work makes this survival precarious, the choice for abortion is also distressing in that she considers it to be "highly introverted—that in this one respect, having an abortion would be going a step backward; going outside to love someone else and having a child would be a step forward." The sense of retrenchment that the severing of connection signifies is apparent in her anticipation of the cost which abortion would entail:

Probably what I will do is I will cut off my feelings, and when they will return or what would happen to them after that, I don't know. So that I don't feel anything at all, and I would probably just be very cold and go through it very coldly. . . . The more you do that to yourself, the more difficult it becomes to love again or to trust again or to feel again. . . . Each time I move away from that, it becomes easier, not more difficult, but easier to avoid committing myself to a relationship. And I am really concerned about cutting off that whole feeling aspect.

Caught between selfishness and responsibility, unable to find in the circumstances of this choice a way of caring which does not at the same time destroy, she confronts a dilemma which reduces to a conflict between morality and survival. Adulthood and femininity fly apart in the failure of this attempt at integration as the choice to work becomes a decision not only to renounce this particular relationship and child but also to obliterate the vulnerability that love and care engender.

The Third Level: The Morality of Nonviolence
In contrast, a twenty-five-year-old woman, facing a similar disappointment, finds a way to reconcile the initially disparate concepts of selfishness and responsibility through a transformed understanding of self and a corresponding redefinition of morality. Examining the assumptions un-

derlying the conventions of feminine self-abnegation and moral self-sacrifice, she comes to reject these conventions as immoral in their power to hurt. By elevating nonviolence—the injunction against hurting—to a principle governing all moral judgment and action, she is able to assert a moral equality between self and other. Care then becomes a universal obligation, the self-chosen ethic of a postconventional judgment that reconstructs the dilemma in a way that allows the assumption of responsibility for choice.

In this woman's life, the current pregnancy brings to the surface the unfinished business of an earlier pregnancy and of the relationship in which both pregnancies occurred. The first pregnancy was discovered after her lover had left and was terminated by an abortion experienced as a purging expression of her anger at having been rejected. Remembering the abortion only as a relief, she nevertheless describes that time in her life as one in which she "hit rock bottom." Having hoped then to "take control of my life," she instead resumed the relationship when the man reappeared. Now, two years later, having once again "left my diaphragm in the drawer," she again becomes pregnant. Although initially "ecstatic" at the news, her elation dissipates when her lover tells her that he will leave if she chooses to have the child. Under these circumstances, she considers a second abortion but is unable to keep the repeated appointments she makes because of her reluctance to accept the responsibility for that choice. While the first abortion seemed an "honest mistake," she says that a second would make her feel "like a walking slaughter-house." Since she would need financial support to raise the child, her initial strategy was to take the matter to "the welfare people" in the hope that they would refuse to provide the necessary funds and thus resolve her dilemma:

In that way, you know, the responsibility would be off my shoulders, and I could say, it's not my fault, you know, the state denied me the money that I would need to do it. But it turned out that it was possible to do it, and so I was, you know, right back where I started. And I had an appointment for an abortion, and I kept calling and cancelling it and then remaking the appointment and cancelling it, and I just couldn't make up my mind.

Confronting the need to choose between the two evils of hurting herself or ending the incipient life of the child, she finds, in a reconstruction of the dilemma itself, a basis for a new priority that allows decision. In doing so, she comes to see the conflict as arising from a faulty construction of reality. Her thinking recapitulates the developmental sequence, as she considers but rejects as inadequate the components of earlier-stage resolutions. An

306 expanded conception of responsibility now reshapes moral judgment and guides resolution of the dilemma, whose pros and cons she considers as follows:

Well, the pros for having the baby are all the admiration that you would get from, you know, being a single woman, alone, martyr, struggling, having the adoring love of this beautiful Gerber baby . . . just more of a home life than I have had in a long time, and that basically was it, which is pretty fantasyland; it is not very realistic. . . . Cons against having the baby: it was going to hasten what is looking to be the inevitable end of the relationship with the man I am presently with. . . . I was going to have to go on welfare, my parents were going to hate me for the rest of my life, I was going to lose a really good job that I have, I would lose a lot of independence . . . solitude . . . and I would have to be put in a position of asking help from a lot of people a lot of the time. Cons against having the abortion is having to face up to the guilt . . . and pros for having the abortion are I would be able to handle my deteriorating relation with S. with a lot more capability and a lot more responsibility for him and for myself . . . and I would not have to go through the realization that for the next twenty-five years of my life I would be punishing myself for being foolish enough to get pregnant again and forcing myself to bring up a kid just because I did this. Having to face the guilt of a second abortion seemed like, not exactly, well, exactly the lesser of the two evils but also the one that would pay off for me personally in the long run because by looking at why I am pregnant again and subsequently have decided to have a second abortion, I have to face up to some things about myself.

Although she doesn't "feel good about having a second abortion," she nevertheless concludes,

I would not be doing myself or the child or the world any kind of favor having this child. . . . I don't need to pay off my imaginary debts to the world through this child, and I don't think that it is right to bring a child into the world and use it for that purpose.

Asked to describe herself, she indicates how closely her transformed moral understanding is tied to a changing self-concept:

I have been thinking about that a lot lately, and it comes up different than what my usual subconscious perception of myself is. Usually paying off some sort of debt, going around serving people who are not really worthy of my attentions because somewhere in my life I think I got the impression that my needs are really secondary to other people's, and that if I feel, if I make any demands on other people to fulfill my needs, I'd feel guilty for it and submerge my own in favor of other people's, which later backfires on me, and I feel a great deal of resentment for other people that I am doing things for, which causes friction and the eventual deterioration of the relationship. And then I start all over again. How would I describe myself to myself? Pretty frustrated and a lot angrier than I admit, a lot more aggressive than I admit.

Reflecting on the virtues which comprise the conventional definition of the feminine self, a definition which she hears articulated in her mother's voice, she says, "I am beginning to think that all these virtues are really not getting me anywhere. I have begun to notice." Tied to this recognition is an acknowledgement of her power and worth, both previously excluded from the image she projected:

I am suddenly beginning to realize that the things that I like to do, the things I am interested in, and the things that I believe and the kind of person I am is not so bad that I have to constantly be sitting on the shelf and letting it gather dust. I am a lot more worthwhile than what my past actions have led other people to believe.

Her notion of a "good person," which previously was limited to her mother's example of hard work, patience, and self-sacrifice, now changes to include the value that she herself places on directness and honesty. Although she believes that this new self-assertion will lead her "to feel a lot better about myself," she recognizes that it will also expose her to criticism:

Other people may say, "Boy, she's aggressive, and I don't like that," but at least, you know, they will know that they don't like that. They are not going to say, "I like the way she manipulates herself to fit right around me." . . . What I want to do is just be a more self-determined person and a more singular person.

While within her old framework abortion had seemed a way of "copping out" instead of being a "responsible person [who] pays for his mistakes and pays and pays and is always there when she says she will be there and even when she doesn't say she will be there is there," now, her "conception of what I think is right for myself and my conception of self-worth is changing." She can consider this emergent self "also a good person," as her concept of goodness expands to encompass "the feeling of self-worth; you are not going to sell yourself short and you are not going to make yourself do things that, you know, are really stupid and that you don't want to do." This reorientation centers on the awareness that

I have a responsibility to myself, and you know, for once I am beginning to realize that that really matters to me . . . instead of doing what I want for myself and feeling guilty over how selfish I am, you realize that that is a very usual way for people to live . . . doing what you want to do because you feel that your wants and your needs are important, if to no one else, then to you, and that's reason enough to do something that you want to do.

308   Once obligation extends to include the self as well as others, the disparity between selfishness and responsibility is reconciled. Although the conflict between self and other remains, the moral problem is restructured in an awareness that the occurrence of the dilemma itself precludes nonviolent resolution. The abortion decision is now seen to be a "serious" choice affecting both self and others: "This is a life that I have taken, a conscious decision to terminate, and that is just very heavy, a very heavy thing." While accepting the necessity of abortion as a highly compromised resolution, she turns her attention to the pregnancy itself, which she now considers to denote a failure of responsibility, a failure to care for and protect both self and other.

As in the first transition, although now in different terms, the conflict precipitated by the pregnancy catches up the issues critical to development. These issues now concern the worth of the self in relation to others, the claiming of the power to choose, and the acceptance of responsibility for choice. By provoking a confrontation with these issues, the crisis can become "a very auspicious time; you can use the pregnancy as sort of a learning, teeing-off point, which makes it useful in a way." This possibility for growth inherent in a crisis which allows confrontation with a construction of reality whose acceptance previously had impeded development was first identified by Coles (1964) in his study of the children of Little Rock. This same sense of possibility is expressed by the women who see, in their resolution of the abortion dilemma, a reconstructed understanding which creates the opportunity for "a new beginning," a chance "to take control of my life."

For this woman, the first step in taking control was to end the relationship in which she had considered herself "reduced to a nonentity," but to do so in a responsible way. Recognizing hurt as the inevitable concomitant of rejection, she strives to minimize that hurt "by dealing with [his] needs as best I can without compromising my own . . . that's a big point for me, because the thing in my life to this point has been always compromising, and I am not willing to do that any more." Instead, she seeks to act in a "decent, human kind of way . . . one that leaves maybe a slightly shook but not totally destroyed person." Thus the "nonentity" confronts her power to destroy which formerly had impeded any assertion, as she considers the possibility for a new kind of action that leaves both self and other intact.

The moral concern remains a concern with hurting as she considers Kohlberg's Heinz dilemma in terms of the question, "who is going to be hurt more, the druggist who loses some money or the person who loses their life?" The right to property and right to life are weighed not in the abstract, in terms of their logical priority, but rather in the particular, in terms of the actual consequences that the violation of these rights would have in the lives of the people involved. Thinking remains contextual and admixed with feelings of care, as the moral imperative to avoid hurt begins to be informed by a psychological understanding of the meaning of nonviolence.

Thus, release from the intimidation of inequality finally allows the expression of a judgment that previously had been withheld. What women then enunciate is not a new morality, but a moral conception disentangled from the constraints that formerly had confused its perception and impeded its articulation. The willingness to express and take responsibility for judgment stems from the recognition of the psychological and moral necessity for an equation of worth between self and other. Responsibility for care then includes both self and other, and the obligation not to hurt, freed from conventional constraints, is reconstructed as a universal guide to moral choice.

The reality of hurt centers the judgment of a twenty-nine-year-old woman, married and the mother of a preschool child, as she struggles with the dilemma posed by a second pregnancy whose timing conflicts with her completion of an advanced degree. Saying that "I cannot deliberately do something that is bad or would hurt another person because I can't live with having done that," she nevertheless confronts a situation in which hurt has become inevitable. Seeking that solution which would best protect both herself and others, she indicates, in her definition of morality, the ineluctable sense of connection which infuses and colors all of her thinking:

[Morality is] doing what is appropriate and what is just within your circumstances, but ideally it is not going to affect—I was going to say, ideally it wouldn't negatively affect another person, but this is ridiculous, because decisions are always going to affect another person. But you see, what I am trying to say is that it is the person that is the center of the decision making, of that decision making about what's right and what's wrong.

The person who is the center of this decision making begins by denying, but then goes on to acknowledge, the conflicting nature both of her own needs and of her various responsibilities. Seeing the pregnancy as a manifestation of the inner conflict between her wish, on the one hand, "to be a college president" and, on the other, "to be making pottery and flowers and having kids and staying at home," she struggles with contradiction between femininity and adulthood. Considering abortion as the "better" choice— because "in the end, meaning this time next year or this time two weeks from now, it will be less of a personal strain on us individually and on us as a family for me not to be pregnant at this time," she concludes that the decision has

got to be, first of all, something that the woman can live with—a decision that the woman can live with, one way or another, or at least try to live with, and that it be based on where she is at and other people, significant people in her life, are at.

At the beginning of the interview she had presented the dilemma in its conventional feminine construction, as a conflict between her own wish to have a baby and the wish of others for her to complete her education. On the basis of this construction she deemed it "selfish" to continue the pregnancy because it was something "I want to do." However, as she begins to examine her thinking, she comes to abandon as false this conceptualization of the problem, acknowledging the truth of her own internal conflict and elaborating the tension which she feels between her femininity and the adulthood of her work life. She describes herself as "going in two directions" and values that part of herself which is "incredibly passionate and sensitive"—her capacity to recognize and meet, often with anticipation, the needs of others. Seeing her "compassion" as "something I don't want to lose" she regards it as endangered by her pursuit of professional advancement. Thus the self-deception of her initial presentation, its attempt to sustain the fiction of her own innocence, stems from her fear that to say that *she* does not want to have another baby at this time would be

an acknowledgement to me that I am an ambitious person and that I want to have power and responsibility for others and that I want to live a life that extends from 9 to 5 every day and into the evenings and on weekends, because that is what the power and responsibility means. It means that my family would necessarily come second . . . there would be such an incredible conflict about which is tops, and I don't want that for myself.

Asked about her concept of "an ambitious person" she says that to be ambitious means to be

power hungry [and] insensitive. [Why insensitive?] Because people are stomped on in the process. A person on the way up stomps on people, whether it is family or other colleagues or clientele, on the way up. [Inevitably?] Not always, but I have seen it so often in my limited years of working that it is scary to me. It is scary because I don't want to change like that.

Because the acquisition of adult power is seen to entail the loss of feminine sensitivity and compassion, the conflict between femininity and adulthood becomes construed as a moral problem. The discovery of the

principle of nonviolence begins to direct attention to the moral dilemma
itself and initiates the search for a resolution that can encompass both
femininity and adulthood.

Developmental Theory Reconsidered

The developmental conception delineated at the outset, which has so
consistently found the development of woman to be either aberrant or
incomplete, has been limited insofar as it has been predominantly a male
conception, giving lip-service, a place on the chart, to the interdependence
of intimacy and care but constantly stressing, at their expense, the importance and value of autonomous judgment and action. To admit to this
conception the truth of the feminine perspective is to recognize for both
sexes the central importance in adult life of the connection between self and
other, the universality of the need for compassion and care. The concept of
the separate self and of the moral principle uncompromised by the constraints of reality is an adolescent ideal, the elaborately wrought philosophy
of a Stephen Daedalus, whose flight we know to be in jeopardy. Erikson
(1964), in contrasting the ideological morality of the adolescent with the
ethics of adult care, attempts to grapple with this problem of integration
but is impeded by the limitations of his own previous developmental
conception. When his developmental stages chart a path where the sole
precursor to the intimacy of adult relationships is the trust established in
infancy and all intervening experience is marked only as steps toward
greater independence, then separation itself becomes the model and the
measure of growth. The observation that, for women, identity has as much
to do with connection as with separation led Erikson into trouble largely
because of his failure to integrate this insight into the mainstream of his
developmental theory (Erikson, 1968).

The morality of responsibility which women describe stands apart from
the morality of rights which underlies Kohlberg's conception of the highest
stages of moral judgment. Kohlberg[4] sees the progression toward these
stages as resulting from the generalization of the self-centered adolescent
rejection of societal morality into a principled conception of individual
natural rights. To illustrate this progression, he cites as an example of
integrated Stage Five judgment, "possibly moving to Stage Six," the follow-

---

4. Kohlberg, L. *Continuities and discontinuities in childhood and adult moral development revisited.*
Unpublished paper, Harvard University, 1973.

312 ing response of a twenty-five-year-old subject from his male longitudinal sample:

> [What does the word morality mean to you?] Nobody in the world knows the answer. I think it is recognizing the right of the individual, the rights of other individuals, not interfering with those rights. Act as fairly as you would have them treat you. I think it is basically to preserve the human being's right to existence. I think that is the most important. Secondly, the human being's right to do as he pleases, again without interfering with somebody else's rights. (p. 29)

Another version of the same conception is evident in the following interview response of a male college senior whose moral judgment also was scored by Kohlberg[5] as at Stage Five or Six:

> [Morality] is a prescription, it is a thing to follow, and the idea of having a concept of morality is to try to figure out what it is that people can do in order to make life with each other livable, make for a kind of balance, a kind of equilibrium, a harmony in which everybody feels he has a place and an equal share in things, and it's doing that—doing that is kind of contributing to a state of affairs that go beyond the individual in the absence of which, the individual has no chance for self-fulfillment of any kind. Fairness; morality is kind of essential, it seems to me, for creating the kind of environment, interaction between people, that is prerequisite to this fulfillment of most individual goals and so on. If you want other people to not interfere with your pursuit of whatever you are into, you have to play the game.

In contrast, a woman in her late twenties responds to a similar question by defining a morality not of rights but of responsibility:

> [What makes something a moral issue?] Some sense of trying to uncover a right path in which to live, and always in my mind is that the world is full of real and recognizable trouble, and is it heading for some sort of doom and is it right to bring children into this world when we currently have an overpopulation problem, and is it right to spend money on a pair of shoes when I have a pair of shoes and other people are shoeless. . . . It is part of a self-critical view, part of saying, how am I spending my time and in what sense am I working? I think I have a real drive to, I have a real maternal drive to take care of someone. To take care of my mother, to take care of children, to take care of other people's children, to take care of my own children, to take care of the world. I think that goes back to your other question, and when I am dealing with moral issues, I am sort of saying to myself constantly, are you taking care of all the things that you think are important and in what ways are you wasting yourself and wasting those issues?

While the postconventional nature of this woman's perspective seems

---

5. Kohlberg, L. Personal communication, August, 1976.

clear, her judgments of Kohlberg's hypothetical moral dilemmas do not meet his criteria for scoring at the principled level. Kohlberg regards this as a disparity between normative and metaethical judgments which he sees as indicative of the transition between conventional and principled thinking. From another perspective, however, this judgment represents a different moral conception, disentangled from societal conventions and raised to the principled level. In this conception, moral judgment is oriented toward issues of responsibility. The way in which the responsibility orientation guides moral decision at the postconventional level is described by the following woman in her thirties:

[Is there a right way to make moral decisions?] The only way I know is to try to be as awake as possible, to try to know the range of what you feel, to try to consider all that's involved, to be as aware as you can be to what's going on, as conscious as you can of where you're walking. [Are there principles that guide you?] The principle would have something to do with responsibility, responsibility and caring about yourself and others. . . . But it's not that on the one hand you choose to be responsible and on the other hand you choose to be irresponsible—both ways you can be responsible. That's why there's not just a principle that once you take hold of you settle—the principle put into practice here is still going to leave you with conflict.

The moral imperative that emerges repeatedly in the women's interviews is an injunction to care, a responsibility to discern and alleviate the "real and recognizable trouble" of this world. For the men Kohlberg studied, the moral imperative appeared rather as an injunction to respect the rights of others and thus to protect from interference the right to life and self-fulfillment. Women's insistence on care is at first self-critical rather than self-protective, while men initially conceive obligation to others negatively in terms of noninterference. Development for both sexes then would seem to entail an integration of rights and responsibilities through the discovery of the complementarity of these disparate views. For the women I have studied, this integration between rights and responsibilities appears to take place through a principled understanding of equity and reciprocity. This understanding tempers the self-destructive potential of a self-critical morality by asserting the equal right of all persons to care. For the men in Kohlberg's sample as well as for those in a longitudinal study of Harvard undergraduates[6] it appears to be the recognition through experience of the need for a more active responsibility in taking care that corrects the potential indifference of a morality of noninterference and turns attention from

6. Gilligan, C., & Murphy, M. *The philosopher and the "dilemma of the fact": Moral development in late adolescence and adulthood.* Unpublished manuscript, Harvard University, 1977.

314 the logic to the consequences of choice. In the development of a postconventional ethic understanding, women come to see the violence generated by inequitable relationships, while men come to realize the limitations of a conception of justice blinded to the real inequities of human life.

Kohlberg's dilemmas, in the hypothetical abstraction of their presentation, divest the moral actors from the history and psychology of their individual lives and separate the moral problem from the social contingencies of its possible occurrence. In doing so, the dilemmas are useful for the distillation and refinement of the "objective principles of justice" toward which Kohlberg's stages strive. However, the reconstruction of the dilemma in its contextual particularity allows the understanding of cause and consequence which engages the compassion and tolerance considered by previous theorists to qualify the feminine sense of justice. Only when substance is given to the skeletal lives of hypothetical people is it possible to consider the social injustices which their moral problems may reflect and to imagine the individual suffering their occurrence may signify or their resolution engender.

The proclivity of women to reconstruct hypothetical dilemmas in terms of the real, to request or supply the information missing about the nature of the people and the places where they live, shifts their judgment away from the hierarchical ordering of principles and the formal procedures of decision making that are critical for scoring at Kohlberg's highest stages. This insistence on the particular signifies an orientation to the dilemma and to moral problems in general that differs from any of Kohlberg's stage descriptions. Given the constraints of Kohlberg's system and the biases in his research sample, this different orientation can only be construed as a failure in development. While several of the women in the research sample clearly articulated what Kohlberg regarded as a postconventional metaethical position, none of them were considered by Kohlberg to be principled in their normative moral judgments of his hypothetical moral dilemmas (n. 4). Instead, the women's judgments pointed toward an identification of the violence inherent in the dilemma itself which was seen to compromise the justice of any of its possible resolutions. This construction of the dilemma led the women to recast the moral judgment from a consideration of the good to a choice between evils.

The woman whose judgment of the abortion dilemma concluded the developmental sequence presented in the preceding section saw Kohlberg's Heniz dilemma in these terms and judged Heinz's action in terms of a choice between selfishness and sacrifice. For Heinz to steal the drug, given the circumstances of his life (which she inferred from his inability to pay two thousand dollars), he would have "to do something which is not in his best interest, in that he is going to get sent away, and that is a supreme sacrifice, a sacrifice which I would say a person truly in love might be willing to make." However, not to steal the drug "would be selfish on his part . . . he would just have to feel guilty about not allowing her a chance to live longer." Heinz's decision to steal is considered not in terms of the logical priority of life over property which justifies its rightness, but rather in terms of the actual consequences that stealing would have for a man of limited means and little social power.

Considered in the light of its probable outcomes—his wife dead, or Heinz in jail, brutalized by the violence of that experience and his life compromised by a record of felony—the dilemma itself changes. Its resolution has less to do with the relative weights of life and property in an abstract moral conception than with the collision it has produced between two lives, formerly conjoined but now in opposition, where the continuation of one life can now occur only at the expense of the other. Given this construction, it becomes clear why consideration revolves around the issue of sacrifice and why guilt becomes the inevitable concomitant of either resolution.

Demonstrating the reticence noted in the first section about making moral judgments, this woman explains her reluctance to judge in terms of her belief

that everybody's existence is so different that I kind of say to myself, that might be something that I wouldn't do, but I can't say that it is right or wrong for that person. I can only deal with what is appropriate for me to do when I am faced with specific problems.

Asked if she would apply to others her own injunction against hurting, she says:

See, I can't say that it is wrong. I can't say that it is right or that it's wrong because I don't know what the person did that the other person did something to hurt him . . . so it is not right that the person got hurt, but it is right that the person who just lost the job has got to get that anger up and out. It doesn't put any bread on his table, but it is released. I don't mean to be copping out. I really am trying to see how to answer these questions for you.

Her difficulty in answering Kohlberg's questions, her sense of strain with the construction which they impose on the dilemma, stems from their divergence from her own frame of reference:

I don't even think I use the words right and wrong anymore, and I know I don't use the word moral, because I am not sure I know what it means. . . . We are talking about an unjust society, we are talking about a whole lot of things that are not right,

316 that are truly wrong, to use the word that I don't use very often, and I have no control to change that. If I could change it, I certainly would, but I can only make my small contribution from day to day, and if I don't intentionally hurt somebody, that is my contribution to a better society. And so a chunk of that contribution is also not to pass judgment on other people, particularly when I don't know the circumstances of why they are doing certain things.

The reluctance to judge remains a reluctance to hurt, but one that stems now not from a sense of personal vulnerability but rather from a recognition of the limitations of judgment itself. The deference of the conventional feminine perspective can thus be seen to continue at the postconventional level, not as moral relativism but rather as part of a reconstructed moral understanding. Moral judgment is renounced in an awareness of the psychological and social determinism of all human behavior at the same time as moral concern is reaffirmed in recognition of the reality of human pain and suffering.

I have a real thing about hurting people and always have, and that gets a little complicated at times, because, for example, you don't want to hurt your child. I don't want to hurt my child but if I don't hurt her sometimes, then that's hurting her more, you see, and so that was a terrible dilemma for me.

Moral dilemmas are terrible in that they entail hurt; she sees Heinz's decision as "the result of anguish, who am I hurting, why do I have to hurt them." While the morality of Heinz's theft is not in question, given the circumstances which necessitated it, what is at issue is his willingness to substitute himself for his wife and become, in her stead, the victim of exploitation by a society which breeds and legitimizes the druggist's irresponsibility and whose injustice is thus manifest in the very occurrence of the dilemma.

The same sense that the wrong questions are being asked is evident in the response of another woman who justified Heinz's actions on a similar basis, saying "I don't think that exploitation should really be a right." When women begin to make direct moral statements, the issues they repeatedly address are those of exploitation and hurt. In doing so, they raise the issue of nonviolence in precisely the same psychological context that brought Erikson (1969) to pause in his consideration of the truth of Gandhi's life.

In the pivotal letter, around which the judgment of his book turns, Erikson confronts the contradiction between the philosophy of nonviolence that informed Gandhi's dealing with the British and the psychology of violence that marred his relationships with his family and with the children of the ashram. It was this contradiction, Erikson confesses, which almost brought *me* to the point where I felt unable to continue writing *this* book because I seemed to sense the presence of a kind of untruth in the very protestation of truth; of something unclean when all the words spelled out an unreal purity; and, above all, of displaced violence where nonviolence was the professed issue. (p. 231)

In an effort to untangle the relationship between the spiritual truth of Satyagraha and the truth of his own psychoanalytic understanding, Erikson reminds Gandhi that "Truth, you once said, 'excludes the use of violence because man is not capable of knowing the absolute truth and therefore is not competent to punish'" (p. 241). The affinity between Satyagraha and psychoanalysis lies in their shared commitment to seeing life as an "experiment in truth," in their being

somehow joined in a universal "therapeutics," committed to the Hippocratic principle that one can test truth (or the healing power inherent in a sick situation) only by action which avoids harm—or better, by action which maximizes mutuality and minimizes the violence caused by unilateral coercion or threat. (p. 247)

Erikson takes Gandhi to task for his failure to acknowledge the relativity of truth. This failure is manifest in the coercion of Gandhi's claim to exclusive possession of the truth, his "unwillingness to learn from *anybody anything* except what was approved by the 'inner voice'" (p. 236). This claim led Gandhi, in the guise of love, to impose his truth on others without awareness or regard for the extent to which he thereby did violence to their integrity.

The moral dilemma, arising inevitably out of a conflict of truths, is by definition a "sick situation" in that its either/or formulation leaves no room for an outcome that does not do violence. The resolution of such dilemmas, however, lies not in the self-deception of rationalized violence—"I was" said Gandhi, "a cruelly kind husband. I regarded myself as her teacher and so harassed her out of my blind love for her" (p. 233)—but rather in the replacement of the underlying antagonism with a mutuality of respect and care.

Gandhi, whom Kohlberg has mentioned as exemplifying Stage Six moral judgment and whom Erikson sought as a model of an adult ethical sensibility, instead is criticized by a judgment that refuses to look away from or condone the infliction of harm. In denying the validity of his wife's reluctance to open her home to strangers and in his blindness to the different reality of adolescent sexuality and temptation, Gandhi compromised in his everyday life the ethic of nonviolence to which in principle and in public he was so steadfastly committed.

The blind willingness to sacrifice people to truth, however, has always

318   been the danger of an ethics abstracted from life. This willingness links Gandhi to the biblical Abraham, who prepared to sacrifice the life of his son in order to demonstrate the integrity and supremacy of his faith. Both men, in the limitations of their fatherhood, stand in implicit contrast to the woman who comes before Solomon and verifies her motherhood by relinquishing truth in order to save the life of her child. It is the ethics of an adulthood that has become principled at the expense of care that Erikson comes to criticize in his assessment of Gandhi's life.

This same criticism is dramatized explicitly as a contrast between the sexes in *The Merchant of Venice* (1598/1912), where Shakespeare goes through an extraordinary complication of sexual identity (dressing a male actor as a female character who in turn poses as a male judge) in order to bring into the masculine citadel of justice the feminine plea for mercy. The limitation of the contractual conception of justice is illustrated through the absurdity of its literal execution, while the "need to make exceptions all the time" is demonstrated contrapuntally in the matter of the rings. Portia, in calling for mercy, argues for that resolution in which no one is hurt, and as the men are forgiven for their failure to keep both their rings and their word, Antonio in turn foregoes his "right" to ruin Shylock.

The research findings that have been reported in this essay suggest that women impose a distinctive construction on moral problems, seeing moral dilemmas in terms of conflicting responsibilities. This construction was found to develop through a sequence of three levels and two transitions, each level representing a more complex understanding of the relationship between self and other and each transition involving a critical reinterpretation of the moral conflict between selfishness and responsibility. The development of women's moral judgment appears to proceed from an initial concern with survival, to a focus on goodness, and finally to a principled understanding of nonviolence as the most adequate guide to the just resolution of moral conflicts.

In counterposing to Kohlberg's longitudinal research on the development of hypothetical moral judgment in men a cross-sectional study of women's responses to actual dilemmas of moral conflict and choice, this essay precludes the possibility of generalization in either direction and leaves to further research the task of sorting out the different variables of occasion and sex. Longitudinal studies of women's moral judgments are necessary in order to validate the claims of stage and sequence presented here. Similarly, the contrast drawn between the moral judgments of men and women awaits for its confirmation a more systematic comparison of the responses of both sexes. Kohlberg's research on moral development has confounded the variables of age, sex, type of decision, and type of dilemma by presenting a single configuration (the responses of adolescent males to hypothetical dilemmas of conflicting rights) as the basis for a universal stage sequence. This paper underscores the need for systematic treatment of these variables and points toward their study as a critical task for future moral development research.

For the present, my aim has been to demonstrate the centrality of the concepts of responsibility and care in women's constructions of the moral domain, to indicate the close tie in women's thinking between conceptions of the self and conceptions of morality, and, finally, to argue the need for an expanded developmental theory that would include, rather than rule out from developmental consideration, the difference in the feminine voice. Such an inclusion seems essential, not only for explaining the development of women but also for understanding in both sexes the characteristics and precursors of an adult moral conception.

References

Broverman, I., Vogel, S., Broverman, D., Clarkson, F., & Rosenkrantz, P. Sex-role stereotypes: A current appraisal. *Journal of Social Issues*, 1972, *28*, 59–78.

Coles, R. *Children of crisis*. Boston: Little, Brown, 1964.

Didion, J. The women's movement. *New York Times Book Review*, July 30, 1972, pp. 1–2; 14.

Drabble, M. *The waterfall*. Hammondsworth, Eng.: Penguin Books, 1969.

Eliot, G. *The mill on the floss*. New York: New American Library, 1965. (Originally published 1860.)

Erikson, E. H. *Insight and responsibility*. New York: W. W. Norton, 1964.

Erikson, E. H. *Identity: Youth and crisis*. New York: W. W. Norton, 1968.

Erikson, E. H. *Gandhi's truth*. New York: W. W. Norton, 1969.

Freud, S. "Civilized" sexual morality and modern nervous illness. In J. Strachey (Ed.), *The standard edition of the complete psychological works of Sigmund Freud* (Vol. 9). London: Hogarth Press, 1959. (Originally published 1908.)

Freud, S. Some psychical consequences of the anatomical distinction between the sexes. In J. Strachey (Ed.), *The standard edition of the complete psychological works of Sigmund Freud* (Vol. 19). London: Hogarth Press, 1961. (Originally published 1925.)

Gilligan, C., Kohlberg, L., Lerner, J., & Belenky, M. Moral reasoning about sexual dilemmas: The development of an interview and scoring system. *Technical Report of the President's Commission on Obscenity and Pornography* (Vol. 1) [415 060-137]. Washington, D.C.: U.S. Government Printing Office, 1971.

Haan, N. Hypothetical and actual moral reasoning in a situation of civil disobedience. *Journal of Personality and Social Psychology*, 1975, *32*, 255–70.

Holstein, C. Development of moral judgment: A longitudinal study of males and females. *Child Development*, 1976, *47*, 51–61.

Horner, M. Toward an understanding of achievement-related conflicts in women. *Journal of Social Issues*, 1972, *29*, 157–74.

Ibsen, H. *A doll's house*. In *Ibsen plays*. Hammondsworth, Eng.: Penguin Books, 1965. (Originally published, 1879.)

Kohlberg, L. From is to ought: How to commit the naturalistic fallacy and get away with it in the study of moral development. In T. Mischel (Ed.), *Cognitive development and epistemology*. New York: Academic Press, 1971.

Kohlberg, L.,& Gilligan, C. The adolescent as a philosopher: The discovery of the self in a postconventional world. *Daedalus*, 1971, *100*, 1051–56.

Kohlberg, L., & Kramer, R. Continuities and discontinuities in childhood and adult moral development. *Human Development*, 1969, *12*, 93–120.

Piaget, J. *The moral judgment of the child*. New York: The Free Press, 1965. (Originally published, 1932.)

Shakespeare, W. *The merchant of Venice*. In *The comedies of Shakespeare*. London: Oxford University Press, 1912. (Originally published 1598.)

Listening to a Different Voice:
A Review of Gilligan's *In a Different Voice*

ANNE COLBY AND WILLIAM DAMON

In a Different Voice has created an unusual excitement within and beyond the field of psychology, no doubt because it is full of exciting ideas. Gilligan writes with force and elegance. Her characterizations of male and female psychological perspectives are intriguing as well as intuitively appealing. The book stimulates thought and discussion about some of the most profound issues of human development and does not shy away from controversy. These reasons alone make it worthwhile reading.

Nevertheless, the book also must be assessed objectively for its contribution to psychological theory and research. How accurate are its claims concerning the prior literature? How sound are the new data that are presented? How original is the view that it presents, and how fruitful is the direction that it marks out? Although the book has been widely reviewed in both the psychological and mass media, it has not been examined with these questions in mind. Instead, most reviews have focused on the ideological implications of Gilligan's statement. In the current review, we shall discuss the scholarly value of this work, giving particular attention to its potential contribution to developmental psychology.

The most striking feature of Gilligan's book is its boldness. It offers no less than a sweeping critique of all major developmental theories on the grounds that they are biased against women. Included in the culpable network are Freud, Piaget, Bettelheim, Levinson, McClelland, Kohlberg, and Erikson, as well as a host of their followers. If Gilligan's charges are justified, developmental psychology must return to the drawing board, since it has misrepresented a majority of the human race.

Gilligan stakes her argument on two main assertions: first, that women

"Listening to a Different Voice: A Review of Gilligan's *In a Different Voice*" by Anne Colby and William Damon, *Merrill-Palmer Quarterly*, 1983, 29 (4), 473–81. Copyright © 1983 by Wayne State University Press. Reprinted by permission.

Dr. Colby is Director of the Henry A. Murray Research Center, Radcliffe College, Harvard University. Dr. Damon is Professor, Department of Psychology, Clark University, Worcester, Massachusetts.

322 are typically different from men in their basic orientations to life; and, second, that many existing psychological theories, in particular developmental theories, devalue the feminine orientation. For the sake of examining Gilligan's position, it is useful to separate the two assertions and to scrutinize Gilligan's defense of each.

The Feminine Orientation toward Relationships

Gilligan claims that there is a very general psychological sex difference that distinguishes women from men throughout life, beginning in infancy. Women, she writes, are oriented toward attachment and "connectedness" to others, whereas men are oriented toward individuation and "separateness" from others. The feminine orientation predisposes women toward interest in human relationships, while the male orientation predisposes men toward interest in individual achievement. One consequence of this difference in orientation is that women find it easier than men to establish intimate relationships. Another is that women's personal identities are likely to be grounded upon their intimate relationships, whereas men's are likely to be grounded upon their occupational choices.

To explain the origin of the differences between male and female psychological orientations, Gilligan adopts the position put forth by Chodorow in her feminist revision of psychoanalytic theory (Chodorow, 1978). According to this position, distinctly male and female orientations are formed early, and irreversibly, with the mother-child relation. Because women are almost universally responsible for early childcare, male children discover themselves through the contrast between themselves and an opposite-sex parent, whereas female children discover themselves through the similarity between themselves and a same-sex parent. Before long, boys have developed the notion that they are essentially different from significant others in their lives; in contrast, girls experience a fundamental similarity between themselves and others. Gilligan quotes Chodorow's (1978) remark that "Girls emerge with a stronger basis for experiencing another's needs and feelings as one's own" (p. 167). Boys, on the other hand, tend toward a "more emphatic individuation" which curtails "their primary love and sense of empathic tie" (p. 150). Gilligan (1982) credits Chodorow's position with replacing psychoanalytic theory's "negative and derivative description of female psychology with a positive and direct account" (p. 8).

Is Gilligan on firm ground in her distinction between typical male and female orientations to life? In order to answer this question, it is necessary to decompose Gilligan's synthetic concept of global masculine and feminine orientations. That is, Gilligan has synthesized research and theory on sex differences in a number of quite different domains of development, claiming that they form a coherent whole, with a common root in the connectedness-separateness difference. A careful review of the literature, however, reveals that some of the differences to which Gilligan refers are better substantiated than others. Furthermore, the implications for Gilligan's thesis of those differences that have been shown to exist are not always clear.

On the positive side, it is true that boys and girls often play differently. Boys tend to prefer organized games with elaborate systems of rules; girls prefer dyadic intimate exchanges and turn-taking games with relatively few players (Maccoby & Jacklin, 1974; Luria & Herzog, 1983). This difference may indicate a sex-linked difference in children's social interactions, with possible implications for the development of moral judgment or identity formation.

It is also clear that differential stereotypes of males and females are widely held, as has been documented by Broverman, Vogel, Broverman, Clarkson, and Rosenkrantz (1972) and others. Males are commonly viewed as more independent, objective, ambitious, and the like, while females are seen as more aware of others' feelings and more tactful and expressive. But the evidence that these stereotypes reflect reality is much less convincing. For example, there is very little support in the psychological literature for the notion that girls are more aware of others' feelings or are more altruistic than boys. Sex differences in empathy are inconsistently found and are generally very small when they are reported (Hoffman, 1977; Mussen & Eisenberg-Berg, 1977; Staub, 1978). The findings on the applicability of Erikson's identity construct to girls and women are also mixed. Marcia (1980), for example, reports some differences in women's versus men's responses to questions concerning occupational identity. But a recent comprehensive review (Waterman, 1982) of research on Erikson's identity theory concludes that "males and females are more similar than different in their use of developmental processes," and, for the great majority of persons, "males and females undergo similar patterns of identity development" (p. 315). There have been few, if any, sex differences reported for measures derived from Piagetian cognitive, developmental theory.

Thus, it must be concluded that evidence in support of Gilligan's distinction between orientations is mixed. Sex differences have been found in some aspects of social behavior, achievement motivation, occupational choices, and so on, and have been described by several theorists and researchers prior to Gilligan (e.g., Bakan, 1966; Deutsch, 1944; Dweck & Bush, 1976; Gutmann, 1965; Horner, 1972; Wyatt, 1967). But there are

324 also a number of areas in which differences are slight or nonexistent, such as many aspects of prosocial and cognitive development. The available research data, therefore, do not reveal a clear picture of a global dichotomy between the life orientations of men and women.

Certainly the male-female distinction that Gilligan advances has some intuitive appeal, as both her literary citations and anecdotal material indicate. This intuitive appeal should not be discounted lightly, since the point of Gilligan's critique is that one must look beyond social scientific research to appreciate fully this difference. If it is true that social science fails to account for women's experience, this may be why Gilligan is able to provide only sporadic scientific documentation for her claim that men and women have distinct orientations to life. The scarcity of consistent data on this issue could be seen as neither surprising nor damaging to Gilligan's thesis, for we could not expect a flawed science to provide an accurate view of reality.

The Claim of Antifeminine Bias in Developmental Theory

Although Gilligan makes a broad indictment in her introduction, her focus on this issue is restricted to moral development. Gilligan believes that men's moral sensibilities reflect a concern for justice, whereas women's reflect a concern for care. This difference is because, Gilligan claims, men begin with an orientation toward separateness, and women toward connectedness. From a separateness perspective, socialized living requires an intricate moral system of rules and rights in order to resolve persons' competing claims to justice. Such a morality is needed to create links between persons, who are assumed to be fundamentally in conflict regarding their rights. In contrast, an orientation toward connectedness requires no such system. All that is needed is a sensitivity to the needs of others and a benevolent attitude, both of which are dominant in the feminine preference for the morality of care.

Gilligan's main argument with contemporary theories of moral development derives from her belief that, when faced with a hypothetical moral dilemma of the Kohlbergian sort, girls and women are at a disadvantage when compared with boys and men. This is because Kohlberg's hypothetical dilemmas pose conflicts of justice, in which the rights of different persons come into conflict. Since women see morality as a problem in care rather than in justice, they are ill-prepared to reason about the focal issues under investigation. Further, Kohlberg's scoring system is calibrated on a sequence of justice values. Women, who value care and responsibility, inevitably will score lower than men when assessed by this justice-bound system. To make matters worse, Gilligan asserts, hypothetical moral dilemmas tap processes of rationalization and logical deduction. Gilligan suggests that such skills come more naturally to men than to women (though, as noted previously, there is no evidence to support this suggestion).

A final problem of Kohlberg's system, writes Gilligan, is its tendency to score all care and responsibility responses as Stage 3. Since Stage 3 is considered a low-normal score for adults within most populations, this scoring bias relegates adult women to a moral status that is somewhat lower than that of men.

Gilligan uses a number of strategies to make her case. First, she quotes some girls' and boys' reasoning about Kohlberg's Heinz dilemma, and draws contrasts between their orientations. For example, eleven-year-old Amy is set against eleven-year-old Jake: Amy sees the story as a "narrative of relationships" whereas Jake sees it as "a math problem with humans." This, Gilligan claims, is a characteristic difference between boys and girls, and the developmental scoring system rewards the boys. Gilligan tells us that Jake would score an entire stage higher than Amy because of his more logical approach to the problem.

Gilligan then goes on to present her own research as further indication of how inadequately Kohlberg's system represents women. Some of the research involves open-ended questions about the self and morality. For example, Gilligan asks males and females questions like, "if you had to say what morality meant to you, how would you sum it up?" and "How would you describe yourself to yourself?" Gilligan uses subjects' answers in an anecdotal manner, selecting cases that illustrate her overall claim that women are more interpersonally oriented, but no less sophisticated, than men. Her consistent implication is that Kohlbergian scoring would undervalue the intellectual and moral worth of the women's statements that she quotes. Gilligan does not attempt, however, to score these quotes herself, either by Kohlberg's scheme or by any replacement system. Nor does she present any empirical data regarding her interview studies.

The more ambitious and intriguing research that Gilligan presents goes beyond the interview technique to study real-life moral decisions of women in crisis. The particular crisis of Gilligan's subjects is unwanted pregnancy. Gilligan extensively questioned twenty-one women who faced the decision of whether or not to have an abortion. The questions focus on the women's choices, and their views of their own lives. Gilligan demonstrates, through extensive quotes from these women, a "caring" orientation to the moral problems entailed in abortion decisions. Unfortunately for the sake of her main thesis, Gilligan did not collect any comparative data in this study.

326 Ideally, the women in Gilligan's study should have been compared with men faced with the same dilemma. For example, the fathers of the unborn children could have been questioned and their responses compared to those of the mothers. Then it could have been ascertained whether women are uniquely caring in response to abortion-type decisions, or whether men also share this orientation when faced with such decisions.

Because of this methodological limitation in Gilligan's abortion study, it is impossible to tell whether or not women differ from men in how they frame moral issues. In fact, research by Smetana (1981) casts doubt on whether people necessarily see moral issues as the primary considerations in deciding whether or not to have an abortion; many women and men think of abortion as a personal or social-conventional dilemma, and act accordingly. Although Gilligan's abortion interviews yield some interesting data on real-life decision-making processes, they do not provide support for her thesis of sex bias in Kohlberg's theory.

Only the question of sex differences in developmental stage scores on Kohlberg's measure bears directly on Gilligan's charge that Kohlberg's theory is sex biased. That is, Kohlberg's system cannot be said to be biased against women unless they score lower than men. In fact, the data on this issue are clear-cut, and quite different than Gilligan's representations of them. Two recent reviews of the literature report that if educational and occupational backgrounds of subjects are controlled, there are no sex differences in moral judgment stage scores (Rest, 1985; Walker, 1984). This finding applies both to Kohlberg's measure and to Rest's Defining Issues Test. The few studies that have found sex differences favoring men have not established statistical controls for education and work experience, variables that correlate significantly with moral judgment within each sex. Such differences disappear entirely when proper controls are established. Furthermore, several recent longitudinal studies of moral judgment (Erickson, 1980; Snarey, 1982) have found that girls' and women's moral judgment develops through the same developmental sequence in the same order as does male subjects' moral reasoning.

As for the particular issue of whether a caring perspective is confused in Kohlberg's system with Stage 3, one must distinguish between Kohlberg's early scoring procedures in which form and content did tend to be confounded, and his current system in which they have been more fully differentiated. In the early procedures, concern with loving relationships and interpersonal trust was indeed scored as indicative of Stage 3. In the current procedures, the issues of affiliation, trust, and social harmony (under the manual headings of "Norms" and "Elements") are represented at every stage, from the first to the last. The current procedures have been in use since 1978. Levels of relationship, caring, and interpersonal trust that are both more and less developmentally advanced than Stage 3 are built into the current Kohlberg scoring system (Colby, Kohlberg, Gibbs, Candee, Speicher-Dubin, Hewer, Kauffman, & Power, in press).

Issues relating to the greater relativity and diffidence of women and their supposed unwillingness to accept the abstractness of Kohlberg's hypothetical dilemmas have not been systematically investigated. Another, more important question is whether the rights and response orientations represent two qualitatively different organizations of thought with different sequences of development, or whether they can both be subsumed within Kohlberg's stage sequence. It is not yet possible to determine whether moral judgment is best described by a single underlying sequence or by two different sequences, since Gilligan has not yet developed empirical criteria by which to code developmentally the judgments in the responsibility mode, and Kohlberg's scoring criteria have not been extended for use with real-life dilemmas.

In summary, Gilligan's arguments are questionable in some respects. While her portrayal of general, sex-linked life orientations is intuitively appealing, the research evidence at this point does not support such a generalized distinction. Further, to the extent that differences of this sort do exist, there is no evidence whatsoever that they are due to early and irreversible emotional experiences between mother and child.

As for moral development specifically, there may be preliminary indications that men and women emphasize different aspects of morality and frame spontaneously chosen dilemmas somewhat differently. But it is just as likely that all men and women use both orientations, and that the type of dilemma being discussed is as influential in determining a person's orientation as is the person's gender.

Because sex differences in moral stage disappear when occupation and education are controlled, and because girls and women pass through the same stages in the same order as men, Gilligan's allegation of gender bias against Kohlberg's theory is unwarranted. Women's thinking in response to Kohlberg's dilemmas cannot be said to be devalued by his stage scheme, because women's judgments consistently are scored as developmentally equivalent to men's.

We must conclude, then, that Gilligan's most important contribution is not her widely acclaimed critique of existing developmental theories, but rather her preliminary extension of moral development theory and method. Her use of situations in which real moral decisions are made could constitute an advance over the use of hypothetical moral dilemmas. It is only through such investigation that the complex processes that characterize

328 actual moral judgment can be identified, and the relation of moral judgment to moral conduct can be illuminated. A description of multiple styles, orientations, and dimensions of moral judgment would enrich our conception of moral development.

A review of this book would be incomplete without some discussion of the ideological position it represents. Gilligan has taken a new perspective on feminine psychological characteristics that have been assumed to reflect women's oppression—their deference, their self-doubt, their dependence—and has chosen to see these characteristics as representing strengths rather than weaknesses. This is, of course, an ideological position rather than an empirically verifiable, social-scientific claim. The argument has been made somewhat differently by others along the following lines: Although there are obvious disadvantageous psychological consequences to being socially subordinate, outside the dominant system, and relatively powerless, there are also some advantages. Outsiders may escape some of the dominant group's weaknesses and may even be able to develop special strengths and insights by virtue of their subordinate position. In questioning some of Gilligan's methods and specific conclusions, we do not mean to diminish the importance of identifying and describing the development of certain traditionally feminine characteristics that have been devalued illegitimately. On the other hand, it is equally important to guard against reinforcing gender stereotypes that in themselves contribute to the maintenance of women's oppression.

References

Bakan, D. *The duality of human existence*. Boston: Beacon Press, 1966.

Broverman, I., Vogel, S., Broverman, D., Clarkson, F., & Rosenkrantz, P. Sex-role stereotypes: A current appraisal. *Journal of Social Issues*, 1972, *28*, 59–78.

Chodorow, N. *The reproduction of mothering*. Berkeley: University of California Press, 1978.

Colby, A., Kohlberg, L., Gibbs, J., Candee, D., Speicher-Dubin, B., Hewer, A., Kauffman, K., & Power, C. *The measurement of moral judgment*. New York: Cambridge University Press, in press.

Deutsch, H. *The psychology of women: A psychoanalytic interpretation*. New York: Grune & Stratton, 1944.

Dweck, C. E., & Bush, E. S. Sex differences in learned helplessness: Differential debilitation with peer and adult evaluators. *Developmental Psychology*, 1976, *12*, 147–56.

Erickson, V. L. The case study method in the evaluation of developmental programs. In L. Kuhmerker, M. Mentkowski, & L. V. Erickson (Eds.), *Evaluating moral development*. New York: Character Research Press, 1980.

Gilligan, C. *In a different voice: Psychological theory and women's development*. Cambridge: Harvard University Press, 1982.

Gutmann, D. L., Women and the conception of ego strength. *Merrill-Palmer Quarterly*, 1965, *11*, 229–40.

Hoffman, M. Sex differences in empathy and related behaviors. *Psychological Bulletin*, 1977, *84*, 712–22.

Horner, M. Toward an understanding of achievement-related conflicts in women. *Journal of Social Issues*, 1972, *28*, 157–76.

Luria, Z., & Herzog, E. Gender segregation and play groups. Paper presented at the meeting of the Society for Research in Child Development, Detroit, April 1983.

Maccoby, E., & Jacklin, C. N. *The psychology of sex differences*. Stanford: Stanford University Press, 1974.

Marcia, J. E. Identity in adolescence. In J. B. Adelson (Ed.), *Handbook of adolescent psychology*. New York: Wiley, 1980.

Mussen, P., & Eisenberg-Berg, N. *Roots of caring, sharing, and helping: The development of prosocial behavior in children*. San Francisco: Freeman, 1977.

Rest, J. Morality. In J. H. Flavell, & E. Markmas (Eds.), *Cognitive development*. New York: Wiley, 1985.

Smetana, J. Reasoning in the personal and moral domains: Adolescent and young adult women's decision-making regarding abortion. *Journal of Applied Developmental Psychology*, 1981, *2*, 211–26.

Snarey, J. The moral development of Kibbutz founders and Sabras: A cross-sectional and ten year longitudinal cross-cultural study. Unpublished doctoral dissertation. Harvard University, 1982.

Staub, E. *Positive social behavior and morality*. New York: Academic Press, 1978.

Walker, L. Sex differences in the development of moral reasoning: A critical review of the literature. *Child Development*, 1984, 55 (3), 677–91.

Waterman, A. S. Identity development from adolescence to adulthood: An extension of theory and a review of research. *Developmental Psychology*, 1982, *18*, 341–58.

Wyatt, F. Clinical notes on the motives of reproduction. *Journal of Social Issues, 1967, 23*, 29–56.

PART IV

Social Issues Affecting Women

Question 10

Can Sex Differences in Math Achievement Be Explained by Biology?

The study of sex differences has had a long and controversial history. Feminist psychologists, dating back to Leta Stetter Hollingworth and Helen Thompson in the early twentieth century, have objected to the distortions and misuse of the research in this field (Rosenberg, 1982). More recent criticism has ranged from charges that the study of sex differences usually reinforces sex stereotypes (Bart, 1971) to condemnation of this line of research as inherently sexist (Grady, 1977). Kay Deaux (1985) notes that the very popularity of the term "sex difference" reflects a strong belief that such differences do exist and are important. When psychologists construct experiments to test for an expected effect and then find it, the results are usually joyfully reported. The problem is that null effects, the failure to find any effect in any direction, are usually viewed as indications that the experiment has gone awry, and results rarely appear in the scientific literature (Gould, 1986; Caplan, 1986).

In their comprehensive survey of empirical research, Eleanor Maccoby and Carol Nagy Jacklin (1974) found four areas in which there was sufficient evidence to document the existence of sex differences: aggression, visual-spatial ability, verbal ability, and mathematical ability. It is the last of these alleged differences that has received the most popular attention in recent years.

A study done by Lucy Sells at the University of California at Berkeley in the early 1970s showed that whereas 57 percent of the incoming male students had four years of high school math, this was true for only 8 percent of the female students. This meant that 92 percent of the first-year female students could not enroll in fifteen of the twenty majors at the university which required a strong mathematics background, such as engineering, *333*

334 computer science, and physics. In effect, mathematics became, in Sells's words, a "critical filter" which served to close off a number of occupations to women (Sells, 1978).

Impressed by Sells's work, which at that point had not yet been published, Sheila Tobias brought the issue to the attention of the public in a 1976 article in *Ms.* magazine in which she traced the problem to "math anxiety" in girls and women. In her book, appropriately titled *Overcoming Math Anxiety* (1978), Tobias argued that girls are encouraged to drop mathematics at an early age while social forces encourage boys to pursue such courses.

Much of the work in the 1970s on sex differences in mathematics concentrated on exploring the environmental factors that discouraged girls from studying mathematics. John Ernest (1976), for example, suggested that the girl's decision to stop taking mathematics courses may actually be her response to social pressures and the lowered expectations that parents, teachers, and the larger society have for female achievement in math.

In 1980, Camilla Persson Benbow and Julian C. Stanley shifted the focus of the discussion when they reported large sex differences in mean scores on a test of mathematical reasoning for mathematically talented seventh- and eighth-graders. Noting that both sexes had similar formal educational training, they suggested that the sex differences resulted from an innate male talent for mathematical ability.

Benbow and Stanley's research has stimulated a wide range of criticism. Some psychologists, while conceding that there may be some difference between the two sexes, argue that the difference is small. Some studies suggest that the sex variance in mathematical ability can be traced to a sex difference in spatial ability. Others, in turn, have attempted to relate the difference in spatial ability to hemispheric specialization of the brain (Henley, 1985).

Benbow and Stanley have conducted additional research in support of their position. Jacquelynne Eccles and Janis Jacobs challenge Benbow and Stanley's conclusions and, in an interesting wrinkle, suggest that in certain cases such studies can actually help create gender stereotypes of mathematical ability.

References

Bart, P. (1971). Sexism and social science: From the gilded cage to the iron cage, or the perils of Pauline. *Journal of marriage and the family, 33*, 734–45.

Benbow, C. P., & Stanley, J. C. (1980). Sex differences in mathematical ability: Fact or artifact? *Science, 210*, 1262–64.

Caplan, P., MacPherson, G. M., & Tobin, P. (1986). The magnified molehill and the 335 misplaced focus: sex-related differences in spatial ability revisited. *American Psychologist, 41* (9), 1016–18.
Deaux, K. (1985). Sex and gender. *Annual Review in Psychology, 36,* 49–81.
Ernest, J. (1976). Mathematics and sex. *American Mathematical Monthly, 83* (8), 595–614.
Gould, S. (1986, September 25). Cardboard Darwinism. *New York Review of Books, 33* (14), 47–54.
Grady, K. (1977, April). The belief in sex differences. Paper presented at the Eastern Psychological Association Meetings, Boston, Mass.
Henley, N. (1985). Psychology and gender. *Signs: Journal of Women in Culture and Society, 11* (1), 101–19.
Maccoby, E. E. & Jacklin, C. H. (1974). *The psychology of sex differences.* Stanford: Stanford University Press.
Rosenberg, R. (1982). *Beyond separate spheres: Intellectual roots of modern feminism.* New Haven: Yale University Press.
Sells, L. W. (1978). Mathematics—A critical filter. *The Science Teacher, 45* (2), 28–29.
Tobias, S. (1976). Math anxiety: Why is a smart girl like you counting on your fingers? *Ms., V* (3), 56–59, 92.
Tobias, S. (1978). *Overcoming math anxiety.* New York: Norton.

Additional Reading

Benbow, C. P. (In press). Sex-related differences in mathematical reasoning ability among intellectually talented preadolescents: Their characterization, consequences, and possible explanations. *Behavioral and Brain Sciences.*
Benbow, C. P., & Stanley, J. C. (1981). Letters. *Science, 212,* 114.
Crockett, L. J., Petersen, A. C. (1984). Biology: Its role in gender-related educational experiences. In E. Fennema & J. J. Ayer (Eds.), *Women and education: Equity or equality?* (pp. 85–116). Berkeley: McCutchan.
Deitsch, I. (1984). A feminist approach to math-anxiety reduction. In C. M. Brody (Ed.), *Women therapists working with women: New theory and process of feminist therapy* (pp. 144–56). New York: Springer.
Eccles, J. (1985). Sex differences in achievement patterns. In T. Sonderegger (Ed.), *Nebraska Symposium on Motivation, 1984: The psychology of gender, 32* (pp. 97–132). Lincoln: University of Nebraska Press.
Entwisle, E. R., & Baker, D. P. (1983). Gender and young children's expectations for performance in arithmetic. *Developmental Psychology, 19* (2), 200–09.
Hogrebe, M. C. (1987). Gender differences in mathematics. *American Psychologist, 42*(3), 265–66.
Hyde, J. S. (1981). How large are cognitive gender differences? A meta-analysis using w and d, *American Psychologist, 36* (8), 892–901.
Meece, J. L., Parsons, J. E., Kaczala, C. M., Goff, S. G., & Futterman, R. (1982). Sex differences in math achievement: Toward a model of academic choice. *Psychological Bulletin, 91* (2), 324–48.
Sells, L. W. (1980). The mathematical filter and the education of women and minorities. In L. H. Fox, L. Brody, & D. Tobin (Eds.), *Women and the mathematical mystique.* Baltimore: Johns Hopkins University Press, 1980.
Wittig, M. A. & Petersen, A. C. (1979). *Sex-related differences in cognitive functioning: Developmental issues.* New York: Academic Press.

Sex Differences in Mathematical Reasoning Ability: More Facts

CAMILLA PERSSON BENBOW AND JULIAN STANLEY

In 1980 we reported large sex differences in mean scores on a test of mathematical reasoning ability for 9,927 mathematically talented seventh and eighth graders who entered the Johns Hopkins regional talent search from 1972 through 1979.[1] One prediction from those results was that there would be a preponderance of males at the high end of the distribution of mathematical reasoning ability. In this report we investigate sex differences at the highest levels of that ability. New groups of students under age thirteen with exceptional mathematical aptitude were identified by means of two separate procedures. In the first, the Johns Hopkins regional talent searches in 1980, 1981, and 1982,[2] 39,820 seventh graders from the Middle Atlantic region of the United States who were selected for high intellectual ability were given the College Board Scholastic Aptitude Test (SAT). In the second, a nationwide talent search was conducted for which any student under thirteen years of age who was willing to take the SAT was eligible. The results of both procedures substantiated our prediction that before age thirteen far more males than females would score extremely high on SAT-M, the mathematical part of SAT.

The test items of SAT-M require numerical judgment, relational thinking, or insightful and logical reasoning. This test is designed to measure the

1. C. Benbow and J. Stanley, *Science* 210, 1262 (1980). Also see letters by C. Tomizuka and S. Tobias; E. Stage and R. Karplus; S. Chipman; E. Egelman et al.; D. Moran; E. Luchins and A. Luchins; A. Kelly; C. Benbow and J. Stanley, ibid. 212, 114 (1981).
2. The Johns Hopkins Center for the Advancement of Academically Talented Youth (CTY) conducts talent searches during January in Delaware, the District of Columbia, Maryland, New Jersey (added in 1980), Pennsylvania, Virginia, and West Virginia. In 1983 coverage expanded northeast to include Connecticut, Maine, Massachusetts, New Hampshire, Rhode Island, and Vermont.

"Sex Differences in Mathematical Reasoning: More Facts" by Camilla Persson Benbow and Julian Stanley, *Science*, 1983, (2, December), 222, 1029–31. Copyright © 1983 by the American Association for the Advancement of Science. Reprinted by permission.

Dr. Benbow is Associate Professor of Psychology and Director of the Study of Mathematically Precocious Youth at Iowa State University, Ames, Iowa; Dr. Stanley is Professor of Psychology and Director of the Study of Mathematically Precocious Youth at Johns Hopkins University.

developed mathematical reasoning ability of eleventh and twelfth graders.[3]
Most students in our study were in the middle of the seventh grade. Few
had had formal opportunities to study algebra and beyond.[4] Our rationale
is that most of these students were unfamiliar with mathematics from
algebra onward, and that most who scored high did so because of extraordinary reasoning ability.[5]

In 1980, 1981, and 1982, as in the earlier study (n. 1), participants in the
Johns Hopkins talent search were seventh-graders, or boys and girls of
typical seventh-grade age in a higher grade, in the Middle Atlantic area.
Before 1980, applicants had been required to be in the top 3 percent
nationally on the mathematics section of any standardized achievement
test. Beginning in 1980, students in the top 3 percent in verbal or overall
intellectual ability were also eligible. During that and the next two years
19,883 boys and 19,937 girls applied and were tested. Even though this
sample was more general and had equal representation by sex, the mean
sex difference on SAT-M remained constant at 30 points favoring males
(males' $\bar{X} = 416$, S.D. $= 87$; females' $\bar{X} = 386$, S.D. $= 74$; $t = 37$; $P <$
0.001). No important difference in verbal ability as measured by SAT-V
was found (males' $\bar{X} = 367$, females' $\bar{X} = 365$).

The major point, however, is not the mean difference in SAT-M scores
but the ratios of boys to girls among the high scorers (table 10.1). The ratio
of boys to girls scoring above the mean of talent-search males was 1.5:1. The
ratio among those who scored ≥ 500 (493 was the mean of 1981–82
college-bound twelfth-grade males) was 2.1:1. Among those who scored $\geq$
600 (the 79th percentile of the twelfth-grade males) the ratio was 4.1:1.
These ratios are similar to those previously reported (n. 1) but are derived
from a broader and much larger data base.

Scoring 700 or more on the SAT-M before age thirteen is rare. We
estimate that students who reach this criterion (the 95th percentile of
college-bound twelfth-grade males) before their thirteenth birthday represent the top one in ten thousand of their age group. It was because of their
rarity that the nationwide talent search was created in November 1980 in
order to locate such students who were born after 1967 and facilitate their
education.[6] In that talent search applicants could take the SAT at any time
and place at which it was administered by the Educational Testing Service

3. T. Donlon and W. Angoff, in *The College Board Admissions Testing Program*, W. Angoff, Ed. (College Board, Princeton, N.J., 1971), pp. 24–25; S. Messick and A. Jungeblut, *Psychol. Bull.* 89, 191 (1982).
4. C. Benbow and J. Stanley, *Gifted Child Q.* 26, 82 (1982): idem, *Am. Educ. Res. J.* 19, 598 (1982).
5. We have found that among the top 10 percent of these students (who are eligible for our fast-paced summer programs in mathematics) a majority do not know even first-year algebra well.
6. J. Stanley, "Searches under way for youths *exceptionally* talented mathematically or verbally," *Roeper Rev.*, in press.

Table 10.1: Number of high scorers on SAT–M among selected seventh graders—19,883 boys and 19,937 girls—tested in the Johns Hopkins regional talent search in 1980, 1981, and 1982, and of scorers of ≥ 700 prior to age 13 in the national search (9).

Score	Number	Percent	Ratio of boys to girls
	Johns Hopkins regional search		
420 or more*			
Boys	9119	45.9	
Girls	6220	31.2	1.5:1
500 or more			
Boys	3618	18.2	
Girls	1707	8.6	2.1:1
600 or more			
Boys	648	3.3	
Girls	158	0.8	4.1:1
	National search		
	In Johns Hopkins talent search region		
700 or more			
Boys	113	†	
Girls	9	†	12.6:1
	Outside Johns Hopkins talent search region		
700 or more			
Boys	147	†	
Girls	11	†	13.4:1

*Mean score of the boys was 416. The highest possible score is 800.
†Total number tested is unknown (9).

or through one of five regional talent searches that cover the United States.[7] Extensive nationwide efforts were made to inform school personnel and parents about our search. The new procedure (unrestricted by geography or previous ability) was successful in obtaining a large national sample of this exceedingly rare population. As of September 1983, the number of such boys identified was 260 and the number of girls 20, a ratio of 13.0:1.[8]

7. The regional talent searches are conducted by Johns Hopkins (begun in 1972), Duke (1981), Arizona State-Tempe (1981), Northwestern (1982), and the University of Denver (1982). Because there was no logical way to separate students who entered through the regional programs from those who entered through the national channel, results were combined. Most students fit into both categories but at different time points, since the SAT could be taken more than once to qualify or could be retaken in the regional talent search programs. The SAT is not administered by the Educational Testing Service between June and October or November of each year. Therefore, entrants who had passed their thirteenth birthday before taking the test were included if they scored 10 additional points for each excess month or a fraction of a month.
8. There is a remarkably high incidence of lefthandedness or ambidexterity (20 percent), immune disorders (55 percent), and myopia (55 percent) in this group (manuscript in preparation).

This ratio is remarkable in view of the fact that the available evidence suggests there was essentially equal participation of boys and girls in the talent searches.

The total number of students tested in the Johns Hopkins regional annual talent searches and reported so far is 49,747 (9,927 in the initial study and 39,820 in the present study). Preliminary reports from the 1983 talent search based on some 15,000 cases yield essentially identical results. In the ten Middle Atlantic regional talent searches from 1972 through 1983 we have therefore tested about 65,000 students. It is abundantly clear that far more boys than girls (chiefly twelve-year-olds) scored in the highest ranges on SAT-M, even though girls were matched with boys by intellectual ability, age, grade, and voluntary participation. In the original study (n. 1) students were required to meet a qualifying mathematics criterion. Since we observed the same sex difference then as now, the current results cannot be explained solely on the grounds that the girls may have qualified by the verbal criterion. Moreover, if that were the case, we should expect the girls to have scored higher than the boys on SAT-V. They did not.

Several "environmental" hypotheses have been proposed to account for sex differences in mathematical ability. Fox et al. and Meece et al.[9] have found support for a social-reinforcement hypothesis which, in essence, states that sex-related differences in mathematical achievement are due to differences in social conditioning and expectations for boys and girls. The validity of this hypothesis has been evaluated for the population we studied earlier (n. 1) and for a subsample of the students in this study. Substantial differences between boys' and girls' attitudes or backgrounds were not found (nn. 4, 10). Admittedly, some of the measures used were broadly defined and may not have been able to detect subtle social influences that affect a child from birth. But it is not obvious how social conditioning could affect mathematical reasoning ability so adversely and significantly, yet have little detectable effect on stated interest in mathematics, the taking of mathematics courses during the high school years before the SAT's are normally taken, and mathematics-course grades (n. 4).

An alternative hypothesis, that sex differences in mathematical reasoning ability arise mainly from differential course-taking,[11] was also not validated,

9. L. Fox, D. Tobin, L. Brody, in *Sex-Related Differences in Cognitive Functioning*, M. Wittig and A. Petersen, Eds. (Academic Press, New York, 1979); J. Meece, J. Parsons, C. Kaczala, S. Goff, R. Futterman, *Psychol. Bull.* 91, 324 (1982).
10. L. Fox, L. Brody, D. Tobin, *The Study of Social Processes that Inhibit or Enhance the Development of Competence and Interest in Mathematics Among Highly Able Young Women* (National Institute of Education, Washington, D.C., 1982); C. Benbow and J. Stanley, in *Women in Science*, M. Steinkamp and M. Maehr, Eds. (JAI Press, Greenwich, Conn., in press); L. Fox, C. Benbow, S. Perkins, in *Academic Precocity*, C. Benbow and J. Stanley, Eds. (Johns Hopkins Univ. Press, Baltimore, 1983).
11. For example, E. Fennema and J. Sherman. *Am. Educ. Res. J.* 14, 51 (1977).

340   either by the data in our 1980 study (n. 1) or by the data in the present study. In both studies the boys and girls were shown to have had similar formal training in mathematics (n. 4).

It is also of interest that sex differences in mean SAT-M scores observed in our early talent searches became only slightly larger during high school. In the selected subsample of participants studied, males improved their scores an average of 10 points more than females (the mean difference went from 40 to 50 points). They also increased their scores on the SAT-V by at least 10 points more than females (n. 4, ref. 2). Previously, other researchers have postulated that profound differences in socialization during adolescence caused the well-documented sex differences in eleventh- and twelfth-grade SAT-M scores (n. 9), but that idea is not supported in our data. For socialization to account for our results, it would seem necessary to postulate (ad hoc) that chiefly early socialization pressures significantly influence the sex difference in SAT-M scores—that is, that the intensive social pressures during adolescence have little such effect.

It is important to emphasize that we are dealing with intellectually highly able students and that these findings may not generalize to average students. Moreover, these results are of course not generalizable to particular individuals. Finally, it should be noted that the boys' SAT-M scores had a larger variance than the girls'. This is obviously related to the fact that more mathematically talented boys than girls were found.[12] Nonetheless, the environmental hypotheses outlined above attempt to explain mean differences, not differences in variability. Thus, even if one concludes that our findings result primarily from greater male variability, one must still explain why.

Our principal conclusion is that males dominate the highest ranges of mathematical reasoning ability before they enter adolescence. Reasons for this sex difference are unclear.[13]

12. Why boys are generally more variable has been addressed by H. Eysenck and L. Kamin [*The Intelligence Controversy* (Wiley, New York. 1981)] and others.
13. For possible endogenous influences see, for example, R. Goy and B. McEwen, *Sexual Differentiation of the Brain* (MIT Press, Cambridge, Mass., 1980); J. Levy, *The Sciences* 21 (No. 3), 20 (1981); T. Bouchard and M. McGue, *Science* 212, 1055 (1981); D. Hier and W. Crawley Jr., *N. Engl. J. Med.* 306, 1202 (1982); C. DeLacoste-Utamsing and R. Holloway, *Science* 216, 1431 (1982); L. Harris, in *Asymmetrical Function of the Brain*. M. Kinsbourne, Ed. (Cambridge Univ. Press, London, 1978); M. McGee, *Psychol. Bull.* 86, 889 (1979); S. Witelsen, *Science* 193, 425 (1976); J. McGlone, *Behav. Brain Sci.* 3, 215 (1980); D. McGuiness, *Hum. Nat.* 2 (No. 2), 82 (1979); R. Meisel and I. Ward, *Science* 213, 239 (1981); F. Naftolin, ibid. 211, 1263 (1981); A. Ehrhardt and H. Meyer-Bahlburg, ibid., p. 1312; J. Inglis and J. Lawson, ibid. 212, 693 (1981); M. Wittig and A. Petersen, Eds., *Sex-Related Differences in Cognitive Functioning* (Academic Press, New York, 1979).

Social Forces Shape Math Attitudes and Performance

JACQUELYNNE S. ECCLES AND JANIS E. JACOBS

Debate has continued throughout the last decade over the existence and possible causes of differences between males' and females' mathematical skills. Several observations recur as the focus of this controversy. First, adolescent boys have been found to score higher than girls on standardized mathematics achievement tests.[1] Second, males are more likely than females to engage in a variety of optional activities related to mathematics, from technical hobbies to careers in which math skills play an important role.[2] Third, adolescent males typically perform better than their female counterparts on spatial-visualization tests.[3] Researchers have attributed these differences to a variety of hereditary and environmental factors without reaching a consensus about their origins.

A significant addition to this controversy came in a 1980 *Science* article by Camilla Benbow and Julian Stanley. Within a sample of highly gifted seventh- and eighth-grade children, the authors found that, on the average, boys scored higher than girls on the College Board's Scholastic Aptitude Test for Mathematics (SAT-M).[4] This difference was especially marked at the extreme upper end of the distribution. These data extend a pattern of

---

1. See, e.g., Lynn Fox, Linda A. Brody, and Dianne Tobin, eds., *Women and the Mathematical Mystique* (Baltimore, Md.: Johns Hopkins University Press, 1980).
2. See, e.g., Lucy Sells, "The Mathematics Filter and the Education of Women and Minorities," and Dianne Tobin and Lynn Fox, "Career Interests and Career Education: A Key to Change," in Fox, Brody, and Tobin, eds., pp. 66–75, and 179–92, respectively: George Dunteman, Joseph A. Wisenbaker, and Mary Ellen Taylor, *Race and Sex Differences in College Science Program Participation* (Research Triangle Park, N.C.: Research Triangle Institute, 1979).
3. See, e.g., Michelle Wittig and Anne Peterson, eds., *Sex-related Differences in Cognitive Functioning* (New York: Academic Press, 1979).
4. Camilla P. Benbow and Julian C. Stanley, "Sex Differences in Mathematical Ability: Fact or Artifact?" *Science*, no. 210 (December 1980), pp. 1262–64, esp. p. 1262.

"Social Forces Shape Math Attitudes and Performance" by Jacquelynne S. Eccles and Janis E. Jacobs, *Signs: Journal of Women in Culture and Society*, 1986, *11* (21), 367–389. Copyright © 1986 by the University of Chicago Press. Reprinted by permission.

Dr. Eccles is Associate Professor of Psychology, University of Michigan, Ann Arbor, Michigan; Dr. Jacobs is Assistant Professor of Psychology, University of Nebraska, Lincoln, Nebraska.

342 commonly found sex differences to a select population of junior high-school students and thus are neither surprising nor particularly novel.[5] What is novel, however, is Benbow and Stanley's interpretation of their data. They argue that "superior male mathematical ability" is the best explanation for the sex differences, since the boys and girls in their sample had essentially identical mathematics training prior to the seventh grade. Furthermore, they suggest that "superior male mathematical ability" is the probable cause of general sex differences in both mathematical achievement and attitudes toward math. These conclusions have sparked renewed controversy in the scientific community and a disturbing response in the mass media. This article questions Benbow and Stanley's underlying assumptions and presents data counter to their conclusions.

Benbow and Stanley base their argument on the following suppositions: (*a*) students' scores on the SAT-M are primarily a measure of their mathematical aptitude; (*b*) students who have taken similar formal educational courses in mathematics have had similar experiences with the discipline; and (*c*) a demonstrated sex difference in mathematical reasoning supports the conclusion that "less well-developed mathematical reasoning contributes to girls' taking fewer mathematics courses and achieving less than boys."[6] In her rebuttal to Benbow and Stanley, Alice Schafer concluded that taking the SAT-M as a measure of mathematical aptitude is unjustifiable. Moreover, Warner Slack and Douglas Porter and Rex Jackson have pointed out that the SAT measures acquired intellectual skills.[7] Thus, one must question Benbow and Stanley's assumption that the SAT-M measures mathematical aptitude. Furthermore, performance on timed tests is influenced by a wide variety of motivational and affective factors such as test anxiety, risk-taking preferences, cognitive style, and confidence in one's abilities. Since males and females differ on some of these factors, it is quite possible that the sex differences reported by Benbow and Stanley reflect these noncognitive differences rather than, or in addition to, true aptitudinal differences.

The authors' assumption that the boys and girls in their sample had equivalent mathematical experiences is also problematic. Assessing stu-

5. Portions of these results have been reported in other sources. See, e.g., Lynn Fox and Sanford Cohn, "Sex Differences in the Development of Precocious Mathematical Talent," in Fox, Brody, and Tobin, eds., pp. 94–112, esp. p. 94; Lynn Fox and Daniel Keating, eds., *Intellectual Talent: Research and Development* (Baltimore, Md.: Johns Hopkins University Press, 1976). The reported pattern of sex differences, in fact, forms part of the collection of results researchers are now seeking to explain.
6. Benbow and Stanley, pp. 1264, 1262.
7. Alice Schafer, "Sex and Mathematics," *Science*, no. 211 (January 1981), p. 392; Warner Slack and Douglas Porter, "Training, Validity, and the Issue of Aptitude: A Reply to Jackson," *Harvard Educational Review* 50, no. 3 (1980): 392–401; Rex Jackson, "The Scholastic Aptitude Test: A Response to Slack and Porter's 'Critical Appraisal,'" ibid., 50, no. 3 (1980): 382–91, esp. 382.

dents' mathematical experiences is extremely difficult. Counting the number of mathematics courses the children have taken is only one possible method, feasible only if the sample is in secondary school. The fact that all the children in Benbow and Stanley's sample had completed the sixth grade does not support the inference that these students had equivalent formal educational experiences with mathematics. Concluding that their informal experiences were equivalent is even more suspect.

To justify such inferences one would need to develop appropriate measures of the quantity and quality of elementary school children's mathematical experiences and then test for sex differences on these measures. Using one such strategy, Gaea Leinhardt, Andria Seewald, and Mary Engel observed the formal teaching practices of thirty-three second-grade teachers and found that teachers spent relatively more time teaching mathematics to boys than to girls. Based on their results, in fact, boys may receive as much as thirty-six more hours of formal mathematics instruction than do girls by the time the children reach the seventh grade. Both Helen Astin and Lynn Fox and her colleagues have investigated participation in less formal activities related to mathematics. According to their studies, boys are more likely than girls to have informal, mathematically related experiences such as playing with scientific toys, participating in mathematical games, and reading mathematics books.[8] Thus, Benbow and Stanley's assumption that their boys and girls have had equivalent mathematical experiences is questionable, precluding definitive conclusions regarding the origin of observed differences on SAT-M scores.[9]

Benbow and Stanley's assumption that their data contribute new insights into the origins of sex differences in mathematical achievement and attitudes is also suspect. The authors in no way establish the power of SAT-M scores to predict a student's subsequent achievement in, attitudes toward, or course enrollment in mathematics. Other investigators have suggested that the link, if any, is weak. For example, Slack and Porter concluded that the SAT-M score is a poorer predictor of a student's mathematics achievement in college than either high school grades or a score on the SAT Mathematical Achievement test. In addition, in a follow-up of the

8. Gaea Leinhardt, Andria Seewald, and Mary Engel, "Learning What's Taught: Sex Differences in Instruction," *Journal of Educational Psychology* 71, no. 3 (1979): 432–39, esp. 432; Helen Astin, "Sex Differences in Mathematical and Scientific Precocity," in *Mathematical Talent: Discovery, Description, and Development*, ed. Julian Stanley, Daniel Keating, and Lynn Fox (Baltimore, Md.: Johns Hopkins University Press, 1974), pp. 70–86, esp. p. 70; Fox and Cohn, p. 94.
9. It is possible that sex differences in innate mathematical aptitude account for boys' greater interest in mathematically related activities. But it is impossible to discern the cause and effect relations among innate aptitude, interest, and subsequent skill without extensive longitudinal testing. Our critical point here is that one cannot assume equivalent mathematical experiences in a population of seventh-grade girls and boys.

344 1976 cohort of Benbow and Stanley's sample, Lynn Fox and Sanford Cohn found no relation between the girls' SAT-M scores and their subsequent educational acceleration. Finally, Laurie Steel and Lori Wise found that although mathematical ability is a significant predictor of subsequent mathematics achievement and course enrollment, it does not account for the sex differences in either high school seniors' mathematics grades or their high school mathematics enrollment patterns.[10] Apparently variations in mathematical reasoning ability contribute little to variations in subsequent course-taking patterns among either the group of gifted girls studied by Benbow and Stanley or more representative samples of mathematically competent high school students.

Predictors of Math Achievement and Math Participation

What does predict the course-taking plans and achievement patterns of mathematically competent (as distinguished from gifted) junior high school students? Contrary to Benbow and Stanley's conclusion, our data suggest that social and attitudinal factors have a greater influence on junior and senior high school students' grades and enrollment in mathematics courses than do variations in mathematical aptitude. Further, our data suggest that sex differences in mathematical achievement and attitudes are largely due to sex differences in math anxiety; the gender-stereotyped beliefs of parents, especially mothers; and the value students attach to mathematics.

Our conclusions are based on a two-year longitudinal study of 250 average and above-average students in the seventh through ninth grades, their parents, and their mathematics teachers. We gave questionnaires to the students in two successive years and examined their mathematics course grades and scores on a standardized achievement test (either the Michigan Educational Assessment Program or the California Achievement Test) for each year of the study. We also gathered questionnaire data from both parents and teachers.

We created our scales by applying exploratory factor analysis to the information in the student and parent questionnaires. Factor analysis is a statistical procedure whereby items are grouped together according to the

---

10. Slack and Porter; Fox and Cohn, p. 94; Laurie Steel and Lori Wise, "Origins of Sex Differences in High School Math Achievement and Participation" (paper presented at the American Educational Research Association, San Francisco, March 1979).

similarity of respondents' answers. For example, because mothers and fathers gave similar estimates of their children's mathematical abilities, we grouped all questions regarding these estimates in one scale rather than analyzing those questions individually.[11]

Four parent factors emerged: mothers' estimates of the difficulty of mathematics for their children, fathers' estimates of the difficulty of mathematics for their children, both-parents' estimates of their children's mathematical abilities, and both parents' estimates of the importance of enrolling in mathematics courses. Three student factors emerged: students' estimates of their own mathematical abilities, their estimates of the difficulty of mathematics, and their rating of the value of mathematics courses. We created three additional scales: one reflecting teacher's estimates of each student's mathematical ability, one reflecting each student's math anxiety, and one reflecting mathematical aptitude/achievement based on each student's previous year's mathematics grade and most recent score on a standardized test of math achievement.

We assume, based on arguments by Slack and Porter and others,[12] that our composite score is at least as good an estimate of mathematical aptitude as is the SAT-M score. To the extent that mathematics achievement scores reflect mathematical aptitude, this measure provides an estimate of individual differences in mathematical aptitude. Moreover, given that this score summarizes the performance information provided to students, parents, and teachers, it is also an indicator of the objective performance differences on which children, parents, and teachers base their estimates of an individual student's math potential and ability.

We entered each of these scores, along with the student's sex, into a multiple regression, recursive path analysis (see fig. 10.1). The total sample size was 164 students, their parents, and their mathematics teachers. Path analysis is a statistical procedure used to assess the direct and indirect relations among a set of scales or variables. It allows us to estimate how strong the influence of one variable is on other variables. For example, it permits an estimate of the extent to which students' grades in sixth-grade mathematics courses influence their parents' estimates of their children's mathematical ability one year later. Path analysis also allows us to test predictions that students' grades in mathematics have an indirect, rather than direct, effect on their confidence in their own abilities and that parents' interpretations of the students' grades mediate this indirect effect.

11. See Karl Joreskog and Dan Sorbon, eds., *Advances in Factor Analyses and Structural Equation Models* (Cambridge, Mass.: ABT Books, 1979). Factor loadings can be obtained from the authors.
12. Slack and Porter, p. 392.

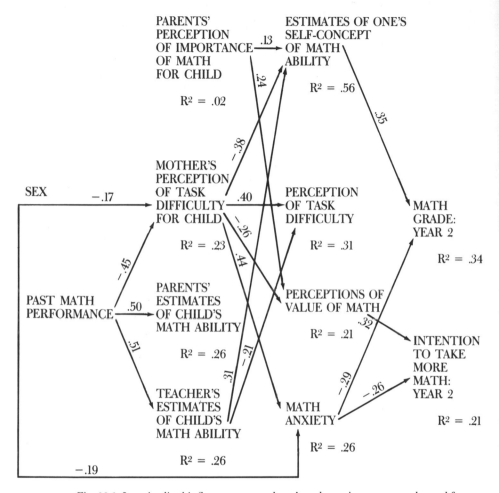

Fig. 10.1. Longitudinal influences on students' mathematics course grades and future course enrollment plans.

Recursive path analysis estimates the direction of efforts in only one direction; in figure 10.1, this direction is always left to right.[13] Only statistically significant paths are depicted in this chart. To make it easier to interpret the direction of impact of these paths, we placed our scales in four columns, left to right, representing the chronological sequence in which we collected the data. Variables in the column on the far left reflect scales of

13. We did not test for effects in the reverse direction, and we did not test for relationships between variables within a given column. We believe such effects exist but did not test for them in this analysis.

students' mathematical performance prior to entry into our study, as well as their sex. Variables in the second column are parent and teacher scales gathered in the first year of our study.[14] With the exception of math anxiety, the variables in the third column are student attitudinal scales based on questionnaires distributed in the first year of our research; math anxiety is a student belief scale gathered in the second year. Variables in the fourth column on the far right represent students' grades and course-taking plans gathered during the study's second year. We estimated all possible paths across columns.[15]

Standardized column-wise multiple regression equation procedures were used to estimate path coefficients. At each step, each of the variables in one column was regressed on the set of all variables in the columns to the left. This procedure yields standardized path coefficients, reflecting the relative predictive power of each variable in comparison to all other variables. These coefficients, printed on each path, can vary from -1 to $+1$.

A high path coefficient (either positive or negative) reflects a relatively strong relationship. A positive path coefficient means that high scores on the variable to the left predict high scores on the variable to the right. Conversely, a negative path coefficient means that the low scores on the variable to the left predict high scores on the variable to the right. We entered sex as a dummy variable, with females equal to 1 and males equal to 2. Thus, the two weak negative path coefficients on the paths leading from the sex variable indicate that females have slightly higher scores on the two related variables; that is, females have slightly higher math anxiety scores, and girls' mothers rate mathematics as slightly more difficult for their children than do boys' mothers.[16]

We used t-tests to calculate the significance of each path coefficient. The R^2 value printed below each scale represents the percent of variance in a measure that is explained by the variables to its left. A large R^2 value indicates that we can predict more about that variable using the variables to its left than we can predict about variables with lower R^2 values.

Grades and plans to continue taking mathematics are predicted most

14. Fathers' estimates of the difficulty of mathematics for their children did not contribute to the prediction of students' mathematics achievement or their course enrollment plans. Including these estimates in the analysis reduced the sample size considerably. Thus this variable is omitted from all our analyses reported here. Fathers' effects in this data set appear to be redundant with, but less powerful than, mothers' effects.

15. Using variables from different years strengthens our conclusions about the direction in which the variables in the columns affect each other but does not rule out the possibility that effects can occur in the opposite direction as well.

16. Specification of the path model, i.e., assignment of variables to particular columns, was based on the theoretical model in Jacquelynne Eccles (Parsons) et al., "Expectations, Values, and Academic Behaviors," in *Achievement and Achievement in Motivation,* ed. Janet Spence (San Francisco: W. H. Freeman & Co., 1983), pp. 75–146.

348 directly by the students' beliefs listed in the third column: their estimates of their mathematical abilities, their perceptions of the value of mathematics courses, and their levels of math anxiety. These students beliefs, in turn, are related most strongly to the students' mothers' beliefs concerning the difficulty of mathematics for their children. Parents' estimates of the importance of mathematics courses for their children and teachers' estimates of each student's mathematical ability also predict some of the students' beliefs.

What does this analysis tell us about boys' and girls' attitudes toward mathematics and their enrollment decisions? To answer this question we need to consider the results of the path analysis in conjunction with the pattern of correlations between the important variables. A correlation is a statistical coefficient (signified by an r value) that indicates the strength of the relationship between two variables; it does not take into account any other variables or possible mediating effects. Like standardized path coefficients, correlation coefficients can range from -1 to $+1$; the higher the number (either positive or negative), the stronger the relationship between the two variables. The closer the coefficient is to zero, the weaker the relationship. A correlation coefficient of zero indicates no relationship between the two variables. In the discussion that follows, we will include the relevant correlation coefficients whenever they aid the interpretation of the path analysis and enhance our understanding of boys' and girls' attitudes toward mathematics.

The path analysis suggests that a student's performance in mathematics has an indirect effect on that student's attitudes toward mathematics and subsequent mathematics grades. While past mathematics aptitude/ achievement scores are related both to a child's subsequent mathematics grades ($r = .40$) and course enrollment plans ($r = .17$), these relationships appear to be mediated by mothers' and teachers' beliefs, by students' estimates of their mathematical abilities, and by students' beliefs about the value of mathematics. Thus, students' grades appear to affect subsequent mathematics performance and course-taking plans only to the extent that these grades influence both parents' confidence in their children's ability to learn mathematics and students' own beliefs, motivation, and math anxiety. Furthermore, the influence of past grades on students' beliefs appears to be mediated by the parents' interpretation of these grades. Finally, when one compares the correlations between girls' and boys' estimates of the value of mathematics and objective indicators of their mathematical ability, an interesting difference emerges. Boys' estimates of the value of mathematics are related to their past performance in mathematics ($r = .33$) and to both their teachers' and parents' estimates of their mathematical ability

($r = .33; r = .28$). In contrast, girls' estimates of the value of mathematics are not related to any of these measures ($r = .06$, $r = .03$, and $r = .06$, respectively). Thus, a student's mathematical aptitude, as measured in this study, can serve only as an indirect predictor of that child's attitudes toward mathematics, future mathematics achievement, and course-enrollment plans. Social and attitudinal factors appear to have much stronger direct effects on these beliefs and plans, especially among girls.

Math anxiety also appears to be an important predictor of both subsequent mathematics grades and course-taking plans, and girls report higher levels of this anxiety than do boys. These results are especially interesting in light of three additional relations. First, in this sample of mathematically competent students, math anxiety is only weakly related to the students' previous performance in mathematics ($r = -.17$). Consequently, the individual variations in math anxiety are not primarily a consequence of objective differences in performance. Second, math anxiety has a stronger and more direct relation to mathematics grades and to students' future plans for taking math courses than does our mathematical aptitude/achievement score. Third, math anxiety is directly and strongly influenced by social factors, in particular by mothers' beliefs about the difficulty of the subject for their children. Thus, math anxiety appears to be a key social/attitudinal variable that might account for sex differences in achievement and enrollment in mathematics courses. Furthermore, given the common finding that anxiety has a debilitating effect on children's scores on standardized achievement tests,[17] one must ask whether the sex differences in math anxiety are strong enough to explain most of the variance in the SAT-M scores that Benbow and Stanley attribute to superior male mathematical ability.

The results of our path analysis also point out parents' importance as critical socializers of sex differences in mathematical achievement and attitudes. While teachers' beliefs are predictive of students' beliefs, teachers in our study estimated that boys and girls had similar mathematical ability. In addition, the impact of teachers' beliefs is not as large as that of parents' beliefs and does not have a direct effect on students' plans to continue taking mathematics. These data suggest that parents' gender-stereotyped beliefs are a key cause of sex differences in students' attitudes toward mathematics.

Although it could be argued that parents' gender-stereotyped beliefs

17. Kennedy Hill, "The Relation of Evaluative Practices to Test Anxiety and Achievement Motivation," *Educator* 19, no. 15 (1977): 15–22; Diane Ruble and Anne Boggiano, "Optimizing Motivation in an Achievement Context," in *Advances in Special Education*, ed. Barbara Keogh (Greenwich, Conn.: JAI Press, 1980), pp. 183–238.

350 about the difficulty of mathematics for their children are veridical, reflecting a real sex difference in children's behaviors, the following additional results suggest that this is not the case. First, girls and boys in this sample had equivalent mathematics grades and standardized math test scores at the start of the study. Second, when asked how much math homework they do, the boys and girls reported equivalent amounts. Third, the teachers' estimates of these girls' and boys' mathematical abilities did not differ. And finally, mothers who endorsed the gender stereotype that boys do better than girls in advanced high school mathematics courses thought that math was harder for their daughters than did the mothers who believed that girls and boys can do equally well in advanced math courses. Thus, the gender stereotypes evident in mothers' and fathers' beliefs do not appear to be grounded in reality. The extent to which they reflect a "real" sex difference in mathematical aptitude remains to be demonstrated.

Thus, Benbow and Stanley's conclusion that sex differences in attitudes toward and achievement in mathematics may result from "superior male mathematical ability" is premature at best. Although the authors may favor a biological explanation, their data do not provide a test of that hypothesis.

Further, one must be concerned about the effect their conclusion may have on girls' future mathematical achievement and attitudes. This concern is especially justified given the distortion of Benbow and Stanley's findings by the popular media (see fig. 10.2) and the strong influence parental beliefs about mathematical ability have in shaping girls' attitudes toward math and their actual achievement. This is not to say that we should rule out the possibility of biological influences on mathematics competence. Biological processes may be important. But the nature, the magnitude, and the malleability of those factors are not yet understood. Our data suggest that, at present, social factors are a major cause of sex differences in both mathematics performance and attitudes toward math in the population at large. And, as noted above, the extensive and biased coverage of the Benbow and Stanley article in the mass media may have provided yet one more social force discouraging female participation in mathematics-related courses and career fields. This is the issue we will now address.

Impact of Media Coverage

Since we were in the midst of a longitudinal study of the socialization of girls' and boys' attitudes toward math when the Benbow and Stanley story broke, we were in a unique position to assess the impact of the media

Study suggests boys may be better at math

WASHINGTON (UPI) — Two psychologists said Friday boys are better than girls in math reasoning, and they urged educators to accept the fact that something more than social factors is re-

Ann Arbor News, December 6, 1980

Do Males Have a Math Gene?

Can girls do math as well as boys? All sorts of recent tests have shown that they cannot. Most educators and feminists

tude Test normally given to high-school seniors. In the results on the math portion of the SAT—there was no appreciable dif-

Newsweek, December 15, 1980

SEX + MATH = ?

Why do boys traditionally do better than girls in math? Many say it's because boys are encouraged to pursue

Family Weekly, January 25, 1981

Are Boys Better At Math?

The New York Times, December 7, 1980

The Gender Factor in Math

A new study says males may be naturally abler than females

Until about the seventh grade, boys and girls do equally well at math. In early high school, when the emphasis

Julian C. Stanley of Johns Hopkins University, males inherently have more mathematical ability than females.

Time, December 15, 1980

Fig. 10.2

352 campaign on parents' stereotypes and beliefs regarding their children's mathematical ability.[18]

We sent the parents in our sample a questionnaire similar to our original one about three months after the research report appeared in *Science*. We added a question, placed on the last page of the form, which described the media coverage of the research and asked if parents had heard about it. Approximately one-quarter of the responding parents (57 out of 200) said yes. While most of these had read about the study in either a magazine or a newspaper, many indicated that they had heard about the report from several sources. We compared the responses of parents who had read the media reports (referred to as the misinformed group) to the responses of those who had not (referred to as the uninformed group).[19]

We first assessed the impact of the media exposure on parents' attitudes about their children's mathematical abilities. The result was different for mothers and fathers. Compared to estimates made by uninformed mothers of girls, responses by misinformed mothers of girls indicated that they felt their daughters had less mathematical ability, would have less success in future math courses, would find mathematics more difficult, and would have to work harder in order to do well in math courses. In addition, the misinformed mothers of girls thought that mathematics was much more difficult for their daughters than did the misinformed mothers of boys. In contrast, uninformed mothers of both girls and boys had similar beliefs about their children's mathematical abilities.

Fathers responded quite differently. Generally, the fathers of girls felt that their daughters had slightly less mathematical ability than did the fathers of sons. However, misinformed fathers of girls were more positive about their daughters' mathematical abilities after reading the media coverage than they had been before reading the reports. In contrast, uninformed fathers of girls had come to feel that their daughters had less mathematical ability than they had estimated one year earlier.

We next assessed the impact of the media reports on parents' stereotypes regarding the utility of mathematics for boys and girls in general. We also asked parents how useful they felt the study of mathematics was for their child. In response to the first question, both misinformed and uninformed

---

18. For more details, see Janis Jacobs and Jacquelynne Eccles, "Gender Differences in Math Ability: The Impact of Media Reports on Parents," *Educational Researcher* 14, no. 3 (1985): 20–25.

19. In order to test the hypothesis that parents in the misinformed group and those in the uninformed group may have had significant differences unrelated to their media exposure, analyses of variance were performed on all pretest variables including the two groups' demographic and attitudinal variables. The parents were similar on all of these measures.

mothers felt that math was more useful for males than for females, regardless of the sex of their child. In addition, the mothers' beliefs had become more gender-stereotyped in the year following our first survey. They now rated math as even more useful for males in their adult lives than they had earlier.

A slightly different pattern emerged for fathers. When fathers were talking about their own children, fathers of sons rated mathematics as more useful for their child than fathers of daughters. In addition, misinformed fathers of sons felt that math was more useful for their sons than did the uninformed fathers of sons. When asked about the usefulness of math for males in general, the misinformed fathers of sons stood out from the other parent groups even more distinctly: they thought mathematics was *much* more important for males than for females. It appears that exposure to the media coverage increased the gender-stereotyped attitudes of fathers of sons.

In summary, media reports of the Benbow and Stanley article did appear to change parents' attitudes. The effect, however, depended on both the sex of the parent and the sex of the child. Misinformed mothers had their gender-stereotypic beliefs confirmed regarding the difficulty of math for females and its comparative ease for males. In contrast, misinformed fathers of girls became more confident in their daughters' mathematical abilities. Unfortunately, while the misinformed fathers of girls came to the defense of their daughters' math abilities, misinformed fathers of boys responded quite differently. They became even more convinced than their uninformed counterparts of the validity of the broader gender stereotypes regarding mathematics abilities. They felt that females in general do not perform as well as males in advanced math classes and that mathematics is more useful to males than to females.

These findings are not surprising. We know that the salience of any event determines how it will be interpreted and remembered. We would expect parents of mathematically able daughters to interpret the news of superior male mathematical ability very differently from parents with sons, and mothers to interpret it differently from fathers. In this case, it appears that exposure to media reports confirmed mothers' beliefs that their daughters are not as able in mathematics as are their sons, while it put fathers of girls in a position of challenging the "evidence" on behalf of their daughters. For fathers the opposite happened for variables measuring general gender-stereotyped beliefs. Fathers of sons had their gender-stereotyped beliefs confirmed and strengthened although their beliefs about their own children did not change.

Conclusions

Our research suggests that sex differences in students' attitudes toward mathematics and in plans to continue taking math courses are influenced substantially by their parents' perceptions of the difficulty of mathematics for their child and by their own attitudes about the value of mathematics. Furthermore, parents' beliefs, especially mothers' beliefs, appear to have a greater influence on students' attitudes than do students' mathematics grades. Doris Entwisle and D. P. Baker recently reported a similar result for children in grades one through three.[20] Although the girls and boys in their study had received similar grades in mathematics and similar scores on a math aptitude measure, the boys had higher expectations for their mathematics performance than did the girls. This sex difference seemed to stem from the different expectations parents held for their sons and for their daughters. Finally, our results suggest that media reports attributing sex differences in mathematics to innate or biological factors have a negative impact on mothers' confidence in their daughters' math abilities.

Even though parents in general held stereotypic beliefs, many parents of daughters spoke of the need to change stereotypic views of women and mathematics. One mother summed up this position succinctly when she said, "For whatever reason, boys in general *seem* to pick up math concepts with more ease and less methodical study. There are exceptions, however, and I would not want *my* daughter to feel she could not do equally well in math as her brothers." She continued, "Perhaps society has encouraged boys in math more than girls. I hope it is changing."

We too hope it will change but fear that change will be very slow, especially given the prevailing biases that influence what is spotlighted and what is ignored in national news coverage. In the meantime, we, as feminists, parents, and teachers, need to do all we can to support and encourage girls in their efforts to develop interests in math and science. In this area, passive nondiscrimination is simply not an adequate intervention strategy.

20. Doris Entwisle and D. P. Baker, "Gender and Young Children's Expectations for Performance," *Developmental Psychology* 19, no. 2 (1983): 200–14, esp. 200.

Question 11

Should Mothers Stay Home with Their Young Children?

Each new report documenting the increase in the number of working mothers touches off another round in the debate over whether this phenomenon has negative effects on children. In a sense, this topic is just one chapter in the voluminous literature on the effects of mothering on infants and children. Even a brief glance at some of the earlier publications on this subject indicates the narrow line mothers have had to walk. On the one hand, they had to avoid providing too little mothering because this could make the child feel rejected. But they also ran the risk of overmothering, what Philip Wylie (1942) referred to as "momism" in his best-selling book *Generation of Vipers*.

The research of the late 1940s and 1950s tended to focus on one side of the line: the effects of maternal deprivation. The work of René Spitz (1945) and John Bowlby (1951) called attention to the negative effects of the separation of infants from their mothers. Early attachment to the mother was considered especially important since it established the model for all future relationships. Paula Caplan and Ian Hall-McCorquodale (1985) have summarized the research that emerged in the 1950s on this topic. Essentially, mothers became the scapegoat for everything that could go wrong in parenting: "all psychopathology, from simple behavior problems to juvenile delinquency to schizophrenia itself" (Chess & Thomas, 1982, pp. 213–14).

Studies in the late 1960s and 1970s pointed out that the Spitz (1945) and Bowlby (1951) data were collected during wartime from barren, understaffed institutions. The conditions in these institutions were hardly analogous to the situation where mothers worked outside the home (Hoffman, 1979). In fact, a nationally representative survey of fifty-five thousand

356 homes found that fewer than 10 percent of the infants of working mothers were in childcare centers (Klein, 1985).

A recent survey of the literature (McCartney & Phillips, in press) found that professional childcare did not harm the mother-child relationship. However, Hoffman (1979) has noted that in "considering the effects of maternal employment on the child, perhaps the period about which it is most difficult to be sanguine is infancy" (p. 860). And, not surprisingly, the issue of infant daycare has now emerged as a major controversy (Gamble & Zigler, 1986; Brazelton, 1986).

Advice books have mirrored the split in the literature. After having advocated full-time mother care in the earlier editions of his book, *Baby and Child Care* (1946, 1968), Dr. Spock included a new section in his 1976 edition on qualities to look for in a parent substitute. In contrast, Selma Fraiberg's *Every Child's Birthright* (1977) continued to support the earlier research in a special section on "the disease of nonattachment." Drawing an analogy between institutionalized children and those in daycare, Fraiberg maintained that it was not until after the age of three that most children could withstand separation from the mother for half a day.

On the other hand, a recent study of pediatricians' attitudes toward maternal employment indicates that more than half of the doctors did not object to mothers of three-month-old babies returning to work (Matlin, Cutler, & Matlin, 1986). Nevertheless, many mothers experience conflicts over this issue. A survey of working women by Daniel Yankelowich in 1983 found that close to half of working mothers believed women who intended to work should not be mothers and, correspondingly, women with young children should not work (McCartney & Phillips, in press).

The following articles highlight the disagreement over whether mothers of young children should work outside the home. Is Burton White correct in asserting that most children will benefit more from care in the family setting than from substitute care-takers? Or does the evidence support Joanne Curry O'Connell's contention that there are "no consistent adverse effects" when children receive daycare outside the home?

References

Bowlby, J. (1951). The nature of the child's tie to his mother. *International Journal of Psychoanalysis, 39*, 350–73.

Brazelton, T. B. (1986). Infant day care: issues for working parents. *American Journal of Orthopsychiatry, 56* (1), 14–25.

Caplan, P. J. & Hall-McCorquodale, I. (1985). Mother blaming in major clinical journals. *American Journal of Orthopsychiatry, 55* (3), 345–53.

Chess, S., & Thomas, A. (Eds.) (1982). Infant bonding: Mystique and reality. *American* 357
    Journal of Orthopsychiatry, 52 (2), 213–22.

Fraiberg, S. (1977). *Every child's birthright: In defense of mothering.* New York: Basic Books.

Gamble, T. & Zigler, E. (1986). Effects of infant day care: Another look at the evidence.
    American Journal of Orthopsychiatry, 56 (1), 26–42.

Hoffman, L. W. (1979). Maternal employment, 1979. *American Psychologist, 34* (10), 859–
    65.

Klein, R. P. (1985). Caregiving arrangements by employed women with children under one
    year of age. *Developmental Psychology, 21* (3), 403–06.

Matlin, M., Cutler, B., & Matlin, A. H. (1986). Pediatricians' attitudes toward maternal
    employment. *Clinical Pediatrics, 25,* 419.

McCartney, K. & Phillips, D. (In press). Motherhood and childcare. In B. Birns & D. Hay,
    The different faces of motherhood. New York: Plenum.

Spitz, R. A. (1945). Hospitalism: An inquiry into the genesis of psychiatric conditions in
    early childhood. In R. S. Eissler (Ed.), *The psychoanalytic study of the child* (Vol. I).
    New York: International Universities Press.

Spock, B. (1946). *Baby and child care.* New York: Pocket Books. Revised and enlarged
    edition published in 1968.

Spock, B. (1976). *Baby and child care* (Revised and updated edition). New York: Pocket
    Books.

Wylie, P. (1942). *Generation of vipers.* New York: Farrar & Rinehart.

Additional Reading

Belsky, J. (In press). The "effects" of infant day care reconsidered. *Early Childhood Research
    Quarterly.*

Easterbrooks, M. A. & Goldberg, W. A. (1985). Effects of early maternal employment on
    toddlers, mothers, and fathers. *Developmental Psychology, 21* (5), 774–83.

Margolis, M. L. (1984). *Mothers and such.* Berkeley: University of California Press.

Scarr, S. (1984). *Mother care / other care.* New York: Basic Books.

Scarr, S. (1985). Constructing psychology: Making facts and fables for our times. *American
    Psychologist, 40,* 499–512.

Zigler, E. & Frank, M. (In press). *The parental leave crisis: Toward a national policy.* New
    Haven: Yale University Press.

Yes

Should You Stay Home with Your Baby?

BURTON L. WHITE

For a long time, it has been traditional for women to assume the primary responsibility for raising their own children, especially during the first years of the child's life. Today, more than ever before, that tradition is being challenged. Today, more infants and toddlers are spending the majority of their waking hours in the care of someone other than a member of the immediate family. As one who has specialized in the study of the development of children for more than twenty years, I am very disturbed by this situation. I'm worried most about the effects on children, but I'm also worried about the pressure being put on women who don't want to join in the trend. I'm also saddened by the thought that many adults stand to miss some of life's sweetest pleasures.

I do not pretend to be expert in all aspects of family life. Rather, I present myself as someone with knowledge of the educational needs of young children. The focus of my message, then, will be the impact on the development of the child of various forms of childrearing. I am writing not only because I feel qualified to do so, but also because, in spite of the many privately expressed concerns, only a few of my colleagues (Fraiberg, 1977; Glickman & Springer, 1978) have spoken out on this topic.

I'd like to state the heart of my position at the outset. Given the current incomplete state of knowledge about children's needs and substitute care, I firmly believe that most children will get off to a better start in life when they spend the majority of their waking hours being cared for by their parents and other family members rather than in any form of substitute care.

Reasons for My Concern

The Needs of Infants and Toddlers

In the eyes of most students of human development, the first three years of life are extremely important and like no other. While experts may differ on many points, there are many areas of agreement. Clearly, what most of us (including parents) worry about most is the emotional development of babies. Few would debate the almost mystical significance of the mother-infant bond. Research from many fields, including psychiatry, child psychology, and studies of other animal species, has confirmed our intuitive respect for the mother-infant bond beyond any doubt. Research has also pointed to the first two years of life as the particular time in life when that bond forms (Scott, 1963; Bowlby, 1958). For obvious reasons, we have not performed experiments with babies to see how far one can deviate from ordinary childrearing practices before that bond is harmfully affected. We have, however, information gained from a few unusual kinds of circumstances. We have information about major deviations from the usual and we have information on lesser deviations from the normal.

During this century, a large number of studies have been performed involving physically normal babies reared in institutions (Bowlby, 1951; Yarrow, 1961). In most such instances, no single adult has had the primary responsibility for a baby. These studies have almost always indicated that the absence of a primary caretaker during a child's first few years produces serious emotional and psychological debilitation. Observing an unattached toddler is a chilling experience for most adults.

Not many people would advocate such institutional childrearing. What about lesser deviations from the usual? Several forms of part-time substitute childrearing of infants and toddlers have existed long enough for us to learn something from them. There is the phenomenon of the British nanny. There is also the experience of the Israeli kibbutz. These and related practices have shown clearly that having an adult other than a baby's mother or father or grandparents assume the primary caretaking role need not lead to any obvious harmful consequences. Indeed, such substitute child care has undoubtedly been in widespread use throughout the world for a long time. Just what the consequences of such practices are is simply not known because no substantial research has (to my knowledge) ever been done on the topic. It is worth pointing out that the selection of

360 substitute caretakers, both in the British system and in the kibbutzim, is done with great care. The caliber of the treatment the baby receives in most such situations appears to be quite good.

Another major source of information about the mother-infant bond and its presumed importance is studies of other animal species (Scott, 1963). Throughout nature the general rule seems to be that nonprecocious, warm-blooded newborns are cared for by their parents during their early developmental stages. Couple this apparent fact of nature with the predominant tendency in diverse human societies for babies to be reared by their mothers, and you have a very imposing argument against full-time substitute care.

Though widespread and longstanding custom is not always correct or beneficial, most people are unwilling to behave in a contrary manner if the stakes are high. Since the stakes here appear to involve a new child's lifelong emotional health, there has been much resistance to any initiatives that would prevent infants from being with their mothers most, if not all, of the time. So, when the U.S. government offered support to low-income families with babies during the 1930s, the first goal was to make it possible for the women in such families to remain the primary caretakers of their children, rather than be obliged to enter the work force. The Aid to Families with Dependent Children program typifies the judgment of policy makers in family services in many Western countries. Setting aside the question of the success or failure of the program, few people disagree with that goal.

Another basis for my objection to the practice of full-time substitute care for infants and toddlers is what I have learned through my research in human development. I've specialized in the study of successful childrearing (White et al., 1973, 1978, 1979). I've had the privilege of being able to compare the everyday experiences of many children getting off to a fine start in life with those not so fortunate. Of particular relevance to this issue is my judgment that, all things being equal, a baby's parents are more likely to meet her most important developmental needs than other people. That kind of statement could be little more than wishful thinking. My experience has convinced me that it is indeed much more.

My favorite example involves one of the many inevitable achievements of all healthy infants, the first steps. The first unaided walking usually takes place when the child is about eleven months old. When a baby is being raised at home, especially if he's a first baby, both parents and all other close family members look forward to the event. There is anticipation and, perhaps, even some mild anxiety. When the time comes, the impact on close family members is powerful and enormously pleasant. The parents of such a child ordinarily become excited to a degree that can be somewhat boring to their friends. The parents' response to the baby is to envelop him in praise and excitement. This is one of a large number of unique pleasures babies can bring to their parents. It is the sheer joy and enthusiasm of such events that impress me the most. Such intensely rewarding experiences seem to me to be important both for the child and his parents. For the parents, these experiences reinforce the commitment to the child and to family life. For the child, they help solidify the sense of personal security and worth. One of the defining characteristics of good early development pinpointed by our research is a sure sense of pride in achievement. Experiences such as the one just described are the basis for that fundamental attribute. Between seven and eleven months of life, as part of the process of mastering the body, most babies learn to sit up, crawl, stand up, climb, walk while supported, and, finally, to walk alone. Each of these achievements is both attainable by all normal infants and, at the same time, an opportunity for parents to make a big fuss over the baby. In doing so, they help generate legitimate pride within the child.

I believe that process is one of several which underlie good development and where parents have a natural advantage over other adults. While first-rate, loving childcare workers will usually enjoy and applaud a baby's achievements, they simply cannot match the enthusiasm and excitement expressed by most parents. After all, when you've seen 200 babies take their first step, your reaction to the 201st cannot reflect the excitement typically present in the response of the baby's parents.

This is one way in which parents have an edge. Another has to do with the satisfaction and encouragement of an infant's curiosity. Once a baby learns to crawl (at about seven months of age), she becomes capable of exploring a much expanded world. Over the next year-and-a-half, a major part of her curriculum consists of close examinations of small objects and their motions, wonder at the way simple mechanisms work, and the study of people and other spectacles. To get the most out of these experiences, nothing seems better than if an infant has ready access to an older person who is especially interested in her and is anxious to serve as a personal consultant. No one fits that definition quite so well as a baby's parents or grandparents.

These are some of the ways to describe the natural advantages parents and other close family members have in raising babies. What about the abilities of substitute caretakers?

Substitute caretakers come in many shapes. They can be well-trained, experienced child development specialists with master's degrees in early education. (If so, the cost of their services is very high.) They can be high

362 school graduates with special training in child development. They can be aunts, cousins, or even older siblings. They may care for a baby or group of babies in an infant's home, in their home, in a nonprofit center, or in a profit-oriented center. It is clear that the variety of substitute care conditions is large. What about the quality of care the baby receives? As you might expect, that varies widely too. It varies from warm and knowledgeable to indifferent and unskilled. How much it varies and what the impact is on babies is not yet known. The practice of full-time substitute care for children younger than three years of age is too new for much research to have been done. The few studies that have been done produced reassuring results (Belsky and Steinberg, 1978). At least in the case of well-financed and well-managed nonprofit programs, no substantial negative impact has been seen. Unfortunately, the programs studied represent only a minority of those operating across the country. As you might imagine, it is a lot easier to do research in a university-affiliated nonprofit center than in some of the many other kinds of programs currently available.

Even though first reports show no obvious harm being done to infants in high quality programs, I am not about to endorse such practices for all families. The reason is that I'm not only concerned with obvious harmful effects, but with what is likely to be very good for infants and toddlers as well. None of the few evaluations performed to date has addressed the question of what is very good for young children. Their focus has naturally been on the more pressing concern about whether any harm is being done, particularly in regard to a child's emotional health. Put simply, after more than twenty years of research on how children develop well, I would not think of putting a child of my own into any substitute care program on a full-time basis, especially a center-based program. If I don't believe full-time substitute care during the first years of life would be in my own child's best interest, how can I recommend it to other parents? The answer is, I can't, except under extraordinary circumstances.

Situations Where Substitute Care Makes Sense

There are three kinds of situations where I think substitute child care not only makes sense but is, in fact, a necessity.

When a Family Cannot Raise Its Own Children

In certain family situations, alcoholism, drug abuse, or some other debilitating condition afflicts parents to such a degree that childrearing is a casualty. The conclusion social workers have come to is that, in many such

families, the situation is so bad that the only hope for the children is to *363*
remove them from the family and place them in foster care.

There are about three million babies born in the United States each year.
Not all the parents are happy, intelligent, in love, and thrilled with their
child. Many babies are born to mothers who are less than eighteen years old
and already have two or three other children. In some of these situations the
prospect for the new baby is grim, and full-time substitute care, if it's of
good quality, may very well make good sense. In fact, there are some good
government-sponsored programs geared to these circumstances.

When a Family Just Does Not Want the Job

At times, for any number of reasons, parents don't want the time-consuming, occasionally stressful job of raising a baby. In such situations, I believe
some substitute arrangement is likely to be preferable.

On a Part-time Basis

I'm a strong advocate of substitute childcare, *on a part-time basis, for all
families who would like it.* In our research, I've met parents for whom the
concept of substitute care is almost unthinkable. They were having such a
good time with their babies, especially during the baby's first year, that they
almost dreaded any separation. Now, I'm not talking about perverted or
bizarre men and women. They were just people extraordinarily happy
about being parents. I would be reluctant to urge such people to use
substitute care, although by the child's second year I believe it would
probably be good for both baby and parents. For most families, however,
part-time care is both desired and desirable.

There are several reasons why *part-time* substitute care might be a good
idea.

- Economics: Part-time substitute care can free up the time of either or
  both parents to hold outside employment.
- Personal development: Part-time substitute care can give parents the
  time to pursue education and avocations.
- Enjoyment: Part-time substitute care can give parents time simply to
  have fun off duty.
- Psychological relief: While this benefit generally comes with the previous
  advantages, it is very important in its own right. Babies are precious and
  vulnerable. For years, young women have been bearing a continuous
  responsibility for the well-being of children. To most people, this situation seems to be perfectly normal and unworthy of comment. If you
  observe women with their infants regularly in their homes, as we have
  done, you can't help but be impressed with the stress that can be gener-

364 ated, particularly if there are two or more young children in the family. One of the most popular features of an early education project I helped initiate was the offer of three hours of no-strings-attached baby-sitting each week. Its purpose was to allow the mother to take a break from the constant responsibility of her children. By combining this service with the provision of a lounge where parents could talk to each other or to child development professionals, we helped overcome a sense of isolation and stress which many at-home mothers feel.

Fathers and Grandparents Make Good "Mothers" Too

No study anywhere has indicated that mothers are the only people capable of raising young babies. We have observed many fathers and grandparents who seem perfectly suited to the task, and are willing or eager to share the job. Furthermore, it has always seemed unfair to me that fathers and grandparents usually have such limited opportunities to share the many exciting and memorable everyday events in babies' lives. To the extent fathers and grandparents assume more of the chores, they will be rewarded by more of the pleasures. These people comprise an enormous underused resource.

Recommendations

For Government

During the last five years or so, tremendous pressure has been put on government at all levels to provide more substitute child care for everyone, including families with babies younger than three years of age. These are my suggestions.

1. Where families (regardless of income level) are unable or unwilling to care for their own infants and toddlers, provide high quality full-time substitute care or foster homes.
2. Resist the cries for free full-time substitute care for babies for all who want it. Good quality care costs more than $3,500 per year per child and, therefore, the cost of such a broad program is prohibitive anyway.
3. In support programs for young parents, provide the option for either or both parents to be the primary caretaker during their child's first three years. Do not deliberately or inadvertently encourage full-time substitute

care for families that do not want it by making out-of-the-home employment mandatory.

For Families

Parents should consider sharing the childrearing function. They might also consider using part-time (up to four hours a day) substitute care, if necessary, as an important resource in meeting their needs for income or self-expression. (Remember, in most cases, substitute child care has been sought to meet the needs of *the parents not the babies.*) High quality, part-time substitute care can make the difference between an oppressive child-rearing situation and a very rewarding one. It can be the means by which a young woman can continue a career or pursue personal interests, without penalty to her child. In general, if you can find and afford high quality substitute care, I encourage you to use it. But sparingly.

Unless you have a very good reason, I also urge you not to delegate the primary childrearing task to anyone else during your child's first years of life. Nothing a young mother or father does out of the home is more important or rewarding than raising a baby. Furthermore, it's a one-time opportunity. Babies form their first human attachment only once. Babies begin to learn language only once. Babies begin to get to know the world only once. The outcomes of these processes play a major role in shaping the future of each new child.

If You Have No Choice, or if I Have Not Convinced You

My suggestions about the types of substitute care are presented here in order of descending preference.

- Individual care in your own home: A warm, intelligent, and experienced person caring for your child in your own home.
- Individual care in someone else's home: A warm, intelligent, and experienced person caring for your child in that person's home.
- Family daycare: The same kind of person caring for no more than three children in her or his own home.
- Nonprofit center-based care: A carefully selected center where the ratio of children to staff is no more than four to one, and where the total number of children in each room is preferably fewer than ten. There should be at least one person with some formal training in early childhood development among the supervisory staff.
- Profit-oriented center-based care: A *very* carefully selected center which meets all the aforementioned requirements.

Summary

If you are the parent of a baby or if you soon will be, I urge you to give serious consideration to the points raised in this analysis. Of course, if you feel you have no option but full-time substitute care for your baby, so be it. For those fortunate enough to have a choice, it is my judgment that the majority of a baby's waking hours should be spent with her parents or grandparents. For most families, I believe that such an arrangement is the surest way to see to it that a baby gets the best beginning in life. Furthermore, when childrearing is shared, it can become one of life's sweetest and most rewarding experiences.

References

Belsky, J., & Steinberg, L. D. "The Effects of Day Care: A Critical Review." *Child Development* 49, no. 4 (1978): 929–49.

Bowlby, J. "The Nature of the Child's Tie to His Mother." *International Journal of Psychoanalysis* 39 (1958): 350–73.

Bowlby, J. *Maternal Care and Mental Health*, Monograph no. 2. Geneva: World Health Organization, 1951.

Fraiberg, S. *Every Child's Birthright: In Defense of Mothering*. New York: Basic Books, 1977.

Glickman, B. M., Springer, N. B. *Who Cares for Baby? Choices in Child Care*. New York: Schocken Books, 1978.

Scott, J. P. "The Process of Primary Socialization in Canine and Human Infants." *Monographs of the Society for Research in Child Development* 28, no. 1 (1963): 1–47.

White, B. L.; Kaban, B.; Attanucci, J.; & Shapiro, B. *Experience and Environment: Major Influences on the Development of the Young Child. Vol. 2*. Englewood Cliffs, N.J.: Prentice-Hall, 1978.

White, B. L.; Watts, J. C.; Barnett, I.; Kaban, B. T.; Marmor, J. R.; & Shapiro, B. B. *Experience and Environment: Major Influences on the Development of the Young Child. Vol. 1*. Englewood Cliffs, N.J.: Prentice-Hall, 1973.

White, B. L. with B. Kaban & J. Attanucci. *The Origins of Human Competence: The Final Report of the Harvard Preschool Project*. Lexington, Mass.: Lexington Books, 1979.

Yarrow, L. J. "Maternal Deprivation: Toward an Empirical and Conceptual Reevaluation." *Psychological Bulletin* 58 (1961): 459–90.

Children of Working Mothers:
What the Research Tells Us

JOANNE CURRY O'CONNELL

Today it is the norm for a child in school to have a mother who is working. During a child's infancy and toddlerhood, the chance is one out of three that the child's mother is employed outside the home; between the ages of three and five, there is almost one chance in two; and for the school age child, there is more than one chance in two that the mother is working. (Women's Bureau 1977, p. 1)

Labor statistics, such as those cited above, provide evidence of the increasing number of mothers who are choosing to work outside the home. The factors influencing this decision are well known and range from the need for additional family income to the need for personal self-fulfillment. The impact of this decision on the family unit, the parents, and the child, however, is not yet fully understood. In fact, the complexity of investigating this issue has eluded even the best researchers.

What is available to early educators in the professional literature developed over the past decade is the attempt to systematically assess the impact of daycare placement on the growth and development of the young child. I would like to review this research as a counterargument to Burton White's position. White advocated that women, with few exceptions, should not work outside the home while their children are young.

This counterviewpoint was undertaken for several reasons. First, White's formulation of a question requiring a yes or no response oversimplified the issue and ignored factors critical to the decision that may be tied to external forces, such as single parent families, economic needs, and so on. Secondly, White's argument was primarily based on institutional research and animal studies of the past (such as Bowlby, 1951, and Yarrow, 1961). Belsky & Steinberg (1978) in their review of the daycare issue noted

"Children of Working Mothers: What the Research Tells Us" by Joanne Curry O'Connell, *Young Children*, 38 (2), 62–70. Copyright © 1983 by the National Association for the Education of Young Children. Reprinted by permission.

Dr. O'Connell is Associate Director of Research at the Institute for Human Development and Associate Professor of Educational Psychology at Northern Arizona University, Flagstaff, Arizona.

368 that negative attitudes toward working mothers are perpetuated by those who rely on research conducted in the 1950s with institutionalized children raised in isolated, unstimulating environments. These studies have led some to make statements about the "obvious harmful effects" of daycare programs (White, 1981, p. 14), while at the same time they neglect a wealth of investigations conducted more recently. Additionally, Etaugh (1980), in a review of feature articles in the popular press on daycare versus homecare, documented a predominantly negative attitude toward today's working mothers. This is, indeed, an emotionally charged issue for the American public for several reasons, and it is incumbent upon professionals in early childhood education to review the *facts*, and form an educated opinion on the effects of daycare.

This review will summarize research related to four popular questions often posed when discussing the effects of daycare on young children's development:

1. How does daycare affect mother/child emotional attachment?
2. How does daycare affect intellectual growth and development?
3. Does daycare help children learn to get along with their peers?
4. What is the effect of maternal attitude toward childcare settings on the child's development?

This information can also assist mothers in making their decisions related to "staying at home with your baby."

How Does Daycare Affect Mother/Child Emotional Attachment?

This question is addressed first because professionals and parents alike have focused much of the daycare versus homecare issue on whether or not daycare disrupts the maternal/child bond. To provide a cogent answer to this question, it is necessary to describe the nature of the investigations and the procedure for assessing maternal attachment and emotional bonding. Most investigations have relied heavily on the Ainsworth and Wittig (1969) strange situation experiment. This procedure assesses the child's proximity-seeking and attention-seeking behavior when separated and reunited with the mother in the presence of a stranger (Heist, 1981). The level of anxiety induced in the child by these strange situations is also noted. This empirical paradigm assumes that the quality of the mother/child relationship can be measured by the approach-avoidance response of the child to her or his mother and to the stranger (Belsky & Steinberg 1978). Other investigators have employed observational techniques in a similar setting to measure behaviors such as crying, smiling, giving, and touching the mother during interaction sessions. The studies using the above-mentioned procedures have generally contrasted groups of children reared exclusively at home to groups of children receiving daily substitute care. The children studied also represent a cross-section of the preschool years, from six months to five years.

Out of ten studies investigating the effects of substitute care on the maternal/child bond, eight reported no significant difference between the home-reared group and the out-of-home group across the variables studied (Doyle, 1975; Caldwell et al., 1970; Cochran, 1977; Hock, 1980; Kagan, Kearsley, & Zelazo, 1977; Moskowitz, Schwarz, & Corsini, 1977; Portnoy & Simmons, 1978; Rubenstein, 1979). In fact, the conclusions drawn by these investigators can best be characterized by Cochran's (1977) summary, in which he stated that the similarities in behavior between the groups far outweighed any observed differences. The mother/child attachment was not found to be weakened or abnormal in the children attending daycare.

The two studies reporting negative findings in terms of the group of children receiving substitute care were Blehar (1974) and Vaughn, Gove, and Egeland (1980). Blehar's study has since been refuted by several investigators who have unsuccessfully attempted to replicate her results. They failed to find that daycare children cried more and interacted less with their mothers than did home-reared children (Moskowitz, Schwarz, & Corsini, 1977; Portnoy & Simmons, 1978). The more recent study (Vaughn, Gove, & Egeland, 1980) looked at a group of infants who were being cared for primarily in an alternate caregiver home. These infants, placed in substitute care prior to their first birthday, exhibited a significantly greater amount of anxious-avoidant behavior than infants remaining at home with their mothers. Although it is difficult to account for these differences without an attempt at replication, the results are not in agreement with the bulk of the research.

An important feature of the eight studies reporting no difference in maternal attachment behaviors is the fact that the age of entry into substitute care situations varied from two months to four years. Thus, even children entering substitute care during infancy were not adversely affected. In fact, one author (Blehar, 1974) has suggested that infants receiving substitute care early in life may not experience the anxiety that separation might produce in older children. Rubenstein (1979) suggests that infants use self-comforting behaviors, and that peers can effectively reduce the effects of separation. One investigation (Portnoy & Simmons, 1979) systematically studied the effects of age of entry into substitute care and found no differences between the groups.

370   *Caretaker Versus Maternal Attachment*

In addition to the assessment of mother/child attachment by studying the child's reaction to a stranger, several investigations have been concerned with the effects the substitute caregiver has on the child's preference for the mother versus the caregiver (Cummings, 1980; Farran & Ramey, 1977; Kagan, Kearsley, & Zelazo, 1977; Ricciuti, 1974). A variation of the attachment paradigm was used in which both the primary caregiver and mother are present in the room and a stressful situation was produced by introducing a stranger to the setting. When children were placed in a conflict situation, they consistently showed an overwhelming preference for their mothers. Although the children were placed daily in a secure environment with a substitute caregiver, the naturally occurring bond between mother and child was not disrupted nor relinquished to the caregiver.

How Does Daycare Affect Intellectual Growth and Development

The early intervention projects of the last decade and a half offer convincing evidence that preschool children from low-income homes can benefit greatly from an enriched daycare environment (Golden et al., 1978; Heber et al., 1972; Ramey & Smith, 1976). Probably the most exciting recent research is provided in several longitudinal, follow-up studies which have evaluated the high-school status of children receiving early intervention during the preschool years (Fredericks, Moore, & Baldwin, 1979; Lazar et al., 1977; Palmer, 1977; Schweinhart & Weikart, 1980). These investigators found that fewer daycare children were placed in special education classes and fewer were retained in later grades. The daycare children had significantly higher expectations and occupational aspirations than children from control groups. These follow-up studies can lay to rest the fears that the intellectual gains which the daycare children exhibited over the control children during the preschool years would not be maintained as they entered public schools. Indeed, the follow-up investigations provide evidence that high-risk children from daycare enrichment programs are more likely to succeed in our society as they reach adulthood.

One must still ask, however, what happens to the low-risk child—the child from the middle- and upper-middle-income homes? Belsky and Steinberg (1978) reported eight studies that found no difference between low-risk daycare-reared children and matched home-reared children on measures of intellectual development.

Differences in Provider Behavior

Although few investigations have systematically compared daycare settings to family group homes, the recent National Day Care Home Study (Davison & Ellis, 1980; Fosburg, 1981; Singer et al., 1980; Stallings & Porter, 1980) provides information on differences within family group home settings by conducting direct behavioral observations of provider behavior. In a recent summary of the study, Stevens (1982) reported that the regulatory status of the homes was related to provider behavior. In the study, family daycare homes were classified as (1) sponsored—requiring affiliation with an external administrative agency; (2) regulated—requiring state licensure or registration; or (3) unregulated—no external control or scrutiny. The providers from sponsored homes spent significantly more time interacting directly with the children than providers of regulated homes, who interacted more with children than providers from unregulated homes. Stevens also notes that "training in early childhood education was strongly associated with more positive and stimulating behaviors." (p. 62). If adult/child interactions are deemed important to growth and development, particularly in the early years, then settings in which the provider spends more time in interaction with children may facilitate children's intellectual and other areas of development.

Does Daycare Help Children Learn to Get Along with Their Peers

The first two questions posed in this review tend to address the concepts about daycare raised by professionals and the popular press. However, when Bronfenbrenner (1970) surveyed a group of Massachusetts parents regarding the most important outcome of substitute care for their child, the majority response could be summarized as: "Help my child get along with others." The issues surrounding this question can be viewed in two ways: (1) daycare promotes peer relationships and behaviors for getting along with others, or (2) group care promotes aggression and negative behaviors directed toward peers.

Belsky and Steinberg (1978) reviewed four studies related to the issue of peer relationships among daycare children (Cornelius & Denney, 1975; Doyle, 1975; Kagan, Kearsley, & Zelazo, 1977; Ricciuti, 1974). Heist (1981) reviewed an additional seven studies (Howes, 1979; Finkelstein, et al. 1978; Johnson, 1979; Macrae & Herbert-Jackson, 1976; McCutcheon & Calhoun, 1976; Rubenstein, 1979; Schwarz, Strickland, & Krolick, 1974).

372 One of the findings consistently reported across studies is the lack of aggression and negative behaviors in center and family daycare settings. Although instances of aggression may occur, they are infrequent and the exception rather than the rule. Heist (1981) has speculated that the degree to which the setting is restrictive may be more important than the type of daycare—highly restrictive homes could result in excessive acting-out behaviors.

Most investigations of the effect of substitute care on social development and peer interactions were based on direct observation. Only two studies used a rating device by which caretaker judgment determined the measure of peer social skills (Macrae & Herbert-Jackson, 1976; Schwarz, Strickland, & Krolick, 1974). Most studies observed the children's behaviors in a small group setting outside the daycare environment (Cornelius & Denney, 1975; Doyle, 1975; Kagan, Kearsley, & Zelazo, 1977). Often, home-reared children were matched with daycare children and observed as pairs (Johnson, 1979; Rubenstein, 1979).

The behaviors that were studied and identified as representative of peer social interactions ranged from frequency counts of behaviors (such as the number of visual regards for peers, joint toy usage, smiling, and hitting); to the proportion of time spent in joint interaction and type of play activity (solitary or cooperative). Although each of the studies may have reported significant differences between the groups on one or two isolated variables, they tended to be balanced in terms of those reporting more favorable social behaviors in daycare children (Rubenstein, 1979; Johnson, 1979; Kagan, Kearsley, & Zelazo, 1977; Ricciuti, 1978) and those reporting more acceptable social skills in home-reared children (Doyle, 1975; Howes, 1979; Schwarz, Strickland, & Krolick, 1974). Finkelstein (1982) recently reported, however, that although no significant problems were found in the social development of their daycare children studied, significant differences in aggressiveness and hostility were found between daycare children and a peer control group upon entry into kindergarten. No reasons were provided for this discrepancy. In reviewing the literature related to daycare issues, the lack of difference between daycare and home-reared children in their behaviors, including social behaviors, is particularly striking. At the very least, no consistent, adverse effects were noted by any investigator, and, in fact, some reported that children in daycare were more skilled socially.

Finkelstein et al. (1978) observed the development of a group of daycare infants at 9, 10, 11, and 12 months of age. They reported that social behaviors in young children were more a function of age and development than of the type of childcare setting. Johnson (1979) reached a similar conclusion, and additionally suggested that social behaviors may be related more to the numbers of peers available to a child than to the setting within which the social interactions occur. It is unclear from current research whether or not mere placement in a group setting will result in a significant change in social abilities. As noted above, for normally developing children, maturation may provide the key ingredient. However, it is incumbent upon daycare providers to be sensitive to their role in facilitating social development. Rather than intervening only when trouble arises, it may be necessary to actively facilitate cooperative play and verbal exchange through modeling and reinforcement. Learning may then occur that will facilitate the maturation process.

What Is the Effect of Maternal Attitude toward Childcare Settings on the Child's Development?

One study (Farel, 1980) approached the issue of the effects of daycare on kindergarten children's development from the perspective of the mother. Farel's study is unique in two ways: first, it assessed the effect of maternal attitude toward her work status on the child's development; and second, it employed a variety of child outcome measures. A questionnaire administered to 212 mothers of kindergarten children was designed to elicit information related to identifying mother's attitudes about the needs of young children, such as (1) whether or not working makes a better or poorer mother, (2) whether or not mothers with preschoolers should work, (3) whether or not children have a negative attitude toward working mothers, and (4) the importance of intrinsic motivation to work for personal satisfaction. Child outcome measures included a classroom adjustment measure (task orientation, persistence, concentration, creativity and curiosity, intelligence, and consideration for others), as well as school achievement data.

Farel concluded that there was no evidence from her data that a mother's working per se interferes with the development of her child. There was no significant relationship between a child's successful school adjustment and whether or not the mother was employed outside the home. Children of mothers whose attitudes toward work and work behavior were congruent (wanted to work and was working, or did not want to work and was not working) scored significantly higher on several measures of adjustment and competence than children of mothers whose behavior and attitudes were not congruent (working and did not want to, or not working and wanted to).

Farel's study contributes a more comprehensive picture because, by

374 looking at maternal attitude, we consider one of the many complex variables that may influence children's development, regardless of where they spend their day.

Summary

A review of research evidence leads to this conclusion: *no consistent adverse effect of out-of-home child daycare has been found by over a dozen child development investigators.* Although professionals in child development are influenced by our own experiences, values, and beliefs, we must also be knowledgeable about the research evidence when we assist parents in making such important decisions. This approach to formulating an opinion is indeed part of what differentiates the professional early childhood educator from the general public. It is our professional responsibility to keep up with the current research, to contribute to the developing knowledge base in our field, and to broaden our understanding about these and other controversial issues.

It is true that much more research needs to be conducted before we have a more complete picture of all the factors involved regarding the influence of daycare, and what components comprise quality care. Several of the major reviews of daycare research cited in this report discuss the current research limitations and future needs. The four critical questions here are still in need of further vigorous investigation. Mothers are choosing to work in increasing numbers, so our professional efforts should be aimed at answering these and other questions, such as

1. What are the critical differences in substitute care that facilitate or inhibit child growth and development?
2. What is the effect of the high turnover rate in substitute care arrangements on the child's adjustment and emotional security?
3. What is the father's influence on the child's success in out-of-home care settings (attitude, sharing of responsibilities, flexibility in assisting with sick children, etc.)?

There are many other pressing questions that can be formulated. We must shift both professional and parent concerns away from the limited question, "Should you stay home with your baby?" to more critical and realistic issues related to the quality of young children's care and the family's impact on the child's development.

References

Ainsworth, M. D., & Wittig, B. A. "Attachment and Exploratory Behavior of One-Year-Olds in a Strange Situation." In *Determinants of Infant Behavior*. Vol. 4, ed. B. M. Foss. New York: Barnes & Noble, 1969.

Belsky, J., & Steinberg, L. D. "The Effects of Day Care: A Critical Review." *Child Development* 49 (1978): 929–49.

Blehar, M. "Anxious Attachment and Defensive Reactions Associated with Day Care." *Child Development* 45 (1974): 683–92.

Bowlby, J. *Maternal Care and Mental Health*. Monograph no. 2. Geneva, Switz.: World Health Organization, 1951.

Bronfenbrenner, U. *Two Worlds of Childhood: U.S. and U.S.S.R.* New York: Sage, 1970.

Caldwell, B. M.; Wright, C. M.; Honig, A. S.; and Tannenbaum, J. "Infant Care and Attachment." *American Journal of Orthopsychiatry* 40 (1970): 397–412.

Cochran, M. "A Comparison of Group Day and Family Child-Rearing Patterns in Sweden." *Child Development* 48 (1977): 702–07.

Cornelius, S., & Denney, N. "Dependency in Day Care and Home Care Children." *Developmental Psychology* 11 (1975): 575–82.

Cummings, E. M. "Caregiver Stability and Day Care." *Developmental Psychology* 16 (1980): 31–37.

Davison, J. L., & Ellis, W. W. *Family Day Care in the United States: Parent Component. Final Report of the National Day Care Home Study. Vol. 4*. Washington, D.C.: U.S. Department of Health and Human Services, Administration for Children, Youth and Families, 1980. (DHHS Publication No. [OHDS] 81-30299)

Doyle, A. "Infant Development in Day Care." *Developmental Psychology* 11 (1975): 655–56.

Etaugh, C. "Effects of Nonmaternal Care on Children: Research Evidence and Popular Views." *American Psychologist* 35 (1980): 309–19.

Farel, A. "Effects of Preferred Maternal Roles, Maternal Employment, and Sociodemographic Status on School Adjustment and Competence." *Child Development* 51 (1980): 1179–86.

Farran, D., & Ramey, C. T. "Infant Day Care and Attachment Behaviors Toward Mothers and Teachers." *Child Development* 48 (1977): 1112–16.

Finkelstein, N. W. "Aggression: Is It Stimulated by Day Care?" *Young Children* 37, no. 6 (September 1982): 3–9.

Finkelstein, N. W.; Dent, C.; Gallagher, K.; & Ramey, C. T. "Social Behavior of Infants and Toddlers in a Day-Care Environment." *Developmental Psychology* 14 (1978): 257–62.

Fosburg, S. *Family Day Care in the United States: Summary of Findings. Final Report of the National Day Care Home Study. Vol. 1*. Washington, D.C.: U.S. Department of Health and Human Services, Administration for Children, Youth and Families, 1981. (DHHS Publication No. [OHDS] 80-30282)

Fredericks, H. D.; Moore, M. G.; & Baldwin, V. L. *The Long-Range Effects of Early Childhood Education on a TMR Population*. Paper presented at the Alice Hayden Symposium, Seattle, Washington, 1979.

Golden, M.; Rosenbluth, L.; Grossi, M.; Policare, H.; Freeman, H.; & Brownlee, E. *The New York City Infant Day Care Study*. New York: Medical and Health Research Association of New York City, 1978.

Heber, R., Garber, H.; Harrington, D.; Hoffman, C.; & Falender, C. *Rehabilitation of*

376   *Families at Risk for Mental Retardation.* Madison: Rehabilitation Research and Training Center in Mental Retardation, University of Wisconsin, 1972.

Heist, M. "The Effects of Day Care: A Literature Review." *Resources in Education* 16 (1981): 120. (ERIC Document Reproduction Service No. 197 812)

Hock, E. "Working and Nonworking Mothers and Their Infants: A Comparative Study of Maternal Caregiving Characteristics and Infants' Social Behavior." *Merrill-Palmer Quarterly* 46 (1980): 79–101.

Howes, C. "Toddler Social Competence in Family and Center Day-Care." *Dissertation Abstracts International* 39, no. 12 (1979): 6097-B. (University Microfilms, No. 7912147, 196)

Johnson, R. L. "Social Behavior of Three Year Old Children in Day Care and Home Settings." *Child Study Journal* 9 (1979): 109–22.

Kagan, J. "Emergent Themes in Human Development." *American Scientist* 64 (1976): 186–96.

Kagan, J.; Kearsley, R.; & Zelazo, P. "The Effects of Infant Day Care on Psychological Development." *Evaluation Quarterly* 1, no. 1 (1977): 109–42.

Lazar, I.; Hubbell, R.; Murray, H.; Rosche, M; & Royce, J. *Preliminary Findings of the Developmental Continuity Longitudinal Study.* Presented at the Office of Child Development Conference, "Parents, Children, and Continuity," El Paso, Texas, 1977.

Macrae, J. W. & Herbert-Jackson, E. "Are Behavioral Effects of Infant Day Care Programs Specific?" *Developmental Psychology* 12 (1976): 269–70.

McCutcheon, B., & Calhoun, K. "Social and Emotional Adjustment of Infants and Toddlers to a Day Care Setting." *American Journal of Orthopsychiatry* 46 (1976): 104–08.

Moskowitz, D. G.; Schwarz, J. C.; & Corsini, D. A. "Initiating Day Care at Three Years of Age: Effects on Attachment." *Child Development* 48 (1977): 1271–76.

Palmer, F. "The Effects of Early Childhood Educational Invervention on School Performance." Paper presented at the President's Commission on Mental Health, 1977.

Portnoy, F. C., & Simmons, C. H. "Day Care and Attachment." *Child Development* 49 (1978): 239–42.

Ramey, C. T., & Smith, B. "Assessing the Intellectual Consequences of Early Intervention with High-Risk Infants." *American Journal of Mental Deficiency* 81 (1976): 318–24.

Ricciuti, H. N. "Fear and the Development of Social Attachments in the First Year of Life." In *The Origins of Human Behavior. Vol. 2. The Origins of Fear,* ed. M. Lewis and L. A. Rosenblum, New York: Wiley, 1974.

Ricciuti, H. N. "Effects of Infant Day Care Experience on Behavior and Development: Research and Implications for Social Policy." *Resources in Education* 13, no. 11 (1978): 149, (ERIC Document Reproduction Service No. 156 340)

Rubenstein, J. "Caregiving and Infant Behavior in Day Care and in Homes." *Developmental Psychology* 15, no. 1 (1979): 1–24.

Schwarz, J. C. "Reconciling Women's Changing Status with Children's Enduring Needs." *Educational Horizons* 59, no. 1 (Fall 1980): 15–21.

Schwarz, J. C.; Strickland, R. G.; & Krolick, G. "Infant Day Care: Behavioral Effects at Preschool Age." *Developmental Psychology* 10 (1974): 502–06.

Schweinhart, L. J., & Weikart, D. P. "Young Children Grow Up: The Effects of the Perry Preschool Program on Youths Through Age 15." *Monographs of the High/Scope Educational Research Foundation* 7 (1980).

Singer, J. D.; Fosburg, S.; Goodson, B. D.; & Smith, J. M. *Family Day Care in the United States: Research Report. Final Report of the National Day Care Home Study. Vol. 2.* Washington, D.C.: U.S. Department of Health and Human Services, Administration for Children, Youth and Families, 1980. (DHHS Publication No. [OHDS] 80-30283)

Stallings, J., & Porter, A. *Family Day Care in the United States: Observation Component. Final Report of the National Day Care Home Study. Vol. 3.* Washington, D.C.: U.S. Depart-

ment of Health and Human Services, Administration for Children, Youth and Fami- 377
lies, 1980. (DHHS Publication No. [OHDS] 80-30284)

Stevens, J. H., Jr. "Research in Review. The National Day Care Home Study: Family Day Care in the United States." *Young Children* 37, no. 4 (May 1982): 59–66.

Vaughn, B. E.: Gove, F. L.; & Egeland, B. "The Relationship Between Out-of-Home Care and the Quality of Infant-Mother Attachment in an Economically Disadvantaged Population." *Child Development* 51, no. 4 (1980): 1203–14.

White, B. L. "Viewpoint. Should You Stay Home with Your Baby?" *Young Children* 37, no. 1 (November 1981): 11–17.

Women's Bureau, "Number of Mothers in the Labor Force Continues to Rise." *Working Mothers and Their Children*. Washington, D.C.: U.S. Department of Labor, 1977. Doc. no. 77-16479.

Yarrow, M. R. "Maternal Deprivation: Toward an Empirical and Conceptual Re-evaluation." *Psychological Bulletin* 58 (1961): 459–90.

Question 12

Does Abortion Cause Psychological Harm to Women?

Although American public opinion is deeply divided over the issue of a woman's right to abortion, a consensus emerged within psychology and psychiatry in the 1970s that abortion had limited, if any, negative emotional outcomes for the woman. This marked a sharp reversal of the position of a large number of psychiatrists and psychologists prior to 1960. Robert Pasnau (1972) notes that before that date most psychiatrists believed that induced abortion led to depression, and some even argued that abortion was implicated in the causes of several neuroses and psychoses.

Many of these early studies rested on poor or nonexistent data and were done by investigators who seemed to have made up their minds about the negative effects of abortion before beginning their research (Simon & Senturia, 1966). A survey of the literature on abortion by Lisa Roseman Shusterman (1976) found a series of flaws in most of the research which raised questions about their findings. One problem was that much of the research was based on the author's clinical experience and therefore was impossible to replicate. Others relied on retrospective data with all the distortions inherent in that approach. Perhaps their greatest weakness was the failure to compare women who underwent abortion with a logical control group: women with unwanted pregnancies who decided to bear children.

Nevertheless, Shusterman (1976) was able to identify several more recent methodologically sound studies on the psychological implications of abortion. She concluded, on the basis of these studies, that abortion on request was a "relatively benign procedure" and that where there were negative sequelae, they were brief and rarely acute.

378   Later studies continued to make similar determinations. In 1978, the

World Health Organization found a substantial amount of data from a variety of countries indicating frequent psychological benefits and a low rate of negative aftereffects from abortion (Watters, 1980). Some recent investigators, however, are taking a second look at women who are stressed by their abortion experiences. Brenda Major (1985), for example, has investigated specific psychological variables which in certain cases may place a woman "at risk" for negative psychological sequelae of abortion.

Joy Osofsky and Howard Osofsky offer support for the consensus that developed in the 1970s: that women experience very few negative reactions as a result of the abortion experience. Karen Lodl, Ann McGettigan, and Janette Bucy, activists in abortion counseling for the past fifteen years, argue that many clinicians avoid mentioning the negative consequences of abortion for fear that they will provide ammunition to the pro-life movement. Minimizing the extent of post-abortion stress, these authors claim, often misleads women, who as a consequence are not prepared to deal with the real problems that occur in some situations.

References

Major, B. (1985). Attributions, expectations, and coping with abortion. *Journal of Personality and Social Psychology, 48* (3), 585–99.

Pasnau, R. O. (1972). Psychiatric complications of therapeutic abortion. *Obstetrics and Gynecology, 40* (2), 252–56.

Shusterman, L. R. (1976). The psychosocial factors of the abortion experience: A critical review. *Psychology of Women Quarterly, 1* (1), 79–106.

Simon, N. M. & Senturia, A. G. (1966). Psychiatric sequelae of abortion. *Archives of General Psychiatry, 15,* 378–89.

Watters, W. W. (1980). Mental health consequences of abortion and refused abortion. *Canadian Journal of Psychiatry, 25,* 68–73.

Additional Reading

Cohen, L., & Roth, S. (1984). Coping with abortion. *Journal of Human Stress, 10* (3), 140–45.

David, H. P., Rasmussen, N. K., & Holst, E. (1981). Postpartum and postabortion psychotic reactions. *Family Planning Perspectives, 13,* 88–92.

Doane, B., & Quigley, B. (1981, September 1). Psychiatric aspects of therapeutic abortion. *Canadian Medical Association Journal, 125,* 427–32.

Faria, G., Barrett, E., & Goodman, L. M. (1985). Women and abortion: Attitudes, social networks, decision-making. *Social Work in Health Care, 2* (1), 85–99.

Freeman, E. W., Rickels, K., Huggins, G. R., Garcia, C.-R., & Polin, J. (1980). Emotional distress patterns among women having first or repeat abortions. *Obstetrics and Gynecology, 55* (5), 630–36.

380 Friedlander, M. L., Kaul, T. J., & Stimel, C. A. (1984). Abortion: Predicting the complexity of the decision-making process. *Women and Health, 9* (1), 43–54.

Gilligan, C., & Belenky, M. F. (1980). A naturalistic study of abortion decisions. In R. L. Selman, R. Yando (Eds.), *New directions for child development: Clinical-developmental psychology*. San Francisco: Jossey-Bass.

Hare, M. J., & Heywood, J. (1981). Counseling needs of women seeking abortion. *Journal of Biosocial Science, 13,* 269–73.

Hodgson, J. E. (Ed.) (1981). *Abortion and sterilization: Medical and social aspects*. New York: Grune & Stratton.

Howe, L. K. (1984). *Moments on Maple Avenue: The reality of abortion*. New York: Macmillan.

Kalmar, R. (1977). *Abortion: The emotional implications*. Dubuque, Iowa: Kendall/Hunt.

Luker, K. (1984a). The war between women. *Family Planning Perspective, 16* (3), 105–10.

Luker, K. (1984b). *Abortion and the politics of motherhood*. Berkeley: University of California Press.

Luker, K. (1975). *Taking chances: Abortion and the decision not to contracept*. Berkeley: University of California Press.

Rogers, J. L., Phifer, J. F., & Nelson, J. A. (1986). Psychological sequelae of abortion: A re-examination of published results. Paper presented at the meeting of the American Psychological Association, Washington, D.C.

The Psychological Reaction of Patients to Legalized Abortion

JOY D. OSOFSKY AND HOWARD J. OSOFSKY

Recent legislative changes have made legal abortion an option for large numbers of women in several states. It is likely that future legislation and court rulings will lead to still further increases in the availability of the procedure. Because of the importance of the legalization of abortion, and because of the impact that has already resulted, it has seemed important to review some of the existent data concerning patients' psychological reactions to abortion and to present early results from a legalized abortion program in New York State.

It is recognized that many of the existent scientific studies will not be completely relevant to the present topic, since the options to unwanted pregnancy were formerly therapeutic or illegal abortion in the United States or legal abortion in other countries. Both therapeutic abortion, requiring a diagnosis of illness substantiated by consultation with several doctors, and illegal abortion, performed under stigmatized and furtive conditions, might be expected to result in different psychological responses and sequelae than would legal abortion. Similarly, procedures performed in other countries, with different cultural traditions and patterns, might be anticipated to have a somewhat different outcome than would those performed in this country. However, at least a portion of the data seems relevant and will be included in this paper. For the sake of pertinence and brevity, an exhaustive review will not be attempted; the interested reader is referred to several good compilations that have appeared in recent years.[17,18,26,37,38,39,40,41] In the presentation of early results from a legal abortion program, special emphasis will be placed upon the patients'

"The Psychological Reaction of Patients to Legalized Abortion" by Joy D. Osofsky and Howard J. Osofsky, *American Journal of Orthopsychiatry*, 1972, *42* (1), 48–60. Copyright © 1972 the American Orthopsychiatric Association, Inc. Reproduced by permission.

Dr. Joy Osofsky is a clinical psychologist and Professor of Pediatrics and Psychiatry, Louisiana State University Medical School, New Orleans, Louisiana; Dr. Howard Osofsky is Head and Professor, Department of Psychiatry, Louisiana State University Medical School, New Orleans.

382 psychological reactions to the procedure and parameters that appear related to these reactions.

Psychological Impact as Determined by Prior Studies

In reviewing the interpretive findings and conclusions of prior studies, one can emerge with a variety of opinions ranging from frequent and severe sequelae,[1, 9, 13, 43] to occasional direct or indirect problems,[3, 27, 35] to no noticeable difficulty.[17, 18, 25, 26] However, almost regardless of the source, the objective data reveal a surprisingly low incidence of psychological complications.

Studies from the United States

Gebhard et al.[14] studied 442 American women who had induced abortions; most of the procedures were performed illegally. Their results demonstrated only rare significant physical or emotional sequelae. The study is perhaps of special note because of the commonly held assumptions concerning the dangers of criminal abortions.

Niswander and Patterson[31] followed 116 patients who underwent therapeutic abortion in one of the affiliated hospitals of the State University of New York at Buffalo from 1963–65. The abortions were performed under a strict law that had been interpreted liberally. The authors found few women who regretted having obtained an abortion. Further, among the small number of individuals who had regrets, the regrets were usually noted shortly after the procedure and tended to disappear by the time of an eight-month followup.

Kummer[25] surveyed the experience of 32 psychiatrists in Los Angeles. He found that, during an average of twelve years experience in practice, 75 percent of the doctors had never seen a patient with any moderate or severe psychiatric sequelae from either illegal or legal induced abortions. The other 25 percent had encountered significant sequelae only rarely.

Peck and Marcus[32] studied 50 women who had therapeutic abortions in New York, half of which were done for psychiatric reasons. Patients were interviewed prior to the surgical procedure and three to six months following the abortion. There was only one case of acute negative reaction to the procedure, which was quickly relieved. Mild guilt occurred in 20 percent of cases but was shortlived and disappeared by the time of followup. Ninety-eight percent of the subjects stated that if they were to make the decision again, they would still prefer the abortion to continuation of the pregnancy.

Kretzschmar and Norris[24] reported on the psychiatric sequelae of 32 therapeutic abortions carried out over a six-year period in Iowa. In a one- to five-year followup study of 24 patients, they found no negative psychological effects or problems.

Early reports from the Colorado experience with liberalized legislation have not stressed psychological information.[8,19] The one exception has been Whittington,[42] who, on the basis of 31 returned followup questionnaires, reported a high incidence of improved symptomatology and only one patient with even possibly worse mental health.

Marder[28] summarized the early results of experience with the 1967 California Therapeutic Abortion Act. This modification of existent legislation represented a liberalization, but not a total legalization. As of September 1969, approximately 600 applications had been received and 550 had been approved. Few serious emotional problems of guilt or remorse were found. It is of some interest, and perhaps related to the continuation of restrictions and technical difficulties in obtaining an abortion, that no reduction in self-induced or criminally induced abortions was noted.

To date, little information is available from Alaska, Hawaii, and New York, all of which have recently enacted new abortion laws.

Scandinavian Studies

Abortion is relatively more freely and legally available in the Scandinavian countries than in most states in this country. However, some restrictions still exist, and considerable difficulty and delay can be encountered in attempting to obtain a legal abortion; this may explain the persistence of a high frequency of illegal abortions.[2,4,15,41] Legal abortions in Scandinavia can be obtained if there exists a serious threat to the mother's life or to her physical or mental health. Disease, bodily defect, and exhaustion are acceptable conditions. Abortions are also granted for eugenic reasons, where severe birth defects are a possibility, and for humanitarian reasons such as rape, incest, or pregnancy in a young female. In Sweden and Denmark, most abortions have been performed under medically oriented indications; in Norway, the law has been more liberal, and social indications have been employed more frequently, including rape, incest, or pregnancy in girls under fifteen or sixteen.[26]

Ekblad[10] studied 479 patients in Sweden who had undergone abortions on psychiatric grounds three to four years previously. He found that 65 percent were satisfied and showed no self-reproach; 10 percent had no self-reproach but felt that the operation was unpleasant; 14 percent felt mild self-reproach; only 11 percent felt serious self-reproach or regretted the operation.

Kolstad,[22] in Norway, followed up 135 individuals three to sixteen years after therapeutic abortion. He reported that 82.8 percent of the women

384 were happy and had no reservation; 9.8 percent were satisfied and had some reservation; 3.7 percent were not happy, but felt that the abortion was necessary; only 3.7 percent felt repentant.

Brekke[2] studied a group of 34 postabortion patients in Norway and found only two who showed even a "slight reaction." The reaction noted was a feeling of stress, which lasted only a few days and then disappeared. It is perhaps worthy of emphasis that the Kolstad and Brekke studies both took place in Norway. Their findings of an extremely low incidence of psychological complications occurred in the Scandinavian country with most liberal social indications for abortion.

In a somewhat different type of report, Höök[20] studied 294 women whose applications for legal abortion were refused by the National Board of Health in Sweden in 1948. The followup examination was carried out 7½ years to 11 years and 11-months after refusal of the application. It is of interest that of 45 women who were excluded from followup, 24 were excluded because their subsequent symptoms allowed them to gain a therapeutic abortion. Höök found that 23 percent of the women who were refused abortion accepted the pregnancy after the refusal and were able to handle the situation satisfactorily; 53 percent of the women finally adjusted themselves after having had a variety of insufficiency reactions during an eighteen-month observation period; the remaining 24 percent found the situation of refusal so unfavorable that the symptoms of insufficiency, which had arisen within eighteen months of the application, were still present at the time of followup. A higher percentage of incapacitating insufficiency was noted among the supposedly healthy women who did not qualify for abortion than among the emotionally and physically disturbed individuals who did qualify.

Forssman and Thuwe,[12] in a still different type of investigation, studied 120 children born after application for therapeutic abortion was refused. Their aim was to determine the mental health, social adjustment, and educational level of such children. All of the subjects were followed until the age of twenty-one. The group was compared with an appropriate control group. The authors found that many more of the unwanted than the control children had not had the advantage of a secure family life during childhood. They more frequently were registered in psychiatric services and more commonly participated in antisocial and criminal behavior. They required public assistance more often than did the control subjects. A greater number were educationally subnormal and far fewer pursued theoretical studies over and above what was obligatory. In general, the social prognosis for the unwanted children was poorer than for the control children.

In 1968 a liberalized abortion act was passed, which allows for abortion with indications similar to those already cited for Scandinavia. While not legalizing abortion, in practice, perhaps related to the existent national mood,[7] it has allowed for marked liberalization. Because of its recency, little psychological data is available. One exception is Gillis,[16] who followed up 31 patients aborted during 1968 and found no significant psychiatric disturbances. In larger national reviews, Diggory et al.[7] have reported data suggesting a decrease in illegal abortions, increased plans for effective contraception[6] and few apparent psychological problems.[6] The psychological data is not based upon in-depth determinations, however, but upon impressions obtained after 1,000 consecutive abortions.

Soviet Union and Eastern European Studies

In the Soviet Union and Eastern Europe, legal abortion has been an option for many years; however, the extent of this option has been differently interpreted in the different countries.[5, 21] In Hungary and the Soviet Union, abortion is available on request (although the abortion law in the Soviet Union has changed several times depending upon differential governmental attitudes and pressures for population growth).[11] Czechoslovakia, Poland, Yugoslavia, and, to some extent, Bulgaria are permissive in authorizing abortion if the pregnant woman persists in her request. Rumania has moved toward more restrictive legislation, but is still more liberal than many Western European countries. The German Democratic Republic has added more liberal instructions to a restrictive law. Only Albania limits abortion to strictly medical indications.

Reasons for the relatively wide availability of abortion in these countries include demographic considerations, inadequate contraception programs, desire to protect women from medically unsafe illegal abortions, and a belief that women have the right to determine family size and pregnancy desirability. Demographically, the effects have been striking,[21] and there is mounting evidence to suggest a diminution in the number of illegal abortions.[30]

From a psychological standpoint, little data is available. Mehlan,[29] in a followup study of 248 East German women, reported that 90 percent felt that abortion had represented the best solution to their problem. Otherwise, information is sparse. One may wonder whether the paucity of data is indicative of the acceptance of the procedure within the countries and the resultant assumption of few specific psychological effects worthy of study.

386 Japanese Studies

In 1948, Japan enacted legislation to make abortions legal for social and economic reasons. In 1949, the law was further liberalized and revised. Perhaps the major concern related to rapid population growth with possible threat to national survival, but considerations were also given to inadequacy of contraceptive utilization and medical complications of illegal abortion. Abortion acceptance has been widespread both because of a desire to limit family size and because of an absence of religious and moral traditions that forbid contraception and abortion.[26,33] As a result, abortion has served as a method of birth and population control, but, contrary to popular misconceptions, contraceptive use has been growing and may eventually lead to a diminution in abortion frequency.[23,34]

As was true for the Soviet Union and Eastern European countries, little Japanese data is available concerning possible psychological sequelae to abortion. Since the procedure is so widely and readily accepted on all levels, few negative sequelae would be anticipated, and this may again account for the lack of studies in the area.

A Legalized Abortion Program in New York State

Description of Program

As a response to the legalization of abortion in July 1970, the State University Hospital in Syracuse, New York, through the Department of Obstetrics and Gynecology, organized a program of education, contraception, and abortion services. Its purpose was to provide individuals with full options and opportunities for controlling their reproductive capacity. The program was designed primarily for a low-income population because of the paucity of meaningful services traditionally available to such individuals, and services were provided at the lowest possible cost to all who requested them. Because it was a medical center program with realistic staff and space limitations, priorities were established, offering care to patients from the immediate geographic area, the seventeen-county area served by the medical center, from the state as a whole, and from out of state, in descending order. The program has been continuously evaluated in order both to improve care and to understand the implications of the offered services.

Operation of the Clinic

Patients are admitted through the out-patient clinic at the State University Hospital in Syracuse, New York. On their first visit, they are seen by a physician, nurse, and social worker. The medical examination and appro-

priate laboratory tests are performed at this time. No patient request for
abortion is refused if the patient is within the limits proscribed for the
procedure. Patients who are more than twelve weeks pregnant are cleared
through a departmental committee. The primary reason for this procedure
relates to a limited number of gynecological beds at the State University
Hospital. Mid-trimester abortions are performed as in-patient procedures
and the committee essentially functions to set priorities when necessary. To
date, no patient has been refused by the committee. At the initial visit, the
patient is scheduled for the procedure, almost always within the same
week. Contraception is discussed both at the initial and at subsequent
visits.

Abortions are performed as an out-patient or in-and-out-patient procedure if the patient is no more than twelve weeks pregnant. Out-patient
procedures are done in the ambulatory services operating room under local
anesthesia and are reserved for uncomplicated cases; approximately 75
percent of the first trimester abortions are performed in this manner. In-
and-out-patient procedures are done in the main operating room suite
under general and local anesthesia and are reserved for patients with
medical problems, marked anxiety, or extreme youth. Suction curettage is
utilized for first trimester and saline induction for mid-trimester abortions.

Shortly after the abortion, the patient is interviewed in order both to
provide her with support and to determine her reactions to the procedure.
Additional information is gathered concerning her perceptions of options
other than legalized abortion, and her attitudes and future plans related to
contraception, marriage, children, and lifestyle.

Patients are seen in the clinic within one month after the abortion for a
followup examination and optional contraceptive prescription. At this time
patients are interviewed to evaluate changes in their attitudes from the time
of the procedure. A longer term followup is currently being planned.

Early Program Findings

Background Information

As of January 1, 1971, 380 abortions had been performed on patients
ranging in age from 12 to 44 years, 84.5% of whom have been from the
central New York area; 9.2% from the remainder of the state; and 6.3%
out-of-state residents. The mean patient age has been 23.5 years, with
highest concentrations in the 21–25 and 16–20-year-old groups. Slightly
over 50% of the group have been single; the remainder have been almost
evenly split between presently married and living with spouse, and sepa-

388 rated or divorced. Of the patients, 71.8% conceived with a boyfriend; 27.3% with their husbands; and only .9% with a stranger. Religious affiliations have been 43.9% Catholic; 46% Protestant; 5.4% other religions; and 4.7% claimed no religion. The high Catholic percentage appears to reflect the religious composition of the community at large. Some 15% of the patients have been nonwhite, a percentage slightly higher than would be expected from figures for the community, but not unusually high when compared to other clinic figures. Educational and occupational data are generally consistent with other clinic data.

Psychological Information

As mentioned previously, psychological interviews are carried out shortly after the abortion. This part of the evaluation was not initiated until after the program was underway, and, as a result, 250 reports are currently available. Table 12.1 presents responses in several categories of over-all ratings. In all categories, markedly negative findings are rare.

Table 12.2 presents information concerning the decision-making process and the reasons for abortion. It shows that 52.5% of the patients reported that the decision to obtain an abortion was not a difficult one.

As is apparent from the data, reasons for obtaining an abortion have most often centered around finances or unmarried status. Approximately one-third of the patients have been very fearful of the abortion procedure, one-third moderately fearful, and one-third not at all fearful. If abortion were still illegal, 58.1% of the patients stated that they would have had the child; 28.5% that they would have had an illegal abortion; and 13.4% that they do not know what they would have done.

Owing to the potential importance of contraception in relationship to abortion, information has been obtained concerning both the patients' past experience with contraception and their plans for contraceptive utilization in the future. It shows that 59.8% of patients reported some knowledge concerning contraception but admitted to not using it at the time of conception; 24.7% claimed contraceptive failure; and 15.5% claimed to have little or no contraceptive knowledge. Some 91.7% of patients plan to use contraception in the future; 54.6% feel even more strongly about using an effective contraceptive after undergoing an abortion. Among unmarried patients, 91.6% hope to be married in the future, and 77.7% of all of patients expressed a desire for children in the future.

Relationships between demographic and psychological variables are presented in table 12.3. With the scaling system employed, older patients have had more prior use of contraception, less fear of the abortion procedure, greater conviction about the future use of contraception, and less desire for future children than have younger women. Married patients have

Table 12.1: *Psychological Evaluation
in 250 Cases*

Affect	Rating[a]	Percent
Predominant Mood		
Very Unhappy	1	4.2%
Moderately Unhappy	2	10.5
Neutral	3	20.7
Moderately Happy	4	20.0
Very Happy	5	44.6
Physical Emotionality		
Much Crying	1	8.2
Moderate Crying	2	7.6
Neutral	3	15.8
Moderate Smiling	4	19.0
Much Smiling	5	49.4
Feelings about Abortion		
Negative: Much Guilt	1	8.2
Moderate Guilt	2	15.6
Neutral	3	13.4
Moderate Relief	4	14.8
Positive: Much Relief	5	48.0
Attitudes toward Self		
Negative: Angry	1	1.5
Moderate Anger	2	7.2
Neutral	3	12.6
Moderate Happiness	4	17.6
Positive: Happy	5	61.1

[a]Ratings from Negative = 1 to Positive = 5.

had more prior use of contraception, less fear of the procedure, and less desire for future children than have unmarried individuals. Married women would have been less likely to obtain an abortion if the procedure were still illegal. Although negative feelings have been uncommon among any group, Catholic patients have felt somewhat more guilt over the abortion, and have had somewhat more difficulty both in making the decision and undergoing the procedure than have non-Catholics; in addition, Catholics have had less prior use of contraception and would have been less likely to obtain an illegal abortion. More highly educated individuals have had greater prior use of contraception and have had less desire for future children; they would have been more likely to obtain an abortion if it were still illegal. Race of the patient has not related significantly to the psychological variables.

Table 12.2: *Decision Making Regarding Abortion*

	Percent
Difficulty of Decision	
Not difficult	52.5
Mildly difficult	19.5
Considerably difficult	28.0
Reason for Difficulty of Decision*	
Desire for the child	32.6
Psychological discomfort	20.1
Physical discomfort	3.3
Reasons for Abortion*	
Single	43.9
Financial	32.2
Wanted child but could not have it	13.4
Wanted to finish school	10.9
No positive feelings for the father	9.2
Medical reasons	8.8
Too many children	6.7
Does not want child	5.9
Too many children close in age	3.3
Parental advice	3.3
Husband not father of child	2.1
Unwilling intercourse	.8

*Some subjects are represented more than once in both the Reasons for Difficulty and Reasons for Abortion categories.

Intercorrelations among the psychological variables are reported in table 12.4. With the scaling system employed, patients who have felt more guilt over the abortion, have had more difficulty in making the decision, have found the procedure more difficult, and have had more fear of the pro-

Table 12.3: *Relationship between Demographic and Psychological Variables*

	Guilt over Abortion	Prior Use of Contraception	Difficulty of Decision	Difficulty of Procedure	Fear of the Procedure	Conviction about Future Use of Contraception	Desire for Future Children	Abortion if Still Illegal
Age	.05	.25[b]	.02	−.05	−.12[a]	−.17[b]	.48[b]	−.00
Marital Status	.10	.23[b]	.04	−.07	−.12[a]	.03	.33[b]	−.12[a]
Religion	.18[b]	.16[b]	−.11[a]	−.12[a]	−.10	−.09	−.01	−.12[a]
Race	.06	.00	−.04	−.04	−.01	−.01	.03	−.10
Education	.01	.22[b]	.05	.07	.01	−.05	−.29[b]	.23[b]

[a]P < .05 level of significance;   [b]P < .01 level of significance

Table 12.4: Intercorrelations among Psychological Variables

	Prior Use of Contraception	Difficulty of Decision	Difficulty of Procedure	Fear of the Procedure	Conviction about Future Use of Contraception	Desire for Future Children	Abortion if Still Illegal
Guilt over Abortion	.05	−.47[b]	−.50[b]	−.14[a]	.09	.17[b]	.17[b]
Prior Use of Contraception		.03	.04	.03	−.16[b]	−.00	.09
Difficulty of Decision			.69[b]	.18[b]	.05	−.19[b]	−.17[b]
Difficulty of Procedure				.20[b]	.04	−.32[b]	−.17[b]
Fear of Procedure					−.14[a]	−.18[b]	−.17[b]
Conviction about Future Use of Contraception						−.09	.10
Desire for Future Children							−.00

[a]P < .05 level of significance; [b]P < .01 level of significance.

cedure have also had more desire for future children and would have been less likely to obtain an abortion if the procedure were illegal. As might be expected from the data, difficulty in making the decision, when present, has correlated with difficulty with the procedure, and both have correlated with fear of the procedure; all three have correlated with a stronger desire for future children and a lessened likelihood of obtaining an abortion if the procedure were illegal. Prior use of contraception has correlated with greater conviction about the future use of contraception.

Discussion

Legalized abortion in this country is of relatively recent origin. As a result, existent data have been obtained from therapeutic and illegal abortion services in the United States and more readily available legal abortion services in other countries. The authors have recognized that conclusions from such studies are not necessarily directly applicable to the current situation in the United States. Therapeutic abortion has been available only to those individuals with significant physical and psychological problems; in addition, it has primarily existed as a service for the affluent. Illegal abortion has been compounded by the problems of societal stigmata, criminality, and questionable medical safety; it also has been more available, especially as a safe procedure, for the affluent. Abortion in other countries raises issues related to cultural, political, and religious dif-

392 ferences. However, it has seemed likely that information could be obtained from these sources which would be of use to the present problem.

Information that has emerged has been of considerable interest. Wherever objective studies have been performed, there has been a low incidence of psychological sequelae. Incidences have varied with samples studied, existence of prior difficulties, relative ease of abortion attainment, and attitudes of the professional staff. However, in no case has the incidence of problems been high, and in most cases, it is questionable whether the abortion or preexistent difficulties provoked the sequelae. The predominant reaction has appeared to be relief.

When one examines the data somewhat indirectly, one finds many interesting points. In the United States, both illegal and therapeutic abortion have been compounded by few psychological sequelae. Psychiatrists have seen almost none of the large numbers of women who have obtained an illegal procedure; when interviewed, the women have reported few problems. Even among individuals obtaining a therapeutic procedure who have had to prove themselves ill to the medical community, significant psychological sequelae have been rare. In this light, it is of interest to note that in Sweden, women too healthy to receive an abortion have had a higher incidence of subsequent emotional incapacitation than have those who were disturbed enough to obtain an abortion. It is also worthwhile to observe that the babies born to mothers who have been denied a therapeutic abortion have a worse developmental and social prognosis than do children in the population at large.

The present study, performed after enactment of liberalized legislation, has revealed some interesting findings. Although there has been slight bias, related to nonrigid priorities, the program has primarily served the area normally encompassed by the Medical Center. Patients have relatively closely reflected the community's religious and racial structure. Catholic women have obtained abortions in spite of church edicts. Contrary to a great many expectations, nonwhites have availed themselves of the procedure in increasing numbers. A higher proportion of young and unmarried patients have received care than is usually reported. However, prior figures in the United States may have been influenced by the more mobile and affluent married women's greater ability to obtain an illegal or therapeutic abortion; similarly, Eastern European and Soviet Union statutes have preferentially encouraged abortion among older married women with children. British data, since the 1968 legislation, have revealed trends similar to those found in the present study.

The contraceptive information would appear to be of interest. As expected, many women have neglected or improperly used contraception. For considerable numbers, however, knowledge has been absent or contraception has failed. It must be remembered that contraception is not foolproof. It must also be remembered that more sex education and contraceptive availability is needed. Again contrary to many expectations, abortion has not been seen by the patients as a preferred or desired form of contraception. It has increased their desire for effective contraception. Such experience is similar to that reported from other countries.

The psychological data is somewhat similar to that reported under other relatively favorable circumstances. Some minor negative feelings have been present, but few women have felt strong guilt, unhappiness, or self-anger; and few have been objectively distressed. Although many have physically feared the procedure, and although a considerable number would have preferred to bear the child if possible, given the existent social and economic circumstances, the predominant moods have been relief and happiness. Physical relief has also been apparent to the staff. It may be anticipated that, if trends from other studies are mirrored here, the few negative feelings noted will diminish as distance from the procedure increases. It may also be anticipated that, as time passes, with greater community and professional acceptance of the procedure, the incidence of negative patient feelings will become even lower.

The correlational data is also consistent with logical expectations and seems worthy of note. Catholic patients have felt somewhat more guilty and have had somewhat more difficulty both in making the decision and in experiencing the procedure; however, even among this group, for whom the social taboo has been strongest, negative feelings have been minimal. Non-Catholic, older, better educated, and married women have utilized more contraception in the past. Single, young, and less educated women have greater desire for children in the future. Catholic and married women would have been less likely to obtain an abortion if the procedure were still illegal. As might be anticipated, among the small number of patients who have experienced such reactions, guilt over abortion, difficulty in decision making, difficulty with the procedure, fear of the procedure, desire for future children, and diminished likelihood of obtaining an abortion if the procedure were illegal have all been related. The data would appear to be of potential importance in thinking through and planning the types and quality of services needed for optimal patient care. However, for perspective, it should again be emphasized that all of the strong negative feelings have occurred relatively infrequently among all groups of patients.

Conclusion

Literature from diverse sources in this country and abroad has indicated that abortion is accompanied by few objective psychological sequelae. The present study is consistent with this overall finding. Relevant patients,

394 regardless of religion or race, have availed themselves of meaningful services. Relief and happiness have been the predominant moods. Convictions about the need for future contraception have been great. Among Catholics, guilt and difficulty with the decision and the procedure have occurred somewhat more frequently; and in general, when present, guilt, fear, and difficulty with the decision and the procedure have been interrelated. However, it is emphasized that negative feelings have been uncommon, occurring in a small percentage of the patients served.

Perhaps one further point should be noted. More studies are needed in this important area, and they should be as objective as possible. But studies should avoid the pitfall that has been all too common in the past—that of applying data to situations for which it is not totally appropriate. Earlier studies, in particular, claimed grave psychological sequelae, and although there was usually little objective substantiation to the conclusions, the opinions were utilized in arguments related to legislative policy. More objective studies, including the present one, have consistently found relatively few psychological sequelae to abortion. However, regardless of the outcome of present or future studies, the women's right to self-control should not be obscured. As is true in other areas, knowledge is desirable, and if there are related or unrelated psychological symptoms, the data should be utilized in an attempt to offer additional, and better, preventative and therapeutic services. Increased information should be used to help the relevant individuals and not to abridge their rights.

References

1. Bolter, S. 1962. The psychiatrist's role in therapeutic abortion: The unwitting accomplice. *Amer. J. Psychiat.* 119:312–16.
2. Brekke, B. 1958. Abortion in the United States. Harper & Row-Hoeber, Inc., New York.
3. Clark, M. et al. 1968. Sequels of unwanted pregnancy. *Lancet* 2:501–03.
4. Clemmesen, C. 1956. State of legal abortion in Denmark. *Amer. J. Psychiat.* 112:662–63.
5. David, H. 1970. Family Planning and Abortion in the Socialist Countries of Central and Eastern Europe. The Population Council, New York.
6. Diggory, P. 1969. Some experiences of therapeutic abortion. *Lancet* 1:873–75.
7. Diggory, P., Peel, J. and Potts, M. 1971. Preliminary assessment of the 1967 abortion act in practice. *Lancet* 1:287–291.
8. Droegemueller, W., Taylor, E. & Drose, V. 1969. The first year of experience in Colorado with the new abortion law. *Amer. J. Obstet. Gynec.* 103:694–702.
9. Ebaugh, F. & Heuser, K. 1947. Psychiatric aspects of therapeutic abortion. *Postgrad. Med.* 2:325–32.
10. Ekblad, M. 1954. Induced abortion on psychiatric grounds: a followup study of 479 women. *Acta Psychiatrica et Neurologica Scand.*, Suppl. 96–100:1–238.
11. Field, M. 1956. The re-legalization of abortion in Soviet Russia. *New Eng. J. Med.* 255:421–27.

12. Forssman, H. & Thuwe, I. 1966. One hundred and twenty children born after application for therapeutic abortion refused. *Acta Psychiat. Scand.* 42:71–88.
13. Galdston, I. 1958. Abortion in the United States. Harper & Row-Hoeber, Inc., New York.
14. Gebhard, P. et al. 1958. Pregnancy, Birth, and Abortion. Harper & Row, New York.
15. Geijerstam, A. 1958. Abortion in the United States. Harper & Row-Hoeber, Inc., New York.
16. Gillis, A. 1969. Follow-up after abortion. *Brit. Med. J.* 1:506.
17. Guttmacher, A. 1967. Abortion: yesterday, today, and tomorrow. *In* The Case for Legalized Abortion Now. Diablo Press, Berkeley, Calif.
18. Hardin, G. 1968. Abortion or compulsory pregnancy? *J. Marr. Fam.* 30:246–51.
19. Heller, A. & Whittington, M. 1968. The Colorado story: Denver General Hospital experience with the change in the law on therapeutic abortion. *Amer. J. Psychiat.* 125:121–28.
20. Höök K. 1963. Refused abortion. *Acta Psychiatrica Scand.*, Suppl. 168, 39:1–152.
21. Klinger, A. 1970. Demographic consequences of the legalization of induced abortion in Eastern Europe. *Int. J. Gynaec. Obstet.* 8:680–91.
22. Kolstad, P. 1957. Therapeutic abortion. *Acta Obstet. Gynec. Scand.* 36:Suppl. 6.
23. Koya, Y. 1954. A study of induced abortion in Japan and its significance. *Milbank Mem. Fund Quart.* 32:282–93.
24. Kretzschmar, R. & Norris, A. 1967. Psychiatric implications of therapeutic abortion. *Amer. J. Obstet. Gynec.* 198:368–73.
25. Kummer, J. 1963. Post-abortion psychiatric illness: a myth? *Amer. J. Psychiat.* 119:980–83.
26. Lader, L. 1966. Abortion. Beacon Press, Boston.
27. Lidz, T. 1958. Abortion in the United States, Harper & Row-Hoeber, Inc., New York.
28. Marder, L. 1970. Psychiatric experience with a liberalized therapeutic abortion law. *Amer. J. Psychiat.* 126(9):1230–36.
29. Mehlan, K. 1957–58. Yearbook of Obstetrics and Gynecology. Yearbook Medical Publishers, Inc., Chicago.
30. Mehlan, K. 1966. Combating illegal abortion in the socialist countries of Europe. *World Med. J.* 13:84–87.
31. Niswander, K. and Patterson, R. 1967. Psychologic reaction to therapeutic abortion. *Obstet. Gynec.* 29:702–706.
32. Peck, A. and Marcus, H. 1966. Psychiatric sequelae of therapeutic interruption of pregnancy. *J. Nerv. Mental Dis.* 143:417–25.
33. Pommerenke, W. 1955. Abortion in Japan. *Obstet. Gynec. Surv.* 10:145–75.
34. Potts, M. 1967. Legal abortion in Eastern Europe. *Eugen. Rev.* 59:232–50.
35. Rosen, H., ed. 1954. Therapeutic Abortion. Julian Press, New York.
36. Rosen, H., ed. 1967. Abortion in America. Beacon Press, Boston.
37. Schwartz, R. A. 1968. Psychiatry and the abortion laws: an overview. *Comprehensive Psychiat.* 9:99–117.
38. Simon, N. & Senturia, A. 1966. Psychiatric sequelae of abortion. *Arch. Gen. Psychiat.* 15:378–89.
39. Sloane, B. 1969. The unwanted pregnancy. *New Eng. J. Med.* 280:1206–13.
40. Walter, G. 1970. Psychologic and emotional consequences of elective abortion: a review. *Obstet. Gynec.* 36:482–91.
41. White, R. 1966. Induced abortions: A survey of their psychiatric implications, complications, and indications. *Texas Rep. Biol. Med.* 24:531–57.
42. Whittington, H. 1970. Evaluation of therapeutic abortion as an element of preventive psychiatry. *Amer. J. Psychiat.* 126(9):1224–29.
43. Wilson, D. 1954. The Abortion Problem in the General Hospital. Julian Press, New York.

Yes

Women's Responses to Abortion: Implications for Post-Abortion Support Groups

KAREN M. LODL, ANN McGETTIGAN, AND
JANETTE BUCY

For many years the decision to have an abortion was between a woman, her psychiatrist, or her illegal abortionist (Pariser, Dixon, & Thatcher, 1978). The decision was made in a context of deviance, criminality, and pathology. Early research based on limited clinical psychiatric impressions described abortion as awful trauma with serious and devastating results for the women involved. Tainted by ideological and value judgments against abortion, most of these early pre-1960 studies were also methodologically deficient, with inadequate samples and poor measurement technology, and were characterized by a plethora of ill-defined psychiatric labels (David, 1978; Figa-Talamanca, 1981; Illsley & Hall, 1978; Zimmerman, 1981).

Liberalization of attitudes and laws restricting abortion in the late sixties and early seventies in Canada, the United States, and Europe resulted in better-designed, more objective research. In general, these studies have concluded that "there is a low incidence of adverse psychiatric sequelae following abortion and a high incidence of beneficial reactions" (Illsey & Hall, 1978, p. 21). Ideological lines, however, continue to be drawn, and this research has been criticized by abortion opponents because of poor follow-up and bias (Hilgers, Horna & Mall, 1981; Mall & Watts, 1979). Although at present the evidence is against the theory of abortion as trauma (Gold, Berger & Andres, 1979; Greenglass, 1976), disagreement still exists in lay and professional sectors over the degree to which women's lives can be disrupted by abortion. Zimmerman (1977) comments on the polarization of this issue: "Perhaps because the 'abortion as crisis' view has been frequently aligned with the anti-abortion movement, and the 'abortion as

"Women's Responses to Abortion: Implications for Post-Abortion Support Groups" by Karen M. Lodl, Ann McGettigan, and Janette Bucy, *Journal of Social Work and Human Sexuality*, 1984–85, 3 (2/3), 119–32. Copyright © 1984–85 by The Haworth Press, Inc. Reprinted by permission.

Ms. Lodl is former President and Education Coordinator, Calgary Birth Control Association, Calgary, Alberta; Ms. McGettigan is Coordinator, YMCA, University of Washington Abortion Birth Control Referral Service, Seattle, Washington; and Ms. Bucy is a counseling psychologist in private practice, Seattle, Washington.

harmless' view has been used by those who favor abortion, this disagreement has tended to be seen as an either/or issue" (p. 3).

This polarization has presented a dilemma for pregnancy and abortion
counselors and referral agencies. Abortion counseling as a field has its roots
in the women's health movement of the late 1960s. Espousing a feminist,
pro-choice perspective, counselors have frequently functioned as advocates
negotiating with the medical system on behalf of their clients as well as
activists in the pro-choice movement. There is a reluctance to call attention
to negative consequences of abortion for fear of being seen as providing
support to anti-abortion and pronatalist pressure groups. The dilemma for
feminist-oriented counseling services lies in the responsibility to provide
preventive counseling predicated on potential stresses without being able
to acknowledge the role such stress might play subsequently in a woman's
life. The working assumption has been that pre-abortion counseling will
minimize this stress (Addelson, 1973; Bracken, 1977; Brashear, 1973; Urman & Meginnis, 1980).

Consequently, the topic of post-abortion counseling has been treated in
a defensive or minimizing manner by service-providers. In practice, abortion counseling agencies are usually limited to short-term crisis intervention (Baker, 1981; Beresford, 1977). Women who do present problems
resolving their abortion experiences may be perceived as having life problems beyond the skills of counselors trained in crisis intervention and are
frequently referred to long-term professional counseling. As a result of this
process, some abortion counselors may have little experience working with
women with post-abortion concerns and may thus feel unable to deal with
the issue except as suspected psychopathology. Women may then be left
feeling abandoned by their counselors and isolated from other women
experiencing similar difficulties (Francke, 1978). This combination of
denial and referral risks discouraging women from revealing their post-
abortion feelings or labeling women with difficulties as deviant and in need
of psychotherapy. Carter (1982) writes poignantly of her own experience of
isolation:

I hadn't heard of anyone who had written about abortion, and didn't know of
anyone who verbally discussed it openly. . . . This information vacuum not only
made me feel alone, but also "weird and sick" for feeling upset. I believed all of the
pro-choice arguments that said abortions are not severely stressful for most wom-
en. "If they were difficult." I reasoned, "somebody would have written about them
already." So I was not only upset about my abortion, but upset about being upset!
(p. 2)[1]

_____

1. From *Getting Beyond An Abortion* (p. 2) by D. L. Carter, 1982. Copyright 1982 by Diana L. Carter.
Quoted by permission.

398   Other professionals have expressed concern about a tendency to minimize post-abortion reactions:

> In my opinion, the woman is entitled to her feelings of depression and loss and as psychiatrists and physicians we need to be sensitive to the ambivalent feelings in reaction to the loss rather than denying the psychological significance of the abortion. (Cherazi, 1979, p. 287)

After more than fifteen years' experience with legalized abortion, family planning and abortion counseling agencies are beginning to reexamine the concept of providing post-abortion services as part of an overall attention to follow-up needs. These concerns are partly a result of the maturing of the pro-choice movement and an increased willingness to look at contentious issues, and partly a factor of the growing evolution of abortion counseling from grassroots activism to the status of a mainstream service area.

Review of the Literature

Consistent with these concerns, themes emphasizing the social and psychological situations and adjustment processes experienced by women undergoing abortion have emerged in the research literature over the past several years. Abortion has been shown to be essentially a positive procedure whose relative negative consequences are mild and self-limiting. For some women, however, abortion can be a stressful and emotionally difficult experience. The proportion of women who experience varying degrees of post-abortion stress ranges from less than 10 percent for possible psychiatric sequelae to 50 percent for feelings of unhappiness or troubled thoughts. The sources of emotional stress have been attributed to ambivalence over the pregnancy or abortion, lack of positive support from significant others, and inadequate coping skills (Adler, 1975; Belsey, Greer, Lal, Lewis & Beard, 1977; Bracken, Klerman & Bracken, 1978; Freeman, 1977; Lask, 1975; Moseley, Follingstad, Harley & Heckel, 1981; Payne, Kravitz, Notman & Anderson, 1976; Shusterman, 1979; Zimmerman, 1977, 1981). All of these factors are informed by a social and political milieu that identifies abortion as a deviant act (Adler, 1975). Illsley and Hall (1978) have commented: "Guilt about abortion has been, and in most societies continues to be, deliberately induced as part of a traditional system of social control. In such circumstances, it is superfluous to ask whether patients experience guilt—it is axiomatic that they will" (p. 12).

Two types of post-abortion stress have been identified in the literature:

socially based emotions that reflect the social stigma and norm violation associated with unwanted pregnancy and abortion; and internally based emotions associated with the abortion experienced as personal loss (Adler, 1975). Socially based emotions include guilt, shame, and fear of disapproval. Younger women, single women, and churchgoing women appear to be most vulnerable to these stresses. Often the guilt experienced by these women is due more to the circumstances surrounding their pregnancies and sexual activity than to the abortion itself:

The woman who had had in her previous life style a rule-oriented and rigid value system and who then because of error in judgment becomes pregnant, is a likely candidate for post-abortion guilt. . . . These women are faced with the situation that they have become what they formerly deplored (Brashear, 1973, p. 434)

Previous negative attitudes toward abortion have been indicated as a risk factor (Adler, 1975; Bogen, 1973; Payne et al., 1976). Many women, however, find that their views on abortion are more positive after having had an abortion themselves (Snegroff & Leff, 1983). How one moves from being a woman "who would never have an abortion" to one who has made that decision depends on the woman's coping skills and her ability to adjust her self-concept in a positive way. Many women are able to negotiate this transition successfully in order to minimize dissonance (Blackburne-Stover, Belenky & Gilligan, 1982; Snegroff & Leff, 1983). An inability to negotiate this change, however, can result in residual guilt and lowered self-esteem (Brashear, 1973), associated with post-abortion depression (Freeman, 1976; Gould, 1980).

Conservative views toward abortion and negative abortion outcomes have been associated with religion. Osofsky and Osofsky (1972) found that women who identified themselves as Catholic experienced more post-abortion stress. Bogen (1974), however, found that negative outcomes were associated more with church attendance than church affiliation. It can probably be safely concluded that while religious affiliation alone may not predict abortion outcomes, the degree of religiosity may reflect other social issues or values that would confound abortion outcomes. Examples would be extent of social support for her decision, ambivalence, religious views on the value of life, and sexual guilt.

Issues related to women's socially approved roles are another source of stress. Important values such as motherhood and the value of life may be sacrificed in order to attain or sustain other beliefs or achievements such as career, self-determination, and independence. Smetana (1982) has described women's thinking as clustering around abortion as a moral issue of life, or a personal issue of autonomy and control over one's body. How a woman resolves these issues can determine the degree of satisfaction she feels with her decision.

Generalizations about the gender-role orientation of women who choose to abort are difficult to make. A woman's judgments about gender-role orientation and self-concept can combine both externally based factors relating to prescribed social roles and internally based factors relating to her own experiences and the personal meanings given to these roles. Rosen and Martindale (1980) found a moderate correlation between acceptance of traditional roles and conflict over the abortion decision. Gold, Berger, and Andres (1979) found that attitudes opposed to sex-role egalitarianism, contraception, abortion, and the expression of sexuality were associated with relatively poor adjustment after an abortion.

Freeman (1977) reported that most women in her sample accepted traditional concepts of women's roles and also displayed high self-esteem. Those groups of women, however, whose personality attributes were described as dependent, valuing emotional-expressive characteristics, and having low self-esteem had the highest incidence of post-abortion depression. These were also women who had most wanted to be pregnant. These women reported that their abortions had been difficult, but they had learned from the experience. Freeman (1977) described this change as part of the personal-growth aspect of the pregnancy-abortion crisis: "She begins to know about herself, who she is, and how she affects her world, as differentiated from social definitions of what she ought to be" (p. 510).

Alter (1984) also found a relationship between self-concept, sex-role orientation, and post-abortion adjustment. She reported that both highly androgynous women, as measured by the Bem scales, and women whose self-perceptions were similar to their perceptions of career women were more likely to have a positive short-term abortion outcome. Women who identified as homemakers also had a positive outcome, but only if they did not differentiate between the roles of career and homemaker. Incongruence between a woman's self-image and her image of a career woman predicted negative abortion outcomes.

Regret, anxiety, depression, doubt and anger can result from a woman's personal sense of loss associated with the pregnancy and abortion (Adler, 1975). Whitlock (1978) referred to this response as existential guilt "experienced in relation to one's own reality or personal meanings and values specifically including those promises and commitments to oneself that one has failed to fulfill" (p. 149).

Reports of grief-related depression tend to come from small clinical samples and to be psychodynamically oriented. Cavenar, Maltbie, and

Sullivan (1978) reported grief reactions experienced on the anniversary date of the abortion or the expected date of delivery. Often these reactions had their roots in unresolved grief from other deaths or losses. Burkle (1977), Gould (1980), and Horowitz (1978) have also described the mourning process as a developmental task of particular importance for adolescents after an abortion. Kumar and Robson (1978) described patients for whom unresolved mourning for the lost fetus became a problem during a subsequent wanted pregnancy. It was suggested that unresolved feelings of grief, loss, and guilt may remain dormant long after an abortion until they are evoked by another pregnancy.

Abortion can generate a mourning process not directly connected with the death of the fetus. Potts (1971) commented that something is taken away even if it is desperately wanted: the pregnancy may be the result of a valued relationship, a final tie to a lover who has left, the end of a teenager's first romance. Carter (1982) suggested that "we can mourn the imperfections in our lives that made the abortion the wiser choice. . . . Mourning an abortion does not necessarily mean that we considered the fetus a living human being" (p. 3).[2]

Women who have difficult or troubled "passages" (Zimmerman, 1977) through abortion may be dealing with loss of several types: loss of the fetus, loss of self-concept based on their perceptions of abortion and of themselves as a certain kind of person, or the loss of a lifestyle or value they had thought was important before the pregnancy or abortion. These issues may be dealt with through repression or denial, or through grief and confusion; or a woman may enter a period of introspection whereby she is engaged in a process of reexamining her life and values and beginning to take control for the first time. Skowronski (1977) commented as follows: "Sometimes an abortion can bring needs and desires to the surface you never knew were there. These feelings may be related to childbearing or may be related to relationships with men, your own mother, your self-worth, or your own unfulfilled expectations" (p. 113).

For many women, the abortion is their first experience of making a decision of any consequence about their own lives. Such a decision can result in what Miller (1976) has called a paradoxical depression following a major step toward taking responsibility. Skowronski notes that "In this case, depression, then, is not a result of the abortion per se but a symptom of a larger growth cycle the woman has initiated" (1977, p. 114).

It is important to remember that the proportion of women experiencing

2. From *Getting Beyond an Abortion* (p. 3) by D. L. Carter, 1982. Copyright 1982 by Diana L. Carter. Quoted by permission.

the negative outcomes described here is small compared to the proportion of women for whom abortion is not extremely stressful. Many of these negative emotions also exist in tandem with relief and renewal. As society as a whole accepts the research confirming the generally positive effects of abortion, attention can be given to the meaning of abortion as a developmental event in a woman's life, as opposed to debating whether or not it is inherently traumatic. In the meantime, the damage to a woman's self-esteem that might result from anti-abortion pressures is still a concern. Even as abortion becomes normalized, women's responses may still be problematic. The impact of this expanded area of choice on women's lives remains an important issue:

> When birth control and abortion provide women with effective means for controlling their fertility, the dilemma of choice enters a central area of women's lives. Then relationships that have traditionally defined women's identities and framed their moral judgments no longer flow inevitably from their reproductive capacity but become matters of decision over which they have control. (Gilligan, 1982, p. 70)

Implications for Post-Abortion Counseling

The literature on post-abortion counseling has focused on two factors: the alleviation of symptoms of grief, depression, anger and guilt, and bringing the abortion experience to positive closure. The emphasis has been on increasing self-esteem and facilitating an appropriate mourning process (Brashear, 1973; Buckles, 1982; Gould, 1980).

Gould (1980) described a three-stage process of managing loss of self-esteem and delayed grief: (1) cognitive restructuring in order to identify and integrate factors that have been distruptive; (2) management of affect through awareness and verbalizing of feelings; and (3) identification and utilization of coping strategies and appropriate outside support. Her ultimate goal is to help the woman overcome her sense of helplessness and understand what it means to ultimately take responsibility for herself.

Buckles (1982) described a similar model of post-abortion therapy, focusing more on the mourning response. She suggested working cognitively to review options and decisions regarding the pregnancy and abortion; encouraging expression of feelings of loss and anger; giving support and reassurance for the choice already made; and providing relevant relationship, contraceptive, and decision-making education. In addition, she advocated a gestalt approach to dealing with grief over the lost fetus in two stages: saying goodbye by expressing regrets, resentments, and appreciations; and then establishing some means of positive remembrance of the significant meaning that the fetus had for the woman.

The value of post-abortion counseling in the form of support groups has been cited by a number of authors as serving a number of purposes: to alleviate alienation and isolation (Brashear, 1974; Freeman, 1977, 1978); to reinforce coping mechanisms (Payne et al., 1976; Urman & Meginnis, 1980); and to facilitate the mourning process (Gould, 1980; Horowitz, 1978).

Surprisingly very little on post-abortion groups has been reported in the professional literature. This review found only two articles dealing specifically with the·topic (Bernstein & Tinkham, 1977; Burnell, Dworsky, & Harrington, 1972). Both articles were written in the early 1970s and described therapy groups run by psychiatrists in hospital settings. The emphasis in these groups was on nonjudgmental sharing of information and feelings. Burnell et al. (1972) report that for the women who attended their groups, the abortion had been a crisis that reactivated "conflicts about femininity, motherhood, self-esteem, self-control, and acceptance or rejection" (p. 136).

A Model for Post-Abortion Support Groups

Beginning in February 1984, post-abortion support groups have been offered by the University of Washington Y.W.C.A. Abortion Birth Control Referral Service in Seattle, Washington. Led by the Seattle-based authors, the closed groups of two to eight women meet for two hours a week for six weeks. Plans for the group developed out of the leaders' observation that women who came to the service requesting a second abortion had often not dealt with feelings and issues from the first.

The approach of the groups has been to alleviate stress related to the abortion and to effect changes in problematic ideas and feelings about the abortion. Goals that have emerged out of the issues discussed by the groups include providing information about the grieving process, understanding the various types of loss that may be represented by the abortion, assessing values and life goals, and experiencing support from other women by sharing differences and commonalities. An important function of the groups has been the exploration of feelings associated with the abortion: reaching an awareness, understanding, and eventual acceptance of present feelings, and moving from negative feelings to beginning positive feelings about the abortion. Some women have shown a need to forgive themselves and to balance self-punishing feelings and self-loving feelings. The empha-

404 sis has been on accepting the various ambivalent feelings, understanding these, and working hard toward a positive self-image.

The therapeutic process has included listening for issues, identifying those issues and using various interventions to facilitate individual expression of feelings. These interventions might include general discussion, empty-chair role plays, simple art therapy and psychodrama techniques. A tentative topic outline has been developed that functions to stimulate issues rather than structure the groups into a particular sequence:

Session 1: Introduction, Education, and Information. Discussion focuses on dispelling myths and misinformation about abortion procedures and consequences of this choice. Introduction of the grieving process as a model for the group to use in exploring feelings.

Session 2: Relationship Concerns. Focus is on how the abortion affects women's relationships with others and self. Discussion of how the abortion decision affects participants as women, especially their sexuality.

Session 3: Religious-Moral Concerns. Discussion of how abortion affects one's religious, spiritual or moral beliefs. Fears or concerns about loss of faith, rejection, or alienation due to choice of abortion.

Session 4: If Only I Had . . . Discussion of some of the reasons participants had for choosing abortion, focus on positive aspects of the decision, and come to a resolution about these reasons.

Session 5: What Now? Discussion of future directions to take, how participants might like to feel about the abortion in the future, how the experience can eventually feel over and past.

Session 6: Closure. Final evaluation of the grieving process and each member's place in that process. Emphasis on self-healing and continued self-appreciation. Evaluation of the group by the group members.

Thus far, three six-week groups have been conducted. The women who attended the groups ranged in age from 17 to 35 years. No clear demographic profile emerges with respect to marital status, number of children, religious background, socioeconomic status, or race. All the participants were heterosexual. The length of time since the abortion ranged from thirteen years to three weeks.

Women came to the groups because they felt alone with their decision, needed to talk about the decision in a safe place, were depressed, felt "stuck" and unable to resolve the abortion, needed affirmation that their feelings were normal, or desired to let go of the experience and achieve final closure. The participants seemed to show marked relief as they began sharing their stories and feelings. Participating in the groups helped the women to validate ambivalent feelings and reduced their sense of isolation.

An important outcome was that participants were able to see the variety of *405* women who have had abortions and experienced ambivalence: women· with different religious and other values; women with different lifestyles, some with partners and others alone; and women from all socioeconomic backgrounds.

Another outcome was that participating in a women's group was, for some members, a step toward individual empowerment. For those who felt angry, out of control, or isolated, the group provided a context for dealing with these feelings and finding ways to take control. Many women came to see the abortion as a major decision they had made. By putting themselves first, a step had been taken toward raising their consciousness about women's societal status, women's assessment of themselves with respect to self-worth, and the nature of the decision-making process with respect to childbearing.

A further issue that surfaced in each group was negativism toward men. In many cases the women felt intense frustration with their partners for a lack of empathy in relation to the abortion. Some felt that their own strong feelings related to the abortion had ended the relationship. In some cases they were able to identify the abortion as a catalyst for pointing out already existing emotional or communication deficits within the relationship. On the other hand, there were some women who found that their relationships had been strengthened by the sharing of emotions related to a difficult choice.

While each of the three groups has identified certain themes, each group has also expanded the definition of what post-abortion intervention encompasses. At this point each group offers new data which will help define the nature of post-abortion counseling.

Summary and Conclusions

The literature on the psychosocial consequences of abortion reveals that whereas for the majority of women abortion can be a positive, growth-producing experience, for a smaller group of women it can be emotionally stressful. For most women these negative affective responses are short-term and self-limiting. A substantial anecdotal literature describing post-abortion trauma focuses on the death of the fetus and violation of norms regarding motherhood and femininity.

There is some evidence that women experiencing emotional difficulty after an abortion would benefit from post-abortion counseling, especially

406 in the form of post-abortion support groups. The rationale for such a group is that women experiencing post-abortion conflict are likely to feel alone in trying to resolve it.

A major concern with the provision of post-abortion groups is that of outreach to the client population. For women who have cast a cloak of secrecy over their abortions, it may be difficult to come forward with their experiences. Often negative feelings are confusing because they can coexist with strong positive feelings. A woman may not want to lend support to the anti-abortion movement by revealing negative reactions, or she may feel alone and isolated because she considers herself to be the "only one." Public education regarding the value of post-abortion groups is an important first step to overcoming these barriers.

From a feminist perspective, a post-abortion group as described here provides not only a safe place for working through personal reactions to the abortion, but also a space in which to understand individual responses to abortion in a broader societal context. A norm of nonjudgmental acceptance of abortion as an individual choice empowers the group participants to examine both internal and external assaults on their self-esteem, freeing each woman to find and resolve the personal meanings the abortion has for her.

It would be difficult in such a group to avoid examination of participants' negative emotions in relation to social structural inequities such as women's traditional responsibility for contraception, decision-making about abortion by the medical profession, and lack of access to abortion facilities. Clearly women have not had a dominant role in developing services related to abortion, and these services are typically not designed to facilitate a woman's belief in herself as a worthwhile person, capable of making a decision. Post-abortion counseling offers women an opportunity to take charge of one facet of the abortion, and if desired, to advocate with other women about the entire abortion process.

References

Addelson,F. (1975). Induced abortion: Source of guilt or growth? *American Journal of Orthopsychiatry, 43,* 815–23.

Adler, N. F. (1975). Emotional responses of women following therapeutic abortion. *American Journal of Orthopsychiatry, 43,* 446–545.

Alter, R. C. (1984). Abortion outcome as a function of sex-role identification. *Psychology of Women Quarterly, 8*(3), 211–33.

Baker, A. (1981). *Training manual for problem pregnancy counseling.* (Available from The Hope Clinic for Women Ltd., 1602-21st Street, Granite City, Illinois, 62040).

Belsey, E. M., Greer, H. S., Lal, S., Lewis, S. C., Beard, R. W. (1977). Predictive factors in 407
emotional response to abortion: King's termination study-IV. *Social Science Medicine*,
11(2), 71–82.
Beresford, T. (1977). *Short-term relationship counseling. A self-instructional manual for use
in family planning clinics*. Baltimore: Planned Parenthood of Maryland.
Bernstein, N. R., & Tinkham, C. B. (1977). Group therapy following abortion. In R.
Kalmar (Ed.). *Abortion: The emotional implications* (pp. 108–124). Dubuque: Ken-
dall/Hunt Publishing Company.
Blackburne-Stover, G., Belenky, M. E., & Gilligan, C. (1982). Moral development and
reconstructive memory: Recalling a decision to terminate an unplanned pregnancy.
Developmental Psychology, *18*(6), 862–70.
Bogen, I. (1974). Attitudes of women who have had abortions. *Journal of Sex Research*,
10(2), 97–109.
Bracken, M. B. (1977). Psychosomatic aspects of abortion: Implications for counseling. *The
Journal of Reproductive Medicine*, *19*, 265–72.
Bracken, M. B., Klerman, L. V., & Bracken, M. (1978). Coping with pregnancy resolution
among never-married women. *American Journal of Orthopsychiatry*, *43*, 320–33.
Brashear, D. B. (1973). Abortion counseling. *Family Coordinator*, *22*(4), 429–35.
Buckles, N. B. (1982). Abortion: A technique for working through grief. *Journal of the
American College Health Association*, *30*(4), 181–82.
Burkle, F. M. (1977). A developmental approach to post-abortion depression. *The Practi-
tioner*, *218*, 217–25.
Burnell, G. M., Dworsky, W. A., & Harrington, R. L. (1972). Post-abortion group therapy.
American Journal of Psychiatry, *129*, 134–37.
Carter, D. L. (1982). *Getting beyond an abortion*. (Available from Diana L. Carter, M. S.,
P. O. Box 2230, Glen Ellyn, Illinois 60137).
Cavenar, J., Maltbie, A., & Sullivan, J. (1978). Aftermath of abortion: Anniversary reaction
and abdominal pain. *Bulletin of the Menninger Clinic*, *42*, 433–38.
Cherazi, S. (1979). Psychological reaction to abortion. *Journal of the American Medical
Women's Association*, *34*, 287–88.
David, H. P. (1978). Psychosocial studies of abortion in the United States. In H. P. David,
H. L. Friedman, J. van der Tak, & M. J. Sevilla (Eds.). *Abortion in psychosocial
perspective* (pp. 77–118). New York: Springer Publishing Company.
Figa-Talamanca, I. (1981). Abortion and mental health. In J. E. Hodgson (Ed.). *Abortion
and sterilization* (pp. 181–208). New York: Academic Press.
Francke, L. B. (1978). *The ambivalence of abortion*. New York: Random House.
Freeman, E. W. (1977). Influence of personality attributes on abortion experiences. *Ameri-
can Journal of Orthopsychiatry*, *47*: 503–13.
Freeman, E. W. (1978). Abortion: Subjective attitudes and feelings. *Family Planning Per-
spectives*, *10*, 150–55.
Gilligan, C. (1982). *In a different voice*. Cambridge, Massachusetts: Harvard University
Press.
Gold, D., Berger, C., Andres, D. (1979). *The abortion choice: Psychological determinants and
consequences*. Montreal: Concordia University. Department of Psychology.
Gould, N. B. (1980). Postabortion depressive reactions in college women. *American College
Health Association*, *28*, 316–21.
Greenglass, E. (1976). *After abortion*. Don Mills: Longman Canada Limited.
Hilgers, T., Horna, D., & Mall, D. (Eds.). (1981). *New perspectives of human abortion*.
Frederick, Maryland: University Publications of America.
Horowitz, M. H. (1978). Adolescent mourning reactions to infant and fetal loss. *Social
Casework*, *59*, 551–59.
Illsley, R., & Hall, M. (1978). Psychosocial research in abortion: Selected issues. In H. P.
David et al. (Ed.). *Abortion in psychosocial perspective* (pp. 11–34). New York: Springer.

408   Kumar, R., & Robson, K. (1978). Previous induced abortion and antenatal depression in primiparae. *Psychological Medicine, 8,* 711–15.

Lask, B. (1975). Short term psychiatric sequelae to therapeutic termination of pregnancy. *British Journal of Psychiatry, 126,* 173–77.

Mall, D., & Watts, W. F. (Eds.). (1979). *The psychological aspects of abortion.* Washington, D.C.: University Publications of America, Inc.

Miller, J. B. (1976). *Toward a new psychology of women.* Boston: Beacon Press.

Moseley, D. T., Follingstad, D. R., Harley, H., Heckel, R. V. (1981). Psychological factors that predict reaction to abortion. *Journal of Clinical Psychology, 37*(2), 276–79.

Osofsky, J. D., & Osofsky, J. J. (1972). The psychological reactions of patients to legalized abortion. *American Journal of Orthopsychiatry, 42,* 48–60.

Pariser, D., Dixon, K., Thatcher, K. (1978). The psychiatric abortion consultation. *The Journal of Reproductive Medicine, 21*(3), 171–76.

Payne, E. C., Kravitz, A. R., Notman, M. T. & Anderson, J. V. (1976). Outcome following therapeutic abortion. *Archives of General Psychiatry, 33*(6), 725–33.

Potts, L. (1971). Counseling women with unwanted pregnancies. In F. Haselkorn (Ed.). *Family planning: A source book and case material for social work education* (pp. 249–266). New York: Council on Social Work Education.

Rosen, R. H., & Martindale, L. J. (1980). Abortion as "deviance," Traditional female roles vs. the feminist perspective. *Social Psychiatry, 15,* 103–08.

Shusterman, L. (1979). Predicting the psychological consequences of abortion. *Social Science and Medicine, 13A,* 683–89.

Skowronski, M. (1977). *Abortion and alternatives.* Millbrae, California: Les Femmes Publishing.

Smetana, J. C. (1982). *Concepts of self and morality: Women's reasoning about abortion.* New York: Praeger.

Snegroff, S., & Leff, I. (1983). Objective measurement of women's post-abortion attitudes and the relationship of selected variables to those attitudes. *Journal of Sex Education and Therapy, 8*(1), 42–49.

Urman, J., & Meginnis, S. K. (1980). The process of problem pregnancy counseling. *Journal of the American College Health Association, 28,* 308–15.

Whitlock, G. E. (1978). *Understanding and coping with real-life crisis.* Monterey, California: Brooks/Cole Publishing Company.

Zimmerman, M. K. (1977). *Passage through abortion. The personal and social reality of women's experiences.* New York: Praeger Publishers.

Zimmerman, M. K. (1981). Psychosocial and emotional consequences of elective abortion. A literature review. In P. Sachev (Ed.). *Abortion: Readings and research* (pp. 63–75). Toronto, Butterworths.

Is Lesbianism a Sickness?

One of the most dramatic changes in psychology and psychiatry in recent years has been the movement away from viewing lesbianism as deviant behavior. Until mid-century, the traditional approach was to treat lesbianism as a disorder that could be "cured" through conversion to heterosexuality.

Freudian theory saw lesbianism as a neurotic defense mechanism arising out of a failure to resolve the oedipal complex. Learning theorists, on the other hand, viewed conditioning and socialization as an explanation for lesbianism. There is, in fact, no consensus on the causes of either female or male homosexuality. As Janet Hyde (1985) notes, "perhaps the failure . . . to uncover a consistent single 'cause' of lesbianism is a result of the fact that there is no single 'cause' just as there is no single 'lesbian personality' " (p. 314).

The shift in the attitude toward homosexuality may have begun with the publication of the research of Kinsey and his associates (Kinsey, Pomeroy, & Martin, 1948; Kinsey, Pomeroy, Martin, & Gebhard, 1953). Homosexuality, along with other behaviors thought to be abnormal, was shown by Kinsey to be fairly widespread. Breaking with past patterns of research, which focused on lesbians who were patients in psychotherapy, investigators began to study lesbians who were not in therapy. Reviews of this literature (Rosen, 1974; Mannion, 1981) indicated that the psychological adjustment of lesbians did not differ significantly from that of heterosexual women.

The changing view of homosexuality is underscored by the reversal of the American Psychiatric Association's position. The 1968 edition of the *Diagnostic and Statistical Manual* (DSM-II), the official list of psychiatric   *409*

410 diagnoses, classified homosexuality, along with disorders such as child molestation, as a "sexual deviance." Five years later, the Board of Trustees of the APA voted to remove "homosexuality per se" from its list of psychiatric disorders.

A new classification, "ego-dystonic homosexuality," was established in 1973 in order to categorize those homosexuals "who are either disturbed by, in conflict with, or wish to change their sexual orientation" (Davison, 1976). Charges that the substitute classification implied that there were a substantial number of disturbed homosexuals led the board to eliminate homosexuality completely from the official diagnostic nomenclature in 1986 (Landers, 1986; "Board Excludes," 1986).

Researchers during the past decade have concentrated on studying how lesbians function in love relationships at work and as parents. Similarly, many therapists have stopped trying to change lesbians' sexual preference and are instead helping them cope with the stresses of living in a homophobic world. A number of therapists who do a great deal of lesbian counseling believe that concealing one's lesbianism makes self-acceptance extremely difficult (Gartrell, 1984).

Nanette Gartrell discusses the special conflicts lesbians face and suggests that "coming out" is a way of resolving some of these problems. Charles Socarides demonstrates that not all therapists accept the 1973 decision of the American Psychiatric Association that homosexuality is not an "emotional disorder."

References

Board excludes new diagnoses from main DSM-III-R text. (1986, July 18.) *Psychiatric News*, *21* (14), pp. 1, 7.

Davison, G. C. (1976). Homosexuality: The ethical challenge. *Journal of Consulting and Clinical Psychology*, *44* (2), 157–62.

Gartrell, N. (1984). Issues in the psychotherapy of lesbians. In P. Rieker & P. Carmen (Eds.), *The gender gap in psychotherapy: Social realities and psychological processes*. New York: Plenum Press.

Hyde, J. S. (1985). *Half the human experience: The psychology of women* (3rd ed.). Lexington, Mass: D. C. Heath.

Kinsey, A. C., Pomeroy, W. B., & Martin, C. E. (1948). *Sexual behavior in the human male*. Philadelphia: Saunders.

Kinsey, A. C., Pomeroy, W. B., Martin, C. E., & Gebhard, P. H. (1953). *Sexual behavior in the human female*. Philadelphia: Saunders.

Landers, S. (1986, August). Semi-final DSM vote both delights, dismays. *APA Monitor*, p. 15.

Mannion, K. (1981). Psychology and the lesbian: A critical view of the research. In S. Cox (Ed.), *Female psychology: The emerging self*, (2nd ed.) (pp. 256–74). New York: St. Martin's Press.

Rosen, D. H. (1974). *Lesbianism: A study of female homosexuality.* Springfield, Ill.: Charles *411*
C. Thomas.

Additional Reading

Altman, D. (1982). *The homosexualization of America.* New York: St. Martin's Press.
Faderman, L. (1985). The "new gay" lesbians. *Journal of Homosexuality, 10* (3/4), 85–97.
Gartrell, N. (1984). Combating homophobia in the psychotherapy of lesbians. *Women and Therapy, 3* (1), 13–29.
Gartrell, N. (1982). Hormones and homosexuality. In C. Nadelson & D. Marcott (Eds.), *Homosexuality as a social issue.* Beverly Hills: Sage Publications.
Gartrell, N. (1981). Reply by Nanette Gartrell, M.D. *American Journal of Psychotherapy, 35* (4), 515–16.
Hancock, K. (1986). Homophobia. *Lesbian and gay issues in psychology.* Washington, D.C.: American Psychological Association.
Harek, G. (1984). Beyond "homophobia": A social psychological perspective on attitudes toward lesbians and gay men. *Journal of Homosexuality, 10,* 1–21.
Hidalgo, H., Peterson, T., & Woodman, N. J. (Eds.) (1985). *Lesbian and gay issues: A resource manual for social workers.* New York: Springer.
Peplau, L. A., & Amaro, H. (1982). Understanding lesbian relationships. In W. Paul, J. D. Weinrich, J. D. Gonsiorek, & M. E. Hotvedt (Eds.), *Homosexuality: Social psychological and biological issues* (pp. 233–47), Beverly Hills, Calif.: Sage.
Peplau, L. A., Padesky, C., & Hamilton, M. (1982). Satisfaction in lesbian relationships. *Journal of Homosexuality, 8,* 23–35.
Rich, A. (1980). Compulsory heterosexuality and lesbian existence. *Signs: Journal of Women in Culture and Society, 5,* 631–60.
Riddle, D. I. & Sang, G. (1979). Psychotherapy with lesbians. *Journal of Social Issues, 34* (3), 84–100.
Socarides, C. W. (1962). Theoretical and clinical aspects of overt female homosexuality. *Journal of the American Psychoanalytic Association, 10* (3), 579–92.
Socarides, C. W. (1975). *Beyond sexual freedom.* New York: Quadrangle/New York Times Book Co.
Woodman, N. J., & Lenna, H. R. (1980). Counseling with gay men and women: A guide for facilitating positive life-styles. San Francisco: Jossey-Bass.

The Lesbian as a "Single" Woman

NANETTE GARTRELL

Historically, lesbianism has been considered evil, sinful, illegal, perverted, deviant, and antisocial. Lesbians were burned as witches during the Middle Ages and sentenced to death in concentration camps during World War II, simply because of their sexual orientation. More recently, lesbians have been subjected to police harassment, blackmail attempts, employment discrimination, and child custody suits because of social prejudice against them.[1,2] In view of this long history of discrimination, it is not surprising that some lesbians have turned to psychiatrists for help in coping with a difficult environment.

For most of the earlier part of this century, psychiatrists viewed lesbianism as a developmental disorder, and conversion to heterosexuality was considered the primary psychotherapeutic goal. In his first detailed case study of a lesbian, "The Psychoanalysis of a Case of Female Homosexuality," Freud hypothesized that mother fixation, penis envy, and maternal indifference contributed to the development of her sexual orientation. Although Freud stated that this patient was "not in any way ill," he did describe her lesbianism as an "abnormality" which was caused by inadequate resolution of the Oedipus complex.[3] Deutsch subsequently proposed a more pathological view of lesbianism in her 1932 paper, "On Female Homosexuality." Her theories were based on the analyses of eleven lesbian patients. She defined lesbianism as a "perversion," which developed in a setting of sadistic mothering and inadequate fathering. She considered lesbianism to be the result of the renunciation of the father in conjunction with the transformation of rage toward the mother into libidinal relationships with other women.[4]

The psychopathological view of lesbianism proposed by Freud and

"The Lesbian as a 'Single' Woman" by Nanette Gartrell, *American Journal of Psychotherapy*, 1981, *35* (4), 502–09. Copyright © 1981 by the *American Journal of Psychotherapy*. Reprinted by permission.

Dr. Gartrell is a psychiatrist in private practice and an Assistant Professor of Psychiatry at the Harvard Medical School.

Deutsch underwent only minor modifications in the literature during the   *413*
next forty years. Caprio in 1954 described lesbianism as a narcissistic
"extension of autoeroticism."[5] Other theorists suggested that clitoral fixation, fear of men, fear of rejection, sexual abuse (including rape and
incest), and ambivalence toward both parents contributed to the development of lesbianism.[6–8] Clinical observations of lesbian patients, as reported in a survey of 150 psychoanalysts by Kaye et al. in 1967, were also
consistent with the "illness" model of lesbianism. Kaye concluded that
psychoanalysts in his study viewed lesbianism as a "massive adaptational
response to a crippling inhibition of normal heterosexual development."[9]

It is important to note that psychoanalytic theories about lesbianism
were based on clinical observations of lesbians who were undergoing psychiatric treatment and not on controlled studies of the general population.
When these theories began to be subjected to rigorous scientific scrutiny in
the early 1960s, their validity was seriously challenged. Armon examined
the Rorschach protocols of lesbians and heterosexual women and found no
differences in their overall level of maturity or psychological adjustment.[10]
Two independent investigators, Hopkins and Siegelman, compared lesbians with heterosexual women on the 16 Personality Factor Questionnaire. The lesbians in the Hopkins study showed no differences from the
heterosexual subjects in the neuroticism profile; in the Siegelman studies,
lesbians scored lower on total neuroticism and higher on both goal-direc-
tedness and self-acceptance than heterosexual women.[11–13] Although
Freedman found no differences in the overall adjustment of lesbians and
heterosexual women to whom he administered the Eysenck Personality
Inventory, he did report that lesbians scored higher on measures of job
stability, job satisfaction, and self-actualization than heterosexual wom-
en.[14] Similarly, lesbians in other studies have scored higher in self-confidence than comparable groups of heterosexual women.[15–16] Although it
would be beyond the scope of this paper to review all of the lesbian studies
of the past two decades, the data have clearly indicated that there are no
major differences between lesbians and heterosexual women in psychological adjustment.[17–22]

As American psychiatry has begun to move away from the "illness"
model of lesbianism, many psychiatrists are finding that they lack sufficient
training in understanding lesbianism as a viable alternative lifestyle. In fact,
relatively little has been written about the risks, stresses, and benefits of
being a lesbian in contemporary society. One issue which has received very
little attention in the literature concerns the psychological impact of marital
status on the life of the lesbian woman. Any woman who is not married is
automatically assumed to be single and heterosexual unless she makes her

414   sexual orientation known. It is important for psychiatrists to be aware of the unique conflict this assumption creates for the lesbian woman, since successful resolution of this conflict is essential for a healthy adaptation to a lesbian lifestyle.

Life in the Closet

Because of widespread discrimination against lesbians, the vast majority of the estimated ten million lesbians in the United States have chosen to keep their sexual orientation hidden, or to remain in the "closet." The closeted lesbian is a woman who feels that she is at risk of a major loss—her job, her home, her economic security, her family, her friends, or her children—if her sexual orientation is disclosed. As a result, the closeted lesbian is forced to lead a double life, constantly denying who she really is and whom she really loves.[23]

Life in the closet can be a very lonely and isolating experience. It is a very constrained life, because the closeted lesbian must constantly monitor her emotional responses in order to conceal her true feelings. During any expedition outside her home—even shopping in a supermarket—the closeted lesbian must be careful not to demonstrate too much affection toward her lover. The closeted lesbian invariably spends much of her time analyzing every social interaction to determine whether she has accidently provided clues about her sexual orientation.[24] She must also be very discriminating in her choice of close friends in order to insure confidentiality about her lifestyle. It is often very difficult for the closeted lesbian to maintain a positive self-image when she must conceal a major part of her life from the rest of the world.

Living a closeted existence involves more than simply being secretive about one's lesbianism. For the unmarried lesbian, being closeted also means that she must deal with constant assumptions that she is a single, heterosexual woman. She finds herself frequently confronted by the dilemma of having to turn down dates with men without giving them an honest explanation for her lack of interest. She often encounters the difficulty of having men experience her disinterest as a personal rejection by a woman whom they view as unattached. The closeted lesbian may also avoid social functions which are work-related, because as a "single" woman, she is encouraged to bring a male escort. She must then tolerate criticism from her colleagues for her seemingly antisocial behavior. And finally, the unmarried lesbian experiences a tremendous amount of pressure from her family to marry and bear children. Concealing her lesbianism from her family is often one of the most difficult problems a lesbian encounters. This is particularly true for the lesbian whose parents interpret her disinterest in marriage as a personal rejection. Parental disappointment about her "failure" to marry contributes to the public image of social inadequacy which the closeted lesbian inevitably maintains.

The difficulties associated with leading a double life make it necessary for some lesbians to seek psychiatric care. It is very important for psychiatrists who are treating closeted lesbians to be in touch with their own attitudes toward lesbianism so that personal biases do not interfere with patient care. Depression, anxiety, loneliness, and isolation in a closeted lesbian must be understood in terms of the social context in which she lives. In many cases, the social climate is so hostile toward lesbianism that psychotherapy can only be supportive for the lesbian patient. In any case, it is important for therapist and patient to explore the patient's environment for sources of interpersonal support which will not contribute to the patient's anxiety about being "found out."

Case 1

Ms. A. was a twenty-six-year-old black woman medical student who presented at the student health service because of depression about her medicine clerkship evaluation. She stated that her medicine resident had asked her out on several occasions, and that she had declined his invitations by explaining that she was already in a relationship. He began calling her at home, and he accused her of lying about being in a relationship because the only other person who ever answered the phone was a woman. At the end of the clerkship, he wrote very negative comments about her ability to relate to her instructors. His comments resulted in her receiving a "marginal pass" in medicine.

A. was involved in a lesbian relationship, but she did not want anyone in the medical school to know about it. She was applying for a gynecology residency, and she was concerned that prejudice against lesbians would prevent her from being selected for a good program. Her medicine evaluation was particularly upsetting to her because she had received "honors" in all her previous clerkships.

The short-term therapeutic intervention for A. consisted of helping her make a decision about filing a complaint in the Department of Medicine. A. informed her therapist that she would like to find other gay medical students who might have experienced similar difficulties in their clerkships. The therapist was able to provide information for A. about a group of gay medical students who had been meeting monthly at her school. Through this group, A. found another lesbian student who had encountered a

416 similar problem during her surgery clerkship. This student had been able to have her evaluation modified without disclosing any information about her lesbianism. With her help, A. was able to file a complaint which resulted in a modification of A.'s medicine evaluation. A. successfully presented her case in such a way that her sexual orientation was never an issue.

Coming Out

"Coming out" means that a lesbian will no longer be secretive about her sexual orientation and lifestyle. Coming out as a lesbian is a process of reintegrating one's life. Coming out implies that a lesbian has improved her self-image to the point that she will no longer allow herself to be mistaken as a "single" heterosexual woman. Coming out involves a highly personal set of choices about how a lesbian perceives herself, how she views her own sexuality, how she structures her life, and how she presents herself in public. Coming out is also a lifelong process in which the lesbian is working toward acceptance of her lesbianism by a resistant and sometimes hostile society.[23–24]

Coming out is political as well as a personal and social process. Lesbianism by its very existence conflicts with traditional role expectations in our society. In asserting her unwillingness to be dependent on men, the lesbian who is "out" represents a threat to traditional cultural assumptions about male supremacy. As such, coming out involves a willingness to combat social, personal, legal, and political discrimination against lesbian women. Because myths about lesbianism are perpetuated in American culture, coming out involves a political decision to have one's lifestyle open to public scrutiny as a means for changing public attitudes about lesbianism.

Coming out is generally viewed as an opportunity to develop more honest personal relationships. Improved communication with family and friends inevitably increases a lesbian's sense of self-confidence and self-worth. Because she no longer has to lie about her sexual orientation, the lesbian who is "out" can share the joyful and positive aspects of her life with those around her. She can also turn to her family and friends for support when she encounters difficulties because of her lesbianism.

Probably the most important benefit of coming out for a lesbian is the opportunity to share a sense of community with other lesbians. The lesbian subculture is a vast network of social, political, artistic, medical, psychotherapeutic, and legal organizations which offer a variety of services and entertainment to lesbians. The availability of an extensive lesbian community ensures that a lesbian who is "out" will no longer feel alienated in a generally hostile society.

The psychotherapeutic concerns of the lesbian who is considering coming out relate primarily to the personal, social, and occupational ramifications of being identified as a lesbian. Anxieties about potential employment discrimination, child custody suits, physical assault, and familial rejection are common concerns at this time. The psychotherapist must be capable of assisting the lesbian in making her own decision about whether the benefits of coming out exceed the difficulties of being open about her lifestyle. The therapist must also be willing to be available for court testimony if a woman encounters legal discrimination because of her lesbianism.

Case 2

Dr. B. was a thirty-year-old white woman intern who had spent two years in psychotherapy working on her decision to come out. She was in the process of applying for psychiatric residencies, and she felt uncomfortable about having to pretend that she was not involved in a significant relationship. She also anticipated difficulties in psychotherapy supervision during her residency if she were unable to be honest about her countertransference feelings toward patients. B. made a decision prior to her residency interviews that she would no longer lie about her personal life. She also decided that she had no desire to enroll in a residency program in which she would feel uncomfortable as a lesbian.

She was offered residency positions in all but one of the prestigious institutions to which she applied. In the residency program by which she was rejected, one of her interviewers was extremely uncomfortable about her lesbianism. He asked her if she was a lesbian because she had unsatisfactory relationships with men or because she secretly wanted to be a man. When she answered negatively to both questions, he asked her if her relationships with women consisted primarily of one-night stands. She replied that she had been involved in an eight-year monogamous relationship with another woman, but that she did not see how that related to her application for a residency position. He informed her that it was important for psychiatric residents to have a history of good object relationships, and that her lesbianism did not qualify her for admission into the program.

Despite this one negative encounter in her interviews, B.'s successful admission to several excellent programs made her confident that she had made the right decision to come out. She was able to enter a training

418 program in which she could not only be open about her personal life, but also educate her peers about the unique psychological conflicts which gay people experience.

Single Lesbians

A single lesbian is a woman who considers herself lesbian, but who is not currently involved in a lesbian relationship. A lesbian may be single for one of several reasons: (1) because she has not yet found a woman with whom she would like to establish a relationship; (2) because she has recently terminated a relationship; (3) because she has chosen for a variety of reasons not to be in a relationship; or (4) because her lover has recently died. How successfully a woman copes with life as a single lesbian will depend on her resources for personal and social support.

Relationships have historically been very important to lesbian women. Prior to the existence of a large lesbian subculture, lesbians had very little access to community support. Lesbians who had been abandoned by their families and excluded from religious worship relied heavily on their lovers for insulation from public discrimination. Lovers were viewed not only as sexual partners and intimate friends, but also as protectors from a generally hostile environment. Consequently, the dissolution of a lesbian relationship was associated with the loss of primary support.

The emergence of a lesbian community has allowed lesbians to develop support networks which extend far beyond their primary relationships. Although losing a relationship continues to be difficult, the availability of a variety of support groups and mental health organizations within the lesbian community has made the transition from being in a relationship to being single considerably less traumatic. Symptoms of unresolved grief, severe depression, and intractable loneliness as a result of losing a relationship are far more common among lesbians who live in rural areas of the country, where access to lesbian community services continues to be minimal.

Recent evidence suggests that lesbians demonstrate greater adaptive capacities after the loss of a relationship than some heterosexual women.[25] Presumably, since lesbians have learned to rely on themselves for economic and social support, they are much less likely to feel completely incapacitated after losing relationships than heterosexual women who have chosen more traditional roles. The financial hardships which divorced or widowed heterosexual women frequently encounter are also less common among lesbian women, because they are generally self-supporting.

A discussion of single lesbians would not be complete without some

consideration of lesbians who choose to remain single. These are women *419*
who enjoy the flexibility of not being confined to a primary relationship.
Single lesbians may seek nurturance and support from several close friends
or from a living collective, but they choose not to be involved in monogamous sexual or emotional relationships. Lesbians who are single by choice
find greater opportunities for personal growth in being able to explore
nontraditional relationships with other women.

Case 3

Dr. C. was a fifty-nine-year-old white woman English professor who
sought psychotherapy after the death of her lesbian lover of twenty years.
She lived in a small university town, where she had few opportunities to
meet or associate with other lesbians. In addition to feeling very sad about
her lover's death, C. felt hopeless about the possibility of ever meeting
another woman with whom she could share her life.

In therapy, C. was able to work through many issues related to the death
of her lover. At the end of three months, C. asked her therapist about the
possibility of joining a support group for older lesbians. The therapist was
able to locate such a group through the women's center in a large city
nearby. Through this group, C. developed several close friendships which
were able to sustain her through the difficult adjustment period after her
lover's death.

Summary

This paper has attempted to provide information about the unique conflicts which social definitions of the "single" woman create for the lesbian
woman. It has explored the stereotypes associated with being a single
woman which the closeted lesbian inevitably encounters. The risks and
benefits of rejecting the label "single woman" and publicly proclaiming
one's lesbianism have also been discussed. The process of coming out is
presented as a means of working through some of the conflicts created by
social discrimination against lesbians. It is important for psychiatrists to
understand the unique stresses of being a lesbian in contemporary society
in order to provide more effective mental health care.

References

1. Vida, G., ed. *Our Right to Love.* Prentice-Hall, New Jersey, 1978.
2. Rule, J. *Lesbian Images.* Doubleday, New York, 1975.

420 3. Freud, S. The Psychoanalysis of a Case of Female Homosexuality. *Int. J. Psychoanal.*, 1:129, 1920.
   4. Deutsch, H. On Female Homosexuality. *Psychoanal. Q.*, 1:484, 1932.
   5. Caprio, F. S. *Female Homosexuality; A Psychodynamic Theory of Lesbianism.* Grove Press, New York, 1962.
   6. Wilbur, C. B. Clinical Aspects of Female Homosexuality. In *Sexual Inversion: The Multiple Roots of Homosexuality.* Marmor, J., Ed., Basic Books, New York, 1965.
   7. Romm, M. E. Sexuality and Homosexuality in Women. In *Sexual Inversion: The Multiple Roots of Homosexuality.*
   8. Socarides, C. W. The Historical Development of Theoretical and Clinical Concepts of Overt Female Homosexuality. *J. Am. Psychoanal. Assoc.*, 11:386, 1963.
   9. Kaye, H. et al. Homosexuality in Women. *Arch. Gen. Psychiatry*, 17:626, 1967.
   10. Armon, V. Some Personality Variables in Overt Female Homosexuality. *J. Proj. Tech.*, 24:292, 1960.
   11. Hopkins, J. The Lesbian Personality. *Brit. J. Psychiatry*, 115:1433, 1969.
   12. Siegelman, M. Adjustment of Homosexual and Heterosexual Women. *Brit. J. Psychiatry*, 120:477, 1972.
   13. Siegelman, M. Adjustment of Homosexual and Heterosexual Women: A Cross-National Replication. Arch. Sex. Behav., 8:121, 1979.
   14. Freedman, M. J. Homosexuality Among Women and Psychological Adjustment. *Diss. Abst. Int.*, 28:347, 1971.
   15. Ohlson, E., & Wilson, M. Differentiating Female Homosexuals from Female Heterosexuals by Use of the MMPI. *J. Sex Roles,* 10:308, 1974.
   16. Thompson, N. et al. Personal Adjustment of Male and Female Homosexuals and Heterosexuals. *J. Abn. Psychol.*, 78:237, 1971.
   17. Wilson, M., & Green, R. Personality Characteristics of Female Homosexuals *Psychol. Reports*, 28:407, 1971.
   18. Saghir, M. J., & Robins, E. *Male and Female Homosexuality.* Williams and Williams, Baltimore, 1973.
   19. Oberstone, A., & Sukoneck, H. Psychological Adjustment and Life Style of Single Lesbians and Single Heterosexual Women. *Psychol. Women Q.*, 2:172, 1976.
   20. Adelman, M. R. A Comparison of Professionally Employed Lesbians and Heterosexual Women on the MMPI. *Arch. Sex. Behav.*, 6:193, 1977.
   21. Bell, A. P. & Weinberg, M. S. *Homosexualities.* Simon and Schuster, New York, 1978.
   22. Hart, M., et al. Psychological Adjustment of Nonpatient Homosexuals: Critical Review of the Research Literature. *J. Clin. Psychiatry*, 39:604, 1978.
   23. National Gay Task Force. *About Coming Out* (Pamphlet), NGTF, New York.
   24. Riddle, D. I. Finding Supportive Therapy. In *Our Right to Love*, Vida, G., Ed., Prentice-Hall, New Jersey, 1978.
   25. Martin, D., & Lyon, P. The Older Woman. In *Positively Gay*, Berzon, B. and Leighton, R., Eds. Berkeley: Bookpeople, Mediamix Assoc.

Psychoanalytic Perspectives on Female Homosexuality: A Discussion of "The Lesbian as a 'Single' Woman"

CHARLES W. SOCARIDES

Dr. Gartrell's interesting paper informs the psychiatric community as to "the unique stresses of being a lesbian in contemporary society." She describes some distressing situations that the female homosexual faces, to which the reader's reaction can only be that of compassion and understanding. Societal prejudice only adds to the painfulness of any emotional disorder. Viewed from this perspective her paper constitutes a useful contribution which well deserves our attention.

Our compassion and concern as regards the external conflicts faced by the female homosexual should not blind us, however, to her *internal* conflicts, conflicts which occur between various conscious and unconscious tendencies within her, which are causative of her disorder. The homosexual, no matter what her/his level of adaptation and function in other areas of life, is severely handicapped in the most vital area—namely, that of her interpersonal relations. She is not only afraid of the opposite sex but has deprived herself of meaningful relations to men as a group and individually. She also harbors considerable aggression against both men and women while simultaneously is in deep need of affection and support so totally denied her in earliest childhood.

Pathology, organically and psychologically, may be defined as a failure to function, with concomitant pain and/or suffering. It is this failure, its significance, and manifold consequences that are so obvious in obligatory homosexuality—a failure in functioning which, if carried to its extreme, would mean the death of the species. Beneath this obvious failure of

"Psychoanalytic Psychotherapeutic Perspectives on Female Homosexuality: Discussion of "The Lesbian as a 'Single' Woman" by Charles Socarides, *American Journal of Psychotherapy*, 35 (4), 510–15. Copyright © 1981 by the *American Journal of Psychotherapy*. Reprinted by permission.

Dr. Socarides is a psychiatrist in private practice and Clinical Professor of Psychiatry, Albert Einstein College of Medicine.

422 function and the secondary *external* conflicts it may provoke lie the agony, sorrow, tragedy, fear, and guilt of a both conscious and unconscious nature which pervades the homosexual's life. Psychiatrists who treat such individuals in depth know this very well. Those who do not practice depth psychotherapy or psychoanalysis often do not observe or may tend to minimize the degree of suffering the homosexual endures—suffering induced by internal conflicts—inasmuch as the homosexuality also provides temporary relief from severe anxiety. Furthermore, obligatory homosexuality may cause such disruption to the equilibrium of the individual that all meaningful relations in life are damaged from the outset and peculiarly susceptible to breakdown. Attitudes toward the opposite sex are often filled with distrust and fear as to render them impossible of any relationship at all except on the most superficial and brittle basis. The obligatory homosexual is unable to function in the most meaningful relationship in life: the male-female sexual union and the affective state of love, tenderness, and joy with a partner of the opposite sex.

The homosexual engages in a compromise adaptation, "choosing" a same-sex partner for sexual gratification in order to save the self from anxiety. In this way she also attains a temporary state of equilibrium which can be so misleading not only to the public but to any investigator who accepts the facade without deep probing. The ability of the homosexual symptom to neutralize anxiety motivates the homosexual to use this as a face-saving rationalization—that is, that she is not suffering from an emotional disorder at all, especially if she is convinced that there is no help for changing her condition. Despite the appearance at any given time of an adequate life performance, internal conflict threatens to disrupt this fragile adjustment.

The author asserts that there are "no major differences between lesbians and heterosexual women in psychological adjustment" (p. 413). Citing questionnaire studies, Eysenck Personality Inventories, and other personality tests, she concludes that homosexual women are as well adjusted, if not better adjusted, than heterosexual women. Evelyn Hooker, Ph.D., was among the first psychologists to conclude from psychological testing that there are no basic psychological differences between homosexuals and heterosexuals. In assessing this type of evidence, the Task Force on Homosexuality of the New York County District Branch of the American Psychiatric Association (1973)[1] reported that: "with regard to her [Hooker's[2,3]] major thesis that there is no evidence to show that homosexuals are maladjusted (ignoring their homosexuality for the time being), her study shows nothing of the kind. It is too full of methodological errors (particularly the spurious 'controls') and confused thinking to warrant any such conclusion. The conclusions that *can* be inferred from her study are: (1) Certain signs and sign complexes in the Rorschach are definitely characteristic of homosexual records. As usual with Rorschach indices, the presence of these signs warrants certain conclusions, but their absence does not. (2) In a TAT-MAPS surface discussion of homosexuality and homosexual problems occur far more frequently in homosexuals than in heterosexuals. (3) With regard to the 'adjustment' of the homosexual, the study proves nothing one way or the other. It was not adequately designed to do so"[1] (p. 475).

The Task Force further noted that psychometric examinations on homosexuals may in many instances reveal quite the opposite of what Dr. Gartrell asserts. For example, Doidge and Holtzman[4] studied a group of Air Force trainees comprised of four groups of twenty each: one markedly homosexual; one composed of men who were predominantly heterosexual but had some limited homosexual experiences; one exclusively homosexual who had been charged with some nonhomosexual offense; one heterosexual, neither charged with an offense nor under disciplinary survey. The most striking finding of these authors was the difference between the first group and the others. They found that "severe pathology is likely to accompany the markedly severe homosexual."[4]

Dr. Gartrell dismisses psychoanalytic theory in connection with the psychogenesis of homosexuality. She is of the opinion that data derived from patients "undergoing psychoanalysis" cannot have validity. (In rebuttal, psychoanalysts might well state that in the final analysis the most important study which can disclose the meaning of a particular piece of behavior or act is that secured by introspective reporting and motivational analysis, for the meaning of an act is its place in a motivational context, i.e., the purpose that it serves.) Dr. Gartrell further notes that psychoanalytic conclusions are arrived at by studying individuals undergoing treatment without "controlled studies of the general population." If this argument were to be taken seriously and applied to other forms of psychopathology such as schizophrenia, hysteria, obsessive-compulsive neurosis, etc., it would mean that all findings in the schizophrenic, for example, could only be termed valid and pathological if a control study of the general population were done simultaneously.

We do not have to take a random sample from the general population to know from our study of our schizophrenic patients that their primary and secondary symptoms are a form of pathology. The notion that the only homosexuals who enter therapy are the "sick homosexuals" and that they represent a special group or skewed sample (i.e., because they have entered psychiatric treatment) is erroneous, as very often these patients are far less masochistic and self-destructive than their partners or associates, who will not even make a realistic attempt to relieve their anguish. My patients and those of most of my colleagues continue to function successfully in many

424 areas of life throughout their therapy. Sometimes they turn to us for help because they perceive that their symptom is a consequence of anxiety, or because of a specific interpersonal crisis; others, particularly those nearing middle age, find the shifting transiency of the homosexual scene no longer "exciting." They have begun to perceive their homosexual mode of existence as meaningless, and in seeking therapy, they feel themselves entitled to attempt a correction of an immature psychosexual state. They long for the rewards made possible by divesting themselves of an emotional condition caused by early life experiences over which they had no control and which prevented their attaining their full gender-defined self-identity. They no longer can resign themselves to the locked-in "gay mythology" and are too intelligent and insightful to explain their situation away on the generalized basis of mere social disapproval. As individuals, they feel entitled to love and be loved—a mutuality they know from experience is extremely hard to achieve in any homosexual relationship on an enduring basis.

Of course female homosexuals should turn to psychiatrists for help in coping with environmental stresses. But they should not be dissuaded or discouraged from turning to psychiatrists if they wish treatment for the underlying psychogenic conflicts which caused their condition to begin with. To place emphasis on the former and to disregard the latter, or to proceed as if homosexuality had no known pathogenesis, no known course or treatment, as if it were not the product of early faulty childrearing, is to mislead our patients and the public.

Lastly, Dr. Gartrell concludes that "new rigorous scrutiny" has seriously challenged the validity of psychoanalytic theories. She implies that "for most of the earliest part of this century psychiatrists have viewed lesbianism as a developmental disorder" but that they no longer do so. Such an impression must of course be corrected.

During the past twenty years an overwhelming amount of psychoanalytic clinical research has been published describing the theoretical, clinical, and therapeutic aspects of homosexuality. An extensive bibliography can be found in my book, *Homosexuality*.[5] Indeed, it is not true that little work has been done since the 1960s as she maintains; rather, major breakthroughs have been made leading to the conclusion that oedipal-phase conflict in certain homosexual patients is always superimposed on deeper, basic pre-oedipal nuclear conflicts. In certain cases of homosexuality it is apparent that object relations pathology contributes more to the development of homosexuality than the vicissitudes of the drives—in other words, that the central conflict of the female homosexual, as well as the male homosexual, is an object-related one rather than a structural one. These views apply to relatively pronounced cases in which the perverse development is clear and definite. In these patients, nonengagement in perverse acts induces anxiety. Because the perverse acts are usually the only avenue for the attainment of sexual gratification and are obligatory for the alleviation of anxieties, and because the intensity of the need for such gratification is relatively pronounced, these cases may be termed the "well-structured" sexual deviation.

Furthermore, psychoanalytic clinical data gathered through the psychoanalysis of adult female and male homosexuals has acquired theoretical underpinning in the work of Mahler and her associates, among others, who have delineated symbiotic and separation-individuation phases of human development. The combination of infant observation studies and developmental theories, and the analytic material derived from adult homosexuals, helps to explain that the fixation of the homosexual lies in all probability in the later phases of the separation-individuation process, producing a disturbance in self-identity as well as in gender identity, a persistence of a primary feminine identification with the mother (in the case of the female, an identification with a mother perceived as malevolent and hateful), separation anxiety, fears of engulfment (restoring the mother-child unity), and disturbance in object relations and associated ego functions. By combining data and theory, major advances into the question of causation have been made. It is quite likely that the significant incidence of homosexuality in the general population is due to the necessity for all human beings to traverse the separation-individuation phase of early childhood, which is decisive for gender-defined self-identity. A substantial number of children fail to successfully complete this developmental process and are therefore unable to form a healthy sexual identity (the core disturbance in all homosexuals) in accordance with their anatomical and biological capacities.

Most recently new problems are being conceptualized and solutions suggested by advances in our knowledge of the pathology of internal object relations, ego developmental psychology (including self-psychology), and new concepts of narcissism. Clinical forms of homosexuality have now been divided into oedipal, pre-oedipal type 1 and 2 (depending upon the degree of pathology of object relations), and schizo-homosexuality (the coexistence of homosexuality and schizophrenia).[5]

The female homosexual *has no choice* as regards her sexual object. In the true obligatory female homosexual the condition is unconsciously determined, as differentiated from the behavior of the person who deliberately engages in female-female sexual contact due to situational factors or the desire for variational experiences. These constitute nonclinical forms of *homosexual behavior*. The nuclear core of true homosexuality is never a conscious choice, an act of will. Rather, it is determined from the earliest period of childhood (in terms of its origins, of course, not its practice). The presence of external conflicts which complicate the lives of female homosexuals should not be allowed to obfuscate the valid clinical data secured through in-depth psychoanalytic studies for this would misinform psychiatrists, the general reader, and an unfortunately vulnerable public.

References

1. Socarides, C. W., Bieber, I., Bychowski, G. et al. Homosexuality in the Male: A Report of a Psychiatric Study Group. Report of the Task Force on Homosexuality, New York County District Branch APA. *Int. J. Psychiatry*, 11:451, 1973.
2. Hooker, Evelyn. The Adjustment of Male Homosexuals." *J. Projective Techniques*, 21:17, 1957.
3. _____. Male Homosexuality and the Rorschach. *J. Projective Techniques*, 22:33–54, 1957.
4. Doidge, W. T. & Holtzman, W. H. Implications of Homosexuality Among Air Force Trainees. *J. Consult. Psychol.*, 24:9–13, 1960.
5. Socarides, C. W. *Homosexuality*. Jason Aronson, New York, 1978.

Question 14

Is Pornography Harmful to Women?

The question of whether pornography has adverse effects on women usually arouses very strong personal opinions. Nevertheless, until President Johnson established the Commission on Obscenity and Pornography in January 1968, relatively little was known about the effects of explicit erotic material on behavior. The summary report of this commission (Commission on Obscenity and Pornography, 1970) and the nine volumes containing the studies it sponsored (Committee on Obscenity and Pornography, 1971) record the first phase of research in this area (Byrne & Kelley 1984). The commission concluded that there was no evidence that the easy availability of pornography played a significant role in sexual crimes.

Although subsequent research in the early 1970s seemed to substantiate the commission's findings, reservations about its methodology and conclusions began to emerge. One of the objections was that the early research was not conducted over the extended time period necessary to prove or disprove changing behavior. Other researchers were concerned about the conflict between the finding that pornographic films did not change behavior and research on modeling behavior showing that subjects tended to imitate the activities of filmed models (Byrne & Kelley, 1984). Feminists in the mid-1970s also began to raise questions about the harmlessness of pornography. Brownmiller (1975), for example, argued that the open display of pornography created a climate of tolerance for sexual assault against women, who were sometimes even portrayed as willing victims.

In spite of the growing amount of research on pornography in the past decade, there is still strong disagreement among social scientists as to its effects on behavior. Many believe that an individual's sexual attitudes are   427

428 determined long before he or she is exposed to pornography. Consequently, their position is that pornographic material either has no effect on behavior or slightly reinforces an already established pattern of sexual behavior.

Others have argued that pornography not only is harmless but provides viewers with an outlet, a cathartic safety net for feelings that might otherwise injure society. In contrast is the conclusion, based on a growing amount of research in recent years, which suggests that sexual behavior is learned behavior. According to these studies, some men learn to imitate the violent behavior they see on the screen.

In 1986, the Meese Commission issued a new governmental report (Attorney General's Commission, 1986) which reversed the findings of the 1970 commission. Noting that the previous report had become obsolete in the face of the increasingly violent and explicit pornography of the 1980s, the Meese Commission stated that there is a causal relationship between violent pornography and violence against women.

Social scientists have charged the Meese Commission with distorting and trivializing the existing research in the field. Moreover, they point out that current research is not designed to evaluate the relationship between exposure to pornography and the commission of sexual crimes (Turkington, 1986).

Psychiatrist Richard Green maintains that the available research does not support the contention that pornography increases sexual violence. Social psychologist Neil Malamuth, on the other hand, argues that we must pay more attention to the indirect influence of the sexually violent media to fully gauge their effects.

References

Attorney General's Commission on Pornography (1986). Final Report of the Commission (Vols. 1 and 2). Washington, D.C.: Government Printing Office.

Byrne, D. & Kelley, K. (1984). Pornography and sex research. In N. M. Malamuth and E. Donnerstein (Eds.), *Pornography and sexual aggression* (pp. 1–15). Orlando, Fla.: Academic Press.

Brownmiller, S. (1975). *Against our will: Men, women and rape.* New York: Simon & Schuster.

Commission on Obscenity and Pornography. (1970). *The report of the commission on obscenity and pornography.* New York: Bantam Books.

Committee on Obscenity and Pornography. (1971). *Presidential Commission on Obscenity and Pornography.* Washington, D.C.: Government Printing Office.

Turkington, C. (1986, August). Pornography and violence. *APA Monitor, 17* (8), 8–9.

Additional Reading

Burstyn, V. (Ed.) (1985). *Women against censorship*. Vancouver/Toronto: Douglas and Macintyre.

Donnerstein, E., & Linz, D. (1984, January). Sexual violence in the media: A warning. *Psychology Today*, 14–15.

Donnerstein, E., & Linz, D. G. (1986, December). The question of pornography. *Psychology Today*, 56–59.

Donnerstein, E., Linz, D. G., & Penrod, S. (1987). *The question of pornography*. New York: Free Press.

Donnerstein, E., Linz, D., & Penrod, S. (in press). Sexualized mass media violence. In P. Shaver and C. Hendrick (Eds.), *Review of Personality and Social Psychology*, Vol. 7, *Sex and Gender*. Beverly Hills: Sage.

FACT Book Committee. (1986). Caught looking: Feminism, pornography and censorship. New York: Caught Looking, Inc.

Gray, S. H. (1982). Exposure to pornography and aggression toward women: The case of the angry male. *Social Problems, 29* (4), 387–98.

Huesmann, L. R., & Malamuth, N. (Eds.) (1986). Media violence and antisocial behavior. *Journal of Social Issues* [Special issue].

Jacobs, C. (1984). Patterns of violence: A feminist perspective on the regulation of pornography. *Harvard Women's Law Journal, 7,* 5–55.

Kappeler, S. (1986). *The pornography of representation*. Minneapolis: University of Minnesota Press.

Soble, A. (1986). Pornography: Marxism, feminism, and the future of sexuality. New Haven: Yale University Press.

Vance, C. (Ed.) (1984). *Pleasure and danger: Exploring female sexuality*. Boston: Routledge & Kegan Paul.

Exposure to Explicit Sexual Materials and Sexual Assault: A Review of Behavioral and Social Science Research

RICHARD GREEN

Definitions

Like beauty, pornography is in the eyes of the beholder. On Labor Day weekend I was in London and spent time with an English couple. The wife lamented her role as the mother of two teenagers. Her children were aficionados of rock and punk video. This woman became most animated during her repeated descriptions of these video materials as "hard-core porn."

I recognize that there is a segment of the American population convinced that the nation is being propelled to hell in consequence of mass exposure to teens tight in jeans, semi-clad females draped across sports cars, and Madonna's midriff. However, the behavioral and social science data I have studied addresses a different sort of material. It involves portrayals in pictures or words of the female breasts and/or genitalia and/or the male genitalia. It usually involves the suggestion or depiction of sexual activity such as masturbation, fellatio, cunnilingus, or vaginal or anal intercourse. Upon this foundation may be superimposed a variety of additional variables, such as intimidation, physical violence, multiplicity of partners, and age of partner.

Social Science Research: Cross-Cultural Analyses

One way of assessing the relationship between the availability of explicit sexual materials and sexual assault is to examine the rates of assault in

"Exposure to Explicit Sexual Materials and Sexual Assault: A review of Behavioral and Social Science Research" by Richard Green. This paper was prepared for a hearing of the Attorney General's Commission on Pornography, Houston, Texas, September 12, 1985.

Dr. Green is a psychiatrist and Professor of Psychiatry at the University of California, Los Angeles, California and Director of the Program in Psychiatry, Law, and Human Sexuality.

countries that have made pornographic materials readily available. Two Western countries that have greatly relaxed laws restricting access to pornography are the Federal Republic of Germany (West Germany) and Denmark. To a lesser degree this has also happened in Great Britain and in regions of the United States.

Denmark

Before 1967, Danish laws against pornography were similar to those of other Western nations. In fact, *Fanny Hill, or Memoirs of a Woman of Pleasure* was successfully prosecuted as late as 1958. From 1961, prosecutions of explicit erotic writing ceased. The production of these materials rapidly increased and peaked in 1967, the year in which the laws against pornographic literature were repealed. By 1967, illegal production of sexually explicit photographic magazines had begun. It peaked in 1969. In that year the Danish Parliament legalized the sale of sexually explicit materials to persons over sixteen years of age (Kutchinsky, 1985).

The rate of reported rape in Denmark remained steady between 1966 and 1972 (it increased by a total of eighteen cases for the entire country over the six-year period). This steady rate is noteworthy in that during the same period there was a sharp increase in the rate of nonsexual assault. It is also noteworthy in that during the same period the Danish women's movement was encouraging rape victims to report attacks. Thus the actual rate may have dropped.

As for child pornography in Denmark, taking pornographic pictures of children remained punishable. However, the reproduction and sale of child pornography was not illegal between 1969 and 1980. Between 1967 and 1973 child molestation or "physical sexual interference with female children" showed a rapid decrease. The drop in the rate of child molestation that occurred with the increased availability of pornography, including "child pornography," was 67 percent (from 24 per 100,000 population to 8 per 100,000 population). The rate has not subsequently increased. There is no evidence that the drop in the rate of sexual assault against children was a product of the Danes' accepting this conduct and not reporting these offenses to police (Kutchinsky, 1985).

Federal Republic of Germany

West Germany legalized pornography in 1973. Between 1972 and 1980 the total number of sex crimes reported to the police decreased by 11 percent. Sex offenses against minors under fourteen years of age also showed a slight decrease during this period. In the police category of sex offenses against victims under six years of age, the decrease was substantially larger. It

432 dropped from 100 per 100,000 population to 40 per 100,000, a decrease of 60 percent. As for rape, the number of reported cases remained the same. Concurrently, however, nonsexual violent offenses increased sharply—127 percent (Polizeiliche Kriminal Statistik, 1983 Bundesrepublik Deutschland. Bundeskriminalamt Wiesbaden).

Great Britain

In 1974, British publishers launched a series of sexually explicit magazines. The market peaked in 1976. While the rate of rape rose during this period, the increase had begun long before the increased availability of pornography. Additionally, during this period, the rates of other offenses against the person increased by a far greater percentage. The British Committee on Obscenity and Film Censorship "unhesitantly reject[ed] the suggestion that the available information for England and Wales lends any support at all to the argument that pornography acts as a stimulus to the commission of sexual violence" (Committee on Obscenity and Film Censorship, 1979, p. 80).

Japan

Before shifting focus to the United States, there is an important point to be made about an Oriental culture, Japan. The most common form of Japanese pornography deals with rape. Yet their reported rape rate is one-sixteenth that of the United States. (Abramson & Hayashi, 1984).

The explanation for these changes in sex-crime rates in association with the increased availability of pornography has been called the "substitution hypothesis." The common male reaction to pornographic pictures is masturbation. The availability of portrayals of a forbidden activity, accompanied by autoerotic behavior, may provide an outlet for antisocial sexual impulses. It may permit the person to experience vicariously or in fantasy what would otherwise have been acted out with a victim.

United States

Data from other nations may not be relevent to the situation in the United States. Therefore it is important to study crime rates, sexual and otherwise, in this country during the period of increased availability of explicit sexual materials. It is also helpful to look at the United States as a group of regional subcultures, in that in some parts of the country sexually explicit materials are much more available than in others. The research question asks, "Do these regions differ in reported sex crimes?"

During 1970–78, when explicit sexual films became widely available, the reported U.S. rape rate rose from 20 per 100,000 to 30 per 100,000 *433* population. By comparison, the rate of aggravated assault rose from 150 per 100,000 to 230 per 100,000 (FBI Uniform Crime Reports, U.S. Department of Justice). This suggests that the rise in reported rape was a nonspecific correllate of the rise in assaultive crimes in general. Further, if through the raising of women's consciousness during the same period a higher percentage of actual rapes were reported, the rape rate may have declined.

Regional analyses of the relation between the availability of sexual materials and sex-crime rates do not support a positive relationship between the two. The availability of explicit sexual materials in adult theaters and bookstores is not significantly correlated with rates of reported rape. Other variables, however, are related to rape. These include alcohol consumption, the percentage of poor, and the circulation of another type of magazine—"outdoor" publications such as *Field and Stream* and *Guns and Ammo* (Scott, 1985).

While another preliminary study found that states with a higher circulation of sex magazines also had higher rape rates, the investigators later found that "legitimate" violence was equally associated with such rates. "Legitimate" violence includes viewing violent television programs, corporate punishment laws, and the sale of hunting licenses. Furthermore, three other variables were found to correlate more with rape. These were the number of divorced men, economic inequality, and urbanization (Baron & Straus, 1984; Baron & Straus, 1985).

Thus, the experience of Western nations, including the United States, contradicts the thesis that the availability of pornography is associated with an increase in sex crimes against women and children. These data are disturbing to those who are convinced, on the basis of their informal "research" or personal views, that increased availability of pornography leads to increased sexual crime. In an effort to discredit these data, false statements have been made. It is not true, for example, that in Denmark the decrease in reported sex crime rates is due to changes in the definition of sex crime and/or to failure to report such crimes. Child molestation and rape, the data reported here, are crimes in Denmark and are reported with the same frequency there as in other Western countries.

The learned critique of these studies is that they are correlational. The results do not prove that increased availability of pornography reduces sex crime. While the concordance of findings across cultures argues against the correlations being spurious, the decrease in sex crime could be related to a third variable. Perhaps the concurrent rise in nonsexual antisocial behavior channels the pernicious energies of a society. Perhaps there is a fixed pool

434 of antisocial potential. While this is mere speculation, scientists must be prepared to consider the possibility of intervening variables before attributing causality to correlation.

Laboratory Research: In Search of the "Real World"

Because sex offenders are not readily available to academic researchers, and because the factors that led to their sexual assault are not easily studied, investigators have taken to the experimental laboratory in their search for valid models of sexual aggression. However, laboratory research of sex crimes presents several formidable, if not insurmountable, obstacles. The first concerns the persons studied. Typically subjects are undergraduate college students who receive academic credit or a fee for serving as "guinea pigs." As students, they may be aware of the research reputation and experimental approaches of faculty and thus may not be naive research subjects. In demographic and psychological background they are often very different from the street sex offender. Importantly, they usually are persons who have never committed a sexual offense and will never do so.

The experimental setting is necessarily artificial. Situations are contrived with varying levels of credibility. In experiments in which subjects are allowed to "aggress" against a putative "victim," they are given permission (if not in fact encouraged) to do so by an authority figure in charge of the experiment. The circumstances of the experiment are often remote from "real world" settings. A typical laboratory model has a male student view a sexually explicit film just after a female has attempted to provoke him to anger. He is now permitted to punish the female by delivering a mock shock, which he believes to be real. The tether to street sexual assault is tenuous. Other studies assess attitudes toward women and toward sexual assault after the subject views sexually violent films. The assessment is usually performed shortly after exposure to the erotic materials. Extending these findings to long-term attitudinal change is problematic. Extending attitudinal change to behavioral change is even more problematic.

Compounding these problems of interpreting laboratory studies is the nonuniformity of experimental findings. Even in the laboratory, a clear picture of the sex offender has not emerged from this research.

Some findings, from studies that seem to me well done and more interesting than most, will be summarized. Contrary to expectation, with mildly erotic nonviolent stimuli, aggression against females in these laboratory settings may decrease (Baron & Bell, 1977). With highly erotic nonviolent stimuli, the level of aggression, while not decreasing, may not increase beyond what is obtained with nonerotic stimuli (Donnerstein et 435 al., 1975). Exposure to more violent pornography, in conjunction with angering the viewer, may increase aggression against the female confederate of the researcher (Donnerstein, 1986). These materials may also increase a viewer's attitudes condoning violence against women. Interestingly, the study that demonstrated this used R-rated, not X-rated, films (Malamuth & Check, 1981).

The "real world" concerns of society may not be so much for the person who rarely views explicit films but for the habitual viewer. Therefore, in some studies, subjects have been exposed to heavy doses of pornographic material, up to thirty-five hours. After this massive exposure, subjects were less supportive of the feminist movement and less punitive toward a hypothetical rapist (Zillmann & Bryant, 1982). Similarly, after viewing violent sexual films (again, R-rated) on a daily basis, subjects became somewhat attenuated to the violence against the women in the film (Linz et al., 1984).

On the other hand, repeated exposure to violent sexual material may reduce sexual arousal by rape depictions. The study that demonstrated this is noteworthy in that prior to exposure to the materials subjects were classified as "force-oriented" or "not force-oriented" depending on their responsiveness to rape stimuli. Thus it could be considered a model for the real-world persons most likely to commit sexual assault. Among the force-oriented subjects, exposure to either violent or nonviolent sexual materials resulted in a reduction in sexual responsiveness to rape portrayals. The authors suggest that repeated exposure to rape stimuli may be therapeutic to rape-prone persons—that is, it may reduce sexual arousal reactions to rape scenes (Ceniti & Malamuth, 1984).

Prison and Clinical Research on Sex Offenders

A study in which I was a co-investigator assessed convicted rapists' and pedophiles' experience with pornography. Their experience was compared with that of normal males. The sex offenders' experience with pornography, both in adolescence and in the year prior to incarceration, was lower (Goldstein et al. 1971). Our findings were similar to those of another study in which incarcerated sex offenders were compared to prisoners who were not sex offenders. The sex offenders reported less exposure to pornography during childhood (Cook et al., 1971). The largest study of sex offenders was conducted at the Kinsey Institute—over 1,300 imprisoned sex offenders were compared with 900 prisoners not convicted of sex crimes and 500 nonprisoners. The groups did not differ significantly in reported exposure

436 to pornography or reported arousal by pornography. If anything, those convicted of sex crimes may have been less responsive to pornography and less interested in it (Gebhard et al., 1965).

A popular argument against taking the findings of these "old" studies seriously today is that the materials available then were bland compared with contemporary pornography. The extent of depicted aggression at the time of these studies and the availability of materials depicting minors are presumed to have been less. While these assumptions of changes in the type of material available have been challenged (Scott, 1985), let us assume, for the sake of argument, that the contentions are true. In that case the data remain significant. They point out that the mere availability of violent or child pornography is not a sufficient condition for sexual assault. The sex offenders in the older studies did not commit their offenses in significant association with exposure to these materials. The data warn against over-simplifying a complex phenomenon.

Atypical Sexuality

A principal societal concern is that exposure to depictions of deviant sexual behavior will promote deviant sexual behavior. Homosexuality is a common concern in our society, and homosexual pornography is seen as promoting this pattern of sexuality.

My area of psychiatric research expertise has been in the development of homosexual orientation in males. For fifteen years, I have been engaged in a study of two groups of young boys as they matured into adolescence and young adulthood. The boys were between four and eleven when initially seen. Today over two-thirds of one group are homosexual or bisexual. No one in the second group is homosexual or bisexual.

What distinguishes these two groups developmentally is their early childhood behavior at ages three through six. One group showed extensive cross-gender or "feminine" behavior. They liked to cross-dress in women's clothes, they liked to role-play as females, they said they wanted to be girls or women, and they preferred the toys and companionship of girls.

The parents of both groups of boys were heterosexual. In some families in both groups, heterosexual pornography such as *Playboy* and *Penthouse* was available to the child. As the boys emerged into adolescence, some sought out or were exposed to a wider range of erotic materials. The boys who were already aware of homosexual attractions found erotic depictions of males sexually arousing. Those aware of heterosexual attractions found depictions of females arousing. Patterns of interest in erotic materials followed the emergence of sexual orientation.

This unique study documents that patterns of sexual orientation have **437** their roots in childhood in a variety of behaviors that do not appear to be sexual (Green, 1986). It also finds that pornography plays little, if any, role in the emergence of sexual preference for male or female partners.

Prosocial Uses of Pornography

Education

Explicit sexual materials are widely used in the sex education of adult students. I have utilized pornography at the State University of New York at Stony Brook and previously at the University of California, Los Angeles. Some of the films I used were commercially made adult films available for general distribution. Others were made specifically for educational or therapeutic purposes. The materials were useful in providing information about sexual practices and in stimulating dialogue about sexual behavior.

Such films with heterosexual or homosexual content have been widely utilized in educational settings for adults during the past fifteen years. Records of the Multi-Media Resource Center in San Francisco show that four thousand institutions were using graphic sexual materials as of 1979.

Therapy

Explicit sexual materials are used in the treatment of sexual dysfunctions (impotency in the male, nonorgasmic response in the female, inhibited sexual desire in both) (Kaplan, 1974). The goals of using pornography are three: to increase knowledge about the range of sexual expression, to facilitate communication about sexuality between partners, and to increase sexual arousal in clinically inhibited persons. The records of the Multi-Media Resource Center show that almost eight thousand individual practitioners and counselors had rented or purchased explicit sexual material during the late 1970s.

General Considerations

At the outset I addressed the difficulty of defining pornography in a manner that suits everyone. Courts have had equal difficulty in defining obscenity. Supreme Court Justice William Brennan threw up his hands in despair after watching the court wrestle with a working definition for years. Former Justice Potter Stewart did not contribute to a picture of clarity with his memorable statement, "I can't define it, but I know it when I see it."

The question of what types of explicit sexual depictions should be permitted or eliminated divides the ranks of our society, even groups otherwise united. Among feminists, there is considerable debate on this

438 issue. For example, one faction asserts that depictions of sadomasochistic activity between two consenting females represent a healthy liberation of female sexuality. Another asserts that these depictions are pernicious by-products of the oppressive male-female role division. Another condemns all male-female erotica, arguing that no female in our society can truly consent to sexual intercourse with a male owing to the inequality of the sexes. This faction sees all heterosexual intercourse as rape. These differing viewpoints are important considerations where the will of one group may be imposed on that of another.

Much of the research summarized here has utilized college students or sex offenders. Another group that is often reported on are the individuals who contribute anecdotal reports about the role of pornography in their lives. Again, as with other research, we must be cautious in interpreting such information. Assessing the relative positive or negative effect on the population from anecdotal reports is problematic. The material we gather, while genuine, may not be representative of those persons not seen. This is a historic difficulty in clinical psychiatric research where troubled patients report earlier life trauma and psychiatrists conclude that the events caused the present difficulty. Clinicians do not see persons for whom the same events did not lead to difficulty.

A major obstacle in weighing the significance of anecdotal reports, whether they be from patients, volunteers at public hearings, or apprehended sex offenders, is that the population on the other side of the balance is invisible. On that side should be placed those persons who flirted with aggressive or deviant sexual acts in fantasy but were repelled by the depiction of these acts in pornography. On the other side should be placed persons who were able to satisfy their interest in antisocial activity by means of pornography rather than acting it out.

We may have seen the shadows of those people—they may be represented by those missing from the numbers who would have been expected to commit sex crimes after the legalization of pornography, if crime rates had not dropped in association with the increased availability of sexual materials.

Both the large volume of pornography available in the United States and survey data on American viewing habits suggest that most persons see explicitly sexual films or magazines at some time. By and large these persons are voluntary viewers. There are two subsamples of Americans for whom seeing explicit sexual films is not entirely voluntary, however. These people are expected to view the material in its entirety, no matter how offensive it is to their tastes. These captive audiences are composed of the jurors in obscenity trials and Supreme Court justices. The late Justice

William Douglas refused to attend these film screenings after many years on the court, declaring that they were boring, offensive, time-consuming, and that the films were (anyway) protected by the Constitution.

No one to my knowledge has reported that anyone in either of these two groups of captive viewers has suffered psychological damage. Nor would I expect them to. I am not pessimistic about the level of responsibility, maturity, and psychiatric health of the average person. I do not believe that the average person is fragile. I do not believe that if an explicit film were shown here now, the pattern of anyone's sexual conduct would be reorganized.

A major social concern, however, is for the more vulnerable members of society. We feel that they must be protected from themselves, and we from them. This concern too is problematic. Millions of people saw the film *Taxi Driver*. One of them harnessed the film to his deranged fantasy life and attempted to assassinate the President. Could it have been predicted that the film would have that effect on anyone? On some? If so, should the film have been banned?

My concern in this essay is not to address the issue of First Amendment rights and whether the danger of censorship of speech and press is greater or less than the danger of pornography. My law classes at Yale have pointed out that this debate is generic. Once again, the protections of the First Amendment are pitted against the punitive villains of a particular period. This issue I will leave to legal scholars. I will only say that many of us who oppose censorship and believe in the rights of women view some parts of the world today with great alarm. The Iranians have no pornography.

The debate over whether pornography is good or bad (or neither) will continue no matter what the outcome of this commission's inquiry. Some will continue to believe that pornography causes social problems, others will believe that it reflects them. Some will believe that pornography (however defined) should be banned. Others will respond that many things in our society are believed to cause more social harm than good but are not banned. In some cases, these things are made available to consenting adults. At the same time, educational efforts are mounted to make them less attractive. More Americans will die this year because they were allowed to purchase cigarettes or alcohol than because they watched a pornographic film.

References

Abramson, P. & Hayashi, H. (1982). Pornography in Japan. In N. Malamuth and E. Donnerstein (eds).. *Pornography and Sexual Aggression.* New York: Academic Press.
Baron, L. (1974). The Aggression-inhibiting influence of heightened sexual arousal. *Journal of Personality and Social Psychology* 30:318–22.

440 Baron, R. A. & Bell, P. A. (1977). Sexual arousal and aggression by males: Effects of type of erotic stimuli and prior provocation. *Journal of Personality and Social Psychology 35*:78–87.

Baron, L. & Straus, M. (1984). Sexual stratification, pornography and rape in the United States. In *Pornography and Sexual Aggression.*

Baron, L. & Straus, M. (1985). Legitimate violence, pornography, and sexual inadequacy as explanations for state and regional differences in rape. Paper read at the annual meeting of the American Association for the Advancement of Science, Los Angeles.

Ceniti, J. & Malamuth, N. (1984). Effects of repeated exposure to sexually violent or non-violent stimuli on sexual arousal to rape and non-rape depictions. *Behavior Research and Therapy 22*:535–48.

Committee on Obscenity and Film Censorship (1979). Report of the Committee on Obscenity and Film Censorship. London: Her Majesty's Printing Office.

Cook, R., Fosen, R. & Pacht, A. (1971). Pornography and the sex offender. *Journal of Applied Psychology 55*:503–11.

Donnerstein, E. (1980). Aggressive erotica and violence against women. *Journal of Personality and Social Psychology 39*:269–77.

Donnerstein, E., Donnerstein, N. & Evans, R. (1975). Erotic stimuli and aggression: Facilitation or inhibition. *Journal of Personality and Social Psychology 32*:237–44.

Gebhard, P., Gagnon, J. Pomeroy, W., & Christenson, H. (1965). *Sex offenders*. New York: Harper and Row.

Goldstein, M. Kant, H., Judd, L., Rice E., & Green, R. (1971). Experience with pornography. *Archives of Sexual Behavior* 1:1–15.

Green, R. (1987). *The "sissy boy syndrome" and the development of homosexuality*. New Haven: Yale University Press.

Kaplan, H. (1974). *The new sex therapy*. New York: Bruner/Mazel, p. 204.

Kutchinsky, B. (1973). The effect of easy availability of pornography on the incidence of sex crimes. *Journal of Social Issues.* 29:163–81.

Kutchinsky, B. (1985). Pornography and its effects in Denmark and the United States. *Comparative Social Research, Vol. 8.*

Linz, D., Donnerstein, E. & Penrod, S., (1984). The effects of multiple exposure to filmed violence against women. Journal of Communication 34:130–47.

Malamuth, N. & Check, J. (1981). The effects of mass media exposure on acceptance of violence against women. *Journal of Research in Personality,* 15:436–46.

Polizeiliche Kriminal Statistik (1983). Bundesrepublik Deutschland. Bundeskriminalamt Weisbaden.

Scott, J. (1985). Violence and erotic material: The relationship between adult entertainment and rape. Paper read at the annual meeting of the American Association for the Advancement of Science, Los Angeles.

Vandervoert, M. & McIlvenna, T. (1979). The use of sexually explicit teaching materials. In R. Green (ed.), *Human sexuality: A health practitioner's text*. 2d ed. Baltimore: Williams and Williams.

Zillmann, D. & Bryant, J. (1982). Pornography, sexual callousness, and the trivialization of rape. *Journal of Communication 32*:1–21.

Do Sexually Violent Media Indirectly Contribute to Antisocial Behavior?

NEIL M. MALAMUTH

Introduction: The Indirect-Effects Perspective

The research described herein focuses on violent sexual media, particularly rape.[1] It demonstrates the importance of analyzing media stimuli by the "messages" or meanings they convey. Meaning is, of course, a function of both the message and the receiver's interpretations of it.

The message given the most attention here involved the consequences of sexual aggression. A series of experiments found that rape depictions that showed the victim ultimately deriving physical pleasure from her experience fostered attitudes more condoning of aggression against women. Rape depictions that portrayed the victim abhorring the experience, on the other hand, were less likely to have such effects.

According to these findings, a PG-rated film showing rape in a positive light could be more socially detrimental than an X-rated film not showing sexual violence. The degree of sexual explicitness, according to this approach, is less relevant than the "message" behind the depiction of sexual aggression.[2]

Besides discriminating among differing "messages" in studying media

---

1. The term *pornography* is used in this essay to refer to sexually explicit media without any pejorative meaning intended. Also, the terms *aggression* and *violence* are used interchangeably herein, as are the terms *sexually violent media* and *violent pornography*.

2. Of course, sexual explicitness in and of itself should not be ignored as a conveyor of messages. Based on cultural and personal background and experience, sexual explicitness may be interpreted in many different ways. For example, the uncovering of a woman's body may be perceived by some as debasing her. Similarly, the public display of sex may break taboos that could be interpreted as sanctioning other restricted behaviors (Malamuth, Jaffe, & Feshbach, 1977). However, such interpretations are not inherent to sexually explicit media, whereas a positive depiction of rape or child molestation is not equally a matter of individual interpretation.

"Do Sexually Violent Media Indirectly Contribute to Antisocial Behavior?" by Neil M. Malamuth. This paper was prepared for the Surgeon General's Workshop on Pornography and Public Health, Arlington, Virginia, June 22–24, 1986.

Dr. Malamuth is a social psychologist and Professor of Communications Studies, University of California, Los Angeles.

442 stimuli, the research differentiates among media consumers. No influence works in a vacuum, and media influences are viewed as combining and interacting with a variety of other influences—sometimes counteracting them, sometimes reinforcing them, and at other times not having much of any effect.

The current strong interest in exploring a possible relationship between pornography and crime has led to a search for direct links between media exposure and deviant behavior. People have sought an immediate causal connection between media action and audience imitation. For example, a civil suit brought against NBC alleged that a rape portrayal in a television movie, *Born Innocent,* resulted in an imitation rape by some juvenile viewers. However, because of the ethical constraints against researchers' creating conditions that might increase serious aggression (e.g., exposing individuals to large doses of violent pornography and seeing if some commit rapes), experimentation to study direct effects is very limited.

Beyond the dramatic popular notion of violent pornography spurring a minority of sexual deviants and "weirdos" to criminal acts lies the far more complex but also potentially far more pervasive area of indirect effects. The evidence presented here suggests that a wide range of media affect the general population in a variety of different ways. It looks at how an aggregate of media sexual violence could affect a person's attitudes, which are concurrently being shaped by family, peers, other media messages, and a host of other influences. Such attitudes might contribute to stranger and date rape, a desire, not acted upon, to be sexually aggressive, sanctioning the sexual aggression of others, or sexist and discriminatory acts. Even when not translated into violent behavior, such effects have wide social implications.

Elsewhere (Malamuth & Briere, 1986), we described an indirect-effects model of the hypothesized development of aggressive behavior against women (see fig. 14.1). To summarize this model briefly, individual conditions and the broader social climate are postulated as the originating influences on the individual. The mass media are considered among the *many* social forces that may, in interaction with a variety of other cultural and individual factors, affect the development of intermediate attributes such as attitudes, arousal patterns, motivations, emotions, and personality characteristics. These intermediate variables, in complex interaction with each other and with situational circumstances such as alcohol or acute arousal, may precipitate behavior ranging from passive support to actual aggression.[3] In addition to contributing to attitude formation, the mass media

3. The focus in this model is on the factors that may contribute to the development of antisocial behavior. Obviously, various factors, including some media portrayals, may lead to the development of attributes stimulating prosocial behavior and reducing antisocial responses. Also, this model does not

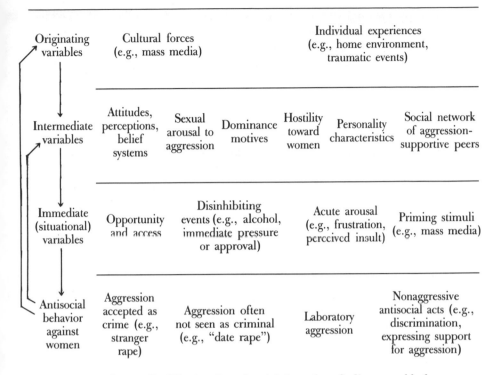

Figure 14.1: Hypothesized Development of Aggression Against Women

Developmental level					
Originating variables	Cultural forces (e.g., mass media)		Individual experiences (e.g., home environment, traumatic events)		
Intermediate variables	Attitudes, perceptions, belief systems	Sexual arousal to aggression	Dominance motives	Hostility toward women	Personality characteristics	Social network of aggression-supportive peers
Immediate (situational) variables	Opportunity and access	Disinhibiting events (e.g., alcohol, immediate pressure or approval)		Acute arousal (e.g., frustration, perceived insult)	Priming stimuli (e.g., mass media)
Antisocial behavior against women	Aggression accepted as crime (e.g., stranger rape)	Aggression often not seen as criminal (e.g., "date rape")		Laboratory aggression	Nonaggressive antisocial acts (e.g., discrimination, expressing support for aggression)

may increase the recall of "prime" antisocial thoughts, feelings, and behavioral urges that were previously formed (Berkowitz, 1984).

For some individuals, antisocial acts may take the form of violence that comes to the attention of the law, such as stranger rape or wife-battering. For others, these same underlying factors may contribute to actions that are not typically prosecuted but instead are manifested as aggression in dating situations or in laboratory settings, a reported desire to commit acts of sexual violence, discrimination against women, and/or expressed support for the sexual aggression of others. We are not lumping illegal violence together with all other antisocial behaviors but we are suggesting that all these behaviors may share some underlying causes, including media influences.

This model indicates possible avenues by which cultural forces such as the media may change a person's intermediate·responses and how such

---

necessarily exclude other possible effects of sexually violent media, some of which may not necessarily be judged harmful by many observers.

444 changes may ultimately affect his or her own aggressive behavior under some circumstances. This model also suggests that attitudinal changes in some people may affect the aggressive behavior of others. If a person becomes more tolerant of violence against women as a result of media exposure or other causal factors, for example, his or her reactions to the sexual aggression of others may change even if his or her own aggressive behavior is not altered.

This general model does not suppose a linear sequence of events but a reciprocating system of mutually influencing factors, as indicated by the upward arrows in figure 14.1. For example, mass media portrayals of sexual violence may contribute to attitudes and perceptions which, in combination with personality characteristics derived from aversive childhood experiences, may result in sexual aggression on a date. This aggression, especially if unpunished, might produce a further alteration in attitudes and perceptions (including perceptions of self) that could attract the individual to a peer network supportive of sexual aggression. These peers, themselves a product of "originating" and "intermediate" variables, might then provide greater support and approval for further sexual aggression.

We have suggested two possible routes culminating in sexual aggression. First, an individual may "progress" through the stages hypothesized to produce sexual violence. Second, mass media stimuli and other cultural influences may impact on individuals who are not sexually violent themselves but who nevertheless, because of their negative attitudes toward women, support and reinforce sexual violence by others. Such support may manifest itself in blaming a rape victim, supporting another man's aggression in a "locker room" conversation, or even one's decision as a jury member in a rape trial. The idea that such thought patterns may encourage sexual violence is reminiscent of the "cultural climate" concept suggested by Brownmiller (1975). It argues that media influences which increase cultural supports for sexual aggression need not directly produce violence to have seriously harmful effects. Of course, the indirect model need not be restricted to sexual aggression but may apply to nonsexual aggression as well. For example, media depictions of violent vigilantes as heroes (for example, the *Death Wish* series of movies) may contribute to a cultural climate condoning similar behavior in "real world" settings.

The indirect-effects model provides the basis for this essay's twin hypotheses that (1) exposure to some sexually violent media may contribute to the development of attitudes that condone aggression against women and (2) such attitudes, in combination with other influences and circumstances, may lead to sexually violent acts.

Hypothesized Processes Leading to Attitude Changes

Obviously, most viewers of media sexual violence distinguish between fantasy and reality and don't necessarily perceive what is depicted in the media as a model for behavior. However, there is considerable research indicating that even when people recognize an event as fictional, it can nonetheless affect some people's perceptions of reality and their attitudes. Such media influences may be more likely to occur when the sexual violence is presented in a positive light or when the audience is sexually aroused by it.

Table 14.1 summarizes several possible processes by which media sexual violence might lead to attitudes that are accepting of violence against women. I adapted these from Bandura's (1977, 1986) description of ways by which normally censured acts become more intellectually and emotionally acceptable. They include:

1. Labeling sexual violence as a sexual rather than a violent act.
2. Adding to perceptions that sexual aggression is normative and culturally acceptable.
3. Altering perceptions of the consequences of sexual aggression; in particular, minimizing the seriousness of the consequences to the victim and reinforcing the myth that victims derive pleasure from sexual assaults.

Table 14.1: Hypothesized Processes Mediating Impact of Media Sexual Violence on Attitudes

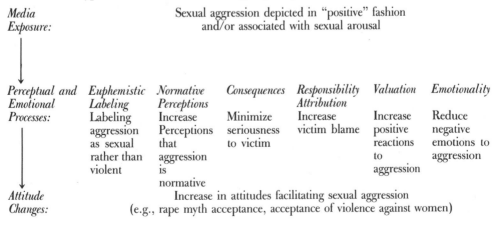

Media Exposure:	Sexual aggression depicted in "positive" fashion and/or associated with sexual arousal					
Perceptual and Emotional Processes:	Euphemistic Labeling	Normative Perceptions	Consequences	Responsibility Attribution	Valuation	Emotionality
	Labeling aggression as sexual rather than violent	Increase Perceptions that aggression is normative	Minimize seriousness to victim	Increase victim blame	Increase positive reactions to aggression	Reduce negative emotions to aggression
Attitude Changes:	Increase in attitudes facilitating sexual aggression (e.g., rape myth acceptance, acceptance of violence against women)					

4. Changing attributions of responsibility to place more blame on the victim.
    5. Elevating the positive value of sexual aggression by associating it with sexual pleasure and a sense of conquest.
    6. Reducing negative emotional reactions to sexually aggressive acts.

Some of the studies discussed later measure these cognitive and emotional processes.

The Anatomy of Media Sexual Violence

A comparison of sexual versus nonsexual media violence helps to isolate the characteristics of sexually violent depictions. Of course, males act against females in the vast majority of sexually aggressive depictions (e.g., Smith, 1976a,b), whereas the victim is usually male in nonsexual portrayals of violence (Gerbner, 1972). Two other important differences distinguish sexual and nonsexual violence. First, victims of nonsexual aggression are usually shown as outraged by their experience and intent on avoiding victimization. They, and also at times the perpetrators of the aggression, suffer from the violence. However, when sexual violence is portrayed, there is frequently the suggestion that, despite initial resistance, the victim secretly desired the abusive treatment and eventually derived pleasure from it. This provides a built-in justification for aggression that would otherwise be considered unjustifiable. Sexual violence is often presented without negative consequences for either the victim or the perpetrator. For example, less than 3 percent of the rapists in "adult" books surveyed by Smith (1976a,b) suffered negative consequences, and their victims were seldom shown to have had regrets about being raped. Similarly, in a recent content analysis of videos, Palys (1986) found that the majority of sexual aggressors were portrayed in a positive fashion and only seldom did their violence result in negative consequences.

The second distinction between sexual and nonsexual violence involves the element of sexual arousal. Such arousal in response to sexually violent depictions might result in subliminal conditioning and cognitive changes in the consumer by associating physical pleasure with violence. Therefore, even sexual aggression depicted negatively may have harmful effects because of the sexual arousal induced by the explicitness of the depiction. For example, a person who views a sexually violent scene might feel that the violence is immoral but may nonetheless be sexually aroused by it. Such

arousal might motivate him to rationalize the aggression or to minimize its *447*
seriousness or its consequences.

Given these issues, particular concern about sexual aggression in the
media is based not only on the frequency of sexual as compared to nonsexual violent portrayals; the positive manner in which sexual violence is
portrayed and its potential to link or reinforce the link between sex and
violence justifies special concern.

The research described below provides some support for the indirect
effects model's two interrelated hypotheses that exposure to media depictions can help form attitudes supportive of real-life sexual aggression and
that such attitudes can in turn contribute to actual aggression against
women.

From Media Exposure to Antisocial Attitudes

Survey Data

Several studies assessed the correlation between the degree of men's exposure to sexually explicit media and their attitudes supportive of violence
against women. Such correlational studies can only reveal associations
between the amount of media people reported consuming and their attitudes. They cannot indicate whether the media were responsible for the
attitudes. Unfortunately, these studies did not distinguish between sexually
violent and sexually nonviolent media. Had they focused exclusively on
sexually violent media rather than on pornography in general, it is likely
that the links to attitudes condoning aggression would have emerged as
strongly, if not more so.

In most studies, higher levels of reported exposure to sexually explicit
media correlated with higher levels of attitudes supportive of violence
against women. For example, in a sample of college men, Malamuth and
Check (1985a) found that a higher level of readership of sexually explicit
magazines was correlated with a stronger belief that women enjoy forced
sex. Similarly, Check (1984) found that the more exposure to pornography
a diverse sample of Canadian men had, the higher their acceptance of rape
myths, violence against women, and general sexual callousness. Briere,
Corne, Runtz, and Malamuth (1984) reported similar correlations in a
sample of college males. On the other hand, the failure to find a statistically
significant correlation in another study led Malamuth (in progress) to
examine other interesting correlations.

That study asked subjects to indicate how much information about

448 sexuality they had obtained in their childhood from various sources, such as peers, parents, church, educational media, educational courses, sexually explicit media, and doctors. Pornography emerged as the second most important source of information, second only to peers. Subjects who reported obtaining more information from pornography also held attitudes more supportive of violence against women. Such a correlation was not found with the other sources of information about sexuality. Information from some, such as educational courses, actually correlated with lower levels of attitudes supportive of violence against women. In fact, pornography's link to antisocial attitudes tended to be stronger when compared to other sources of sexual information than when measured alone.

Focusing only on quantity of exposure, therefore, may be an oversimplified approach. Pornography's degree of influence on a person may depend largely on how that exposure interacts with other influences. People raised with little education about sexuality or in families where sex was treated as "taboo" may be more susceptible to the influences of pornography than those reared with considerable education about sex (Malamuth, 1978; Malamuth & Billings, 1985). It makes sense that those with other sources of sex information can more accurately assess the myths about women and sexuality portrayed in some pornography. However, those without much sex education might be more apt to use pornography as a primary source of information.

Experimental Research

A growing body of experimental research complements the survey data linking media exposure to attitudes. The studies described below have shown connections between sexually violent media and attitudes supportive of sexual aggression but have not revealed similar relations with equally explicit, nonviolent stimuli which portrayed both sexes in equal power roles. Here it is possible to consider a causal link between exposure and attitudes because other factors have been controlled. Still, caution must be exercised in generalizing findings from controlled situations to naturally occurring settings.

Research has examined the impact of "positive" vs. "negative" rape portrayals in two ways. One series of studies assessed how either victim arousal or abhorrence at the end of a rape depiction changed the way in which the assault was perceived when the rape itself remained identical in the two versions. When the rape victim became aroused, male subjects labeled the assault more as a sexual act. They also perceived greater justification for it, reported a greater likelihood that they and other men would

commit such an act, and saw the victim as more responsible for what had   *449*
occurred (Donnerstein, 1984; Rapaport, 1984). These effects were particularly pronounced for more sexually aggressive men.

These experiments show that changing the outcome of a rape affects the
way it is perceived. They do not show that these perceptions carry over to
actual rape. In another series of studies, the carryover effects of perceptions
of and attitudes toward rape were directly examined. These studies assessed whether rapes depicting victim arousal changed subjects' perceptions of other rapes, altered beliefs about women's reactions to sexual
assaults, and increased the acceptance of violence against women.

In three experiments, male subjects were exposed either to depictions of
mutually consenting sex, to rape in which the female victim eventually
became aroused, or to rape abhorred by the victim. Afterwards, the subjects were shown a rape depiction and asked about their perceptions of the
act and the victim. In two of the studies, those subjects exposed to the
"positive" rape portrayal perceived the second rape as less negative than
those first exposed to the other depictions (Malamuth, Haber, & Feshbach,
1980; Malamuth & Check, 1980). One of these studies also found that the
rape depicting victim arousal led men to perceive rape as a more normative
act (Malamuth & Check, 1980). Subjects in the third experiment were
asked how women in general would react to being victimized by sexual
violence (Malamuth & Check, 1985a). Those exposed to a "positive" rape
portrayal believed that a higher percentage of women would derive pleasure from being sexually assaulted. This effect of the portrayal was particularly apparent in men with higher inclinations to aggress against women.

A fourth experiment conducted outside the laboratory yielded similar
results (Malamuth & Check, 1981). Male and female undergraduates were
randomly assigned to one of two exposure conditions. Participants in the
experimental condition were given free tickets to view feature-length films
on two different evenings that included portrayals of women as victims of
aggression in sexual and nonsexual scenes. These films suggested that the
aggression was justified and/or had "positive" consequences. Subjects in
the control condition were given tickets to other films on the same evenings
which did not contain any sexual violence. The movies shown in both
exposure conditions have been aired with some editing on national television. Subjects viewed these films with moviegoers who purchased tickets
and were not part of the research. Classmates of the recruited subjects who
did not see the films were also studied as an "untreated" control group.
Several days after the films were viewed, a "Sexual Attitude Survey" was
administered to the entire classes. (Subjects were not aware of the rela-

450 tionship between this survey—purportedly administered by a polling agency—and the earlier movies some students had seen as part of an ostensibly unrelated study.)

Subject responses were assessed by scales developed by Burt (1980). They included Acceptance of Interpersonal Violence (AIV) against women (e.g., acceptance of sexual aggression and wife battering), Rape Myth Acceptance (RMA) (e.g., the belief that women secretly desire to be raped), and Adversarial Sexual Beliefs (ASB) (e.g., the notion that women act sly and manipulating when out to attract a man). These measures were embedded within many irrelevant items intended to disguise the purpose of the survey.

Exposure to the films portraying "positive" effects significantly increased the scores of male but not female subjects on the AIV scale.[4] A similar pattern was observed on the RMA scale. Only the ASB scores were not at all affected. Taken together, the data demonstrated effects sustained over time of sexually violent movies on men's acceptance of violence against women.[5] Moreover, the results were obtained in a nonlaboratory setting seemingly devoid of "demand characteristics," that is, researchers' subtly conveying their hypotheses to subjects. Recently, Demare (1985) replicated these results using very similar procedures.

An earlier experiment by Malamuth, Reisin, and Spinner (1979) found no attitude changes following exposure to media sexual violence that did not depict victim arousal. In the experiments showing significant media effects, the stimuli were specifically selected because they clearly depicted violence against women as having "positive" consequences. These findings suggest that certain antisocial effects may be limited to media stimuli depicting "positive" consequences of sexual aggression.

Still, sexually violent films that do not portray "positive" consequences may nonetheless affect consumers in undesirable ways. For example, Linz (1985) studied the effects of repeated exposure to X- and R-rated feature-length films portraying sexual violence with primarily negative consequences to victims. He found that these movies had desensitizing effects on

4. Some might argue that the use of college students in these and similar studies limits the ability to generalize from the findings. That implies that college students are more susceptible to media influences than non-college students or younger people. In fact, less educated and younger groups might be more susceptible to such influences.

5. It would be desirable to examine the effects of sexually violent media over longer time periods than a week. However, ethics committees have in certain instances refused to permit such delays, requiring that subjects be debriefed soon after the media exposures. These debriefings are intended to mitigate the negative effects of exposure to sexually violent media. They appear to have been effective (e.g., Donnerstein & Berkowitz, 1981; Linz, 1985; Malamuth & Check, 1984). They point to the need for further research on the efficacy of educational interventions, including those presented via the mass media, designed to reduce attitudes supportive of violence against women and to reduce susceptibility to the possible negative impact of sexually violent portrayals.

viewers. In one experiment, male college students who viewed five such movies had fewer negative emotional reactions to such films. There was even a tendency for the subjects' "desensitization" to carry over to their judgments of a rape victim in a simulated trial presented following their exposure to the films. In a second experiment, Linz (1985) again found that males exposed to several R-rated, sexually violent films became less sympathetic to a rape victim in a simulated trial and were less able to empathize with rape victims in general.

From Attitudes to Antisocial Behavior

Although psychologists have demonstrated that there is seldom a strong direct link between attitudes and behavior (Ajzen & Fishbein, 1977), several researchers have contended that attitudes accepting or justifying sexual aggression are an important cause of aggression against women (e.g., Brownmiller, 1975; Russell, 1984). Burt has presented the most influential theoretical perspective in this area (1978; 1980; 1983). She contends that a cultural matrix which encourages rigid sex roles and supports male dominance over females generates attitudes supportive of rape. These attitudes act as "psychological releasers or neutralizers, allowing potential rapists to turn off social prohibitions against injuring or using others" (1978, p. 282). To assess such attitudes and beliefs, Burt (1980) developed the scales used in the experiments described earlier, including the AIV, RMA, and ASB.

Studies by Malamuth and his colleagues provide some support for Burt's perspective. They show a significant relationship between Burt's rape-condoning attitude scales and men's self-reported likelihood of engaging in a wide range of violenct acts against women as long as the men suffered no negative consequences (e.g., Briere & Malamuth, 1983; Malamuth, 1981; 1984a). However, some commentators have contended that the linkage between attitudes and actual aggressive behavior is assumed too facilely in such studies (e.g., Vance, 1985). Fortunately, several studies have recently examined this connection and have found consistently that the attitude scales can predict actual aggressive behavior. This, of course, does not mean that everyone with attitudes condoning aggression will act on them.

Laboratory Aggression

Malamuth (1983) tested whether men's attitudes could predict their aggressive behavior in a laboratory setting. He also examined whether men's arousal to rape depictions compared to their arousal to consensual sex depictions predicted laboratory aggression.

452   About a week after both attitudes (on the AIV and RMA scales) and sexual arousal to rape were measured, subjects participated in what they believed was a totally unrelated "extrasensory perception" experiment. In that session, they were angered by a female aide of the experimenter who pretended to be another subject. Later in the session, subjects could vent their aggression against her by administering unpleasant noise as punishment for her incorrect responses. They were told that punishment was thought to impede rather than aid extrasensory transmission, but they were given the option of trying it out. Subjects were also asked how much they wanted to hurt their co-subject with the noise. Men with attitudes more condoning of aggression and with higher levels of sexual arousal to rape were more aggressive against the woman and wanted to hurt her to a greater extent.

Malamuth and Check (1982) successfully replicated these results in a similar experiment that did not consider the subjects' arousal to rape but did assess attitudes toward aggression. Later, Malamuth (1984b) examined the extent to which several measures related to violence against women (including attitudes) predicted laboratory aggression against both female and male targets. While strong relations between the predictor measures and aggressive behavior were found for female targets, only weak relations were obtained for male targets. Taken together, these three experiments consistently showed that attitudes condoning aggression against women related to objectively observable behavior—laboratory aggression against women.

Although such laboratory assessments of aggression have the advantage of being an objective measurement not relying on subjects' self-reports, they have the disadvantage of using a setting that some researchers argue is artificial and lacking in ecological validity (e.g., Kaplan, 1983). The case for linking attitudes condoning aggression with actual aggressive behavior is strengthened by studies that have measured naturally occurring behavior.

Aggression in Naturalistic Settings

These studies have used samples of men from the general population as well as convicted rapists. The importance of attitudes toward violence is confirmed by data showing that men's aggression against women is linked with their own attitudes as well as those of their peers.

Ageton (1983) gauged the extent to which a variety of measures predicted levels of sexual aggression. Eleven- to seventeen-year-old subjects, drawn from a representative national sample, were interviewed in five consecutive years between 1976 and 1981. Based on subjects' self-reported behavior, they were categorized as sexually aggressive or nonaggressive.

The results showed that involvement with delinquent peers at a young age was the strongest factor in predicting sexual aggression later in life. Personal attitudes toward sexual assault was another factor found to differentiate significantly between those who became sexually aggressive and those who did not. Ageton therefore concluded that "peer-group support for sexually aggressive behavior does appear to be relevant to the performance of this behavior, as do attitudes supportive of rape myths."

Another study was recently reported by Alder (1985). She used a subsample from a larger representative sample of men from a particular county in Oregon. Variables potentially predictive of sexual aggression were assessed. These included family, social class, educational attainment, war experience, peer behavior, and personal attitudes toward sexual aggression. The findings suggested that the most important factor relating to sexual aggression was having sexually aggressive friends. The other two factors found likely to contribute to sexual aggression were attitudes legitimizing such aggression and military service in the Vietnam war.

Several studies using samples of college men also reported significant links between attitudes and actual sexual aggressiveness (Briere, Corne, Runtz, & Malamuth, 1984; Koss, Leonard, Beezley, & Oros, 1985; Mosher & Anderson, 1986; Rapaport & Burkhart, 1984). These studies measured self-reported sexual aggression on a continuum of behaviors ranging from psychological pressure on women to rape. Similar results were reported by Kanin (1985) who compared the attitudes of 71 university students who admitted committing rape with a control group of nonaggressive college males. He found that a much higher percentage of rapists than control subjects justified rape in general. Moreover, he found that rapists were far more likely to believe their reputations would be enhanced among their peers by aggressive behavior toward women, particularly women perceived as "pick-ups," "loose," "teasers," or "economic exploiters."

In a study of 155 men who were mostly college students, Malamuth (1986) broke down the variables thought to set the stage for sexual aggression into three classes. Motivation for sexual aggression included sexual arousal to aggression, hostility toward women, and dominance as a motive for sex. Disinhibition to commit sexual aggression included attitudes condoning aggression and antisocial personality characteristics. Opportunity to aggress sexually was assessed by sexual experience. These rape "predictors" were then correlated with self-reports of sexual aggression. While the "predictors" related individually to sexual aggression, interactive combinations of these variables allowed far more accurate prediction of varying levels of sexual aggression. Subjects who had relatively high scores on all of the predictor variables were also highly aggressive sexually. These data

454 have been successfully replicated by Malamuth and Check (1985b) in an independent sample of 297 males. The findings suggest that a person's attitudes accepting of violence against women may be one of several important contributors to sexually aggressive acts, but that none alone is sufficient for serious sexual aggression.

Taken together, the data on unincarcerated subjects point clearly to a relationship between sexual aggression and attitudes supportive of violence against women, although they also highlight the importance of other contributing factors. One of these other factors, peer support, might also be influenced by the impact of media exposure on the audience's attitudes. The findings on unincarcerated men are reinforced by research on incarcerated rapists.

Convicted Rapists

Many clinical studies report that convicted rapists frequently hold callous attitudes about rape and believe in rape myths to a relatively high degree (e.g., Gager & Schurr, 1976). Data from more systematic studies of rapists' attitudes tend to collaborate the clinical reports. For example, Wolfe and Baker (1980) studied the beliefs and attitudes of 86 convicted rapists and reported that virtually all believed that their actions did not constitute rape or were justified by the circumstances. Unfortunately, these investigators did not distinguish between general endorsement of rape myths and rationalizations of the rapists' own crimes. Burt (1983) found that although rapists perceived the same degree of violence as the general public in vignettes describing aggression against women, they were less likely to perceive the violence as "bad" and more likely to justify it. Finally, Scully and Marolla (1984, 1985) found that rapists tended to believe in rape myths, particularly those justifying violence against women, more than control groups composed of other felons.

Other Relevant Data

Nonsexual Media Violence

Although research on nonsexual media violence has not devoted much attention to the formation and importance of attitudes (Rule & Ferguson, 1986), some relevant findings exist. The research of Huesmann, Eron, Klein, Brice, and Fischer (1983) attempts the most direct assessment of cause and effect relations in this area. After involving elementary school children in a program designed to change their attitudes about television violence, the researchers studied whether changed attitudes translated into less aggressive behavior. The students were randomly divided into experimental and control groups. Over a two-year span, the experimental group was educated about the harmful aspects of television violence while the control group received neutral treatments. Although the frequency of the children's free-time viewing of violence did not change, their attitudes about the violence did. In addition, their peers reported reduced aggression in the experimental group but no change in the behavior of the control group. These data suggest that changed attitudes about TV violence led to a reduction in personal aggression by children, as reported by their peers.

Another relevant study by Van der Voort (1986) assessed whether individual differences in children's perceptual, emotional, and attitudinal reactions to TV violence predicted peer-reported aggression. Significant relations were found between the predictors (measured one year earlier) and actual aggression. The more children approved of the violence of "good guys" on TV, the higher their aggression, even after factors such as socioeconomic levels and school achievement were controlled. Van der Voort also found that parents who were less concerned about their children viewing violence had more aggressive children. While these findings suggest a relation between attitudes and behavior, they do not enable us to draw cause-and-effect conclusions.

Jury Studies

One aspect of the model presented in figure 14.1 is the idea that changes in attitudes may be of importance even if these attitudes do not increase the likelihood that the person himself will commit aggressive acts. Jury decisions, for example, involve attitudes about whether particular behavior is aggressive.

Feild and Bienen (1980) examined the impact of personal juror characteristics on reactions to a simulated rape case. The "jurors" in the simulated trials were groups of citizens, police officers, rape counselors, and rapists. Juror attitudes about rape were found to be highly predictive of their decisions in the rape trial. For example, people who believed that rape victims often precipitate rape were more lenient toward the rapist than those not holding such an attitude. If attitudes condoning of violence against women can result in milder punishment of rapists, the deterrence against rape may be reduced by social attitudes.

The research presented has provided support for the model hypothesizing indirect causal influences of media sexual violence on antisocial behavior against women. Data were described which indicate (1) linkages between exposure to media portrayals of sexual violence and resultant

456 attitudes supportive of sexual aggression; and (2) a relationship between such attitudes and a variety of antisocial behaviors against women. The data suggest that such attitudes may lead to high levels of sexual aggression if combined with other factors such as peer support for aggression, sexual arousal to aggression, antisocial personality characteristics, and hostility toward women. Clearly, much additional research is needed to further develop and test this model.

As with many behaviors, it is apparent that antisocial behavior against women is a function of several interacting causal factors. It is very difficult to gauge the relative influence of media exposure alone, but it would appear that, by itself, it exerts a small influence. But this appears to be true to some degree for all the contributing causes. Only in interaction with other factors might they be substantially influential. The reduction of antisocial behavior against women, therefore, requires attention to all potentially contributing factors, including the mass media.

References

Ageton, S. S. (1983). *Sexual assault among adolescents*. Lexington, Mass.: Lexington Books.

Ajzen, I., & Fishbein, M. (1977). Attitude-behavior relations: A theoretical analysis and review of empirical research. *Psychological Bulletin, 84*, 888–918.

Alder, C. (1985). An exploration of self-reported sexually aggressive behavior. *Crime and Delinquency, 31*, 306–31.

Bandura, A. (1977). *Social learning theory*. Englewood Cliffs, N.J.: Prentice-Hall.

Bandura, A. (1986). *Social foundations of thought action: A social cognitive theory*. Englewood Cliffs, N.J.: Prentice-Hall.

Berkowitz, L. (1984). Some effects of thoughts on anti- and pro-social influence of media events: A cognitive neoassociation analysis. *Psychological Bulletin, 95*, 410–27.

Briere, J., Corne, S., Runtz, M., & Malamuth, N. M. (1984, August). The Rape Arousal Inventory: Predicting actual and potential sexual aggression in a university population. Paper presented at the annual meeting of the American Psychological Association, Toronto, Canada.

Briere, J., & Malamuth, N. M. (1983). Self-reported likelihood of sexually aggressive behavior: Attitudinal versus sexual explanations. *Journal of Research in Personality, 17*, 315–23.

Brownmiller, S. (1975). *Against our will: Men, women and rape*. New York: Simon & Schuster.

Burt, M. R. (1978). Attitudes supportive of rape in American culture. *House Committee on Science and Technology, Subcommittee Domestic and International Scientific Planning, Analysis, and Cooperation, Research into violent behavior: Sexual assaults* (Hearing, 95th Congress, 2d session, January 10–12, 1978) (pp. 277–322). Washington, D.C.: U.S. Government Printing Office.

Burt, M. R. (1980). Cultural myths and support for rape. *Journal of Personality and Social Psychology, 38*, 217–30.

Burt, M. R. (1983). Justifying personal violence: A comparison of rapists and the general public. *Victimology: An International Journal, 8*, 131–50.

Check, J. (1984). *The effects of violent and nonviolent pornography* (Contract No. 95SV 19200-3-0899). Ottawa, Ontario: Canadian Department of Justice.

Dietz, P. E., & Evans, B. (1982). Pornographic imagery and prevalence of paraphilia. *American Journal of Psychiatry, 139,* 1493–95.

Demare, D. (1985). The effects of erotic and sexually violent mass media on attitudes toward women and rape. Unpublished manuscript, University of Winnipeg, Winnipeg, Manitoba, Canada.

Donnerstein, E. (1984). Pornography: Its effects on violence against women. In N. M. Malamuth & E. Donnerstein (Eds.), *Pornography and sexual aggression* (pp. 53–81). Orlando, Fla.: Academic Press.

Donnerstein, E., & Berkowitz, L. (1981). Victim reactions in aggressive-erotic films as a factor in violence against women. *Journal of Personality and Social Psychology, 41,* 710–24.

Feild, H., & Bienen, L. (1980). *Jurors and rape: A study in psychology and the law.* Lexington, Mass.: D. C. Heath.

Gager, N., & Schurr, C. (1976). *Sexual assault: Confronting rape in America.* New York: Grosset & Dunlap.

Gerbner, G. (1972). Violence in television drama: Trends and symbolic functions. In G. A. Comstock and E. A. Rubinstein (Eds.), *Television and social behavior* (Vol. 1). *Media content and control* (pp. 28–187). Washington, D.C.: U.S. Government Printing Office.

Huesmann, L. R., Eron, L. D., Klein, R., Brice, P., & Fischer, P. (1983). Mitigating the imitation of aggressive behaviors by changing children's attitudes about media violence. *Journal of Personality and Social Psychology, 44,* 899–910.

Kanin, E. J. (1985). Date rapists: Differential sexual socialization and relative deprivation. *Archives of Sexual Behavior, 14,* 219–31.

Kaplan, R. (1983). The measurement of human aggression. In R. Kaplan, V. Koencni, & R. Novaco (Eds.), *Aggression in children and youth.* Rijn, Netherlands: Sijthoff & Noordhuff International Publishers.

Koss, M. P., Leonard, K. E., Beezley, D. A., & Oros, C. J. (1985). Nonstranger sexual aggression: A discriminant analysis of psychological characteristics of nondetected offenders. *Sex Roles, 12,* 981–92.

Koss, M. P., & Oros, C. J. (1982). Sexual experiences survey: A research instrument investigating sexual aggression and victimization. *Journal of Consulting and Clinical Psychology, 50,* 455–57.

Linz, D. (1985). Sexual violence in the media: Effects on male viewers and implications for society. Unpublished doctoral dissertation, University of Wisconsin, Madison.

Malamuth, N.M. (1978, September). Erotica, aggression and perceived appropriateness. Paper presented at the meeting of the American Psychological Association, Toronto, Canada.

Malamuth, N. M. (1981). Rape proclivity among males. *Journal of Social Issues, 37,* 138–57.

Malamuth, N. M. (1983). Factors associated with rape as predictors of laboratory aggression against women. *Journal of Personality and Social Psychology, 45,* 432–42.

Malamuth, N. M. (1984a). Aggression against women: Cultural and individual causes. In N. M. Malamuth and E. Donnerstein (Eds.), *Pornography and sexual aggression* (pp. 19–52). Orlando, Fla.: Academic Press.

Malamuth, N. M. (1984b). Violence against women: Cultural, individual, and inhibitory-disinhibitory causes. Paper presented at the annual meeting of the American Psychological Association, Toronto, Canada.

Malamuth, N. M. (1986). Predictors of naturalistic sexual aggression. *Journal of Personality and Social Psychology, 50,* 953–62.

Malamuth, N. M. (in progress). Sources of information about sexuality and their correlates: With particular focus on pornography.

458 Malamuth, N. M., & Billings, V. (1985). The functions and effects of pornography: Sexual communication versus the feminist models in light of research findings. In J. Bryant & D. Zillmann (Eds.), *Perspectives on media effects*. Hillsdale, N.J.: Erlbaum Publishers.

Malamuth, N. M., & Briere, J. (1986). Sexual violence in the media: Indirect effects on aggression against women. *Journal of Social Issues, 42* (3), 75–92.

Malamuth, N., & Check, J. (1980). Penile tumescence and perceptual responses to rape as a function of victim's perceived reactions. *Journal of Applied Social Psychology, 10*, 528–47.

Malamuth, N. M., & Check, J. V. P. (1981). The effects of mass media exposure on acceptance of violence against women: A field experiment. *Journal of Research in Personality, 15*, 436–46.

Malamuth, N. M., & Check, J. V. P. (1982, June). Factors related to aggression against women. Paper presented at the annual meeting of the Canadian Psychological Association, Montreal, Canada.

Malamuth, N. M., & Check, J. V. P. (1984). Debriefing effectiveness following exposure to rape depictions. *The Journal of Sex Research, 20*, 1–13.

Malamuth, N. M., & Check, J. V. P. (1985a). The effects of aggressive pornography on beliefs in rape myths: Individual differences. *Journal of Research in Personality, 19*, 299–320.

Malamuth, N. M., & Check, J. V. P. (1985b). Predicting naturalistic sexual aggression: A replication. Unpublished manuscript, University of California, Los Angeles.

Malamuth, N. M., Check, J. V. P., & Briere, J. (1986). Sexual arousal in response to aggression: Ideological, aggressive, and sexual correlates. *Journal of Personality and Social Psychology, 50*, 330–40.

Malamuth, N. M., Feshbach, S., & Jaffe, Y. (1977). Sexual arousal and aggression: Recent experiments and theoretical issues. *Journal of Social Issues, 33*, 110–33.

Malamuth, N. M., Haber, S., & Feshbach, S. (1980). Testing hypotheses regarding rape: Exposure to sexual violence, sex differences, and the "normality" of rapists. *Journal of Research in Personality, 14*, 121–37.

Malamuth, N. M., Reisin, I., & Spinner, B. (1979). Exposure to pornography and reactions to rape. Paper presented at the meeting of the American Psychological Association, New York.

Mosher, D. L., & Anderson, R. D. (1986). Macho personality, sexual aggression, and reactions to guided imagery of realistic rape. *Journal of Research in Personality, 20*, 77–94.

Palys, P. S. (1986). Testing the common wisdom: The social content of video pornography. *Canadian Psychology, 27*, 22–35.

Rapaport, K. (1984). Sexually aggressive males: Characterological features and sexual responsiveness to rape depictions. Unpublished doctoral dissertation, Auburn University, Auburn, Alabama.

Rapaport, K., & Burkhart, B. R. (1984). Personality and attitudinal characteristics of sexually coercive college males. *Journal of Abnormal Psychology, 93*, 216–21.

Rule, B., & Ferguson, T. (1986). The effects of media violence on attitudes, emotions and cognitions. *Journal of Social Issues*.

Russell, D. E. H. (1984). *Sexual exploitation: Rape, child sexual abuse and workplace harassment*. Beverly Hills: Sage Publications.

Scully, D., & Marolla, J. (1984). Convicted rapists' vocabulary of motive: Excuses and justifications. *Social Problems, 31*, 530–44.

Scully, D., & Marolla, J. (1985). Riding the bull at Gilley's: Convicted rapists describe the rewards of rape. *Social Problems, 32*, 251–63.

Smith, D. G. (1976a). Sexual aggression in American pornography: The stereotype of rape. Paper presented at the annual meeting of the American Sociological Association, New York.

Smith, D. G. (1976b). The social content of pornography. *Journal of Communication, 26,* **459** 16–33.

Vance, C. S. (1985, April). What does the research prove? *Ms. Magazine,* Vol. XIII, No. 10 (p. 40).

Van der Voort, T. H. A. (1986). *Television violence: A child's-eye view.* Amsterdam: Elsevier Science Publishing Co.

Wolfe, J., & Baker, V. (1980). Characteristics of imprisoned rapists and circumstances of the rape. In C. G. Warner (Ed.), *Rape and sexual assault.* Germantown, Md.: Aspen Systems.

Name Index

Prepared by E. Alice Moore

Subject Index

Prepared by E. Alice Moore

Abortion, 378–408; contraception use, 386, 387, 388–389, 392–393, 406; demographics of patients, 387–388; decision making, 388–390; illegal, 381, 382–383, 385–386, 391–392; legal, 381–394; methods, 387; as moral choice, 288–311, 325–326; psychoanalytic view of, 55; therapeutic, 381, 382–385, 391–392

—counseling, 396–408; cognitive restructuring, 402; consciousness-raising, 405; gestalt approach, 402–403; long-term counseling, 397; models of, 402–405; short-term crisis intervention, 397; support groups, 403–405, 406

—psychological effects, 11, 378–408; anger, 389, 400; anxiety, 400; cross-cultural research, 382–386; denial response, 401; depression, 399, 400, 401; factors involved, 399–400; grief reactions, 400–401, 403; guilt, 389, 390, 391, 400; low incidence of negative effects, 378–379, 381–395, 396, 398, 402, 405; minimizing negative reactions, 397–398; research overview, 378–379, 382–383, 396; stress, 379, 384, 398–399, 403; summary of controversy, 11, 378–380

Achievement: masochism and, 92; negative attitudes toward, 174; negative attitudes toward women's, 171

—motivation: research overview, 165; sex differences in, 323

Aggression: conflict with femininity, 169; effect of daycare on children's, 371–372; in batterers, 63; in lesbians, 421; masochism and, 83, 86, 92; sex differences in, 333

American Psychiatric Association, 60, 128, 409

American Psychological Association: recognition of the psychology of women, 4; status of women in, 3–4

Analogue studies, 109, 124

Androgyny, 203–225, 244–245; benefits of, 209; clinical applications, 204; criticisms of, 204, 244–245; definition of, 207–208; description of androgynous individuals, 219–220; description of sex-typed individuals, 219–221, 233–236; equated with mental health, 203; independence and, 214–215, 216; measurement of, 203, 209–212; nurturance and, 214, 215–219; popularity of, 203–204; relation to post-abortion adjustment, 400; research overview, 203–204, 208–209; summary of controversy, 9, 203–205

Anger, post-abortion, 389, 400

Anxiety: fear of success and, 192, 193; in lesbians, 415, 417; post-abortion, 400

Assertiveness: masochism and, 64, 92

Attribution theory, 140

Autonomy: moral development and, 279, 289

Bem Sex Role Inventory, 203, 209–212

Bisexuality, 35

Black women, 7

Bladder infections, after menopause, 154

Blame-the-victim approach: in fear of success, 166, 200; in masochism, 59, 66; in rape, 444; in wife abuse, 59, 66; in women's mental illness, 121

Bonding, traumatic, 87

Brain syndromes: exclusion from mental illness definition, 105

Cancer: endometrial, 148, 151, 152, 158; uterine, 155

Castration anxiety/complex: definition of, 33; entry into oedipal phase, 27, 29; masochism and, 83–84

Catharsis theory, and pornography, 428

475

List of Contributors

SANDRA LIPSITZ BEM is Professor of Psychology and Women's Studies, Cornell University, Ithaca, New York.

CAMILLA PERSSON BENBOW is Associate Professor of Psychology and Director of the Study of Mathematically Precocious Youth at Iowa State University, Ames, Iowa.

JANETTE BUCY is a counseling psychologist in private practice, Seattle, Washington.

PENNY WISE BUDOFF is a physician and Medical Director of the Women's Medical Center in Bethpage, New York.

PAULA J. CAPLAN is a clinical psychologist and Professor of Applied Psychology, Ontario Institute for Studies in Education, Toronto, Canada.

SHAHLA CHEHRAZI is a psychiatrist and Assistant Clinical Professor, Department of Psychiatry, University of California, San Francisco.

NANCY CHODOROW is Associate Professor, Department of Sociology, University of California, Berkeley.

ANNE COLBY is Director of the Henry A. Murray Research Center, Radcliffe College, Harvard University.

KATHARINA DALTON is a physician specializing in gynecology and endocrinology in London, England.

WILLIAM DAMON is Professor, Department of Psychology, Clark University, Worcester, Massachusetts.

JACQUELYNNE S. ECCLES is Associate Professor of Psychology, University of Michigan, Ann Arbor, Michigan.

NANETTE GARTRELL is a psychiatrist in private practice and an Assistant Professor of Psychiatry at the Harvard Medical School.

CAROL GILLIGAN is Professor, Harvard Graduate School of Education, Harvard University.

WALTER R. GOVE is a sociologist and Professor of Sociology and Anthropology, Vanderbilt University, Nashville, Tennessee.

RICHARD GREEN is a psychiatrist and Professor of Psychiatry at the University of California, Los Angeles, and Director of the Program in Psychiatry, Law, and Human Sexuality.

484   MATINA S. HORNER is President of Radcliffe College and Associate Professor, Department of Psychology, Harvard University.

JANIS E. JACOBS is Assistant Professor of Psychology, University of Nebraska, Lincoln, Nebraska.

MARILYN JOHNSON is a counseling psychologist and Director of the Student Counseling Center and Assistant Professor of Psychology and Social Sciences, Rush-Presbyterian-St. Luke's Medical Center, Chicago, Illinois.

RANDI DAIMON KOESKE is a Research Psychologist in the Psychology Department at the University of Pittsburgh.

HANNAH LERMAN is a clinical psychologist in private practice in Los Angeles.

KAREN M. LODL is former President and Education Coordinator, Calgary Birth Control Association, Calgary, Alberta.

ANN MCGETTIGAN is Coordinator, YMCA, University of Washington Abortion Birth Control Referral Service, Seattle, Washington.

JOHN B. MCKINLAY is a medical sociologist and Professor, Department of Sociology, Boston University.

SONJA M. MCKINLAY is an epidemiologist and Associate Professor (Research), Department of Community Health, Brown University, Providence, Rhode Island.

NEIL M. MALAMUTH is a social psychologist and Professor of Communications Studies, University of California, Los Angeles.

JOANNE CURRY O'CONNELL is Associate Director of Research at the Institute for Human Development and Associate Professor of Educational Psychology at Northern Arizona State University, Flagstaff, Arizona.

HOWARD J. OSOFSKY is Head and Professor, Department of Psychiatry, Louisiana State University Medical School, New Orleans, Louisiana.

JOY D. OSOFSKY is a clinical psychologist and Professor of Pediatrics and Psychiatry, Louisiana State University Medical School, New Orleans, Louisiana.

MICHELE A. PALUDI is Associate Professor, Department of Psychology, Kent State University, Kent, Ohio.

ALICE S. ROSSI is Professor, Department of Sociology, University of Massachusetts.

NATALIE SHAINESS is a psychiatrist in private practice in New York City.

CHARLES W. SOCARIDES is a psychiatrist in private practice and Clinical Professor of Psychiatry, Albert Einstein College of Medicine.

JULIAN STANLEY is Professor of Psychology and Director of the Study of Mathematically Precocious Youth at Johns Hopkins University.

MARY ROTH WALSH is Professor of Psychology at the University of Lowell, Lowell, Massachusetts.

BURTON L. WHITE is Director and Trustee, Center for Parent Education, Newton, Massachusetts.